W R Mensen
May 1984   Central Reference Dept
Milwaukee

.75

JOINT STEERING COMMITTEE FOR REVISION OF AACR

Chair: Peter R. Lewis

Secretary: Carol R. Kelm

Editors: Michael Gorman and Paul W. Winkler

AMERICAN LIBRARY ASSOCIATION

Representative: John D. Byrum
Deputy representative: Frances Hinton

BRITISH LIBRARY

Representative: Peter R. Lewis
Deputy representative: J.C. Downing

CANADIAN COMMITTEE ON CATALOGUING

Representative: Jean Lunn (1974–1975)
        Edwin Buchinski (1975–1978)
Deputy representative: Ronald Hagler

LIBRARY ASSOCIATION

Representative: Philip K. Escreet
Deputy representative: G.E. Hamilton

LIBRARY OF CONGRESS

Representative: C. Sumner Spalding (1974)
        Elizabeth Tate (1974–1976)
        Ben R. Tucker (1976–1978)
Deputy representative: Robert M. Hiatt

ANGLO-AMERICAN CATALOGUING RULES

ANGLO-AMERICAN CATALOGUING RULES

SECOND EDITION

Prepared by

THE AMERICAN LIBRARY ASSOCIATION
THE BRITISH LIBRARY
THE CANADIAN COMMITTEE ON CATALOGUING
THE LIBRARY ASSOCIATION
THE LIBRARY OF CONGRESS

Edited by

MICHAEL GORMAN *and* PAUL W. WINKLER

AMERICAN LIBRARY ASSOCIATION / *Chicago*

CANADIAN LIBRARY ASSOCIATION / *Ottawa*

Published 1978 by

AMERICAN LIBRARY ASSOCIATION
50 East Huron Street, Chicago, Illinois 60611
ISBN 0-8389-3210-X
ISBN 0-8389-3211-8 (Pbk)

CANADIAN LIBRARY ASSOCIATION
151 Sparks Street, Ottawa, Ontario K1P 5E3
ISBN 0-88802-121-6
ISBN 0-88802-122-4 (Pbk)

THE LIBRARY ASSOCIATION
7 Ridgmount Street, London WC1E 7AE
ISBN 0-85365-681-9
ISBN 0-85365-691-6 (Pbk)

Library of Congress Cataloging in Publication Data

Main entry under title:

Anglo-American cataloguing rules.
   Includes index.
   1. Descriptive cataloging—Rules. I. Gorman,
Michael, 1941–   II. Winkler, Paul Walter.
III. American Library Association.
Z694.A5 1978   025.3′2   78-13789
ISBN 0-8389-3210-X
ISBN 0-8389-3211-8 pbk.

Set in 10 on 12 pt. Times Roman
by the University of Chicago Printing Department

Printed and bound in the United States of America
by R. R. Donnelley & Sons Co., Chicago

PREFACE

The first edition of the *Anglo-American Cataloguing Rules,* in its separately published North American and British texts, was the product of the inspired editorship successively of Seymour Lubetzky and C. Sumner Spalding and the culmination of many years' activity by a large number of individuals, to whom credit and acknowledgment were given in that edition. This second edition does not supersede their work, but continues it: for, in spite of the changes in presentation and content which it introduces, these are still the *Anglo-American Cataloguing Rules,* having the same principles and underlying objectives as the first edition, and being firmly based on the achievement of those who created the work, first published in 1967.

The starting point for this new edition is, indeed, the very clear success of the 1967 texts in meeting the needs of large numbers—and many different kinds—of libraries during a period in which there have been considerable growth in libraries and extensions of catalogue processes, bibliographic services, and national library services; not only in the three "Anglo-American" countries for which AACR was established, but throughout the world. AACR has been adopted by major libraries and agencies in most English-speaking countries, and has had a considerable influence on the formation or revision of local and national cataloguing rules in a number of others. For ten years it has thus been subjected to the critical test of application over a very wide range of professional practice across the world.

During this time mechanization, the growth of centralized and cooperative bibliographic services and networks, the development and unification of services in the national libraries (especially, in the AACR context, those of the United Kingdom and Canada)—all these have had, as they continue to have, significant effects on the assembly, transmission, and catalogue exploitation of bibliographic information, both within libraries and between libraries. And the introduction into most libraries of increasing numbers of the new media that have established themselves in the same period as having a parallel importance, for many library users, with the paper-based and printed documents traditionally the staple of the processing and cataloguing department, has created or intensified integrative problems on a scale unpredictable by those who wrought the 1967 texts.

A "memorandum of agreement" of 1966 between the American Library Association (ALA) and the [British] Library Association provided a means of continuing review by these two bodies of the 1967 texts after publication, so that appropriate action by amendment and addition might be taken to deal with any problems encountered by users on account either of errors and ambiguities or of changing circumstances. The forum for that review was the Descriptive Cataloging Committee (DCC) of the ALA Resources and Technical Services Division; and from 1969 to 1974 regular meetings of DCC were attended by representatives of the Cataloguing Rules Committee established by the Library Association, with formal representation also of the Library of Congress and the Canadian Library Association. At these meetings a number of amendments and changes of the 1967 texts were agreed and promulgated; and some of the problems arising from changing circumstances were addressed for the first time, particularly those of the treatment of nonbook materials. However, the memorandum did not stipulate agreement among all parties as a condition of amendment to either text and, while in one or two important respects the differences between the two texts were diminished, there were some not unimportant issues on which they seemed in some danger of moving further apart. Furthermore, some significant problems were identified on which, although all parties were agreed on the line of development needed, the procedural mechanisms provided by the memorandum were not wholly adequate for thorough examination and effective action.

At this stage, two new factors made it both propitious and desirable to find a new means of consolidating development since 1967 and of providing for the ascertainable requirements of bibliographic control in the 1980s and beyond. These were, first, the proposed conclusion by the Library of Congress of the policy of "superimposition" by which its adoption of AACR had been limited; and, second, the establishment by the newly formed British Library of its policies of working alongside the Library of Congress, the National Library of Canada, and other libraries and agencies, in the framework of national and international networks and standards for bibliographic records. Another contributory factor was the emergence, from the International Meeting of Cataloguing Experts held in Copenhagen in 1969, of a programme of International Standard Bibliographic Description (ISBD) under the aegis of the International Federation of Library Associations and Institutions (IFLA). This programme commenced with a standard for monographs, ISBD(M), which was incorporated into the two texts of AACR in 1974 by means of separately published revisions of chapter 6.

For these reasons, and on the initiatives of ALA and the British Library, there took place at ALA headquarters in Chicago, in March 1974, a tripartite meeting—consisting of one delegate each from the three "Anglo-American" countries, representing in each case both the library association and the national library—to draw up a new memorandum of agreement and to complete the planning of the project for a second edition of AACR.

OBJECTIVES AND POLICIES

The objectives established in the memorandum of the tripartite meeting may be briefly stated as follows:

1) To reconcile in a single text the North American and British texts of 1967
2) To incorporate in the single text all amendments and changes already agreed and implemented under the previous mechanisms
3) To consider for inclusion in AACR all proposals for amendment currently un-

der discussion between the American Library Association, the Library Association, the Library of Congress, and the Canadian Library Association; any new proposals put forward by these bodies and the British Library; and any proposals of national committees of other countries in which AACR is in use

4) To provide for international interest in AACR by facilitating its use in countries other than the United States, Canada, and the United Kingdom. This final objective was later intensified, as a condition of funding by the Council on Library Resources, to one of making a contribution to the development of an international cataloguing code.

The tripartite meeting set up a Joint Steering Committee for Revision of AACR (JSCAACR), consisting of one voting and one nonvoting representative of each of the five participating organizations, and provided for two editors, one from either side of the Atlantic. JSCAACR's function has been to appoint the editors, to consider all proposals and determine questions of policy with the editors, to assess for approval the rules framed by the editors, and to present the final text for publication; and thus to be the ultimate authority for the content and presentation of this second edition.

An early result of JSCAACR's consideration of the objectives and its own terms of reference was its declaration of the guidelines by which policy questions and new proposals were to be determined. These guidelines were stated publicly at the commencement of the project; they have been sustained throughout the two and a half years of its completion, and they may be summarized as follows:

1) Maintenance of general conformity with the Paris Principles of 1961, as manifested in the first edition

2) Particular attention to developments in the machine processing of bibliographic records

3) Continuance of conformity with the ISBD(M) as a basis for the bibliographic description of monographs, and commitment to the principle of standardization in the bibliographic description of all types of materials

4) Determination of the treatment of nonbook materials primarily from a consideration of the published cataloguing rules of the Canadian Library Association, the Library Association, and the Association for Educational Communications and Technology; and of the ALA revision of chapter 12 of the 1967 text.[1]

With regard to the first of the guidelines, the second edition continues to reflect the tendency to closer conformity with the Paris Principles that was already embodied in amendments to the 1967 texts promulgated before work on the edition began, specifically the abandonment of entry under the name of a place of certain institutional bodies, as related to section 9.4 of the Paris Principles[2]; and some other

---

1. See "Sources" on page xi for full citations.

2. See the Introduction to the 1967 edition of AACR (pp. 2–4 North American Text, pp. 2–3 British Text) for a summary statement on the initial relationship with the Paris Principles; and *Statement of Principles . . . Paris . . . 1961. Annotated Edition* (full citation at "Sources," below, p. xi) for an extensive commentary with texts of the Principles.

shortfalls in conformity have been made good during the course of approving new proposals, notably by the substitution of uniform titles for form subheadings in relation to section 9.5.

With regard to the second guideline, the single most important contribution of this edition to meeting the needs of machine processing resides, in the submission of the authors, in the achievement of an integrated and standardized framework for the systematic description of all library materials, as presented by Part I. This achievement, being also the first such comprehensive systematization to be related to the goals of international standardization, is also presented by the authors as the principal fulfilment of the undertaking (in objective 4 above) to make a contribution to the development of an international cataloguing code, and as a major development in its own right.

It is also the principal means by which the third and fourth guidelines have been sustained, and by which resolution has been achieved of the conflict that was soon apparent between them and the programme initiated by IFLA, under the general heading of Universal Bibliographical Control (UBC), for the development of separate ISBDs for such materials as serials, maps, and nonbook materials.

Seeking to establish means of uniform description for all materials, JSCAACR could not easily reconcile AACR users' needs with those of the UBC programme on two counts: (1) the timetables of AACR revision and UBC were not in phase with each other; and (2) although harmonized in general terms with ISBD(M), the available drafts from the new ISBD working groups contained indications that in their final forms they would be insufficiently uniform in their relations with ISBD(M) and with each other; and thus they might be neither anticipated nor utilized in AACR as an integrated code.

Mindful of its undertaking to the Council on Library Resources, JSCAACR took the initiative of proposing to the IFLA Committee on Cataloguing that a standardized general framework, drawn up by joint editor Michael Gorman after scrutiny of the four main sources for nonbook materials and of other sources, should be developed jointly by JSCAACR and IFLA as a constraint within which both AACR and the evolving special-material ISBDs should be held; so that the fullest uniformity might be achieved within AACR, within ISBDs, and between ISBDs and AACR. The first meeting between JSCAACR (represented by all but one of its voting members and by both editors) and the IFLA committee with the chairpersons of all the then established ISBD working groups was held in Paris in October 1975, and substantial agreement was reached on the implementation of a general framework, to be known as ISBD(G). Further agreement on some modifications was reached at subsequent meetings, and Part I of this edition is based on the ISBD(G) framework determined by these agreements.

STRUCTURE AND WORKING METHODS

In each of the three participating countries the Joint Steering Committee's work has been supported and stimulated by a national committee, which initiated and/or screened very many of the proposals for revision and then reviewed and commented on the draft texts before their final form in this edition was settled.

In the United States the ALA/RTSD Catalog Code Revision Committee (CCRC) organized rule review and revision proposal teams to identify systematically the rules needing attention and to make their own proposals in respect of them, as well as to process those of other bodies. CCRC established working relations with other ALA/RTSD groups, notably the Serials Section's AACR Revision Study Committee, the Filing Committee, and with the Interdivisional Committee on Representation in Machine-Readable Form of Bibliographic Information (MARBI); and the entire membership of the Descriptive Cataloging Committee also participated in its work. Thirty organizations outside ALA were invited either to designate representatives to CCRC or to receive and comment on the Committee's documents.

In the United Kingdom a joint Library Association/British Library Committee on Revision of AACR, having equal representation from both organizations, performed a similar task in respect of the British Text. A close relationship was maintained with the Library Association Cataloguing and Indexing Group, under whose aegis consultations and meetings with representatives of numerous other interest groups and organizations were held; and a joint conference was convened with AACR-oriented library representatives of the Nordic countries of Europe. The formal input of comments and proposals from these and other countries outside the "Anglo-American" triangle was processed for JSCAACR by its Library of Congress representative; but the British committee was responsible for arranging and monitoring the review of final drafts by those other English-speaking countries who contributed to the input. This wider input and review were greatly assisted by the good offices of the Director of the IFLA International Office for UBC.

In Canada the Canadian Committee on Cataloguing/Comité canadien de catalogage (CCC) expressed the interests of the three national bodies that appoint its members: L'Association pour l'avancement des sciences et des techniques de la documentation, the Canadian Library Association, and the National Library of Canada. The committee called on the Canadian Association of Law Libraries, the Association of Canadian Map Libraries, and the Joint Advisory Committee for Nonbook Materials throughout the revision project for assistance in formulating its positions.

The input from these sources, from the Library of Congress's discussions among its own staff, and from the editors, was considered by JSCAACR at seven meetings between January 1975 and December 1976; five in the United States (New York, Washington (2), Chicago, and Princeton University), and one each in Canada (Toronto) and the United Kingdom (London). In January 1977 a draft of the emergent text of Part I was distributed for review to the national committees and by them to a wide range of outside organizations. This draft was followed by drafts of Part II in April 1977, in which month a special meeting of JSCAACR in Washington planned the concluding stages of drafting and copy preparation. The ninth and final meeting, to consider all proposals and comments of reviewers, to approve the whole text, and to authorize its presentation for publication, was held in Washington in August 1977.

ADOPTION STRATEGIES

In fulfilling their brief the Joint Steering Committee and the editors have striven to maintain as conservative an approach to revision as the demands of text reconciliation and closer uniformity, and the evidence of new needs from new circumstances, will allow. Most of what is here was already in the first edition, only made (if the attempt has been successful in this respect) more accessible to cataloguers and bibliographers in language and articulation, and more nearly related to what are seen as the normal sequences of cataloguing decision making in current practice, than before.

Some of the contents of the first edition (AACR 1) are not now included. They are those in which were provided options or alternatives inappropriate to the objectives of reconciliation and uniformity and those that treated of matters at a level of detail more appropriate to the interpretations and "in-house" rules of a single institution than to a code for all types and sizes of institutions. The absence of such details does not necessarily mean that observances of them by particular libraries should be abandoned.

Some of what is new does no more than extend the coverage of AACR to the newer categories of library materials with which cataloguers and bibliographers nowadays have to deal; and in this respect there should be little difficulty in adopting the new text.

But there are also some areas in which—looking ahead from current developments and seeking resolution of problems that, for all its excellence, AACR 1 did not entirely resolve—AACR 2 has introduced some changes and new directions that will lead to differences in the bibliographic record and in the types and forms of heading at which it is displayed. The treatment of description, corporate headings, uniform titles, and fullness of names are instanced.

Such changes have not been introduced without awareness of the difficulties that they raise for libraries with large retrospective files. Indeed, these difficulties were acknowledged to be at the heart of the compromises and occasional inconsistencies in AACR 1 of which, from the sheer weight of evidence of the need for better resolution, JSCAACR has felt most strongly impelled to attempt amelioration for the sake of future practice. It has also been felt that, with the increased flexibility of modern systems for processing bibliographic data and of catalogue formats, the inertia of the retrospective file is much less than it has been in the past. Many of the larger research libraries have, or may expect soon to have, the capability of relatively inexpensive conversion of at least part of their catalogues to more flexible forms of storage; and, too, there appears generally a much wider acceptance in libraries of the propriety and utility of simply closing old catalogues when they become too large to respond easily to new requirements of their users and starting new ones alongside them.

JSCAACR therefore envisions libraries and bibliographic agencies adopting first those rules (principally in Part I) the application of which has no significant effect on the arrangement and collocation of existing bibliographic records, even though some differences of style and content may occur between one record and another. The remaining provisions, where they differ from AACR 1 or from previous local practice, may then be most easily adopted at the time when newly designed cataloguing and bibliographic systems allow earlier records to be converted or reconciled or when a new sequence or catalogue is to come into being. In this connection there is a chronological checkpoint in the announced intention, earlier in 1978, of the Library of Congress, the National Library of Canada, the British Library, and the Australian National Library to adopt AACR2 as of January 1981, so that cumulations of their published bibliographic records from that date will reflect the new rules.

SOURCES

The principal published sources for this edition include, in addition to the texts for the first edition itself, the amendments and changes to the North American Text published in the Library of Congress *Cataloging Service* and to the British Text published in the Library Association *Anglo-American Cataloguing Rules Amendment Bulletin,* 1969 through 1975; the two revised texts of chapter 6 published respectively by ALA and the Library Association in 1974; and the North American Text revision of chapter 12 (ALA, 1975).

The other three primary sources for the development of rules for nonbook materials are *Non-book Materials Cataloguing Rules* / prepared by the Library Association Media Cataloguing Rules Committee. — London : National Council for Educational Technology, 1973. — (Working paper ; no. 11) ; *Nonbook Materials* : *the Organization of Integrated Collections* / by Jean Riddle Weihs, Shirley Lewis, Janet Macdonald. — 1st ed. — Ottawa : Canadian Library Association, 1973; and *Standards for Cataloging Nonprint Materials* : *an Interpretation and Practical Application* / by Alma Tillin and William J. Quinly. — 4th ed. — Washington : Association for Educational Communications and Technology, [1976].

Relevant sections of Part I, as of the revised chapter 6 above, are based on *ISBD(M)* : *International Standard Bibliographic Description for Monographic Publications*. — 1st standard ed. — London : IFLA Committee on Cataloguing, 1974; and, as noted above, Part I as a whole is closely related to *ISBD(G)* : *General International Standard Bibliographic Description* : *Annotated Text* / prepared by the Working Group on the General International Standard Bibliographic Description set up by the IFLA Committee on Cataloguing. — London : IFLA International Office for UBC, 1977.

In consideration of Part II, a principal reference source has been *Statement of Principles Adopted at the International Conference on Cataloguing Principles, Paris, October 1961*. — Annotated ed. with commentary and examples / by Eva Verona, assisted by . . . [others]. — London : IFLA Committee on Cataloguing, 1971. JSCAACR and the editors also acknowledge their debt to Eva Verona's *Corporate Headings* : *Their Use in Library Catalogues and National Bibliographies* : *a Comparative and Critical Study*. — London : IFLA Committee on Cataloguing, 1975.

ACKNOWLEDGMENTS

In his prefatorial acknowledgment of all those who contributed to the first edition, the chairman of the then Catalog Code Revision Committee observed that "rules are not lightly made or changed." Working on this edition, though with more limited objectives and occupying fewer years of their lives, has proved no less arduous for the many individuals who have been engaged in it. The members of the ALA Catalog Code Revision Committee, the Library Association/British Library Committee on Revision of AACR, and the Canadian Committee on Cataloguing, and the senior staff of the Library of Congress deserve very special thanks for the formidable accomplishment of their contributions: and their names are on the following pages. Our thanks extend to the many organizations and committees in several countries whose members are not listed in the following pages, but who have devoted time and trouble to assist in this, a truly international enterprise; and, of course, to the members of the Joint Steering Committee for Revision of AACR themselves, with an admirable record of 100 percent attendance through all the long and often weary meetings at which this edition has taken shape.

Our debt to the editors, for the commitment and inspiration they brought to their task, is obvious; but to the acknowledgment they will surely receive from those who discover the merits of their work by applying it, an addition of particular gratitude from those for whom they toiled is commanded for their achievement in meeting the very onerous deadlines that the schedule of the project required of them. A similar encomium is deserved by Carol Kelm, then executive secretary of ALA/RTSD, who acted as secretary to the Joint Steering Committee and without whose organizational, documentational, and administrative talents the committee's work could scarcely have been accomplished in this time. Mention must also be made of the special documentational contributions of Helen Schmierer and Robert M. Hiatt, both being important factors in the completion on schedule of the review of draft texts.

Finally, grateful acknowledgment is made to the American Library Association, the British Library, the Library Association, the Library of Congress, and the National Library of Canada for the financial and other supportive resources with which they sustained the project at both national and international levels; and to the Council on Library Resources, without whose generous financial support of the Joint Steering Committee and the editors this edition could not have been undertaken.

PETER R. LEWIS, *Chair*
Joint Steering Committee for Revision of AACR

AMERICAN LIBRARY ASSOCIATION
RESOURCES AND TECHNICAL SERVICES DIVISION
CATALOG CODE REVISION COMMITTEE

Chair: John D. Byrum

Lizbeth Bishoff
Winifred Duncan
Neal L. Edgar
Barbara Gates (1977–1978)
Doralyn J. Hickey
Frances Hinton
Carol Ishimoto (1974–1976)

Paul Kebabian (1974–1976)
Åke Koel
Joan Marshall (1977–1978)
Marian Sanner (1974)
Helen Schmierer (1976–1978)
Edith Scott
Gordon Stevenson (1974–1976)

Resource person: C. Sumner Spalding (1975–1977)
Recording secretary: Ann Murphy (1974–1976)
Marilyn Jones (1977–1978)

SUBCOMMITTEE ON RULES

FOR CATALOGING MACHINE-READABLE DATA FILES

Chair: Elizabeth Herman

Laurence W.S. Auld
Geraldine Dobbin (1974–1976)
Walter J. Fraser
Carolyn Kacena

Judith Rowe
Henriette D. Avram
Sharon Chapple Henry (1975–1978)

Consultants

AACR Revision Study Committee, Resources and Technical Services Division, ALA, Judith Cannan (1975–1978)
American Association of Law Librarians, Cecilia Kwan (1975–1978)
American Association of School Librarians, Robert Little
American Library History Round Table, ALA, Constance Rinehart
American Library Trustee Association, ALA, Lee Brawner (1974)
American National Standards Institute (1975–1976)
American Theological Library Association, Lydia Lo (1975–1978)
Art Libraries Society of North America, Nancy John
Association for Asian Studies (1975–1978)
Association for Educational Communications and Technology, Alma Tillin (1975–1976); William Quinly (1976–1978)
Association of American Library Schools, Constance Rinehart (1975–1978)
Association of College and Research Libraries, ALA, LeRoy Ortopan
Audiovisual Committee, ALA, Evelyn G. Clement (1975)
Catholic Library Association, Arnold M. Rzepecki (1975); Rev. Thomas Pater (1975–1978)

Children's Services Division, ALA, Annette Shockey (1974–1976)

Church and Synagogue Library Association (1975)

Committee on Computer Filing, Resources and Technical Services Division, ALA, Joseph Rosenthal (1975–1976)

Council on Library Resources (1975–1978)

Educational Media Council, Carolyn Whitenack (1975–1976)

Federal Librarians Round Table, ALA, Mary Sauer

Government Documents Round Table, ALA, Bernadine Hoduski

Health and Rehabilitative Library Services Division, ALA, Dallas R. Shawkey (1974); Marilyn Jones (1975–1978)

Information Science and Automation Division, ALA, Barbara Gates

Intellectual Freedom Round Table, Sanford Berman (1974); James R. Dwyer (1974–1978)

Joint Advisory Committee on Nonbook Materials, Margaret Chisholm (1975); Suzanne Massonneau (1975–1978)

Library Administration Division, ALA, Morris Schertz (1974–1976)

Library Research Round Table, ALA, Lawrence Leonard (1974); Helen Schmierer (1975–1978)

Medical Library Association, Emilie Wiggins (1975–1978)

Middle East Librarians Association, John A. Eilts (1975–1978)

Music Library Association, Katherine Skrobela (1975–1978)

National Federation of Abstracting and Indexing Services (1975–1978)

Reference and Adult Services Division, ALA, Concetta Sacco (1974–1976); David F. Kohl (1976–1978)

Representation in Machine-Readable Form of Bibliographic Information Committee, ALA, Ruth Tighe (1975); John Knapp (1975–1977)

Social Responsibilities Round Table, Sanford Berman (1974–1975); Joan Marshall (1975–1978)

Society of American Archivists (1975–1978)

Special Libraries Association (1975–1978)

Young Adult Services Division, ALA, Mary K. Chelton (1974)

DESCRIPTIVE CATALOGING COMMITTEE

Chair: Carolyn J. McMillen (*to* 1976)
Michael J. Fitzgerald (*from* 1976)

Allen Cohen (1977–   )
Arlene T. Dowell (1977–   )
Oliver T. Field (1974–1978)
Eugene R. Hanson (1973–1977)
Frances R. Ladd (1975–   )
Shirley Lewis (1975–1977)

Frances R.L. Needleman (1974–1976)
Leila Payne (1976–1978)
Carolyn A. Small (1975–   )
Gordon Stevenson (*to* 1975)
Donald E. Talkington (*to* 1975)
Alma Tillin (*to* 1975)

CANADIAN COMMITTEE ON CATALOGUING
COMITÉ CANADIEN DE CATALOGAGE

Chair: Jean Lunn (1974–1975)
Edwin Buchinski (1975–1978)

Jack Cain
Clarisse Cardin (*Executive
Secretary*)
Pierre Deslauriers

Ronald Hagler
Paule Rolland-Thomas
Hlib Sirko

LIBRARY ASSOCIATION–BRITISH LIBRARY
COMMITTEE ON REVISION OF AACR

Chair: Geoffrey E. Hamilton

Joyce E. Butcher
Richard E. Christophers
(*Secretary*)
Joel C. Downing
Philip K. Escreet
Robert J. Fulford

Eric J. Hunter
Alan E. Jeffreys
Mary E. Jesper
Peter R. Lewis
Christopher Ravilious
Malcolm R. Shifrin

CONTENTS

GENERAL INTRODUCTION

0.1. These rules are designed for use in the construction of catalogues and other lists in general libraries of all sizes. They are not specifically intended for specialist and archival libraries, but it is recommended that such libraries use the rules as the basis of their cataloguing and augment their provisions as necessary. The rules cover the description and entry of all library materials commonly collected at the present time, and the integrated structure of the text will facilitate the use of the general rules as a basis for cataloguing uncommonly collected materials of all kinds and library materials yet unknown.

0.2. This edition of the rules incorporates numerous agreements on the development of rules in the first edition and is based on a reconciliation of the British and North American texts of that edition. The reconciliation extends to style, which in this edition is generally in accordance with the University of Chicago Press *A Manual of Style*,[1] and to spellings, which are those of *Webster's New International Dictionary*.[2] Where Webster's gives as a permitted alternative a British spelling (e.g., *catalogue, centre*), this has been adopted; where the American usage is the only one specified (e.g., *capitalize*), it has been used in these rules. Agreement on terminology has similarly resulted sometimes in the use of an American term (e.g., *membership in*) and sometimes in a British term (e.g., *full stop*).

STRUCTURE OF THE RULES

0.3. The rules follow the sequence of cataloguers' operations in most present-day libraries and bibliographic agencies, in that Part I deals with the provision of information describing the item being catalogued and Part II deals with the determination and establishment of headings, or access points in the catalogue, under which the descriptive information is to be presented to catalogue users, and with the making

---

1. *A Manual of Style for Authors, Editors, and Copywriters.* — 12th ed. rev. — Chicago ; London : University of Chicago Press, 1969.

2. *Webster's Third New International Dictionary of the English Language, Unabridged* / editor in chief, Philip Babcock Gove and the Merriam-Webster editorial staff. — Springfield [Mass.] : Merriam ; London : Bell, 1961.

of references to those headings. Separate introductions to Parts I and II begin on page 7 and page 277 respectively.

0.4. In both parts the rules proceed from the general to the specific. In Part I the specificity relates to the physical medium of the item being catalogued, to the level of detail required for each element of the description, and to the analysis of an item containing separate parts.

MAIN ENTRY AND ALTERNATIVE HEADINGS

0.5. In Part II the rules are based on the proposition that one *main entry* is made for each item described, and that this is supplemented by *added entries*. The question of the use of *alternative heading* entries (i.e., sets of equal entries for each item described) was discussed but has not been embodied in the rules, largely because of the lack of time to explore the considerable implications of such a change. It is recognized, however, that many libraries do not distinguish between the main entry and other entries. It is recommended that such libraries use chapter 21 as guidance in determining all the entries required in particular instances. It will be necessary, however, for all libraries to distinguish the main entry from the others when:

        a) making a single entry listing
or b) making a single citation for a work (as required for entries for
        related works and for some subject entries).

In addition, the concept of main entry is considered to be useful in assigning uniform titles and in promoting the standardization of bibliographic citation.

STRUCTURE OF ENTRIES

0.6. The headings and/or uniform titles assigned to a description must be distinguished from the descriptive data either:

        a) by giving them on separate lines above the description
or b) by separating them from the description by a full stop and spaces.

If an entry begins with a title proper (i.e., the first element of the description) either:

        a) the title proper is repeated on a separate line above the description
or b) the description is given alone.

ALTERNATIVES AND OPTIONS

0.7. Some rules are designated as *alternative rules* or as *optional additions*, and some other rules or parts of rules are introduced by the word *optionally*. These provisions arise from the recognition that different solutions to a problem and differing levels of detail and specificity are appropriate in different contexts. Some alternatives and options should be decided as a matter of cataloguing policy for a particular catalogue or bibliographic agency and should therefore be exercised either always or never. Other alternatives and options should be exercised case by case. It is recommended that all cataloguing agencies distinguish between these two types of options and keep a record of their policy decisions and of the circumstances in which a particular option may be applied.

0.8. The word *prominently* (used in such phrases as *prominently named* and *stated prominently*) means that a statement to which it applies must be a formal statement found in one of the prescribed sources of information (see 1.0A) for areas 1 and 2 for the class of material to which the item being catalogued belongs.

0.9. The necessity for judgement and interpretation by the cataloguer is recognized in these rules. Such judgement and interpretation may be based on the requirements of a particular catalogue or upon the use of the items being catalogued. The need for judgement is indicated in these rules by words and phrases such as *if appropriate, important,* and *if necessary.* These indicate recognition of the fact that uniform legislation for all types and sizes of catalogues is neither possible nor desirable, and encourages the application of individual judgement based on specific local knowledge. This statement in no way contradicts the value of standardization. Such judgements must be applied consistently within a particular context and must be recorded by the cataloguing agency.

APPENDICES

0.10. Certain matters (abbreviations, capitalization, and the treatment of numerals) are considered to be of general application and are, therefore, dealt with in appendices. The instructions given in those appendices are, however, of the same force as the rules themselves and should be applied consistently. A glossary is given as the final appendix.

STYLE

0.11. In matters of style not covered by the rules (including the appendices), e.g., matters of punctuation other than prescribed punctuation, the University of Chicago Press *A Manual of Style* should be followed.

LANGUAGE PREFERENCES

0.12. The rules contain some instances in which a decision is made on the basis of languages and in which English is preferred. It is expected that users of the rules who do not use English as their working language will replace the specified preference for English by a preference for their working language. Authorized translations will be allowed to do the same.

0.13. The ALA/LC romanization tables[3] are used in examples in which romanization is called for. This usage is based on the recognition that these tables are used

---

3. *Cataloging Service* / Processing Department, Library of Congress. — Bull. 118 (summer 1976)–   . — Washington : Cataloging Distribution Service, Library of Congress, 1976–   .

by the overwhelming majority of libraries in Canada, the United Kingdom, and the United States. It is expected that authorized translations will, in examples, substitute romanizations derived from the standard romanization tables prevailing in libraries in the countries or areas for which the translation is intended.

EXAMPLES

0.14. The examples used throughout these rules are illustrative and not prescriptive. That is, they are intended to illuminate the provisions of the rule to which they are attached, rather than to extend those provisions. Neither the examples nor the form in which they are presented should be taken as instructions unless the accompanying text specifically states that they should.

Examples often have explanatory notes in italics added to them. These are not to be confused with notes to be added to the description by the cataloguer (see 1.7). In Part I of the rules, notes to be added to the description are indicated in the examples by the word *Note*. This word is not to be included in the actual description.

PART I. DESCRIPTION

INTRODUCTION

0.21. This part of the rules contains instructions on the formulation of descriptions of library materials. These descriptions need (in most instances) headings and/or uniform titles added to them before they are usable as catalogue entries. For instructions on the formulation of such access points, see Part II.

0.22. The rules for description are based on the general framework for the description of library materials, the General International Standard Bibliographic Description (ISBD(G)[1]), agreed between the International Federation of Library Associations and Institutions (IFLA) and the Joint Steering Committee for Revision of AACR. It follows that framework exactly in the order of elements and their prescribed punctuation. It was agreed with IFLA that it is not necessary for codes of rules to follow the terminology of the ISBD(G) exactly.

IFLA has developed, and is developing, specialized ISBDs for specific types of material, also on the basis of the ISBD(G). Close correspondence will therefore exist between chapters in Part I and the corresponding ISBD.

STRUCTURE OF PART I

0.23. The basic rules for the description of all library materials are to be found in chapter 1, which sets out all the rules that are of general applicability. Then follow rules for specific types of material (chapters 2–10) and rules of partial generality (chapters 11–13). There are no chapters numbered 14–20; Part II begins with chapter 21, the paragraphs of the Introduction to Part II being numbered 20.1, 20.2, etc.

The general chapter contains those rules that apply to all library materials. For example, rule 1.4B deals with the place of publication, distribution, etc., and all subsequent chapters refer the user to that rule for guidance on that topic. Where types of material demand specific treatment of a certain element, the general chapter contains only brief guidance and the user of the rules will find specific guidance in the

---

1. *ISBD(G) : General International Standard Bibliographic Description : Annotated Text* / prepared by the Working Group on the General International Standard Bibliographic Description set up by the IFLA Committee on Cataloguing. — London : IFLA International Office for UBC, 1977.

appropriate specific chapter. For example, rule 1.5 contains an indication of the type of information found in the physical description area; and detailed guidance on the physical description of sound recordings will be found in rule 6.5, on the physical description of motion pictures and video recordings in rule 7.5, and so on. The chapters in Part I can be used alone or in combination as the specific problem demands. For example, a difficult problem in describing a serial sound recording might lead the user to consult chapters 1, 6, and 12. The majority of problems, however, can be solved, once the rules have been studied comprehensively, by a single reference to a single rule.

Within the chapters the rule numbering has a mnemonic structure. Each rule number consists of the number of the chapter followed by a full stop and the number of the area within the description; in general the first (lettered) subdivision of each area denotes the element concerned. For example, rule 1.4C is concerned with the place of publication, etc., for all materials, rule 2.4C is concerned with the place of publication, etc., for printed monographs, rule 3.4C is concerned with the place of publication, etc., for cartographic materials, and so on. If a particular rule appearing in chapter 1 is not applicable to the material treated in a subsequent chapter, the rule is omitted from that chapter. For example, there are no rules numbered 2.7B15 and 2.7B16 because rules 1.7B15 and 1.7B16 are not applicable to books, etc.

METHODS OF PROCEDURE

0.24. It is a cardinal principle of the use of Part I that the description of a physical item should be based in the first instance on the chapter dealing with the class of materials to which that item belongs. For example, a printed monograph in microform should be described as a microform (using the rules in chapter 11). There will be need in many instances to consult the chapter dealing with the original form of the item, especially when constructing notes. So, using the same example, the chapter dealing with printed books (chapter 2) will be used to supplement chapter 11. In short, the starting point for description is the physical form of the item in hand, not the original or any previous form in which the work has been published.

In describing serials, chapter 12 should be consulted in conjunction with the chapter dealing with the physical form in which the serial is published. So, in describing serial motion pictures, both chapters 12 and 7 should be used.

0.25. An innovation of the ISBD(G) is the introduction of an area for details that are special to a particular class of material or type of publication. This area (area 3) is used in these rules for cartographic materials (see chapter 3) and for serials (see chapter 12). Area 3 is not to be used for any other materials treated in these rules. In describing a serial that consists of cartographic materials (e.g., a map series), area 3 may be repeated. In such case, give the area 3 details relating to the cartographic materials before those relating to the serial.

OPTIONS AND OMISSIONS

0.26. Although the rules for description are based upon a standard (the ISBD(G)), it is recognized that certain materials do not require every element of that standard. For this reason there are differences between the treatment of some materials and some others. For example, the physical description area is called the "extent of file area" in dealing with machine-readable data files. Again, the place of publication, etc., and the name of publisher, etc., elements are not used for manuscripts, some art originals, and some three-dimensional objects and artefacts.

0.27. All notes described in the chapters of Part I may be considered to be optional in that their inclusion in the entry depends on the nature of the item described and the purpose of the entry concerned. In addition, the wording of notes in the examples is not prescriptive (i.e., another wording may be chosen provided that it meets the general requirements of brevity and clarity).

0.28. The measurements prescribed in Part I for library materials are not all metric. They are the normal measurements used at this time in libraries in Canada, the United Kingdom, and the United States. Where no predominant system of measurement exists, metric measurements have been used. Metric measurements may be substituted for the nonmetric measurements when:

either   a)   in the course of time a metric measurement becomes the normal measurement for the materials in question

or   b)   the rules are being used in a country where only metric measurements are used.

0.29. Rule 1.0D contains a specification of three levels of description. Each of these levels is to be considered as a minimum in that, when appropriate, further information may be added to the required set of data. The three levels of description allow libraries flexibility in their cataloguing policy, because they prescribe an entry that is in conformity with bibliographic standards and yet allow some materials to be described in more detail than others. Libraries may choose to use the three levels of description:

either   a)   by choosing a level of description for all items catalogued in that library

or   b)   by drawing up guidelines for the use of all three levels in one catalogue depending on the type of item being described.

This standardization at three levels of description will help in achieving uniformity of cataloguing, and it is recommended that each record in a machine system carry an indication of the level at which the item has been described.

GENERAL RULES FOR DESCRIPTION

Contents

Contents

1.10   ITEMS MADE UP OF SEVERAL TYPES OF MATERIAL

1.11   FACSIMILES, PHOTOCOPIES, AND OTHER REPRODUCTIONS

1.0. GENERAL RULES

1.0A. Sources of information

1.0A1. Each chapter in Part I contains a specification of the chief source of information for each material or type of publication covered by that chapter. A source of information may be unitary in nature (e.g., a title page) or may be collective (e.g., the credits sequence of a motion picture). Prefer information found in that chief source to information found elsewhere. When the other sources of information are placed in a ranking order by specific chapters, follow that order. For each area of the description one or more sources of information are prescribed. Enclose in square brackets information taken from outside the prescribed source or sources.

1.0A2. Items lacking a chief source of information. If no part of the item supplies data that can be used as the basis of the description, take the necessary information from any available source, whether this be a reference work or the content of the item itself. This technique may be necessary for printed works, the title pages of which are lost; collections of pamphlets or other minor material assembled by the library or by a previous owner and which are to be catalogued as a single item; unprocessed sound recordings, etc. In all such cases give in a note the reason for and/or source of the supplied data.

1.0B. Organization of the description
The description is divided into the following areas:

> Title and statement of responsibility
> Edition
> Material (or type of publication) specific details
> Publication, distribution, etc.
> Physical description
> Series
> Note
> Standard number and terms of availability

Each of these areas is divided into a number of elements as set out in the rules in this and in following chapters.

1.0C. Punctuation
Precede each area, other than the first area, or each occurrence of a note or standard number, etc., area, by a full stop, space, dash, space (. —) unless the area begins a new paragraph.

1.0D *Levels of detail in the description*

Precede or enclose each occurrence of an element of an area with standard punctuation prescribed at the head of each section of this chapter.

Precede each mark of prescribed punctuation by a space and follow it by a space, except for the comma, full stop, hyphen (see 12.3A1), and opening and closing parentheses and square brackets. The comma, full stop, hyphen, and closing parenthesis and square bracket are not preceded by a space; the hyphen and the opening parenthesis and square bracket are not followed by a space.

Precede the first element of each area, other than the first element of the first area or the first element of an area beginning a new paragraph, by a full stop, space, dash, space. When that element is not present in a description, precede the first element that is present by a full stop, space, dash, space instead of the prescribed preceding punctuation for that element.

Indicate an interpolation (i.e., data taken from outside the prescribed source(s) of information) by enclosing it in square brackets. Indicate a conjectural interpolation by adding a question mark within the square brackets. Indicate the omission of part of an element by the mark of omission (. . .). Precede and follow the mark of omission by a space. Omit any area or element that does not apply in describing an individual item; also omit its prescribed preceding or enclosing punctuation. Do not indicate the omission of an area or element by the mark of omission.

When adjacent elements within one area are to be enclosed in square brackets, enclose them in one set of square brackets unless one of the elements is a general material designation, which is always enclosed in its own set of brackets.

Skaterdater [GMD] / [produced by] Marshal Backlar
but   [London : Phipps, 1870]

When adjacent elements are in different areas, enclose each element in a set of square brackets.

[2nd ed.]. — [London] : Thomsons, 1973

When an element ends with an abbreviation followed by a full stop or ends with the mark of omission and the punctuation following that element either is or begins with a full stop, omit the full stop that constitutes or begins the prescribed punctuation.

261 p. ; 24 cm. — (Canadian Ethnic Studies Association series ; v. 4)
not   261 p. ; 24 cm.. — (Canadian Ethnic Studies Association series ; v. 4)

When punctuation occurring within or at the end of an element is retained, give it with normal spacing. Prescribed punctuation is always added, even though double punctuation may result.

Quo vadis? : a narrative from the time of Nero

1.0D. Levels of detail in the description

The elements of description provided in the rules in this and in following chapters constitute a maximum set of information. This rule sets out three recommended levels of description containing those elements that must be given as a minimum by libraries and other cataloguing agencies choosing the level of description. Base the choice of a level of description on the purpose of the catalogue or catalogues for

14

which the entry is constructed. Include this minimum set of elements for all items catalogued at the chosen level when the elements are applicable to the item being described and when, in the case of *optional additions*, the library has chosen to include an optional element. If the rules in Part I specify other pieces of information in place of any of the elements set out below, include those other pieces of information. Consult individual rules in this chapter and in those following for the content of elements to be included. (See also 0.29.)

1.0D1. First level of description. For the first level of description, include at least the elements set out in this schematic illustration:

> Title proper / first statement of responsibility, if different from main entry heading in form or number or if there is no main entry heading. — Edition statement. — Material (or type of publication) specific details. — First publisher, etc., date of publication, etc. — Extent of item. — Note(s). — Standard number.

See 1.1B, 1.1F, 1.2B, 1.3, 1.4D, 1.4F, 1.5B, 1.7, 1.8B.

1.0D2. Second level of description. For the second level of description, include at least the elements set out in this schematic illustration:

> Title proper [general material designation] = parallel title : other title information / first statement of responsibility ; each subsequent statement of responsibility. — Edition statement / first statement of responsibility relating to the edition. — Material (or type of publication) specific details. — First place of publication, etc. : first publisher, etc., date of publication, etc. — Extent of item : other physical details ; dimensions. — (Title proper of series / statement of responsibility relating to series, ISSN of series ; numbering within the series. Title of subseries, ISSN of subseries ; numbering within subseries). — Note(s). — Standard number.

1.0D3. Third level of description. For the third level of description, include all elements set out in the following rules that are applicable to the item being described.

1.0E. Language and script of the description

In the following areas, give information transcribed from the item itself in the language and script (wherever practicable) in which it appears there:

> Title and statement of responsibility
> Edition
> Publication, distribution, etc.
> Series

Replace symbols or other matter that cannot be reproduced by the typographical facilities available with a cataloguer's description in square brackets. Make an explanatory note if necessary. (Cf. 1.1B1, 1.1F9, 1.2B2.)

1.0F *Inaccuracies*

In general, give interpolations into these areas in the language and script of the other data in the area. Exceptions to this are:

1) prescribed interpolations and abbreviations
2) general material designations (see 1.1C)
3) other forms of the place of publication (see 1.4C2)
4) statements of function of the publisher, distributor, etc. (see 1.4E)

If the other data are romanized, give interpolations according to the same romanization.

Give all elements in the other areas (other than the key-title (see 1.8C) and titles and quotations in notes) in the language and script of the cataloguing agency.

1.0F. Inaccuracies

Transcribe an inaccuracy or a misspelled word as it appears in the item. Follow such an inaccuracy either by [sic] or by the abbreviation *i.e.* and the correction within square brackets. Supply a missing letter or letters in square brackets.

> Some of me pomes [sic]

> The Paul Anthony Buck [i.e. Brick] lectures

> What your child really wants to know about sex, and why / by Will[i]am A. Block

1.0G. Accents and other diacritical marks

Add accents and other diacritical marks that are omitted from data found in the source of information in accordance with the usage of the language used in the context.

1.0H. Items with several chief sources of information

Single part items. Describe an item in one physical part from the first occurring chief source of information or that one that is designated as first, unless one of the following applies:

1) In cataloguing sound recordings, treat two or more chief sources of information as if they were a single source.
2) Prefer a chief source of information bearing a later date of publication, distribution, etc.
3) If the chief sources present the item in different aspects (e.g., as an individual item and as part of a multipart item), prefer the one that corresponds to the aspect in which the item is to be treated.
4) For items that contain written, spoken, or sung words for which there are chief sources of information in more than one language or script, prefer (in this order):
   a) the source in the language or script of the written, spoken, or sung words if there is only one such language or script or only one predominant language or script
   b) the source in the original language or script of the work if the words are

in more than one language or script, unless translation is known to be the purpose of the publication, in which case use the source in the language of the translation

c) the source in the language or script that occurs first in the following list: English, French, German, Spanish, Latin, any other language using the roman alphabet, Greek, Russian, any other language using the cyrillic alphabet, Hebrew, any other language using the Hebrew alphabet, any other language.

Multipart items. Describe an item in several physical parts from the chief source of information for the first part. If the first part is not available, use the first part that is. If there is no discernible first part, use the part that gives the most information. Failing this, use any part or a container that is a unifying element. Show variations in the chief sources of information of subsequent parts in notes, or by incorporating the data with those derived from the first part.

1.1. TITLE AND STATEMENT OF RESPONSIBILITY AREA

Contents:

1.1A. Preliminary rule

1.1A1. Punctuation

For instructions on the use of spaces before and after prescribed punctuation, see 1.0C.

Precede the title of a supplement or section (see 1.1B9) by a full stop.

Enclose the general material designation in square brackets.

Precede each parallel title by an equals sign.

Precede each unit of other title information by a colon.

Precede the first statement of responsibility by a diagonal slash.

Precede each subsequent statement of responsibility by a semicolon.

For the punctuation of this area for items without a collective title, see 1.1G2.

1.1A2. Sources of information.
Take information recorded in this area from the chief source of information for the material to which the item being described belongs. Enclose information supplied from any other source in square brackets.

Record the elements of data in the prescribed order, even if this means transposing data, unless case endings are affected, or the grammatical construction of the data would be disturbed, or one element is inseparably linked to another. In the latter cases, transcribe the data as found.

1.1B. Title proper

1.1B1. Transcribe the title proper exactly as to wording, order, and spelling, but not necessarily as to punctuation and capitalization. Give accentuation and other diacritical marks that are present in the chief source of information (see also 1.0G).

> Speedball technique charts
>
> Les misérables
>   (*Diacritic supplied*)
>
> The materials of architecture
>
> Supplement to The conquest of Peru and Mexico
>
> The 1919/20 Breasted Expedition to the Near East
>
> λ-calculus and computer theory
>
> Fourteen hours
>
> IV informe de gobierno

An alternative title is part of the title proper (see Glossary, Appendix D). Follow the first part of the title and the word *or* (or equivalent) with commas and capitalize the first word of the alternative title.

> Marcel Marceau, ou, L'art du mime

However, if the title proper as given in the chief source of information includes the punctuation marks . . . or [ ], replace them by — and (   ), respectively.

> If elected—
>   (*Source of information reads:* If elected . . .)

If the title proper as given in the chief source of information includes symbols that cannot be reproduced by the typographic facilities available, replace them with a cataloguer's description in square brackets. Make an explanatory note if necessary.

> Tables of the error function and its derivative, [reproduction of
> equations for the functions]

1.1B2. If the title proper includes a statement of responsibility or the name of a publisher, distributor, etc., and the statement or name is an integral part of the title proper (i.e., connected by a case ending or other grammatical construction), transcribe it as such.

> Marlowe's plays
>
> Eileen Ford's A more beautiful you in 21 days
>
> Ernst Günther läser Balzac
>
> La route Shell

1.1B3. If the title proper consists solely of the name of a person or body responsible for the item, give such a name as the title proper.

> Georges Brassens
>
> Conference on Industrial Development in the Arab Countries

1.1B4. Abridge a long title proper only if this can be done without loss of essential information. Never omit the first five words of the title proper (excluding the alternative title). Indicate omissions by the mark of omission.

1.1B5. If a letter or word appears only once but the design of the chief source of information makes it clear that it is intended to be read more than once, repeat the letter or word without the use of square brackets.

> *Chief source of information*
> Canadian BIBLIOGRAPHIES canadiennes

> *Transcription*
> Canadian bibliographies = Bibliographies canadiennes

If the first level of description is used (see 1.0D1), the transcription is:

> Canadian bibliographies

1.1B6. If a title proper includes separate letters or initials without full stops between them, record such letters without spaces between them.

> ALA rules for filing catalog cards

If such letters or initials have full stops between them, record them with full stops but without any internal spaces.

> T.U.E.I. occasional papers in industrial relations

> The most of S.J. Perelman

1.1B7. Supply a title proper for an item lacking the prescribed chief source of information or its substitute from the rest of the item, or a reference source, or elsewhere. If no title can be found in any source, devise a brief descriptive title. Enclose such a supplied or devised title in square brackets.

> [Carte de la lune]

> [Photograph of Theodore Roosevelt]

1.1B8. If the title proper appears in two or more languages or scripts, record as the title proper the one in the language or script of the main written, spoken, or sung content of the item. If this criterion is not applicable, choose the title proper by reference to the order of titles on, or the layout of, the chief source of information. Record the other titles as parallel titles (see 1.1D).

1.1B9. If the title proper for an item that is supplementary to, or a section of, another item appears in two or more parts not grammatically linked, record the title of the main work first, followed by the title(s) of the supplementary item(s) or section(s) in order of their dependence. Separate the parts of the title proper by full stops.

> Journal of biosocial science. Supplement
> (*Title appears on item as:* JOURNAL OF BIOSOCIAL SCIENCE
> Supplement . . .)

> Faust. Part one

1.1C. *Optional addition.* **General material designation**

1.1C1. Choose one of the lists of general material designations given below.

The following general material designations are recommended for British and North American use. If general material designations are to be used in cataloguing, British agencies should use terms from list 1 and North American agencies, terms from list 2.

LIST 1	LIST 2[1]
cartographic material	{ map { globe
graphic	⎧ art original ⎪ chart ⎪ filmstrip ⎪ flash card ⎨ picture ⎪ slide ⎪ technical drawing ⎩ transparency
machine-readable data file	machine-readable data file
manuscript	manuscript
microform	microform
motion picture	motion picture
multimedia	kit
music	music
object	⎧ diorama ⎪ game ⎨ microscope slide ⎪ model ⎩ realia
sound recording	sound recording
text	text
videorecording	videorecording

Use the terms from the list chosen in all descriptions for which general material designations are desired.[2]

1.1C2. If an item consists of material falling within one category in the list chosen, add the appropriate designation immediately following the title proper.

---

1. The following rules apply to list 2: (1) use *map* for cartographic charts, not *chart;* (2) for material treated in chapter 8, use *picture* for any item not subsumed under one of the other terms in list 2; (3) use *technical drawing* for items fitting the definition of this term in the Glossary, Appendix D; for architectural renderings, however, use *art original* or *picture*, not *technical drawing;* (4) use *kit* for any item containing more than one type of material if the relative predominance of components is not easily determinable and for the single-medium packages sometimes called "lab kits."

2. In all subsequent examples, other than those directly illustrating general material designations, the general material designation when indicated is given as ₍GMD₎. The use of ₍GMD₎ in examples does not imply that a designation is required.

How the poor view their health ₁machine-readable data file₁

British masters of the albumen print ₁microform₁

In the case of items having no collective title, add the appropriate designation immediately following the last title of a group of titles by the same author. If there are several authors, add the designation following the last statement of responsibility appertaining to a group of titles by the different·authors (see 1.1G2).

1.1C3. If the item is a reproduction in one material of a work originally presented in another material (e.g., a text as microform; a map on a slide), give the general material designation appropriate to the material being described (e.g., in the case of a map on a slide, give the designation appropriate to the slide).

1.1C4. If an item contains parts belonging to materials falling into two or more categories in the list chosen and if none of these is the predominant constituent of the item, give the designation *multimedia* or *kit* (see 1.1C1 and 1.10).

> Changing Africa ₁multimedia₁
> *or* Changing Africa ₁kit₁

1.1D. Parallel titles

1.1D1. Record parallel titles in the order indicated by their sequence on, or by the layout of, the chief source of information.

1.1D2. In preparing a second-level description (see 1.0D2), give the first parallel title. Give any subsequent parallel title that is in English. If no title is in English and the title proper is in a nonroman script, give the parallel title that is (in order of preference) in French, German, Spanish, Latin, or any other roman alphabet language.

> Wood Cree ₁GMD₁ = Les Cris des forêts
>
> Einführung in die Blutmorphologie ₁GMD₁ = Introduction to the morphology of blood
>
> Strassenkarte der Schweiz ₁GMD₁ = Carte routière de la Suisse = Road map of Switzerland

In preparing a third-level description (see 1.0D3), transcribe all parallel titles appearing in the chief source of information according to the instructions in 1.1B.

> Wood Cree ₁GMD₁ = Les Cris des forêts
>
> Einführung in die Blutmorphologie ₁GMD₁ = Introduction to the morphology of blood = Введение в морфологию крови
>
> Strassenkarte der Schweiz ₁GMD₁ = Carte routière de la Suisse = Road map of Switzerland = Carte stradale della Svizzera

1.1D3. Record an original title in a language different from that of the title proper appearing in the chief source of information as a parallel title if the item contains all or some of the text in the original language, or if the original title appears before the title proper in the chief source of information. Record an original title in the same language as the title proper, as other title information (see 1.1E). In all other cases give the original title in a note.

> Twenty love poems and a song of despair ₁GMD₁ = 20 poemas de
> amor y una canción desesperada
> (*Contains parallel Spanish text and English translation*)

1.1D4. Record parallel titles appearing outside the chief source of information in a note (see 1.7B5).

1.1E. Other title information

1.1E1. Transcribe all other title information appearing in the chief source of information according to the instructions in 1.1B.

> Edgar Wallace ₁GMD₁ : the man who made his name
>
> Winterthur ₁GMD₁ : an adventure in the past
>
> SPSS primer ₁GMD₁ : statistical package for the social sciences primer

1.1E2. Record other title information in the order indicated by the sequence on, or the layout of, the chief source of information.

> Distribution of the principal kinds of soil ₁GMD₁ : orders, suborders,
> and great groups : National Soil Survey classification of 1967

1.1E3. Lengthy other title information. If the other title information is lengthy, either give it in a note (see 1.7B5) or abridge it.

Abridge other title information only if this can be done without loss of essential information. Never omit the first five words of the other title information. Indicate omissions by the mark of omission.

1.1E4. If the other title information includes a statement of responsibility or the name of a publisher, distributor, etc., and the statement or name is an integral part of the other title information, transcribe it as such.

> The devil's dictionary ₁GMD₁ : a selection of the bitter definitions
> of Ambrose Bierce
>
> Robert Owen's American legacy ₁GMD₁ : proceedings of the Robert
> Owen Bicentennial Conference, Thrall Opera House, New Harmony,
> Indiana, October 15 and 16, 1971

1.1E5. Transcribe other title information following the title proper or parallel title to which it pertains.

> Love ₁GMD₁ : a novel = L'envers de l'histoire contemporaine : roman

If there are no parallel titles and if other title information appears in more than one language or script, give the other title information that is in the language or script of the title proper. If this criterion does not apply, give the other title information that appears first. *Optionally,* add the other title information in other languages.

Variants on a Czech love song ₁GMD₁ : for piano solo and woodwind choir : pour piano soliste et ensemble de bois

1.1E6. If the title proper needs explanation, make a brief addition as other title information, in the language of the title proper.

Longfellow ₁GMD₁ : ₁selections₁. —

Conference on Industrial Development in the Arab Countries ₁GMD₁ : ₁proceedings₁. —

1.1F. Statements of responsibility

1.1F1. Record statements of responsibility appearing prominently in the item in the form in which they appear there. If a statement of responsibility is taken from a source other than the chief source of information, enclose it in square brackets.

All that jazz ₁GMD₁ / Fats Waller

Stereogram book of fossils ₁GMD₁ : photographs of invertebrate fossils in 3 dimensions / by Philip A. Sandberg

Obiter dicta ₁GMD₁ / ₁A. Birrell₁
(*Statement appears on spine and cover only*)

Handley Cross ₁GMD₁ : a sporting tale / by the author of "Jorrocks' jaunts and jollities"

George Gissing and H.G. Wells ₁GMD₁ : their friendship and correspondence / edited, with an introduction, by Royal A. Gettmann

Map catalogue ₁GMD₁ / Ordnance Survey

Common service book of the Lutheran church ₁GMD₁ / authorized by the United Lutheran Church of America

1.1F2. If no statement of responsibility appears prominently in the item, neither construct one nor extract one from the content of the item.

Do not include statements of responsibility that do not appear prominently in the item in the title and statement of responsibility area. If such a statement is necessary, give it in a note.

1.1F3. If a statement of responsibility precedes the title proper in the chief source of information, transpose it to its required position unless case endings would be affected by the transposition. In the latter instance, see 1.1B2.

1.1F4. Record a single statement of responsibility as such whether the two or more persons or corporate bodies named in it perform the same function or different functions.

Thinking and reasoning ₁GMD₁ : selected readings / edited by P.C. Wason and P.N. Johnson-Laird

Puzzled people ₁GMD₁ : a study in popular attitudes to religion, ethics, progress, and politics in a London borough / prepared for the Ethical Union by Mass-Observation

1.1F5. When a single statement of responsibility names more than three persons or corporate bodies performing the same function, or with the same degree of responsibility, omit all but the first of each group of such persons or bodies. Indicate the omission by the mark of omission (. . .) and add *et al.* (or its equivalent in non-roman scripts) in square brackets.

>America's radical right ₍GMD₎ / Raymond Wolfinger . . . ₍et al.₎

>Dickens 1970 ₍GMD₎ : centenary essays / by Walter Allen . . . ₍et al.₎ ; edited by Michael Slater

>A short-title catalogue of books printed in England, Scotland & Ireland . . . 1475–1640 ₍GMD₎ / compiled by A.W. Pollard & G.R. Redgrave with the help of G.F. Barwick . . . ₍et al.₎
>   (*Ten other collaborators are named*)

>Proceedings of the Workshop on Solar Collectors for Heating and Cooling of Buildings, New York City, November 21–23, 1974 ₍GMD₎ / sponsored by the National Science Foundation, RANN—Research Applied to National Needs ; coordinated by University of Maryland . . . ₍et al.₎

1.1F6. If there is more than one statement of responsibility, record them in the order indicated by their sequence on, or by the layout of, the chief source of information. If the sequence and layout are ambiguous or insufficient to determine the order, record the statements in the order that makes the most sense. If statements of responsibility appear in sources other than the chief source, record them in the order that makes the most sense.

>Bits of paradise ₍GMD₎ : twenty-one uncollected stories / by F. Scott and Zelda Fitzgerald ; selected by Scottie Fitzgerald Smith and Matthew J. Bruccoli ; with a foreword by Scottie Fitzgerald Smith

>A saint in Philadelphia ₍GMD₎ : John Neumann / Raymond C. Kammerer and Carl R. Steinbecker ; made by Creative Sights & Sounds

>Exploration of the solar system ₍GMD₎ / prepared by members of the AIAA Technical Committees on Space Systems and Space Atmospheric Physics ; edited by Arthur Henderson, Jr., and Jerry Grey

1.1F7. Include titles and abbreviations of titles of nobility, address, honour, and distinction, initials of societies, qualifications, etc., with the names of persons in statements of responsibility if:

a) such a title is necessary grammatically

>. . . prólogo del Excmo. Sr. D. Manuel Fraga Iribarne

b) the omission would leave only the person's given name or surname

>. . . / by Miss Jane

>. . . / by Dr. Johnson

c) the title is necessary to identify the person

>. . . / by Mrs. Charles H. Gibson

d) the title is a title of nobility or is a British title of honour (Sir, Dame, Lord, or Lady).

Omit all other titles, etc., from the names of persons in statements of responsibility. Do not use the mark of omission.

> . . . / by Harry Smith
> (*Source of information reads:* by Dr. Harry Smith)

1.1F8. Add an explanatory word or short phrase to the statement of responsibility if the relationship between the title and the person(s) or body (bodies) named in the statement is not clear.

> Baijun ballads ₁GMD₁ / ₁collected by₁ Chet Williams
>
> Piers Plowman ₁GMD₁ / ₁edited by₁ Elizabeth Salter

but

> Bleak House ₁GMD₁ / Charles Dickens
>
> Brief guide ₁GMD₁ / National Gallery of Art
>
> Beggars banquet ₁GMD₁ / the Rolling Stones

1.1F9. Replace symbols or other matter that cannot be reproduced by the typographic facilities available with the cataloguer's description in square brackets. Make an explanatory note if necessary.

> Over the border ₁GMD₁ : Acadia, the home of "Evangeline"/ by ₁E.B.C.₁
> *Note:* Author's initials represented by musical notes on title page

1.1F10. If an item has parallel titles but a statement or statements of responsibility in only one language or script, give the statement of responsibility after all the parallel titles or other title information.

> Jeux de cartes pour enfants ₁GMD₁ = Children's playing cards / par Giovanni Belgrado et Bruno Munari

1.1F11. If an item has parallel titles and a statement or statements of responsibility in more than one language or script, give each statement after the title proper, parallel title, or other title information to which it relates.

> Familias norte-americanas ₁GMD₁ : los De Stefano / colaborador de educación, Beryl L. Bailey = American families : the De Stefanos / educational collaborator, Beryl L. Bailey

If it is not practicable to give the statements of responsibility after the titles to which they relate, give the statement of responsibility in the language or script of the title proper and omit the others.

> Concerto in c-Moll für Cembalo (Klavier) und Streicher ₁GMD₁ = Concerto in C minor for harpsichord (piano) and strings / Carl Philipp Emanuel Bach ; herausgegeben von György Balla
> (*Statement about editor appears in German and English*)

1.1F12. Treat a noun phrase occurring in conjunction with a statement of responsibility as other title information if it is indicative of the nature of the work.

> Characters from Dickens [GMD] : dramatised adaptations / by
> Barry Campbell

If the noun or noun phrase is indicative of the role of the person(s) or body (bodies) named in the statement of responsibility rather than of the nature of the work, treat it as part of the statement of responsibility.

> Roman Britain ₍GMD₎ / research and text by Colin Barham

In case of doubt, treat the noun or noun phrase as part of the statement of responsibility.

1.1F13. When a name associated with responsibility for the item is transcribed as part of the title proper (see 1.1B2) or other title information (see 1.1E4), do not make any further statement relating to that name unless such a statement is required for clarity, or unless a separate statement of responsibility including or consisting of that name appears in the chief source of information.

> Goethes Stücke ₍GMD₎. —

but

> Feminism and Vivian Gornick ₍GMD₎ / Vivian Gornick
> (*Name of author appears separately in the chief source of
> information as well as in the title proper*)

> Malo's complete guide to canoeing and canoe-camping ₍GMD₎ /
> by John Malo

> The John Franklin Bardin omnibus ₍GMD₎ / John Franklin Bardin
> (*Name of author appears separately in the chief source of
> information as well as in the title proper*)

1.1F14. Transcribe a statement of responsibility even if no person or body is named in that statement.

> Korean phrases ₍GMD₎ / by a group of students with a Korean
> resource person

> Call of love ₍GMD₎ / translated from the Danish

1.1F15. Omit statements found in the chief source of information that neither constitute other title information nor form part of statements of responsibility. A phrase such as "with a spoken commentary by the artist" is a statement of responsibility. Statements of responsibility may include words or phases which are neither names nor linking words (e.g., . . . / written by Jobe Hill in 1812).

1.1G. Items without a collective title

1.1G1. If, in an item lacking a collective title, one work is the predominant part of the item, treat the title of that part as the title proper and name the other parts in a note (see 1.7B18).

1.1G2. If, in an item lacking a collective title, no one part predominates, record the titles of the individually titled parts in the order in which they are named in the chief source of information, or in the order in which they appear in the item if there is no single chief source of information. Separate the titles of the parts by semicolons if the parts are all by the same person(s) or body (bodies), even if the titles are linked by a connecting word or phrase. If the individual parts are by different persons or bodies, or in case of doubt, follow the title of each part by its parallel titles, other title information, and statements of responsibility and a full stop followed by two spaces.

> Clock symphony (no. 101) ; Surprise symphony (no. 94) ₍GMD₎ / Haydn

> Lord Macaulay's essays ; and, Lays of ancient Rome ₍GMD₎

> Saudades do Brasil : suite de danses pour orchestre / Darius Milhaud. Symphonie concertante pour trompette et orchestre / Henry Barraud ₍GMD₎

> Le prince / Machiavel. Suivi de L'anti-Machiavel de Frédéric II ₍GMD₎
>> (*At head of title:* Machiavel)
>> (*Title:* Le prince, suivi de L'anti-Machiavel de Frédéric II)

1.1G3. Make the relationship between statements of responsibility and titles clear by additions, as instructed in 1.1F8.

1.1G4. If, in an item lacking a collective title, more than one (but not all) of the separately titled parts predominate, treat the predominating parts as instructed in 1.1G2, and name the other parts in a note (see 1.7B18).

1.2. EDITION AREA

Contents:

1.2A. Preliminary rule
1.2B. Edition statement
1.2C. Statements of responsibility relating to the edition
1.2D. Subsequent edition statement
1.2E. Statements of responsibility relating to a subsequent edition statement

1.2A Preliminary rule

1.2A1. Punctuation

For instructions on the use of spaces before and after prescribed punctuation, see 1.0C.

Precede this area by a full stop, space, dash, space.

Precede a subsequent edition statement by a comma.

Precede the first statement of responsibility following an edition or subsequent edition statement by a diagonal slash.

Precede each subsequent statement of responsibility by a semicolon.

1.2A2. Sources of information. Record in this area information taken from the chief source of information or from any other source specified for this area in the following chapters. Enclose any information supplied from any other source in square brackets.

1.2B. Edition statement

1.2B1. Transcribe the edition statement as found on the item. Use standard abbreviations (see Appendix B) and numerals in place of words (see Appendix C).

> *Source of information*
> Ny udgave

> *Transcription*
> Ny udg.

> *Source of information*
> Second edition

> *Transcription*
> 2nd ed.

1.2B2. If the edition statement consists solely or chiefly of characters that are neither numeric nor alphabetic, record the statement in words in the language and script of the title proper and enclose them in square brackets.

> [Three asterisks] ed.

If the edition statement consists of a letter or letters and/or a number or numbers without accompanying words, add an appropriate word or abbreviation.

> 3e [éd.]

> [State] B

1.2B3. In case of doubt about whether a statement is an edition statement, take the presence of such words as *edition, issue, version* (or their equivalents in other languages) as evidence that such a statement is an edition statement, and record it as such.

> South-west gazette [GMD]. — Somerset ed.

> Subbuteo table soccer [GMD]. — World Cup ed.

1.2B4. *Optional addition.* If an item lacks an edition statement but is known to contain significant changes from previous editions, supply a suitable brief statement in the language and script of the title proper and enclose it in square brackets.

> [New ed.]

> [3e éd.]

> [2nd ed., partly rev.]

1.2B5. If an edition statement appears in more than one language or script, record the statement that is in the language or script of the title proper. If this criterion does not apply, record the statement that appears first (but see also 12.2B3).

1.2B6. If an item lacking a collective title contains one or more works with an associated edition statement(s), record such statements following the titles and statements of responsibility to which they relate, separated from them by a full stop.

> Le western / textes rassemblés et présentés par Henri Agel. Nouv.
> éd. Évolution et renouveau du western (1967–1968) / par Jean
> A. Gili ₍GMD₎

1.2C. Statements of responsibility relating to the edition

1.2C1. Record a statement of responsibility relating to one or more editions, but not to all editions, of a given work following the edition statement if there is one. Follow the instructions in 1.1F for the transcription and punctuation of such statements.

> The nether world ₍GMD₎ : a novel / George Gissing. — ₍New ed.,
> repr.₎ / edited, with an introduction, by John Goode

> Shachiapang ₍GMD₎ : a modern revolutionary Peking opera. —
> May 1970 script / revised collectively by the Peking Opera Troupe
> of Peking

1.2C2. In case of doubt about whether a statement of responsibility applies to all editions or only to some, or if there is no edition statement, give such a statement in the title and statement of responsibility area. When describing the first edition, give all statements of responsibility in the title and statement of responsibility area (see 1.1F).

> The prelude, 1798–1799 ₍GMD₎ / by William Wordsworth ; edited
> by Stephen Parrish

1.2D. Subsequent edition statement

1.2D1. If an item is designated as a reissue containing changes from a particular edition, give that statement following the edition statement and its statements of responsibility.

> The pocket Oxford dictionary of current English ₍GMD₎ / compiled
> by F.G. Fowler & H.W. Fowler. — 4th ed. / revised by H.G. Le
> Mesurier and E. McIntosh, Repr. with corrections

> The natural history of Selborne in the county of Southampton
> ₍GMD₎ / by Gilbert White. — World's classics ed., New ed., rev., reset,
> and illustrated

1.2E. Statements of responsibility relating to a subsequent edition statement

1.2E1. Record a statement of responsibility relating to one or more designated subsequent editions (but not to all subsequent editions) of a particular edition following the subsequent edition statement. Follow the instructions in 1.1F for the transcription and punctuation of such statements of responsibility.

The elements of style ₍GMD₎ / by William Strunk, Jr. — Rev. ed.
/ with revisions, an introduction, and a chapter on writing by E.B.
White, 2nd ed. / with the assistance of Eleanor Gould Packard

1.3. MATERIAL (OR TYPE OF PUBLICATION) SPECIFIC DETAILS AREA

Precede this area with a full stop, space, dash, space.

This area will be used in the description of cartographic materials (chapter 3) and serial publications (chapter 12). See those chapters for the contents of this area and its internal prescribed punctuation.

1.4. PUBLICATION, DISTRIBUTION, ETC., AREA

Contents:

1.4A. Preliminary rule
1.4B. General rules
1.4C. Place of publication, distribution, etc.
1.4D. Name of publisher, distributor, etc.
1.4E. Statement of function of publisher, distributor, etc.
1.4F. Date of publication, distribution, etc.
1.4G. Place of manufacture, name of manufacturer, date of manufacture

1.4A. Preliminary rule

1.4A1. Punctuation

For instructions on the use of spaces before and after prescribed punctuation, see 1.0C.

Precede this area by a full stop, space, dash, space.

Precede a second or subsequently named place of publication, distribution, etc., by a semicolon.

Precede the name of a publisher, distributor, etc., by a colon.

Enclose a supplied statement of function of a publisher, distributor, etc., in square brackets.

Precede the date of publication, distribution, etc., by a comma.

Enclose the details of manufacture (place, name, date) in parentheses.

Precede the name of a manufacturer by a colon.

Precede the date of manufacture by a comma.

1.4A2. Sources of information. Record in this area information taken from the chief source of information or from any other source specified for this area in the following chapters. Enclose information supplied from any other source in square brackets.

1.4B. General rules

1.4B1. This area is used to record all information about the place, name, and date of all types of publishing, distributing, releasing, and issuing activities.

1.4B2. Information relating to the manufacture of the item is also recorded in this area.

1.4B3. The places, names, and dates relating to publication, distribution, etc., may be repeated in any order that is appropriate to the item being described (see 1.4B8).

1.4B4. Give names of places, persons, or bodies as they appear, omitting accompanying prepositions unless case endings would be affected.

> Berolini
>
> Den Haag
>
> . . . : Im Deutschen Verlag

but Paris

not A Paris

1.4B5. If the publication, distribution, etc., details appear in more than one language or script, record the details that are in the language or script of the title proper. If this criterion does not apply, record the details that appear first.

1.4B6. If the original publication details are covered by a label containing publication details relating to a reproduction, give the publication details of the reproduction in this area. Give the publication details of the original in a note if they can be easily ascertained.

1.4B7. If an item is known to have fictitious publication, distribution, etc., details, record these in the conventional order. Supply the real publication, distribution, etc., details as a correction if these are known.

> Belfast ₁i.e. Dublin₁
>
> Paris : Impr. Vincent, 1798 ₁i.e. Bruxelles : Moens, 1883₁

1.4B8. If an item has two or more places of publication, distribution, etc., and/or names of publishers, distributors, etc., named in it, describe it in terms of the first named place of publication, distribution, etc., and the corresponding publisher, distributor, etc. Always add the place and name of a publisher if the first named place refers to a distributor, releasing agency, etc. If any subsequent place or name is distinguished by the layout of the source of information as being that of the principal publisher, etc., add that place and name.

Follow this rule for items issued in more than one physical part when the place of publication, etc., and/or the name of the publisher, etc., changes in the course of publication.

If a place in the country of the cataloguing agency, with or without a corresponding publisher, etc., is named in a secondary position, add the information relating to it.

> London ; New York : Longmans, Green
>   *(For a cataloguing agency in the United States)*
>
> Paris : Gauthier-Villars ; Chicago : University of Chicago Press
>   *(For a cataloguing agency in the United States)*
>
> New York ; London : McGraw-Hill
>   *(For a cataloguing agency in the United Kingdom)*

31

1.4C *Place of publication, distribution, etc.*

> New York : Dutton ; Toronto : Clarke, Irwin
> (*For a cataloguing agency in Canada*)
>
> London : Macmillan for the University of York

1.4C. Place of publication, distribution, etc.

1.4C1. Record the place of publication, etc., in the form and the grammatical case in which it appears.

> Köln
>
> Lugduni Batavorum

1.4C2. Add another form of the name of the place if such an addition is considered desirable as an aid to identifying the place.

> Lerpwl ₍Liverpool₎
>
> Christiania ₍Oslo₎

1.4C3. Add the name of the country, state, province, etc., to the name of the place if it is considered necessary for identification, or if it is considered necessary to distinguish the place from others of the same name. Use the English form of name if there is one (see 23.2A). Use abbreviations appearing in Appendix B.

> *City alone appears in prescribed source of information*
> Waco ₍Tex.₎
>
> London ₍Ont.₎
>
> Santiago ₍Chile₎
>
> Renens ₍Switzerland₎
>
> *City and country, etc., appear in prescribed source of information*
> Tolworth, England
>
> Carbondale, Ill.

1.4C4. If a place name is found only in an abbreviated form in the prescribed source of information, give it as found, and add the full form or complete the name.

> Mpls ₍i.e. Minneapolis₎
>
> Rio ₍de Janeiro₎

1.4C5. If a publisher, distributor, etc., has offices in more than one place and these are named in the item, always give the first named place, and the first of any subsequently named places that is in the home country of the cataloguing agency or is given prominence by the layout of the source of information. Omit all other places.

> London ; New York
> (*For a cataloguing agency in the United States*)
>
> Montréal ; Toronto
> (*Toronto given prominence by typography*)

1.4C6. If the place of publication, distribution, etc., is uncertain, give the probable place in the language of the chief source of information, with a question mark.

> ₍Hamburg?₎

If no probable place can be given, give the name of the country, state, province, etc. If, in such a case, the country, state, province, etc., is not certain, give it with a question mark.

> ₍Canada₎

> ₍Chile?₎

If no place or probable place can be given, give the abbreviation *s.l.* (sine loco), or its equivalent in nonroman scripts.

> ₍S.l.₎

1.4C7. *Optionally,* add the full address of a publisher, distributor, etc., to the name of the place. Enclose such an addition in parentheses. Do not add the full address for major trade publishers.

> London (35 Notting Hill Gate, London, W. 11)

1.4D. Name of publisher, distributor, etc.

1.4D1. Give the name of the publisher, distributor, etc., following the place(s) to which it relates.

> London : Macmillan

> New York ; London : McGraw-Hill

> London : Sussex Tapes ; Wakefield : Educational Productions

1.4D2. Give the name of a publisher, distributor, etc., in the shortest form in which it can be understood and identified internationally.

> : Penguin

> *not* : Penguin Books

> : W. H. Allen

> *not* : Allen

> > (*Avoids confusion with other publishers called Allen*)

1.4D3. Do not omit from the phrase naming a publisher, distributor, etc.:

a) words or phrases indicating the function (other than solely publishing) performed by the person or body

> : Printed for the CLA by the Morriss Print. Co.

> : Distributed by New York Graphic Society

> : In Kommission bei O. Harrassowitz

> *but* : Allen & Unwin

> *not* : Published by Allen & Unwin

33

    b) parts of the name required to differentiate between publishers, distributors, etc.

> : Longmans, Green

> : Longmans Educational

not   : Longmans

1.4D4. If the name of the publisher, distributor, etc., appears in a recognizable form in the title and statement of responsibility area, give it in the publication, distribution, etc., area in a shortened form. If, in such a case, the publisher, distributor, etc., is a person rather than a corporate body, give the initials and the surname of the person.

> The wonder of new life ₍GMD₎ / Cleveland Health Museum. — Cleveland : The Museum, 1971

> Fichier de terminologie ₍GMD₎ / Office de la langue française, Centre de terminologie. — Québec : O.L.F., 1972–

> Even the waitresses were poets ₍GMD₎ / Daisy Warren. — Iowa City : D. Warren, 1971

1.4D5. If two or more agencies are named as performing the same function, always include the first named agency and add any agency given prominence by typography.

> Toronto : McClelland and Stewart : World Crafts Council
> (*Second publisher given prominence by typography*)

1.4D6. If the name of the publisher, distributor, etc., is unknown, give the abbreviation *s.n.* (sine nomine) or its equivalent in nonroman scripts.

> Paris : ₍s.n.₎

1.4D7. In case of doubt about whether a named agency is a publisher or a manufacturer, treat it as a publisher.

1.4E. *Optional addition.* **Statement of function of publisher, distributor, etc.**

1.4E1. Add to the name of a publisher, distributor, etc., one of the terms below:

> distributor
> publisher
> producer
>   (*used for a producing entity other than a production company*)
> production company

unless:
    a) the phrase naming the publisher, distributor, etc., includes words that indicate the function performed by the person(s) or body (bodies) named

or b) the function of the publishing, distributing, etc., agency is clear from the context.

> Montréal : National Film Board of Canada ₍production company₎ ;
> London : Guild Sound and Vision ₍distributor₎

London : Macmillan : Educational Service ₍distributor₎

but

New York : Released by Beaux Arts

Oliver Twist ₍GMD₎ / Charles Dickens. — London : Chapman and Hall, 1939

1.4F. Date of publication, distribution, etc.

1.4F1. Give the date of publication, distribution, etc., of the edition named in the edition area. If there is no edition statement, give the date of the first edition. Give dates in Western-style arabic numerals. If the date found in the item is not of the Gregorian or Julian calendar, give the date as found and follow it with the year(s) of the Gregorian or Julian calendar.

, 1975

, 4308 ₍1975₎

, ₍4308 i.e. 1975₎

, 5730 ₍1969 or 1970₎

, anno 18 ₍1939₎ (*not* anno XVIII)

, 1976 (*not* ۱۹۷۶)

1.4F2. Give the date as found in the item even if it is known to be incorrect. If a date is known to be incorrect, add the correct date.

, 1697 ₍i.e. 1967₎

If necessary, explain any discrepancy in a note.

, 1963 ₍i.e. 1971₎
Note: Originally issued as a sound disc in 1963; issued as a cassette in 1971.

1.4F3. Give the date of a particular reissue of an edition as the date of publication only if the reissue is specified in the edition area (see 1.2D). In this case, give only the date of the reissue.

1.4F4. If the publication date differs from the date of distribution, add the date of distribution if it is considered to be significant by the cataloguing agency. If the publisher and distributor are different, give the date(s) after the name(s) to which they apply.

London : Macmillan, 1971 ₍distributed 1973₎

London : Educational Records, 1973 ; New York : Edcorp ₍distributor₎, 1975

Toronto : Royal Ontario Museum, 1971 ; Beckenham ₍Kent₎ : Edward Patterson ₍distributor₎
(*Distribution date known to be different but not recorded*)

35

If the publication and distribution dates are the same, give the date after the last named publisher, distributor, etc.

> New York : American Broadcasting Co. ₁production company₁ :
> Released by Xerox Films, 1973

1.4F5. *Optional addition.* Add the latest date of copyright following the publication, distribution, etc., date if it is different.

> , 1967, c1965

1.4F6. If the dates of publication, distribution, etc., are unknown, give the copyright date or, in its absence, the date of manufacture (indicated as such) in its place.

> , c1967

> , 1967 printing

1.4F7. If no date of publication, distribution, etc., copyright date, or date of manufacture can be assigned to an item, give an approximate date of publication.

, ₁1971 or 1972₁	*One year or the other*
, ₁1969?₁	*Probable date*
, ₁between 1906 and 1912₁	*Use only for dates less than 20 years apart*
, ₁ca. 1960₁	*Approximate date*
, ₁197–₁	*Decade certain*
, ₁197–?₁	*Probable decade*
, ₁18—₁	*Century certain*
, ₁18—?₁	*Probable century*

1.4F8. If two or more dates are found on the various parts of a multipart item (e.g., if such an item is published in parts over a number of years), give the earliest and latest dates.

> , 1968–1973

In describing a multipart item that is not yet complete, give the earliest date only, and follow it with a hyphen and four spaces.

> , 1968–

Optionally, when the item is complete, add the latest date.

1.4G. Place of manufacture, name of manufacturer, date of manufacture

1.4G1. If the name of the publisher is unknown, give the place and name of the manufacturer if they are found in the item.

> ₁S.l. : s.n.₁, 1970 (London : High Fidelity Sound Studios)

1.4G2. In recording the place and name of the manufacturer, follow the instructions in 1.4B–1.4D.

1.4G3. If the date of manufacture is given in place of an unknown date of publication, distribution, etc. (see 1.4F6), do not repeat it here.

1.4G4. *Optional addition.* Give the place, name of manufacturer, and/or date of manufacture if they differ from the place, name of publisher, distributor, etc., and date of publication, distribution, etc., and are found in the item and are considered important by the cataloguing agency.

> London : Arts Council of Great Britain, 1976 (Twickenham : CTD Printers, 1974)

> Harmondsworth : Penguin, 1949 (1963 printing)

1.5. PHYSICAL DESCRIPTION AREA

Contents:
- 1.5A. Preliminary rule
- 1.5B. Extent of item (including specific material designation)
- 1.5C. Other physical details
- 1.5D. Dimensions
- 1.5E. Accompanying material

1.5A. Preliminary rule

1.5A1. Punctuation

For instructions on the use of spaces before and after prescribed punctuation, see 1.0C.

Precede this area by a full stop, space, dash, space *or* start a new paragraph.
Precede other physical details (i.e., other than extent or dimensions) by a colon.
Precede dimensions by a semicolon.
Precede a statement of accompanying material by a plus sign.
Enclose physical details of accompanying material in parentheses.

1.5A2. Sources of information. Take information for this area from any source. Take explicitly or implicitly stated information from the item itself. Enclose information in square brackets only when specifically instructed by the following chapters.

1.5A3. If an item is available in different formats (e.g., as text and microfilm; as sound disc and sound tape reel), give the physical description of the format in hand. *Optionally,* make a note describing other formats in which it is available (see 1.7B16).

1.5B. Extent of item (including specific material designation)

1.5B1. Record the number of physical units of the item being described by giving the number of parts in arabic numerals and the specific material designation as detailed in the following chapters.

> 3 microscope slides
>
> 1 jigsaw puzzle
>
> 3 v.
>
> 1 hand puppet

1.5B2. Describe single-part printed text items as detailed in chapter 2.

> 327 p.

1.5B3. Specify, in addition, the number of components as detailed in the following chapters.

> 1 microfiche (150 fr.)
>
> 3 v. (1397 p.)

1.5B4. If the material being described has a playing time, specify the latter as detailed in the following chapters.

> 2 sound discs (1 hr., 30 min.)
>
> 1 film loop (5 min., 30 sec.)
>
> 1 sound tape reel (25 min.)

1.5B5. In describing a multipart item that is not yet complete, give the specific material designation alone preceded by three spaces.

> ₍3 spaces₎ microscope slides
>
> ₍3 spaces₎ v.

Optionally, when the item is complete, add the number of physical units.

1.5C. Other physical details

1.5C1. Give physical data (other than extent or dimensions) about an item as instructed in the following chapters.

> 1 filmstrip (70 fr.) : b&w
>
> 321 p. : ill. (some col.)
>
> 5 microscope slides : stained
>
> 1 sound disc (20 min.) : 33⅓ rpm, mono.
>
> 1 model (4 pieces) : polystyrene

1.5D. Dimensions

1.5D1. Give the dimensions of an item as instructed in the following chapters.

> 1 wall chart : col. ; 24 × 48 cm.
>
> 321 p. : ill. (some col.) ; 23 cm.
>
> 6 microreels ; 35 mm.
>
> 1 sound disc (20 min.) : 33⅓ rpm, stereo. ; 12 in.

1.5E. Accompanying material

1.5E1. There are four ways of recording information about accompanying material:

a) record the details of the accompanying material in a separate entry *rarely do this*

or b) record the details of the accompanying material in a multilevel description (see chapter 13) *LC won't ever do this* *Keep it together!*

or c) record the details of the accompanying material in a note (see 1.7B11)

> Accompanied by atlas "A demographic atlas of North-west Ireland" (39 p. : col. maps ; 36 cm.), previously published separately in 1956

> Teacher's guide (24 p.) by Robert Garry Shirts

> Accompanied by filmstrip entitled: Mexico and Central America

or d) record the name of accompanying material at the end of the physical description.

> 387 p. : ill. ; 27 cm. + teacher's notes

> 32 p. : col. ill. ; 28 cm. + 3 maps

> 271 p. : ill. ; 21 cm. + 1 atlas

Optional addition. If method *d* is applicable and further physical description is desired, add a statement of the extent, other physical details, and dimensions of the accompanying material as appropriate. Formulate such additional descriptions in accordance with the rules for the material or type of publication to which the accompanying material belongs.

> . . . 21 cm. + 1 atlas (301 p. : ill. (some col.) ; 23 cm.)

> . . . 18 cm. + 20 slides (col.)

1.6. SERIES AREA

Contents:

1.6A. Preliminary rule
1.6B. Title proper of series
1.6C. Parallel titles of series
1.6D. Other title information of series
1.6E. Statements of responsibility relating to series
1.6F. ISSN of series
1.6G. Numbering within series
1.6H. Subseries
1.6J. More than one series statement

1.6A. Preliminary rule

1.6A1. Punctuation

For instructions on the use of spaces before and after prescribed punctuation, see 1.0C.

Precede this area by a full stop, space, dash, space.

Enclose each series statement (see 1.6J) in parentheses.

Precede parallel titles of series or subseries by an equals sign.

Precede other title information relating to series or subseries by a colon.

Precede the first statement of responsibility relating to a series or subseries by a diagonal slash.

Precede subsequent statements of responsibility relating to a series or subseries by a semicolon.

Precede the ISSN of a series or subseries by a comma.

Precede the numbering within a series or subseries by a semicolon.

Precede the title of a subseries by a full stop.

1.6A2. Sources of information. Take information recorded in this area from the chief source of information or from any other source specified for this area in the following chapters. Enclose any information supplied from other sources in square brackets, within the parentheses enclosing each series statement.

1.6B. Title proper of series

1.6B1. If an item is one of a series, record the title proper of the series as instructed in 1.1B (see also 12.1B2).

> The World of folk dances
>
> Great newspapers reprinted

1.6B2. If variant forms of the title of the series (other than parallel titles) appear, choose the title given in the chief source of information as the title proper of the series. Give the variant form(s) in the note area if it is of value in identifying the item.

If variant forms of the title of the series (other than parallel titles) appear in the chief source of information, use the variant that identifies the series most adequately and succinctly.

If the title of the series does not appear in the chief source of information and variant forms appear elsewhere in the publication, choose the variant that identifies the series most adequately and succinctly, preferring a variant that appears in the other preliminaries.

1.6C. Parallel titles of series

1.6C1. Follow the instruction in 1.1D (second level of description) when recording the parallel titles of a series.

> Jeux visuels = Visual games

1.6D. Other title information of series

1.6D1. Include other title information of a series only if it provides valuable information identifying the series. Follow the instructions in 1.1E when recording other title information of a series.

English linguistics, 1500–1750 : a collection of facsimile reprints

Words : their origin, use, and spelling

1.6E. Statements of responsibility relating to series

1.6E1. Give statements of responsibility appearing in conjunction with the series title if they are considered to be necessary for identification of the series. Follow the instructions in 1.1F when recording a statement of responsibility relating to a series.

Map supplement / Association of American Geographers

Technical memorandum / Beach Erosion Board

Research monographs / Institute of Economic Affairs

Sämtliche Werke / Thomas Mann

1.6F. ISSN of series

1.6F1. Record the International Standard Serial Number (ISSN) of a series if it appears in the item being described (see also 1.6H4). Record the ISSN in the standard manner, i.e., ISSN followed by a space and two groups of four digits separated by a hyphen.

Western Canada series report, ISSN 0317-3127

1.6G. Numbering within series

1.6G1. Record the numbering of the item within the series in the terms given in the item. Use standard abbreviations (see Appendix B) and substitute arabic numerals for other numerals or spelled out numbers (see Appendix C).

Historic instruments at the Victoria and Albert Museum ; 4

Beatrix Potter jigsaw puzzles ; no. 1

Environment science research ; v. 6

Russian titles for the specialist, ISSN 0305-3741 ; no. 78

1.6G2. If the parts of a multipart item are separately numbered within a series, give the first and the last numbers if the numbering is continuous; otherwise, give all the numbers. For numbering of a periodical series, see 12.6B.

; v. 11–15

; v. 131, 145, 152

1.6G3. If the item has a designation other than a number, give the designation as found.

; v. A

; 1971

1.6H. Subseries

1.6H1. If an item is one of a subseries (a series within a series, whether or not it has a dependent title) and both the series and the subseries are named in the item, give the details of the main series (see 1.6A–1.6G) first and follow them with the name of the subseries and the details of that subseries.

>   Biblioteca del lavoro. Serie professionale

>   Geological Survey professional paper ; 683-D. Contributions to palaeontology

1.6H2. If the subseries has an alphabetic or numeric designation and no title, give the designation. If such a subseries has a title as well as a designation, give the title after the designation.

>   Music for today. Series 2 ; no. 8

>   Viewmaster science series. 4, Physics

1.6H3. Add parallel titles, other title information, and statements of responsibility relating to subseries as instructed in 1.6C, 1.6D, and 1.6E.

>   World films. France today = La France d'aujourd'hui

>   Papers and documents of the I.C.I. Series C, Bibliographies ; no. 8 = Travaux et documents de l'I.C.I. Série C, Bibliographies ; no 8

1.6H4. Add the ISSN of a subseries if it appears in the item being described; in such a case, omit the ISSN of the main series.

>   Janua linguarum. Series maior, ISSN 0075-3114

> *not*   Janua linguarum, ISSN 0446-4796. Series maior, ISSN 0075-3114

1.6H5. Add the numbering within a subseries as instructed in 1.6G.

>   Sciences. Physics ; TSP 1

>   Biblioteca de arte hispánico ; 8. Artes aplicadas ; 1

1.6J. More than one series statement

1.6J1. The information relating to one series or series and subseries constitutes collectively one series statement. If an item belongs to two or more series and/or series and subseries, make separate series statements and enclose each statement in parentheses. Follow the instructions in 1.6A–1.6H in recording each series statement. If the criterion applies, give the more specific series first.

>   (Video marvels ; no. 33) (Educational progress series ; no. 3)

If parts of an item belong to different series and this relationship cannot be stated clearly in the series area, give details of the series in a note (see 1.7B12).

1.7. NOTE AREA
Contents:
1.7A. Preliminary rule
1.7B. Notes

1.7A. Preliminary rule

1.7A1. Punctuation

Precede each note by a full stop, space, dash, space *or* start a new paragraph for each note.

Separate introductory wording from the main content of a note by a colon and a space.

1.7A2. Sources of information.
Take data recorded in notes from any suitable source. Use square brackets only for interpolations within quoted material. See also 1.0E.

1.7A3. Form of notes

Order of information. If data in a note correspond to data found in the title and statement of responsibility, edition, material (or type of publication) specific details, publication, etc., physical description, and series areas, give the elements of the data in the order in which they appear in those areas. In such a case, use prescribed punctuation, except substitute a full stop for a full stop, space, dash, space.

> Translation of: Germinie Lacerteux / Edmond et Jules de Goncourt
>
> Originally published: London : Gray, 1871
>
> Revision of: 3rd ed. London : Macmillan, 1953

When giving in notes names or titles originally in nonroman scripts, use the original script whenever possible rather than a romanization.

> Based on: Братья Карамазовы / Ф. М. Достоевский

Quotations. Give quotations from the item or from other sources in quotation marks. Follow the quotation by an indication of its source, unless that source is the chief source of information. Do not use prescribed punctuation in quotations.

> "Published for the Royal Institute of Public Administration"
>
> "A textbook for 6th form students"—Pref.
>
> "Generally considered to be by William Langland"—Oxford companion to English literature

References. Make reference to passages in the item, or in other sources, if these either support the cataloguer's own assertions or save repetition in the catalogue entry of information readily available from other sources.

> Introd. (p. xxix) refutes attribution to John Bodenham
>
> Detailed description in: Supplement to Hain's Repertorium bibliographicum / W.A. Copinger

Formal notes. Use formal notes employing an invariable introductory word or phrase or a standard form of words when uniformity of presentation assists in the recognition of the type of information being presented or when their use gives economy of space without loss of clarity.

1.7A4 *Notes citing other editions and works*

Informal notes. When making informal notes, use statements that present the information as briefly as clarity, understandability, and good grammar permit.

1.7A4. Notes citing other editions and works

Other editions. In citing another edition of the same work, give enough information to identify the edition cited.

> Revision of: 2nd ed., 1973

Other works and other manifestations of the same work. In citing other works and other manifestations of the same work (other than different editions with the same title), always give the title and (when applicable) the statement(s) of responsibility. Give the citation in the form, author, title proper; or in the form, title proper / statement of responsibility. When necessary, add the edition and/or date of publication of the work cited.

> Continues: Poetry in London. 1931–1947
>
> Translation of: Le deuxième sexe
>
> Previously published as: Mike. 1909
>
> Adaptation of: Wells, H.G. Kipps
>
> *or*   Adaptation of: Kipps / by H.G. Wells

1.7A5. Notes contain useful descriptive information that cannot be fitted into other areas of the description. A general outline of notes is given in 1.7B. Specific applications of 1.7B are provided in other chapters in Part I. When appropriate, combine two or more notes to make one note.

1.7B. Notes

Give notes in the order in which they are listed here.

1.7B1. Nature, scope, or artistic form of the item

> Comedy in two acts
>
> Documentary

1.7B2. Language of the item and/or translation or adaptation

> Commentary in English
>
> Based on music by Schubert
>
> Spanish version of: Brushing away tooth decay

1.7B3. Source of title proper

> Title from container
>
> Title from descriptive insert

1.7B4. Variations in title

Cover title: Giovanni da Firenze

Original title: L'éducation sentimentale

1.7B5. Parallel titles and other title information

Title on container: The four seasons

Subtitle: An enquiry into the present state of medicine including several recommendations as to how it may be improved and a discussion of the merits of the proposals of other persons

1.7B6. Statements of responsibility

Attributed to Thomas Dekker

Based on the novel by Thomas Hardy

1.7B7. Edition and history

Formerly available as: CAS 675

Microreproduction of original published: London : Macmillan, 1883

Continues: Monthly Scottish news bulletin

Rev. ed. of: The portable Dorothy Parker

1.7B8. Material specific details

Scale of original: ca. 1:6000

Military grid

Vol. numbering irregular

Numbering begins each year with no. 1

1.7B9. Publication, distribution, etc.

Distributed in the U.K. by: EAV Ltd.

1.7B10. Physical description

Printed area measures 30 × 46 cm.

Consists of head and torso made of clear plastic, ⅛ life size

Magnetic sound track

1.7B11. Accompanying materials and supplements

Set includes booklet (16 p.): The new mathematics guide

Every 3rd issue includes supplement: EEC facts and statistics

Slides with every 7th issue

1.7B12. Series

Originally issued in the series: Our world of today

Pts. 1 and 2 in series: African perspective. Pts. 3 and 4 in series: Third World series. Pt. 5 in both series

1.7B13 *Dissertations*

1.7B13. Dissertations

> Thesis (M.A.)—University of Illinois at Urbana-Champaign

1.7B14. Audience

> Intended audience: Elementary grades
>
> For children aged 7–9
>
> Intended audience: Clinical students and postgraduate house officers

1.7B15. Reference to published descriptions

> References: HR6471; GW9101; Goff D-403

1.7B16. Other formats available

> Also available on cassette and cartridge tapes
>
> Also available in 16 mm. format

1.7B17. Summary

> Summary: Pictures the highlights of the play "Julius Caesar" using photographs of an actual production

1.7B18. Contents

> Partial contents: Introduction / Howard H. Brinton — William I. Hull : a biographical sketch / Janet Whitney — George Fox as a man / Frank Aydelotte
>
> Contents: v. 1. Plain tales from the hills — v. 2–3. Soldiers three and military tales — v. 4. In black and white — v. 5. The phantom 'rickshaw and other stories — v. 6. Under the deodars. The story of the Gadsbys. Wee Willie Winkie ₍etc.₎

1.7B19. Numbers borne by the item (other than those covered in 1.8)

> Supt. of Docs. no.: I 19.16:818
>
> Warner Bros.: K56151

1.7B20. Copy being described and library's holdings

> Ms. notes by author on endpapers
>
> Library set lacks slides 7–9

1.7B21. "With" notes

> With: Symphony no. 5 / Beethoven
>
> With: Candles at night / Alexandra Napier

1.8. STANDARD NUMBER AND TERMS OF AVAILABILITY AREA

Contents:
>> 1.8A. Preliminary rule
>> 1.8B. Standard number

1.8C. Key-title
1.8D. Terms of availability
1.8E. Qualification

1.8A. Preliminary rule

1.8A1. Punctuation

For instructions on the use of spaces before and after prescribed punctuation, see 1.0C.

Precede this area by a full stop, space, dash, space *or* start a new paragraph.

Precede each repetition of this area by a full stop, space, dash, space.

Precede a key-title by an equals sign.

Precede terms of availability by a colon.

Enclose a qualification to the standard number or terms of availability in parentheses.

1.8A2. Sources of information. Take information included in this area from any source. Do not enclose any information in brackets.

1.8B. Standard number

1.8B1. Give the International Standard Book Number (ISBN), or International Standard Serial Number (ISSN), or any other internationally agreed standard number for the item being described. Give such numbers with the agreed abbreviation and with the standard spacing or hyphenation.

> ISBN 0-552-67587-3
>
> ISSN 0002-9769

1.8B2. If an item bears two or more such numbers, record the one which applies to the whole item, or applies to the item being described.

Optionally, record more than one number and add a qualification as prescribed in 1.8E. Give a number for a complete set before the number(s) for the part(s). Give numbers for parts in the order of the parts.

> ISBN 0-379-00550-6 (set). — ISBN 0-379-00551-4 (v. 1)

1.8B3. If it is desired to include any number of an item other than an International Standard Number, include such a number in a note (see 1.7B19).

1.8B4. If a number is known to be incorrectly printed in the item, give the correct number if it can be easily ascertained and add *(corrected)* to it.

> ISBN 0-340-16427-1 (corrected)

1.8C. Key-title

1.8C1. Add the key-title of a serial, if it is found on the item or is otherwise readily available, after the International Standard Serial Number (ISSN). Give the key-title

1.8D *Terms of availability*

even if it is identical with the title proper. If no ISSN is given, do not record the key-title.

> ISSN 0340-0352 = IFLA journal

1.8D. *Optional addition.* **Terms of availability**

1.8D1. Give the terms on which the item is available. These terms consist of the price (given in numerals with standard abbreviations) if the item is for sale, or a brief statement of other terms if the item is not for sale.

> : £2.50

> : Free to students of the college

> : For hire

1.8E. Qualification

1.8E1. Add after the standard number or terms of availability, as appropriate, a brief qualification when an item bears two or more standard numbers

> ISBN 0-435-91660-2 (cased). — ISBN 0-435-91661-0 (pbk.)

> ISBN 0-387-08266-2 (U.S.). — ISBN 3-540-08266-2 (Germany)

> ISBN 0-684-14258-9 (bound) : $12.50. — ISBN 0-684-14257-0 (pbk.) : $6.95

and *optionally* when the terms of availability (see 1.8D) need qualification.

> : £1.00 (£0.50 to members)

> : $12.00 ($6.00 to students)

1.8E2. If there is no standard number, give the terms of availability before any qualification.

> $1.00 (pbk.)

1.9. SUPPLEMENTARY ITEMS

Contents:
  1.9A. Supplementary items described independently
  1.9B. Supplementary items described dependently

1.9A. Describe supplementary items which are to be catalogued separately (see 21.28) as separate items. For instructions on the recording of the title proper of supplementary items, the titles proper of which consist of two or more parts, see 1.1B9.

1.9B. Choose one of the following methods of describing supplementary items described dependently:

> 1) record the supplementary item as accompanying material (see 1.5E)

> 5 v. : ill., facsims., ports. ; 32 cm. + 1 index (135 p. ; 32 cm.)

48

or 2) record minor supplementary items in the note area (see 1.7B11)

Accompanied by supplement (37 p.) issued in 1971

or 3) use the multilevel description (see 13.6). *LC will never do this*

The Nonesuch Dickens / published under the editorial direction of Arthur Waugh . . . [et al.]. — Bloomsbury [London] : Nonesuch, 1937–1938. — 23 v. : ill. ; 26 cm.

The Nonesuch Dickens. Retrospectus and prospectus. — 1937. — 130 p. : ill., facsims. ; 26 cm. — Contains facsim. pages from previous eds. of the Pickwick papers.

1.10. ITEMS MADE UP OF SEVERAL TYPES OF MATERIAL

1.10A. This rule applies to items that are made up of two or more components, two or more of which belong to distinct material types (e.g., a sound recording and a printed text).

1.10B. If an item has one predominant component, describe it in terms of that component and give details of the subsidiary component(s) as accompanying material following the physical description (see 1.5E) or in a note (see 1.7B11).

47 slides : col. ; 5 × 5 cm. + 1 sound cassette

3 v. : ill. ; 30 cm.
Note: Sound disc (12 min. : 45 rpm, mono. ; 7 in.) in pocket at end of v. 3

1.10C. If an item has no predominant component, follow the rules below in addition to the rules in this chapter and the rules in the appropriate following chapters.

1.10C1. General material designation. If general material designations are used (see 1.1C):

For an item without a collective title, give the appropriate designation after each title.

The Valley of the Kings [GMD] / James Merriman. Treasures of ancient Egypt [GMD]

For an item with a collective title, follow the instructions in 1.1C4.

. . . [kit]

. . . [multimedia]

1.10C2. Physical description. Apply whichever of the following three methods is appropriate to the item being described:

a) Give the extent of each part or group of parts belonging to each distinct class of material as the first element of the physical description (do this if no further physical description of each item is desired), ending this element with *in container,* if there is one, and following it with the dimensions of the container.

400 lesson cards, 40 answer key booklets, student record, teacher's handbook, placement test ; in container, 18 × 25 × 19 cm. — Lesson cards arranged in 100 steps with 4 lessons at each level

or b) Give separate physical descriptions for each part or group of parts belonging to each distinct class of material (do this if a further physical description of each item is desired). Give each physical description on a separate line.

Beyond the reading list ₍multimedia₎ : guidelines for research in the humanities / C.P. Ravilious ; University of Sussex Library. — Brighton : University of Sussex Library, Audio-Visual Materials Room ₍distributor₎, 1975
46 slides : col.
1 sound cassette (15 min.) : 3¾ ips, mono.
Summary: The bibliographic control of the humanities, with special reference to literature. A typical research project is followed through.
— Intended audience: Postgraduates and research students

or c) For items with a large number of heterogeneous materials, give a general term as the extent (see also 1.5B). Give the number of such pieces unless it cannot be ascertained.

various pieces

27 various pieces

1.10C3. Notes. Give notes on particular parts of the item all together following the series area or following the physical description(s) if no series area is present.

Tape cassette also available as disc. — Slides photographed in Death Valley, Calif.

1.10D. Multilevel description. In describing a single part of a multimedia item, follow the instructions in chapter 13.

1.11. FACSIMILES, PHOTOCOPIES, AND OTHER REPRODUCTIONS

1.11A. In describing a facsimile, photocopy, or other reproduction of printed texts, maps, manuscripts, printed music, and graphic items, give all the data relating to the facsimile, etc., in all areas except the note area. Give data relating to the original in the note area (but give numeric and/or alphabetic, chronological, etc., designations of serials in the material [or type of publication] specific details area). If a facsimile, etc., is in a form of library material different from that of the original (e.g., a manuscript reproduced as a book), use the chapter on the form of the facsimile, etc., in determining the sources of information (e.g., for a manuscript reproduced as a book, use chapter 2). In addition to instructions given in the relevant chapters, follow the instructions in this rule.

1.11B. If the facsimile, etc., has a title different from the original, give the title of the facsimile, etc., as the title proper. Record the original title as other title information if it appears on the chief source of information of the facsimile, etc. (see 1.1D3). Otherwise, give the title of the original in the note area (see 1.11F).

1.11C. If the facsimile, etc., has the edition statement, publication details, or series data of the original as well as those of the facsimile, etc., give those of the facsimile, etc., in the edition, publication, distribution, etc., and series areas. Give the details of the original in the note area (see 1.11F).

1.11D. Give the physical description of the facsimile, etc., in the physical description area. Give the physical description of the original in the note area (see 1.11F).

1.11E. If the facsimile, etc., has a standard number, give it in the standard number and terms of availability area, together with the key-title and terms of availability of the facsimile, etc. Give the standard number and key-title of the original in the note area (see 1.11F).

1.11F. Give all the details of the original of a facsimile, etc., in a single note. Give the details of the original in the order of the areas of the description.

> The baby's bouquet : a fresh bunch of old rhymes and tunes / arranged and decorated by Walter Crane ; the tunes collected and arranged by L.C. — London : Pan, 1974. — 56 p.: col. ill. ; 16 × 17 cm. — (A Piccolo book)
> Facsim. of: 2nd ed., rev. London : Routledge, 1877
> ISBN 0-330-24089-7 : £0.60

> Alice's adventures under ground / by Lewis Carroll ; with a new introduction by Martin Gardner. — New York : Dover, 1965. — xiii, 91, [17] p. : ill., facsims. ; 22 cm.
> Contents: Complete facsimile of the British Museum manuscript of Alice's adventures under ground — Front matter of the Macmillan 1886 edition — Back matter of the Macmillan 1886 edition.

> Pre-Raphaelite drawings [GMD] / by Dante Gabriel Rossetti ; [selected and introduced by] Andrea Rose. — Chicago : University of Chicago Press, 1977. — 3 microfiches (251 fr.) : all ill. ; 10 × 15 cm. + 1 booklet (48 p. ; 18 cm.)
> Reproductions of 251 drawings from Birmingham City Museums

CHAPTER 2

BOOKS, PAMPHLETS, AND PRINTED SHEETS

Contents

2.0. GENERAL RULES

2.0A. Scope

The rules in this chapter cover the description of separately published monographic printed items of all kinds (referred to hereafter in this chapter as *printed monographs*). These items comprise books, pamphlets, and single sheets. For microform reproductions of printed texts, see chapter 11. For serial printed texts, see chapter 12.

2.0B. Sources of information

2.0B1. Chief source of information. The chief source of information for printed monographs is the title page or, if there is no title page, the source from within the publication that is used as a substitute for it. For printed monographs published without a title page, or without a title page applying to the whole work (as in the case of some editions of the Bible and some bilingual dictionaries), use the part of the item supplying the most complete information, whether this be the cover (excluding a separate book jacket), half title page, caption, colophon, running title, or other part. Specify the part used as a title page substitute[1] in a note (see 2.7B3). If no part of the item supplies data that can be used as the basis of the description, take the necessary information from any available source. If information traditionally given on the title page is given on two facing pages or on pages on successive leaves, with or without repetition, treat those pages as the title page.

2.0B2. Prescribed sources of information. The prescribed source(s) of information for each area of the description of printed monographs is set out below. Enclose information taken from outside the prescribed source(s) in square brackets.

AREA	PRESCRIBED SOURCES OF INFORMATION
Title and statement of responsibility	Title page
Edition	Title page, other preliminaries, and colophon
Publication, distribution, etc.	Title page, other preliminaries, and colophon
Physical description	The whole publication
Series	The whole publication
Note	Any source
Standard number and terms of availability	Any source

2.0C. Punctuation

For the punctuation of the description as a whole, see 1.0C.

For the prescribed punctuation of elements, see the following rules.

2.0D. Levels of detail in the description

See 1.0D.

---

1. Hereafter in this chapter the term *title page* is used to include any substitute.

2.0E. Language and script of the description
See 1.0E.

2.0F. Inaccuracies
See 1.0F.

2.0G. Accents and other diacritical marks
See 1.0G.

2.0H. Items with several title pages
See 1.0H.

2.1. TITLE AND STATEMENT OF RESPONSIBILITY AREA
Contents:
2.1A. Preliminary rule
2.1B. Title proper
2.1C. General material designation
2.1D. Parallel titles
2.1E. Other title information
2.1F. Statements of responsibility
2.1G. Items without a collective title

2.1A. Preliminary rule

2.1A1. Punctuation
For instructions on the use of spaces before and after prescribed punctuation, see 1.0C.
Precede the title of a supplement or section (see 1.1B9) by a full stop.
Enclose the general material designation in square brackets.
Precede each parallel title by an equals sign.
Precede each unit of other title information by a colon.
Precede the first statement of responsibility by a diagonal slash.
Precede each subsequent statement of responsibility by a semicolon.
For the punctuation of this area for items without a collective title, see 1.1G.

2.1B. Title proper

2.1B1. Record the title proper as instructed in 1.1B.

The articulate mammal

Why a duck?

Classification décimale de Dewey et index

Memoirs of the life of the late John Mytton, Esq.

The ballroom of romance and other stories

The first Rex Stout omnibus

The most of P.G. Wodehouse

2.1C *General material designation*

> Marlowe's plays
>
> Linda Goodman's Sun signs
>
> Larousse's French-English dictionary
>
> Harriet said—
>> (*Title page reads:* Harriet said . . .)
>
> Under the hill, or, The story of Venus and Tannhäuser
>
> 4.50 from Paddington
>
> Advanced calculus. Student handbook
>> (*Title proper consists of title of main work and title of handbook. See 1.1B9*)
>
> Instructor's guide and key for The American economy
>
> Bank officer's handbook of commercial banking law, fourth edition, by Frederick K. Bentel. 1975 supplement
>> (*Title proper consists of title, author statement, and edition statement of main work and designation of supplement*)

2.1B2. If the title page bears both a collective title and the titles of individual works, give the collective title as the title proper and give the titles of the individual works in a contents note (see 2.7B18).

> Three notable stories
> *Note:* Contents: Love and peril / the Marquis of Lorne — To be or not to be / Mrs. Alexander — The melancholy hussar / Thomas Hardy

2.1C. *Optional addition.* **General material designation**

2.1C1. Add, immediately following the title proper, the appropriate general material designation as instructed in 1.1C.

2.1C2. If an item contains parts belonging to materials falling into two or more categories, and if none of these is the predominant constituent of the item, give either *multimedia* or *kit* as the designation (see 1.1C1 and 1.10).

2.1D. Parallel titles

2.1D1. Record parallel titles as instructed in 1.1D.

> Tyres and wheels = Pneus et roues = Reifen und Räder
>
> Thumbelina = Tommelise

2.1E. Other title information

2.1E1. Record other title information as instructed in 1.1E.

> A Laodicean : a story of to-day

The age of neo-classicism : the fourteenth exhibition of the Council of Europe : the Royal Academy and the Victoria & Albert Museum, 9 September–19 November 1972

Private eyeballs : a golden treasury of bad taste

Letters to an intimate stranger : a year in the life of Jack Trevor Story

2.1F. Statements of responsibility

2.1F1. Record statements of responsibility relating to persons or bodies as instructed in 1.1F.

Shut up in Paris / by Nathan Sheppard

Great Britain : handbook for travellers / by Karl Baedeker

Le père Goriot / Honoré de Balzac

Statistics of homelessness / Home Office

Tynan right & left : plays, films, people, places, and events / Kenneth Tynan

Vas-y, Charlie Brown / par Charles M. Schulz

Dan Russel the fox : an episode in the life of Miss Rowan / by E.Œ. Somerville and Martin Ross

The world of the lion / by Samuel Devend . . . [et al.]

Eventyr og historier / H.C. Andersen

A modern herbal / by Mrs. M. Grieve ; edited and introduced by Mrs. C.F. Leyel
  (*Lengthy other title information omitted*)

Eldorado : a story of the Scarlet Pimpernel / by the Baroness Orczy

Letters from AE / selected and edited by Alan Denson ; with a foreword by Monk Gibbon

The diary of a country parson, 1758–1802 / by James Woodforde ; passages selected and edited by John Beresford

Hadrian the Seventh / Fr. Rolfe (Frederick, Baron Corvo)

Underwater acoustics : a report / by the Natural Environment Research Council Working Group on Underwater Acoustics

Proceedings / International Symposium on the Cataloguing, Coding, and Statistics of Audio-Visual Materials ; organised by ISO/TC46 Documentation in collaboration with IFLA and IFTC, 7–9 January 1976 in Strasbourg

American Ballet Theatre : thirty-six years of scenic and costume design, 1940–1976 / presented by Ballet Theatre Foundation, Inc., and the International Exhibitions Foundation

Scientific policy, research, and development in Canada : a bibliography / prepared by the National Science Library = La politique des sciences, la recherche et le développement au Canada : bibliographie / établie par la Bibliothèque nationale des sciences

Teach yourself Irish / Myles Dillon, Donncha Ó Cróinín

Swedenborgs korrespondenslära / av Inge Jonsson ; with a summary in English

Book of bores / drawings by Michael Heath

Sanditon / Jane Austen and another lady

2.1F2. Do not include statements of responsibility taken from outside the publication in the title and statement of responsibility area. If such a statement is considered to be necessary, give it in a note (see 2.7B6).

2.1F3. Add a word or short phrase to the statement of responsibility if the relationship between the title of the work and the person(s) or body (bodies) named in the statement is not clear.

Morte Arthure / ₍edited by₎ John Finlayson

The great ideas of Plato / ₍selected by₎ Eugene Freeman and David Appel

Research in human geography / by Michael Chisholm ; ₍for the₎ Social Science Research Council

Palava Parrot / ₍illustrations by₎ Tamasin Cole ; story by James Cressey

Antologija hrvatske poezije dvadesetog stoljeća od Kranjčevića do danas / ₍sastavili₎ Slavko Mihalić, Josip Pupačić, Anton Šoljan

2.1G. Items without a collective title

2.1G1. If a printed monograph lacks a collective title, record the titles of the individual parts as instructed in 1.1G.

The listing attic ; The unstrung harp / by Edward Gorey

Flash and filigree ; and, The magic Christian / by Terry Southern

Henry Esmond : a novel / by Thackeray. Bleak House : a novel / by Dickens

Humanismens krise / af H.C. Branner. Eneren og massen / af Martin A. Hansen

2.1G2. Make the relationship between statements of responsibility and the parts of an item lacking a collective title clear by additions as instructed in 2.1F3.

Man Friday : a play ; Mind your head : a return trip with songs / Adrian Mitchell ; music ₍for Man Friday₎ by Mike Westbrook ; music ₍for Mind your head₎ by Andy Roberts

2.2. EDITION AREA

Contents:

2.2A. Preliminary rule

2.2A1. Punctuation

For instructions on the use of spaces before and after prescribed punctuation, see 1.0C.

Precede this area by a full stop, space, dash, space.

Precede a subsequent edition statement by a comma.

Precede the first statement of responsibility following an edition or subsequent edition statement by a diagonal slash.

Precede each subsequent statement of responsibility by a semicolon.

2.2B. Edition statement

2.2B1. Transcribe a statement relating to an edition of a work that contains differences from other editions of that work, or that is a named reissue of that work, as instructed in 1.2B.

> 2nd ed.
>
> New ed., rev. and enl.
>
> 1st American ed.
>
> 1st illustrated ed.
>
> Household ed.
>
> 6. Aufl.
>
> Draft
>
> Facsim. ed.
>
> New Wessex ed.
>
> [3rd ed.]
>
> [New ed.]
>
> 3ª ed.

2.2B2. In case of doubt about whether a statement is an edition statement, follow the instructions in 1.2B3.

2.2B3. *Optional addition.* If an item lacks an edition statement but is known to contain significant changes from previous editions, supply a suitable brief statement in the language and script of the title proper and enclose it in square brackets.

ₜNew ed.ₜ

ₜ5ᵉ éd.ₜ

2.2B4. If an edition statement appears in more than one language or script, record the statement that is in the language or script of the title proper. If this criterion does not apply, record the statement that appears first.

2.2B5. If an item lacking a collective title and described as a unit contains one or more parts with an associated edition statement, record such statements following the titles and statements of responsibility to which they relate, separated from them by a full stop.

2.2C. Statements of responsibility relating to the edition

2.2C1. Record a statement of responsibility relating to one or more editions, but not to all editions, of a work as instructed in 1.2C.

Economic history of England : a study in social development / by
H.O. Meredith. — 5th ed. / by C. Ellis

The well-beloved : a sketch of a temperament / Thomas Hardy.
— New Wessex ed. / introduction by J. Hillis Miller ; notes by
Edward Mendelson

A short history of the Catholic Church / by Philip Hughes. —
8th ed. / with a final chapter (1966–1974) by E.E.Y. Hales

2.2D. Subsequent edition statement

2.2D1. If the item is a designated reissue of a particular edition containing changes from that edition, give the subsequent edition statement as instructed in 1.2D.

Selected poems / D.H. Lawrence. — ₜNew ed.ₜ / edited, with
an introduction, by Keith Sagar, Reprinted with minor revisions

Ireland / edited by L. Russel Muirhead. — 3rd ed., 2nd (corr.)
impression

Do not record statements relating to impressions or printings that contain no changes unless the item is considered to be of particular bibliographic importance to the cataloguing agency.

2.2E. Statements of responsibility relating to a subsequent edition statement

2.2E1. Record a statement of responsibility relating to one or more designated subsequent editions, but not to all subsequent editions, of a particular edition as instructed in 1.2E.

2.3. MATERIAL (OR TYPE OF PUBLICATION) SPECIFIC DETAILS AREA

This area is not used for printed monographs.

2.4. PUBLICATION, DISTRIBUTION, ETC., AREA

Contents:

2.4A. Preliminary rule

2.4A1. Punctuation

For instructions on the use of spaces before and after prescribed punctuation, see 1.0C.

Precede this area by a full stop, space, dash, space.

Precede a second or subsequently named place of publication, distribution, etc., by a semicolon.

Precede the name of a publisher, distributor, etc., by a colon.

Enclose a supplied statement of function of a distributor in square brackets.

Precede the date of publication, distribution, etc., by a comma.

Enclose the details of printing (place, name, date) in parentheses.

Precede the name of a printer by a colon.

Precede the date of printing by a comma.

2.4B. General rule

For items with multiple or fictitious places and name of publishers, distributors, etc., follow the instructions in 1.4B.

2.4C. Place of publication, distribution, etc.

2.4C1. Record the place of publication, distribution, etc., as instructed in 1.4C.

2.4D. Name of publisher, distributor, etc.

2.4D1. Record the name of the publisher, distributor, etc., as instructed in 1.4D.

London : Macmillan

London : H.M.S.O.

Taunton, Somerset : Barnicotts

London : The Society : Sold by Longman

London : Oxford University Press

London : John Lane, the Bodley Head

Geneva : WHO

[Hove, East Sussex] : Fox

2.4E *Statement of function of distributor*

> Göttingen : Vandenhoeck & Ruprecht
>
> Urbana : University of Illinois Press
>
> London : Benn ; Chicago : Rand McNally
> (*For a cataloguing agency in the United States*)
>
> Freiburg : Baedeker ; London : Allen & Unwin
> (*For a cataloguing agency in the United Kingdom*)
>
> New York : Dutton ; Toronto : Clarke, Irwin
> (*For a cataloguing agency in Canada*)
>
> London : T. Wall and Sons
> (*Title page reads:* Published in celebration of life's minor
> pleasures by T. Wall and Sons (Ice-Cream) Ltd.)

2.4E. *Optional addition.* **Statement of function of distributor**

2.4E1. Add to the name of a distributor a statement of function as instructed in 1.4E.

> New York : Dover ; London : Constable [distributor]

2.4F. Date of publication, distribution, etc.

2.4F1. Record the date of publication, distribution, etc., as instructed in 1.4F.

> London : Gollancz, 1951
>
> New York : Dover, 1970 ; London : Constable [distributor], 1972
>
> London : Collins, c1957

2.4G. Place of printing, name of printer, date of printing

2.4G1. If the name of the publisher is unknown, give the place and name of the printer if they are found in the item, as instructed in 1.4G.

> London : [s.n.], 1971 (London : HiTimes Press)
>
> [S.l. : s.n.], 1971 (London : Wiggs)

2.4G2. *Optional addition.* Give the place, name of printer, and/or date of printing if they differ from the place, name of publisher, etc., and date of publication, etc., and are found in the item and are considered important by the cataloguing agency.

> London : The Society, 1971 (London : Ploughshare Press)
>
> London : J. Lane, 1902 (1907 printing)

2.5. PHYSICAL DESCRIPTION AREA

Contents:
- 2.5A. Preliminary rule
- 2.5B. Number of volumes and/or pagination
- 2.5C. Illustrative matter

2.5D. Size
2.5E. Accompanying material

2.5A. Preliminary rule

2.5A1. Punctuation

For instructions on the use of spaces before and after prescribed punctuation, see 1.0C.

Precede this area by a full stop, space, dash, space *or* start a new paragraph.

Precede details of illustrations by a colon.

Precede the size by a semicolon.

Precede a statement of accompanying material by a plus sign.

Enclose physical details of accompanying material in parentheses.

2.5B. Number of volumes and/or pagination

Single volumes

2.5B1. Record the number of pages or leaves in a publication in accordance with the terminology suggested by the volume. That is, describe a volume with leaves printed on both sides in terms of pages, describe a volume with leaves printed on one side only in terms of leaves, and describe a volume that has more than one column to a page and is numbered in columns rather than pages in terms of columns. If a publication contains sequences of leaves and pages, or pages and columns, or leaves and columns, record each sequence. Describe a volume printed without numbering in terms of leaves or pages, but not of both. For the treatment of unnumbered leaves of plates, see 2.5B10. Describe a broadside as such. Describe a folder and other single sheets as *sheet*. Describe a case or portfolio as such.

2.5B2. Record the number of pages, leaves, or columns in terms of the numbered or lettered sequences in the volume. Record the last numbered page, leaf, or column in each sequence[2] and follow it with the appropriate term or abbreviation.

> 327 p.
>
> 321 leaves
>
> 381 columns
>
> xvii, 323 p.
>
> 27 p., 300 leaves
>
> 1 broadside
>
> 1 sheet
>
> 1 portfolio

---

2. A sequence of pages or leaves is (1) a separately numbered group of pages, etc., (2) an unnumbered group of pages, etc., that stands apart from the other groups in the publication, or (3) a number of pages or leaves of plates distributed throughout the publication.

Record pages, etc., that are lettered as inclusive lettering in the form *A–K p., a–d leaves,* etc. Designate pages, etc., that are numbered in words or characters other than arabic or roman in arabic figures.

> A–Z p.
>   *(Pages lettered A–Z)*
>
> 32 p.
>   *(Pages numbered in words)*

2.5B3. Disregard unnumbered sequences, unless such a sequence constitutes the whole (see 2.5B7) or a substantial part (see also 2.5B8) of the publication, or unless an unnumbered sequence includes page(s), etc., that are referred to in a note. When recording the number of unnumbered pages, etc., either give the estimated number preceded by *ca.,* without square brackets, or enclose the exact number in square brackets.

> 8, vii, ca. 300, 73 p.
>
> 33, ₍31₎ leaves
>
> ₍8₎, 155 p.
> *Note:* Bibliography: 6th prelim. page

Disregard unnumbered sequences of inessential matter (advertising, blank pages, etc.).

2.5B4. If the number printed on the last page or leaf of a sequence does not represent the total number of pages or leaves in that sequence, let it stand uncorrected unless it gives a completely false impression of the extent of the item, as, for instance, when only alternate pages are numbered or when the number on the last page or leaf of the sequence is misprinted. Supply corrections in such cases in square brackets.

> 48 ₍i.e. 96₎ p.
>
> 329 ₍i.e. 392₎ p.

2.5B5. If the numbering within a sequence changes (e.g., from roman to arabic numerals), ignore the numbering of the first part of the sequence.

> 176 p.
>   *(Publication numbered i–xii, 13–176)*

2.5B6. If the pages, etc., are numbered as part of a larger sequence (e.g., one volume of a multivolume publication) or if the item appears to be incomplete (see also 2.5B16), give the first and last numbers of the pages or leaves, preceded by the appropriate term or abbreviation.

> leaves 81–149
>
> p. 713–797

2.5B7. If the volume is printed without pagination or foliation, ascertain the total number of pages, etc., and give the number in square brackets. For larger items, estimate the number of pages and give the estimated number preceded by *ca.*, without square brackets.

> [93] p.
>
> [55] leaves
>
> ca. 600 p.

2.5B8. If the volume has complicated or irregular paging, record the pagination using one of the following methods, depending upon the nature or extent of the complications:

a) Record the total number of pages or leaves (excluding those which are blank or contain advertising or other inessential matter) followed by the words *in various pagings* or *in various foliations*.

> 1000 p. in various pagings
>
> 256 leaves in various foliations

b) Record the number of pages or leaves in the main sequences of the pagination and add the total number, in square brackets, of the remaining variously paged sequences.

> [93] p.
>
> 226, [44] p.
>
> 366, 98, [99] p.

c) Describe the volume simply as *1 v. (various pagings)*, *1 case,* or *1 portfolio,* as appropriate (see 2.5B18).

2.5B9. Describe all loose-leaf publications that are designed to receive additions as *1 v. (loose-leaf)*, *2 v. (loose-leaf)*, etc.

2.5B10. Leaves or pages of plates. Record the number of leaves or pages of plates at the end of the sequence(s) of pagination, whether the plates are found together or distributed throughout the publication, or even if there is only one plate. For volumes consisting of unnumbered leaves or pages of plates, follow the instructions in 2.5B7. If the numbering of the leaves or pages of plates is complex or irregular, follow the instructions in 2.5B8.

> 246 p., 32 p. of plates
>
> xvi, 249 p., [12] leaves of plates
>
> x, 32, 73 p., [1] leaf of plates
>
> [16] p., [40] leaves of plates
>
> [80] p. of plates
>
> xii, 24 p., 212, [43] leaves of plates

If the volume contains both leaves and pages of plates, record the number in terms of whichever is predominant.

> 323 p., ₁19₁ p. of plates
>> (*Contains 16 pages and 3 leaves of plates*)

2.5B11. Describe folded leaves as such.

> 122 folded leaves
>
> 230 p., 25 leaves of plates (some folded)
>
> 25 folded leaves of plates

2.5B12. If numbered pages or leaves are printed on a double leaf (e.g., books in the traditional oriental format), record them as pages or leaves according to their numbering. If they are unnumbered, count each double leaf as two pages.

2.5B13. If the paging is duplicated, as is sometimes the case with books having parallel texts, record both pagings and make an explanatory note (see 2.7B10).

> xii, 35, 35 p.
> *Note:* Opposite pages bear duplicate numbering

2.5B14. If a volume has a pagination of its own and also bears the pagination of a larger work of which it is a part, record the paging of the individual volume in this area and record the continuous paging in a note (see 2.7B10).

> 328 p.
> *Note:* Pages also numbered 501–828

2.5B15. If the volume has groups of pages numbered in opposite directions, as is sometimes the case with books having texts in two languages, record the pagings of the various sections in order, starting from the title page selected for cataloguing.

> ix, 155, 127, x p.

2.5B16. If the last part of a publication is missing and the paging of a complete copy cannot be ascertained, give the paging in the form *234 + p.*, and make a note of the imperfection (see 2.7B20).

> xxiv, 179 + p.
> *Note:* Library's copy imperfect: all after p. 179 wanting

Publications in more than one volume

2.5B17. If a printed monograph is in more than one physical volume, record the number of volumes.

> 3 v.

2.5B18. If the term *volume* is not appropriate for a multipart item, use one of the following terms:

> *Parts.* Use for bibliographic units intended to be bound several to a volume, especially if so designated by the publisher.

Pamphlets. Use for collections of pamphlets bound together or assembled in a portfolio for cataloguing as a collection.

Pieces. Use for items of varying character (pamphlets, broadsides, clippings, maps, etc.) published, or assembled for cataloguing, as a collection.

Case(s). Use for either boxes containing bound or unbound material or containers of fascicles.

Portfolio(s). Use for containers holding loose papers, illustrative materials, etc. A portfolio usually consists of two covers joined together at the back and tied at the front, top, and/or bottom.

2.5B19. If the number of bibliographic volumes differs from the number of physical volumes, record the fact in the form [*bibliographic*] *v. in* [*physical*].

> 8 v. in 5

2.5B20. If a set of volumes is continuously paged, give the pagination in parentheses after the number of volumes. Ignore separately paged sequences of preliminary matter in volumes other than the first.

> 2 v. (xxxxi, 999 p.)
>
> 3 v. (xx, 800 p.)
> (*Pages numbered xx, 1–201; xx, 202–513; xxi, 514–800*)

2.5B21. *Optional addition.* If the volumes in a multivolume set are individually paged, give the pagination of each volume in parentheses after the number of volumes.

> 2 v. (xvi, 329; xx, 412 p.)

2.5B22. If a publication was planned to be in more than one volume, but not all have been published and it appears that publication will not be continued, describe the incomplete set as appropriate (i.e., give paging for a single volume or number of volumes for multiple volumes), and make a note (see 2.7B10) to the effect that no more volumes have been published.

2.5B23. Braille or other raised types. If an item consists of leaves of braille or another tactile writing system, add, to the statement of the number of volumes or leaves, *of braille, of Moon type,* etc., as appropriate.

> 310 leaves of braille

Use *of jumbo braille* or *of microbraille* when appropriate.

> 4 v. of jumbo braille

If an item contains press braille pages, add *of press braille* to the statement of the number of pages or volumes.

> 300 p. of press braille
>
> 5 v. of press braille

If an item consists of eye-readable print and braille, add *of print/braille* or *of print /press braille*, as appropriate, to the statement of the number of pages or volumes.

> 300 p. of print/braille

2.5C. Illustrative matter

2.5C1. Describe an illustrated printed monograph as *ill.* unless the illustrations are all of one or more of the particular types mentioned in the next paragraph. If only some of the illustrations belong to these types, give the abbreviation *ill.* first. Tables are not illustrations. Disregard illustrated title pages and minor illustrations (decorations, vignettes, etc.).

> 327 p. : ill.

2.5C2. If the illustrations are of one or more of the following types, and are considered to be important, designate them by the appropriate term or abbreviation (in this order): charts, coats of arms, facsimiles, forms, genealogical tables, maps, music, plans, portraits (use for both single and group portraits), samples. Designate all other types as *ill.*

> 333 p. : maps
>
> 333 p. : ill., maps
>
> xvii, 333 p. : maps, ports.

2.5C3. Describe coloured illustrations (i.e., those in two or more colours) as such.

> : col. ill.
>
> : ill., col. maps, ports. (some col.)
>
> : ill. (some col.), maps, plans

2.5C4. Specify the number of illustrations if their number can be easily ascertained (e.g., when the illustrations are listed and their numbers stated).

> : 48 ill.
>
> : ill., 12 maps
>
> : ill., 3 forms, 1 map

2.5C5. If some or all of the illustrations appear on the lining papers, make a note of this fact (see 2.7B10).

> : ill., maps
> *Note:* Maps on lining papers

2.5C6. If the publication consists wholly or predominantly of illustrations, use the terms *all ill.* or *chiefly ill.*, as appropriate. If those illustrations are all of one type (see 2.5C2), use *all [name of type]* or *chiefly [name of type]*.

> : all ill.
>
> : chiefly maps

2.5C7. Include illustrative matter issued in a pocket inside the cover of an item in the physical description. Specify the number of items and their location in a note (see 2.7B10).

> : ill., col. maps
> *Note:* Four maps on 2 folded leaves in pocket

2.5C8. If rules 2.5C1–2.5C7 give a misleading impression of the relative extent of the illustrations and text, combine the statements of pagination and of illustrative matter.

> 74 p. of ill., 15 p.
>
> 74 p., 15 leaves of ill.

2.5D. Size

2.5D1. Give the height of the volume(s) in centimetres, to the next whole centimetre up (e.g., if a volume measures 17.2 centimetres, record it as 18 cm.). Measure the height of the binding if the volume is bound. Otherwise, measure the height of the item itself. If the volume measures less than 10 centimetres, give the height in millimetres.

2.5D2. If the width of the volume is either less than half the height or greater than the height, give the width following the height preceded by a multiplication sign.

> ; 20 × 8 cm.
>
> ; 20 × 32 cm.

2.5D3. If the volumes in a multivolume set differ in height and the difference is less than two centimetres, give the largest size. If the difference is more than two centimetres, give the smallest size and the largest size, separated by a hyphen.

> ; 24–28 cm.

2.5D4. In cataloguing single sheets, give the height and the width. If such a sheet is designed for issue folded, add the dimensions of the sheet when folded.

> ; 48 × 30 cm. folded to 24 × 15 cm.

If the sheet is designed to be used only in the folded form, describe it as *1 folded sheet* and give the number of imposed pages and the height of the sheet when folded.

> 1 folded sheet (8 p.) ; 18 cm.

2.5D5. If the volume consists of items of varying height bound together, give the height of the binding only.

2.5E. Accompanying material

2.5E1. Record the name, and *optionally* the physical description, of any material that is issued with the item and is intended to be used in conjunction with it, as instructed in 1.5E.

> 271 p. : ill. ; 21 cm. + 1 answer book
>
> 271 p. : ill. ; 21 cm. + 1 atlas (37 p., 19 leaves : col. maps ; 37 cm.)
>
> 27 p. : ill. ; 21 cm. + 1 sound disc (25 min. : 33⅓ rpm, mono. ; 12 in.)

2.5E2. If the accompanying material is issued in a pocket inside the cover of the publication, specify its location in a note (see 2.7B11).

2.6. SERIES AREA

Contents:
>   2.6A. Preliminary rule
>   2.6B. Series statements

2.6A. Preliminary rule

2.6A1. Punctuation

For instructions on the use of spaces before and after prescribed punctuation, see 1.0C.

Precede this area by a full stop, space, dash, space.

Enclose each series statement (see 1.6J) in parentheses.

Precede parallel titles of series or subseries by an equals sign.

Precede other title information relating to series or subseries by a colon.

Precede the first statement of responsibility relating to a series or subseries by a diagonal slash.

Precede subsequent statements of responsibility relating to a series or subseries by a semicolon.

Precede the ISSN of a series or subseries by a comma.

Precede the numbering within a series or subseries by a semicolon.

Precede the title of a subseries by a full stop.

2.6B. Series statements

2.6B1. Record each series statement as instructed in 1.6.

> (Typophile chap books ; 7)
>
> (Britain advances ; 10)
>
> (The King Penguin books)
>
> (Special paper / Geological Society of America)
>
> (Publicación / Universidad de Chile, Departamento de Geología ; no. 28)
>
> (Occasional papers / University of Sussex Centre for Continuing Education, ISSN 0306-1108 ; no. 4)
>
> (Department of State publication ; 8583. East Asian and Pacific series ; 199)
>
> (Olympia Press traveller's companion series ; no. 105)

(Acta Universitatis Stockholmiensis. Stockholm studies in the history of literature ; 10)

(Acta Universitatis Stockholmiensis. Studia Hungarica Stockholmiensia ; 6)

(Treaty series ; no. 66 (1976)) (Cmnd. ; 6580)
(*Numbering of first series follows official usage*)

(Graeco-Roman memoirs, ISSN 0306-9222 ; no. 62)

(Scríbhinni Gaeilge na mBráthar Mionúr ; imleabhar 11)

(S266 ; block 6)

(Works / Charles Dickens ; v. 12)

2.7. NOTE AREA

Contents:
2.7A. Preliminary rule
2.7B. Notes

2.7A. Preliminary rule

2.7A1. Punctuation

Precede each note by a full stop, space, dash, space *or* start a new paragraph for each.

Separate introductory wording from the main content of a note by a colon and a space.

2.7A2. In making notes, follow the instructions in 1.7A.

2.7B. Notes

Make notes as set out in the following subrules and in the order given there.

2.7B1. Nature, scope, or artistic form. Make notes on these matters unless they are apparent from the rest of the description.

"Collection of essays on economic subjects"

Arabic reader

Play in 3 acts

Scenario of film

2.7B2. Language of item and/or translation or adaptation. Make notes on the language of the item, or on the fact that it is a translation or adaptation, unless this is apparent from the rest of the description.

Translation of: La muerte de Artemio Cruz

Author's adaptation of his Russian text

Latin text, parallel English translation

Adaptation of: The taming of the shrew

2.7B3. Source of title proper. Make notes on the source of the title proper if it is other than the chief source of information.

> Caption title

> Spine title

2.7B4. Variations in title. Make notes on titles borne by the item other than the title proper. If considered desirable, give a romanization of the title proper.

> Added t. p. in Russian

> Previously published as: Enter Psmith

> Cover title: The fair American

2.7B5. Parallel titles and other title information. Give parallel titles and other title information not recorded in the title and statement of responsibility area if they are considered to be important.

> Subtitle: The medicinal, culinary, cosmetic and economic properties, cultivation, and folklore of herbs, grasses, fungi, shrubs, and trees, with all their modern scientific uses

> Title on added t. p.: Les rats

2.7B6. Statements of responsibility. Make notes on variant names of persons or bodies named in statements of responsibility if these are considered to be important for identification. Give statements of responsibility not recorded in the title and statement of responsibility area. Make notes on persons or bodies connected with a work, or significant persons or bodies connected with previous editions, not already named in the description.

> At head of title: ₍name not used in the main entry and with indeterminate responsibility for the work₎

> "Also attributed to Jonathan Swift"—Introd.

> "Begun by Jane Austen in 1817 . . . completed, some 160 years later, by another lady"—Cover

2.7B7. Edition and history. Make notes relating to the edition being described or to the bibliographic history of the work.

> "This issue is founded on the second edition, printed by Rudolf Ackermann in the year 1837 (with considerable additions) from the New sporting magazine"—T. p. verso

> Previous ed.: Harmondsworth : Penguin, 1950

> Sequel to: Mémoires d'un médecin

2.7B9. Publication, distribution, etc. Make notes on publication, distribution, etc., details that are not included in the publication, distribution, etc., area and that are considered to be important.

Imprint under label reads: Humanitas-Verlag Zürich

"Privately printed"

Published simultaneously in Canada

2.7B10. Physical description. Make notes on important physical details that are not already included in the physical description area. Make notes on braille or other raised type books.

Captions on verso of plates

Printed on vellum

Limited ed. of 60 signed and numbered copies

Alternate pages blank

No more published

Two charts on folded leaves in pocket

Tables on 4 leaves in pocket

Grade 3 braille

Alternate leaves of print and braille

2.7B11. Accompanying material. Make notes on the location of accompanying material if appropriate. Give details of accompanying material not mentioned in the physical description area or given a separate entry or separate description according to the rules for multilevel description (see 13.6).

Slides in pocket

"Tables I, II, and III omitted by error from report" published as supplement (5 p.) and inserted at end

Accompanied by atlas "A demographic atlas of North-west Ireland" (39 p. : col. maps ; 36 cm.), previously published separately in 1956

2.7B12. Series. Make notes on series data that cannot be given in the series area.

Series title romanized: Min hady al-Islām

Also issued without series statement

Original issued in series: English life in English literature
(*For reprint edition*)

Originally issued in series: Environmental science series
(*For another edition*)

2.7B13. Dissertations. If the item being described is a dissertation or thesis presented in partial fulfillment of the requirements for an academic degree, give the designation of the thesis (using the English word *thesis*) followed by a brief statement of the degree for which the author was a candidate (e.g., M.A. or Ph.D., or, for theses to which such abbreviations do not apply, *doctoral* or *master's*), the name of the institution or faculty to which the thesis was presented, and the year in which the degree was granted.

    Thesis (Ph.D.)—University of Toronto, 1974

    Thesis (M.A.)—University College, London, 1969

    Thesis (doctoral)—Freie Universität, Berlin, 1973

If the publication is a revision or abridgement of a thesis, state this.

    Abstract of thesis (Ph.D.)—University of Illinois at Urbana-Champaign, 1974

If the thesis is a text edited by the candidate, include the candidate's name in the note.

    Karl Schmidt's thesis (doctoral)—München, 1965

If the publication lacks a formal thesis statement, give a bibliographic history note.

    Originally presented as the author's thesis (doctoral—Heidelberg)
    under the title:

2.7B14. Audience. Make a brief note of the intended audience for, or intellectual level of, an item if this information is stated in the item.

    For 9–12 year olds

    Undergraduate text

    Intended audience: Preschool children

2.7B17. Summary. Give a brief objective summary of the content of an item unless another part of the description gives enough information.

    Summary: Kate and Ben follow their rabbit into a haunted house
    and discover the source of the house's ghostly sound

2.7B18. Contents. Make a note of the contents of an item, either selectively or fully, if it is considered necessary to show the presence of material not implied by the rest of the description, or to stress items of particular importance, or to list the contents of a collection. When recording titles formally, take them from the head of the part to which they refer rather than from contents lists, etc.

    Bibliography: p. 859–910

    Includes bibliographies

    Includes index

    Statistical tables cover periods between 1849 and 1960

    Contents: Love and peril / the Marquis of Lorne — To be or not
    to be / Mrs. Alexander — The melancholy hussar / Thomas Hardy

    Partial contents: Recent economic growth in historical perspective
    / by K. Ohkawa and H. Rosovsky — The place of Japan . . . in world
    trade / by P.H. Tresize

    Contents: How these records were discovered — A short sketch
    of the Talmuds — Constantine's letter

2.7B19. Numbers borne by the item. Make notes of important numbers borne by the item other than ISBNs (see 2.8B).

> Supt. of Docs. no.: HE20.8216:11

2.7B20. Copy being described and library's holdings. Make notes on any peculiarities or imperfections of the copy being described that are considered to be important. If the library does not hold a complete set of a multipart item, give details of the library's holdings. Make a temporary note if the library hopes to complete the set.

> Library's copy lacks Appendices, p. 245–260
>
> Library has v. 1, 3–5, and 7 only
>
> Library's copy signed and with marginalia by the author

2.7B21. "With" notes. If the description is of a separately titled part of an item lacking a collective title, make a note beginning *With:* listing the other separately titled parts of the item in the order in which they appear there.

> With: The reformed school / John Drury. London : Printed for R. Wadnothe, [1650]
>
> With: Out of the depths / Mary Ryan. [New York? : s.n., 1945?] — Label your luggage / Robert Nash. [New York? : s.n. 1945?]
>
> With: Of the sister arts / H. Jacob. New York : [s.n.], 1970

2.8. STANDARD NUMBER AND TERMS OF AVAILABILITY AREA

Contents:

> 2.8A. Preliminary rule
> 2.8B. International Standard Book Number
> 2.8C. Terms of availability
> 2.8D. Qualification

2.8A. Preliminary rule

2.8A1. Punctuation

For instructions on the use of spaces before and after prescribed punctuation, see 1.0C.

Precede this area by a full stop, space, dash, space *or* start a new paragraph.

Precede each repetition of this area by a full stop, space, dash, space.

Precede terms of availability by a colon.

Enclose a qualification to the International Standard Book Number (ISBN) or terms of availability in parentheses.

2.8B. International Standard Book Number (ISBN)

2.8B1. Record ISBNs as instructed in 1.8B.

> ISBN 0-904576-17-5
>
> ISBN 0-8352-0875-3 (corrected)

2.8C *Terms of availability*

2.8B2. Give any other number in a note (see 2.7B19).

2.8C. *Optional addition.* **Terms of availability**

2.8C1. Record the price or other terms on which the item is available. Give the price in symbols and numbers, and other terms as concisely as possible.

  ISBN 0-85435-332-1 (pbk.) : £0.60

  ISBN 0-902573-45-4 : Subscribers only

  ISBN 0-7043-3100-4 : $1.95

2.8D. Qualification

2.8D1. Add qualifications to the ISBN and/or terms of availability as instructed in 1.8E. Additionally, if volumes in a set have different ISBNs, follow each ISBN with the designation of the volume to which it applies.

  ISBN 0-901212-04-0 (v. 38)

  ISBN 0-19-212192-8 (cased). — ISBN 0-19-281123-1 (pbk.)

  ISBN 0-08-019857-0 (set). — ISBN 0-08-019856-2 (v. 1 : pbk.)

  ISBN 0-900002-92-1 (limited ed.) : £35.00 (£30.00 to members of the association)

2.8D2. *Optional addition.* Record the type of binding as a qualification of the ISBN.

  ISBN 0-7225-0344-X (pbk.)

2.9. SUPPLEMENTARY ITEMS
Describe supplementary items as instructed in 1.9.

2.10. ITEMS MADE UP OF SEVERAL TYPES OF MATERIAL
Describe items made up of several types of material as instructed in 1.10.

2.11. FACSIMILES, PHOTOCOPIES, AND OTHER REPRODUCTIONS
Describe facsimiles, photocopies, and other reproductions as instructed in 1.11.

EARLY PRINTED MONOGRAPHS

2.12. SCOPE
The following rules (2.12–2.18) are extra rules for the description of books, pamphlets, and broadsides published before 1821 in countries following European conventions in bookmaking. In general, follow the instructions in chapter 1 and in 2.1–2.11 for describing those materials and use the additional and modifying rules given below only when the conditions they state apply to the early book, etc., or when, as in 2.16, they contain instructions different from the previous rules.

2.13. CHIEF SOURCE OF INFORMATION
If the early book, etc., has a title page, use it as the chief source of information. If it has no title page, use the following sources (in this order of preference):

> half title
> caption
> colophon
> cover
> running title
> incipit *or* explicit
> privilege *or* imprimatur
> other sources

Make a note indicating the source used if the item has no title page (see 2.18B).

2.14. TITLE PROPER

2.14A. If the item has no title page and if none of the sources named in 2.13 furnishes a title proper, record as the title proper as many of the opening words of the text as are sufficient to identify the item uniquely.

2.14B. In abridging a long title proper (see 1.1B4), omit first any alternative title and the connecting word (*or*, etc.), then omit inessential words or groups of words. Indicate omissions by the mark of omission.

> *Title appears as*
> Revelation examined with candour. Or a fair enquiry into the sense
> and use of the several revelations expressly declared or sufficiently
> implied to be given to mankind from the Creation as they are found
> in the Bible
>
> *Title proper recorded as*
> Revelation examined with candour . . .

2.14C. Always omit mottoes, quotations, dedications, statements, etc., appearing on the title page that are separate from the title proper.

2.14D. Do not treat additions to the title, even if they are linked to it by a preposition, conjunction, prepositional phrase, etc., as part of the title proper.

> The English Parliament represented in a vision : with an
> after-thought upon the speech delivered to His Most Christian
> Majesty by the deputies of the states of Britany on the 29th day
> of February last . . . : to which is added at large the memorable
> representation of the House of Commons to the Queen in the year
> 1711/12 . . .

2.14E. Transcription of certain letters

Transcribe Latin capitals that are to be converted to lowercase as follows:

> U is transcribed as u.
> V is transcribed as u, provided the text does not distinguish between u and v.
> V is transcribed as u or as v when the text does distinguish between the two.

> J is transcribed as j.
>
> I is transcribed as i, provided the text does not distinguish between i and j.
>
> I is transcribed as i or as j when the text does distinguish between the two.

Transcribe the gothic capitals J and U as i and v.

For languages other than Latin, convert capitals to lowercase according to the orthography of the language, e.g., transcribe TVTTO as tutto.

2.14F. Abridge lengthy other title information and statements of responsibility by omitting inessential words or groups of words. Include as many words of a statement of responsibility as are necessary to identify the person(s) concerned.

2.15. EDITION STATEMENT

2.15A. In general, record an edition statement as it is found in the item. If an exact transcription is not desired, use standard abbreviations and arabic numerals in place of words as instructed in 1.2B.

> Nunc primum in lucem aedita
>
> Editio secunda auctior et correctior
>
> Cinquième édition
>
> *or* 5e éd.

2.15B. If the edition statement is an integral part of the title proper, other title information, or statement of responsibility, or if it is grammatically linked to any of these, record it as such and do not make a further edition statement.

> Chirurgia / nunc iterum non mediocri studio atque diligentia a pluribus mendis purgata

2.16. PUBLICATION, ETC., AREA

2.16A. If the item lacks a publisher statement, give the details of the bookseller, bookseller-printer, or printer as a publisher statement if it appears that this person acted as publisher, seller, or distributor of the item.

2.16B. Give the place of publication, etc., as it is found in the item. Add the modern name of the place if it is considered necessary for identification.

> Augustae Treverorum [Trier]

2.16C. If the full address or the sign of the publisher, etc., appears in the prescribed sources of information, add it to the place if it aids in identifying or dating the item.

> Augsburg, in S. Katharinen Gassen
>
> London, Fleete Streate at the signe of the Blacke Elephant

2.16D. If the only indication in the item of the place of publication, etc., is an address, publisher's sign, etc., or a fictitious designation, add the known or probable name of the town.

>A l'enseigne de l'éléphant ₁Paris₁

>Impressum in Utopia ₁Basel?₁

2.16E. If more than one place of publication, etc., is found in the item, always record the first, and *optionally,* record the others in the order in which they appear. If second or subsequent places are omitted, add ₁*etc.*₁.

>Londres ; et se trouve à Paris

>London ₁etc.₁

2.16F. Record the rest of the details relating to the publisher, etc., as they are given in the item. Separate the parts of a complex publisher, etc., statement only if they are presented separately in the item. If the publisher, etc., statement includes the name of a printer, record it here. Omit words in the publisher, etc., statement that do not aid in the identification of the item and do not indicate the role of the publisher, etc. Indicate omissions by the mark of omission.

>London : R. Barker

>London : Printed for the author and sold by J. Roberts

>London : Imprinted . . . by Robt. Barker . . . and by the assigns of John Bill

>Birmingham : Printed by John Baskerville for R. and J. Dodsley . . .

>Paris : Chez Testu, imprimeur-libraire

>Paris : Ex officina Ascensiana : Impendio Joannis Parvi

2.16G. If there is more than one statement relating to publishers, etc., always record the first statement, and *optionally,* record the other statements in the order in which they appear. If subsequent statements are omitted, add ₁*etc.*₁.

>London : Printed for the author and sold by J. Parsons ₁etc.₁

2.16H. Give the date of publication or printing, including the day and month, as found in the item. Change roman numerals indicating the year to arabic numerals unless they are misprinted, in which case record the roman numerals and add a correction. Add the date in the modern chronology if this is considered to be necessary.

>1716

>iv Ian 1497

>xii Kal. Sept. ₁21 Aug.₁ 1473

>In vigilia S. Laurentii Martyris ₁9 Aug.₁ 1492

>iii Mar. 1483 ₁i.e. 1484₁

>1733
>> (*Date in book:* MDCCXXXIII)

>DMLII ₁i.e. 1552₁

Optionally, formalize the date if the statement appearing in the book is very long.

> xviii Mai. 1507
>> (*not* Anno gratiae millesimo quingentesimo septimo die vero decimoctavo Maij)

2.16J. If the item is undated and the date of publication is unknown, give an approximate date.

> ₍1492?₎
>
> ₍not after Aug. 21, 1492₎
>
> ₍between 1711 and 1719₎

2.16K. If the printer of an early printed monograph is named separately in the item and the function as printer can be clearly distinguished from that of the publisher or bookseller, give the place of printing and the name of the printer as instructed in 1.4G.

2.17. PHYSICAL DESCRIPTION AREA

2.17A. Extent

In recording the pagination of single volume or multivolume (see 2.5B) early printed monographs, record each sequence of leaves, pages, or columns in the terms and form presented in the item. If it is desired to give more precise information about pagination, blank leaves, or other aspects of collation, either expand the extent statement (if this can be done succinctly) or use the note area.

> xi, 31 p.
>
> XII, 120 leaves
>
> x, 32 p., 90 leaves
>
> xi, ₍79₎ leaves
>
> ₍160₎ p.
>
> 40 leaves, ₍8₎ p.

Describe broadsides as such and other single sheets as *sheets.*

> 1 broadside
>
> 1 sheet
>
> ₍2₎ sheets
>
> VIII sheets

2.17B. Illustrations

Describe an illustrated item as instructed in 2.5C. *Optionally,* add *woodcuts, metal cuts,* or, in doubtful cases, *cuts,* as appropriate.

> : ill. (woodcuts)
>
> : 30 ill. (cuts)

: ill. (woodcuts, some col.)

: ill. (woodcuts), ports.

: ports. (woodcuts)

If the item is illustrated by hand or if the illustrations are hand coloured, give a note (see 2.18E).

2.17C. Dimensions

Record the dimensions of the item as instructed in 2.5D. Add the format to the dimensions of a volume in an abbreviated form (e.g., fol., 4to, 8vo, 12mo, etc.).

; 23 cm. (4to)

; 20 cm. (8vo)

; 33 cm. (fol.)

; 23 cm. (4to)

1 sheet ; 48 × 27 cm.

2.18. NOTE AREA

2.18A. Make notes as instructed in 2.7 and follow the instructions given below. Always make the notes below for incunabula.

If the formalized description of the areas preceding the note area does not clearly identify the edition or issue being catalogued, make all notes necessary for unambiguous identification. When appropriate, refer to a detailed description in a standard catalogue or bibliography (see 2.18C), or use both notes and the reference to a catalogue or bibliography.

2.18B. Source of title proper

Give the source of the title proper if it is not the title page.

Title from colophon

Title from: Incipit leaf [2]^a

2.18C. Bibliographic references

For incunabula, and *optionally* for other early printed monographs, give the place in standard lists where a description of the item being described is to be found. Make this note in standard and abbreviated form.

References: HR 6471; GW9101; Goff D-403

References: BMC (XV cent.) II, p. 346 (IB.5874); Schramm, v. 4, p. 10, 50, and ill.

2.18D. Signatures and foliation

Make a note giving details of the signatures and foliation of a volume.

Signatures: a–v^8, x^6

2.18E. Physical description

Give the number of columns or lines and the type measurements if these aid in identifying the printer or if the item is considered to be of bibliographic interest. Give fuller details of the illustrations if these are considered necessary. Make a note on colour printing.

> 24 lines; type 24G
>
> Woodcuts on leaves B2ᵇ and C5ᵇ signed: b
>
> Woodcuts: ill., initials, publisher's and printer's devices
>
> Title and headings printed in red

2.18F. Copy being described

Make notes on special features of the copy in hand. These include rubrication, illumination and other hand colouring, manuscript additions, binding (if noteworthy), provenance, and imperfections.

> Leaves I5–6 incorrectly bound between h3 and h4
>
> Imperfect: wanting leaves 12 and 13 (b6 and c1); without the blank last leaf (S8)
>
> On vellum. Illustrations and part of borders hand coloured. With illuminated initials. Rubricated in red and blue
>
> Contemporary doeskin over boards; clasp. Stamp: Château de La Roche Guyon, Bibliothèque
>
> Blind stamped pigskin binding with initials C.S.A.C. 1644
>
> Inscription on inside of front cover: Theodorinis ab Engelsberg
>
> Signed: Alex. Pope

CARTOGRAPHIC MATERIALS

Contents

Contents

3.0. GENERAL RULES

3.0A. Scope

The rules in this chapter cover the description of cartographic materials of all kinds. Cartographic materials include all materials that represent, in whole or in part, the earth or any celestial body. These include two- and three-dimensional maps and plans (including maps of imaginary places); aeronautical, navigational, and celestial charts; atlases; globes; block diagrams; sections; aerial photographs with a cartographic purpose; bird's-eye views (map views); etc. They do not cover in detail the description of early or manuscript cartographic materials, though the use of an additional term in the physical description (see 3.5B) and the use of the specific instructions in chapter 4 will furnish a sufficiently detailed description for the general library catalogue.

3.0B. Sources of information

3.0B1. For sources of information for an atlas, see 2.0B.

3.0B2. Chief source of information. The chief source of information (in order of preference) is:

    a) the cartographic item itself; when an item is in a number of physical parts, treat all the parts (including a title sheet) as the cartographic item itself

    b) container (portfolio, cover, envelope, etc.) or case, the cradle and stand of a globe, etc.

If information is not available from the chief source, take it from any accompanying printed material (pamphlets, brochures, etc.).

3.0B3. Prescribed sources of information. The prescribed source(s) of information for each area of the description of cartographic materials is set out below. Enclose information taken from outside the prescribed source(s) in square brackets.

AREA	PRESCRIBED SOURCES OF INFORMATION
Title and statement of responsibility	Chief source of information
Edition	Chief source of information, accompanying printed material
Mathematical data	Chief source of information, accompanying printed material
Publication, distribution, etc.	Chief source of information, accompanying printed material
Physical description	Any source
Series	Chief source of information, accompanying printed material
Note	Any source
Standard number and terms of availability	Any source

3.0C. Punctuation

For punctuation of the description as a whole, see 1.0C.

For the prescribed punctuation of elements, see the following rules.

3.0D. Levels of detail in the description

Follow the instructions in 1.0D. Additionally, in a first-level description include the scale in the mathematical data area. In a second-level description, include all the data specified in 3.3.

3.0E. Language and script of the description

See 1.0E.

3.0F. Inaccuracies

See 1.0F.

3.0G. Accents and other diacritical marks

See 1.0G.

3.0H. Items with several chief sources of information

See 1.0H.

3.0J. Description of whole or part

In describing a collection of maps, describe the collection as a whole *or* describe each map (giving the name of the collection as the series), according to the needs of the cataloguing agency. If the collection is catalogued as a whole, but descriptions of the individual parts are considered desirable, see chapter 13. If in doubt about whether to describe the collection as a whole or to describe each part separately, describe the collection as a whole.

> *Description of the collection as a whole*
> Ordnance Survey of Great Britain one inch to one mile map
> : seventh series. — Scale 1:63,360. — Southampton : Ordnance
> Survey, 1952–1974. — 145 maps : col. ; 76 × 68 cm.
>
> ₁Plans of the Rideau Canal from Kingston Bay to Ottawa / signed
> by₁ John By . . . ₁et al.₁. — Scales vary. — 1827–1828. — 28 ms.
> maps : col. ; 74 × 234 cm. or smaller. — Provenance stamps: Board of
> Ordnance, Inspector General of Fortifications; sheets AA3–6,
> 9–11, 13–32
>
> Portfolio of Ghana maps. — Scale 1:2,000,000. — Accra : Survey
> of Ghana, ₁ca. 1962₁. — 12 maps : col. ; 36 × 24 cm.
>
> *Description of one map—separate description*
> Banbury / Ordnance Survey. — ₁State₁ B. — Scale 1:63,360. —
> Southhampton : The Survey, 1968. — 1 map : col. ; 76 × 68
> cm. — (Ordnance Survey of Great Britain one inch to one mile map
> : seventh series ; sheet 145). — "Fully revised 1965–66"

Locks and dams at Merrick Mills, sect. no. 5 / ₁signed by₁ John By. — Scale ₁1:1,050₁. — 1827 Oct. 25. — 1 ms. map : col. ; 65 × 75 cm. — (₁Plans of the Rideau Canal from Kingston to Ottawa / signed by₁ John By ; sheet AA29)·

Ghana vegetation zones / compiled, drawn, and photolithographed by the Survey of Ghana. — Scale 1:2,000,000. — Accra : The Survey, ₁ca. 1962₁. — 1 map : col. ; 36 × 24 cm. — (Portfolio of Ghana maps ; 3)

Description of one map—multilevel description
Ordnance Survey of Great Britain one inch to one mile map : seventh series. — Scale 1:63,360. — Southampton : Ordnance Survey, 1952–1974.

Sheet 145: Banbury. — ₁State₁ B. — 1968. — 1 map : col. ; 76 × 68 cm. — "Fully revised 1965–66"

₁Plans of the Rideau Canal from Kingston Bay to Ottawa / signed by₁ John By . . . ₁et al.₁. — Scales vary. — 1827–1828.

Sheet AA29: Locks and dams at Merrick Mills, sect. no. 5. — 1827. — 1 ms. map : col. ; 65 × 75 cm.

Portfolio of Ghana maps. — Scale 1:2,000,000. — Accra : Survey of Ghana, ₁ca. 1962₁

Sheet 3: Ghana vegetation zones / compiled, drawn, and photolithographed by the Survey of Ghana. — 1 map : col. ; 36 × 24 cm.

3.1. TITLE AND STATEMENT OF RESPONSIBILITY AREA

Contents:
3.1A. Preliminary rule
3.1B. Title proper
3.1C. General material designation
3.1D. Parallel titles
3.1E. Other title information
3.1F. Statements of responsibility
3.1G. Items without a collective title

3.1A. Preliminary rule

3.1A1. Punctuation

For instructions on the use of spaces before and after prescribed punctuation, see 1.0C.

Precede the title of a supplement or section (see 1.1B9) by a full stop.

Enclose the general material designation in square brackets.

Precede each parallel title by an equals sign.

Precede each unit of other title information by a colon.

Precede the first statement of responsibility by a diagonal slash.

Precede each subsequent statement of responsibility by a semicolon.

For the punctuation of this area for items without a collective title, see 1.1G.

3.1B. Title proper

3.1B1. Record the title proper as instructed in 1.1B.

> Historical north England
>
> A map of the county of Essex
>
> Road map of 50 miles around London
>
> England & Wales
>
> The Edinburgh world atlas, or, Advanced atlas of modern geography
>
> Bouguer gravity anomaly map of Tennessee
>
> Františkovy Lázně orientačni plán
>
> British maps of the American Revolution
>
> The Faber atlas
>
> Map of Middle Earth
>
> Geographia marketing and sales maps of Europe

3.1B2. If the title proper includes a statement of the scale, include it in the transcription.

> Topographic 1:500,000 low flying chart
>
> New "half-inch" cycling road maps of England and Wales

3.1B3. If the chief source of information bears more than one title, choose the title proper as instructed in 1.1B8. If both or all of the titles are in the same language and script, choose the title proper on the basis of the sequence or layout of the titles. If these are insufficient to enable the choice to be made or are ambiguous, choose the most comprehensive title.

3.1B4. If the item lacks a title, supply one as instructed in 1.1B7. Always include the name of the area covered in the supplied title.

> [Map of Ontario]
>
> [Lunar globe]
>
> [Gravity anomaly map of Canada]

3.1C. *Optional addition.* **General material designation**

3.1C1. Add, immediately following the title proper, the appropriate general material designation as instructed in 1.1C.

> Central Europe [GMD]
>
> Camden's Britannia, 1695 [GMD]
>
> Decca aeronautical plotting chart [GMD]

3.1C2. If an item contains parts belonging to materials falling into two or more categories, and if none of these is the predominant constituent of the item, give either *multimedia* or *kit* as the designation (see 1.1C1 and 1.10).

3.1D. Parallel titles

3.1D1. Record parallel titles as instructed in 1.1D.

> Suomi ₍GMD₎ = Finland

> International map of natural gas fields in Europe ₍GMD₎ = Carte internationale des champs de gaz naturel en Europe

> Mobil street map of Durban ₍GMD₎ = Straatkaart van Durban

3.1E. Other title information

3.1E1. Record other title information as instructed in 1.1E.

> Canada ₍GMD₎ : a pictorial & historical map

> Ethelreda's Isle ₍GMD₎ : a pictorial map of the Isle of Ely to commemorate the 1300th anniversary of the founding of Ely's conventual church

> Motor road map of south-east England ₍GMD₎ : showing truck and other classified roads

> Kaunispää–Kopsusjärvi ₍GMD₎ : ulkoilukartta

3.1E2. If neither the title proper nor the other title information includes an indication of the geographic area covered by the item, or if there is no other title information, add, as other title information, a word or brief phrase indicating the area covered.

> Vegetation ₍GMD₎ : ₍in Botswana₎

3.1F. Statements of responsibility

3.1F1. Record statements of responsibility as instructed in 1.1F.

> Football history map of England and Wales ₍GMD₎ : showing . . . the colours and locations of all the clubs in the Football League . . . / compiled by John Carvosso

> The English pilot, the fifth book ₍GMD₎ / J. Seller & C. Price

> A map book of West Germany ₍GMD₎ / A.J.B. Tussler, A.J.L. Alden

> Road atlas Europe ₍GMD₎ / Bartholomew

> World atlas ₍GMD₎ / compiled by Rand McNally International

> The Wills south coast yachting guide ₍GMD₎ / edited by the Daily express

> Flugbild Schweiz ₍GMD₎ = Vue aérienne Suisse = Air view Switzerland / Swissair Photo + Vermessungen AG

> Maps & plans of the operations, movements, battles & sieges of the British Army, during the campaigns in Spain, Portugal, and the south

of France, from 1808 to 1814 ₁GMD₁ / compiled by Lieut. Godwin
; engraved by Jas. Wyld

Glacial map of Tasmania ₁GMD₁ / compiled by E. Derbyshire . . .
₁et al.₁

₁Pocket terrestrial globe₁ ₁GMD₁ / J. Moxon

Mondmapo ₁GMD₁ / laŭ la decidoj de Internacia Komisiono por
Ordigo de Geografiaj Nomoj ; redaktis, Tibor Sekelj

Wheaton's atlas of British and world history ₁GMD₁ / by the late
T.A. Rennard ; editors, H.E.L. Mellersh and B.S. Trinder ; maps
prepared by David A. Hoxley

3.1F2. Add a word or short phrase to the statement of responsibility if the relationship between the title of the item and the person(s) or body (bodies) named in the
statement is not clear.

Maps of the Mid-west ₁GMD₁ : ₁edited by₁ D.M. Bagley

3.1G. Items without a collective title

3.1G1. If a cartographic item lacks a collective title, *either* describe the item as a
unit (see 3.1G2 and 3.1G3), *or* make a separate description for each separately
titled part (see 3.1G4), *or* (in certain circumstances) supply a collective title (see
3.1G5).

3.1G2. In describing a cartographic item lacking a collective title as a unit, record
the titles of the individual parts as instructed in 1.1G.

Grand Teton ; Yellowstone National Park ₁GMD₁
(*Both maps produced by the same body*)

Daily mail motor road map of London and twelve miles round.
Motor road map of south-east England ₁GMD₁
(*Maps produced by different bodies*)

Dissegno della fabrica fatta ad uso delle fiere di Verona nell'anno
1722 Pierantonio Berno forma in Verona. Pianta della fiera di
Verona ₁GMD₁

3.1G3. Make the relationship between statements of responsibility and the parts of
an item lacking a collective title and described as a unit clear by additions as instructed in 3.1F2.

France ; Germany ₁GMD₁ / drawn by L. Scott ₁France₁ &
P. McComb ₁Germany₁

3.1G4. If desired, make a separate description for each separately titled part of an
item lacking a collective title. For the description of the extent in each of the descriptions, see 3.5B4. Link the separate descriptions with a note (see 3.7B21).

3.1G5. If a cartographic item lacking a collective title consists of a large number of physically separate parts, supply a collective title as instructed in 3.1B4.

〔Maps of Denmark〕

〔Collection of tourist maps of Thailand published by various authorities〕

〔Ontario county and district maps colour series〕

3.2. EDITION AREA

Contents:
  3.2A. Preliminary rule
  3.2B. Edition statement
  3.2C. Statements of responsibility relating to the edition
  3.2D. Subsequent edition statement
  3.2E. Statements of responsibility relating to a subsequent edition statement

3.2A. Preliminary rule

3.2A1. Punctuation

For instructions on the use of spaces before and after prescribed punctuation, see 1.0C.

Precede this area by a full stop, space, dash, space.

Precede a subsequent edition statement by a comma.

Precede the first statement of responsibility following an edition or subsequent edition statement by a diagonal slash.

Precede each subsequent statement of responsibility by a semicolon.

3.2B. Edition statement

3.2B1. Transcribe a statement relating to an edition of a work that contains differences from other editions, or that is a named revision of that work, as instructed in 1.2B.

2nd ed.

1974 new ed.

Rev. et corr.

Facsim. ed.

2e éd.

3.2B2. In case of doubt about whether a statement is an edition statement, follow the instructions in 1.2B3.

3.2B3. *Optional addition.* If an item lacks an edition statement but is known to contain significant changes from previous editions, supply a suitable brief statement in the language and script of the title proper and enclose it in square brackets.

3.2C *Statements of responsibility relating to the edition*

> [5th ed.]
>
> [Nouv. éd.]

3.2B4. If an edition statement appears in more than one language or script, record the statement that is in the language or script of the title proper. If this criterion does not apply, record the statement that appears first.

> Carte géologique internationale de l'Europe [GMD] = International geological map of Europe. — 3e éd.

3.2B5. If an item lacking a collective title and described as a unit contains one or more parts with an associated edition statement, record such statements following the titles and statements of responsibility to which they relate, separated from them by a full stop.

3.2C. Statements of responsibility relating to the edition

3.2C1. Record a statement of responsibility relating to one or more editions, but not to all editions, of a cartographic item as instructed in 1.2C.

> 3rd ed. / with maps redrawn by N. Manley

3.2D. Subsequent edition statement

3.2D1. If the item is a designated revision of a particular edition, containing changes from that edition, give the subsequent edition statement as instructed in 1.2D.

> 9th ed., Reprinted with summary of the 1961 census and supplement of additional names and amendments

> 4th ed., Roads rev.

> [State] A, [Three bars, one star]
> (*Appears on map as A*≡★)

Do not record statements relating to reissues that contain no changes unless the item is considered to be of particular bibliographic importance to the cataloguing agency.

3.2E. Statements of responsibility relating to a subsequent edition statement

3.2E1. Record a statement of responsibility relating to one or more designated subsequent editions, but not to all subsequent editions, of a particular edition as instructed in 1.2E.

3.3. MATHEMATICAL DATA AREA

Contents:
      3.3A. Preliminary rule
      3.3B. Statement of scale
      3.3C. Statement of projection
      3.3D. Statement of coordinates and equinox

3.3A. Preliminary rule

3.3A1. Punctuation

For instructions on the use of spaces before and after prescribed punctuation, see 1.0C.

Precede this area by a full stop, space, dash, space.

Precede the projection statement by a semicolon.

Enclose the statement of coordinates and equinox in one pair of parentheses.

If both coordinates and equinox are given, precede the statement of equinox by a semicolon.

3.3A2. Use English words and abbreviations in this area.

3.3B. Statement of scale

3.3B1. Give the scale of a cartographic item as a representative fraction expressed as a ratio (1:   ). Precede the ratio by the word *scale*. Give the scale even if it is already recorded as part of the title proper or other title information.

> Geologic map of southeast Kalimantan ₁GMD₁ = Peta geologi Kalimantan tenggara / compiled by the Geological Survey of Indonesia. — Scale 1:500,000

> Bartholomew one inch map of the Lake District ₁GMD₁. — Rev. — Scale 1:63,360

If a verbal scale statement is found on the item, record it as a representative fraction in square brackets.

> Scale ₁1:253,440₁
> (*Verbal scale statement reads:* One inch to four miles)

If a representative fraction or a verbal scale statement is found in a source other than the chief source of information, the scale is given in square brackets in the form of a representative fraction.

> Scale ₁1:63,360₁

If no statement of scale is found on the item, its container or case, or accompanying material, compute a representative fraction from a bar graph, a grid or by comparison with a map of known scale. Give the scale preceded by *ca.*

> Scale ca. 1:63,360

If the scale cannot be determined by any of the above means, give the statement *Scale indeterminable.*

3.3B2. *Optional addition.* Give additional scale information that is found on the item (such as a statement of comparative measures or limitation of the scale to particular parts of the item). Use standard abbreviations and numerals in place of words. Precede such additional information by a full stop.

> Scale 1:250,000. 1 in. to 3.95 miles. 1 cm. to 2.5 km.

3.3C *Statement of projection*

Quote the additional scale information directly if (a) the statement presents unusual information that cannot be verified by the cataloguer; *or* (b) a direct quotation is more precise than a statement in conventional form; *or* (c) the statement on the item is in error or contains errors.

> Scale 1:59,403,960. "Along meridians only, 1 inch = 936 statute miles"

> Scale ca. 1:90,000 not "1 inch to the mile"

3.3B3. If the scale within one item varies and the outside values are known, give both scales connected by a hyphen.

> Scale 1:15,000–1:25,000

If the values are not known, give the statement *Scale varies.*

3.3B4. If the description concerns a multipart item with two scales, give both. Give the larger scale first.

> Scale 1:100,000 and 1:200,000

3.3B5. If the description concerns a multipart item with three or more scales, give the statement *Scales vary.*

3.3B6. In describing a cartographic item in which all the main maps are of one or two scales, give the scale or both scales (in the latter case give the larger scale first). Otherwise, give the statement *Scales vary.*

3.3B7. Give a statement of scale for celestial charts, maps of imaginary places, views (bird's-eye views or map views) and maps with nonlinear scales only if the information appears on the item. If the item is not drawn to scale, give the statement *Not drawn to scale.*

> Scale 1' per 2 cm.

3.3B8. In describing a relief model or other three-dimensional item, give the vertical scale (specified as such) after the horizontal scale if the vertical scale can be ascertained.

> Scale 1:744,080. 1 in. to ca. 28 miles. Vertical scale ca. 1:96,000

> Vertical exaggeration 1:5

3.3C. Statement of projection

3.3C1. Give the statement of projection if it is found on the item, its container or case, or accompanying printed material. Use standard abbreviations (see Appendix B) and numerals in place of words (see Appendix C).

> Conic equidistant proj.

3.3C2. *Optional addition.* Add associated phrases connected with the projection statement if they are found on the item, its container or case, or accompanying printed material. Such associated phrases concern, for example, meridians, parallels, and/or ellipsoid.

> Transverse Mercator proj. Everest spheroid

> Azimuthal equidistant proj. centered on Nicosia, N 35°10′, E 33°22′

3.3D. *Optional addition.* **Statement of coordinates and equinox**

3.3D1. Give the coordinates in the following order:

> westernmost extent of area covered by item (longitude)
> easternmost extent of area covered by item (longitude)
> northernmost extent of area covered by item (latitude)
> southernmost extent of area covered by item (latitude)

Express the coordinates in degrees (°), minutes (′), and seconds (″) of the sexagesimal system (360° circle) taken from the Greenwich prime meridian. Precede each coordinate by W, E, N, or S, as appropriate. Separate the two sets of latitude and longitude by a diagonal slash, and separate each longitude or latitude from its counterpart by a dash.

> (E 79°—E 86°/N 20°—N 12°)

> (E 15°00′00″—E17°30′45″/N 1°30′12″—S 2°30′35″)

> (W 74°50′—W 74°40′/N 45°05′—45°00′)

Optionally, give other meridians found on the item in the note area (see 3.7B8).

3.3D2. For celestial charts, give the declination of the centre of the chart or of its northern and southern limits in degrees with a plus sign (for the Northern Hemisphere) or a minus sign (for the Southern Hemisphere). Precede the declination by the word *zone.* Give the right ascension of the centre of the chart or of its eastern and western limits in hours and, if necessary, minutes.

> (Zone +30°, 2 hr. 18 min.)

> (Zone +30°, 2 hr.–2 hr. 30 min.)

> (Zone −25° −85°)

Give the equinox or epoch as a date preceded by the abbreviation *eq.*

> (Eq. 1971)

3.4. PUBLICATION, DISTRIBUTION, ETC., AREA

Contents:
- 3.4A. Preliminary rule
- 3.4B. General rules
- 3.4C. Place of publication, distribution, etc.
- 3.4D. Name of publisher, distributor, etc.

>**3.4E.** Statement of function of publisher, distributor, etc.
>
>**3.4F.** Date of publication, distribution, etc.
>
>**3.4G.** Place of printing, etc., name of printer, etc., date of printing, etc.

3.4A. Preliminary rule

3.4A1. Punctuation

For instructions on the use of spaces before and after prescribed punctuation, see 1.0C.

Precede this area by a full stop, space, dash, space.

Precede a second or subsequently named place of publication, distribution, etc., by a semicolon.

Precede the name of a publisher, distributor, etc., by a colon.

Enclose a supplied statement of function of a publisher, distributor, etc., in square brackets.

Precede the date of publication, distribution, etc., by a comma.

Enclose the details of printing, etc. (place, name, date) in parentheses.

Precede the name of a printer, etc., by a colon.

Precede the date of printing, etc., by a comma.

3.4B. General rules

3.4B1. Follow the instructions in 1.4B for items with multiple or fictitious places and names of publishers, distributors, etc.

3.4B2. Early cartographic items

Record the publication, etc., details of early cartographic items, when appropriate, as instructed in 2.16.

3.4C. Place of publication, distribution, etc.

3.4C1. Record the place of publication, distribution, etc., as instructed in 1.4C.

3.4D. Name of publisher, distributor, etc.

3.4D1. Record the name of the publisher, etc., and *optionally* the distributor, as instructed in 1.4D.

>Southampton : Ordnance Survey
>
>Point Reyes, Calif. : Drake Navigators Guild
>
>Paris : Institut géographique national
>
>[London] : Royal Geographical Society
>
>Montréal : Éditions FM
>
>[Chicago] : Chicago Area Transportation Study
>
>Amsterdam ; London : North-Holland Pub. Co.
> (*For a cataloguing agency in the United Kingdom*)

London : Royal Geographical Society ; Lympne Castle, Kent :
H. Margary
> (*Second publisher given prominence by layout*)

Southampton : Ordnance Survey for the Institute of Geological
Sciences

Tananarive : Service géographique de Madagascar

3.4E. *Optional addition.* **Statement of function of publisher, distributor, etc.**

3.4E1. Add to the name of the publisher, distributor, etc., a statement of function
as instructed in 1.4E.

København : Geodætisk Institut ; ₁London₁ Stanford ₁distributor₁

3.4F. Date of publication, distribution, etc.

3.4F1. Record the date of publication, distribution, etc., as instructed in 1.4F.

Washington, D.C. : Secretaría General de la Organización de los
Estados Americanos, 1969

Sevenoaks, Kent : Geographers' Map Co., ₁1973₁

Zürich : Orell Füssli, c1973

Helsinki : Maanmittaushallitus, 1965–1967

3.4G. Place of printing, etc., name of printer, etc., date of printing, etc.

3.4G1. If the name of the publisher is unknown, give the place and name of the
printer or manufacturer, if they are found on the item, its container or case, or
accompanying printed material, as instructed in 1.4G.

Paris : ₁s.n., ca. 1898₁ (Paris : LeBrun)

3.4G2. *Optional addition.* Give the place, name of printer, etc., and/or date of
printing, etc., if they differ from the place, name of publisher, etc., and date of
publication, etc.; and are found on the item, its container or case, or accompanying
printed material; and are considered important by the cataloguing agency.

London : Laurie & Whittle, 1804 (1810 printing)

3.5. PHYSICAL DESCRIPTION AREA

Contents:
3.5A. Preliminary rule
3.5B. Extent of item (including specific material designation)
3.5C. Other physical details
3.5D. Dimensions
3.5E. Accompanying material

3.5A. Preliminary rule

3.5A1. Punctuation
For instructions on the use of spaces before and after prescribed punctuation, see 1.0C.

Precede this area by a full stop, space, dash, space *or* start a new paragraph.

Precede other physical details by a colon.

Precede dimensions by a semicolon.

Precede a statement of accompanying material by a plus sign.

Enclose physical details of accompanying material in parentheses.

3.5B. Extent of item (including specific material designation)

3.5B1. Record the number of physical units of a cartographic item by giving the number of units in arabic numerals and one of the following terms, as appropriate. If the item is in manuscript, add *ms.* to the term used.

aerial chart

aerial remote sensing image

anamorphic map

atlas

bird's-eye view *or* map view

block diagram

celestial chart

celestial globe

chart

globe

 (*for globes other than celestial globes*)

hydrographic chart

imaginative map

map

map profile

map section

orthophoto

photo mosaic (controlled)

photo mosaic (uncontrolled)

photomap

plan

relief model

remote-sensing image

space remote-sensing image

terrestrial remote-sensing image

topographic drawing

topographic print

1 aerial chart

1 atlas

1 celestial globe

1 imaginative map

1 ms. map

3 plans

2 topographic prints

If the parts of the item are very numerous and the exact number cannot be readily ascertained, give an approximate number.

ca. 800 maps

If the cartographic item is not comprehended by one of the above terms, use an appropriate term (preferably taken from rule 5B of one of the chapters of Part I).

> 7 wall charts
>
> 52 playing cards

3.5B2. If there is more than one map, plan, etc., on a sheet, specify the number of maps, etc.

> 6 maps on 1 sheet

If maps, plans, etc., are printed in two or more sections but so designed that they could be fitted together to form a single map, plan, etc., or more than one map, plan, etc., give the number of complete maps, plans, etc., followed by the number of sections.

> 1 map in 4 sections
>
> 2 plans in 6 sections
>
> 1 hydrographic chart in 4 sections

If the item consists of a number of sheets each of which has the characteristics of a complete map, plan, etc., treat it as a collection and describe it as instructed in 3.5B1.

3.5B3. Add, to the statement of extent for an atlas, the pagination or number of volumes as instructed in 2.5B.

> 1 atlas (3 v.)
>
> 1 atlas (xvii, 37 p., 74 leaves of plates)

3.5B4. If the description is of a separately titled part of a cartographic item lacking a collective title (see 3.1G4) and the part is physically separate from the rest of the item, give the statement of extent as instructed in 3.5B1–3.5B3.

> 1 globe

If the description is of a separately titled part of a cartographic item lacking a collective title (see 3.1G4) and if the part is not physically separate from the rest of the item, express the fractional extent in the form *on sheet 3 of 4 maps* (if the parts are numbered in a single sequence) or *on 1 side of 4 plans* (if there is no single numbering).

> on side 1 of 1 map
>
> on 1 side of 1 plan
>
> in 2 sections of 2 maps in 6 sections

3.5C. Other physical details

3.5C1. Give the following details, as appropriate, in the order set out here:

> number of maps in an atlas   material
> colour   mounting

3.5C3 *Colour*

3.5C2. Specify the number of maps in an atlas as instructed in 2.5C.

> 1 atlas (xvi, 97, 100 p.) : 35 col. maps
>
> 1 atlas (330 p.) : 100 col. maps (some folded)

3.5C3. Colour. If the item is coloured or partly coloured, indicate this. Disregard coloured matter outside a map, etc., border.

> 1 map : col.
>
> 4 maps : 2 col.
>
> 1 globe : col.
>
> 1 ms. map : pencil drawing, col.

3.5C4. Material. Record the material of which the item is made if it is considered to be significant (e.g., if a map is printed on a substance other than paper).

> 1 map : col., plastic
>
> 1 map : col., silk
>
> 1 globe : col., wood
>
> 1 ms. map : ink drawing, col., vellum

3.5C5. Mounting. If the item is mounted or has been mounted subsequent to its publication, indicate this.

> 1 map : col., mounted on linen
> *Note:* Originally published on 4 sheets
>
> 1 globe : col., wood, mounted on brass stand
>
> 1 celestial globe : plastic, mounted on metal stand

3.5D. Dimensions

3.5D1. Maps, plans, etc. For two-dimensional cartographic items, give the height × width in centimetres, to the next whole centimetre up (e.g., if a measurement is 37.1 centimetres, record it as 38 cm.); *optionally,* for early and manuscript cartographic items, give the dimensions to the nearest millimetre. Give the measurements of the face of the map, etc., measured between the neat lines. Give the diameter of a circular map, etc., and specify it as such. If a map, etc., is irregularly shaped, or if it has no neat lines, or if it has bleeding or damaged edges, give the greater or greatest dimensions of the map itself. If it is difficult to determine the points for measuring the height and the width of the map, etc. (e.g., when the shape is extremely irregular, or when it was printed without one or more of its borders, or when it lacks one or more of its borders), give the height × width of the sheet specified as such.

> 1 map : col. ; 25 × 35 cm.
>
> 1 topographic drawing ; 40 × 23 cm.
>
> 1 ms. map ; 123.5 × 152.4 cm.
>
> 1 map : col. ; 45 cm. in diam.

1 plan ; 78 × 80 cm.
   (*Irregularly shaped*)

1 map : col. ; on sheet 45 × 33 cm.

Measure a single map, etc., drawn in sections at a consistent scale as if it were joined. Add the sheet size. If the sections have irregular outlines, give the sheet size alone. If such a map, etc., has been mounted, give the dimensions of the whole map, etc., alone.

1 map ; 10 × 60 cm. on sheet 25 × 35 cm.

1 map in 9 sections ; 264 × 375 cm., sections each 96 × 142 cm.

1 plan in 4 sections ; sections each 30 × 40 cm.

If the size of either dimension of a map, etc., is less than half the same dimension of the sheet on which it is printed or if there is substantial additional information on the sheet (e.g., text), give the sheet size as well as the size of the map, etc.

1 map ; 20 × 31 cm. on sheet 42 × 50 cm.

If a map, etc., is printed with an outer cover within which it is intended to be folded or if the sheet itself contains a panel or section designed to appear on the outside when the sheet is folded, give the sheet size in folded form as well as the size of the map, etc.

1 map ; 80 × 57 cm. folded to 21 × 10 cm.

1 map : col. ; 9 × 20 cm. on sheet 40 × 60 cm. folded to
   21 × 10 cm.

If a map, etc., is printed on both sides of a sheet at a consistent scale, give the dimensions of the map, etc., as a whole, and give the sheet size. If such a map, etc., cannot conveniently be measured, give the sheet size alone.

1 map ; 45 × 80 cm. on sheet 50 × 44 cm.
   (*Printed on both sides of sheet with line for joining indicated*)

1 map ; on sheet 45 × 30 cm.
   (*Printed on both sides of sheet*)

If the maps, etc., in a collection are of two sizes, give both. If they are of more than two sizes, give the greatest height of any of them followed by greatest width of any of them and the words *or smaller*.

60 maps ; 44 × 55 cm. and 48 × 75 cm.

60 maps ; 60 × 90 cm. or smaller

10 charts in 25 sections : col. ; sections each 100 × 90 cm. or smaller

3.5D2. Atlases. For atlases, give the dimensions as instructed in 2.5D.

1 atlas (xii, 100, 32 p.) : 100 col. maps ; 29 cm.

3.5D3. Relief models. For relief models, give the height × width in centimetres as instructed in 3.5D1, and *optionally* add the depth.

1 relief model : col., plastic ; 45 × 35 × 2 cm.

3.5D4 *Globes*

3.5D4. Globes. For globes, give the diameter, specified as such.

> 1 globe : col., wood, mounted on metal stand ; 12 cm. in diam.

3.5D5. *Optional addition.* **Containers.** Add the dimensions of a container, specified as such, to the dimensions of the item.

> 1 globe : col., plastic, mounted on a metal stand ; 20 cm. in diam.
> in box, 40 × 12 × 12 cm.

> 1 map : col. ; 200 × 350 cm. folded to 20 × 15 cm. in plastic case,
> 25 × 20 cm.

3.5E. Accompanying material

3.5E1. Record the name, and *optionally* the physical description, of any material that is issued with the item and is intended to be used in conjunction with it, as instructed in 1.5E.

> 17 hydrographic charts ; 90 × 96 cm. + 1 book (xvii, 272 p. ;
> 25 cm.)

3.6 SERIES AREA

Contents:
> 3.6A. Preliminary rule
> 3.6B. Series statements

3.6A. Preliminary rule

3.6A1. Punctuation

For instructions on the use of spaces before and after prescribed punctuation, see 1.0C.

Precede this area by a full stop, space, dash, space.

Enclose each series statement (see 1.6J) in parentheses.

Precede parallel titles of series or subseries by an equals sign.

Precede other title information relating to series or subseries by a colon.

Precede the first statement of responsibility relating to a series or subseries by a diagonal slash.

Precede subsequent statements of responsibility relating to a series or subseries by a semicolon.

Precede the ISSN of a series or subseries by a comma.

Precede the numbering within a series or subseries by a semicolon.

Precede the title of a subseries by a full stop.

3.6B. Series statements

3.6B1. Record each series statement as instructed in 1.6.

> (Climatological studies ; no. 8)

> (A1 street atlas series)

102

(Carte géographique de l'Angleterre ; no 16)

(Deutscher Planungsatlas ; Bd. 8)

(Bartholomew world travel series)

(Nouvelle collection / Maurice Le Lannou)

(Communications of the Dublin Institute for Advanced Studies. Series D, Geophysical bulletin ; no. 29)

(Series of atlases in facsimile / Theatrum Orbis Terrarum. 6th series ; v. 1)

(Saggi e memorie di storia dell'arte ; v. 7)

(Graeco-Roman memoirs, ISSN 0306-9992 ; no. 93)

(₁Geological Survey of Canada A series₁ ; 1245A)

(Military city map : series A902 = Carte militaire de la ville : série A902 1:25,000 / Mapping and Charting Establishment, Department of National Defence ; MCE 329)

3.7. NOTE AREA

Contents:
3.7A. Preliminary rule
3.7B. Notes

3.7A. Preliminary rule

3.7A1. Punctuation
Precede each note by a full stop, space, dash, space *or* start a new paragraph for each.

Separate introductory wording from the main content of a note by a colon and a space.

3.7A2. In making notes, follow the instructions in 1.7A.

3.7B. Notes
Make notes as set out in the following subrules and in the order given there.

3.7B1. Nature and scope of the item. If the nature or scope of a cartographic item is not apparent from the rest of the description, indicate it in a word or brief phrase. Also give a note on unusual or unexpected features of the item.

Shows all of western Europe and some of eastern Europe
(*Item entitled:* Germany)

Maps dissected and pasted onto the sides of 42 wooden blocks to form an educational game

Shows the routes of Amundsen, Byrd, and Gould

Shows southernmost extent of the midnight sun

> Shows the main battles of 1944–1945
> (*Item entitled:* The Asian struggle)

> Free ball globe in transparent plastic cradle with graduated horizon circle and "geometer"

> Shows dioceses

3.7B2. Language. Give the language or languages of captions, etc., and text unless they are apparent from the rest of the description.

> In Esperanto

> Includes text in Finnish, Swedish, English, and German

> Place names in Italian

> Legend in English and Afrikaans

> Except for title and "La mer du Nord" the map is in English

3.7B3. Source of title proper. Make notes on the source of the title proper if it is other than the chief source of information.

> Title from container

> Title from separate wrapper

> Title from: A list of maps of America / P.L. Phillips. p. 502

3.7B4. Variations in title. Make notes on titles borne by the item other than the title proper. If considered desirable, give a romanization of the title proper.

> Panel title: Welcome to big Wyoming

> Title in left margin: Ville de Aix-les-Bains, Savoie

> Romanized title: Moskovskaia oblast′

3.7B5. Parallel titles and other title information. Give parallel titles and other title information not recorded in the title and statement of responsibility area if they are considered to be important.

> Added title in Spanish

> Subtitle on wrapper: Showing population changes 1951–60

3.7B6. Statements of responsibility. Make notes on variant names of persons or bodies named in statements of responsibility if these are considered to be important for identification. Give statements of responsibility not recorded in the title and statement of responsibility area. Make notes on persons or bodies connected with a work, or significant persons or bodies connected with previous editions, not already named in the description.

> Engraved by T.J. Newman

> "Ch. Smith sculp."—Cover

> "Plotted . . . by G. Petrie and D.P. Nicol, University of Glasgow, 1965. Field reconnaissance, 1962, and geomorphological interpretation

by R.J. Price as part of project no. 1469 of the Institute of Polar
Studies, the Ohio State University"

Attributed to Blaeu in: Atlantes Neerlandici / C. Koeman, vol.
. . . , p. . . .

3.7B7. Edition and history. Make notes relating to the edition being described or
to the history of the cartographic item.

First ed. published 1954

Sheets of various eds.

A later state of the map first published in 1715 and later in 1745.
This state has the additions of "King's roads" and an advertisement
for Overton's large map of the British Isles, dated 1746

Facsim. of: "The 52 countries [sic] of England and Wales described
in a pack of cards. Sold by Robert Morton . . . [et al.] in 1676"

The map plates, printed in Leipzig in English, derive from
R. Andree's "Allgemeiner Handatlas," 1887. The plates were later
published in the first ed. of the "Times atlas," 1895

Copied from:

Based on:

Red overprinting on the author's "Greater Germany, administrative
divisions 1 July 1944 (no. 3817-R&A, OSS)"

"Roads and railways fully revised, 1971"—Wrapper

A later state of the map first published in 1772

From: Atlas élémentaire de géographie physique et politique /
E. Mentelle et P.G. Chanlaire. [1798]

First ed. published as: Philips modern school atlas of comparative
geography. 1903

3.7B8. Mathematical and other cartographic data. For celestial charts, give the
magnitude.

Limiting magnitude 3.5

For remote-sensing imagery, give mathematical data not already included in the
mathematical data area.

f5.944, alt. 12,000 ft.

Give other mathematical and cartographic data additional to or elaborating on
that given in the mathematical data area.

Scale of original: ca. 1:1300

Oriented with north to right

Prime meridians: Ferro and Paris

3.7B9 *Publication, distribution, etc.*

> Scale departure graph: "Statute miles Mercator projection"
>
> Military grid

3.7B9. Publication, distribution, etc. Make notes on publication, distribution, etc., details that are not included in the publication, distribution, etc., area and are considered to be important.

> All previous eds. published by:
>
> Based on 1961 statistics
>
> Maps dated between 1780 and 1813
>
> The imprint of Gerard Valck has been substituted for the erased imprint of Joan. Blaeu, who probably first published the map ca. 1672
>
> Imprint of W. & S. Jones pasted onto the terrestrial and celestial globe gores

3.7B10. Physical description. Indicate any physical details that are considered to be important and have not been included in the physical description area. If the item is a photoreproduction, indicate this by the term *Photocopy* followed by the method of reproduction if this is likely to affect use of the item (e.g., when it is a blue or blue line print).

> Irregularly shaped
>
> Hand coloured
>
> Printed on both sides of sheet
>
> Photocopy
>
> Photocopy, blue line print
>
> Photocopy, negative
>
> Watermark: C. & I. Honig
>
> In wooden case bearing, on its inner faces, representations of the celestial hemispheres
>
> Bound in vellum

3.7B11. Accompanying material. Make notes on the location of accompanying material if appropriate. Give details of accompanying material not mentioned in the physical description area or given a separate entry or separate description according to the rules for multilevel description (see 13.6).

> Accompanied by filmstrip entitled: Mexico and Central America
>
> Accompanied by the same maps in sheet form first published in: Géographie générale / M.J.C. Barbié Du Bocage. 1842
>
> Each sheet accompanied by a sheet of geological sections

3.7B12. Series. Make notes on series data that cannot be given in the series area.

> Original issued in series:
>
> Some sheets have series designation:

3.7B13. Dissertations. If a cartographic item is a dissertation, make a note about this as instructed in 2.7B13.

3.7B14. Audience. Make a brief note of the intended audience for, or intellectual level of, an item if this information is stated in the item.

> Intended audience: Primary schools

3.7B18. Contents. If a collection of maps is described as a unit (see 3.0J), make notes on the state of the collection at the time of description and indicate the composition of the complete collection if possible. Give variations between sheets in the collection. Complete this note when the collection is complete.

> Complete in 174 sheets. Set includes various editions of some sheets including some reissued by the U.S. Army Map Service. Some sheets, prepared under the direction of the Chief of Engineers, U.S. Army, have series designation "Provisional G.S. G.S. 4145"

Make notes describing the contents of an item (either partially or fully), including: parts; insets; maps, etc., printed on the verso of a map, etc., sheet; illustrations, etc. Give insets, etc., on the recto before maps, etc., on the verso of a sheet. Give the scale of insets, etc., if it is consistent. If the insets, etc., are numerous and minor, give a note in general terms.

> Includes index

> Includes "Glossary"

> Includes key to 140 place names

> With two additional unnumbered parts: The stars in six maps. 1830 — The terrestrial globe in six maps. 1831

> Includes an index and illustrations of the Wangapeka Track

> Insets: Connaught Place — Chanakyapuri — Delhi & New Delhi City. Scale ca. 1:23,000

> Insets: Political and economic alliances — Air distances from London — Membership of international organisations

> On verso: New map of South Hadley, Mass. Scale ca. 1:15,000

> On verso: Indiana ; Iowa ; Missouri. Scale 1:60,000

> Insets: Harrow ; Wembley ; Ruislip. On verso: Map of N.W. London

> Includes 7 insets

> Parts: Ancient Orient before the rise of the Greeks. Scale 1:4,752,000 — Palestine about 860 B.C. Scale 1:506,880

> Parts: The world in 3000 B.C. — The world in 1500 B.C. — The world in 500 B.C. — The world in A.D. 1

> Parts: Colonial organization of the world 1937 — Achievement of independence 1958–1966

3.7B19. Numbers. Give important numbers borne by the item other than ISBNs or ISSNs (see 3.8B).

> Publisher's no.: LB 3721-9

3.7B20. Copy being described and library's holdings. Make notes on any peculiarities or imperfections of the copy being described that are considered important. If the library does not hold a complete set of a multipart item, give details of the library's holdings. Make a temporary note if the library hopes to complete the set.

> Library's copy annotated in red ink to show land owners
>
> Library's copy imperfect: Upper left corner missing
>
> Library's set lacks sheets 9–13 and sheet 27

3.7B21. "With" notes. If the description is of a separately titled part of a cartographic item lacking a collective title, make a note listing the other separately titled parts of the item in the order in which they appear there.

> With a separate map on same sheet: Queen Maud Range
>
> With (on verso): Motor road map of south-east England
>
> Mounted on a wooden stand to form a pair with: Bale's New celestial globe, 1845
>
> With: Atlas de France. Paris : Desnos, 1775

3.8. STANDARD NUMBER AND TERMS OF AVAILABILITY AREA

Contents:
- 3.8A. Preliminary rule
- 3.8B. Standard number
- 3.8C. Key-title
- 3.8D. Terms of availability
- 3.8E. Qualification

3.8A. Preliminary rule

3.8A1. Punctuation

For instructions on the use of spaces before and after prescribed punctuation, see 1.0C.

Precede this area by a full stop, space, dash, space *or* start a new paragraph.

Precede each repetition of this area by a full stop, space, dash, space.

Precede a key-title by an equals sign.

Precede terms of availability by a colon.

Enclose a qualification to the standard number or terms of availability in parentheses.

3.8B. Standard number

3.8B1. Give the International Standard Book Number (ISBN) or the International Standard Serial Number (ISSN) assigned to an item. Record these numbers as instructed in 1.8B.

> ISBN 0-85152-392-7
>
> ISSN 0085-4859

3.8B2. Give any other number in a note (see 3.7B19).

3.8C. Key-title

3.8C1. Give the key-title of a serial item as instructed in 1.8C.

3.8D. *Optional addition.* **Terms of availability**

3.8D1. Give the terms on which the item is available as instructed in 1.8D.

> £4.40 (complete collection). — £0.55 (individual sheets)

3.8E. Qualification

3.8E1. Add qualifications to the standard number and/or to the terms of availability as instructed in 1.8E.

3.9. SUPPLEMENTARY ITEMS

Describe supplementary items as instructed in 1.9.

3.10. ITEMS MADE UP OF SEVERAL TYPES OF MATERIAL

Describe items made up of several types of material as instructed in 1.10.

3.11. FACSIMILES, PHOTOCOPIES, AND OTHER REPRODUCTIONS

Describe facsimiles, photocopies, and other reproductions as instructed in 1.11.

CHAPTER 4

MANUSCRIPTS (INCLUDING MANUSCRIPT COLLECTIONS)

Contents

4.0. GENERAL RULES

4.0A. Scope

The rules in this chapter cover the description of manuscript (including type-script) texts of all kinds, including manuscript books, dissertations, letters, speeches, etc., legal papers (including forms completed in manuscript), and collections of such manuscript texts. For reproductions of manuscript texts published in multiple copies, see chapter 2 or chapter 11, as appropriate. For manuscript cartographic items, see also chapter 3. For manuscript music, see also chapter 5.

4.0B. Sources of information

4.0B1. Chief source of information. The chief source of information for a manuscript text is the manuscript itself. Within manuscripts prefer information found on a title page, in the colophon, then information found in a caption, heading, etc., and lastly, the text itself. Prefer a source, however, that is part of the original manuscript to sources that have been supplied later. If information is not available from the chief source, take it from the following sources (in this order of preference):

> another manuscript copy of the item
> a published edition of the item
> reference sources
> other sources

For collections of manuscripts, treat the whole collection as the chief source.

4.0B2. Prescribed sources of information. The prescribed source(s) of information for each area of the description of manuscript texts is set out below. Enclose information taken from outside the prescribed source(s) with square brackets.

AREA	PRESCRIBED SOURCES OF INFORMATION
Title and statement of responsibility	Chief source of information and manuscript or published copies
Date	Chief source of information and manuscript or published copies
Physical description	Any source
Note	Any source

4.0C. Punctuation

For punctuation of the description as a whole, see 1.0C. For the prescribed punctuation of elements, see the following rules.

4.0D. Levels of detail in the description

See 1.0D.

4.0E. Language and script of the description

See 1.0E.

4.0F. Inaccuracies

See 1.0F.

4.0G. Accents and other diacritical marks

See 1.0G.

4.1. TITLE AND STATEMENT OF RESPONSIBILITY AREA

Contents:

    4.1A. Preliminary rule
    4.1B. Title proper
    4.1C. General material designation
    4.1D. Parallel titles
    4.1E. Other title information
    4.1F. Statements of responsibility
    4.1G. Items without a collective title

4.1A. Preliminary rule

4.1A1. Punctuation

For instructions on the use of spaces before and after prescribed punctuation, see 1.0C.

Enclose the general material designation in square brackets.

Precede each parallel title by an equals sign.

Precede each unit of other title information by a colon.

Precede the first statement of responsibility by a diagonal slash.

Precede each subsequent statement of responsibility by a semicolon.

For the punctuation of this area for items without a collective title, see 1.1G.

4.1B. Title proper

4.1B1. Record the title proper as instructed in 1.1B.

> Life of Romney

> A declaration of the representatives of the United States of America in Congress assembled

> The waste land

> Death in Leamington Spa

4.1B2. If a manuscript text or manuscript collection lacks a title or lacks some of the data prescribed for the material below, supply one as instructed below.

Manuscript volumes and similar material. This section applies to literary manuscripts, diaries, journals, memorandum books, account books, etc. Supply a brief title indicating the nature of the material. For manuscripts of subsequently published works, supply the title by which the work is known.

> [Diary]

> [Seventeen poems]

Ancient, medieval, and Renaissance manuscripts.[1] For these manuscripts and for oriental manuscripts lacking a title page, follow, when appropriate, the provisions for early printed monographs (see 2.14). Otherwise, supply a title by which the work is known or a title indicating the nature of the material.

> [De re militari]

> [Treatise on arithmetic]

Letters, etc. This section applies to single letters, postcards, telegrams, radiograms, etc. Supply a title consisting of the word *Letter* (or *Postcard, Telegram,* etc.), the date of writing (expressed as year, month, day), the place of writing, the name of the addressee, and place to which addressed. Enclose any details not taken from the letter, etc., its envelope, or enclosures, in square brackets.

> [Letter] 1901 March 6, Dublin [to] Henrik Ibsen, Kristiania [Oslo]

> [Letter, ca. 1898 Jan. 1] Worcester Park, Surrey [to] George Gissing, Rome

> [Postcard] 1898 March 1, Rome [to] H.G. Wells, Worcester Park, Surrey

> [Telegram] 1889 Feb. 8, London [to] James McNeill Whistler, Chelsea, London

Speeches, sermons, etc. Supply a title for a speech, sermon, etc., consisting of an appropriate word (*Speech, Address,* etc.) followed by the place and/or the occasion of the delivery.

> [Lecture, Royal College of Medicine, London]

---

1. This rule is intended for general guidance only.

[Address, before Goucher College, Baltimore, Md., in the First Methodist Episcopal Church]

Legal documents. This section applies to legal documents such as wills, deeds, mortgages, leases, warrants, commissions, etc. Supply a title for a legal document consisting of a word or brief phrase characterizing the document, the date of signing (expressed as year, month, day) the name(s) of persons concerned other than those responsible for the document, and the occasion for the document if it can be expressed concisely. Enclose any details not taken from the document in square brackets.

[Will] 1943 Feb. 8

[Commission, ca. 1851 Apr. 9] appointing J.E. Bradshaw to command the Peshawar Battalion

[Lease, 1937 Oct. 17, of shop in Bridge St., Harrow, Middlesex]

Collections of manuscripts. This section applies to collections of manuscript materials formed by or around a person, family, corporate body, or subject. The materials may be in their original form or reproductions, and may include photographs and printed materials. Supply a title by which the collection is known, or a title indicating the nature of the collection. Unless more specific terms are used, use *Letters* for letters by an individual, *Correspondence* for letters between persons or to a person or persons, *Papers* for miscellaneous personal or family material, and *Records* for materials relating to a corporate body.

[Letters]

[Records]

[Mercantile records]

[Indian papers]

[Literary remains]

Miscellaneous single manuscripts. For manuscript texts not covered by the above sections, supply a title by which the manuscript is known, or supply a title indicating the nature of the material.

[Chart for Tender is the night]

Indicate the source of a supplied title in the note area (see 4.7B3).

4.1C. *Optional addition.* **General material designation**

4.1C1. Add, immediately following the title proper, the appropriate general material designation as instructed in 1.1C.

Gondal poems [GMD]

4.1D. Parallel titles

4.1D1. Record parallel titles as instructed in 1.1D.

4.1E. Other title information

4.1E1. Record other title information as instructed in 1.1E.

> The need of redirected rural schools ₍GMD₎ : address, before the Iowa State Teachers' Association, ₍Des Moines₎, Oct. 4, 1910

4.1E2. If a letter, etc., speech, sermon, etc., or legal document has a title lacking the information specified for supplied titles for those documents (see 4.1B2), add the information as other title information.

> Why no Baal? ₍GMD₎ : ₍sermon, Westminster Cathedral₎

> In place of uncertainty ₍GMD₎ : a speech ₍delivered to the Peace Pledge Union and Society of Friends, Friends Hall, London₎

4.1F. Statements of responsibility

4.1F1. Record statements of responsibility appearing on the manuscript as instructed in 1.1F.

> Exil ₍GMD₎ / St.-J. Perse

> ₍Letter₎ 1899 Jan. 3, Dorking, Surrey ₍to₎ H.G. Wells, Worcester Park, Surrey ₍GMD₎ / George Gissing

> Three sonnets of Shakespeare ₍GMD₎ / written in the italic hand by Pamela Thomson

4.1F2. *Optional addition.* If the name appended to, or the signature on, a manuscript is incomplete, add to it the name of the person concerned.

> ₍Letter₎ 1929 Feb. 8, New York ₍to₎ F. Scott Fitzgerald, Wilmington, Del. ₍GMD₎ / Zelda ₍Fitzgerald₎

> ₍Letter₎ 1898 July 19, Dorking, Surrey ₍to₎ H.G. Wells, Worcester Park, Surrey ₍GMD₎ / G.G. ₍George Gissing₎

4.1F3. If a manuscript lacks a signature or statement of responsibility, supply the name(s) of the person(s) responsible for it, if known.

> Speech, Trafalgar Square, London ₍GMD₎ / ₍William Morris₎

> The waste land ₍GMD₎ / T.S. Eliot ; ₍with ms. amendments by Ezra Pound₎

4.1G. Items without a collective title

4.1G1. If a single manuscript lacks a collective title, record the titles of the individual parts as instructed in 1.1G.

> Gold shoes ; The other world ₍GMD₎ / J.M. Morgan

> Speculum regum / Godefridus Viterbiensis. Tractatus de occultatione vitiorum sub specie virtutum ₍GMD₎

4.2. EDITION AREA

This area is not used for manuscript texts.

4.3. MATERIAL (OR TYPE OF PUBLICATION) SPECIFIC DETAILS AREA

This area is not used for manuscript texts.

4.4. DATE AREA

Contents:
>   4.4A. Preliminary rule
>   4.4B. Date of the manuscript

4.4A. Preliminary rule

4.4A1. Punctuation

For instructions on the use of spaces before and after prescribed punctuation, see 1.0C.

Precede this area by a full stop, space, dash, space.

4.4B. Date of the manuscript

4.4B1. Give the date or inclusive dates of the manuscript or manuscript collection unless it is already included in the title (as with letters and legal documents). Give the date as a year or years, and *optionally* the month and day (in the case of single manuscripts), in that order.

>   Exil ₁GMD₁ / St.-J. Perse. — 1941

>   Correspondence ₁GMD₁ / William Allen. — 1821–1879

>   Records ₁GMD₁ / American Colonization Society. — 1816–1908

>   Alice's adventures under ground ₁GMD₁ : a Christmas gift to a dear child in memory of a summer day / ₁Lewis Carroll (Rev. C.L. Dodgson)₁. — 1864

>   Sonnet, To Genevra ₁GMD₁ / ₁Lord Byron₁. — 1813 Dec. 17

4.4B2. If the date of delivery of a speech, sermon, etc., differs from the date of the manuscript, record the date of delivery in a note (see 4.7B5) unless this date is part of the title information.

>   ₁Speech₁ Glasgow Labour Club ₁GMD₁ / James Maxton. — 1928 Jan. 13
>   *Note:* Delivered Feb. 8, 1928

4.5. PHYSICAL DESCRIPTION AREA

Contents:
>   4.5A. Preliminary rule
>   4.5B. Statement of extent
>   4.5C. Other physical details
>   4.5D. Dimensions

4.5A. Preliminary rule

4.5A1. Punctuation

For instructions on the use of spaces before and after prescribed punctuation, see 1.0C.

Precede this area by a full stop, space, dash, space *or* start a new paragraph.

Precede other physical details by a colon.

Precede the dimensions by a semicolon.

4.5B. Statement of extent

4.5B1. Single manuscripts. Record sequences of leaves or pages, whether numbered or not, as instructed in 2.5B.

> 23 leaves
>
> iv, 103 leaves
>
> ₍63₎ leaves
>
> ₍4₎ p.
>
> ₍4₎, 103 p.
>
> leaves 51–71

If the manuscript has been bound, add *bound* at the end of the pagination.

> ₍70₎ leaves, bound
>
> 4, ₍20₎, 30 p., bound

Add, to the pagination, etc., of ancient, medieval, and Renaissance manuscripts, the number of columns (if more than one) and the average number of lines to the page.

> ₍208₎ leaves (41 lines)
>
> ₍26₎ leaves (2 columns, 45–47 lines)

Optional addition. Add, to the pagination, the number of leaves if this is different from the number of pages.

> ₍2₎ p. on 1 leaf
>
> ₍5₎ p. on 3 leaves

4.5B2. Collections of manuscripts. If a collection occupies one linear foot or less of shelf space, record the extent in terms of the number, or approximate number of items[2] (the number of bound and unbound items separately expressed), or the number of containers or volumes. *Optionally,* if the number of volumes or containers is recorded, add the number or approximate number of items.

> 123 items
>
> ca. 400 items

---

2. *Item* here means a separate manuscript. For example, a letter with several leaves and an enclosure is counted as one item.

4.5C *Other physical details*

> 37 items, 30 items bound
>
> 6 v.
>
> 12 boxes
>
> 3 v. (183 items)
>
> 12 boxes (ca. 1000 items)

If the collection occupies more than one linear foot of shelf space, record the extent in terms of the number of linear feet occupied. *Optionally,* add the number or approximate number of items or containers or volumes.

> 40 ft.
>
> 3 ft. (ca. 2250 items)
>
> 6 ft. (75 v.)

4.5C. Other physical details

4.5C1. If the material on which a single manuscript is written is not paper, record the name of the type of material.

> ₁1₁ leaf : parchment
>
> ₁20₁ leaves : vellum

4.5C2. If a manuscript is illustrated or if a collection of manuscripts includes illustrated items, record this as instructed in 2.5 C. If a manuscript consists of illustration(s), record this as instructed in 8.5C.

> 30 p. : ill.
>
> ₁3₁, 20 leaves : vellum, ill., maps
>
> 30 p. : col. ill.
>
> 6 v. : ill.
>
> 3 v. (183 items) : some ill. (some col.)

4.5D. Dimensions

4.5D1. Single manuscripts. Give the height of single unbound manuscripts in centimetres to the next whole centimetre up. Add the width if it is less than half the height or greater than the height. If the manuscript is kept folded, add the dimensions when folded.

> 6 p. ; 24 cm.
>
> ₁7₁ p. ; 24 × 30 cm.
>
> 12 leaves : ill. ; 20 cm. folded to 10 × 12 cm.
>
> ₁1₁ leaf : parchment ; 35 × 66 cm. folded to 10 × 19 cm.

Give the dimensions of a bound volume or case as instructed in 2.5D.

> 131 leaves in case ; 26 cm.
>
> ₁70₁ p. in case ; 20 × 24 cm.

4.5D2. Collections of manuscripts. If the size of the items, containers, or volumes (depending on the terms of the first statement of extent) is uniform, give that size in centimetres. *Optionally,* if the size is not uniform, give the size of the largest followed by *or smaller.*

> 20 items ; 20 × 30 cm.
>
> 6 v. ; 30 cm.
>
> 12 boxes ; 40 × 15 × 10 cm.
>
> 6 v. ; 28 cm. or smaller

4.6. SERIES AREA

This area is not used for manuscript texts.

4.7. NOTE AREA

Contents:
    4.7A. Preliminary rule
    4.7B. Notes

4.7A. Preliminary rule

4.7A1. Punctuation

Precede each note by a full stop, space, dash, space *or* start a new paragraph for each.

Separate introductory wording from the main content of a note by a colon and a space.

4.7A2. In making notes, follow the instructions in 1.7A.

4.7B. Notes

Make notes as set out in the following subrules and in the order given there. For notes on ancient, medieval, and Renaissance manuscripts, see also 4.7B22.

4.7B1. Nature, scope, or form of manuscript(s).
Make notes on the nature of a manuscript or the manuscripts in a collection unless it is apparent from the rest of the description. Use one of the following terms, as appropriate:

> holograph(s) — *for manuscripts handwritten by the author*
> ms. — *for all other handwritten manuscripts*
> mss. — *for all other collections of handwritten manuscripts*
> typescripts(s)

If the item or collection being described is a copy or consists of copies, add (*carbon copy*), (*photocopy*), (*transcript*), or the plural of these, as appropriate. To *transcript,* add *handwritten* or *typewritten.*

> Holograph
>
> **Ms.**

Typescripts

Holograph (carbon copy)

Ms. (photocopy, negative)

Mss. (transcripts, handwritten)

Typescript (photocopy)

If the items in a collection are not all of the same nature, word the qualification to indicate this.

Mss. (some photocopies)

Mss. (transcripts, handwritten, and photocopies)

Mss. (photocopies, some negative)

If the item is signed, indicate this.

Holograph signed

Ms. signed (photocopy)

If the item is a copy, add the location of the original if this can be readily ascertained.

Ms. (photocopy), original in the British Library Reference Division

Holograph signed (photocopy), original in possession of the author

Indicate the scope or form of a manuscript item if it is not apparent from the rest of the description.

Poem

Journal and account book

Typescript of sound recording

In describing a collection of manuscripts, name the types of papers, etc., constituting the collection and mention any other features that characterize it. If the collection is of personal papers, give enough data to identify the person, either as a brief initial statement or as part of the summary of the nature of the collection. If necessary, give the contents (see also 4.7B18) as part of that summary.

Paleontologist and educator. Correspondence, reports, notes, articles, maps, printed matter, and other papers, mainly relating to the Carnegie Institution, the National Academy of Sciences, the National Research Council, and national parks

Papers covering (in the main) Allen's service as U.S. senator, 1837–1848, and as governor of Ohio, 1873–1874. Includes some of his speeches, drafts of his letters, and letters from various correspondents on political matters in Ohio

Includes records of the Banking Board, 1911–1939, and those of of the Bureau of Insurance, 1897–1943

Writer. Personal papers, letters, etc., drafts of some poems, including the complete text of the verse drama "The Pierrot of the minute"

4.7B2. Language(s). Give the language or languages of the item unless they are apparent from the rest of the description.

> In Swedish
>
> Latin with English marginalia
>
> Some items in English, some in French
>
> English with typewritten French translation

4.7B3. Source of title proper. Make notes on the source of the title proper if it is other than the chief source of information.

> Title from cover
>
> Title from: Guide to manuscript collections in the William L. Clements Library / compiled by H.H. Peckham. 1942

4.7B4. Variations in title. Make notes on titles borne by the item other than the title proper. If considered desirable, give a romanization of the title proper.

> Also known as: The Thynne papers

4.7B5. Parallel titles and other title information. Give parallel titles and other title information not recorded in the title and statement of responsibility area if they are considered to be important.

4.7B6. Statements of responsibility. Make notes on variant names of persons or bodies named in statements of responsibility if these are considered to be important for identification. Give statements of responsibility not recorded in the title and statement of responsibility area. Make notes on persons or bodies connected with a work not already named in the description.

> Original, signed by John Hancock
>
> Marginalia by Robert Graves
>
> Collection made by P.M. Townshend
>
> Dictated to Clare Wheeler

4.7B7. Donor, source, etc., and previous owner(s). Make notes on the donor or source of a manuscript or manuscript collection, and on previous owners if they can be easily ascertained. Add the year or years of accession to the name of the donor or source, and add the years of ownership to the name of a previous owner.

> Gift of Worthington C. Ford, 1907
>
> Purchase, 1951–1968
>
> Purchased from the Del Monte collection, 1901
>
> Gift of Mr. Wright, 1938–1954
>
> Previously owned by L. McGarry, 1951–1963

4.7B8. Place of writing. If the manuscript carries an indication of the place in which it was written, record this and the source of the information in a note.

> At end: Long Beach Island
>
> On t.p.: London-Zagreb-Trieste

4.7B9. Published versions. If the work contained in a manuscript or the content of a manuscript collection has been, or is being, published, give the publication details.

> Published as: The life of George Romney. London : T. Payne, 1809
>
> Published in: Poetry : a magazine of verse. Vol. 59, 1942. p. 295–308
>
> Entire collection, with Jefferson papers from the Library of Congress and elsewhere, is being published in: Papers of Thomas Jefferson / edited by J.P. Boyd. 1950–

4.7B10. Physical description. Give physical details not given elsewhere in the description that are considered to be important.

> Paper watermarked:
>
> Two seals, pendant
>
> Ms. torn in half and rejoined
>
> Lacks top right corner
>
> Some papers stained by water
>
> Red ink on yellow paper

4.7B11. Accompanying material. Give details of materials accompanying a manuscript or manuscript collection, especially (for letters) envelopes, enclosures, and endorsements; (for legal documents) accompanying papers and endorsements; and (for collections) unpublished guides.

> Accompanied by autobiographical sketch (2 p., holograph)
>
> Accompanied by slip containing emendations
>
> In envelope, with enclosure (4 p. on 2 leaves, holograph signed)
>
> Endorsement: Thomas Kitchen to Ellen Montgomery Jones
>
> Accompanied by photocopies of documents relating to the probate of the will
>
> Unpublished guide in the library
>
> Indexed in the library's catalogue

4.7B13. Dissertations. If a manuscript is a dissertation, give this as instructed in 2.7B13.

4.7B14. Access and literary rights. Indicate as specifically as possible all restrictions on the access to a manuscript or manuscript collection.

> Accessible after 1983
>
> Open to researchers under library restrictions

If the literary rights in a collection have been reserved for a specified period or are dedicated to the public and a document stating this is available, make the following note:

> Information on literary rights available

4.7B15. Reference to published descriptions. Make a note on the best or fullest published description of a manuscript or manuscript collection and published indexes or calendars.

> Calendar: Spanish manuscripts concerning Peru, 1531–1651.
> Washington, D.C. : Library of Congress, 1932

> Described in:

4.7B17. Summary. Give a brief objective summary of the content of an item unless another part of the description gives enough information.

4.7B18. Contents. Give the contents of an item, either selectively or fully, if it is considered necessary to show the presence of material not implied by the rest of the description, or to stress items of particular importance, or to list the contents of a collection. When recording titles formally, take them from the head of the part to which they refer rather than from contents lists, etc.

> Includes petition to the King from the citizens of London, 1783,
> in scroll form

> Also contains two short prose pieces dated 1937

> Contains letters to Mrs. Wells and Gabrielle Gissing

4.7B22. Ancient, medieval, and Renaissance manuscripts. In addition to the notes specified above, give the following notes for ancient, medieval, and Renaissance manuscripts and collections of such manuscripts.

Style of writing. Give the script used in a manuscript or the predominant script in a collection.

> Semigothic script with marginal corrections in roman script

Illustrative matter. Give ornamentation, rubrication, illumination, etc., and important details of other illustrative matter.

> Rubricated

> Headings in red, with sepia drawings

> Col. drawing of Jacob's dream on leaf [23][a]

Collation. Give the number of gatherings with mention of blank, damaged, or missing leaves, and any earlier foliation.

> Signatures (with catchwords at the end of each): [4] leaves (on vellum), $_{[}a_{]}^{10}$, b^{10+2} (1st and last leaves on vellum), $c–f^{10}$, g^{10+2}, $h–p^{10}$, q^{10+2} (2nd and 11th leaves on vellum), $r–t^{10}$, v^{8} (the last 2 leaves blank)

Other physical details. Give details of owner's annotations, the binding, and any other important physical details.

>Annotated by previous owner, signed M. B.

>Bound in calf, gold stamped, with Bellini arms on spine

Opening words. If the manuscript is given a supplied title, quote as many of the opening words of the main part of the text as will enable the item to be identified.

>Tractatus begins (on leaf ₁17₁ᵃ): Est via que videtʳ homī rcta nouissima . . .

MUSIC

Contents

5.0. GENERAL RULES

5.0A. Scope

The rules in this chapter cover the description of published music. They do not cover manuscript or other unpublished music in detail, though the use of an additional term in the physical description (see 5.5B) and the use of the specific provisions of chapter 4 will furnish a sufficiently detailed description for the general library catalogue. For the description of recorded music, see chapter 6. For microform reproductions of music, see chapter 11.

5.0B. Sources of information

5.0B1. Chief source of information. If the title page consists of a list of titles including the title of the item being catalogued, use as the chief source of information whichever of the "list" title page, the cover, or the caption furnishes the fullest information. In all other cases use the title page (see 2.0B1) as the chief source of information.

If information is not available from the chief source, take it from the following sources (in this order of preference):

> caption
> cover
> colophon
> other preliminaries
> other sources

5.0B2. Prescribed sources of information. The prescribed source(s) of information for each area of the description of published music is set out below. Enclose information taken from outside the prescribed source(s) in square brackets.

AREA	PRESCRIBED SOURCES OF INFORMATION
Title and statement of responsibility	Chief source of information
Edition	Chief source of information, caption, cover, colophon, other preliminaries
Publication, distribution, etc.	Chief source of information, caption, cover, colophon, other preliminaries, first page of music
Physical description	Any source
Series	Chief source of information, caption, cover, colophon, other preliminaries
Note	Any source
Standard number, etc.	Any source

5.0C. Punctuation

For the punctuation of the description as a whole, see 1.0C.

For the prescribed punctuation of elements, see the following rules.

5.0D. Levels of detail in the description

See 1.0D.

5.0E. Language and script of the description
See 1.0E.

5.0F. Inaccuracies
See 1.0F.

5.0G. Accents and other diacritical marks
See 1.0G.

5.0H. Items with several chief sources of information
See 1.0H.

5.1. TITLE AND STATEMENT OF RESPONSIBILITY AREA

Contents:
5.1A. Preliminary rule
5.1B. Title proper
5.1C. General material designation
5.1D. Parallel titles
5.1E. Other title information
5.1F. Statements of responsibility
5.1G. Items without a collective title

5.1A. Preliminary rule

5.1A1. Punctuation
For instructions on the use of spaces before and after prescribed punctuation, see 1.0C.

Precede the title of a supplement or section (see 1.1B9) by a full stop.

Enclose the general material designation in square brackets.

Precede each parallel title by an equals sign.

Precede each unit of other title information by a colon.

Precede the first statement of responsibility by a diagonal slash.

Precede each subsequent statement of responsibility by a semicolon.

For the punctuation of this area for items without a collective title, see 1.1G.

5.1B. Title proper

5.1B1. Record the title proper as instructed in 1.1B.

Die Meistersinger von Nürnberg

Georgia moon

Beethoven for ten little fingers

Violin-Sonaten 1, 2, 3

Gigi

3 D.H. Lawrence love poems

String quartet 5

Songs & folk music

Hymne à la joie

Charles Aznavour présente ses plus grands succès

The vocal score and libretto of The merry widow

The Beatles song book

5.1B2. If the title, exclusive of the medium of performance, the key, or the opus numbering of the work, consists of a generic term (e.g., trio, symphony, string quartet), treat the statements of medium of performance, the key, and/or the opus numbering as part of the title proper.

Sonate en ré majeur, opus 3, pour violon

Scherzo for two pianos, four hands

Symphony no. 3, A major, op. 56

Symphony no. 1, in E flat major

Four suites in 3 parts with organ

String quintet no. 1, A major, op. 18

Otherwise, treat such a statement as other title information (see 5.1E).

Easter fresco [GMD] : for soprano, flute, horn, harp, and piano

In case of doubt, treat such a statement as part of the title proper.

5.1B3. If a title proper has to be devised by the cataloguer (see 1.1B7), give all the elements prescribed for uniform titles for music (see 25.25–25.36) in the order prescribed there.

Trios, piano, strings, no. 2, op. 66, C minor

5.1C. *Optional addition.* **General material designation**

5.1C1. Add, immediately following the title proper, the appropriate general material designation as instructed in 1.1C.

Sonata for viola and piano, op. 147 [GMD]

Fugue for 6 cellos on themes by Beethoven [GMD]

Sechs Partiten für Flöte [GMD]

Sunday morning coming down [GMD]

5.1C2. If an item contains parts belonging to materials falling into two or more categories, and if none of these is the predominant constituent of the item, give either *multimedia* or *kit* as the designation (see 1.1C1 and 1.10).

The call of Isaiah [multimedia]

or The call of Isaiah [kit]

5.1D. Parallel titles

5.1D1. Record parallel titles as instructed in 1.1D.

> Gold und Silber ₍GMD₎ = L'or et l'argent = Gold and silver

> Album for the young ₍GMD₎ = Album für die Jugend

> Concerto, D-Dur, für Horn und Orchester ₍GMD₎ = Concerto, D major, for horn and orchestra = Concerto, ré majeur, pour cor et orchestre

5.1E. Other title information

5.1E1. Record other title information as instructed in 1.1E.

> Angelo mio ₍GMD₎ : valse

> 6 succès d'Elvis Presley ₍GMD₎ : album : piano, chant et guitare

> Fugue on "Hey diddle diddle" ₍GMD₎ : for SATB unaccompanied

> Kleine Meditationen ₍GMD₎ : für Streichtrio und Harfe = Short meditations : for string trio and harp

> Officium pastorum ₍GMD₎ = The shepherds at the manger : an acting version of a 13th-century liturgical music drama : for six soloists (three sopranos and three basses, or two sopranos, one tenor, and three basses) and treble (or soprano) chorus with suggested accompaniment for chamber organ and chime bells

5.1F. Statements of responsibility

5.1F1. Record statements of responsibility as instructed in 1.1F.

> Traces ₍GMD₎ : pour violoncelle seul / Jacques Lenot

> Overture from La sultane suite ₍GMD₎ / by François Couperin

> La vie parisienne ₍GMD₎ : operetta in three acts / Jacques Offenbach ; music adapted and arranged by Ronald Hanmer ; new book and lyrics by Phil Park

> Door number three ₍GMD₎ / Steve Goodman, Jimmy Buffett

> The Liber usualis ₍GMD₎ : with introduction and rubrics in English / edited by the Benedictines of Solesmes

> Song to the Virgin Mary ₍GMD₎ : for mixed chorus a capella or 6 solo voices / by Andrzej Panufnik ; words anonymous

> Three songs for America ₍GMD₎ : bass voice and instruments (woodwind quintet and string quintet) / David Amram ; piano reduction by the composer ; words by John F. Kennedy, Martin Luther King, and Robert F. Kennedy

5.1F2. Add a word or short phrase to the statement of responsibility if the relationship between the title of the work and the person(s) or body (bodies) named in the statement is not clear.

A Collection of ancient piobaireachd or Highland pipe music ₍GMD₎ / ₍collected₎ by Angus Mackay

Der Prozess ₍GMD₎ / ₍Musik von₎ Gottfried von Einem ; ₍Text von₎ Boris Blacher und Heinz von Cramer

5.1G. Items without a collective title

5.1G1. If an item lacks a collective title, record the titles of the individual works as instructed in 1.1G.

Four small dances ; and, Six Hungarian folksongs ₍GMD₎ / Béla Bartók ; arranged for junior string orchestra by Gábor Darvas

Her silver will ; Looking back at Sposalizio ₍GMD₎ : medium voice / Gordon Binkerd ; poems by Emily Dickinson

Neosa : march / Phil B. Catelinet. The wonder of Christmas : suite / Leslie Condon. I come to thee : meditation / Stuart Johnson. Rejoicing every day / selection by Neville McFarlane ₍GMD₎

5.1G2. Make the relationship between statements of responsibility and the parts of an item lacking a collective title clear by additions as instructed in 5.1F2.

5.2. EDITION AREA

Contents:
5.2A. Preliminary rule
5.2B. Edition statement
5.2C. Statements of responsibility relating to the edition
5.2D. Subsequent edition statement
5.2E. Statements of responsibility relating to a subsequent edition statement

5.2A. Preliminary rule

5.2A1. Punctuation
For instructions on the use of spaces before and after prescribed punctuation, see 1.0C.
Precede this area by a full stop, space, dash, space.
Precede a subsequent edition statement by a comma.
Precede the first statement of responsibility following an edition or subsequent edition statement by a diagonal slash.
Precede each subsequent statement of responsibility by a semicolon.

5.2B. Edition statement

5.2B1. Transcribe a statement relating to an edition of a work that contains differences from other editions or that is a named reissue of that work as instructed in 1.2B.

2nd ed.

2ᵉ éd. du recueil noté

6. udg.

Urtextausg.

Ed. for 2 pianos

Ausg. für 2 Klaviere

5.2B2. In case of doubt about whether a statement is an edition statement, follow the instructions in 1.2B3.

5.2B3. *Optional addition.* If an item lacks an edition statement but is known to contain significant changes from previous editions, supply a suitable brief statement in the language and script of the title proper and enclose it in square brackets.

₍3rd ed.₎

₍Nouv. éd. augm. des Lectures chantées, parue en 1968₎

5.2B4. If an edition statement appears in more than one language or script, record the statement that is in the language or script of the title proper. If this criterion does not apply, record the statement that appears first.

5.2B5. If an item lacking a collective title and described as a unit contains one or more parts with an associated edition statement, record such statements following the titles and statements of responsibility to which they relate, separated from them by a full stop.

5.2C. Statements of responsibility relating to the edition

5.2C1. Record a statement of responsibility relating to one or more editions, but not to all editions, as instructed in 1.2C.

Nolo mortem peccatoris ₍GMD₎ / Thomas Morley ; edited by Sylvia Townsend Warner. — Rev. ed. / by John Morehen

Piano concerto, A major, K.414 ₍GMD₎ / Wolfgang Amadeus Mozart. — Rev. ed. / foreword by Paul Badura-Skoda

5.2D. Subsequent edition statement

5.2D1. If the item is a named revision of a particular edition containing changes from that edition, give the subsequent edition statement as instructed in 1.2D.

Do not record statements relating to subsequent editions that contain no changes unless the item is considered to be of particular importance to the cataloguing agency.

5.2E. Statements of responsibility relating to a subsequent edition statement

5.2E1. Record a statement of responsibility relating to one or more designated subsequent editions, but not to all subsequent editions, of a particular edition as instructed in 1.2E.

5.3. MATERIAL (OR TYPE OF PUBLICATION) SPECIFIC DETAILS AREA

This area is not used for music.

5.4. PUBLICATION, DISTRIBUTION, ETC., AREA

Contents:

5.4A. Preliminary rule

5.4A1. Punctuation

For instructions on the use of spaces before and after prescribed punctuation, see 1.0C.

Precede this area by a full stop, space, dash, space.

Precede a second or subsequently named place of publication, distribution, etc., by a semicolon.

Precede the name of a publisher, distributor, etc., by a colon.

Enclose a supplied statement of function of the publisher, distributor, etc., in square brackets.

Precede the date of publication, distribution, etc., by a comma.

Enclose the details of printing (place, name, date) in parentheses.

Precede the name of a printer by a colon.

Precede the date of printing by a comma.

5.4B. General rules

5.4B1.
Follow the instructions in 1.4B for items with multiple or fictitious places and names of publishers, distributors, etc.

5.4B2. Early printed music.
Record the publication, etc., details of items published before 1821, when appropriate, as instructed in 2.16.

5.4C. Place of publication, distribution, etc.

5.4C1.
Record the place of publication, distribution, etc., as instructed in 1.4C.

5.4D. Name of publisher, distributor, etc.

5.4D1.
Record the name of the publisher, etc., and *optionally* the distributor, as instructed in 1.4D.

London : Faber Music

5.4D2 *Plate numbers and publishers' numbers*

>Leipzig : Breitkopf & Härtel
>
>Mainz ; London : Schott

5.4D2. Plate numbers and publishers' numbers. Record plate numbers and publishers' numbers in the note area (see 5.7B19).

5.4E. *Optional addition.* **Statement of function of publisher, distributor, etc.**

5.4E1. Add to the name of a publisher, distributor, etc., a statement of function as instructed in 1.4E.

>New York : Warner ; [London] : Blossom [distributor]

5.4F. Date of publication, distribution, etc.

5.4F1. Record the date of publication, distribution, etc., as instructed in 1.4F. If the copyright date is found only on the first page of the music, do not enclose it in square brackets.

>New York ; London : Peters, 1975
>
>Leipzig : Peters, c1971

5.4G. Place of printing, name of printer, date of printing

5.4G1. If the name of the publisher is unknown, give the place and name of the printer if they are found in the item as instructed in 1.4G.

>[London? : s.n.], 1871 (London : Lord's Press)

5.4G2. *Optional addition.* Give the place, name of printer, and/or date of printing if they differ from the place, name of publisher, distributor, etc., and date of publication, distribution, etc., and are found in the item and are considered important by the cataloguing agency.

>Madrid : Real Academia de Bellas Artes de San Fernando, [1890] (Madrid : Tip. de las Huérfanos)

5.5. PHYSICAL DESCRIPTION AREA

Contents:
>5.5A. Preliminary rule
>5.5B. Extent of item (including specific material designation)
>5.5C. Illustrations
>5.5D. Dimensions
>5.5E. Accompanying material

5.5A. Preliminary rule

5.5A1. Punctuation

For instructions on the use of spaces before and after prescribed punctuation, see 1.0C.

Precede this area by a full stop, space, dash, space *or* start a new paragraph.
Precede details of illustrations by a colon.
Precede dimensions by a semicolon.
Precede a statement of accompanying material by a plus sign.
Enclose physical details of accompanying material in parentheses.

5.5B. Extent of item (including specific material designation)

5.5B1. Record the number of physical units of an item by giving the number of scores or parts in arabic numerals and one of the following terms as appropriate:

> score
> condensed score
> close score
> miniature score[1]
> piano [violin, etc.] conductor part
> vocal score
> piano score
> chorus score
> part

For special types of music, use an appropriate specific term (e.g., choir book, table book).

If none of the terms above is appropriate, use *v. of music,* or *p. of music,* or *leaves of music* unless a general material designation appears in the description, in which case use *v.,* or *p.,* or *leaves.*

If the item is a manuscript, add *ms.* to the appropriate term. Give the number of scores and/or parts issued by the publisher. Record differences in the library's holdings and the number of copies of each score or part held by the library in the note area (see 5.7B20).

> 1 score
>
> 1 vocal score
>
> 4 parts
>
> 1 ms. score
>
> 1 score and part
> (*Part printed on p. 5 of the score*)

5.5B2. If the item consists of different types of scores, or a score and parts, or different types of score and parts, record the details of each in the order of the list in 5.5B1, separated from each other by a space, plus sign, space.

5.5B3. Add, to the statement of extent of an item, the pagination or number of volumes as instructed in 2.5B.

> 1 score (vi, 27 p.)
>
> 1 score (2 v.)

---

1. Use for scores reduced in size and therefore not primarily intended for performance.

5.5C *Illustrations*

    1 miniature score (3 v.)

    1 score (viii, 278 p.) + 24 parts

    1 score (23 p.) + 1 piano conductor part (8 p.) + 16 parts

    1 score (2 sheets)

5.5C. Illustrations

5.5C1. Record details of illustrations as instructed in 2.5C.

    1 score (vi, 27 p.) : ill.

    1 score (23 p.) : port.

    1 score (23 p.) : ill. + 16 parts

5.5D. Dimensions

5.5D1. Record the dimensions of the item as instructed in 2.5D. If the item consists of score(s) and parts, give the dimensions after all the details of the score(s) and parts. If the dimensions of the score(s) and parts differ, give the dimensions of each after the details to which they apply.

    1 miniature score (34 p.) ; 18 cm.

    1 score (20 p.) + 1 part ; 28 cm.

    1 score (vi, 63 p.) ; 20 cm. + 16 parts ; 32 cm.

5.5E. Accompanying material

5.5E1. Record the name, and *optionally* the physical description, of any material that is issued with the item and is intended to be used in conjunction with it, as instructed in 1.5E.

    1 score (32 p.) + 5 parts ; 26 cm. + 1 sound tape reel

    1 score (vii, 32 p.) ; 28 cm. + 1 sound tape reel (60 min. : 7½ ips, mono. ; 7 in., ½ in. tape)

    1 score (30 p.) + 4 parts ; 24 cm. + 1 booklet

5.6. SERIES AREA

    Contents:

        5.6A. Preliminary rule

        5.6B. Series statements

5.6A. Preliminary rule

5.6A1. Punctuation

For instructions on the use of spaces before and after prescribed punctuation, see 1.0C.

Precede this area by a full stop, space, dash, space.

Enclose each series statement (see 1.6J) in parentheses.

Precede parallel titles of series or subseries by an equals sign.

Precede other title information relating to series or subseries by a colon.

Precede the first statement of responsibility relating to a series or subseries by a diagonal slash.

Precede subsequent statements of responsibility relating to a series or subseries by a semicolon.

Precede the ISSN of a series or subseries by a comma.

Precede the numbering within a series or subseries by a semicolon.

Precede the title of a subseries by a full stop.

5.6B. Series statements

5.6B1. Record each series statement as instructed in 1.6.

(Master choruses for Lent and Easter)

(Early English church music ; no. 7)

(Concertino : Werke für Schul- und Liebhaber Orchester)

(Music for today. Series 2 ; no. 8)

(The Salvation Army brass band journal. General series ; no. 1565–1568)

(Ashdown vocal duets ; no. 384)

(Yesterday's music, ISSN 4344-1277 ; no. 56)

5.7. NOTE AREA

Contents:
> 5.7A. Preliminary rule
> 5.7B. Notes

5.7A. Preliminary rule

5.7A1. Punctuation

Precede each note by a full stop, space, dash, space *or* start a new paragraph for each.

Separate introductory wording from the main content of a note by a colon and a space.

5.7A2. In making notes, follow the instructions in 1.7A.

5.7B. Notes

Make notes as set out in the following subrules and in the order given there.

5.7B1. Form of composition and medium of performance. If the musical form of a work is not apparent from the rest of the description, give such a form in a word or brief phrase.

Carol

Opera in two acts

Name the medium of performance for which a musical work is intended unless it has already been named in the rest of the description in English or in foreign language terms that can be readily understood. Name voices before instruments. Name the voices and instruments in the order of the item being described. Name the voices and instruments in English unless there is no satisfactory English term.

If the work is for solo instruments, name them all if not more than eleven must be named. If the work is for an orchestra, band, etc., do not list the instruments involved. In describing ensemble vocal music, add to the appropriate term a parenthetical statement of the component voice parts, using the abbreviations *S* (soprano), *Mz* (mezzo-soprano), *A* (alto), *T* (tenor), *Bar* (baritone), and *B* (bass). Repeat the abbreviations, if necessary, to indicate the number of parts.

For organ

For unacc. child's voice

For voice and piano

For voice, 2 violins, and violoncello

Arr. for guitar

Electronic music

For alto saxophone and piano

For soprano and electronic tape

Reduction for clarinet and piano

For piano, 4 hands

For soprano and piano

For voice and sitar

For solo voices (SATB), chorus (SSATB), and orchestra

For 2 treble recorders, 2 oboes, 2 violins, and basso continuo

For superius, contratenor, tenor, and bassus

If the information relating to the medium of performance given in the rest of the description is ambiguous or insufficient, record supplementary information here.

Part for piano only

Score for violoncello and piano, part for clarinet
(*Title page reads:* For violoncello or clarinet or viola and piano)

5.7B2. Text. Give the language or languages of the textual content of the work, unless they are apparent from the rest of the description. Indicate vocal texts published with part of the music.

French and English words

Latin words

Russian, German, and English words

Words in Hebrew (romanized)

Arbitrary syllables as text

Original text with English translation

Macaronic text (Latin and German)

French words, English translation on p. v–xxii

English words, includes principal melodies

5.7B3. Source of title proper. Make notes on the source of the title proper if it is other than the chief source of information.

Title from publisher's catalogue

5.7B4. Variations in title. Make notes on titles borne by the item other than the title proper. If considered desirable, give a romanization of the title proper.

Title on cover: Love songs of Lennon & McCartney

5.7B5. Parallel titles and other title information. Give parallel titles and other title information not recorded in the title and statement of responsibility area if they are considered to be important.

5.7B6. Statements of responsibility. Make notes on variant names of persons or bodies named in statements of responsibility if these are considered to be important for identification. Give statements of responsibility not recorded in the title and statement of responsibility area. Make notes on persons or bodies connected with a work, or significant persons or bodies connected with previous editions, not already named in the description.

Arr. by Charles Graveney

Previously attributed to Handel

"Based on themes in the poems of Thomas Hardy"—T.p. verso

Transcriptions of recordings made by Alan Lomax

The libretto is by Arrigo Boito, based on Victor Hugo's "Angelo"

5.7B7. Edition and history. Make notes relating to the edition being described or to the bibliographic history of the work.

Reprinted from the 1712 ed.

Reprint in reduced format of the full score originally published: Berlin : Harmonie, 1910

Rev. ed. of "Complete organ works." London : Schott, 1958

Facsim. reprint. Originally published: London : I. Walsh, ca. 1734

5.7B8. Notation. Give the notation used in an item if it is not the notation normally found in that type of item.

> Lute tablature and staff notation on opposite pages
>
> Plainsong notation
>
> Modern staff notation
> (*Used to describe a work that would normally be in plainsong notation*)
>
> Tonic sol-fa notation
>
> Graphic notation
>
> Melody in both staff and tonic sol-fa notation

5.7B9. Publication, distribution, etc. Make notes on publication, distribution, etc., details that are not included in that area and are considered to be important.

> Distributed by: London : Peters

5.7B10. Duration of performance and physical description. Give the duration of performance if it is stated in the item being described. Give the duration in English and in abbreviated form.

> Duration: 18 min.
>
> Duration: about 1 hr., 10 min.

Indicate any physical details considered to be important that have not already been included in the physical description area.

> Bound in green doeskin
>
> Each copy signed by the composer and numbered

5.7B11. Accompanying material. Make notes on the location of accompanying material if appropriate. Record details of accompanying material not mentioned in the physical description area or given a separate entry or separate description according to the rules for multilevel description (see 13.6).

> Three photos. of first performance in pocket inside each cover

5.7B12. Series. Make notes on series data that cannot be given in the series area.

> Originally issued in series:

5.7B13. Dissertations. If the item being described is a dissertation, give this information as instructed in 2.7B13.

> Thesis (M. Mus.)—University of Western Ontario, 1972
>
> Thesis (M.M.A.)—McGill University, 1971

5.7B14. Audience. Make a brief note of the intended audience for, or intellectual level of, an item, if this information is stated in the item.

> For 7–9 year old children
>
> Intended audience: first year undergraduate students

5.7B18. Contents. Give a list of the separately titled works contained in an item. Add to the titles opus numbers (if they are necessary to identify the works named) and statements of responsibility not already included in the title and statement of responsibility area. If the works in a collection are all in the same musical form and that form is named in the title proper of the item, do not repeat the musical form in the titles in the contents note.

> Contents: Sailing homeward — People call me the Pied Piper — The piper's theme

> Contents: The matron cat's song / words by Ruth Pitter — My cat Jeffry / words by Christopher Smart — The song of the Jellicles / words by T. S. Eliot

> Contents: Komm Heiliger Geist, Herre Gott = Come, O Holy Ghost, God and Lord / by Lucas Osiander ; text by Lucas Osiander — Psalm 121 / by Heinrich Schütz ; freely translated by Cornelius Becker

> Contents: Sonata in D major, op. 6 — Three marches, op. 45 — Variations in C major, op. 23 — Variations in C major, op. 34

> Sonatas for flute and piano ₍GMD₎ / Handel . . . . — Contents: v. 1. No. 1 (op. 1, no. 1b) E minor. No. 2 (op. 1, no. 2) G minor. No. 3 (op. 1, no. 5) G major. No. 4 (op. 1, no. 7) C major — v. 2. No. 5 (op. 1, no. 11) F major. No. 6 (op. 1, no. 9) B minor. No. 7 (op. 1, no. 4) A minor. No. 8, A minor

Make notes on additional or partial contents when appropriate.

> Includes a song by George Harrison

5.7B19. Plate numbers and publishers' numbers. Record the plate number(s) if they are given on the item. Record publishers' numbers only if the plate number is not given. Designate them as *Pl. no.* or *Publisher's no.* as appropriate.

In describing an item in several volumes, give inclusive numbers if the numbering is consecutive, otherwise give individual numbers or, if there are more than three of these, the first number and the last number separated by a diagonal slash. Give letters preceding a number before the first number, letters following a number after the last number, but letters preceding and following numbers in conjunction with each number.

> Pl. no.: S. & B. 4081

> Publisher's no.: 6139

> Pl. no.: B. & H. 8797–8806

> Pl. no.: B. M. Co. 10162, 10261, 10311

> Publisher's no.: 6201/9935
> (*The complete set of numbers is 6201, 6654, 7006, 7212, 7635, 7788, 8847, 9158, 9664, 9935*)

> Pl. no.: 9674–9676 H.L.

> Pl. no.: R.10150E.–R.10155E.

5.7B20 *Copy being described and library's holdings*

In describing a reprint, give the plate or publisher's number(s) together with the statement that the item is a reprint (see 5.7B7).

> Reissued from Brandus plates. Pl. no.: B. et Cie 4520

5.7B20. Copy being described and library's holdings. Give details of peculiarities or imperfections of the copies held. Give details of the number of copies held by the library. Always give the holdings if they affect the use of the item in performance. If the library does not hold a complete set of a multipart item, give this information. Make a temporary note if the library hopes to complete the set.

> Library has 6 parts
>
> Library's copy signed by the composer
>
> Three copies of each score, 2 copies of each part

5.7B21. "With" notes. If the description is of a separately titled part of an item lacking a collective title, make a note beginning *With:* listing the other separately titled parts of the item in the order in which they appear there.

> With: Die Mittagshexe; and, Das goldene Spinnrad / Antonín Dvořák

5.8. STANDARD NUMBER AND TERMS OF AVAILABILITY AREA

Contents:

5.8A.   Preliminary rule
5.8B.   Standard number
5.8C.   Key-title
5.8D   Terms of availability
5.8E.   Qualification

5.8A. Preliminary rule

5.8A1. Punctuation

For instructions on the use of spaces before and after prescribed punctuation, see 1.0C.

Precede this area by a full stop, space, dash, space *or* start a new paragraph.

Precede each repetition of this area by a full stop, space, dash, space.

Precede a key-title by an equals sign.

Precede terms of availability by a colon.

Enclose a qualification to the standard number or terms of availability in parentheses.

5.8B. Standard number

5.8B1. Give the International Standard Book Number (ISBN) or International Standard Serial Number (ISSN) assigned to an item. Record these numbers as instructed in 1.8B.

> ISBN 0-19-341508-9

5.8B2. Give any other number in a note (see 5.7B19).

5.8C. Key-title

5.8C1. Give the key-title of a serial item as instructed in 1.8C.

5.8D. *Optional addition.* **Terms of availability**

5.8D1. Give the terms on which the item is available as instructed in 1.8D.

> ISBN 0-333-17848-3 : £4.50

> Free to students and members of the association

5.8E. Qualification

5.8E1. Add qualifications to the standard number and/or terms of availability as instructed in 1.8E.

> ISBN 0-573-08042-9 (pbk.)

5.9. SUPPLEMENTARY ITEMS

Describe supplementary items as instructed in 1.9.

5.10. ITEMS MADE UP OF SEVERAL TYPES OF MATERIAL

Describe items made up of several types of material as instructed in 1.10.

5.11. FACSIMILES, PHOTOCOPIES, AND OTHER REPRODUCTIONS

Describe facsimiles, photocopies, and other reproductions as instructed in 1.11.

CHAPTER 6

SOUND RECORDINGS

Contents

6.0. GENERAL RULES

6.0A. Scope

The rules in this chapter cover the description of sound recordings in all media, i.e., discs, tapes (open reel-to-reel, cartridges, cassettes), piano rolls (and other rolls), and sound recordings on film (other than those intended to accompany visual images, for which see chapter 7). They do not cover specifically recordings in other forms (wires, cylinders, etc.) or in various experimental media, though the use of appropriate specifications in the physical description (see 6.5) and special notes will furnish a sufficiently detailed description for such items.

6.0B. Sources of information

6.0B1. Chief source of information. The chief source of information for each major type of sound recording is set out here.

TYPE	CHIEF SOURCE
Disc	Label[1]
Tape (open reel-to-reel)	Reel and label
Tape cassette	Cassette and label
Tape cartridge	Cartridge and label
Roll	Label
Sound recording on film	Container and label

If there are two or more chief sources of information as defined above (e.g., two labels on a disc) treat these as a single chief source.

Treat accompanying textual material or a container as the chief source of information if it furnishes a collective title and the parts themselves and their labels do not. Make a note (see 6.7B3) indicating the source of information.

If information is not available from the chief source, take it from the following sources (in this order of preference):

> accompanying textual material
> container (sleeve, box, etc.)
> other sources

---

1. In this list *label* means any permanently affixed paper, plastic, etc., label as opposed to the container itself, which may have data embossed or printed on it.

Prefer textual data to sound data. For example, if a sound disc has a label and also information presented in sound form on the disc, prefer the label information.

6.0B2. Prescribed sources of information. The prescribed source(s) of information for each area of the description of sound recordings is set out below. Enclose information taken from outside the prescribed source(s) in square brackets.

AREA	PRESCRIBED SOURCES OF INFORMATION
Title and statement of responsibility	Chief source of information
Edition	Chief source of information, accompanying textual material, container
Publication, distribution, etc.	Chief source of information, accompanying textual material, container
Physical description	Any source
Series	Chief source of information, accompanying textual material, container
Note	Any source
Standard number and terms of availability	Any source

6.0C. Punctuation

For the punctuation of the description as a whole, see 1.0C.
For the prescribed punctuation of elements, see the following rules.

6.0D. Levels of detail in the description
See 1.0D.

6.0E. Language and script of the description
See 1.0E.

6.0F. Inaccuracies
See 1.0F.

6.0G. Accents and other diacritical marks
See 1.0G.

6.0H. Items with several chief sources of information
See 1.0H.

6.1. TITLE AND STATEMENT OF RESPONSIBILITY AREA

Contents:
    6.1A. Preliminary rule
    6.1B. Title proper

6.1A1 *Punctuation*

6.1A. Preliminary rule

6.1A1. Punctuation

For instructions on the use of spaces before and after prescribed punctuation, see 1.0C.

Precede the title of a supplement or section (see 1.1B9) by a full stop.

Enclose the general material designation in square brackets.

Precede each parallel title by an equals sign.

Precede each unit of other title information by a colon.

Precede the first statement of responsibility by a diagonal slash.

Precede each subsequent statement of responsibility by a semicolon.

For the punctuation of this area for items without a collective title, see 1.1G.

6.1B. Title proper

6.1B1. Record the title proper as instructed in 1.1B. For data to be included in titles proper for musical items, see 5.1B2.

> Music from Fiddler on the roof
>
> Greatest hits
>
> The little match girl and other tales
>
> Living and dying in ¾ time
>
> Symphony no. 3, A major, op. 56
>
> The very best of Melanie
>
> Braverman's condensed cream of Beatles
>
> Antoine de Saint-Exupéry
>
> The Beatles
>
> Institute on International Standards as Related to Universal Bibliographic Control

6.1B2. If a title proper for a musical work has to be devised by the cataloguer (see 1.1B7), give all the elements prescribed for uniform titles for music (see 25.25–25.36) in the order prescribed there.

> [Sonatas, piano, no. 17, op. 31, no. 2, D minor]

6.1C. *Optional addition.* General material designation

6.1C1. Add immediately following the title proper the appropriate general material designation (see 1.1C).

Faustus [GMD]

Music for flute and tape [GMD]

Elite Hotel [GMD]

Woody Guthrie [GMD]

6.1C2. If an item contains parts belonging to materials falling into two or more categories, and if none of these is the predominant constituent of the item, give either *multimedia* or *kit* as the designation (see 1.1C1 and 1.10).

6.1D. Parallel titles

6.1D1. Record parallel titles as instructed in 1.1D.

Quattro concerti per l'organo ed altri stromenti [GMD] = Vier Orgelkonzerte = Four organ concertos = Quatre concertos pour orgue

Русские народные песни [GMD] = Russian folk songs

6.1E. Other title information

6.1E1. Record other title information as instructed in 1.1E.

Hello Dolly! [GMD] : original motion picture soundtrack

Valedictory [GMD] : for computer and soprano

6.1F. Statements of responsibility

6.1F1. Record statements of responsibility relating to writers of spoken words, composers of performed music, and collectors of field material for sound recordings as instructed in 1.1F. If the participation of the person(s) or body (bodies) named in a statement found in the chief source of information goes beyond that of performance, execution, or interpretation of a work (as is commonly the case with "popular," rock, and jazz music), record such a statement as a statement of responsibility. If, however, the participation is confined to performance, execution, or interpretation (as commonly the case with "serious" or classical music and recorded speech), give the statement in the note area (see 6.7B6).

Prometheus bound [GMD] : a play for radio / Robert Lowell

Famous overtures [GMD] / Offenbach

Melville [GMD] / written and narrated by Thomas S. Klise

Texas country [GMD] / Willie Nelson . . . [et al.]

Bury my heart at Wounded Knee [GMD] / by Dee Brown
Note: "Dramatically presented by Harry Madden and Manu Tupon"
—Accompanying leaflet

Subterranean homesick blues [GMD] / Bob Dylan

Piano rags ₍GMD₎ / Scott Joplin
Note: Piano: Joshua Rifkin

The Afro-American's quest for education ₍GMD₎ : a Black odyssey /
produced by Pepsi-Cola Co. ; script writer, Norman McRae

Natty dread ₍GMD₎ / Bob Marley and the Wailers

Beach Boys greatest hits ₍GMD₎ / Beach Boys

6.1F2. If the members of a group, ensemble, company, etc., are named in the chief
source of information as well as the name of the group, etc., give them in the note
area (see 6.7B6) if they are considered important. Otherwise omit them.

Quartet in F major ₍GMD₎ / Ravel
Note: Budapest String Quartet (J. Roisman and A. Schneider, violins;
B. Kroyt, viola; M. Schneider, cello)

6.1F3. Add a word or short phrase to the statement of responsibility if the relationship between the title of the item and the person(s) or body (bodies) named in the
statement is not clear.

Born to run ₍GMD₎ / ₍written and performed by₎ Bruce Springsteen

6.1G. Items without a collective title

6.1G1. If a sound recording lacks a collective title, *either* describe the item as a unit
(see 6.1G2 and 6.1G3) *or* make a separate description for each separately titled
work (see 6.1G4).

6.1G2. In describing as a unit a sound recording lacking a collective title, record
the titles of the individual works as instructed in 1.1G.

La mer ; Khamma ; Rhapsody for clarinet and orchestra ₍GMD₎ /
Claude Debussy

How come? ; Tell everyone ; Done this one before ₍GMD₎ / Ronnie
Lane ; accompanied by the band Slim Chance

Prelude, The afternoon of a faun / Claude Debussy. Peer Gynt
(Suite) no. 1–2 / Edvard Grieg. Till Eulenspiegels lustige Streiche
/ Richard Strauss ₍GMD₎

6.1G3. Make the relationship between statements of responsibility and the parts of
an item lacking a collective title and described as a unit clear by additions as instructed in 6.1F3.

6.1G4. If desired, make a separate description for each separately titled work on a
sound recording. For the description of the extent in each of these descriptions, see
6.5B3. Link the separate descriptions with a note (see 6.7B21). For instructions on
sources of information, see 6.0B.

6.2. EDITION AREA

Contents:

6.2A. Preliminary rule

6.2A1. Punctuation

For instructions on the use of spaces before and after prescribed punctuation, see 1.0C.

Precede this area by a full stop, space, dash, space.

Precede a subsequent edition statement by a comma.

Precede the first statement of responsibility following an edition or subsequent edition statement by a diagonal slash.

Precede each subsequent statement of responsibility by a semicolon.

6.2B. Edition statement

6.2B1. Transcribe a statement relating to an edition of a sound recording that contains differences from other editions or that is a named reissue of that recording as instructed in 1.2B.

6.2B2. In case of doubt about whether a statement is an edition statement, follow the instructions in 1.2B3.

> Viens vers le Père [GMD] / Office catéchistique provincial du
> Québec. — Éd. spéciale

6.2B3. *Optional addition.* If a sound recording lacks an edition statement but is known to contain significant changes from previous editions, supply a suitable brief statement in the language and script of the title proper and enclose it in square brackets.

6.2B4. If an edition statement appears in more than one language or script, record the statement that is in the language or script of the title proper. If this criterion does not apply, record the statement that appears first.

6.2B5. If an item lacking a collective title and described as a unit contains one or more parts with an associated edition statement, record such statements following the titles and statements of responsibility to which they relate, separated from them by a full stop.

6.2C. Statements of responsibility relating to the edition

6.2C1. Record a statement of responsibility relating to one or more editions, but not to all editions, of a sound recording as instructed in 1.2C.

6.2D. Subsequent edition statement

6.2D1. If the item is a named revision of a particular edition containing changes from that edition, give the subsequent edition statement as instructed in 1.2D.

Do not record statements relating to subsequent editions that contain no changes unless the item is considered to be of particular importance to the cataloguing agency.

6.2E. Statements of responsibility relating to a subsequent edition statement

6.2E1. Record a statement of responsibility relating to one or more designated subsequent editions, but not to all subsequent editions, of a particular edition as instructed in 1.2E.

6.3. MATERIAL (OR TYPE OF PUBLICATION) SPECIFIC DETAILS AREA

This area is not used for sound recordings.

6.4. PUBLICATION, DISTRIBUTION, ETC., AREA

Contents:
- 6.4A. Preliminary rule
- 6.4B. General rule
- 6.4C. Place of publication, distribution, etc.
- 6.4D. Name of publisher, distributor, etc.
- 6.4E. Statement of function of publisher, distributor, etc.
- 6.4F. Date of publication, distribution, etc.
- 6.4G. Place of manufacture, name of manufacturer, date of manufacture

6.4A. Preliminary rule

6.4A1. Punctuation

For instructions on the use of spaces before and after prescribed punctuation, see 1.0C.

Precede this area by a full stop, space, dash, space.

Precede a second or subsequently named place of publication, distribution, etc., by a semicolon.

Precede the name of a publisher, distributor, etc., by a colon.

Enclose a supplied statement of function of a publisher, distributor, etc., in square brackets.

Precede the date of publication, distribution, etc., by a comma.

Enclose the details of manufacture (place, name, date) in parentheses.

Precede the name of a manufacturer by a colon.

Precede the date of manufacture by a comma.

6.4B. General rule

For items with multiple places and names of publishers, distributors, etc., follow the instructions in 1.4B.

6.4C. Place of publication, distribution, etc.

6.4C1. Record the place of publication, distribution, etc., as instructed in 1.4C.

6.4D. Name of publisher, distributor, etc.

6.4D1. Record the name of the publisher, etc., as instructed in 1.4D. *Optionally, record the name of the distributor as instructed in 1.4D.*

> ₁London₁ : Warner
>
> New York : RCA Victor
>
> London : Gandolf Records : Distributed by Middle Earth Co.

6.4D2. If a sound recording bears both the name of the publishing company and the name of a subdivision of that company or a trade name or brand name used by that company, record the name of the subdivision or the trade name or brand name as the name of the publisher.

> *Sound disc label reads*
> Decca Record Company / Ace of Diamonds
>
> *Recorded as*
> London : Ace of Diamonds

6.4D3. If, however, a trade name appears to be the name of a series rather than of a publishing subdivision, record it as a series (see 6.6). In case of doubt, treat the name as a series.

> *Sound disc label reads*
> Disney Storyteller. Walt Disney Productions
>
> *Recorded as*
> London : Walt Disney Productions. . . . — (Disney storyteller)

6.4E. *Optional addition.* Statement of function of publisher, distributor, etc.

6.4E1. Add to the name of a publisher, distributor, etc., a statement of function as instructed in 1.4E.

> New York : Sunflower ; ₁London₁ : Virgin Records ₁distributor₁

6.4F. Date of publication, distribution, etc.

6.4F1. Record the date of publication, distribution, etc., as instructed in 1.4F.

> ₁Los Angeles₁ : CREDR Corp., c1976
>
> Chicago : Mercury, 1973

6.4F2. Give a date of recording appearing on the item in a note (see 6.7B7).

6.4G *Place of manufacture, name of manufacturer, date*

ₜNew Yorkₗ : Music Guild, 1971
Note: Recorded in 1961

6.4G. Place of manufacture, name of manufacturer, date of manufacture

6.4G1. If the name of the publisher is unknown, give the place and name of the manufacturer, if they are found in the item, as instructed in 1.4G.

ₜS.l. : s.n.ₗ, 1970 (London : High Fidelity Sound Studios)

6.4G2. *Optional addition.* Give the place, name of manufacturer, and/or date of manufacture if they differ from the place, name of publisher, etc., and date of publication, etc., and are found in the item and are considered important by the cataloguing agency.

6.5. PHYSICAL DESCRIPTION AREA

Contents:
    6.5A. Preliminary rule
    6.5B. Extent of item (including specific material designation)
    6.5C. Other physical details
    6.5D. Dimensions
    6.5E. Accompanying material

6.5A. Preliminary rule

6.5A1. Punctuation

For instructions on the use of spaces before and after prescribed punctuation, see 1.0C.
    Precede this area by a full stop, space, dash, space *or* start a new paragraph.
    Precede other physical details by a colon.
    Precede dimensions by a semicolon.
    Precede a statement of accompanying material by a plus sign.
    Enclose physical details of accompanying material in parentheses.

6.5B. Extent of item (including specific material designation)

6.5B1. Record the number of physical units of a sound recording by giving the number of parts in arabic numerals and one of the following terms as appropriate:

    sound cartridge   sound tape reel
    sound cassette   sound track film
    sound disc

Use the terms *piano roll, organ roll,* etc., as appropriate, for rolls.
Add to *sound track film* one of the terms *reel, cassette,* etc., as appropriate.

    1 sound cartridge

    2 piano rolls

    2 sound cassettes

    1 sound track film reel

Optionally, if general material designations are used and the general material designation includes the word *sound,* drop the word *sound* from all of the above terms except the last.

6.5B2. Add to the designation the stated total playing time of the sound recording in minutes (to the next minute up) unless the duration is less than 5 minutes, in which case give the time in minutes and seconds.

> 1 sound disc (50 min.)
>
> 3 sound cassettes (120 min.)
>
> 1 sound disc (3 min., 15 sec.)

If no indication of duration appears on the item, its container, or its accompanying textual material, give an approximate time if it can be readily established.

> 1 sound tape reel (ca. 60 min.)
>
> 2 sound track film reels (ca. 90 min.)

6.5B3. If the description is of a separately titled part of a sound recording lacking a collective title (see 6.1G4), express the fractional extent in the form *on side 3 of 2 sound discs, on reel 3 of 4 sound tape reels,* etc. (if the physical parts are numbered or lettered in a single sequence) or *on 1 side of 2 sound discs, on 1 reel of 3 sound tape reels,* etc. (if there is no single numbering). Follow such a statement by the duration of that part.

> on 1 side of 1 sound disc (13 min.)
>
> on cassettes 3–4 of 4 sound cassettes (67 min.)
>
> on 1 side of 2 sound discs (ca. 25 min.)

6.5C. Other physical details

6.5C1. Give the following details, as appropriate, in the order set out here:

> type of recording (sound track films)
> playing speed
> groove characteristic (discs)
> track configuration (sound track films)
> number of tracks (tape cartridges, cassettes, and reels)
> number of sound channels
> recording and reproduction characteristics (tapes)

6.5C2. Type of recording. Give, for a sound track film, the type of recording (either *optical* or *magnetic*) or the name of a unique recording system (e.g., *Phillips-Miller*).

> 1 sound track film reel (10 min.) : magnetic
>
> 1 sound track film reel (15 min.) : Phillips-Miller

6.5C3. Playing speed. Give the playing speed of a disc in revolutions per minute (rpm).

6.5C4 *Groove characteristic*

> 1 sound disc (45 min.) : 33⅓ rpm

Give the playing speed of a tape in inches per second (ips).

> 1 sound cassette (60 min.) : 3¾ ips

Give the playing speed of a sound track film in frames per second (fps).

> 1 sound track film reel (10 min.) : magnetic, 24 fps

6.5C4. Groove characteristic. Give the groove characteristic of a disc if it is not standard for the type of disc.

> 1 sound disc (7 min.) : 78 rpm, microgroove

6.5C5. Track configuration. For sound track films, give the track configuration (*centre track, edge track,* etc.).

> 1 sound track film reel (10 min.) : magnetic, 24 fps, centre track

6.5C6. Number of tracks. For tape cartridges, cassettes, and reels, give the number of tracks, unless the number of tracks is standard for that item.[2]

6.5C7. Number of sound channels. Give one of the following terms as appropriate:

> mono.
> stereo.
> quad.

> 1 sound disc (20 min.) : 33⅓ rpm, stereo.
> 1 sound tape reel (ca. 60 min.) : 1⅞ ips, 2 track, mono.

6.5C8. *Optional addition.* **Recording and reproduction characteristics.** For sound recordings, give the recording and reproduction characteristics (e.g., *Dolby processed, NAB standard*).

> 1 sound cassette (60 min.) : 1⅞ ips, stereo., Dolby processed

6.5D. Dimensions

6.5D1. Give the dimensions of a sound recording as set out in the following rules.

6.5D2. Sound discs. Give the diameter of the disc in inches.

> 1 sound disc (20 min.) : 33⅓ rpm, stereo. ; 12 in.

6.5D3. Sound track films. Give the gauge (width) of the film in millimetres.

> 1 sound track film reel (10 min.) : magnetic, 25 fps, centre track
> ; 16 mm.

---

2. The standard number of tracks for a cartridge is 8, for a cassette 4.

6.5D4. Sound cartridges. Give the dimensions of the cartridge if they are other than the standard dimensions (5¼ × 3⅞ in.) in inches, and the width of the tape if other than the standard width (¼ in.) in fractions of an inch.

6.5D5. Sound cassettes. Give the dimensions of the cassette if they are other than the standard dimensions (3⅞ × 2½ in.) in inches, and the width of the tape if other than the standard width (⅛ in.) in fractions of an inch.

> 1 sound cassette (85 min.) : 3¾ ips, mono. ; 7¼ × 3½ in., ¼ in. tape

6.5D6. Sound tape reels. Give the diameter of the reel in inches, and the width of the tape if other than the standard width (¼ in.) in fractions of an inch.

> 1 sound tape reel (60 min.) : 7½ ips, mono. ; 7 in., ½ in. tape

6.5D7. Rolls. Do not give any dimensions.

6.5E. Accompanying material

6.5E1. Record the name, and *optionally* the physical description, of any accompanying material as instructed in 1.5E.

> 1 sound disc (50 min.) : 33⅓ rpm, stereo. ; 12 in. + 1 pamphlet (11 p. : col. ill. ; 32 cm.)

6.6. SERIES AREA

Contents:
> 6.6A. Preliminary rule
> 6.6B. Series statements

6.6A. Preliminary rule

6.6A1. Punctuation

For instructions on the use of spaces before and after prescribed punctuation, see 1.0C.

Precede this area by a full stop, space, dash, space.

Enclose each series statement (see 1.6J) in parentheses.

Precede parallel titles of series or subseries by an equals sign.

Precede other title information relating to series or subseries by a colon.

Precede the first statement of responsibility relating to a series or subseries by a diagonal slash.

Precede subsequent statements of responsibility relating to a series or subseries by a semicolon.

Precede the ISSN of a series or subseries by a comma.

Precede the numbering within a series or subseries by a semicolon.

Precede the title of a subseries by a full stop.

6.6B. Series statements

6.6B1. Record each series statement as instructed in 1.6.

> (Historic instruments at the Victoria and Albert Museum ; 2)
>
> (Standard radio super sound effects. Trains)
>
> (Audio-cassette library for professional librarians ; L-510)
>
> ([Development digest. Premier series])
>
> (Disney storyteller)
>
> (Sounds of the seventies, ISSN 3344-5566 ; no. 54)

6.7. NOTE AREA
Contents:
> 6.7A. Preliminary rule
> 6.7B. Notes

6.7A. Preliminary rule

6.7A1. Punctuation
Precede each note by a full stop, space, dash, space *or* start a new paragraph for each.

Separate introductory wording from the main content of a note by a colon and a space.

6.7A2. In making notes, follow the instructions in 1.7A.

6.7B. Notes
Make notes as set out in the following subrules and in the order given there.

6.7B1. Nature or artistic form and medium of performance. Make notes on the form of a literary work or the type of musical work or other description of a recording unless it is apparent from the rest of the description.

> Play for child actors
>
> Opera in two acts
>
> Field recording of birdsong

Name the medium of performance when necessary, as instructed in 5.7B1.

> Singer, bass, 2 electric guitars, drums

6.7B2. Language. Give the language or languages of the spoken or sung content of the recording unless they are apparent from the rest of the description.

> Sung in French
>
> In French, introduced in English

6.7B3. Source of title proper. Make notes on the source of the title proper if it is other than the chief source of information.

Title from container

Title from typewritten notes (4 p.) inserted

6.7B4. Variations in title. Give titles borne by the item other than the title proper. If considered desirable, give a romanization of the title proper.

Title on container: The four seasons

6.7B5. Parallel titles and other title information. Give parallel titles and other title information not recorded in the title and statement of responsibility area if they are considered to be important.

Subtitle: Songs of redemption

6.7B6. Statements of responsibility. Give the names of performers and the medium in which they perform if they have not already been named in the statements of responsibility and if they are judged necessary for the bibliographic description. Give also statements relating to any other persons or bodies connected with a work that are not named in the statements of responsibility if they are considered important.

Based on music by Franz Schubert

Genevieve Warner, Lois Hunt, Genevieve Rowe, sopranos ;
Elizabeth Brown, Virginia Paris, contraltos ; Frank Rogier, baritone ;
Columbia Chamber Orchestra, Leon Engel, conductor

Backing by Coral Reefer Band

Recordings by Willie Nelson (side 1), Bob Wills and his Texas
Playboys (side 2), Asleep at the Wheel (side 3), and Freddy Fender
(side 4)

Piano: Joshua Rifkin

Combine performers' names with the contents note if appropriate (see 6.7B18).

6.7B7. Edition and history. Make notes relating to the edition being described or to the history of the recording.

Reissue of: Caedmon TC 1125 (1952)

Ed. recorded: New York : Farrar, 1937

Recorded in Vienna in 1961, previously released as Westminster
WST 17035

"The twenty-four songs on these two discs are drawn from sessions
that took place between June and October 1967 in the basement
of Big Pink-West Saugherties, New York"—Container notes

An abridgement of: Bury my heart at Wounded Knee / by Dee
Brown. Text originally published: New York : Holt, Rinehart &
Winston, 1971

6.7B9. Publication, distribution, etc. Make notes on publication, distribution, etc., details that are not included in the publication, etc., area and are considered to be important.

      Distributed in the U.K. by:

6.7B10. Physical description. Indicate important physical details that are not already included in the physical description area. Do not give any physical details that are standard to the item being described (e.g., assume that all discs are electrically recorded, laterally cut, and designed for playing from the outside inward).

    Discs
        In 2 containers

        Acoustic recording

        Impressed on rectangular surface 20×20 cm.

        Vertically cut. Reproduces from inside outward

    Roll
        For 65-note player piano

    Tape
        Paper tape

        Recording made with stacked heads

        Recorded on both sides

        Recorded on 1 track

  Give the duration of each part of a multipart item without a collective title and described as a unit (see 6.1G2–6.1G3).

      Durations: 17 min. ; 23 min. ; 9 min.

6.7B11. Accompanying material. Make notes on the location of accompanying material if appropriate. Give details of accompanying material not mentioned in the physical description area or given a separate entry or separate description, according to the rules for multilevel description (see 13.6).

      Programme notes on container

6.7B12. Series. Make notes on series data that cannot be given in the series area.

      Originally issued in series: Sound effects

6.7B13. Dissertations. If the item being described is a dissertation, give a note as instructed in 2.7B13.

6.7B14. Audience. Give a brief note of the intended audience for, or intellectual level of, a sound recording if one is stated on the item, its container, or accompanying textual material.

      Intended audience: First year undergraduates

      Intended audience: G.C.E. "A" level students

6.7B16. Other formats available. Make notes on other formats in which a sound recording is available.

>Available as cassette or cartridge

6.7B17. Summary. Give a brief objective summary of the content of a sound recording (other than one that consists entirely or predominantly of music) unless another part of the description provides enough information.

>Summary: Episodes from the novel, read by Ed Begley

>Summary: A brief historical account up to the introduction of wave mechanics

6.7B18. Contents. Give a list of the titles of individual works contained on a sound recording. Add to the titles statements of responsibility not included in the title and statement of responsibility area and of the duration of individual pieces if known.

>Contents: The golden age of rock'n'roll — Born late 58 — Trudi's song — Pearl'n'Roy — Roll away the stone — Marionette — Alice — Crash Street kids — Through the looking glass

>Contents: The fourth millennium / Henry Brant (9 min.) — Music for brass quintet (14 min.)

>Contents: Louise : Depuis le jour / G. Charpentier (Mary Garden, soprano, with orchestra) — Tosca : Vissi d'arte / Puccini (Maria Jeritza, soprano, with piano)

Give additional contents or partial contents when appropriate.

>With musical extracts from the works of the composer

6.7B19. Notes on publishers' numbers. Give the publisher's alphabetic and/or numeric symbol as found on the item. Precede the number(s) by the label name and a colon.

>Tamla Motown: STMA 8007

>Island: ILPS 9281

If the item has two or more numbers, give the principal number if one can be ascertained, otherwise give both or all. If one of the numbers applies to the set as a whole, give it first.

>A. & M. SP4561–SP4877

If an item consists of two or more separately numbered units, give inclusive numbering if the units are numbered consecutively. Give all numbers if the units are not numbered consecutively.

6.7B20. Copy being described and library's holdings. Make notes on any peculiarities or imperfections of the copy being described that are considered important. If the library does not hold a complete set of a multipart item, give details of the library's holdings. Make a temporary note if the library hopes to complete the set.

6.7B21. "With" notes. If the description is of a separately titled part of a sound recording lacking a collective title, make a note beginning *With:* and listing the other separately titled parts of the item in the order in which they appear there. If the individual items are not titled, use devised titles as instructed in 6.1B2.

> With: Peer Gynt (Suite) no. 1–2 / Edvard Grieg — Till Eulenspiegels lustige Streiche / Richard Strauss

6.8. STANDARD NUMBER AND TERMS OF AVAILABILITY AREA

Contents:
- 6.8A. Preliminary rule
- 6.8B. Standard number
- 6.8C. Key-title
- 6.8D. Terms of availability
- 6.8E. Qualification

6.8A. Preliminary rule

6.8A1. Punctuation

For instructions on the use of spaces before and after prescribed punctuation, see 1.0C.

Precede this area by a full stop, space, dash, space *or* start a new paragraph.

Precede each repetition of this area by a full stop, space, dash, space.

Precede a key-title by an equals sign.

Precede terms of availability by a colon.

Enclose a qualification to the standard number or terms of availability in parentheses.

6.8B. Standard number

6.8B1. Give the International Standard Book Number (ISBN) or International Standard Serial Number (ISSN) assigned to an item. Record these numbers as instructed in 1.8B.

6.8B2. Give any other number in a note (see 6.7B19).

6.8C. Key-title

6.8C1. Give the key-title of a serial sound recording as instructed in 1.8C.

6.8D. *Optional addition.* Terms of availability

6.8D1. Give the terms on which the item is available as instructed in 1.8D.

> £2.99

> Free with the Dec. issue

6.8E. Qualification

6.8E1. Add qualifications to the standard number and/or terms of availability as instructed in 1.8E.

6.9. SUPPLEMENTARY ITEMS

Describe supplementary items as instructed in 1.9.

6.10. ITEMS MADE UP OF SEVERAL TYPES OF MATERIAL

Describe items made up of several types of material as instructed in 1.10.

6.11. NONPROCESSED SOUND RECORDINGS[3]

6.11A. Follow the rules for sound recordings (6.1–6.10) as far as possible in describing nonprocessed recordings.

6.11B. If the recording has no title proper, formulate a title as instructed in 1.1B7.

[Address to high school students, discussing good writing]

6.11C. Do not give any information in the publication, etc., area. Give the date of recording in a note.

6.11D. Make notes on the participants in such a recording and the available details of the event recorded, as well as other notes prescribed in 6.7.

---

3. *Nonprocessed sound recordings* are noncommercial instantaneous recordings, generally existing in unique copies.

CHAPTER 7

MOTION PICTURES AND VIDEORECORDINGS

Contents

7.0. GENERAL RULES

7.0A. Scope

The rules in this chapter cover the description of motion pictures and videorecordings of all kinds, including complete films and programmes, compilations, trailers, newscasts and newsfilms, stock shots, and unedited material. For other visual material, see chapter 8. For sound track film not accompanied by visual material, see chapter 6.

7.0B. Sources of information

7.0B1. Chief source of information. The chief source of information for motion pictures and videorecordings is the film itself (e.g., the title frames) and its container (and its label) if the container is an integral part of the piece (e.g., a cassette).

If the information is not available from the chief source, take it from the following sources (in this order of preference):

> accompanying textual material (e.g., scripts, shot lists, publicity material)
> container (if not an integral part of the piece)
> other sources

7.0B2. Prescribed sources of information. The prescribed source(s) of information for each area of the description of motion pictures and videorecordings is set out below. Enclose information taken from outside the prescribed source(s) in square brackets.

AREA	PRESCRIBED SOURCES OF INFORMATION
Title and statement of responsibility	Chief source of information
Edition	Chief source of information and accompanying material
Publication, distribution, etc.	Chief source of information and accompanying material
Physical description	Any source
Series	Chief source of information and accompanying material
Note	Any source
Standard number and terms of availability	Any source

7.0C. Punctuation

For the punctuation of the description as a whole, see 1.0C.
For the prescribed punctuation of elements, see the following rules.

7.0D. Levels of detail in the description
See 1.0D.

7.0E. Language and script of the description
See 1.0E.

7.0F. Inaccuracies

See 1.0F.

7.0G. Accents and other diacritical marks

See 1.0G.

7.0H. Items with several chief sources of information

See 1.0H.

7.1. TITLE AND STATEMENT OF RESPONSIBILITY AREA

Contents:

7.1A. Preliminary rule
7.1B. Title proper
7.1C. General material designation
7.1D. Parallel titles
7.1E. Other title information
7.1F. Statements of responsibility
7.1G. Items without a collective title

7.1A. Preliminary rule

7.1A1. Punctuation

For instructions on the use of spaces before and after prescribed punctuation, see 1.0C.

Precede the title of a supplement or section (see 1.1B9) by a full stop.

Enclose the general material designation in square brackets.

Precede each parallel title by an equals sign.

Precede each unit of other title information by a colon.

Precede the first statement of responsibility by a diagonal slash.

Precede each subsequent statement of responsibility by a semicolon.

For the punctuation of this area for items without a collective title, see 1.1G.

7.1B. Title proper

7.1B1. Record the title proper as instructed in 1.1B.

Jules et Jim

How to steal a diamond in four uneasy lessons

Pulse generator basics

Lost by a hare on my terra pin pin

Gullible's travails, or, How the meter met her match

Little Roquefort in Good mousekeeping

Walt Whitman's Civil War

7.1B2. If an item lacks a title, supply one as instructed in 1.1B7 and also follow these particular instructions.

Commercials. Supply a title for a short advertising film consisting of the name of the product, service, or other interest advertised, and the word *advertisement*.

> ₁Manikin cigar advertisement₁

> ₁Road safety campaign advertisement₁

Unedited material and newsfilm. Include in a supplied title for unedited material, stock shots, and newsfilm all the major elements present in the picture in order of their occurrence (e.g., place, date of event, date of shooting (if different), personalities, and subjects).

> ₁Phantom jet landing at R.A.F. Leuchars, July 1971₁

Optionally, give a description of the action and length of each shot in a note (see 7.7B18).

7.1C. *Optional addition.* **General material designation**

7.1C1. Add immediately following the title proper the appropriate general material designation as instructed in 1.1C.

> The Pickwick papers ₁GMD₁

> The administration of justice ₁GMD₁

7.1C2. If an item contains parts belonging to materials falling into two or more categories, and if none of these is the predominant constituent of the item, give either *multimedia* or *kit* as the designation (see 1.1C1 and 1.10).

N.B. Treat a sound track (recorded sound physically integrated or synchronized with the item and intended to be played with it) as an integral part of the motion picture or videorecording, and give the general material designation appropriate to the motion picture or videorecording alone. See also 7.5C3 and 7.7B10a.

7.1D Parallel titles

7.1D1. Record parallel titles as instructed in 1.1D.

> Clima de la calle ₁GMD₁ = Climate in the streets

7.1D2. Record an original title in another language appearing in the chief source of information as a parallel title.

> Breathless ₁GMD₁ = A bout de souffle

7.1E. Other title information

7.1E1. Record other title information as instructed in 1.1E.

> Jury and juror ₁GMD₁ : function and responsibility

> Le tambou ₁GMD₁ : drum of Haiti

7.1E2. If the item is a trailer containing extracts from a larger film, add ₁*trailer*₁ as other title information.

> Annie Hall ₁GMD₁ : ₁trailer₁

7.1F. Statements of responsibility

7.1F1. Record statements of responsibility relating to those persons or bodies credited in the chief source of information with participation in the production of a film (e.g., as producer, director, animator) who are considered to be of major importance to the film and the interests of the cataloguing agency. Give all other statements of responsibility in notes.

> Flowering and fruiting of papaya ₍GMD₎ / Department of Botany, Iowa State University

> Classroom control ₍GMD₎ / University of London Audio Visual Centre ; produced, directed, and edited by N.C. Collins

> Food ₍GMD₎ : green grow the profits / ABC News ; producer and writer, James Benjamin ; director, Al Niggemeyer

> Square pegs, round holes ₍GMD₎ / director, Dan Bessie ; writer, Phyllis Harvey ; animation, B. Davis ; editor, I. Dryer

7.1F2. Add a word or short phrase to the statement of responsibility if the relationship between the title of the work and the person(s) or body (bodies) named in the statement is not clear.

> Skaterdater ₍GMD₎ / ₍produced by₎ Marshal Backlar

7.1F3. If a statement of responsibility names both the agency responsible for the production of a motion picture or videorecording and the agency for which it is produced, give the statement as found.

> New readers begin here ₍GMD₎ / University of Salford Audiovisual Media for University of Salford Library

7.1G. Items without a collective title

7.1G1. If a motion picture or videorecording lacks a collective title, *either* describe the item as a unit (see 7.1G2 and 7.1G3) *or* make a separate description for each separately titled work (see 7.1G4).

7.1G2. In describing as a unit a motion picture or videorecording lacking a collective title, record the titles of individual works as instructed in 1.1G.

> Infancy ; Childhood ₍GMD₎ / ₍written by₎ J. Thornton Wilder

> The Truman story. They're in the army now ₍GMD₎

7.1G3. Make the relationship between statements of responsibility and the parts of an item lacking a collective title and described as a unit clear by additions as instructed in 7.1F2.

7.1G4. If desired, make a separate description for each separately titled work on a motion picture or videorecording. For the description of the extent in each of these descriptions, see 7.5B3. Link the separate descriptions with a note (see 7.7B21).

7.2. EDITION AREA

Contents:

7.2A. Preliminary rule

7.2A1. Punctuation

For instructions on the use of spaces before and after prescribed punctuation, see 1.0C.

Precede this area by a full stop, space, dash, space.

Precede a subsequent edition statement by a comma.

Precede the first statement of responsibility following an edition or subsequent edition statement by a diagonal slash.

Precede each subsequent statement of responsibility by a semicolon.

7.2B. Edition statement

7.2B1. Transcribe a statement relating to an edition of a motion picture or videorecording that contains differences from other editions of that film, or that is a named reissue of that film, as instructed in 1.2B.

> 2nd ed.

7.2B2. In case of doubt about whether a statement is an edition statement, follow the instructions in 1.2B3.

7.2B3. *Optional addition.* If a motion picture or videorecording lacks an edition statement but is known to contain significant changes from previous editions, supply a suitable brief statement in the language and script of the title proper and enclose it in square brackets.

7.2B4. If an edition statement appears in more than one language or script, record the statement that is in the language or script of the title proper. If this criterion does not apply, record the statement that appears first.

7.2B5. If an item lacking a collective title and described as a unit contains one or more parts with an associated edition statement, record such statements following the titles and statements of responsibility to which they relate, separated from them by a full stop.

7.2C. Statements of responsibility relating to the edition

7.2C1. Record a statement of responsibility relating to one or more editions, but not to all editions, of a motion picture or videorecording as instructed in 1.2C.

170

7.2D. Subsequent edition statement

7.2D1. If the item is a named revision of a particular edition containing changes from that edition, give the subsequent edition statement as instructed in 1.2D.

Do not record statements relating to subsequent editions that contain no changes unless the item is considered to be of particular importance to the cataloguing agency.

7.2E. Statements of responsibility relating to a subsequent edition statement

7.2E1. Record a statement of responsibility relating to one or more designated subsequent editions, but not to all subsequent editions, of a particular edition as instructed in 1.2E.

7.3. MATERIAL (OR TYPE OF PUBLICATION) SPECIFIC DETAILS AREA
This area is not used for motion pictures and videorecordings.

7.4. PUBLICATION, DISTRIBUTION, ETC., AREA

Contents:
    7.4A. Preliminary rule
    7.4B. General rule
    7.4C. Place of publication, distribution, etc.
    7.4D. Name of publisher, distributor, etc.
    7.4E. Statement of function of publisher, distributor, etc.
    7.4F. Date of publication, distribution, etc.
    7.4G. Place of manufacture, name of manufacturer, date of manufacture

7.4A. Preliminary rule

7.4A1. Punctuation
For instructions on the use of spaces before and after prescribed punctuation, see 1.0C.

Precede this area by a full stop, space, dash, space.

Precede a second or subsequently named place of publication, distribution, etc., by a semicolon.

Precede the name of a publisher, distributor, etc., by a colon.

Enclose a supplied statement of function of a publisher, distributor, etc., in square brackets.

Precede the date of publication, distribution, etc., by a comma.

Enclose the details of manufacture (place, name, date) in parentheses.

Precede the name of a manufacturer by a colon.

Precede the date of manufacture by a comma.

7.4B. General rule
For items with multiple or fictitious places and names of publishers, distributors, etc., follow the instructions in 1.4B.

7.4C. Place of publication, distribution, etc.

7.4C1. Record the place of publication, distribution, etc., as instructed in 1.4C.

7.4D. Name of publisher, distributor, etc.

7.4D1. Record the name of the publisher, distributor, releasing agency, etc., and of a production agency or producer not named in the statements of responsibility (see 7.1F) as instructed in 1.4D.

> New York : National Society for the Prevention of Blindness
>
> Rochester, N.Y. : Modern Learning Aids

7.4E. *Optional addition.* **Statement of function of publisher, distributor, etc.**

7.4E1. Add to the name of the publisher, distributor, releasing agency, etc., or production agency or producer a statement of function as instructed in 1.4E.

> Manchester : University of Manchester, Dept. of Medical
> Biochemistry ₁distributor₁
>
> San Francisco : Davidson Films ₁production company₁ ;
> Morristown, N.J. : Silver Burdett ₁publisher₁

7.4F. Date of publication, distribution, etc.

7.4F1. Record the date of publication, distribution, release, etc., as instructed in 1.4F.

> Santa Ana, Calif. : Doubleday Multimedia, 1973
>
> Big Spring, Tex. : Creative Visuals, ₁197–?₁

7.4F2. *Optionally,* give a date of original production differing from the date of publication, distribution, etc., in the note area (see 7.7B9).

> Santa Monica ₁Calif.₁ : Pyramid Films ₁distributor₁, 1971
> *Note:* Made in 1934

7.4G. Place of manufacture, name of manufacturer, date of manufacture

7.4G1. If the name of the publisher is unknown, give the place and name of the manufacturer if they are found in the item, as instructed in 1.4G.

7.4G2. *Optional addition.* Give the place, name of manufacturer, and/or date of manufacture if they differ from the place, name of publisher, etc., and date of publication, etc., and are found in the item and are considered important by the cataloguing agency.

7.5. PHYSICAL DESCRIPTION AREA

Contents:
7.5A. Preliminary rule
7.5B. Extent of item (including specific material designation)

7.5C. Other physical details
7.5D. Dimensions
7.5E. Accompanying material

7.5A. Preliminary rule

7.5A1. Punctuation

For instructions on the use of spaces before and after prescribed punctuation, see 1.0C.

Precede this area by a full stop, space, dash, space *or* start a new paragraph.
Precede other physical details by a colon.
Precede dimensions by a semicolon.
Precede a statement of accompanying material by a plus sign.
Enclose physical details of accompanying material in parentheses.

7.5B. Extent of item (including specific material designation)

7.5B1. Record the number of physical units of a motion picture or videorecording by giving the number of parts in arabic numerals and one of the following terms as appropriate:

film cartridge	videocartridge
film cassette	videocassette
film loop	videodisc
film reel	videoreel

1 film cassette

3 film reels

2 videodiscs

Optionally, if general material designations are used and the general material designation indicates that the item is a motion picture or videorecording, drop *film* or *video* from all of the above terms.

1 reel

If the videorecording being described is in the library in two or more formats (e.g., as a cassette tape and a reel),

a) use the term *videorecording* and give the alternative forms in the note area (see 7.7B16)

4 videorecordings
Note: Available as cassette or reel

or b) use multilevel description (see 13.6)
or c) make a separate description for each.

Add a trade name or other technical specification to the term for a videorecording if the use of the item is conditional upon this information and if it is only available in that particular form. Otherwise, give such data in the note area (see 7.7B16).

1 videoreel (Ampex 7003)

> 1 videocassette
> *Note:* Available for purchase as Philips VCR or Sony U-Matic
>
> 1 videorecording
> *Note:* Available in the library as cassette (Philips VCR or Sony U-Matic) or reel (Sony CV $\frac{1}{2}$ in. or Sony AV $\frac{1}{2}$ in. or IVC 1 in. or Quadruplex 2 in.)

7.5B2. Add to the statement of extent the stated total playing time of the item in minutes unless the duration is less than five minutes, in which case give the duration in minutes and seconds.

> 14 film reels (157 min.)
>
> 1 film loop (4 min., 30 sec.)

If no indication of duration appears on the item, its container, or its accompanying textual material, give an approximate time if it can be readily established.

> 1 videoreel (Quadruplex) (ca. 75 min.)

If the parts of a multipart item are of uniform playing time or of approximately the same playing time, use the form *3 film reels (20 min. each)* or *2 film reels (ca. 20 min. each)*, as appropriate. Otherwise, give the total duration.

> 2 film cassettes (25 min. each)
>
> 2 videoreels (Ampex 7003) (50 min.)

7.5B3. If the description is of a separately titled part of a motion picture or videorecording lacking a collective title (see 7.1G4), express the fractional extent in the form *on reel 3 of 4 film reels* (if the parts are numbered in a single sequence) or *on 1 cassette of 3 videocassettes* (if there is no single numbering). Follow such a statement by the duration of that part.

> on reel 1 of 2 film reels (13 min.)
>
> on 2 cassettes of 4 videocassettes (50 min.)

7.5C. Other physical details

7.5C1. Give the following details, as appropriate, in the order set out here:

> aspect ratio and special projection characteristics (motion pictures)
> sound characteristics
> colour
> projection speed (motion pictures)
> playing speed (videodiscs)

7.5C2. Aspect ratio and special projection characteristics. If a film has special projection requirements, record them as succinctly as possible (e.g., Cinerama, Panavision, multiprojector, etc.; and whether anamorphic, techniscope, stereoscopic, or multiscreen).

> 14 film reels (157 min.) : Panavision

7.5C3. Sound characteristics. Indicate the presence or absence of a sound track by the abbreviations *sd.* (sound) or *si.* (silent). If a silent film is known to be photographed at the speed of sound film, use *si. at sd. speed.*

> 1 videoreel (Ampex 7003) (15 min.) : sd.

7.5C4. Colour. Indicate whether an item is in colour or black and white (using the abbreviations *col.* or *b&w*). Describe a sepia print as *b&w* (see also 7.7B10).

> 1 film reel (10 min.) : sd., col.

If an item is in a combination of colour and black and white, indicate this succinctly.

> 1 film reel (30 min.) : sd., col. with b&w sequences

> 1 videocassette (24 min.) : sd., b&w with col. introductory sequence

7.5C5. Projection speed. For a film give the projection speed in frames per second (fps) if this information is considered important.

> 1 film reel (1 min., 17 sec.) : si., col., 25 fps

7.5C6. Playing speed. Give the playing speed of a videodisc in revolutions per minute (rpm).

> 1 videodisc (4 min.) : sd., col., 1500 rpm

7.5D. Dimensions

7.5D1. Give the dimensions of a motion picture or videorecording as set out in the following rules.

7.5D2. Give the gauge (width) of a motion picture in millimetres. If 8 mm., state whether single, standard, super, or Maurer.

> 1 film reel (12 min.) : sd., b&w ; 16 mm.

> 1 film cassette (21 min.) ; sd., col. ; standard 8 mm.

7.5D3. Give the gauge (width) of a videotape in inches.

> 1 videoreel (30 min.) : sd., b&w ; ½ in.

7.5D4. Give the diameter of a videodisc in inches.

> 1 videodisc (5 min.) : sd., b&w, 1500 rpm ; 8 in.

7.5E. Accompanying material

7.5E1. Record the name, and *optionally* the physical description, of any accompanying material as instructed in 1.5E.

> 1 film cassette (21 min.) : sd., col. ; standard 8 mm. + 1 teacher's guide

7.6. SERIES AREA

Contents:
    7.6A. Preliminary rule
    7.6B. Series statements

7.6A. Preliminary rule

7.6A1. Punctuation

For instructions on the use of spaces before and after prescribed punctuation, see 1.0C.

Precede this area by a full stop, space, dash, space.

Enclose each series statement (see 1.6J) in parentheses.

Precede parallel titles of series or subseries by an equals sign.

Precede other title information relating to series or subseries by a colon.

Precede the first statement of responsibility relating to a series or subseries by a diagonal slash.

Precede subsequent statements of responsibility relating to a series or subseries by a semicolon.

Precede the ISSN of a series or subseries by a comma.

Precede the numbering within series or subseries by a semicolon.

Precede the title of a subseries by a full stop.

7.6B. Series statements

7.6B1. Record each series statement as instructed in 1.6.

(Allstate simulation film library)

(Ecology : communities in nature)

(Automotive damage correction series. Set 5)

(Mathematics for elementary school students—whole numbers ; no. 10)

(Fant anthology of literature in Ameslan)

(Welding series. Gas metal arc (mig) welding)

(Images of the seventies, ISSN 7745-2251 ; no. 22)

7.7. NOTE AREA

Contents:
    7.7A. Preliminary rule
    7.7B. Notes

7.7A. Preliminary rule

7.7A1. Punctuation

Precede each note by a full stop, space, dash, space *or* start a new paragraph for each.

Separate introductory wording from the main content of a note by a colon and a space.

7.7A2. In making notes follow the instructions in 1.7A.

7.7B. Notes

Make notes as set out in the following subrules and in the order given there.

7.7B1. Nature or form. Make notes on the nature or form of a motion picture or videorecording unless it is apparent from the rest of the description.

> Documentary
>
> TV play

7.7B2. Language. Give the language or languages of the spoken, sung, or written content of a motion picture or videorecording unless they are apparent from the rest of the description.

> In French
>
> French dialogue, English subtitles
>
> Dubbed into English

7.7B3. Source of title proper. Make notes on the source of the title proper if it is other than the chief source of information.

> Title from script

7.7B4. Variations in title. Give titles borne by the item other than the title proper. If considered desirable, give a romanization of the title proper.

> Title on container: Papaya and guava
>
> Title in English on title frame: 400 blows
>
> Title on containers of parts 3, 5–6 varies slightly

7.7B5. Parallel titles and other title information. Give parallel titles and other title information not recorded in the title and statement of responsibility area if they are considered to be important.

> Subtitle: Les fleurs anglaises

7.7B6. Statements of responsibility

Cast. List featured players, performers, narrators, or presenters.

> Presenter: Jackie Glanville
>
> Cast: Laurence Harvey, Mia Farrow, Lionel Stander, Harry Andrews
>
> Cast: Gilles Behat (Charles IV), Jean Deschamps (Charles de Valois), Hélène Duc (Mahaut d'Artois)

Combine the cast note with the contents note if appropriate (see 7.7B18).

Credits. List persons (other than the cast) who have contributed to the artistic and technical production of a motion picture or videorecording and who are not named in the statements of responsibility (see 7.1F). Do not include assistants, associates, etc., or any other persons making only a minor contribution. Preface each name or group of names with a statement of function.

7.7B7 *Edition and history*

Credits: Screenplay, Harold Pinter ; music, John Dankworth ; camera, Gerry Fisher ; editor, Reginald Beck

Credits: Script, John Taylor ; calligraphy and design, Alan Haigh ; commentator, Derek G. Holroyde

7.7B7. Edition and history. Make notes relating to the edition being described or to the history of the motion picture or videorecording.

Shorter version of the 1969 motion picture of the same name

Censored version. 3 min. sequence missing on reel 3. Censorship certificate C-132, May 4, 1946

Spanish version of the 1956 motion picture entitled: Jenny's birthday book. — Based on: Jenny's birthday book / by Esther Averill

Remake of the 1933 motion picture of the same name

Based on the novel by Nicolas Mosley

7.7B9. Publication, distribution, etc., and date. Give details of the publication, distribution, etc., of the item or the date of the item if these have not already been given in the publication, etc., area. Give a date of original production differing from the date of publication, distribution, etc.

Distributed in the U.S. by: Stamford, Conn. : Educational Dimensions

Made in 1927

Give the country of original release if it is not stated or implied elsewhere in the description.

First released in Yugoslavia

7.7B10. Physical description

Make the following notes on the physical description when appropriate and if this level of detail is desired:

a) *Sound characteristics.* Give any special characteristics of the sound component of a motion picture or videorecording (e.g., optical or magnetic, whether the sound track is physically integrated with the film or the sound is separate on a synchronized recording).

Magnetic sound track

b) *Length of film or tape.* Give the length in feet of a motion picture (from first frame to last) or videotape (from first programme signal to last).

Film: 14,139 ft.

c) *Colour.* Give the process or colour recording system of a motion picture or videorecording, or any other details of the colour.

Technicolor

Colour recording system: SECAM

Sepia print

178

d) *Form of print*. Give the form of print of a film (i.e., negative, positive, reversal, reversal internegative, internegative, interpositive, colour separation, duplicate, fine grain duplicating positive or negative). For master material held in checkerboard cutting form, state if A, B, C, etc., roll.

e) *Film base*. Give the film base (i.e., nitrate, acetate, or polyester).

f) *Videorecording system*. Give the system(s) used for a videorecording if not already named in the statement of extent.

> Teldec disc

> For two-inch videotape, give the number of lines and fields, followed by the modulation frequency (high band, low band, etc.)

> Standard: 405 lines, 50 field, high band

g) *Generation of copy*. For videotapes, give the generation of the copy and whether it is a master copy or show copy.

> Second generation, show copy

h) *Special projection requirements*. Give special projection requirements not already given in the physical description area (see 7.5C2).

> Three-dimensional film

j) Give any other physical details that are important to the use or storage of the motion picture or videorecording.

7.7B11. Accompanying material. Make notes on the location of accompanying material if appropriate. Give details of accompanying material not mentioned in the physical description area or given a separate entry or separate description, according to the rules for multilevel description (see 13.6).

> With shot list

> With instruction manual

> Cast list and credits on box

7.7B12. Series. Make notes on series data that cannot be given in the series area.

> Originally issued in series:

7.7B13. Dissertations. If a motion picture or videorecording is a dissertation, make a note as instructed in 2.7B13.

7.7B14. Audience. Make a brief note of the intended audience for a motion picture if one is stated on the item, its container, or accompanying textual material.

> Intended audience: Elementary grades

7.7B16. Other formats available. Make notes on other formats in which a motion picture or videorecording is available (see also 7.5B1).

> Available as cassette (Philips VCR or Sony U-Matic) or reel (Sony CV $\frac{1}{2}$ in. or Sony AV $\frac{1}{2}$ in. or IVC 1 in. or Quadruplex 2 in.)

7.7B17. Summary. Give a brief objective summary of the content of an item unless another part of the description provides enough information.

> Summary: Presents several brief sketches showing communication problems in a family, in a business, and in school in order to analyze and correct failures in interpersonal relations

7.7B18. Contents. Give a list of the individual works contained in, or parts of, a motion picture or videorecording. Add to the titles any statements of responsibility not already included in the title and statement of responsibility area, and the duration of individual pieces if known.

> Contents: pt. 1. The cause of liberty (24 min.) — pt. 2. The impossible war (25 min.)

Make notes on additional contents or partial contents when appropriate.

> Also contains newsfilm on the trooping of the colour

Unedited material and newsfilm. Give a description, using standard abbreviations, of the action and length of each shot on unedited material, newsfilm, or stock shots.

> Shots: LS through heat haze of jet landing towards camera. CU front view of jet as it taxis towards camera (40 ft.). CU fuselage turning right to left through picture (30 ft.). CU braking parachute as it is discarded (52 ft.). CU nose and engines (57 ft.)

7.7B19. Numbers borne by the item. Give important numbers borne by the item other than ISBNs or ISSNs (see 7.8B).

7.7B20. Copy being described and library's holdings. Give any peculiarities and imperfections of the copy being described that are considered to be important. If the library does not hold a complete set of a multipart item, give details of the library's holdings. Make a temporary note if the library hopes to complete the set.

7.7B21. "With" notes. If the description is of a separately titled part of a motion picture or videorecording lacking a collective title, make a note beginning *With:* and listing the other separately titled parts of the item in the order in which they appear there.

> With: The Truman story

> With: Frilly follies — The shy mouse — The night hawk — No more cheese!

7.8. STANDARD NUMBER AND TERMS OF AVAILABILITY AREA

Contents:
    7.8A. Preliminary rule
    7.8B. Standard number
    7.8C. Key-title
    7.8D. Terms of availability
    7.8E. Qualification

7.8A. Preliminary rule

7.8A1. Punctuation

For instructions on the use of spaces before and after prescribed punctuation, see 1.0C.

Precede this area by a full stop, space, dash, space *or* start a new paragraph.

Precede each repetition of this area by a full stop, space, dash, space.

Precede a key-title by an equals sign.

Precede terms of availability by a colon.

Enclose a qualification to the standard number or terms of availability in parentheses.

7.8B. Standard number

7.8B1. Give an International Standard Book Number (ISBN) or International Standard Serial Number (ISSN) assigned to a motion picture or videorecording. Record these numbers as instructed in 1.8B.

7.8B2. Give any other number in a note (see 7.7B19).

7.8C. Key-title

7.8C1. Give the key-title of a serial motion picture as instructed in 1.8C.

7.8D. *Optional addition.* Terms of availability

7.8D1. Give the terms on which the item is available as instructed in 1.8D.

> For hire or sale (£15.00)

> Free to universities and colleges

7.8E. Qualification

7.8E1. Add qualifications to the standard number and/or terms of availability as instructed in 1.8E.

7.9. SUPPLEMENTARY ITEMS
Describe supplementary items as instructed in 1.9.

7.10. ITEMS MADE UP OF SEVERAL TYPES OF MATERIAL
Describe items made up of several types of material as instructed in 1.10.

CHAPTER 8

GRAPHIC MATERIALS

Contents

8.0. GENERAL RULES

8.0A Scope

The rules in this chapter cover the description of graphic materials of all kinds, whether opaque (e.g., two-dimensional art originals and reproductions, charts, photographs, technical drawings) or intended to be projected or viewed (e.g., filmstrips, radiographs, slides), and collections of such graphic materials. For visual material recorded on film and intended to be projected so as to create the illusion of movement, see chapter 7. For microforms, see chapter 11. For maps, etc., see chapter 3. For microscope slides, see chapter 10.

8.0B. Sources of information

8.0B1. Chief source of information. The chief source of information for graphic materials is the item itself including any labels, etc., that are permanently affixed to the item and a container that is an integral part of the item. If the item being described consists of two or more separate physical parts (slide set, etc.), treat a container that is the unifying element as the chief source of information if it furnishes a collective title and the items themselves and their labels do not. If the information is not available from the chief source, take it from the following sources (in this order of preference):

> container (box, frame, etc.)
> accompanying textual material (manuals, leaflets, etc.)
> other sources

In describing a collection of graphic materials as a unit, treat the whole collection as the chief source.

8.0B2. Prescribed sources of information. The prescribed source(s) of information for each area of the description of graphic materials is set out below. Enclose information taken from outside the prescribed source(s) in square brackets.

	PRESCRIBED SOURCES
AREA	OF INFORMATION
Title and statement of responsibility	Chief source of information
Edition	Chief source of information, container, and accompanying material
Publication, distribution, etc.	Chief source of information, container, and accompanying material
Physical description	Any source
Series	Chief source of information, container, and accompanying material
Note	Any source
Standard number and terms of availability	Any source

8.0C. Punctuation

For the punctuation of the description as a whole, see 1.0C.

For the prescribed punctuation of elements, see the following rules.

8.0D. Levels of detail in the description

See 1.0D.

8.0E. Language and script of the description

See 1.0E.

8.0F. Inaccuracies

See 1.0F.

8.0G. Accents and other diacritical marks

See 1.0G.

8.0H. Items with several chief sources of information

See 1.0H.

8.1. TITLE AND STATEMENT OF RESPONSIBILITY AREA

Contents:

8.1A1 *Punctuation*

8.1A. Preliminary rule

8.1A1. Punctuation

For instructions on the use of spaces before and after prescribed punctuation, see 1.0C.

Precede the title of a supplement or section (see 1.1B9) by a full stop.

Enclose the general material designation in square brackets.

Precede each parallel title by an equals sign.

Precede each unit of other title information by a colon.

Precede the first statement of responsibility by a diagonal slash.

Precede each subsequent statement of responsibility by a semicolon.

For the punctuation of this area for items without a collective title, see 1.1G.

8.1B. Title proper

8.1B1. Record the title proper as instructed in 1.1B.

Searching British patent literature

Ancient Greek coins

Napoleon

19th century development in art

Walt Disney's Disneyland

Advanced diagnostic ultrasound (two-dimensional ultrasonography)

8.1B2. If a single graphic item lacks a title, supply one as instructed in 1.1B7.

[Birds of Jamaica]

[Photograph of Alice Liddell]

Collections of graphic materials. Supply a title by which the collection is known or a title indicating the nature of the collection.

[Dance posters, 1909–1970]

8.1C. *Optional addition.* General material designation

8.1C1. Add immediately following the title proper the appropriate general material designation as instructed in 1.1C.

8.1C2. If a graphic item contains parts belonging to materials falling into two or more categories and if none of these is the predominant constituent of the item, give either *multimedia* or *kit* as the designation (see 1.1C1 and 1.10).

8.1D. Parallel titles

8.1D1. Record parallel titles as instructed in 1.1D.

French colonies in America [GMD] = Colonies françaises d'Amérique

8.1E. Other title information

8.1E1. Record other title information as instructed in 1.1E.

> Basic principles in chemistry—stoichiometry ₁GMD₁ : atomic weights, molecular weights, and the mole concept

> Bulgaria ₁GMD₁ : my country

> Personal communication ₁GMD₁ : gestures, expressions, and body English

8.1F. Statements of responsibility

8.1F1. Record statements of responsibility as instructed in 1.1F.

> The beach ₁GMD₁ / Walt Smith

> Searching British patent literature ₁GMD₁ / British Library, Science Reference Library

> The histomap of religion ₁GMD₁ : the story of man's search for spiritual unity / John B. Sparks

> A picture study of the settlement of the West ₁GMD₁ / prepared by Historical Services and Consultants under the direction of John T. Saywell and John C. Ricker

> Two dancers on a stage ₁GMD₁ / Degas

> A girl with a broom ₁GMD₁ / Rembrandt ; National Gallery of Art

8.1F2. Add a word or short phrase to the statement of responsibility if the relationship between the title of the item and the person(s) or body (bodies) named in the statement is not clear.

8.1G. Items without a collective title

8.1G1. If a graphic item lacks a collective title, record the titles of the individual parts as instructed in 1.1G.

> The great big enormous turnip / Alexei Tolstoy ; with pictures by Helen Oxenbury. The three poor tailors / Victor G. Ambrus ₁GMD₁
> (*A filmstrip based on two children's books*)

8.1G2. Make the relationship between statements of responsibility and the parts of an item lacking a collective title clear by additions as instructed in 8.1F2.

8.2. EDITION AREA

Contents:

8.2A. Preliminary rule

8.2A1. Punctuation

For instructions on the use of spaces before and after prescribed punctuation, see 1.0C.

Precede this area by a full stop, space, dash, space.

Precede a subsequent edition statement by a comma.

Precede the first statement of responsibility following an edition or subsequent edition statement by a diagonal slash.

Precede each subsequent statement of responsibility by a semicolon.

8.2B. Edition statement

8.2B1. Transcribe a statement relating to an edition of a graphic item that contains differences from other editions, or that is a named reissue of that item, as instructed in 1.2B.

> Britain's government at work [GMD] / by John A. Hawgood. — 3rd ed.

8.2B2. In case of doubt about whether a statement is an edition statement, follow the instructions in 1.2B3.

8.2B3. *Optional addition.* If a graphic item lacks an edition statement but is known to contain significant changes from previous editions, supply a suitable brief statement in the language and script of the title proper and enclose it in square brackets.

> Wooded landscape with church, cow, and figure [GMD] / T. Gainsborough fecit aqua forte ; J. Wood perfecit. — [3rd state]

> The story of the Pied Piper [GMD] / Encyclopaedia Britannica Educational Corporation. — [New ed.]

8.2B4. If an edition statement appears in more than one language or script, record the statement that is in the language or script of the title proper. If this criterion does not apply, record the statement that appears first.

8.2B5. If an item lacking a collective title and described as a unit contains one or more works with an associated edition statement, record such statements following the titles and statements of responsibility to which they relate, separated from them by a full stop.

8.2C. Statements of responsibility relating to the edition

8.2C1. Record a statement of responsibility relating to one or more editions, but not to all editions, of a graphic item as instructed in 1.2C.

> Precambrian and older Palaeozoic eras [GMD] / by Knud Dreyer Jorgenson. — [New issue] / re-edited in Great Britain by D.E. Owen

8.2D. Subsequent edition statement

8.2D1. If the item is a named revision of a particular edition containing changes from that edition, give the subsequent edition statement as instructed in 1.2D.

Do not record statements relating to subsequent editions that contain no changes unless the item is considered to be of particular importance to the cataloguing agency.

8.2E. Statements of responsibility relating to a subsequent edition statement

8.2E1. Record a statement of responsibility relating to one or more designated subsequent editions, but not to all subsequent editions, of a particular edition as instructed in 1.2E.

8.3. MATERIAL (OR TYPE OF PUBLICATION) SPECIFIC DETAILS AREA

This area is not used for graphic materials.

8.4. PUBLICATION, DISTRIBUTION, ETC., AREA

Contents:
    8.4A. Preliminary rule
    8.4B. General rule
    8.4C. Place of publication, distribution, etc.
    8.4D. Name of publisher, distributor, etc.
    8.4E. Statement of function of publisher, distributor, etc.
    8.4F. Date of publication, distribution, etc.
    8.4G. Place of manufacture, name of manufacturer, date of manufacture

8.4A. Preliminary rule

8.4A1. Punctuation

For instructions on the use of spaces before and after prescribed punctuation, see 1.0C.

Precede this area by a full stop, space, dash, space.

Precede a second or subsequently named place of publication, distribution, etc., by a semicolon.

Precede the name of a publisher, distributor, etc., by a colon.

Enclose a supplied statement of function of a publisher, distributor, etc., in square brackets.

Precede the date of publication, distribution, etc., by a comma.

Enclose the details of manufacture (place, name, date) in parentheses.

Precede the name of a manufacturer by a colon.

Precede the date of manufacture by a comma.

8.4A2. Art originals, unpublished photographs, etc. For art originals and unpublished photographs and other unpublished graphic materials, give only the date in this area (see 8.4F2).

8.4A3. Collections of graphic materials. For collections of graphic materials, give only the inclusive dates of the materials in this area (see 8.4F3).

8.4B. General rule

For items with multiple places and names of publishers, distributors, etc., follow the instructions in 1.4B.

8.4C. Place of publication, distribution, etc.

8.4C1. Record the place of publication, distribution, etc., as instructed in 1.4C.

8.4D. Name of publisher, distributor, etc.

8.4D1. Record the name of the publisher, distributor, etc., as instructed in 1.4D.

> Trowbridge, Wiltshire : Micro Colour (International)
>
> ₁Fullerton, Calif.₁ : Ruhle and Associates
>
> ₁Leeds₁ : University of Leeds, Dept. of Spanish

8.4E. *Optional addition.* **Statement of function of publisher, distributor, etc.**

8.4E1. Add to the name of a publisher, distributor, etc., a statement of function as instructed in 1.4E.

> London : Rickett Encyclopedia of Slides ₁publisher₁ : Voluntary Committee on Overseas Aid & Development ₁distributor₁

8.4F. Date of publication, distribution, etc.

8.4F1. Record the date of publication, distribution, etc., as instructed in 1.4F.

> Melbourne : University of Melbourne ; London : EFVA ₁distributor₁, 1966
>
> Toronto : Royal Ontario Museum, ₁197–₁
>
> New York : Personality Posters, c1966

8.4F2. Record the date of creation of an art original, unpublished photograph, or other unpublished graphic item.

> Fair Rosamund ₁GMD₁ / E. Burne-Jones. — 1863
> (*Dated gouache*)
>
> Portrait of Charles Dickens [GMD]. — ₁1861?₁
> (*Undated photograph*)

8.4F3. Record the inclusive dates of a collection of graphic materials.

> ₁Pen drawings of birds and flowers of Dorset₁ ₁GMD₁. — ₁1910–1937₁

8.4G. Place of manufacture, name of manufacturer, date of manufacture

8.4G1. If the name of the publisher is unknown, give the place and name of the manufacturer as instructed in 1.4G, if they are found in the item and have not been recorded in a statement of responsibility.

> ₁S.l. : s.n., 1966?₁ (London : Curwen Press)

190

8.4G2. *Optional addition.* Give the place of manufacture, name of manufacturer, and/or date of manufacture if they differ from the place and name of publisher, etc., and date of publication, etc., and are found on the item and are considered important by the cataloguing agency.

8.5. PHYSICAL DESCRIPTION AREA

Contents:
    8.5A. Preliminary rule
    8.5B. Extent of item (including specific material designation)
    8.5C. Other physical details
    8.5D. Dimensions
    8.5E. Accompanying material

8.5A. Preliminary rule

8.5A1. Punctuation

For instructions on the use of spaces before and after prescribed punctuation, see 1.0C.

Precede this area by a full stop, space, dash, space *or* start a new paragraph.

Precede other physical details by a colon.

Precede dimensions by a semicolon.

Precede a statement of accompanying material by a plus sign.

Enclose physical details of accompanying material in parentheses.

8.5B. Extent of item (including specific material designation)

8.5B1. Record the number of physical units of a graphic item by giving the number of parts in arabic numerals and one of the following terms as appropriate:

art original	postcard
art print	poster
art reproduction	radiograph
chart	slide
filmslip	stereograph
filmstrip	study print
flash card	technical drawing
flip chart	transparency
photograph	wall chart
picture	

Add to filmstrip and stereograph the words *cartridge* or *reel* when appropriate.

Add the trade name or other technical specification to the term for a stereograph.

    1 wall chart

    3 wall charts

    100 slides

    1 filmstrip cartridge

    12 transparencies

    3 stereograph reels (Viewmaster)

8.5C *Other physical details*

If the parts of the item are very numerous and the exact number cannot be easily ascertained, give an approximate number.

       ca. 1,000 photos.

Optionally, substitute or add a term more specific than those listed above.

8.5B2. Add to the designation for a filmslip, filmstrip, or stereograph the number of frames or pairs of frames, the latter designated *double frames.*

       1 filmstrip (36 fr.)

       1 stereograph reel (Viewmaster) (7 double fr.)

       1 filmstrip (10 double fr.)

If the frames are unnumbered and are too numerous to count, give an approximate figure.

       1 filmstrip (ca. 100 fr.)

If the title frames are separately numbered, give separate totals of title frames and other frames.

       1 filmstrip (41 fr., 4 title fr.)

8.5B3. Add to the designation for flip charts the number or approximate number of sheets.

       1 flip chart (8 sheets)

8.5B4. Add to the designation for transparencies the number or approximate number of overlays. If the overlays are attached, indicate this.

       1 transparency (5 overlays)

       1 transparency (5 attached overlays)

8.5B5. If the parts of a multipart filmslip, filmstrip, stereograph, flip chart, or transparency have the same number of components (frames, sheets, etc.) or approximately the same number of components, use the form *3 filmstrips (50 fr. each)* or *3 transparencies (ca. 10 overlays each)*, etc. Otherwise, give the total number of components if they are consecutively numbered or omit the statement of the number of components.

       4 filmstrips (50 double fr. each)

       2 transparencies (20 overlays)

       4 flip charts

8.5C. Other physical details

8.5C1. Art originals. Give the medium (chalk, oil, pastel, etc.) and the base (board, canvas, fabric, etc.).

       1 art original : oil on canvas

8.5C2. Art prints. Give the process in general terms (engraving, lithograph, etc.) or

192

specific terms (copper engraving, chromolithograph, etc.) and an indication of the colour (b&w, sepia, col., etc.).

> 2 art prints : engraving, tinted
>
> 1 art print : sugar lift aquatint

8.5C3. Art reproductions. Give the method of reproduction (photogravure, collotype, etc.) and an indication of the colour (b&w, col., etc.).

> 1 art reproduction : photogravure, col.

8.5C4. Filmstrips and filmslips. Give an indication of sound if the sound is integral. If the sound is not integral, describe the accompanying sound as accompanying material (see 8.5E). Give an indication of the colour (col. or b&w).

> 1 filmstrip (41 fr., 4 title fr.) : sd., col.
>
> 3 filmslips : col.

8.5C5. Flash cards. Give an indication of colour (col. or b&w).

> 16 flash cards : col.

8.5C6. Flip charts. If the charts are double sided, indicate this. Give an indication of the colour (col. or b&w).

> 1 flip chart (8 sheets) : double sides, col.

8.5C7. Photographs. If the photograph is a transparency not designed for projection or a negative print, indicate this. Give an indication of the colour (col., b&w. etc.). *Optionally*, give the process used.

> 1 photo. : tinted
>
> 3 photos. : negative, b&w
>
> 1 photo. : photogravure, col.
>
> 1 photo. : glass photonegative

8.5C8. Pictures. Give an indication of the colour (col., b&w, etc.).

> 1 picture : col.

8.5C9. Postcards. Give an indication of the colour (col., b&w, etc.).

> 8 postcards : sepia

8.5C10. Posters. Give an indication of the colour (col., b&w, etc.).

> 7 posters : b&w
>
> 7 posters : blue and white

8.5C11. Radiographs. Do not give any other physical details.

8.5C12. Slides. Give an indication of sound if the sound is integral. Add the name of the system (e.g., 3M Talking Slide) after the indication of sound. If the sound is not integral, describe the accompanying sound as accompanying material (see 8.5E). Give an indication of the colour (col., b&w, etc.).

> 12 slides : sd. (3M Talking Slide), col.

8.5C13. Stereographs. Give an indication of the colour (col., b&w, etc.).

> 1 stereograph reel (Viewmaster) (7 double fr.) : col.

8.5C14. Study prints. Give an indication of the colour (b&w or col.).

> 1 study print : col.

8.5C15. Technical drawings. Give the method of reproduction if any (blueprint, photocopy, etc.).

> 1 technical drawing : blueprint

8.5C16. Transparencies. Give an indication of the colour (col. or b&w).

> 3 transparencies (5 overlays each) : col.

8.5C17. Wall charts. Give an indication of the colour (col., b&w, etc.).

> 1 wall chart : col.

8.5D. Dimensions

8.5D1. Give for all graphic materials except filmstrips, filmslips, and stereographs the height and the width in centimetres to the next whole centimetre up. For additional instructions on the dimensions of art works, slides, technical drawings, transparencies, and wall charts, see 8.5D4–8.5D6.

> 16 flash cards : col. ; 28 × 10 cm.
>
> 1 flip chart : double sides, col. ; 23 × 18 cm.
>
> 24 photos. : b&w ; 13 × 8 cm.
>
> 1 picture : b&w ; 20 × 25 cm.
>
> 1 radiograph ; 38 × 38 cm.
>
> 1 study print : col. ; 34 × 47 cm.
>
> 1 technical drawing : blueprint ; 87 × 87 cm.

8.5D2. Filmstrips and filmslips. Give the gauge (width) of the film in millimetres.

> 1 filmstrip (50 fr.) : col. ; 35 mm.

8.5D3. Stereographs. Do not give any dimensions.

8.5D4. Art originals, art prints, art reproductions, transparencies. Give the height and the width of the item, excluding any frame or mount. (See also 8.7B10.)

1 art print : lithograph, col. ; 28 × 36 cm.

3 transparencies (15 overlays) : b&w ; 26 × 22 cm.

8.5D5. Slides. Give the height and the width only if the dimensions are other than 5 × 5 cm. (2 × 2 in.).

1 slide : col.

1 slide : b&w ; 7 × 7 cm.

8.5D6. Technical drawings and wall charts. Give the height and the width when extended and (when appropriate) folded.

1 wall chart : col. ; 244 × 26 cm. folded to 30 × 26 cm.

8.5E. Accompanying material

8.5E1. Record the name, and *optionally* the physical description, of any accompanying material as instructed in 1.5E. Indicate integral sound systems as part of "other physical details" (see 8.5C4 and 8.5C12).

1 stereograph reel (12 double fr.) : col. + 1 booklet

40 slides : col. + 1 sound disc (30 min. : 33⅓ rpm, mono. ; 12 in.)

1 filmstrip (70 fr.) : sd., col. ; 35 mm. + 1 teacher's guide

8.6. SERIES AREA

Contents:
    8.6A. Preliminary rule
    8.6B. Series statements

8.6A. Preliminary rule

8.6A1. Punctuation

For instructions on the use of spaces before and after prescribed punctuation, see 1.0C.

Precede this area by a full stop, space, dash, space.

Enclose each series statement (see 1.6J) in parentheses.

Precede parallel titles of series or subseries by an equals sign.

Precede other title information relating to series or subseries by a colon.

Precede the first statement of responsibility relating to a series or subseries by a diagonal slash.

Precede subsequent statements of responsibility relating to a series or subseries by a semicolon.

Precede the ISSN of a series or subseries by a comma.

Precede the numbering within series or subseries by a semicolon.

Precede the title of a subseries by a full stop.

8.6B. Series statements

8.6B1. Record each series statement as instructed in 1.6.

> (Listening, looking, and feeling)
>
> (At-a-flash time line cards ; set 1)
>
> (Ward's solo-learn system)
>
> (The Sciences. Man and his environment ; TSB 3)
>
> (Viewmaster science series. 4, Physics)
>
> (How the health are you? ; no. 3)
>
> (Environmental studies, ISSN 8372-7639 ; v. 32)

8.7. NOTE AREA

Contents:
8.7A. Preliminary rule
8.7B. Notes

8.7A. Preliminary rule

8.7A1. Punctuation
Precede each note by a full stop, space, dash, space *or* start a new paragraph for each.

Separate introductory wording from the main content of a note by a colon and a space.

8.7A2. In making notes, follow the instructions in 1.7A.

8.7B. Notes
Make notes as set out in the following subrules and in the order given there.

8.7B1. Nature or artistic form. Make notes on the nature or artistic form of a graphic item unless it is apparent from the rest of the description.

> A cross-cultural survey

8.7B2. Language. Give the language or languages of the spoken or written content of a graphic item and its accompanying sound unless they are apparent from the rest of the description.

> Captions in Spanish
>
> Sound tape in Spanish and English

8.7B3. Source of title proper. Make notes on the source of the title proper if it is other than the chief source of information.

> Title from manufacturer's catalogue

8.7B4. Variations in title. Make notes on titles borne by the item other than the title proper. If considered desirable, give a romanization of the title proper.

Also known as: The blue boy

Title on container:

8.7B5. Parallel titles and other title information. Give parallel titles and other title information not recorded in the title and statement of responsibility area if they are considered to be important.

Subtitle:

8.7B6. Statements of responsibility. Make notes on variant names of persons or bodies named in statements of responsibility if these are considered to be important for identification. Give statements of responsibility not recorded in the title and statement of responsibility area. Make notes on persons or bodies connected with a work, or significant persons or bodies connected with previous editions, not already named in the description.

Narrator: Rod Serling

Teacher's guide by M. McComb

Variously attributed to Mathew B. Brady, to Dan Adams, and to Anthony, Edwards & Co.

Donor, source, etc., and previous owner(s). Make notes on the donor or source of a graphic item and on previous owners if they can be easily ascertained. Add the year or years of accession to the name of the donor or source, and add years of ownership to the name of a previous owner.

8.7B7. Edition and history. Make notes relating to the edition being described or to the history of the item.

Originally released in 1965 with sound disc

Spanish version of: Your mouth speaking

Based on the fairy tale by H.C. Andersen

8.7B8. Characteristics of original of art reproduction, poster, postcard, etc. Give the location (if known) of, and other information about, the original of a reproduced art work.

Original in Prado Museum, Madrid

Original measures: 93 × 98 cm.

8.7B9. Publication, distribution, etc. Make notes on publication, distribution, etc., details that are not included in the publication, etc., area and are considered to be important.

First released in 1969

197

8.7B10. Physical description. Give important physical details that have not been included in the physical description area, especially if these affect the use of the item.

> Scales vary
>
> Composite photo.
>
> Collage of wood, fabric, and paper
>
> Filmslip mounted in rigid format for use with [brand name] viewer
>
> Images placed in frame both horizontally and vertically
>
> Text on verso
>
> Unmounted
>
> Size when framed: 40 × 35 cm.

8.7B11. Accompanying material. Make notes on the location of accompanying material if appropriate. Give details of accompanying material not mentioned in the physical description area or given a separate entry or separate description according to the rules for multilevel description (see 13.6).

> With 2 exhibition catalogues: 19th century America : furniture and other decorative arts / by Marilynn Johnson, Marvin D. Schwartz, and Suzanne Boorsch — 19th century America : paintings and sculpture / by John K. Howat and others

8.7B12. Series. Make notes on series data that cannot be given in the series area.

> Originally issued in series:

8.7B13. Dissertations. If the item being described is a dissertation, make a note as instructed in 2.7B13.

8.7B14. Audience. Make a brief note of the intended audience for a graphic item if one is stated on the item, its container, or accompanying material.

> Intended audience: Elementary grades
>
> For remedial reading programmes

8.7B16. Other formats available. Make notes on other formats in which a graphic item is available.

> Also available with sound (75 fr.)
>
> Also available with double frames

8.7B17. Summary. Give a brief objective summary of the content of an item unless another part of the description provides enough information.

> Aerial view of Champaign-Urbana, Ill.
>
> Summary: Uses the children's tale of Goldilocks and the three bears in a programme of Spanish language instruction

Summary: A reading exercise which presents some little-known facts about gopher snakes, crocodiles, and sea turtles

8.7B18. Contents. Give a list of the individually named parts of a graphic item. Add to the titles statements of responsibility not already included in the title, etc., area, and the number of cards, frames, slides, etc., when appropriate.

Contents: Penny, nickel, dime, quarter — Nickel, dime, quarter, half-dollar — Dollar — Use of cent and dollar notation — Addition and subtraction — Making change — Story problems

Contents: Getting ahead of the game (81 fr.) — Decisions, decisions (55 fr.) — Your money (72 fr.) — How to be a loser (65 fr.) — The law and your pocketbook (70 fr.) — The all-American consumer (63 fr.)

Make notes on additional contents or partial contents when appropriate.

End frames reproduce 5 famous Spanish paintings

8.7B19. Numbers. Give important numbers borne by the item other than ISBNs or ISSNs (see 8.8B).

8.7B20. Copy being described and library's holdings. Make notes on any peculiarities or imperfections of the copy being described that are considered to be important. If the library does not hold a complete set of a multipart item, give details of the library's holdings. Make a temporary note if the library hopes to complete the set.

8.8. STANDARD NUMBER AND TERMS OF AVAILABILITY AREA

Contents:
    8.8A. Preliminary rule
    8.8B. Standard number
    8.8C. Key-title
    8.8D. Terms of availability
    8.8E. Qualification

8.8A. Preliminary rule

8.8A1. Punctuation

For instructions on the use of spaces before and after prescribed punctuation, see 1.0C.

Precede this area by a full stop, space, dash, space *or* start a new paragraph.

Precede each repetition of this area by a full stop, space, dash, space.

Precede a key-title by an equals sign.

Precede terms of availability by a colon.

Enclose a qualification to the standard number or terms of availability in parentheses.

8.8B. Standard number

8.8B1. Give an International Standard Book Number (ISBN) or International Standard Serial Number (ISSN) assigned to an item. Record these numbers as instructed in 1.8B.

8.8C *Key-title*

8.8B2. Give any other number in a note (see 8.7B19).

8.8C. Key-title

8.8C1. Give the key-title of a serial graphic item as instructed in 1.8C.

8.8D. *Optional addition.* **Terms of availability**

8.8D1. Give the terms on which the item is available as instructed in 1.8D.

> Free loan to students

> For rent or sale ($10.00)

8.8E. Qualification

8.8E1. Add qualifications to the standard number and/or terms of availability as instructed in 1.8E.

8.9. SUPPLEMENTARY ITEMS
Describe supplementary items as instructed in 1.9.

8.10. ITEMS MADE UP OF SEVERAL TYPES OF MATERIAL
Describe items made up of several types of material as instructed in 1.10.

8.11. FACSIMILES, PHOTOCOPIES, AND OTHER REPRODUCTIONS
Describe facsimiles, photocopies, and other reproductions as instructed in 1.11.

CHAPTER 9

MACHINE-READABLE DATA FILES

Contents

9.0 *General rules*

9.0. GENERAL RULES

9.0A. Scope

The rules in this chapter cover the description of machine-readable data files of all types and their accompanying documentation. A machine-readable data file is defined as a body of information coded by methods that require the use of a machine (typically a computer) for processing. Examples are files stored on magnetic tape, punched cards (with or without a magnetic tape strip), aperture cards, punched paper tapes, disk packs, mark sensed cards, and optical character recognition font documents.

The term *machine-readable data file* embraces both the data stored in machine-readable form and the programs used to process that data.

9.0B. Sources of information

9.0B1. Chief source of information. The chief source of information for a machine-readable data file with an adequate internal user label[1] is such an internal user label. If the information required is not available from the chief source, take it from the following sources (in this order of preference):

> documentation issued by the creator, etc., of the file
> other published descriptions of the file
> other sources (including the container of the file and its labels)

The chief source of information for a machine-readable data file lacking an adequate internal user label is the documentation issued by the agency or person(s) responsible for creating, compiling, editing, or producing the file. If the information required is not available from the chief source, take it from the following sources (in this order of preference):

> other published descriptions of the file
> other sources (including the container of the file and its labels)

9.0B2. Prescribed sources of information. The prescribed source(s) of information for each area of the description of machine-readable data files is set out below. Enclose information taken from outside the prescribed source(s) in square brackets.

AREA	PRESCRIBED SOURCES OF INFORMATION
Title and statement of responsibility	Chief source of information and documentation issued by the creator, etc., of the file
Edition	Chief source of information, documentation issued by the creator, etc., of the file, any other published description of the file
Publication, production, distribution, etc.	Chief source of information, documentation issued by the creator, etc., of the file, any other published description of the file
File description	Any source
Series	Chief source of information, documentation issued by the creator, etc., of the file, any other published description of the file
Note	Any source
Standard number and terms of availability	Any source

9.0C. Punctuation

For the punctuation of the description as a whole, see 1.0C.

For the prescribed punctuation of elements, see the following rules.

---

1. A machine-readable identifier containing alphabetic and/or numeric characters providing information about the file.

9.0D. Levels of detail in the description

See 1.0D.

9.0E. Language and script of the description

See 1.0E.

9.0F. Inaccuracies

See 1.0F.

9.0G. Accents and other diacritical marks

See 1.0G.

9.0H. Items with several chief sources of information

See 1.0H.

9.1. TITLE AND STATEMENT OF RESPONSIBILITY AREA

Contents:
> 9.1A. Preliminary rule
> 9.1B. Title proper
> 9.1C. General material designation
> 9.1D. Parallel titles
> 9.1E. Other title information
> 9.1F. Statements of responsibility
> 9.1G. Items without a collective title

9.1A. Preliminary rule

9.1A1. Punctuation

For instructions on the use of spaces before and after prescribed punctuation, see 1.0C.

Precede the title of a supplement or section (see 1.1B9) by a full stop.

Enclose the general material designation in square brackets.

Precede each parallel title by an equals sign.

Precede each unit of other title information by a colon.

Precede the first statement of responsibility by a diagonal slash.

Precede each subsequent statement of responsibility by a semicolon.

For the punctuation of this area for items without a collective title, see 1.1G.

9.1B. Title proper

9.1B1. Record the title proper as instructed in 1.1B. Record the source of the title proper if taken from outside the file itself in the note area (see 9.7B3).

> Redistricting program

> How the poor view their health

> The Washington lobbyists survey

9.1B2. Do not treat a locally assigned data set name as a title proper, unless the creator, etc., of the file has assigned a data set name that is also the title of the file. If desired, record a data set name in a note (see 9.7B4).

9.1B3. If neither the internal user label nor the documentation supplied by the creator, etc., of the file contains a title for the file, supply a brief descriptive title (see 1.1B7) and enclose it in square brackets. Indicate in a note that the title has been supplied (see 9.7B3).

> [Library catalogue, 1969–1975]

9.1C. *Optional addition.* **General material designation**

9.1C1. Add immediately following the title proper the appropriate general material designation as instructed in 1.1C.

> U.S. economic data tapes, 2477 series [GMD]

9.1C2. If an item contains parts belonging to materials falling into two or more categories, and if none of these is the predominant constituent of the item, give either *multimedia* or *kit* as the designation (see 1.1C1 and 1.10).

9.1D. Parallel titles

9.1D1. Record parallel titles as instructed in 1.1D.

> Citizen participation in non-work-time activities [GMD] = Participation des citoyens aux activités hors des heures de travail

9.1E. Other title information

9.1E1. Record other title information as instructed in 1.1E.

> The family and population control [GMD] : a Puerto-Rican experiment in social change

> Dutch continuous survey [GMD] : wave 1, January 1972

9.1F. Statements of responsibility

9.1F1. Record statements of responsibility relating to those persons or bodies responsible for the content of the file as instructed in 1.1F. Give statements relating to those persons or bodies responsible for the preparation of the file in machine-readable form in the note area (see 9.7B6).

> Retrospective UK MARC file, 1950–1974 [GMD] / British Library Bibliographic Services Division

> The China study [GMD] / principal investigator, Angus Campbell

> Supreme Court justices biographical data [GMD] / principal investigator, John R. Schmidhauser

9.1G *Items without a collective title*

>Public policy, dynamics of political choice ₍GMD₎ / developed by Marvin K. Hoffman

>The suburbia study ₍GMD₎ / principal investigator, Louis Harris and Associates, Inc.

9.1F2. Add a word or short phrase to the statement of responsibility if the relationship between the title of the work and the person(s) or body (bodies) named in the statement is not clear.

>Redistricting program ₍GMD₎ / ₍prepared by₎ Stuart Nagel ₍for the₎ Inter-University Consortium for Political Research

9.1G. Items without a collective title

9.1G1. If an item lacks a collective title, record the titles of the individual parts as instructed in 1.1G.

9.1G2. Make the relationship between statements of responsibility and the parts of an item lacking a collective title clear by additions as instructed in 9.1F2.

9.2. EDITION AREA

Contents:
>9.2A. Preliminary rule
>9.2B. Edition statement
>9.2C. Statements of responsibility relating to the edition
>9.2D. Subsequent edition statement
>9.2E. Statements of responsibility relating to a subsequent edition statement

9.2A. Preliminary rule

9.2A1. Punctuation

For instructions on the use of spaces before and after prescribed punctuation, see 1.0C.

Precede this area by a full stop, space, dash, space.

Precede a subsequent edition statement by a comma.

Precede the first statement of responsibility following an edition or subsequent edition statement by a diagonal slash.

Precede each subsequent statement of responsibility by a semicolon.

9.2B. Edition statement

9.2B1. Transcribe a statement relating to an edition of a machine-readable data file that contains differences from other editions, or that is a named reissue of that file, as instructed in 1.2B.

>1974 issue

>OSIRIS ed.

>Rev. ICPR ed.

9.2B2. In case of doubt about whether a statement is an edition statement, follow the instructions in 1.2B3.

9.2B3. *Optional addition.* If a machine-readable data file lacks an edition statement but is known to contain significant changes from previous editions, supply a suitable brief statement in the language and script of the title proper and enclose it in square brackets.

    [1976 ed.]

9.2B4. Do not treat a file in which the records have undergone minor corrections (e.g., of misspellings, incorrectly transcribed data) as a new edition. If desired, give details of such changes in the note area (see 9.7B7). Do not treat a change in the physical form of the file as a new edition.

9.2B5. If an edition statement appears in more than one language or script, record the statement that is in the language or script of the title proper. If this criterion does not apply, record the statement that appears first.

9.2B6. If a file lacking a collective title and described as a unit contains one or more parts with an associated edition statement, record such statements following the titles and statements of responsibility to which they relate, separated from them by a full stop.

9.2C. Statements of responsibility relating to the edition

9.2C1. Record a statement of responsibility relating to one or more editions, but not to all editions, of a machine-readable data file as instructed in 1.2C.

9.2D. Subsequent edition statement

9.2D1. If the item is a named revision of a particular edition containing changes from that edition, give the subsequent edition statement as instructed in 1.2D.

    Do not record statements relating to subsequent editions that contain no changes unless the item is considered to be of particular importance to the cataloguing agency.

9.2E. Statements of responsibility relating to a subsequent edition statement

9.2E1. Record a statement of responsibility relating to one or more designated subsequent editions, but not to all subsequent editions, of a particular edition as instructed in 1.2E.

9.3. MATERIAL (OR TYPE OF PUBLICATION) SPECIFIC DETAILS AREA
This area is not used for machine-readable data files.

9.4. PUBLICATION, PRODUCTION, DISTRIBUTION, ETC., AREA
Contents:
    9.4A. Preliminary rule
    9.4B. General rule

9.4C. Place of publication, production, distribution, etc.

9.4D. Name of publisher, producer, distributor, etc.

9.4E. Statement of function of publisher, producer, distributor, etc.

9.4F. Date of publication, production, distribution, etc.

9.4A. Preliminary rule

9.4A1. Punctuation

For instructions on the use of spaces before and after prescribed punctuation, see 1.0C.

Precede this area by a full stop, space, dash, space.

Precede a second or subsequently named place of publication, production, distribution, etc., by a semicolon.

Precede the name of a publisher, producer, distributor, etc., by a colon.

Enclose a supplied statement of function of a publisher, producer, distributor, etc., in square brackets.

Precede the date of publication, production, distribution, etc., by a comma.

9.4B. General rule

For items with multiple places and names of publishers, producers, distributors, etc., follow the instructions in 1.4B.

9.4C. Place of publication, production, distribution, etc.

9.4C1. Record the place of publication, production, distribution, etc., as instructed in 1.4C.

9.4D. Name of publisher, producer, distributor, etc.

9.4D1. Record the name of the publisher, distributor, etc., and of any agency responsible for the production or dissemination of a machine-readable data file (data archives, project groups, etc.) as instructed in 1.4D.

> Rosslyn, Va. : DUALabs
>
> London : University College Hospital Medical School
>
> Philadelphia : Independent Productions ; London : Unicorn
> Productions
> *(For a cataloguing agency in the United Kingdom)*

9.4E. *Optional addition.* Statement of function of publisher, producer, distributor, etc.

9.4E1. Add to the name of the publisher, producer, distributor, etc., a statement of function as instructed in 1.4E.

> Chicago : National Opinion Research Center [publisher] : Roper
> Public Opinion Research Center [distributor]
>
> Ames, Iowa : University of Iowa ; Ann Arbor, Mich. :
> Inter-University Consortium for Political Research [distributor]

9.4F. Date of publication, production, distribution, etc.

9.4F1. Record the date of publication, production, distribution, etc., as instructed in 1.4F.

> Ann Arbor, Mich. : University of Michigan, Institute for
> Social Research, 1968

> Chicago : University of Chicago, 1961–1962

> Washington, D.C. : Brookings Institution, 1958 ; Ann Arbor,
> Mich. : Inter-University Consortium for Political Research ₍distributor₎

9.4F2. Give any other useful dates (e.g., dates of collection of data and dates of supplementary files) in the note area (see 9.7B7).

9.5. FILE DESCRIPTION AREA

Contents:
> 9.5A. Preliminary rule
> 9.5B. Extent of file (including specific material designation)
> 9.5C. Other file details
> 9.5D. Accompanying material

9.5A. Preliminary rule

9.5A1. Punctuation

For instructions on the use of spaces before and after prescribed punctuation, see 1.0C.

Precede this area by a full stop, space, dash, space *or* start a new paragraph.

Precede a statement of accompanying material by a plus sign.

Enclose details of accompanying material in parentheses.

9.5B. Extent of file (including specific material designation)

9.5B1. Record the number of files making up a machine-readable data file by giving the number of parts in arabic numerals and one of the following terms as appropriate:

> data file
> program file
> object program

> 1 data file

> 2 program files

> 1 object program

9.5B2. Add in parentheses to the designation for a data file the number of logical records. Add in parentheses to the designation for a program file the number of statements and the name of the programming language. Do not add the number of statements to the designation of an object program.

> 1 data file (1,613 logical records)
>
> 1 program file (300 statements, COBOL)

9.5B3. Add to the designation for a multipart file the number of logical records or statements in each file.

> 2 data files (1,000, 12,000 logical records)
>
> 2 program files (300 statements each, COBOL)

9.5B4. Add to the designation for an object program the name, number, etc., of the machine on which it runs.

> 1 object program (IBM 360/40)

9.5B5. If the number of logical records or statements in a large file is unknown, give the approximate number of records or statements, or, if this cannot be done, omit such data and give a note (see 9.7B10).

> 2 data files (ca. 15,000 logical records)
>
> 2 data files
> *Note:* Size of file unknown

9.5C. Other file details

9.5C1. Give other characteristics of the file in the note area (see 9.7B10).

9.5D. Accompanying material

9.5D1. Record the designation for a program accompanying a data file or for a file accompanying a program as accompanying material (see 1.5E). *Optionally*, add to the designation the number of statements or logical records in such accompanying programs or files.

> 1 data file (3,000 logical records) + 1 program file
>
> 1 program file (300 statements, COBOL) + 1 data file (1,000 logical records)

9.5D2. Record the name, and *optionally* the physical description, of any other accompanying material (e.g., codebooks, manuals) as instructed in 1.5E.

> 1 program file (5,000 statements, FORTRAN IV) + 1 manual (100 p. ; 25 cm.)

9.5D3. If a file is accompanied by both an eye-readable and a machine-readable codebook, give details of both.

> 1 data file (30,000 logical records) + 1 codebook (24 p. ; 25 cm.) + 1 codebook (990 logical records)

9.5.D4. If a variety of documentation consisting of items that are individually of minor importance accompanies a file, use the term *associated documentation*.

> 2 data files (1,000, 10,000 logical records) + associated documentation

9.6. SERIES AREA

Contents:
9.6A. Preliminary rule
9.6B. Series statements

9.6A. Preliminary rule

9.6A1. Punctuation

For instructions on the use of spaces before and after prescribed punctuation, see 1.0C.

Precede this area by a full stop, space, dash, space.

Enclose each series statement (see 1.6J) in parentheses.

Precede parallel titles of series or subseries by an equals sign.

Precede other title information relating to series or subseries by a colon.

Precede the first statement of responsibility relating to a series or subseries by a diagonal slash.

Precede subsequent statements of responsibility relating to a series or subseries by a semicolon.

Precede the ISSN of a series or subseries by a comma.

Precede the numbering within a series or subseries by a semicolon.

Precede the title of a subseries by a full stop.

9.6B. Series statements

9.6B1. Record each series statement as instructed in 1.6.

(Interactive digital computer teaching models)

(SETUPS ; no. 6)

(Zentralarchiv ; no. 556) (ICPR study ; no. 7103)

9.7. NOTE AREA

Contents:
9.7A. Preliminary rule
9.7B. Notes

9.7A. Preliminary rule

9.7A1. Punctuation

Precede each note by a full stop, space, dash, space *or* start a new paragraph for each.

Separate introductory wording from the main content of a note by a colon and a space.

9.7A2. In making notes, follow the instructions in 1.7A.

9.7B. Notes

Make notes as set out in the following subrules and in the order given there.

9.7B1. Nature and scope. Make notes on the nature or scope of a machine-readable data file unless it is apparent from the rest of the description.

>Records relate to books published in the U.K.

9.7B2. Language, etc. Give an indication of the language, script, and/or type of characters that make up the content of a data file unless this is apparent from the rest of the description.

>ASCII characters

>Contains roman and Cyrillic characters

>In German

9.7B3. Source of title proper. Make notes on the source of the title proper if it has been taken from anywhere other than the data file itself.

>Title from codebook

>Title from: DUALabs technical document ST-5

>Title supplied in correspondence by creator of file

>Title from: A guide to the resources and services of the Inter-University Consortium for Political Research. 1971/72 ed. p. 76

>Title supplied by cataloguer

9.7B4. Variations in title. Give other titles found on the file or in its accompanying documentation or in other descriptions of the file. *Optionally*, record a data set name differing from the title proper.

>Title on codebook: New Democratic Party of Ontario, 1967

>Data set name: MACPEE

9.7B5. Parallel titles and other title information. Give parallel titles and other title information not recorded in the title and statement of responsibility area if they are considered to be important.

9.7B6. Statements of responsibility. Give statements relating to collaborators, sponsors, commissioning agents, programmers, systems analysts, etc., and persons or bodies responsible for the preparation of the file in machine-readable form if they are not named elsewhere in the description and are judged necessary for the bibliographic description.

>Associate investigators: Jack Dennis, John David Jackson, Judith Torney

>Prepared for the Manpower Administration, U.S. Dept. of Labor (contract no.   )

>Simulation rev. and reprogrammed in BASIC by John Smith for use in an on-line time-sharing environment

9.7B7. Edition and history. Make notes relating to the edition being described or to the history of an item. Cite other works upon which the file depends for its content.

File first issued in 1970

Updated version of 1971 program

Mnemonic tags substituted for numeric tags

1961 ed. corr. 1975 using update program received 1972

Based on: C. Valerii Catulli "Carmina" / edited by R.A.B. Mynors. London : Oxford University Press, 1960

Source of data: Human relations area file

Give the following dates if they are considered to be relevant to the content, use, or condition of the file:

a) the date when data were copied from an outside source

Copied on-line from State University Computer Center, June 1975

b) the date(s) covered by the data content of a file

Data for 1945–1960

c) the date(s) when data were collected

Data collected May–Aug. 1971

d) the date(s) of supplementary files if these are not described separately.

Includes supplementary files issued 1971 and 1973

9.7B8. Program. Give the program version and/or level.

SPSS 5.2

FORTRAN IV, level H

9.7B9. Publication, production, distribution, etc. Make notes on publication, production, distribution, etc., details that are not included in the publication, etc., area and are considered to be important.

Distributed in the U.K. by: ILIP Services

9.7B10. File description and physical description

If the number of records or statements in a file has not been verified, indicate this.

Size of file not verified

If the file consists of exemplars retained for their physical characteristics, give a concise physical description of the file.

75 plastic credit cards with magnetic strip on back

If the number of records or statements in a file cannot be ascertained (even approximately), give a concise description of the file as received.

Received as 2,000 reels of magnetic tape, 800 bpi

If, in the context of a particular catalogue or other list, a physical description of the medium in which the file has been received is judged necessary, give the number of physical entities, the name of the physical medium, and other necessary physical details such as quantitative properties, trade name, dimensions, etc.

> 1 tape reel : 7 tracks, blocked BCDs, 40 records per block, 90 characters per record, 800 bpi, odd parity, standard label ; 31 cm.

> 150 punched cards : 80 columns, IBM System 3

9.7B11. Accompanying material. Give details of accompanying material not mentioned in the file description area (see 9.5D). If a codebook has an ISBN, give it here.

> Data accompanied by a series of 5 programs in PL/1, with assembler subroutines

> Codebook numbered: ISBN . . .

9.7B12. Series. Make notes on series data that cannot be given in the series area.

9.7B13. Dissertations. If a machine-readable data file is a dissertation, give this fact as instructed in 2.7B13.

9.7B14. Audience and restrictions on access. Make a brief note of the intended audience for, or intellectual level of, a data file if one is stated on the item or in its documentation.

> Intended audience: Clinical students and postgraduate house officers

If the material is not available to all users of the catalogue or other list, indicate this. If possible, word the note in general terms so as to avoid recataloguing when the restriction is lifted.

> File closed until Jan. 1979

> Available only to students, faculty, and staff of . . .

> Not generally available

9.7B15. Mode of use. If the file cannot be used on all facilities available to the user of the catalogue or other list, specify its mode of use.

> Mode of use: On-line video or teletype terminal or with a small dedicated computer (e.g., PDP 8)

9.7B16. Other formats. If the documentation indicates that the data content of a file is available in another format, indicate this.

> Also available in microform

9.7B17. Summary. Give a brief objective summary of the content of the file unless another part of the description gives enough information.

> Summary: Responses of New York City adults to Harris study questionnaire (no. 1,925) used during Apr. and May 1969

9.7B18. Contents. Make a list of the titles of the individually named parts of a file. Add to the titles the number of logical records or statements in each part.

Contents: file 1. Idaho (985 logical records) — file 2. Montana (1,102 logical records) — file 3. Oregon (1,158 logical records) — file 4. Washington (2,544 logical records)

Contents: Summaries for 3-digit ZIP code areas (1,000 logical records) — Summaries for 5-digit ZIP code areas completely within standard metropolitan statistical areas (12,000 logical records)

Make informal, additional, or partial contents notes when appropriate.

Trip record includes travel data and demographic data. Records from no-trip households include demographic data only

Includes some records relating to serial holdings

Contains information on all 50 states

9.7B19. Numbers borne by the item. Give important numbers borne by the item other than ISBNs and ISSNs (see 9.8B).

9.7B20. Copy being described and library's holdings. Make notes on any peculiarities or imperfections of the copy being described that are considered to be important. If the library does not hold a complete set of a multipart item, give details of the library's holdings. Make a temporary note if the library hopes to complete the set.

9.8. STANDARD NUMBER AND TERMS OF AVAILABILITY AREA

Contents:
9.8A. Preliminary rule
9.8B. Standard number
9.8C. Key-title
9.8D. Terms of availability
9.8E. Qualification

9.8A. Preliminary rule

9.8A1. Punctuation

For instructions on the use of spaces before and after prescribed punctuation, see 1.0C.

Precede this area by a full stop, space, dash, space *or* start a new paragraph.

Precede each repetition of this area by a full stop, space, dash, space.

Precede a key-title by an equals sign.

Precede terms of availability by a colon.

Enclose a qualification to the standard number or terms of availability in parentheses.

9.8B. Standard number

9.8B1. Give the International Standard Book Number (ISBN) or International Standard Serial Number (ISSN) assigned to a machine-readable data file as instructed in 1.8B.

215

9.8C *Key-title*

9.8B2. Give any other number in a note (see 9.7B19).

9.8C. Key-title

9.8C1. Give the key-title of a serial machine-readable data file as instructed in 1.8C.

9.8D. *Optional addition.* **Terms of availability**

9.8D1. Give the terms on which the item is available as instructed in 1.8D.

$800.00

Free to universities and colleges, for hire to others

9.8E. Qualification

9.8E1. Add qualifications to the standard number and/or terms of availability as instructed in 1.8E.

9.9. SUPPLEMENTARY ITEMS

Describe supplementary items as instructed in 1.9.

9.10. ITEMS MADE UP OF SEVERAL TYPES OF MATERIAL

Describe items made up of several types of material as instructed in 1.10.

CHAPTER 10

THREE-DIMENSIONAL ARTEFACTS AND REALIA

Contents

Contents

10.0. GENERAL RULES

10.0A. Scope

The rules in this chapter cover the description of three-dimensional artefacts of all kinds (other than those covered in previous chapters), including models, dioramas, games (including puzzles and simulations), sculptures and other three-dimensional art works, exhibits, machines, and clothing. They also cover the description of naturally occurring objects, including microscope specimens (or representations of them) and other specimens mounted for viewing. For the description of three-dimensional cartographic materials (relief models, globes, etc.), see chapter 3.

10.0B. Sources of information

10.0B1. Chief source of information. The chief source of information for the materials covered in this chapter is the object itself together with any accompanying textual material and container issued by the "publisher" or manufacturer of the item. Prefer information found on the object itself (including any permanently affixed labels) to information found in accompanying textual material or on a container.

10.0B2. Prescribed sources of information. The prescribed source of information for each area of the description of these materials is set out below. Enclose information taken from outside the prescribed source(s) in square brackets.

AREA	PRESCRIBED SOURCES OF INFORMATION
Title and statement of responsibility	Chief source of information
Edition	Chief source of information
Publication, distribution, etc.	Chief source of information
Physical description	Any source
Series	Chief source of information
Note	Any source
Standard number and terms of availability	Any source

10.0C. Punctuation

For the punctuation of the description as a whole, see 1.0C.

For the prescribed punctuation of elements, see the following rules.

10.0D. Levels of detail in the description

See 1.0D.

10.0E. Language and script of the description

See 1.0E.

10.0F. Inaccuracies

See 1.0F.

10.0G. Accents and other diacritical marks

See 1.0G.

10.0H. Items with several chief sources of information

Multipart items with a container that is a unifying element. Prefer information found on a container that is the unifying element of a multipart item to information found on the objects.

Multipart items without a container that is a unifying element. See 1.0H.

Single part items. See 1.0H.

10.1. TITLE AND STATEMENT OF RESPONSIBILITY AREA

Contents:
10.1A. Preliminary rule
10.1B. Title proper
10.1C. General material designation
10.1D. Parallel titles
10.1E. Other title information
10.1F. Statements of responsibility
10.1G. Items without a collective title

10.1A. Preliminary rule

10.1A1. Punctuation

For instructions on the use of spaces before and after prescribed punctuation, see 1.0C.

Enclose the general material designation in square brackets.

Precede each parallel title by an equals sign.

Precede each unit of other title information by a colon.

Precede the first statement of responsibility by a diagonal slash.

Precede each subsequent statement of responsibility by a semicolon.

For the punctuation of this area for items without a collective title, see 1.1G.

10.1B. Title proper

10.1B1. Record the title proper as instructed in 1.1B.

Human development models

Solar system simulator

Muscular dynamism, or, Unique forms of continuity in space

1787

Adventure with sea-shells

[Woman's dress, ca. 1830]

Tooth development

[United States silver dollar]

Pet rock

10.1C. *Optional addition.* **General material designation.**

10.1C1. Add immediately following the title proper the appropriate general material designation as instructed in 1.1C.

10.1C2. If an item contains parts belonging to materials falling into two or more categories, and if none of these is the predominant constituent of the item, give either *multimedia* or *kit* as the designation (see 1.1C1 and 1.10).

10.1D. Parallel titles

10.1D1. Record parallel titles as instructed in 1.1D.

> Tarot cards ₍GMD₎ = L'ancien tarot

10.1E. Other title information

10.1E1 Record other title information as instructed in 1.1E.

> The language arts box ₍GMD₎ : 150 games, activities, manipulatives

10.1F. Statements of responsibility

10.1F1. Record statements relating to persons or bodies responsible for the creation of the item, or for its display or selection, as instructed in 1.1F.

> Hang-up ₍GMD₎ / developed by W.J. Gordon and T. Poze
>
> Rosetta Stone unit ₍GMD₎ / consultant, Edward L.B. Terrace
>
> A trip to the zoo ₍GMD₎ / created by the fourth grade class of Washington Elementary School, Berkeley, CA

10.1F2. Add a word or short phrase to the statement of responsibility if the relationship between the title of the work and the person(s) or body (bodies) named in the statement is not clear.

10.1G. Items without a collective title

10.1G1. If an item lacks a collective title, record the titles of the individual works as instructed in 1.1G.

10.1G2. Make the relationship between statements of responsibility and the parts of an item lacking a collective title clear by additions as instructed in 10.1F2.

10.2. EDITION AREA

Contents:

10.2A. Preliminary rule

10.2A1. Punctuation

For instructions on the use of spaces before and after the prescribed punctuation, see 1.0C.

Precede this area by a full stop, space, dash, space.

Precede a subsequent edition statement by a comma.

Precede the first statement of responsibility following an edition or subsequent edition statement by a diagonal slash.

Precede each subsequent statement of responsibility by a semicolon.

10.2B. Edition statement

10.2B1. Transcribe a statement relating to an edition of an artefact that contains differences from other editions or that is a named reissue of that artefact as instructed in 1.2B.

> The fable game ₍GMD₎ = Il gioco delle favole / Enzo Mari. — 2nd ed., with cards re-drawn in colour

> Subbuteo table soccer ₍GMD₎. — World Cup ed.

10.2B2. In case of doubt about whether a statement is an edition statement, follow the instructions in 1.2B3.

10.2B3. *Optional addition.* If an item lacks an edition statement but is known to contain significant changes from previous editions, supply a suitable brief statement in the language and script of the title proper and enclose it in square brackets.

> ₍New ed.₎

> ₍5ᵉ éd.₎

10.2B4. If an edition statement appears in more than one language or script, record the statement that is in the language or script of the title proper. If this criterion does not apply, record the statement that appears first.

10.2B5. If an item lacking a collective title and described as a unit contains one or more parts with an associated edition statement, record such statements following the titles and statements of responsibility to which they relate, separated from them by a full stop.

10.2C. Statements of responsibility relating to the edition

10.2C1. Record a statement of responsibility relating to one or more editions, but not to all editions, of an artefact as instructed in 1.2C.

10.2D. Subsequent edition statement

10.2D1. If the item is a named revision of a particular edition, containing changes from that edition, give the subsequent edition statement as instructed in 1.2D.

Do not record statements relating to subsequent editions that contain no changes unless the item is considered to be of particular importance to the cataloguing agency.

10.2E. Statements of responsibility relating to a subsequent edition statement

10.2E1. Record a statement of responsibility relating to one or more designated subsequent editions, but not to all subsequent editions, of a particular edition as instructed in 1.2E.

10.3. MATERIAL (OR TYPE OF PUBLICATION) SPECIFIC DETAILS AREA
This area is not used for three-dimensional artefacts and realia.

10.4. PUBLICATION, DISTRIBUTION, ETC., AREA
Contents:
    10.4A. Preliminary rule
    10.4B. General rule
    10.4C. Place of publication, distribution, etc.
    10.4D. Name of publisher, distributor, etc.
    10.4E. Statement of function of publisher, distributor, etc.
    10.4F. Date of publication, distribution, etc.
    10.4G. Place of manufacture, name of manufacturer, date of manufacture

10.4A. Preliminary rule

10.4A1. Punctuation
For instructions on the use of spaces before and after prescribed punctuation, see 1.0C.

Precede this area by a full stop, space, dash, space.

Precede a second or subsequently named place of publication, distribution, etc., by a semicolon.

Precede the name of a publisher, distributor, etc., by a colon.

Enclose a supplied statement of function of a publisher, distributor, etc., in square brackets.

Precede the date of publication, distribution, etc., by a comma.

Enclose the details of manufacture (place, name, date) in parentheses.

Precede the name of a manufacturer by a colon.

Precede the date of manufacture by a comma.

10.4B. General rule
Follow the instructions in 1.4B for items with multiple places and names of publishers, distributors, etc.

10.4C. Place of publication, distribution, etc.

10.4C1. Record the place of publication, distribution, etc., as instructed in 1.4C.

10.4D *Name of publisher, distributor, etc.*

10.4C2. In the case of naturally occurring objects (other than those mounted for viewing or packaged for presentation) and artefacts not intended primarily for communication, do not record any place of publication, etc.

10.4D. Name of publisher, distributor, etc.

10.4D1. Record the name of the publisher, distributor, etc., as instructed in 1.4D.

> Philadelphia : DCA Educational Products
>
> Circle Pines, Minn. : American Guidance Service

10.4D2. In the case of naturally occurring objects (other than those mounted for viewing or packaged for presentation) and artefacts not intended primarily for communication, do not record any name of publisher, distributor, etc.

10.4E. *Optional addition.* **Statement of function of publisher, distributor, etc.**

10.4E1. Add to the name of a publisher, distributor, etc., a statement of function as instructed in 1.4E.

10.4F. Date of publication, distribution, etc.

10.4F1. Record the date of publication, distribution, etc., as instructed in 1.4F.

> Chicago : Science Research Associates, 1971
>
> Cambridge, Mass. : Synetics Education Systems, c1969

10.4F2. In the case of naturally occurring objects (other than those mounted for viewing or packaged for presentation), do not give a date. In the case of artefacts not intended primarily for communication, give the date of manufacture as the first element of this area.

> ₍English Victorian costume₎ ₍GMD₎. — ₍186–?₎
>
> ₍United States silver dollar₎ ₍GMD₎. — 1931

10.4G. Place of manufacture, name of manufacturer, date of manufacture

10.4G1. If the name of the publisher, distributor, etc., is unknown or not applicable (see 10.4C2 and 10.4D2), give the place and the name of the manufacturer, if known, as instructed in 1.4G.

> ₍Wooden chair₎ ₍GMD₎. — 1881 (Chiswick : Morris & Co.)
>
> ₍Millefiori paperweight₎ ₍GMD₎. — ₍1890?₎ (Paris : Reynaud frères)

10.4G2. If the person or body responsible for the manufacture of the object has been named in the statements of responsibility (see 10.1F), do not repeat the place and name here.

> ₍Appliqué quilt, album style, Baltimore, Md.₎ ₍GMD₎ / Anna Putney Farrington. — 1857
> > (*Quilt is signed and dated*)

10.4G3. *Optional addition.* Give the place, name of manufacturer, and/or date of manufacture if they differ from the place, name of publisher, etc., and date of publication, etc., and are found on the item or in accompanying textual material or on a container, and are considered important by·the cataloguing agency.

10.5. PHYSICAL DESCRIPTION AREA

Contents:
10.5A. Preliminary rule
10.5B. Extent of item (including specific material designation)
10.5C. Other physical details
10.5D. Dimensions
10.5E. Accompanying material

10.5A. Preliminary rule

10.5A1. Punctuation

For instructions on the use of spaces before and after prescribed punctuation, see 1.0C.

Precede this area by a full stop, space, dash, space *or* start a new paragraph.

Precede other physical details by a colon.

Precede dimensions by a semicolon.

Precede a statement of accompanying material by a plus sign.

Enclose physical details of accompanying material in parentheses.

10.5B. Extent of item (including specific material designation)

10.5B1. Record the number of physical units of a three-dimensional artefact or object by giving the number of parts in arabic numerals and one of the terms listed below, as appropriate. If none of these terms is appropriate, give the specific name of the item or the names of the parts of the item as concisely as possible.

diorama
exhibit
game
microscope slide
mock-up
model

1 game

2 dioramas

1 microscope slide

6 microscope slides

2 jigsaw puzzles

3 hand puppets

2 feather headbands, 1 pair beaded moccasins

3 quilts

10.5C Other physical details

Optionally, if general material designations are used and the general material designation consists of one of the above listed terms, drop that term and give the number of pieces alone (see 10.5B2).

10.5B2. Add to the designation, when appropriate, the number and the name(s) of the pieces.

> 1 jigsaw puzzle (1,000 pieces)
>
> 1 game (2 players' manuals, board, cards, role cards, 2 dice)

If the pieces cannot be named concisely or cannot be ascertained, add the term *various pieces*, and *optionally* give the details of the pieces in a note (see 10.7B10).

> 1 diorama (various pieces)
> *Note:* Contains 1 small stage, 5 foreground transparencies, 2 backgrounds, 5 story sheets, and 1 easel
>
> 2 games (various pieces)

10.5C. Other physical details

10.5C1. Material. When appropriate, give the material(s) of which the object is made If the material(s) cannot be stated concisely, either omit them or give them in a note. Give the material of which a microscope slide is made if it is other than glass.

> 2 models (various pieces) : polystyrene
>
> 1 diorama (various pieces) : plywood and papier mâché
>
> 1 statue : marble
>
> 2 paperweights : glass
>
> 1 quilt : cotton
>
> 1 jigsaw puzzle : wood
>
> 1 microscope slide : plastic

10.5C2. Colour. When appropriate, give the abbreviation *col.* for multicoloured objects, or name the colour(s) of the object if it is in one or two colours, or give the abbreviation *b&w*. If a microscope slide is stained, state this.

> 1 bowl : porcelain, blue and white
>
> 1 model : wood, blue
>
> 1 paperweight : glass, col.
>
> 1 model : balsa wood and paper, b&w
>
> 1 microscope slide : stained

10.5D. Dimensions

10.5D1. Give the dimensions of the object, when appropriate, in centimetres, to the next whole centimetre up. If necessary, add a word to indicate which dimension is being given. If multiple dimensions are given, record them as height × width × depth (for microscope slides, length × width).

1 sculpture : polished bronze ; 110 cm. high

6 microscope slides : stained ; 8 × 3 cm.

10.5D2. If the object is in a container, name the container and give its dimensions either after the dimensions of the object or as the only dimensions.

1 model (10 pieces) : col. ; 16 × 32 × 3 cm. in case, 17 × 34 × 6 cm.

1 diorama (various pieces) : col. ; in box, 30 × 25 × 13 cm.

1 jigsaw puzzle : wood, col. ; in box, 25 × 32 × 5 cm.

10.5E. Accompanying material

10.5E1. Record the name, and *optionally* the physical description, of any accompanying material as instructed in 1.5E.

5 models : col. ; in box, 20 × 20 × 12 cm. + 1 teacher's guide
(3 v. ; 30 cm.)

1 hand puppet : red and blue ; 20 cm. long + 1 sound disc
(20 min. : 33 1/3 rpm, mono. ; 12 in.)

10.6. SERIES AREA

Contents:
10.6A. Preliminary rule
10.6B. Series statements

10.6A. Preliminary rule

10.6A1. Punctuation

For instructions on the use of spaces before and after prescribed punctuation, see 1.0C.

Precede this area by a full stop, space, dash, space.

Enclose each series statement (see 1.6J) in parentheses.

Precede parallel titles of series or subseries by an equals sign.

Precede other title information relating to series or subseries by a colon.

Precede the first statement of responsibility relating to a series or subseries by a diagonal slash.

Precede subsequent statements of responsibility relating to a series or subseries by a semicolon.

Precede the ISSN of a series or subseries by a comma.

Precede the numbering within a series or subseries by a semicolon.

Precede the title of a subseries by a full stop.

10.6B. Series statements

10.6B1. Record each series statement as instructed in 1.6.

(Dioramas of American history ; 7)

(Beatrix Potter jigsaw puzzles ; no. 3)

10.7. NOTE AREA

Contents:
    10.7A. Preliminary rule
    10.7B. Notes

10.7A. Preliminary rule

10.7A1. Punctuation

Precede each note by a full stop, space, dash, space *or* start a new paragraph for each.

Separate introductory wording from the main content of a note by a colon and a space.

10.7A2. In making notes, follow the instructions in 1.7A.

10.7B. Notes

Make notes as set out in the following subrules and in the order given there.

10.7B1. Nature of the item. Give the nature of the item unless it is apparent from the rest of the description.

    Study of a figure in motion

    Section of fetal pig mandible

10.7B3. Source of title proper. Make notes on the source of the title proper if it is other than the chief source of information.

    Title supplied by cataloguer

    Title taken from sales catalogue

10.7B4. Variations in title. Make notes on titles borne by the item other than the title proper. If considered desirable, give a romanization of the title proper.

    Title on container: DNA-RNA protein synthesis model kit

10.7B5. Parallel titles and other title information. Give parallel titles and other title information not recorded in the title and statement of responsibility area if they are considered important.

    Title on container: Elementary dental model

10.7B6. Statements of responsibility. Make notes on variant names of persons or bodies named in statements of responsibility if these are considered to be important for identification. Give statements of responsibility not recorded in the title and

228

statement of responsibility area. Make notes on persons or bodies connected with a work, or significant persons or bodies connected with previous editions, not already named in the description.

> Notes by Jack Megenity

> "Developed by Frederick A. Rasmussen of E₍ducational₎ R₍esearch₎ C₍ouncil of America₎"

10.7B7. Edition and history. Make notes relating to the edition being described or to the history of the item. Cite other works upon which the item depends for its intellectual or artistic content.

> Recast in bronze from artist's plaster original of 1903

> Game based on: Lateral thinking / by M. Freedman

10.7B9. Publication, distribution, etc. Make notes on publication, distribution, etc., details that are not included in the publication, etc., area and are considered to be important.

10.7B10. Physical description. Give important physical details that have not been included in the physical description area, especially if these affect the use of the item. If the physical description includes the term *various pieces* and a description of the pieces is considered to be useful, give such a description.

> Four times actual size. — The parts of the ear are painted to show anatomical structure

> Includes headdress, beaded shirt, trousers, and moccasins

> Pattern: Pennsylvania wild goose

> Contains 1 small stage, 5 foreground transparencies, 2 backgrounds, 5 story sheets, and 1 easel

10.7B11. Accompanying material. Make notes on the location of accompanying material if appropriate. Give details of accompanying material not mentioned in the physical description area or given a separate entry or separate description according to the rules for multilevel description (see 13.6).

> Teacher's guide (24 p.) by Robert Garry Shirts

> With instructor and student guides, 16 taped lectures, cassette recorder, and course guide (4 v.)

> Book entitled: The adventure book of shells / by Eva Knox Evans (in container)

10.7B12. Series. Make notes on series data that cannot be given in the series area.

10.7B14. Audience. Make a brief note of the intended audience for, or intellectual level of, an item if this information is stated in the item.

> For medical students

> Intended audience: Junior high and up

10.7B17. Summary. Give a brief objective summary of the content of an item unless another part of the description gives enough information.

> Summary: Illustrations of animals and background scenery, with stands, which may be rearranged to create various scenes of animals at the zoo

> Summary: Puppets from a set designed to dramatize real-life situations

10.7B18. Contents. Make a list of the individually named parts of an object. Make notes on additional or partial contents when appropriate.

> Contents: Colony — Frontier — Reconstruction — Promotion — Intervention — Development

> Contents: Sperm cell in uterus — 2-week embryo — 7- to 8-week fetus — 13-week fetus — 18- to 20-week fetus

> Includes a simplified version of the game

10.7B19. Numbers. Give important numbers borne by the item other than ISBNs or ISSNs (see 10.8B).

10.7B20. Copy being described and library's holdings. Make notes on any peculiarities or imperfections of the copy being described that are considered to be important. If the library does not hold a complete set of a multipart item, give details of the library's holdings. Make a temporary note if the library hopes to complete the set.

10.8. STANDARD NUMBER AND TERMS OF AVAILABILITY AREA

Contents:
> 10.8A. Preliminary rule
> 10.8B. Standard number
> 10.8C. Key-title
> 10.8D. Terms of availability
> 10.8E. Qualification

10.8A. Preliminary rule

10.8A1. Punctuation

For instructions on the use of spaces before and after prescribed punctuation, see 1.0C.

Precede this area by a full stop, space, dash, space *or* start a new paragraph.

Precede each repetition of this area by a full stop, space, dash, space.

Precede a key-title by an equals sign.

Precede terms of availability by a colon.

Enclose a qualification to the standard number or terms of availability in parentheses.

10.8B. Standard number

10.8B1. Give an International Standard Book Number (ISBN) or an International Standard Serial Number (ISSN) assigned to an artefact as instructed in 1.8B.

10.8B2. Give any other number in a note (see 10.7B19).

10.8C. Key-title

10.8C1. Give the key-title of a serial artefact as instructed in 1.8C.

10.8D. *Optional addition.* **Terms of availability**

10.8D1. Give the terms on which the item is available as instructed in 1.8D.

> Free loan to medical students

> $9.00 (medical students only)

10.8E. Qualification

10.8E1. Add qualifications to the standard number and/or terms of availability as instructed in 1.8E.

10.9. SUPPLEMENTARY ITEMS

Describe supplementary items as instructed in 1.9.

10.10. ITEMS MADE UP OF SEVERAL TYPES OF MATERIAL

Describe items made up of several types of material as instructed in 1.10.

CHAPTER 11

MICROFORMS

Contents

11.0. GENERAL RULES

11.0A. Scope

The rules in this chapter cover the description of all kinds of material in microform. Microforms include microfilms, microfiches, microopaques, and aperture cards. Microforms may be reproductions of existing textual or graphic materials or they may be original publications.

11.0B. Sources of information

11.0B1. Chief source of information. The chief source of information for microfilms is the title frame (i.e., a frame, usually at the beginning of the item, bearing the full title and, normally, publication details of the item). The chief source of information for aperture cards is, in the case of a set of cards, the title card, or, in the case of a single card, the card itself. The chief source of information for microfiches and microopaques is the title frame. If there is no such information or if the information is insufficient, treat the eye-readable data printed at the top of the fiche or opaque as the chief source of information. If information normally presented on the title frame or title card is presented on successive frames or cards, treat these frames or cards as the chief source of information.

If information is not available from the chief source, take it from the following sources (in this order of preference):

the rest of the item (including a container that is an integral part of the item)
container
accompanying eye-readable material
any other source

11.0B2. Prescribed sources of information. The prescribed source(s) of information for each area of the description of microforms is set out below. Enclose information taken from outside the prescribed source(s) in square brackets.

AREA	PRESCRIBED SOURCES OF INFORMATION
Title and statement of responsibility	Chief source of information
Edition	Chief source of information, the rest of the item, the container
Special data for cartographic materials and serials	Chief source of information, the rest of the item, the container
Publication, distribution, etc.	Chief source of information, the rest of the item, the container
Physical description	Any source
Series	Chief source of information, the rest of the item, the container
Note	Any source
Standard number and terms of availability	Any source

11.0C. Punctuation

For the punctuation of the description as a whole, see 1.0C.

For the prescribed punctuation of elements, see the following rules.

11.0D. Levels of detail in the description

See 1.0D.

11.0E. Language and script of the description

See 1.0E.

11.0F. Inaccuracies

See 1.0F.

11.0G. Accents and other diacritical marks

See 1.0G.

11.0H. Items with several chief sources of information

See 1.0H.

11.1. TITLE AND STATEMENT OF RESPONSIBILITY AREA

Contents:

11.1A. Preliminary rule
11.1B. Title proper
11.1C. General material designation
11.1D. Parallel titles
11.1E. Other title information
11.1F. Statements of responsibility
11.1G. Items without a collective title

11.1A. Preliminary rule

11.1A1. Punctuation

For instructions on the use of spaces before and after prescribed punctuation, see 1.0C.

Precede the title of a supplement or a section (see 1.1B9) by a full stop.

Enclose the general material designation in square brackets.

Precede each parallel title by an equals sign.

Precede each unit of other title information by a colon.

Precede the first statement of responsibility by a diagonal slash.

Precede each subsequent statement of responsibility by a semicolon.

For the punctuation of this area for items without a collective title, see 1.1G.

11.1B. Title proper

11.1B1. Record the title proper as instructed in 1.1B.

Early narratives of the Northwest

Grimm's fairy tales

11.1C *General material designation*

> Library resources & technical services
>
> Records of the Socialist Labor Party of America
>
> Index to Sussex parish registers and bishops transcripts
>
> Beethoven's symphonies
>
> British masters of the albumen print

11.1C. *Optional addition.* **General material designation**

11.1C1. Add immediately following the title proper the appropriate general material designation as instructed in 1.1C.

> A history of Dalhousie University Main Library, 1867–1931 ₁GMD₁

11.1C2. If an item contains parts belonging to materials falling into two or more categories, and if none of these is the predominant constituent of the item, give either *multimedia* or *kit* as the designation (see 1.1C1 and 1.10).

11.1D. Parallel titles

11.1D1. Record parallel titles as instructed in 1.1D.

> Deutschland ₁GMD₁ = Allemagne = Germany

11.1E. Other title information

11.1E1. Record other title information as instructed in 1.1E.

> The gentleman of Venice ₁GMD₁ : a tragi-comedie presented at the private house in Salisbury Court by Her Majesties servants
>
> A collection in the making ₁GMD₁ : works from the Phillips Collection

11.1F. Statements of responsibility

11.1F1. Record statements of responsibility as instructed in 1.1F.

> The principles of psychology ₁GMD₁ / William James
>
> Books in English ₁GMD₁ / British Library Bibliographic Services Division
>
> Selections from the permanent collection ₁GMD₁ / Whitney Museum of American Art

11.1F2. Add a word or short phrase to the statement of responsibility if the relationship between the title of the item and the person(s) or body (bodies) named in the statement is not clear.

11.1G. Items without a collective title

11.1G1. If a microform lacks a collective title, *either* describe the item as a unit (see 11.1G2 and 11.1G3) *or* make a separate description for each separately titled work (see 11.1G4).

236

11.1G2. In describing as a unit a microform lacking a collective title, record the titles of the individual works as instructed in 1.1G.

> Don Juan ; and, Childe Harold ₍GMD₎ / Lord Byron

> Analysis of the results of the general population census 1964 ; The supply of labour in Libya ₍GMD₎ / Libya, Ministry of Economy and Commerce, Census and Statistical Department

> The Wilson papers. The Colt-Hatt papers ₍GMD₎

11.1G3. Make the relationship between statements of responsibility and the parts of an item lacking a collective title and described as a unit clear by additions as instructed in 11.1F2.

11.1G4. If desired, make a separate description for each separately titled work on a microform. For the description of the extent in each of these descriptions, see 11.5B2. Link the separate descriptions with a note (see 11.7B21).

11.2. EDITION AREA

Contents:
11.2A. Preliminary rule
11.2B. Edition statement
11.2C. Statements of responsibility relating to the edition
11.2D. Subsequent edition statement
11.2E. Statements of responsibility relating to a subsequent edition statement

11.2A. Preliminary rule

11.2A1. Punctuation
For instructions on the use of spaces before and after prescribed punctuation, see 1.0C.
Precede this area by a full stop, space, dash, space.
Precede a subsequent edition statement by a comma.
Precede the first statement of responsibility following an edition or subsequent edition statement by a diagonal slash.
Precede each subsequent statement of responsibility by a semicolon.

11.2B. Edition statement

11.2B1. Transcribe a statement relating to an edition of a microform that contains differences from other editions, or that is a named reissue of that microform, as instructed in 1.2B.

> 2nd ed.

> New ed.

> Memorial ed.

> Micro ed.

11.2C *Statements of responsibility relating to the edition*

11.2B2. In case of doubt about whether a statement is an edition statement, follow the instructions in 1.2B3.

11.2B3. *Optional addition.* If a microform lacks an edition statement but is known to contain significant changes from previous editions, supply a suitable brief statement in the language and script of the title proper and enclose it in square brackets.

> ₁New ed.₁
>
> ₁3rd ed.₁

11.2B4. If an edition statement appears in more than one language or script, record the statement that is in the language or script of the title proper. If this criterion does not apply, record the statement that appears first.

11.2B5. If an item lacking a collective title and described as a unit contains one or more parts with an associated edition statement, record such statements following the titles and statements of responsibility to which they relate, separated from them by a full stop.

> Finnegans wake. 2nd ed. ; Ulysses ₁GMD₁ / James Joyce

11.2C. Statements of responsibility relating to the edition

11.2C1. Record a statement of responsibility relating to one or more editions, but not to all editions, of a microform as instructed in 1.2C.

> 3rd ed. / with an introduction by Tom Barbellion

11.2D. Subsequent edition statement

11.2D1. If the item is a named reissue of a particular edition containing changes from that edition, give the subsequent edition statement as instructed in 1.2D.

> 3rd ed., Corr.

11.2E. Statements of responsibility relating to a subsequent edition statement

11.2E1. Record a statement of responsibility relating to one or more named subsequent editions, but not to all subsequent editions, of a particular edition as instructed in 1.2E.

11.3. SPECIAL DATA FOR CARTOGRAPHIC MATERIALS AND SERIALS

11.3A. Cartographic materials
Record the mathematical data of a cartographic item in microform as instructed in 3.3.

11.3B. Serials
Record the numeric and/or chronological or other designation of a serial microform or a serial reproduced in microform as instructed in 12.3.

Library resources & technical services ₍GMD₎. — Vol. 16, no. 1
(winter 1972)–

The Yellow book ₍GMD₎ : an illustrated quarterly. — Vol. 1 (Apr.
1894)–v. 13 (Apr. 1897)

11.4. PUBLICATION, DISTRIBUTION, ETC., AREA

Contents:
11.4A. Preliminary rule
11.4B. General rule
11.4C. Place of publication, distribution, etc.
11.4D. Name of publisher, distributor, etc.
11.4E. Statement of function of publisher, distributor, etc.
11.4F. Date of publication, distribution, etc.

11.4A. Preliminary rule

11.4A1. Punctuation
For instructions on the use of spaces before and after prescribed punctuation,
see 1.0C.
Precede this area by a full stop, space, dash, space.
Precede a second or subsequently named place of publication, distribution, etc.,
by a semicolon.
Precede the name of a publisher, distributor, etc., by a colon.
Enclose a supplied statement of function of a publisher, distributor, etc., in square
brackets.
Precede the date of publication, distribution, etc., by a comma.

11.4B. General rule
For items with multiple places and names of publishers, distributors, etc., follow
the instructions in 1.4B.

11.4C. Place of publication, distribution, etc.

11.4C1. Record the place of publication, distribution, etc., as instructed in 1.4C.

11.4D. Name of publisher, distributor, etc.

11.4D1. Record the name of the publisher, distributor, etc., as instructed in 1.4D.

Los Angeles : University of Southern California

London : Grossman

New York : Readex Microprint

Ann Arbor, Mich. : Xerox University Microfilms
(*For a cataloguing agency in the United States*)

Ann Arbor, Mich. ; Tylers Green, Buckinghamshire : Xerox
University Microfilms
(*For a cataloguing agency in the United Kingdom*)

11.4E *Statement of function of publisher, distributor, etc.*

11.4E. *Optional addition.* **Statement of function of publisher, distributor, etc.**

11.4E1. Add to the name of a publisher, distributor, etc., a statement of function as instructed in 1.4E.

> New York : Charles & Brown ; London : Salemis ₁distributor₁

11.4F. Date of publication, distribution, etc.

11.4F1. Record the date of publication, distribution, etc., of a microform as instructed in 1.4F.

> New York : Readex Microprint, 1953
>
> London : Challon, 1969
>
> Ann Arbor, Mich. : Xerox University Microfilms, 1973–
>
> Chicago : Library Resources, c1970

11.5. PHYSICAL DESCRIPTION AREA

Contents:
>   11.5A. Preliminary rule
>   11.5B. Extent of item (including specific material designation)
>   11.5C. Other physical details
>   11.5D. Dimensions
>   11.5E. Accompanying material

11.5A. Preliminary rule

11.5A1. Punctuation

For instructions on the use of spaces before and after prescribed punctuation, see 1.0C.

Precede this area by a full stop, space, dash, space *or* start a new paragraph.

Precede other physical details by a colon.

Precede dimensions by a semicolon.

Precede a statement of accompanying material by a plus sign.

Enclose physical details of accompanying material in parentheses.

11.5B. Extent of item (including specific material designation)

11.5B1. Record the number of physical units of a microform item by giving the number of parts in arabic numerals and one of the following terms as appropriate:

> aperture card   microfilm
> microfiche   microopaque

Optionally, if the general material designation *microform* is used, drop the prefix *micro* from these terms.

Add to *microfilm* one of the terms *cartridge, cassette,* or *reel*, as appropriate. Add to *microfiche* the term *cassette* if appropriate.

240

25 aperture cards

1 microfilm cassette

2 microfilm reels

3 microfiches

10 microopaques

Add the number of frames of a microfiche if it can be easily ascertained. Make the addition in parentheses.

1 microfiche (120 fr.)

11.5B2. If the description is of a separately titled part of a microform lacking a collective title (see 11.1G4), express the fractional extent in the form *on reel 2 of 3 microfilm reels, on no. 4 of 5 microfiches*, etc. (if the parts are numbered in a single sequence) or *on 1 reel of 3 microfilm reels, on 1 of 5 microfiches*, etc. (if there is no single numbering).

on no. 3 of 4 microfilm cassettes

on 3 of 5 microopaques

11.5C. Other physical details

11.5C1. If a microform is negative, indicate this.

1 microfilm reel : negative

11.5C2. If a microform contains, or consists of, illustrations, indicate this as instructed in 1.5C.

1 microfilm cassette : ill.

1 microfiche : all ill.

1 microfiche : ill., music

1 microfiche : chiefly music

1 microfilm reel : negative, ill.

11.5C3. If a microform is wholly or partly coloured, indicate this by using *col.* (for a coloured microform without illustrations), or *col. & ill.* (for a coloured microform with illustrations), or *col. ill.*, etc. (for a microform on which only the illustrations are coloured).

1 microfilm reel : col.

1 microfilm reel : col. & ill.

1 microfilm reel : col. ill., col. maps

11.5D. Dimensions

11.5D1. Give the dimensions of a microform item as set out in the following rules. Record a fraction of a centimetre or inch as the next whole centimetre or inch up.

241

11.5D2. Aperture cards. Give the height × width of an aperture card mount in centimetres.

> 20 aperture cards ; 9 × 19 cm.

11.5D3. Microfiches. Give the height × width of a microfiche in centimetres.

> 3 microfiches ; 10 × 15 cm.

11.5D4. Microfilms. If the diameter of a microfilm reel is other than three inches, give the diameter in inches. Give the width of a microfilm in millimetres.

> 1 microfilm reel ; 16 mm.
>
> 1 microfilm reel ; 5 in., 35 mm.
>
> 1 microfilm cartridge ; 35 mm.

11.5D5. Microopaques. Give the height × width of a microopaque in centimetres.

> 5 microopaques ; 8 × 13 cm.

11.5E. Accompanying material

11.5E1. Record the name, and *optionally* the physical description, of any accompanying material as instructed in 1.5E.

> 1 microfilm reel ; 16 mm. + 1 pamphlet (30 p. : ill. ; 22 cm.)

11.6. SERIES AREA

Contents:
>11.6A. Preliminary rule
>11.6B. Series statements

11.6A. Preliminary rule

11.6A1. Punctuation

For instructions on the use of spaces before and after prescribed punctuation, see 1.0C.

Precede this area by a full stop, space, dash, space.

Enclose each series statement (see 1.6J) in parentheses.

Precede parallel titles of series or subseries by an equals sign.

Precede other title information relating to series or subseries by a colon.

Precede the first statement of responsibility relating to a series or subseries by a diagonal slash.

Precede subsequent statements of responsibility relating to a series or subseries by a semicolon.

Precede the ISSN of a series or subseries by a comma.

Precede the numbering within a series or subseries by a semicolon.

Precede the title of a subseries by a full stop.

11.6B. Series statements

11.6B1. Record each series statement relating to a microform as instructed in 1.6. If the original was published in a series, record it in a note (see 11.7B12).

> (Bibliotheca Asiatica ; v. 9)
>
> (PCMI collection)
>
> (AIP-DRP ; 63-2)
>
> (Three centuries of drama. English, 1642–1700)
>
> (Wright American fiction ; reel A-4)

11.7. NOTE AREA

Contents:
11.7A. Preliminary rule
11.7B. Notes

11.7A. Preliminary rule

11.7A1. Punctuation

Precede each note by a full stop, space, dash, space *or* start a new paragraph for each.

Separate introductory wording from the main content of a note by a colon and a space.

11.7A2. In making notes, follow the instructions in 1.7A.

11.7B. Notes

In describing an original reproduced in microform, give the notes set out in the following subrules, and then the notes relating to the original. (For exceptions, see 11.7B12 below and chapter 12.) Combine the notes relating to the original in one note, giving the details in the order of the areas to which they relate.

11.7B1. Nature, scope, or artistic or other form of an item. Make notes on these matters if they are not already apparent from the rest of the description.

> Collection of 18th century mss.

11.7B2. Language. Make notes on the language(s) of the item, unless this is apparent from the rest of the description.

> Latin, with English translations

11.7B3. Source of title proper. Make notes on the source of the title proper if it is other than the chief source of information.

> Title from container

11.7B4. Variations in title. Give titles borne by the item other than the title proper. If considered desirable, give a romanization of the title proper.

> Also known as: NICEM index to educational slides

11.7B5. Parallel titles and other title information. Give parallel titles and other title information not recorded in the title and statement of responsibility area if they are considered to be important.

>Subtitle:

11.7B6. Statements of responsibility. Make notes on variant names of persons or bodies named in statements of responsibility, if these are considered to be important for identification. Give statements of responsibility not recorded in the title and statement of responsibility area. Make notes on persons or bodies connected with a work, or significant persons or bodies connected with previous editions, not already named in the description.

>"Edited . . . by T.N. Jackson"—Pref.

11.7B7. Edition and history. Make notes relating to the edition being described or to the history of the microform.

>Previous ed.: 1971

11.7B9. Publication, distribution, etc. Make notes on publication, distribution, etc., details that are not included in the publication, etc., area and are considered important.

>Distributed in the U.K. by:

11.7B10. Physical description. Make the following physical description notes:

Reduction ratio. Give the reduction ratio if it is outside the $16\times$–$30\times$ range. Use one of the following terms:

Low reduction	*For less than $16\times$*
High reduction	*For $31\times$–$60\times$*
Very high reduction	*For $61\times$–$90\times$*
Ultra high reduction	*For over $90\times$; for ultra high reduction give also the specific ratio, e.g.,* Ultra high reduction, $150\times$

>Reduction ratio varies

Reader. Give the name of the reader on which a cassette or cartridge microfilm is to be used if it affects the use of the item.

>For Information Design reader

Film. *Optionally*, give details of the nature of the film used.

>Silver based film

11.7B11. Accompanying material. Make notes on the location of accompanying material if appropriate. Give details of accompanying material not mentioned in the physical description area or given a separate entry or separate description according to the rules for multilevel description (see 13.6).

>With brief notes (3 p.)

>In container with facsim. reproductions of p. 1–8 of original

11.7B12. Series. Make notes on series data that cannot be given in the series area.

> Original issued in series:
> *(For a reproduction in microform)*

> Originally issued in series:
> *(For a microform previously issued as such in a series)*

11.7B13. Dissertations. If the item being described is a dissertation, make a note as instructed in 2.7B13.

> John Stuart Stowe's thesis (M.A.)—University of New Brunswick, 1975

11.7B14. Audience. Make a brief note of the intended audience for, or intellectual level of, a microform if one is stated on the item, its container, or accompanying eye-readable material.

> For high school students

11.7B16. Other formats available. Make notes on other formats in which a microform is available.

11.7B17. Summary. Give a brief objective summary of the content of an item unless another part of the description gives enough information.

11.7B18. Contents. Give the contents of an item, either selectively or fully, if it is considered necessary to show the presence of material not implied by the rest of the description, or to stress items of particular importance, or to list the contents of a collection. When recording titles formally, take them from the head of the part to which they refer rather than from contents lists, etc.

> Includes bibliography

> Contents: Surrey — Kent — Middlesex — Essex

> Annual reports for 1957–1971

11.7B19. Numbers. Give important numbers borne by the item other than ISBNs or ISSNs (see 11.8B).

11.7B20. Copy being described and library's holdings. Make notes on any peculiarities or imperfections of the copy being described that are considered to be important. If the library does not hold a complete set of a multipart item, give details of the library's holdings. Make a temporary note if the library hopes to complete the set.

11.7B21. "With" notes. If the description is of a separately titled part of a microform lacking a collective title, make a note beginning *With:* listing the other separately titled parts of the item in the order in which they appear there.

> With: General Sherman / M. Force — Life and campaigns of
> Major-General J.E.B. Stuart / H. McClennan — General Butler in
> New Orleans / J. Parton — Life and public services of Ambrose E.
> Burnside / B. Poore — Life of General George G. Meade / R. Bache

11.8. STANDARD NUMBER AND TERMS OF AVAILABILITY AREA

Contents:
11.8A. Preliminary rule
11.8B. Standard number
11.8C. Key-title
11.8D. Terms of availability
11.8E. Qualification

11.8A. Preliminary rule

11.8A1. Punctuation

For instructions on the use of spaces before and after prescribed punctuation, see 1.0C.

Precede this area by a full stop, space, dash, space *or* start a new paragraph.

Precede each repetition of this area by a full stop, space, dash, space.

Precede a key-title by an equals sign.

Precede terms of availability by a colon.

Enclose a qualification to the standard number or terms of availability in parentheses.

11.8B. Standard number

11.8B1. Give an International Standard Book Number (ISBN) or an International Standard Serial Number (ISSN) assigned to a microform item. Record these numbers as instructed in 1.8B.

11.8B2. Give any other number in a note (see 11.7B19).

11.8C. Key-title

11.8C1. Give the key-title of a serial item as instructed in 1.8C.

11.8D. *Optional addition.* Terms of availability

11.8D1. Give the terms on which the item is available as instructed in 1.8D.

11.8E. Qualification

11.8E1. Add qualifications to the standard number and/or terms of availability as instructed in 1.8E.

11.9. SUPPLEMENTARY ITEMS

Describe supplementary items as instructed in 1.9.

11.10. ITEMS MADE UP OF SEVERAL TYPES OF MATERIAL

Describe items made up of several types of material as instructed in 1.10.

SERIALS

Contents

Contents

12.0. GENERAL RULES

12.0A. Scope
The rules in this chapter cover the description of serial publications of all kinds and in all media.

12.0B. Sources of information

12.0B1. Sources of information. Printed serials.

Chief source of information. The chief source of information for a printed serial is the title page (whether published with the issues or published later) or the title page substitute of the first issue of the serial. Failing this, the chief source of information is the first issue that is available. The title page substitute for an item lacking a title page is (in this order of preference) the cover, caption, masthead, editorial pages, colophon, other pages. If information traditionally given on the title page is given on facing pages, with or without repetition, treat the two pages as the title page.

Prescribed sources of information. The prescribed source(s) of information for each area of the description of printed serials is set out below. Enclose information taken from outside the prescribed source(s) in square brackets.

AREA	PRESCRIBED SOURCES OF INFORMATION
Title and statement of responsibility	Chief source of information
Edition	Chief source of information, other preliminaries, colophon
Numeric and/or alphabetic, chronological, or other designation	Chief source of information, other preliminaries, colophon
Publication, distribution, etc.	Chief source of information, other preliminaries, colophon
Physical description	The serial itself
Series	Anywhere in the serial
Note	Any source
Standard number and terms of availability	Any source

12.0B2. Sources of information. Nonprinted serials
Follow the instructions given at the beginning of the relevant chapter in Part I (e.g., for sources of information for a serial sound recording, see chapter 6).

12.0C. Punctuation
For the punctuation of the description as a whole, see 1.0C.
For the prescribed punctuation of elements, see the following rules.

12.0D. Levels of detail in the description
See 1.0D.

12.0E. Language and script of the description
See 1.0E.

12.0F. Inaccuracies
See 1.0F.

12.0G. Accents and other diacritical marks
See 1.0G.

12.0H. Items with several chief sources of information
See 1.0H.

12.1. TITLE AND STATEMENT OF RESPONSIBILITY AREA

Contents:
12.1A. Preliminary rule
12.1B. Title proper
12.1C. General material designation
12.1D. Parallel titles
12.1E. Other title information
12.1F. Statements of responsibility

12.1A. Preliminary rule

12.1A1. Punctuation
For instructions on the use of spaces before and after prescribed punctuation, see 1.0C.
Precede the title of a supplement or section (see 1.1B9) by a full stop.
Enclose the general material designation in square brackets.
Precede each parallel title by an equals sign.
Precede each unit of other title information by a colon.
Precede the first statement of responsibility by a diagonal slash.
Precede each subsequent statement of responsibility by a semicolon.

12.1B. Title proper

12.1B1. Record the title proper as instructed in 1.1B.

Gallia

Bulletin

Le Monde

Boston evening transcript

Champaign-Urbana news-gazette

Transactions for the year

Catalogue & index

Q

Willing's press guide

IAVRI bulletin

Bulletin of the Malaysia-Singapore Commercial Association (Inc.)

941.1

Biblioteca di Critica sociale

Thesis theological cassettes

Supplement to the Journal of physics and chemistry of solids

12.1B2. In case of doubt about whether a corporate body's name or an abbreviation of that name is part of the title proper, treat the name as such only if it is consistently so presented in various locations in the serial (cover, caption, masthead, editorial pages, etc.) and/or, when cataloguing retrospectively, in indexes, abstracts, or other lists.

12.1B3. If a serial is a separately published section of, or supplement to, another serial and its title proper as presented in the chief source of information consists of (a) the title common to all sections (or the title of the main serial) and (b) the title of the section or supplement, and if these two parts are grammatically independent of each other, record the common title first, and then the section or supplement title preceded by a full stop. In such a case disregard the order in which the parts of the title proper are presented in the chief source of information.

Acta Universitatis Carolinae. Philologica

Key abstracts. Industrial power and control systems

Journal of the American Leather Chemists' Association. Supplement

Études et documents tchadiens. Série B

12.1B4. If the title of a section or supplement, as dealt with in 12.1B3, is preceded by an enumeration or alphabetic designation, record the common title first, then the designation preceded by a full stop, and then the section or supplement title preceded by a comma.

Journal of polymer science. Part A, General papers

Progress in nuclear energy. Series 2, Reactors

For enumeration reflecting chronological series designation, see 12.3G.

12.1B5. If the title of a section or supplement is presented in the chief source of information without the title that is common to all sections, give the title of the section or supplement as the title proper. In the case of a section, give the title that is common to all sections as the title proper of the series (see 12.6B). In the case of a supplement, give the title of the main serial in a note (see 12.7B7k).

British journal of applied physics . . . . — (Journal of physics ; D)
(Section title only presented in chief source of information. Common title given as series)

12.1B6. If the title proper includes a date or numbering that varies from issue to issue, omit this date or numbering and replace it by the mark of omission, unless it occurs at the beginning of the title proper, in which case do not include the mark of omission.

12.1C *General material designation*

      Report on the . . . Conference on Development Objectives and Strategy

      Supply estimates for the year ending 31st March . . .

      Annual report

  not . . . Annual report

12.1C. *Optional addition.* General material designation

12.1C1. Add immediately following the title proper the appropriate general material designation as instructed in 1.1C.

      Yoga for health [GMD]

      Pathé pictorial [GMD]

      Audio arts [GMD]

12.1D. Parallel titles

12.1D1. Record parallel titles as instructed in 1.1D.

      Bank of Canada review = Revue de la Banque du Canada

      Internationale volkskundliche Bibliographie = International folklore bibliography = Bibliographie internationale des arts et traditions populaires

      Bulletin of the Association of African Universities = Bulletin de l'Association des universités africaines

12.1D2. If, in the case of a serial with a title proper made up of a title common to a number of sections and a section title, the common title has a parallel title and the section title has a parallel title, transcribe the common title and the section title that make up the title proper followed by the parallel common title and the parallel section title (see 12.1B3).

      Trade of Canada. Exports by commodities = Commerce du Canada. Exportations par marchandises

12.1E. Other title information

12.1E1. Record other title information as instructed in 1.1E. Treat the full form of an acronym or initialism that is, or is part of, the title proper as other title information if it is given in the chief source of information.

      Red herring : lesbian newsletter

      REED : review of environmental educational developments

      Q : question : the independent political review : arts, business, science

      12 millions d'immigrés : feuille de lutte des travailleurs immigrés en Europe = 12 milhões de imigrados : folha de luta dos operarios imigrados na Europa

The greenwood tree : newsletter of the Somerset and Dorset Family
History Society

941.1 : newsletter of AAL in Scotland

12.1F. Statements of responsibility

12.1F1. Record statements of responsibility relating to persons or bodies as instructed
in 1.1F.

Quarterly review / Soil Association

Sussex essays in anthropology / Anthropology Society of Sussex

Serie de culturas mesoamericanas / Universidad Nacional Autónoma de
México, Instituto de Investigaciones Históricas

Bieler Jahrbuch = Annales biennoises / Herausgeber,
Bibliotheksverein Biel

Moot / Eunice Wilson

Statistics of energy / Organisation for Economic Co-operation and
Development = Statistiques de l'énergie / Organisation de coopération et
de développement économiques

Application statistics / [prepared by] the Research Division of the
Council of Ontario Universities and the Ontario Universities'
Application Centre

12.1F2. If a statement of responsibility has appeared, in full or in abbreviated form,
as part of the title proper or other title information, do not give a further statement
of responsibility unless such a statement appears separately in the chief source of
information.

British Library news

ARC research review

Ethnic minorities and employment : quarterly journal of the
Employment Section, Community Relations Commission

but

League review / League of St. George

EmPHASis / Public Health Advisory Service

The K-H newsletter service / Stephen King-Hall

12.1F3. Do not record as statements of responsibility statements relating to personal
editors of serials. If a statement relating to an editor is considered necessary by the
cataloguing agency, give it in a note (see 12.7B6).

La Cause du peuple
Note: Founded, edited, and published by Jean-Paul Sartre

R.L.C.'s museum gazette
Note: Compiled and edited by Richard L. Coulton with the assistance of
voluntary aid

12.1F4. In the case of a serial with a title proper made up of a title common to a number of sections and a section or supplement title, give statements of responsibility after the part of the title proper (common title or section title) to which they refer. In case of doubt, give the statements of responsibility after the whole title proper.

> Bulletin / Institute of Classical Studies, University of London. Supplement
>
> Länderkurzberichte. Thailand / Statistisches Bundesamt

12.2. EDITION AREA

Contents:
- 12.2A. Preliminary rule
- 12.2B. Edition statement
- 12.2C. Statements of responsibility relating to the edition
- 12.2D. Subsequent edition statement
- 12.2E. Statements of responsibility relating to a subsequent edition statement

12.2A. Preliminary rule

12.2A1. Punctuation

For instructions on the use of spaces before and after prescribed punctuation, see 1.0C.

Precede this area by a full stop, space, dash, space.

Precede a subsequent edition statement by a comma.

Precede the first statement of responsibility following an edition or subsequent edition statement by a diagonal slash.

Precede each subsequent statement of responsibility by a semicolon.

12.2B. Edition statement

12.2B1. Record an edition statement as instructed in 1.2B if it belongs to one of the following types:

a) local edition statements

> Cambridgeshire farmers journal. — Northern ed.

b) special interest edition statements

> Éd. pour le médecin

c) special format or physical presentation statements

> Airmail ed.
>
> Braille ed.
>
> Library ed.
>
> Microform ed.

d) language edition statements

> English ed.
>
> Éd. française

e) reprint or reissue statements indicating a reissue or revision of a serial as a whole.

> Reprint ed.
>
> 2nd ed.

12.2B2. Do not treat the following types of statements as edition statements:

a) statements indicating volume numbering, or designation, or chronological coverage (e.g., 1st ed., 1916 ed.); give these in the numeric and/or alphabetic, chronological, or other designation area (see 12.3)

b) statements indicating regular revision (e.g., revised edition issued every 6 months); give these in the note area.

12.2B3. If an edition statement appears in two or more languages or scripts, give the statement that is in the language or script of the title proper, *or*, if this criterion does not apply, the statement appearing first, and *optionally* the parallel statement(s), each preceded by an equals sign.

> Canadian ed. = Éd. canadienne

12.2B4. For serials published in numerous editions, see 12.7B7j.

12.2C. Statements of responsibility relating to the edition

12.2C1. Record a statement of responsibility relating to one or more editions, but not to all editions, of a serial as instructed in 1.2C.

12.2D. Subsequent edition statement

12.2D1. Record a subsequent edition statement as instructed in 1.2D.

> English ed., 2nd ed.

12.2E. Statements of responsibility relating to a subsequent edition statement

12.2E1. Record a statement of responsibility relating to one or more designated subsequent editions, but not to all subsequent editions, of a particular edition as instructed in 1.2E.

12.3. NUMERIC AND/OR ALPHABETIC, CHRONOLOGICAL, OR OTHER DESIGNATION AREA

Contents:

12.3A. Preliminary rule
12.3B. Numeric and/or alphabetic designation
12.3C. Chronological designation
12.3D. No designation on first issue
12.3E. More than one system of designation
12.3F. Completed serials
12.3G. Successive designations

12.3A. Preliminary rule

12.3A1. Punctuation

For instructions on the use of spaces before and after prescribed punctuation, see 1.0C.

Precede this area by a full stop, space, dash, space.

Follow the numeric and/or alphabetic designation and/or the date of the first issue of a serial by a hyphen.

Enclose a date following a numeric and/or alphabetic designation in parentheses.

Precede an alternative numbering, etc., system by an equals sign when more than one system of designation is used.

Precede a new sequence of numbering, etc., by a semicolon.

12.3B. Numeric and/or alphabetic designation

12.3B1. Give the numeric and/or alphabetic designation of the first issue of a serial as given in that issue. Use standard abbreviations (see Appendix B) and numerals in place of words (see Appendix C). In describing a facsimile or other reprint, give the numeric and/or alphabetic designation of the original. Follow the hyphen with four spaces (see also 12.3F).

> Population trends. — 1–
>
> Papers on formal linguistics. — No. 1–
>
> Policy publications review. — Vol. 1, no. 1–
>
> Poetry North-east. — Issue no. 1–
>
> Magic touch : the new weekly encyclopedia of fashion and home crafts. — Pt. 1–
>
> OPCS monitor. Population estimates. — PPL, 75/1–

12.3B2. If the numeric and/or alphabetic designation appears in two or more languages or scripts, give only the designation that is in the language or script of the title proper. If this criterion does not apply, give the designation appearing first.

12.3B3. If a serial has changed its title but has continued the sequence of numbering, etc., used under the previous title, record the numbering, etc., of the first issue under the new title.

> Word processing report. — International ed. — Vol. 1, no. 6–

12.3C. Chronological designation

12.3C1. If the first issue of a serial is identified by a chronological designation, record it in the terms used in the item. Use standard abbreviations (see Appendix B) and numerals in place of words (see Appendix C).

> Annual report on consumer policy in OECD member countries / Organisation for Economic Co-operation and Development. — 1975–
>
> Buck Jones annual. — 1957–

Prince Edward Island tourist exit survey. — 1967–

Commonwealth immigration : a monthly summary of news items from national and local papers relating to immigrants in the United Kingdom. — Jan./Feb. 1964–

International commercial television rate and data book. — 1961-2–

Länderberichte. Ecuador / Statistisches Bundesamt. — 1965–

12.3C2. If the chronological designation includes dates not of the Gregorian or Julian calendar, add the corresponding dates of the Gregorian or Julian calendar in square brackets.

مجلة الاقتصاد والادارة . — العدد 1.
–(‪1975‬ يوليو‪ ‬1395 رجب)

12.3C3. If the chronological designation appears in two or more languages or scripts, give only the designation that is in the language or script of the title proper. If this criterion does not apply, give the designation appearing first.

May 1977–

not May 1977 = Mai 1977

12.3C4. If the first issue of a serial is identified both by numbering, etc., and a chronological designation, give the numbering, etc., before the chronological designation.

SPEL : selected publications in European languages. — No. 1 (Feb. 1973)–

New locations. — No. 1 (Apr./May 1973)–

Renewable energy bulletin. — Vol. 1, no. 1 (Jan./Mar. 1974)–

The Musical mainstream / Division for the Blind and Physically Handicapped, Library of Congress. — Vol. 1, no. 1 (Jan.–Feb. 1977)–

IEEE transactions on acoustics, speech, and signal processing. — Vol. ASSP-22, no. 1 (Feb. 1974)–

12.3D. No designation on first issue

If the first issue of a serial lacks a numeric, alphabetic, chronological, or other designation, record ‪No. 1‬– or its equivalent in the language of the title proper. If, however, subsequent issues adopt a numbering, follow that.

‪No. 1‬–

‪Pt. 1‬–
(Subsequent issues numbered Part 2, Part 3, etc.)

12.3E. More than one system of designation

If a serial has more than one separate system of designation, record the systems in the order in which they are presented in the chief source of information. Precede the alternative numbering by an equals sign.

12.3F *Completed serials*

Vol. 3, no. 7–   = No. 31–

Bd. 6, Nr. 2–   = 3.–   Jahrg. = Nr. 32–

12.3F. Completed serials

In describing a completed serial, give the designation of the first issue followed by the designation of the last issue.

News magazine / Regina Chamber of Commerce. — Vol. 3, no. 6 (Aug./Sept. 1970)–v. 5, no. 3 (Mar. 1972)

12.3G. Successive designations

If a serial starts a new designation system without changing its title proper, give the designation of the first and last issues under the old system, followed by the designation of the first issue under the new system.

Inside Interior / Department of the Interior. — Vol. 1, no. 1 (Nov. 1943)–v. 10, no. 12 (June 1953) ; No. 1 (July 1974)–

Distinguish between a serial with a common title and a section title (see 12.1B3) and a serial with a new designation system indicated by *new series* or similar wording.

If the title proper of a serial changes, make a new description (see 21.2C).

12.4. PUBLICATION, DISTRIBUTION, ETC., AREA

Contents:

12.4A. Preliminary rule
12.4B. General rule
12.4C. Place of publication, distribution, etc.
12.4D. Name of publisher, distributor, etc.
12.4E. Statement of function of publisher, distributor, etc.
12.4F. Date of publication, distribution, etc.
12.4G. Place of manufacture, name of manufacturer, date of manufacture

12.4A. Preliminary rule

12.4A1. Punctuation

For instructions on the use of spaces before and after prescribed punctuation, see 1.0C.

Precede this area by a full stop, space, dash, space.

Precede a second or subsequently named place of publication, distribution, etc., by a semicolon.

Precede the name of a publisher, distributor, etc., by a colon.

Enclose a supplied statement of function of a publisher, distributor, etc., in square brackets.

Precede the date of publication, distribution, etc., by a comma.

Enclose the details of manufacture (place, name, date) in parentheses.

Precede the name of a manufacturer by a colon.

Precede the date of manufacture by a comma.

12.4B. General rule

Follow the instructions in 1.4B for items with multiple or fictitious places and names of publishers, distributors, etc.

12.4C. Place of publication, distribution, etc.

12.4C1. Record the place of publication, distribution, etc., as instructed in 1.4C.

12.4D. Name of publisher, distributor, etc.

12.4D1. Record the name of the publisher, distributor, etc., as instructed in 1.4D.

> London : On Target Publications
>
> Edinburgh : Palingenesis Press
>
> London : ₍s.n.₎
>
> Ottawa : The Association
>
> London : Iron and Steel Board : British Iron and Steel Federation

12.4E. *Optional addition.* **Statement of function of publisher, distributor, etc.**

12.4E1. Add to the name of a publisher, distributor, etc., a statement of function as instructed in 1.4E.

> New York : Wiley ; Oxford : Pergamon ₍distributor₎

12.4F. Date of publication, distribution, etc.

12.4F1. Record the date of publication of the first issue as instructed in 1.4F. Follow the date with a hyphen and four spaces.

> Windsor, Berkshire : Wax & Wane, 1975–

12.4F2. Record the date of publication even if it coincides, wholly or in part, with the date given as the chronological coverage.

> Social history. — 1 (Jan. 1976)–   . — London : Methuen, 1976–

12.4F3. In describing a completed serial, give the dates of publication of the first issue and the last issue, separated by a hyphen.

> Membership list / Canadian Association of Geographers = Liste des membres / Association canadienne des géographes. — 1968–1969. — Montréal : The Association, 1968–1969

12.4G. Place of manufacture, name of manufacturer, date of manufacture

12.4G1. If the name of the publisher is unknown, give the place and name of the manufacturer if they are found in the serial, as instructed in 1.4G.

12.4G2. *Optional addition.* Give the place of manufacture, name of manufacturer, and/or date of manufacture if they differ from the place and name of publisher, etc., and date of publication, etc., and are found in the serial and are considered important by the cataloguing agency.

12.5. PHYSICAL DESCRIPTION AREA

Contents:
12.5A. Preliminary rule
12.5B. Extent of item (including specific material designation)
12.5C. Other physical details
12.5D. Dimensions
12.5E. Accompanying material

12.5A. Preliminary rule

12.5A1. Punctuation

For instructions on the use of spaces before and after prescribed punctuation, see 1.0C.

Precede this area by a full stop, space, dash, space *or* start a new paragraph.
Precede other physical details by a colon.
Precede dimensions by a semicolon.
Precede a statement of accompanying material by a plus sign.
Enclose physical details of accompanying material in parentheses.

12.5B. Extent of item (including specific material designation)

12.5B1. For a serial that is still in progress, give the relevant specific material designation (taken from rule .5B in the chapter dealing with the type of material to which the serial belongs, e.g., 11.5B for microform serials) preceded by three spaces. In the case of printed serials, the specific material designation is *v.*

wall charts
filmstrips
v.
microfiches

12.5B2. For a completed serial, precede the appropriate specific material designation .by the number of parts in arabic numerals.

27 posters

16 microreels

103 v.

12.5C. Other physical details

12.5C1. Give the other physical details appropriate to the item being described as instructed in rule .5C in the chapter dealing with the type of material to which the serial belongs (e.g., 2.5C for printed serials).

v. : ill. (some col.)

filmstrips : sd., col.

posters : b&w

12.5D. Dimensions

260

12.5D1. Give the dimensions of the serial as instructed in rule .5D in the chapter dealing with the type of material to which the serial belongs (e.g., 2.5D for printed serials).

> v. : ill. ; 25 cm.
>
> filmstrips : col. ; 35 mm.
>
> film cassettes : sd., col. ; standard 8 mm.

12.5E. Accompanying material

12.5E1. Record the name, and *optionally* the physical description, of any material that is intended to be issued regularly and is intended to be used in conjunction with the serial, as instructed in 1.5E.

> v. : ill. ; 21 cm. + slides
>
> filmstrips : col. ; 35 mm. + booklet

Give a note on the frequency, etc., of accompanying material (see 12.7B11). If accompanying material is issued irregularly or is issued only once, describe it in a note or ignore it.

12.6. SERIES AREA

> Contents:
>
> 12.6A. Preliminary rule
>
> 12.6B. Series statements

12.6A. Preliminary rule

12.6A1. Punctuation

For instructions on the use of spaces before and after prescribed punctuation, see 1.0C.

Precede this area by a full stop, space, dash, space.

Enclose each series statement (see 1.6J) in parentheses.

Precede parallel titles of series or subseries by an equals sign.

Precede other title information relating to series or subseries by a colon.

Precede the first statement of responsibility relating to a series or subseries by a diagonal slash.

Precede subsequent statements of responsibility relating to a series or subseries by a semicolon.

Precede the ISSN of a series or subseries by a comma.

Precede the numbering within a series or subseries by a semicolon.

Precede the title of a subseries by a full stop.

12.6B. Series statements

12.6B1. Record each series statement as instructed in 1.6. Do not give series numberings if each issue is separately numbered within the series.

> (Acta Universitatis Stockholmiensis)
>
> (H.C.)

12.7 *Note area*

(Quellenwerke der Schweiz = Statistiques de la Suisse)

(Public Health Service publication ; no. 1124)

(Bulletin of the Iowa Highway Research Board) (Iowa State University bulletin)

(West Virginia University bulletin. Engineering Experiment Station bulletin, ISSN 0083-8640)

12.7. NOTE AREA

Contents:
>12.7A. Preliminary rule
>12.7B. Notes

12.7A. Preliminary rule

12.7A1. Punctuation

Precede each note by a full stop, space, dash, space *or* start a new paragraph for each note.

Separate introductory wording from the main content of a note by a colon and a space.

12.7A2. In making notes, follow the instructions in 1.7A.

12.7B. Notes

Make notes as set out in the following subrules and in the order given there. In referring to another serial, use the title or heading-title under which that serial is entered in the catalogue. Otherwise, i.e., (1) if the serial is not in the catalogue *or* (2) if main entry is not used, use the title proper and statement of responsibility of the serial.

12.7B1. Frequency. Make notes on the frequency of the serial unless it is apparent from the content of the title and statement of responsibility area or is unknown. Also make notes on changes in frequency. The examples given here do not constitute an exhaustive list.

>Annual
>
>Quarterly
>
>Issued every month except Aug.
>
>Issued several times a week
>
>Issued twice a month
>
>Six issues yearly
>
>Irregular
>
>Six issues yearly (1950–1961), monthly (1962–   )
>
>Frequency varies

12.7B2. Languages. Make a note on the language(s) of the serial unless this is apparent from the foregoing description.

Text in French and English

Text in Swedish, English summaries

Text in English and French; French text on inverted pages

12.7B3. Source of title proper. Make notes on the source of the title proper if it is other than the chief source of information.

12.7B4. Variations in title. Make notes on titles borne by the serial other than the title proper. If it is considered desirable, give a romanization of the title proper.

Cover title: Proceedings of the . . . Annual Glass Symposium

Sometimes published as:

Title varies slightly

Added t.p. title: Bulletin / Société canadienne d'histoire orale & sonore

Added t.p. in Uzbek

If individual issues of a serial (other than a monographic series) have special titles, make a note about this. Specify the individual titles if they are considered important.

Each issue has a distinctive title

Each volume separately titled: 1939, Government, the citizens' business; 1940, Explorations in citizenship; 1941, Self-government under war pressure

12.7B5. Parallel titles and other title information. Give notes on parallel titles and other title information not recorded in the title and statement of responsibility area if they are considered to be important. Make notes on variations in parallel titles and other title information.

Titles also in the organization's other official languages

Subtitle varies

12.7B6. Statements of responsibility. Give notes on statements of responsibility that do not appear in the title and statement of responsibility area.

Official journal of: the Concrete Products Association, Oct. 1920– Apr. 1930

Give expansions of the names of persons or bodies that appear only in abbreviated form in the rest of the description if they are considered to be necessary.

Journal of the Professional Institute . . . . —
Note: Full name of the institute: Professional Institute of the Public Service of Canada

Occasional newsletter / Alra . . . . —
Note: Issued by: the Abortion Law Reform Association

Give the name of any editor considered to be an important means of identifying the serial (e.g., if a particular person edited the serial for all or most of its existence; if the person's name is likely to be better known than the title of the serial).

Editor: Wyndham Lewis

Editor: 1939–1945, H.L. Mencken

Founded, edited, and published by Jean-Paul Sartre

12.7B7. Relationships with other serials. Make notes on the relationship between the serial being described and any immediately preceding, immediately succeeding, or simultaneously published serial.

a) *Translation.* If a serial is a translation of a previously published serial (as opposed to a different language edition of a serial, for which see 12.2B1), give the name of the original.

Translation of: Радиохимия

b) *Continuation.* If a serial continues a previously published serial, whether the numbering continues or is different, give the name of the preceding serial.

Continues: Monthly Scottish news bulletin

c) *Continued by.* If a serial is continued by a subsequently published serial, whether the numbering continues or is different, give the name of the succeeding serial, and, *optionally*, the date of the change.

Continued by: Regina

Continued by a section in: Canadian Association of Geographers' newsletter

d) *Merger.* If a serial is the result of the merger of two or more other serials, give the names of the serials that were merged.

Merger of: British abstracts. B1, Chemical engineering, fuels metallurgy, applied electrochemistry, and industrial inorganic chemistry; and, British abstracts. B2, Industrial organic chemistry

If a serial is merged with one or more other serials to form a serial with a new title, give the title of the new serial and the title(s) of the serial(s) with which it has merged.

Merged with: Journal / British Ceramic Society, to become: Transactions and journal of the British Ceramic Society

e) *Split.* If a serial is the result of the split of a previous serial into two or more parts, give the name of the serial that has been split, and *optionally* the name(s) of the other serial(s) resulting from the split.

Continues in part: Proceedings / the Institution of Mechanical Engineers

If a serial splits into two or more parts, give the names of the serials resulting from the split.

Split into: Report on research and development / Department of Energy; and, Report on research and development / Department of Industry

Continued by: Journal of environmental science and health. Part A, Environmental science & engineering; and, Journal of environmental science and health. Part B, Pesticides, food contaminants, and agricultural wastes; and, Journal of environmental science and health. Part C, Environmental health sciences

If a serial has separated from another serial, give the name of the serial of which it was once a part.

Separated from: Farm journal and country gentleman

f) *Absorption.* If serial absorbs another serial, give the name of the serial absorbed, and *optionally* the date of absorption.

Absorbed: The Morning post

Absorbed: The Worker's friend, 1936

Absorbed: Metals technology; and, in part, Mining and metallurgy

If a serial is absorbed by another serial, give the name of the absorbing serial, and *optionally* the date of absorption.

Absorbed by: Quarterly review of marketing

g) *Reproduction.* If a serial is a reproduction (photographic or other) of another serial, give the title (if it is different from the title of the reproduction), the original place of publication and name of publisher, the frequency of the original, and the ISSN of the original (if known and if different).

Reprint. Originally published monthly: London : MacAllister

h) *Edition.* If a serial is a subsidiary edition differing from the main edition in partial content and/or in language, give the name of the principal edition.

English ed. of: Bulletin critique du livre français

If the title of the main serial is not known, give a general note.

Also published in French and German editions

j) *Numerous editions.* If a serial is published in numerous editions, give the note *Numerous editions.*

k) *Supplements.* If a serial is a supplement to another serial, give the name of the main serial.

Supplement to: Philosophical magazine

If a serial has supplement(s) that are separately described, give these.

Supplement: Journal of the Royal Numismatic Society

Make brief notes on irregular, informal, numerous, or unimportant supplements that are not separately described.

Supplements accompany some numbers

Numerous supplements

12.7B8. Numbering and chronological designation. Make notes on complex or irregular numbering, etc., not already specified in the numeric and/or alphabetic, chronological, or other designation area. Give notes on peculiarities in the numbering, etc.

> Issues for Aug. 1973–Dec. 1974 called also v. 1, no. 7–v. 2, no. 12
>
> Vol. numbering irregular: Vols. 15–18 omitted, v. 20–21 repeated
>
> Introductory no., called v. 1, no. 0, issued Nov. 30, 1935
>
> Numbering begins each year with v. 1
>
> Numbering irregular

If the period covered by a volume, issue, etc., of an annual or less frequent serial is other than a calendar year, give the period covered.

> Report year ends June 30
>
> Report year irregular
>
> Each issue covers: Apr. 1–Mar. 31
>
> Each issue covers: Every two years since 1961–1962

If a serial suspends publication with the intention of resuming at a later date, give this fact. If publication is resumed, give the dates or designation of the period of suspension.

> Suspended with v. 11
>
> Suspended 1939–1945

12.7B9. Publication, distribution, etc. Give variations, peculiarities, irregularities, etc., in the publication details of the serial. If these have been numerous, give them in general terms.

> No. 4 published in 1939, no. 5 in 1946
>
> Published: Rotterdam : Nijgh & Van Ditman, 1916–1940
>
> Imprint varies

12.7B10. Physical description. Give variations in the physical description of issues of a serial.

> Vols. 3–6: 30 cm.
>
> Some issues illustrated

12.7B11. Accompanying material. Make notes on accompanying materials that are not a regular feature of the serial (see also 12.5E). Give the frequency of accompanying materials that are a regular feature of the serial.

> Vol. 7, no. 6 contains wall chart (col. ; 26 × 40 cm.)
>
> Slides with every 7th issue

12.7B12. Series. Give details of a series in which the original of a reproduction was issued. Give details of the numbering within a series when the numbering varies from issue to issue.

Original issued in series:

Each issue numbered 10, 20, 30, etc., in series

Each issue individually numbered in series

12.7B14. Audience. Make a brief note of the intended audience for, or intellectual level of, a serial if this information is stated in the serial.

12.7B16. Other formats available. Make notes on other formats in which a serial is available.

12.7B17. Indexes. Make notes on the presence of cumulative indexes. When possible, give the kind of index, the volumes, etc., of the serial indexed, the dates of the serial indexed, and the location of the index in the set or the numbering of the index if it is issued separately. Make a note also on separately published indexes.

Indexes: Vols. 1 (1927)–25 (1951) *in* v. 26, no. 1

Indexes: Vols. 10–17 *issued as* v. 18, no. 3

Index published separately every Dec.

Indexes: Subject index, v. 1–11 *in* v. 13
Author-title index, v. 1–11 *in* v. 14

Every third volume is an index to all preceding volumes

Indexes covering every 5 v. (beginning with v. 71 and excluding financial volumes) issued with title: Consolidated index-digest of reports of the Interstate Commerce Commission involving motor carrier operating rights

12.7B18. Contents. Give details of inserts, other serials included in the serial, and important special items with specific titles, unless they are catalogued separately. Do not give contents notes for monographic series.

Includes: Bibliography of Northwest materials

"Liaison" as pullout insert in each issue

Issues for 1922–1931 include: The woman voter : official organ of the League of Women Voters

12.7B19. Numbers. Give notes on important numbers borne by the item other than ISSNs (see 12.8B).

12.7B20. Copy being described and library's holdings. Make notes on any peculiarities or imperfections of the copy being described that are considered to be important. If the library does not hold a complete set of a multipart item, give details of the library's holdings. Make a temporary note if the library hopes to complete the set.

12.7B21. "With" notes. If the description is of a separately titled part of another serial, or of a serial issued with another, make a note beginning *With:* listing the other serials.

12.7B22 *Item described*

    With: Journal of environmental science and health. Part B, Pesticides, food contaminants, and agricultural wastes; and, Journal of environmental science and health. Part C, Environmental health sciences

12.7B22. Item described. If the description is not based on the first issue, give the item(s) described.

    Description based on: Vol. 3, no. 3 (May/June 1975)

12.8. STANDARD NUMBER AND TERMS OF AVAILABILITY AREA

Contents:
    12.8A. Preliminary rule
    12.8B. International Standard Serial Number (ISSN)
    12.8C. Key-title
    12.8D. Terms of availability
    12.8E. Qualification

12.8A. Preliminary rule

12.8A1. Punctuation
    For instructions on the use of spaces before and after prescribed punctuation, see 1.0C.
    Precede this area by a full stop, space, dash, space *or* start a new paragraph.
    Precede each repetition of this area by a full stop, space, dash, space.
    Precede a key-title by an equals sign.
    Precede terms of availability by a colon.
    Enclose a qualification to the standard number or terms of availability in parentheses.

12.8B. International Standard Serial Number (ISSN)

12.8B1. Record the ISSN as instructed in 1.8B.

    ISSN 0075-2363

    ISSN 0027-7495 (corrected)

12.8B2. Give any other number in a note (see 12.7B19).

12.8C. Key-title

12.8C1. Give the key-title of the serial assigned according to the rules of the International Serials Data System (ISDS) if it is found on the serial or is otherwise readily available. Give the key-title even if it is identical with the title proper.

    ISSN 0479-7469 = Volunteer (Washington)

    ISSN 0308-230X = British Library Bibliographic Services Division newsletter

    ISSN 0319-3012 = Image. Niagara edition

12.8D. *Optional addition.* **Terms of availability**

12.8D1. Give the terms on which the serial is available as instructed in 1.8D.

> £0.50 per issue
>
> $6.45 per year

12.8E. Qualification

12.8E1. *Optional addition.* Add qualifications to the terms of availability as instructed in 1.8E.

> $30.00 per year ($25.00 to association members)
>
> £3.00 to individuals (£8.40 to libraries)

12.9. SUPPLEMENTS

Describe supplements as instructed in 1.9.

12.10. SECTIONS OF SERIALS

Do not use the "multilevel" structure, described in chapter 13, for the description of sections of a serial. Record these as separate serials (see 12.1B3–12.1B5).

ANALYSIS

Contents

13.1. SCOPE

Analysis is the process of preparing a bibliographic record that describes a part or parts of a larger item. The rules in this chapter offer various ways of achieving analysis. Some of these methods of analysis are related to provisions found in other chapters, but all the methods are collected here with general guidelines to assist in the selection of one of the means of analysis. Cataloguing agencies have their own policies affecting analysis; in particular, a policy predetermining the creation of separate bibliographic records may override any other consideration.

13.2. ANALYTICS OF MONOGRAPHIC SERIES AND MULTIPART MONOGRAPHS

If the item is a part of a monographic series or a multipart monograph and has a title not dependent on that of the comprehensive item, prepare an analytical entry in terms of a complete bibliographic description of the part. Give details of the comprehensive item in the series area (see 1.6).

> English history, 1914–1945 / A.J.P. Taylor. — Oxford :
> Clarendon Press, 1965. — xxvii, 709 p., ₁1₁ folded leaf of plates
> : ill., maps ; 23 cm. — (The Oxford history of England ; v. 15). —
> Bibliography: p. 602–639

13.3. NOTE AREA

If a comprehensive entry for a larger work is made, this entry may contain a display of parts in the note area (normally in a contents note). This technique is the simplest means of analysis; the bibliographic description of the part is usually limited to a citation of title or name and title.

> The art of Van Gogh . . . . — Contents: v. 1. Plates — v. 2 Text

> The English Bible : essays / by various writers . . . . — Contents:
> The noblest monument of English prose / by John Livingston Lowes
> — The English Bible / by W. Macneile Dixon — The English Bible
> / by A. Clutton-Brock — On reading the Bible / by Arthur
> Quiller-Couch

13.4. ANALYTICAL ADDED ENTRIES

If a comprehensive entry for a larger work is made that shows the part either in the title and statement of responsibility area or in the note area, an added entry for the part may also be made. The heading for this added entry consists of the part's main entry heading plus uniform title (see 21.30M). This method is appropriate when direct access to the part is wanted without creating an additional bibliographic record for the part.

13.5. "IN" ANALYTICS

If more bibliographic description is needed for the part than can be obtained by displaying it in the note area, the "In" analytic entry may be considered.

13.5A. The descriptive part of an "In" analytic entry consists of a description of the part analyzed followed by a short citation of the whole item in which the part occurs.

The description of the part analyzed consists of:

1) elements of the title and statement of responsibility area that apply to the part
2) elements of the edition area that apply to the part
3) numeric or other designation, if a serial
4) elements of the publication, distribution, etc., area, if the part is a monographic item and if the elements differ from those of the whole item
5) extent and specific material designation of the part (when appropriate, in terms of its physical position within the whole item)
6) other physical details
7) dimensions
8) notes.

The citation of the whole item (the "In" analytic note) begins with the word *In* (italicized, underlined, or otherwise emphasized) and consists of the main entry heading and uniform title (in square brackets) as appropriate (see Part II) of the whole item, together with its title proper, edition statement, numeric or other designation (of a serial), or publication details (of a monographic item).

> Miss Mapp / E.F. Benson. — 310 p. ; 23 cm.
>
> *In* ₍Heading₎. All about Lucia. — New York : Sun Dial Press, 1940

> The moving toyshop : a detective story / by Edmund Crispin. — p. 210–450 ; 30 cm.
>
> *In* The Gollancz detective omnibus. — London : Gollancz, 1951

> The loved one / by Evelyn Waugh. — p. 78–159 ; 17 cm.
>
> *In* Horizon. — Vol. 17, no. 98 (Feb. 1948)

> Index numbers of road traffic and inland goods transport. — Feb. 1960–
>
> *In* Monthly digest of statistics. — No. 170 (Feb. 1960)–

> A view of Hampstead from the footway next the Great Road, Pond Street ₍GMD₎ = Vue de Hampstead de la chaussée près du Grand Chemin, rue du Bassin. — ₍Reprint₎. — 1 art reproduction : b&w ; 30 × 35 cm. — Reprint of engraving originally published: London : Robert Sayer, 1745
>
> *In* Twelve views of Camden, 1733–1875. — London : London Borough of Camden, Libraries and Arts Dept., 1971

> Bob Wills and his Texas Playboys ₍GMD₎. — side 4 of 2 sound discs (ca. 17 min.) : 33⅓ rpm, stereo. ; 12 in.
>
> *In* Texas country. — Los Angeles : United Artists, c1976

> Nonbook materials (NBM) ₍GMD₎ / Ronald Hagler. — on side B of tape 2 of 3 sound cassettes : 1⅞ ips, mono.
>
> *In* ₍Heading₎. Institute on International Standards as Related to Universal Bibliographic Control. — ₍Los Angeles₎ : Development Digest, c1976

13.5B. Parts of "In" analytics

If an "In" analytic entry is made for a part of an item that is itself catalogued by means of an "In" analytic entry, the "In" analytic note contains information about the whole item and about the part containing the part being analyzed. Give information about the smaller item first, and then information about the comprehensive item in the form of a series statement.

The Tâo teh king, or, The Tâo and its characteristics. — p. ₍45₎–124 ; 23 cm.

In The Sacred books of China. — Oxford : Clarendon Press, 1891. — pt. 1. — (The Sacred books of the East ; v. 39)

13.6. MULTILEVEL DESCRIPTION

Multilevel description is normally used by national bibliographies and those cataloguing agencies that prepare entries needing complete identification of both part and comprehensive whole in a single record that shows as its primary element the description of the whole. It may sometimes be used as an alternative to "In" analytic entries.

Divide the descriptive information into two or more levels. Record at the first level only information relating to the multipart item as a whole. Record at the second level information relating to a group of parts or to the individual part being described. If information at the second level relates to a group of parts, record information relating to the individual part at a third level. Make the levels distinct by layout or typography.

The Sacred books of the East / translated by various oriental scholars and edited by F. Max Müller. — Oxford : Clarendon Press, 1879–1910. — 50 v. ; 23 cm.

Vol. 39–40: The Sacred books of China : the texts of Tâoism / translated by James Legge

Pt. 1: The Tâo teh king. The writings of Kwang-tsze, Books I–XVII. — 1891. — xxii, 396 p.

American folklore ₍GMD₎ / co-ordinated for the Voice of America by Tristram Coffin. — Washington : United States Information Agency ₍production company₎. —   sound tape reels : 7½ ips, mono. ; 7 in. — (Forum series)

8: The American traditional ballad ₍GMD₎ / G.M. Laws. — 1967. — 1 sound tape reel (35 min.). — Includes illustrative excerpts

Remembrance of things past / Marcel Proust ; translated by C.K. Scott Moncrieff. — London : Chatto & Windus. — Translation of: A la recherche du temps perdu

Vol. 1–   : Swann's way / illustrated by Philippe Jullian.— Translation of: Du côté de chez Swann. — This translation originally published in 1922

Pt. 1: 1957 (1973 printing). — 303 p., 4 leaves of plates : ill. ; 19 cm. — ISBN 0-7011-1048-1 : £2.00

Complete any element left open when all the parts are received.

PART II. HEADINGS, UNIFORM TITLES, AND REFERENCES

INTRODUCTION

20.1. When a standard description for an item has been established according to the rules in Part I, headings and/or uniform titles are normally added to that description to create catalogue entries. The only exception is when an entry is made under title proper, in which case the entry may be made under the first words of the description. In this connection, see also 0.6.

The rules in Part II deal with the choice of main and added entries (chapter 21), with the form of headings and uniform titles (chapters 22–25), and with references (chapter 26). In each chapter, general rules precede special rules. Where no specific rule exists for a specific problem, the more general rules should be applied.

The rules in Part II apply to works and not generally to physical manifestations of those works, though the characteristics of an individual item are taken into account in some instances.

The rules in Part II apply to all library materials, irrespective of the medium in which they are published or of whether they are serial or nonserial in nature.

20.2. The second edition of AACR contains a separate chapter (23) on geographic names. Though normally used as part of corporate headings, these names pose a separate problem. Care must be taken to distinguish between the problem of establishing geographic names in a standard form and the related but separate problem of establishing corporate headings involving such names.

20.3. In chapters 22, 23, and 24 there are rules for additions to names used as headings (see 22.18, 23.4, and 24.4C). Such additions must be made if they are necessary to distinguish between otherwise identical names in a catalogue. In addition to making such necessary additions, cataloguing agencies can exercise the option of adding these elements to all headings in anticipation of future conflicts. In machine systems such optional additions will always be recorded in the machine-readable record, but need not necessarily form part of headings in printed entries derived from those records.

EXAMPLES

20.4. As with the examples in Part I, those in Part II are illustrative and not prescriptive. Moreover, they illustrate only the solutions to the problems dealt with in the rule to which they are appended. This procedure does not imply that other added entries (in chapter 21) or references (in chapters 22–25) may not be necessary in the actual instances cited.

When an example prescribes main (or added) entry under title, it is to be understood as meaning title proper or uniform title as appropriate in the particular case. When a rule or example prescribes a name-title added entry, an additional title added entry under the title concerned may also be made when appropriate.

The presentation of the examples (their layout and typography) is only intended to help in the use of the rules. It is not to be taken as implying a prescribed layout or typography for headings and uniform titles.

In chapters 22–25, x is used to indicate the necessity for a *see* reference and xx the necessity for a *see also* reference.

CHOICE OF ACCESS POINTS

Contents

Contents

280

Contents

Certain religious publications

21.0. INTRODUCTORY RULES

21.0A. Main and added entries

The rules in this chapter are rules for determining the choice of access points (headings) under which a bibliographic description (see Part I) is entered in a catalogue. The rules give instructions on the choice of one of these access points as the main entry heading, the others being added entry headings.

In general, each rule gives instructions on only those access points that are explicitly covered by the rule. Certain general points (e.g., series entries and title added entries) are dealt with in the rules on added entries (see 21.29–21.30).

21.0B. Sources for determining access points

Determine the access points for the item being catalogued from the chief source of information (see 1.0A) for that item or any part of the item that is being used as its substitute. Take other statements prominently stated in the item into account (see 0.8). Use information appearing only in the content of an item (e.g., the text of a book; the sound content of a sound recording) or appearing outside the item only when the statements appearing in the chief source of information are ambiguous or insufficient.

21.0C. Form of examples

The examples, in general, follow ISBD conventions (including ISBD punctuation). However, in some cases, a transcription of the data is given without those conventions and punctuation. In particular, some of the names of persons or corporate bodies and other data occurring before the title proper are given first followed by a full stop.

The access points to be made are indicated without showing their forms. Determine the forms of these access points as instructed in chapters 22–25. When an example is followed by *Main (or Added) entry under title,* it means that the entry should be made under the title proper or uniform title (see chapter 25), as appropriate.

Title added entries (see 21.30J) are indicated only when the rule involves consideration of the title as a possible main entry heading.

21.0D. *Optional addition.* **Designations of function**

In the cases noted below, add an abbreviated designation of function to an added entry heading for a person.

FUNCTION PERFORMED	DESIGNATION
compiler	*comp.*
editor	*ed.*
illustrator	*ill.*
translator	*tr.*

Other designations to be added to headings are indicated in particular rules.

21.1. BASIC RULE

21.1A. Works of personal authorship

21.1A1. Definition. A personal author is the person chiefly responsible for the creation of the intellectual or artistic content of a work. For example, writers of books and composers of music are the authors of the works they create; compilers of bibliographies are the authors of those bibliographies; cartographers are the authors of their maps; and artists and photographers are the authors of the works they create. In addition, in certain cases performers are the authors of sound recordings, films, and videorecordings.

21.1A2. General rule. Enter a work by one or more persons under the heading for the personal author (see 21.4A), the principal personal author (see 21.6), or the probable personal author (see 21.5B). In some cases of shared personal authorship (see 21.6) and mixed personal authorship (see 21.8–21.27), enter under the heading for the person named first. Make added entries as instructed in 21.29–21.30.

21.1B. Entry under corporate body

21.1B1. Definition. A corporate body is an organization or a group of persons that is identified by a particular name and that acts, or may act, as an entity. Consider a corporate body to have a name if the words referring to it are a specific appellation rather than a general description. If, in a script and language using capital letters for proper names, the initial letters of the words referring to a corporate body are consistently capitalized, and/or if, in a language using articles, the words are always associated with a definite article, consider the body to have a name. Typical examples of corporate bodies are associations, institutions, business firms, nonprofit enterprises, governments, government agencies, projects and programmes, religious bodies, local churches, and conferences.[1]

Note that some corporate bodies are subordinate to other bodies (e.g., the Peabody Museum of Natural History is subordinate to Yale University).

---

1. Conferences are meetings of individuals or representatives of various bodies for the purpose of discussing and acting on topics of common interest, or meetings of representatives of a corporate body that constitute its legislative or governing body.

Consider ad hoc events (such as athletic contests, exhibitions, expeditions, fairs, and festivals) and vessels (e.g., ships and spacecraft) to be corporate bodies.

21.1B2. General rule. Enter a work emanating[2] from one or more corporate bodies under the heading for the appropriate corporate body if it falls into one or more of the following categories:

a) those of an administrative nature dealing with the corporate body itself
 or   its internal policies, procedures, and/or operations
 or   its finances
 or   its officers and/or staff
 or   its resources (e.g., catalogues, inventories, membership directories)
b) some legal and governmental works of the following types:[3]
  laws (see 21.31)
  decrees of the chief executive that have the force of law (see 21.31)
  administrative regulations (see 21.32)
  treaties, etc. (see 21.35)
  court decisions (see 21.36)
  legislative hearings
c) those that record the collective thought of the body (e.g., reports of commissions, committees, etc.; official statements of position on external policies)
d) those that report the collective activity of a conference (proceedings, collected papers, etc.), of an expedition (results of exploration, investigation, etc), or of an event (an exhibition, fair, festival, etc.) falling within the definition of a corporate body (see 21.1B1), provided that the conference, expedition, or event is prominently named in the item being catalogued
e) sound recordings, films, and videorecordings resulting from the collective activity of a performing group as a whole where the responsibility of the group goes beyond that of mere performance, execution, etc. (For corporate bodies that function solely as performers on sound recordings, see 21.23.)

In some cases of shared responsibility (see 21.6) and mixed responsibility (see 21.8–21.27), enter such a work under the heading for the first named corporate body. Make added entries as instructed in 21.29–21.30.

In case of doubt about whether a work falls into one or more of these categories, treat it as if it did not.

21.1B3. When determining the main entry heading for works that emanate from one or more corporate bodies but that fall outside the categories given in 21.1B2, treat them as if no corporate body were involved. Make added entries under the headings for prominently named corporate bodies as instructed in 21.30E.

21.1B4. If a work falls into one or more of the categories given in 21.1B2 and if a subordinate unit of a corporate body is responsible for it, apply the following provisions:

---

2. Consider a work to have emanated from a corporate body if it is issued by that body *or* has been caused to be issued by that body *or* if it originated with that body.

3. Some legal and governmental works are entered under bodies other than the body from which they emanate (see rules 21.34–21.36).

a) if the responsibility of the named subordinate unit is stated prominently, enter the work under the heading for the subordinate unit

b) if the responsibility of the named subordinate unit is not stated prominently, or if the parent body is named in the chief source of information and the subordinate unit is not, or if the subordinate unit has no name, enter the work under the heading for the parent body.

21.1C. Entry under title

Enter a work under its title when:

1) the personal authorship is unknown (see 21.5), diffuse (see 21.6C2), or cannot be determined, and the work does not emanate from a corporate body

or 2) it is a collection or a work produced under editorial direction (see 21.7)

or 3) it emanates from a corporate body but does not fall into one or more of the categories given in 21.1B2 and is not of personal authorship

or 4) it is accepted as sacred scripture by a religious group (see 21.37)

Make added entries as instructed in 21.29–21.30.

For the use of uniform titles, see chapter 25.

21.2. CHANGES IN TITLES PROPER

21.2A. Definition

Consider a title proper to have changed if:

1) any change occurs in the first five words (other than an initial article in the nominative case)

or 2) any important words (nouns, proper names or initials standing for proper names, adjectives, etc.) are added, deleted, or changed (including changes in spelling)

or 3) there is a change in the order of words.

All other changes, including changes in punctuation and capitalization, do not constitute a change in the title proper. Record such minor changes in the note area (see 1.7B4).

21.2B. Monographs

21.2B1. Monographs in one physical part. If the title proper of a monograph in one physical part changes between one edition and another, make a separate main entry for each edition. Follow the instructions in 25.2 in deciding whether to use uniform titles to assemble all the editions.

21.2B2. Monographs in more than one physical part. If the title proper of a monograph in more than one physical part changes between parts, give the title proper of the first part as the title of the whole monograph. If, however, another title proper appearing on later parts predominates, change the title proper of the whole monograph to the later title proper. If the title proper of a multipart monograph changes between editions, follow the instructions in 21.2B1.

21.2C. Serials

If the title proper of a serial changes, make a separate main entry for each title.

21.3. CHANGES OF PERSONS OR BODIES RESPONSIBLE FOR A WORK

21.3A. Monographs

21.3A1. If a monograph is modified by a person or corporate body other than the person or body under which the original edition was entered, enter it as instructed in 21.9–21.23.

21.3A2. If there is a change in responsibility between the parts of a multipart monograph, enter the monograph under the heading appropriate to the first part. If, however, a different person or corporate body responsible for later parts predominates, change the heading to that appropriate to the later parts and make an added entry under the heading for the earlier person or body. If more than three persons or corporate bodies are responsible for the completed work and no one is predominantly responsible, change to entry under title (see 21.6).

21.3B. Serials

Make a new entry for a serial when one or more of the following conditions arise, even if the title proper remains the same:

1) if the name of a person or corporate body under which a serial is entered changes (see 22.2B or 24.1B)

or 2) if the main entry for a serial is under a personal or corporate heading and the person or corporate body responsible for the serial changes.

21.4. WORKS FOR WHICH A SINGLE PERSON OR CORPORATE BODY IS RESPONSIBLE

21.4A. Works of single personal authorship

Enter a work, a collection of works, or selections from a work or works by one personal author (or any reprint, reissue, etc., of such a work) under the heading for that person whether named in the work or not.

> The sun also rises / by Ernest Hemingway
> *Main entry under the heading for Hemingway*

> The doom fulfilled / Sir Edward Burne-Jones
> *Main entry under the heading for Burne-Jones*

> I.F. Stone's newsletter
> *Main entry under the heading for Stone*

> De bello Germanico . . . / written in 1918 by the author of
>   Undertones of war
> *Main entry under the heading for the author of Undertones of war,*
>   *known to be Edmund Blunden*

> The poetic and dramatic works of Alfred, Lord Tennyson
> *Main entry under the heading for Tennyson*

Virginia Woolf : selections from her essays
Main entry under the heading for Woolf

Symphony no. 4, E minor, for orchestra, op. 98 / by Johannes
    Brahms
Main entry under the heading for Brahms

The ecological crisis / Richard Felger
    (*A filmstrip*)
Main entry under the heading for Felger

Diagnosis and management of abdominal emergencies / LeRoy H.
    Stahlgren
    (*A set of slides*)
Main entry under the heading for Stahlgren

A short title catalogue of French books, 1601–1700, in the Library
    of the British Museum / by V.F. Goldsmith. — Folkestone :
    Dawsons
    (*An unofficial catalogue*)
Main entry under the heading for Goldsmith

Fifty years of modern art, 1916–1966 / Edward B. Henning. —
    ₁Cleveland₁ : Cleveland Museum of Art
    (*Catalogue of a loan exhibition held at the museum*)
Main entry under the heading for Henning

The Tate Gallery / John Rothenstein. — New York : Abrams
    (*A description of selected works from the gallery's collections*)
Main entry under the heading for Rothenstein

The indispensable Earl Hines
    (*A selection of recordings by the jazz pianist*)
Main entry under the heading for Hines

A tale of a tub : written for the universal improvement of mankind . . .
    (*Published anonymously; by Jonathan Swift*)
Main entry under the heading for Swift

Ecstasy and me : my life as a woman / Hedy Lamarr
    (*The "ghosted" autobiography of a movie star; "ghostwriter"*
    not named)
Main entry under the heading for Lamarr

21.4B. Works emanating from a single corporate body
Enter a work, a collection of works, or selections from a work or works emanating from one corporate body (or any reprint, reissue, etc., of such a work) under the heading for the body if the work or collection falls into one or more of the categories given in 21.1B2.

Association of State Library Agencies, Board of Directors meeting,
    1972, ALA Annual Conference
    (*Minutes of the meeting*)
Main entry under the heading for the association's board

M-Step today : interim report of project activities. — Baltimore :
Multi-State Teacher Education Project
Main entry under the heading for the project

The log of the Bon Homme Richard
(*See 21.1B2a*)
Main entry under the heading for the ship

The book of discipline of the United Methodist Church, 1972
Main entry under the heading for the church

The book of common prayer and administration of the sacraments
and other rites and ceremonies of the church, according to the use
of the Church of England . . .
Main entry under the heading for the church

Codex juris canonici / Pii X pontificis maximi iussu digestus
Benedicti papae XV auctoritate . . .
Main entry under the heading for the Catholic Church

American Bar Association, Section of Patent, Trademark, and
Copyright Law. Directory, 1964
Main entry under the heading for the association's section

Constitution of the American Society of Zoologists . . .
(*The work emanates from the society itself*)
Main entry under the heading for the society

A room-to-room guide to the National Gallery / by Michael Levey. —
₁London₁ : Publications Dept., the National Gallery
(*See 21.1B2a*)
Main entry under the heading for the gallery

The art collection of the First National Bank of Chicago. — Chicago :
The Bank
(*Catalogue of the collection; see 21.1B2a*)
Main entry under the heading for the bank

John W. Hayes. Roman and pre-Roman glass in the Royal Ontario
Museum : a catalogue. — Toronto : The Museum
(*See 21.1B2a*)
Main entry under the heading for the museum

Rembrandt in the National Gallery of Art. — Washington, D.C. :
The Gallery
(*Catalogue of an exhibition of the gallery's holdings*)
Main entry under the heading for the gallery

Library, University of California, Berkeley. Author-title catalog. —
Boston : G.K. Hall
Main entry under the heading for the library

Oversight hearings on the Service Contract Act of 1965, as amended :
hearings before the Subcommittee on Labor-Management Relations
of the Committee on Education and Labor, House of

Representatives, Ninety-fourth Congress, second session . . .
Main entry under the heading for the subcommittee

Twelfth interim report of the Committee on Court Practice and
Procedure. Courts organization. — Dublin : Stationery Office
(*Committee established to investigate the operations of the courts
and to recommend changes in practice, procedure, etc.*)
Main entry under the heading for the committee

Firm action for a fair Britain : the Conservative manifesto, 1974. —
ₜWestminster : Conservative Central Officeₗ
Main entry under the heading for the Conservative Party

Hydrogen sulfide health effects and recommended air quality
standard / prepared for the Illinois Institute of Environmental
Quality by the Environmental Health Resource Center
Main entry under the heading for the center

Northern communities consultation on local responsible government :
a consideration of the possible revision of the Northern Affairs Act
to allow thirty-six unincorporated communities a larger role in local
government responsibilities : a report / prepared for the Honourable
Minister of Northern Affairs, Ron McBryde, by the Manitoba
Human Relations Centre
(*Recommendations with supporting data*)
Main entry under the heading for the centre

General safety standard for installations using non-medical X-ray and
sealed gamma-ray sources, energies up to 10 MeV : approved May
24, 1974, American National Standards Institute . . . / American
National Standards Subcommittee N43-5 . . .
Main entry under the heading for the institute's subcommittee

Capital and equality : report of a Labour Party study group
(*Recommends policies to the party; the study group is not named
prominently*)
Main entry under the heading for the party

Institute on International Standards as Related to Universal
Bibliographic Control : [proceedings]
(*A sound cassette*)
Main entry under the heading for the institute

Proceedings of the Symposium on Talc, Washington, D.C., May 8,
1973
Main entry under the heading for the symposium

Ceramics for high-performance applications : proceedings of the
Second Army Materials Technology Conference, held at Hyannis,
Massachusetts, November 13–16, 1973
(*See 21.1B2d*)
Main entry under the heading for the conference

Canones et decreta sacrosancti oecvmenici et generalis Concilii
   Tridentini
Main entry under the heading for the council

High tide and green grass / the Rolling Stones
   (*Songs written and performed by the group*)
Main entry under the heading for the group

The Royal Society International Geophysical Year Antarctic
   Expedition. Halley Bay, Coats Land, Falkland Island Dependencies,
   1955–1959
Main entry under the heading for the expedition

Salzburger Festspiele. Salzburg Festival. Festival de Salzbourg, 1967,
   26.VII–20.VIII. 1967. Offizielles Programm
Main entry under the heading for the festival

Catalogo della 35ª esposizione biennale internazionale d'arte,
   Venezia
Main entry under the heading for the exhibition

21.4C. Works erroneously or fictitiously attributed to a person or corporate body

21.4C1. If responsibility for a work is erroneously or fictitiously attributed to a person, enter under the actual personal author or under title if the actual personal author is not known. Make an added entry under the heading for the person to whom the authorship is attributed, unless he or she is not a real person.

The autobiography of Alice B. Toklas
   (*The life of Gertrude Stein written by herself as though it were an
   autobiography of her secretary, Alice B. Toklas*)
Main entry under the heading for Stein
Added entry under the heading for Toklas

The hums of Pooh / by Winnie the Pooh
   (*Written by A.A. Milne*)
Main entry under the heading for Milne

The adventure of the peerless peer / by John H. Watson, M.D. ;
   edited by Philip José Farmer
   (*Written by Farmer as if by the fictitious Dr. Watson*)
Main entry under the heading for Farmer

21.4C2. If responsibility for a work is erroneously or fictitiously attributed to a corporate body, enter the work under the actual personal author, or under the actual corporate body responsible if the work falls into one of the categories given in 21.1B2. Make an added entry under the heading for the corporate body to which responsibility is attributed, unless it is not a real body.

21.4D. Works by heads of state, other high government officials, popes, and other high ecclesiastical officials

21.4D1. Official communications. Enter under the corporate heading for the official (see 24.20 and 24.27B) works that fall into the following categories:

a) official communications from heads of state, heads of government, and heads of international bodies (e.g., messages to legislatures, proclamations, and executive orders other than those covered by 21.31)

b) official communications from popes, patriarchs, bishops, etc. (e.g., orders; decrees; pastoral letters; official messages to councils, synods, etc.; bulls; encyclicals; and constitutions)

Make an added entry under the personal heading for the person.

> A proclamation of Queen Anne for settling and ascertaining the
>   current rates for foreign coins in America
> *Main entry under the corporate heading for Queen Anne as sovereign*
> *Added entry under the personal heading for Queen Anne*

> New York City at war : emergency services : report / by F.H. La
>   Guardia, mayor
> *Main entry under the corporate heading for La Guardia as mayor*
> *Added entry under the personal heading for La Guardia*

> Proclamations and executive orders by the President, under, and by
>   virtue of, the Food Control Act of August 10, 1917 : November
>   25, 1918
> (*Communications of President Wilson*)
> *Main entry under the corporate heading for Wilson as President*
> *Added entry under the personal heading for Wilson*

> Fulgens Corona : on the Marian Year and the dogma of the
>   Immaculate Conception : encyclical letter of His Holiness,
>   Pope Pius XII
> *Main entry under the corporate heading for Pius XII as Pope*
> *Added entry under the personal heading for Pius XII*

> Carta pastoral sobre cursilhos de Cristandade / Antonio de Castro
>   Mayer, bispo de Campos
> *Main entry under the corporate heading for Mayer as Bishop*
> *Added entry under the personal heading for Mayer*

> Our vocation as children of Saint Francis : being the encyclical letter
>   Divina Providentia of the Most Rev. Fr. General Pacific M.
>   Perantoni, O.F.M.
> *Main entry under the corporate heading for Perantoni as Minister*
>   *General of the order*
> *Added entry under the personal heading for Perantoni*

Enter a communication that merely accompanies and transmits a document under the heading for the document that it accompanies. Make an added entry under the corporate heading for the transmitting official.

> 66th Congress, 2d session. Senate. Document no. 159. Explosives
>   Regulation Act : message from the President of the United States,

transmitting to the Vice President a letter from the Secretary of
the Interior, recommending an amendment to the Explosives
Regulation Act
(*Message of President Wilson*)
Main entry under the heading for the Interior Department
Added entry under the corporate heading for Wilson as President

Enter a collection of official communications of more than one holder of one of
the offices listed above under the heading for the office. Make an added entry under
the heading for an openly named compiler.

Economic report of the President, transmitted to the Congress
(*An annual*)
Main entry under the corporate heading for the President

Tutte le encicliche dei sommi pontefici / raccolte e annotate da
Eucardio Momigliano
Main entry under the heading for the office of Pope
Added entry under the heading for Momigliano

21.4D2. Other works. Enter all other works of such a person under the personal
heading. Make an explanatory reference from the corporate heading to the personal
heading (see 26.3C1).

Address of President Roosevelt to the Deep Waterway Convention
at Memphis, Tennessee, October 4, 1907
Main entry under the personal heading for Roosevelt

The second inaugural address of Abraham Lincoln
Main entry under the personal heading for Lincoln

Non-citizen Americans in the war emergency / by Fiorello H. La
Guardia, mayor
(*A radio address*)
Main entry under the personal heading for La Guardia

Pope Pius XII. Science and the existence of God ₍(November 22,
1951) ; and, Science and philosophy (September 14, 1955) : two
addresses₎
Main entry under the personal heading for Pius XII

21.4D3. Collections of official communications and other works. Enter a collection
of official communications and other works by one person under the personal heading. Make an added entry under the corporate heading.

The King to his people : being the speeches and messages of His
Majesty King George the Fifth delivered between July 1911 and
May 1935
Main entry under the personal heading for George V
Added entry under the corporate heading for George V as sovereign

Discorsi, messaggi, colloqui del Santo Padre Giovanni XXIII : 28
ottobre 1958–3 giugno 1963
Main entry under the personal heading for John XXIII
Added entry under the corporate heading for John XXIII as Pope

Enter a collection of official communications and other works by more than one holder of an office as a collection (see 21.7). Make an added entry under the heading for the office held.

> Papal thought on the state : excerpts from encyclicals and other
>> writings of recent popes / edited by Gerard F. Yates
>> (*Includes texts of public addresses*)
> *Main entry under title*
> *Added entry under the heading for the office of Pope*

> A compilation of the messages and papers of the Presidents . . . /
>> by James D. Richardson
> *Main entry under title*
> *Added entry under the corporate heading for the President*

21.5. WORKS OF UNKNOWN OR UNCERTAIN AUTHORSHIP OR BY UNNAMED GROUPS

21.5A. If a work is of unknown or uncertain personal authorship or if it emanates from a body that lacks a name, enter it under title.

> The Secret expedition : a farce (in two acts) as it has been represented
>> upon the political theatre of Europe
>> (*Author unknown*)
> *Main entry under title*

> A Memorial to Congress against an increase of duties on importations /
>> by citizens of Boston and vicinity
> *Main entry under title*

> Orthogonal expansions and their continuous analogues : proceedings
>> of a conference held at Southern Illinois University, Edwardsville,
>> April 27–29, 1967 / edited by Deborah Tepper Haimo
> *Main entry under title*

If such a work has been attributed to one or more persons or corporate bodies, either in editions of the work or in reference sources, make added entries under the headings for these persons or corporate bodies.

> The Law scrutiny, or, Attornies' guide
>> (*Variously attributed to Andrew Carmichael and William Norcott*)
> *Main entry under title*
> *Added entries under the headings for Carmichael and Norcott*

> La Capucinière, ou, Le bijou enlevé à la course : poème
>> (*Possibly by Pierre-François Tissot; erroneously attributed to*
>> *Pierre-Jean-Baptiste Nougaret*)
> *Main entry under title*
> *Added entries under the headings for Tissot and Nougaret*

21.5B. If reference sources indicate that a person is the probable author of such a work, enter under the heading for that person and make an added entry under title.

If a work falling into one or more of the categories given in 21.1B2 probably emanates from a particular corporate body, enter under the heading for that body.

Make added entries under the headings for other persons or bodies to which the work has been attributed.

> A true character of Mr. Pope
> (*Author uncertain; generally attributed to John Dennis*)
> *Main entry under the heading for Dennis*
> *Added entry under title*

> Portrait of Andrew Jackson
> (*A daguerreotype once attributed to Mathew Brady but generally thought to be by Edward Anthony*)
> *Main entry under the heading for Anthony*
> *Added entries under the heading for Brady and under title*

21.5C. If the name of a personal author is unknown and the only indication of authorship is the appearance in the chief source of information of a characterizing word or phrase or of a phrase naming another work by the person, enter under the word or phrase in the form given in 22.11D. Make an added entry under title.

> Memoir of Bowman Hendry . . . / by a physician
> (*Name of author unknown*)
> *Main entry under the characterizing word*

> The unveiled heart : a simple story / by the author of Early impressions
> (*Name of author unknown*)
> *Main entry under the phrase*

If the only indication of authorship is a predominantly nonalphabetic and nonnumeric device, enter under title. Do not make an added entry under the device.

> Angry thoughts / by *!*!*
> (*Name of author unknown*)
> *Main entry under title*

> L'Inondation : poésie / par M***
> (*Name of author unknown*)
> *Main entry under title*

For the form of headings for persons identified by initials, numerals, phrases, etc., see 22.10–22.11. For corporate bodies identified by initials, see 24.2D.

21.6. WORKS OF SHARED RESPONSIBILITY

21.6A. Scope

Apply this rule to:

1) works produced by the collaboration of two or more persons
2) works for which different persons have prepared separate contributions
3) works consisting of an exchange between two or more persons (e.g., correspondence, debates)

4) works falling into one or more of the categories given in 21.1B2 that emanate from two or more corporate bodies
5) works listed in 1–3 above that also contain contributions emanating from one or more corporate bodies
6) works resulting from a collaboration or exchange between a person and a corporate body.

Apply it also to cases of shared responsibility among adapters, arrangers, commentators, reporters, etc., when rules 21.8–21.27 prescribe main entry under the headings for such persons.

Do not apply this rule to works that result from the work of contributors working under the direction of an editor or to works that are collections of previously existing works (see 21.7).

For special types of collaboration, see the rules on mixed responsibility (21.8–21.27).

21.6B. Principal responsibility indicated

21.6B1. If, in a work of shared responsibility, principal responsibility is attributed (by the wording or the layout of the chief source of information) to one person or corporate body, enter under the heading for that person or body. If the name of another person or corporate body appears first in the chief source of information, make an added entry under the heading for that person or body. Make added entries under the headings for other persons or bodies involved if there are not more than two.

> The humanities and the library . . . / by Lester Asheim and associates
> *Main entry under the heading for Asheim*

> Lady sings the blues / Billie Holiday with William Dufty
> *Main entry under the heading for Holiday*
> *Added entry under the heading for Dufty*

> Animal motivation : experimental studies on the albino rat / by
> C.J. Warden with the collaboration of T.N. Jenkins, L.H. Warner,
> E.L. Hamilton, and H.W. Nissen
> *Main entry under the heading for Warden*

> Faustus : a musical romance . . . / composed by T. Cooke, Charles
> E. Horn, and Henry R. Bishop
> (*Bishop's name is displayed more prominently than the others*)
> *Main entry under the heading for Bishop*
> *Added entries under the headings for Cooke and Horn*

> "Aaron, r. f." / by Henry Aaron as told to Furman Bisher
> *Main entry under the heading for Aaron*
> *Added entry under the heading for Bisher*

21.6B2. If principal responsibility is attributed to two or three persons or bodies, enter under the heading for the first named of these. Make added entries under the headings for the others. If a work is by two principal persons or corporate bodies and one collaborating person or body, make an added entry also for the third person or body.

> Calcium montmorillonite (fuller's earth) in the Lower Greensand
>   of the Baulking area, Berkshire / E.G. Poole and B. Kelk with
>   contributions from J.A. Bain, D.J. Morgan, G.M. McKissock,
>   B.R. Young, and R.J. Merriman
> *Main entry under the heading for Poole*
> *Added entry under the heading for Kelk*

> The United Nations and economic and social co-operation / by
>   Robert E. Asher, Walter M. Kotschnig, William Adams Brown, Jr.,
>   and associates
> *Main entry under the heading for Asher*
> *Added entries under the headings for Kotschnig and Brown*

> The geology of the southern part of the south Staffordshire coalfield
>   . . . / by Talbot H. Whitehead & T. Eastwood with contributions
>   by T. Robertson
> *Main entry under the heading for Whitehead*
> *Added entries under the headings for Eastwood and Robertson*

21.6C. Principal responsibility not indicated

21.6C1. If responsibility is shared between two or three persons or bodies and principal responsibility is not attributed to any of them by wording or layout, enter under the heading for the one named first. Make added entries under the headings for the others.

> Health for effective living : a basic health education text for college
>   students / Edward Johns, Wilfred C. Sutton, Lloyd E. Webster
> *Main entry under the heading for Johns*
> *Added entries under the headings for Sutton and Webster*

> The basement tapes / Bob Dylan & the Band
>   (*Songs written and performed by Dylan and the rock group the
>   Band*)
> *Main entry under the heading for Dylan*
> *Added entry under the heading for the Band*

> Mail order and trade-paper advertising / by Homer J. Buckley,
>   G.D. Crain, Jr., and Maxwell Droke. Mail order advertising /
>   by Homer J. Buckley. Industrial and trade-paper advertising / by
>   G.D. Crain, Jr. Advertising letters / by Maxwell Droke
> *Main entry under the heading for Buckley*
> *Added entries under the headings for Crain and Droke*

> Bibliography in an age of science / Louis N. Ridenour, Ralph R.
>   Shaw, Albert G. Hill
>   (*"Second annual Windsor lectures"; contains a lecture by each
>   person*)

> *Main entry under the heading for Ridenour*
> *Added entries under the headings for Shaw and Hill*

> The correspondence between Benjamin Harrison and James G. Blaine,
>   1882–1893 . . .
> *Main entry under the heading for Harrison*
> *Added entry under the heading for Blaine*

> Debate : subject, resolved that the United States continue the policy
>   of prohibition as defined in the Eighteenth Amendment / Clarence
>   Darrow, negative, versus John Haynes Holmes, affirmative
> *Main entry under the heading for Darrow*
> *Added entry under the heading for Holmes*

If the persons or bodies are not named in the work, enter under the one named
first in a previous edition or, if there is no previous edition, under the one whose
heading comes first in English alphabetic order.

21.6C2. If responsibility is shared between more than three persons or corporate
bodies and principal responsibility is not attributed to any one, two, or three, enter
under title. Make an added entry under the heading for the first person or corporate
body named. If the persons or bodies are not named in the item, make an added
entry under the one named first in a previous edition, or, if there is no previous
edition, under the one whose heading comes first in English alphabetic order.

> Texas country / Willie Nelson, Freddy Fender, Asleep at the Wheel,
>   Bob Wills and his Texas Playboys
>   (*A sound disc set*)
> *Main entry under title*
> *Added entry under the heading for Nelson*

> Antônio de Castro Mayer, Geraldo de Proença Sigaud, Plinio Corrêa
>   de Oliveira, Luiz Mendonça de Freitas. Reforma agrária
> *Main entry under title*
> *Added entry under the heading for Mayer*

> Mélanges d'histoire du moyen âge : offerts à M. Ferdinand Lot par
>   ses amis et ses élèves
> *Main entry under title*

21.6D. Shared pseudonyms
If two or more persons collaborate and use a single pseudonym, use the pseudonym as the heading for the works produced by their collaboration. Refer to the
pseudonym from their names. If headings for one or more of the persons are also
established in the catalogue, refer from the pseudonym to those headings.

> Deadly weapon / Wade Miller
>   (*Wade Miller is the joint pseudonym of Bill Miller and Bob Wade*)
> *Main entry under the pseudonym*
> *References to the pseudonym from the headings for Miller and Wade*

> The detective short story : a bibliography / by Ellery Queen
>   (*Ellery Queen is the joint pseudonym of Frederic Dannay and*

> *Manfred B. Lee; Dannay also wrote a work under his earlier name,*
> *Daniel Nathan*)
> *Main entry under the pseudonym*
> *References to the pseudonym from the headings for Dannay and Lee*
> *Reference to the heading for Dannay from the pseudonym*

> Philip : the story of a boy violinist / by T.W.O.
> (*Initials are the joint pseudonym of Mary C. Hungerford and*
> *Virginia C. Young*)
> *Main entry under the initials*
> *References to the pseudonym from the headings for Hungerford and*
> *Young*

> Rowntree's Elect cocoa / Beggarstaff Brothers
> (*A poster*)
> (Beggarstaff Brothers *is the joint pseudonym of the artists James*
> *Pryde and Sir William Nicholson, who did work under their own*
> *names*)
> *Main entry under the heading for the Beggarstaff Brothers*
> *References to the pseudonym from the headings for Pryde and*
> *Nicholson*
> *References to the headings for Pryde and Nicholson from the*
> *pseudonym*

21.7. COLLECTIONS AND WORKS PRODUCED UNDER EDITORIAL DIRECTION

21.7A. Scope
Apply this rule to:

1) collections of independent works by different persons or bodies
2) collections consisting of extracts from independent works by different persons or bodies
3) works consisting of contributions by different persons or bodies, produced under editorial direction
4) works consisting partly of independent works by different persons or bodies and partly of contributions produced under editorial direction.

Do not apply this rule to works emanating from a corporate body that fall into one or more of the categories given in 21.1B2. For papers or proceedings of named conferences, see 21.1B2.

21.7B. With collective title
Enter a work falling into one of the categories given in 21.7A under its title if it has a collective title. Make added entries under the headings for the compilers/editors if there are not more than three and if they are named prominently. If there are more than three compilers/editors named prominently, make an added entry under the heading for the principal compiler/editor and/or for the one named first.

A Dictionary of music and musicians (A.D. 1450–1889) / by
  eminent writers . . . ; edited by Sir George Grove
Main entry under title
Added entry under the heading for Grove

A Dictionary of American English on historical principles / compiled
  at the University of Chicago under the editorship of Sir William
  A. Craigie and James R. Hulbert
Main entry under title
Added entries under the headings for Craigie and Hulbert

Working class stories of the 1890's / edited, with an introduction,
  by P.J. Keating
Main entry under title
Added entry under the heading for Keating

Larousse de la musique / publié sous la direction de Norbert Dufourcq
  avec la collaboration de Félix Raugel, Armand Machabey
Main entry under title
Added entries under the headings for Dufourcq, Raugel, and Machabey

The Hamish Hamilton book of giants / edited by William Mayne
Main entry under title
Added entry under the heading for Mayne

Economics of the environment : selected readings / edited by Robert
  Dorfman and Nancy S. Dorfman
Main entry under title
Added entries under the headings for R. Dorfman and N. Dorfman

The Oxford dictionary of quotations
  (*". . . under the general editorship of Miss Alice Mary Smyth, who
  worked, for purposes of selection, with a small committee formed
  of members of the Press itself"—p. xiii*)
Main entry under title

Journal of research of the U.S. Geological Survey
  (*Contains research papers written by staff members*)
Main entry under title
Added entry under the heading for the survey

Motor bus laws and regulations : a complete code of all motor bus
  regulatory laws . . . / compiled and edited by John M. Meighan
Main entry under title
Added entry under the heading for Meighan

Constitutions of nations / [compiled by] Amos J. Peaslee
Main entry under title
Added entry under the heading for Peaslee

Treaty series : treaties and international agreements registered or
 filed and recorded with the Secretariat of the United Nations . . .
Main entry under title

Conciliorum oecumenicorum decreta
 (*Decrees of councils from the 1st Council of Nicaea to the 1st
 Vatican Council*)
Main entry under title

Codex canonum ecclesiae universae = The canons of the first four
 general councils of the church, and those of the early local Greek
 synods : in Greek, with Latin and revised English translations . . . /
 by William Lambert
Main entry under title
Added entry under the heading for Lambert

The Ethiopic Didascalia, or, The Ethiopic version of the Apostolical
 constitutions received in the Church of Abyssinia
Main entry under title

If such a work includes two or three contributions or independent works, make
name-title added entries for each of them.

Classic Irish drama / introduced by W.A. Armstrong
 (*Contents: The Countess Cathleen / W.B. Yeats — The playboy
 of the western world / J.M. Synge — Cock-a-doodle dandy /
 Sean O'Casey*)
Main entry under title
*Added entries (name-title) under the headings for Yeats, Synge,
 and O'Casey*

If there are more than three contributions or independent works but only two or
three contributors, make an added entry (or name-title added entry when appropriate) under the heading for each contributor.

Regency poets : Byron, Shelley, Keats / compiled by C.R. Bull
Main entry under title
Added entries under the headings for Byron, Shelley, Keats, and Bull

A Cornish quintette : five original one-act plays from the Cornwall
 Drama Festivals, 1970–2
 (*Contents: A skeleton in the cupboard ; and, The happening at
 Botathen / by Donald R. Rawe — Wheal Judas ; and, The
 Christmas widow / by Burness Bunn — Shadows of men / by
 Gwen Powell Jones*)
Main entry under title
Added entries under the headings for Rawe and Bunn
Added entry (name-title) under the heading for Jones

Traffic laws, city and state
 (*Contains ordinances of the city of Houston and laws of the state
 of Texas*)
Main entry under title

> *Added entries under the headings for Houston and Texas with uniform titles for the ordinances and laws*

If there are more than three contributors and they are named in the chief source of information, make an added entry under the first-named contributor.

> Cricket '74 / contributors include Mike Brearley . . . ₁and seven others₁
> (*Editors, J.A. Bailey and P.J. Roe, named on first page of text*)
> *Main entry under title*
> *Added entry under the heading for Brearley*

21.7C. Without collective title

If a work falling into one of the categories given in 21.7A lacks a collective title, enter it under the heading appropriate to the first work or contribution named in the chief source of information. If it lacks a collective chief source of information, enter it under the heading appropriate to the first work or contribution in the item. Make added entries for editors/compilers and for the other works or contributors as instructed in 21.7B, insofar as it applies to works without a collective title.

> In praise of older women / Stephen Vizinczey. Feramontov / Desmond Cory. The graveyard shift / Harry Patterson
> *Main entry under the heading for Vizinczey*
> *Added entries (name-title) under the headings for Cory and Patterson*

> History of the elementary school contest in England / Francis Adams. Together with The struggle for national education / John Morley ; edited, with an introduction, by Asa Briggs
> *Main entry under the heading for Adams*
> *Added entry (name-title) under the heading for Morley*
> *Added entry under the heading for Briggs*

Works of mixed responsibility

21.8. WORKS OF MIXED RESPONSIBILITY

21.8A. Scope

A work of mixed responsibility is one to which different persons or bodies make intellectual or artistic contributions by performing different kinds of activity (e.g., writing, adapting, illustrating, editing, arranging, translating).

There are two basic categories of mixed responsibility:

a) a previously existing work that has been modified (e.g., a translation, a musical arrangement, an adaptation)

b) a new work to which different persons or bodies have made different kinds of contributions (e.g., a collaborative work by a writer and an artist (see 21.24), a work that reports an interview (see 21.25))

The rules in this section are divided into these two categories.

WORKS THAT ARE MODIFICATIONS OF OTHER WORKS

21.9. GENERAL RULE

Enter a work that is a modification of another under the heading appropriate to the new work if the modification has substantially changed the nature and content of the original or if the medium of expression has been changed. If, however, the modification is an updating, abridgement, revision, rearrangement, etc., enter under the heading appropriate to the original. In some cases the wording of the chief source of information is taken into account; in other cases the nature of the work itself is the basis for the decision on entry.

For specific applications of this general rule, see 21.10–21.23.

Modifications of texts

21.10. ADAPTATIONS OF TEXTS

Enter a paraphrase, rewriting, adaptation for children, or version in a different literary form (e.g., novelization, dramatization) under the heading for the adapter. If the name of the adapter is unknown, enter under title. Make a name-title added entry for the original work. In case of doubt about whether a work is an adaptation, enter under the heading for the original work.

> The science of education : a paraphrase of Dr. Karl Rosenkranz's
>   Paedagogik als System / by Anna C. Brackett
> *Main entry under the heading for Brackett*
> *Added entry (name-title) under the heading for Rosenkranz*

> Sinclair Lewis's Dodsworth / dramatized by Sidney Howard
> *Main entry under the heading for Howard*
> *Added entry (name-title) under the heading for Lewis*

> The green goddess / by Louise Jordan Miln . . . ; based on the play
>   The green goddess by William Archer
> *Main entry under the heading for Miln*
> *Added entry (name-title) under the heading for Archer*

> Sam Weller, or, The Pickwickians : a farcical comedy . . . / arranged
>   from Charles Dickens's work by W.T. Moncrieff
>   (*Dramatization of scenes from The Pickwick papers*)
> *Main entry under the heading for Moncrieff*
> *Added entry (name-title) under the heading for Dickens*

> Adventures of Tom Sawyer / by Mark Twain ; rewritten for young
>   readers by Felix Sutton
> *Main entry under the heading for Sutton*
> *Added entry (name-title) under the heading for Twain*

> Harp and psaltery : a group of paraphrases of favorite Psalms / by
>   Frank P. Fletcher
> *Main entry under the heading for Fletcher*
> *Added entry under the heading for the Psalms*

> The Pilgrim's progress : for the young . . .
> (*Adapter unknown*)
> *Main entry under title*
> *Added entry (name-title) under the heading for the author of the original work, John Bunyan*

> Gottfried von Strassburg. Tristan / translated . . . With the surviving fragments of the "Tristan" of Thomas, newly translated . . .
> (*Both works are versions of the basic Tristan story*)
> *Main entry under the heading for Gottfried von Strassburg*
> *Added entry (name-title) under the heading for Thomas*
> *Added entry under the heading for the Tristan story*

21.11. ILLUSTRATED TEXTS

21.11A. General rule

Enter a work that consists of a text for which an artist has provided illustrations under the heading appropriate to the text. Make an added entry under the heading for the illustrator if appropriate under the provisions of 21.30K2. For instructions on works of collaboration between a writer and an artist, see 21.24.

> The bedside manner, or, No more nightmares / by Robert Benchley ; with drawings by Gluyas Williams
> *Main entry under the heading for Benchley*

> British butterflies / by E.B. Ford ; with . . . colour plates by Paxton Chadwick
> (*Illustrations occupy more than half the item*)
> *Main entry under the heading for Ford*
> *Added entry under the heading for Chadwick*

> Stories from the Arabian nights / retold by Laurence Housman ; with drawings by Edmund Dulac
> (*Dulac is a famous book illustrator*)
> *Main entry under the heading for Housman*
> *Added entry under the heading for Dulac*

21.11B. Illustrations published separately

If the illustrations for a text, or for several texts, by one artist are published separately, enter them under the heading for the artist. Make an added entry for the work(s) illustrated if there are not more than three. If, however, the illustrations are for more than three works by one writer, make an added entry under the heading for the writer.

> The Doré illustrations for Dante's Divine comedy : 136 plates / by Gustave Doré
> *Main entry under the heading for Doré*
> *Added entry (name-title) under the heading for Dante*

21.12. REVISIONS OF TEXTS

21.12A. Enter an edition that has been revised, enlarged, updated, abridged, condensed, etc., under the heading for the original if the person or body responsible for the original is named in a statement of responsibility or in the title, or if the wording of the chief source of information indicates that that person or body is still considered to be responsible for the work. Make an added entry under the heading for the reviser, abridger, etc.

> Anatomy of the human body / by Henry Gray. — 25th ed. / edited
>   by Charles Mayo Goss
> *Main entry under the heading for Gray*
> *Added entry under the heading for Goss*

> Guide to the study and use of reference books / by Alice Bertha
>   Kroeger. — 3rd ed. / revised throughout and much enlarged by
>   Isadore Gilbert Mudge
> *Main entry under the heading for Kroeger*
> *Added entry under the heading for Mudge*

> Salmond on the law of torts. — 12th ed. / by R.F.V. Heuston
> *Main entry under the heading for Salmond*
> *Added entry under the heading for Heuston*

> John Evelyn's diary : a selection from the diary / edited by Philip
>   Francis
> *Main entry under the heading for Evelyn*
> *Added entry under the heading for Francis*

> Leaves from our Tuscan kitchen . . . / Janet Ross and Michael
>   Waterfield
>   (*A revision by Waterfield of Ross's book of the same title*)
> *Main entry under the heading for Ross*
> *Added entry under the heading for Waterfield*

> The people's Marx. — Abridged popular ed. of the three volumes
>   of "Capital" / edited by Julian Borchardt ; translated by Stephen
>   L. Trask
> *Main entry under the heading for Marx*
> *Added entry under the heading for Borchardt*

21.12B. If the wording of the chief source of information indicates that the person or body responsible for the original is no longer considered to be responsible for the work, enter under the reviser, etc. Make a name-title added entry under the heading for the original.

> Guide to reference books. — 7th ed. / by Constance M. Winchell ;
>   based on the Guide to reference books, 6th ed., by Isadore Gilbert
>   Mudge
> *Main entry under the heading for Winchell*
> *Added entry (name-title) under the heading for Mudge*

21.13. TEXTS PUBLISHED WITH COMMENTARY

21.13A. Scope

Apply this rule to works consisting of a text or texts by the same person or body and a commentary, interpretation, or exegesis by a different person or body.

21.13B. Commentary emphasized

If the chief source of information presents the item as a commentary, enter it as such (see 21.1–21.7). Make an added entry under the heading appropriate to the text.

> Commentary on the Rule of St. Augustine / by Robertus Richardinus
> > (*Includes the text of the* Regula)
> *Main entry under the heading for Richardinus*
> *Added entry (name-title) under the heading for St. Augustine*

> Averrois Cordubensis Commentarium magnum in Aristotelis De anima libros
> > (*Includes a Latin text of Aristotle's work*)
> *Main entry under the heading for Averroës*
> *Added entry (name-title) under the heading for Aristotle*

> The Federal Expropriation Act : a commentary / by Eric C.E. Todd
> > (*Includes the text of the act*)
> *Main entry under the heading for Todd*
> *Added entry under the heading for the act*

21.13C. Edition of the work emphasized

If the chief source of information presents the item as an edition of the original work, enter it as such (see 21.1–21.7). Make an added entry under the heading appropriate to the commentary.

> Demosthenes : with an English commentary / by Robert Whiston
> *Main entry under the heading for Demosthenes*
> *Added entry under the heading for Whiston*

> The interpreter's Bible : the Holy Scriptures in the King James and Revised Standard versions with general articles and introduction, exegesis, exposition for each book of the Bible
> *Main entry under the heading for the* Bible

> The Employment Protection Act, 1975 : with annotations / by Brian Bercusson
> *Main entry under the heading for the act*
> *Added entry under the heading for Bercusson*

> Bundesbaugesetz : mit Kommentar / H. Knaup, H. Ingenstau
> *Main entry under the heading for the law*
> *Added entries under the headings for Knaup and Ingenstau*

21.13D. Chief source of information ambiguous

If the information given in the chief source of information is ambiguous, enter the work as a commentary or edition in accordance with the aspect emphasized by (in this order of preference):

1) the prefatory material
2) the typographic presentation of the text and commentary
3) the relative extent of the text and the commentary.

In case of doubt, enter the work as an edition and make an added entry under the heading appropriate to the commentary.

21.14. TRANSLATIONS

21.14A. Enter a translation under the heading appropriate to the original. Make an added entry under the heading for the translator if appropriate under the provisions of 21.30K1.

> The philosopher in the kitchen / Jean-Anthelme Brillat-Savarin ;
>   translated by Anne Drayton
>   (*Only English translation*)
> *Main entry under the heading for Brillat-Savarin*

> The Christmas carol / Charles Dickens ; ₁a Tamil translation by
>   V.A. Venkatachari₁
>   (*Only Tamil translation*)
> *Main entry under the heading for Dickens*

> Fathers and sons / Ivan Turgenev ; translated by Rosemary Edmonds
>   (*One of several English translations*)
> *Main entry under the heading for Turgenev*
> *Added entry under the heading for Edmonds*

> The Mabinogion / translated by Gwyn Jones and Thomas Jones
>   (*An ancient collection*)
> *Main entry under the heading for the* Mabinogion
> *Added entries under the headings for G. Jones and T. Jones*

If the translation involves adaptation or is described as a "free" translation, treat it as an adaptation (see 21.10).

21.14B. Enter a collection of translations of works by different authors as a collection (see 21.7).

21.15. TEXTS PUBLISHED WITH BIOGRAPHICAL/CRITICAL MATERIAL

21.15A. If a work consisting of a work or works by a writer accompanied by (or interwoven with) biographical or critical material by another person is presented in the chief source of information as a biographical/critical work, enter it as such (see 21.1–21.7). Make an added entry under the heading appropriate to the work or works included.

> Life and letters of Mrs. Jason Lee . . . / by Theressa Gay
> *Main entry under the heading for Gay*
> *Added entry under the heading for Lee*

21.15B. If the biographer/critic is represented as editor, compiler, etc., enter under the heading appropriate to the work or works included. Make an added entry under the heading for the biographer/critic.

> Life and letters of Catharine M. Sedgwick / edited by Mary E. Dewey
> *Main entry under the heading for Sedgwick*
> *Added entry under the heading for Dewey*

Art works

21.16. ADAPTATIONS OF ART WORKS[4]

21.16A. Enter an adaptation from one medium of the graphic arts to another under the heading for the person responsible for the adaptation. If the name of the adapter is not known, enter under title. Make a name-title added entry for the original work.

> Children crying forfeits / engr. by C. Turner from an original painting by Joshua Reynolds
> *Main entry under the heading for Turner*
> *Added entry (name-title) under the heading for Reynolds*
>
> A Summer night / by Albert Moore
> (*An anonymous lithograph of Moore's painting*)
> *Main entry under title*
> *Added entry (name-title) under the heading for Moore*

21.16B. Enter a reproduction of an art work (e.g., a photograph, a photomechanical reproduction, or a reproduction of sculpture) under the heading for the original work. Make an added entry under the heading for the person or body responsible for the reproduction.

> Child with a straw hat / Mary Cassatt
> (*A photomechanical reproduction issued by the National Gallery of Art, Washington*)
> *Main entry under the heading for Cassatt*
> *Added entry under the heading for the gallery*
>
> Cat and butterfly : detail from a Japanese handscroll . . . / by Katsushika Hokusai
> (*A photomechanical reproduction*)
> *Main entry under the heading for Hokusai*
>
> Michelangelo's David
> (*A plaster reproduction of Michelangelo's David*)
> *Main entry under the heading for Michelangelo*

21.17. REPRODUCTIONS OF TWO OR MORE ART WORKS

---

4. By *art works* is meant paintings, engravings, photographs, drawings, sculptures, etc., and any other creative work that can be represented pictorially (e.g., ceramic designs, tapestries, fabrics).

21.17A. Without text

Enter a work consisting of reproductions of the works of an artist without accompanying text under the heading for the artist.

> The paintings of Alma-Tadema
> (*Twelve coloured reproductions in a folder*)
> *Main entry under the heading for Alma-Tadema*

21.17B. With text

If a work consists of reproductions of the works of an artist and text about the artist and/or the works reproduced, enter under the heading appropriate to the text if the person who wrote it is represented as the author of the work in the chief source of information. Make an added entry under the heading for the artist. Otherwise, enter under the heading for the artist. In case of doubt, enter under the heading for the artist. If the work is entered under the heading for the artist, make an added entry under the heading for the person who wrote the text if his or her name appears in the chief source of information.

> Mr. Lincoln's camera man, Mathew B. Brady / by Roy Meredith
> *Main entry under the heading for Meredith*
> *Added entry under the heading for Brady*

> Van Gogh / Palma Buccarelli
> *Main entry under the heading for Buccarelli*
> *Added entry under the heading for Van Gogh*

> Van Gogh / par A.-M. Rosset
> *Main entry under the heading of Rosset*
> *Added entry under the heading for Van Gogh*

> Renoir : paintings, drawings, lithographs, and etchings / selected and
>   introduced by Nigel Lambourne
> *Main entry under the heading for Renoir*
> *Added entry under the heading for Lambourne*

> The landscapes of George Frederick Watts
>   (*Author of text, Walter Bayes, named in contents list*)
> *Main entry under the heading for Watts*

> Garden flowers : from plates by Jane Loudon / with an introduction
>   and notes on the plates by Robert Gathorne-Hardy
> *Main entry under the heading for Loudon*
> *Added entry under the heading for Gathorne-Hardy*

Musical works

21.18. GENERAL RULE

21.18A. Scope

Apply this rule to:

1) arrangements, transcriptions, versions, settings, etc., in which music for one medium of performance has been rewritten for another

2) simplified versions
3) arrangements described as "freely transcribed," "based on . . . ," etc., and other arrangements incorporating new material
4) arrangements in which the harmony or musical style of the original has been changed.

21.18B. Arrangements, transcriptions, etc.

Enter an arrangement, transcription, etc., of one or more works of one composer (or of parts of one composer's works) under the heading for the composer. If the original composer is unknown, enter under title. Make an added entry under the heading for the arranger or transcriber. *Optionally,* add *arr.* to the added entry heading.

> Divertimento, op. 12, no. 2 / L. van Beethoven ; transcribed for
>   woodwind by George J. Trinkaus
> *Main entry under the heading for Beethoven*
> *Added entry under the heading for Trinkaus*

> Suite from The art of fugue / J.S. Bach ; arranged for chamber
>   orchestra by Anthony Lewis
> *Main entry under the heading for Bach*
> *Added entry under the heading for Lewis*

> Michael, row the boat ashore : traditional / arranged by James Burt
>   (*An anonymous spiritual*)
> *Main entry under title*
> *Added entry under the heading for Burt*

21.18C. Adaptations

Enter the following types of adaptations of music under the heading for the adapter:

1) a distinct alteration of another work (e.g., a free transcription)
2) a paraphrase of various works or of the general style of another composer
3) a work merely based on other music (e.g., variations on a theme)

If the name of the adapter is not known, enter under title.

If the work is related to one other work or to a part of a work with its own title or designation (e.g., a movement, an aria), make a name-title added entry for that work or part of a work. If the work is otherwise related to the music of another composer, make an added entry under the heading for that composer.

In case of doubt about whether a work is an arrangement, etc., or an adaptation, treat it as an arrangement, etc. (see 21.18B).

> Grande fantaisie de bravoure sur La clochette de Paganini : pour
>   le piano-forte : œuvre 2 / par Fr. Liszt
>   (*Based on a rondo from a concerto*)
> *Main entry under the heading for Liszt*
> *Added entry* (*name-title*) *under the heading for Paganini*

> Du alter Stefansturm : Viennese folk tune : free transcription for
>   string orchestra / by J.M. Coopersmith

Main entry under the heading for Coopersmith
Added entry under title

Nouvelles soirées de Vienne : valses-caprices d'après J. Strauss /
    Ch. Tausig
Main entry under the heading for Tausig
Added entry under the heading for Strauss

Variationen über "Là ci darem la mano" : für das Pianoforte mit
    Begleitung des Orchesters / von Friedrich Chopin
    (*Based on an aria from Mozart's* Don Giovanni)
Main entry under the heading for Chopin
Added entry (name-title) under the heading for Mozart

Rapsodie sur un thème de Paganini : op. 43, pour piano et orchestre /
    S. Rachmaninoff
Main entry under the heading for Rachmaninoff
Added entry under the heading for Paganini

21.19. MUSICAL WORKS THAT INCLUDE WORDS

21.19A. General rule

Enter a musical work that includes words (a song, opera, musical comedy) under
the heading for the composer. For librettos, see 21.28. Make added entries under
the headings for the writers of the words if their work is fully represented in the item
being catalogued (e.g., a full score, a vocal score). If the words are based on another
text, make a name-title added entry under the heading for the original.

Dedication = Widmung : op. 25, no. 1 / Robert Schumann ; original
    poem by Friedrich Rückert
Main entry under the heading for Schumann
Added entry under the heading for Rückert

Rigoletto : opera in three acts / libretto by Francesco Maria Piave ;
    music by Giuseppe Verdi
    (*A vocal score; libretto based on* Le roi s'amuse *by Victor Hugo*)
Main entry under the heading for Verdi
Added entry under the heading for Piave
Added entry (name-title) under the heading for Hugo

South Pacific : a musical play / music by Richard Rodgers ; lyrics
    by Oscar Hammerstein, 2nd ; book by Oscar Hammerstein, 2nd,
    and Joshua Logan
    (*A vocal score; libretto based on* Tales of the South Pacific *by*
    James A. Michener)
Main entry under the heading for Rodgers
Added entries under the headings for Hammerstein and Logan
Added entry (name-title) under the heading for Michener

21.19B. Pasticcios, ballad operas, etc.

21.19B1. If the music of a pasticcio, ballad opera, etc., consists of previously existing ballads, songs, arias, etc., by various composers, enter the work under title. Make an added entry under the heading for the person who adapted or arranged the music and under the heading for the dramatist.

> The Beggar's opera / written by Mr. Gay ; to which is prefix'd the
> musick to each song
> (*The music for this work was adapted by John Christopher Pepusch*)
> *Main entry under title*
> *Added entries under the headings for Gay and Pepusch*

> The Beggar's opera : vocal score / written by John Gay ; the overture
> composed and the songs arranged by John Christopher Pepusch . . .
> *Main entry under title*
> *Added entries under the headings for Gay and Pepusch*

Enter a collection of musical excerpts from such a work under the title of the larger work. Enter a single song under the heading for its own composer or under title if the composer is unknown. Make a title added entry for the larger work.

> Songs in the opera call'd the Beggar's wedding, as it is perform'd
> at the theatres
> *Main entry under the title of the opera*

21.19B2. If the music of a pasticcio, ballad opera, etc., was especially composed for it, enter the work as instructed in 21.6.

> The most favourite songs in the opera of Muzio Scaevola / composed
> by three famous masters . . .
> (*The composers are Amadei, Bononcini, and Handel*)
> *Main entry under the heading for Amadei*
> *Added entries under the headings for Bononcini and Handel*

> Faustus : a musical romance . . . / composed by T. Cooke, Charles
> E. Horn, and Henry R. Bishop
> (*Bishop's name is displayed more prominently than the others*)
> *Main entry under the heading for Bishop*
> *Added entries under the headings for Cooke and Horn*

21.19C. Writer's works set by several composers

Enter a collection of musical settings of songs, etc., by one writer made by two or more composers as a collection (see 21.7). Make an added entry under the heading for the writer.

> Songs from Shakespeare's tragedies : a collection of songs for concert
> or dramatic use / edited from contemporary sources by Frederick
> Sternfeld
> *Main entry under title*
> *Added entry under the heading for Shakespeare*

Et voici mes chansons / Minou Drouet ; mises en musique par Jean
   Françaix, Pierre Duclos, Paul Misraki, Bernard Boesch, Marc
   Lanjean
   (*Drouet is the poet*)
   Main entry under title
   Added entries under the headings for Drouet and Françaix

21.20. MUSICAL SETTINGS FOR BALLETS, ETC.

Enter a musical setting for a ballet, pantomime, etc., under the heading for the
composer. Make added entries under the headings for choreographers and writers of
scenarios, librettos, etc., whose names appear in the chief source of information.

Robot : ballet / choreography by Stanislaw Povitch ; music by
   Walter L. Rosemont
   Main entry under the heading for Rosemont
   Added entry under the heading for Povitch

Coppélia, ou, La fille aux yeux d'émail : ballet en 2 actes et 3 tableaux
   de Ch. Nuitter et Saint-Léon : musique de Léo Delibes
   Main entry under the heading for Delibes
   Added entries under the headings for Nuitter and Saint-Léon

La fête chez Thérèse : ballet-pantomime / scénario de Catulle
   Mendès ; musique de Reynaldo Hahn
   Main entry under the heading for Hahn
   Added entry under the heading for Mendès

21.21. ADDED ACCOMPANIMENTS, ETC.

Enter a musical work to which an instrumental accompaniment or additional parts
have been added under the heading for the original work. Make an added entry under
the heading for the composer of the accompaniment or the additional parts.

Sechs Sonaten für Violine solo / von Joh. Seb. Bach ; herausgegeben
   von J. Hellmesberger ; Klavierbegleitung von Robert Schumann
   Main entry under the heading for Bach
   Added entries under the headings for Hellmesberger and Schumann

O rosa bella . . .
   (*By John Dunstable, with optional contratenors and 3 additional
   voices by John Bedingham*)
   Main entry under the heading for Dunstable
   Added entry under the heading for Bedingham

21.22. LITURGICAL MUSIC

Enter music that is officially prescribed as part of a liturgy as instructed in 21.39.

The Liber usualis : with introduction and rubrics in English / edited
   by the Benedictines of Solesmes
   Main entry under the heading for the Catholic Church

The restored Holy Week liturgy : practical arrangement of the
   prescribed music for the average church choir / by Carlo Rossini
   Main entry under the heading for the Catholic Church

313

21.23. ENTRY OF SOUND RECORDINGS

21.23A. Enter a sound recording of one work (music, text, etc.) under the heading appropriate to that work. Make added entries under the headings for the principal performers[5] (singers, readers, orchestras, etc.) unless there are more than three. If there are more than three principal performers, make an added entry under the one named first.

> How many miles to Babylon? / author, Alison Uttley
> > (*Read by David Davis*)
> *Main entry under the heading for Uttley*
> *Added entry under the heading for Davis*

> The trout quintet : piano quintet in A major, op. 114 . . . / Schubert
> > (*Smetana Quartet, Jan Panenka, piano, František Pošta, double bass*)
> *Main entry under the heading for Schubert*
> *Added entries under the headings for the quartet, Panenka, and Pošta*

> Bury my heart at Wounded Knee / by Dee Brown
> > (*An abridgement of Dee Brown's book, dramatically presented by Henry Madden and Manu Tupon*)
> *Main entry under the heading for Brown*
> *Added entries under the headings for Madden and Tupon*

21.23B. Enter a sound recording of two or more works all by the same person(s) or body (bodies) under the heading appropriate to those works. Make added entries under the headings for the principal performers unless there are more than three. If there are more than three principal performers, make an added entry under the one named first.

> Piano rags / Scott Joplin
> > (*Joshua Rifkin, piano*)
> *Main entry under the heading for Joplin*
> *Added entry under the heading for Rifkin*

> Any day now : songs of Bob Dylan
> > (*Sung by Joan Baez*)
> *Main entry under the heading for Dylan*
> *Added entry under the heading for Baez*

> The best of Lennon and McCartney
> > (*Songs by Lennon and McCartney sung by Tommy James*)
> *Main entry under the heading for Lennon*
> *Added entries under the headings for McCartney and James*

> The railway stories / W. Awdry
> > (*Read by Johnny Morris*)

---

5. Principal performers are those given prominence (by wording or layout) in the chief source of information.

Main entry under the heading for Awdry
Added entry under the heading for Morris

A tribute to Woody Guthrie
    (*Songs and prose by Woody Guthrie, performed at a concert by*
    Arlo Guthrie and others)
Main entry under the heading for W. Guthrie
Added entry under the heading for A. Guthrie

21.23C. Enter a sound recording containing works by different persons under the heading for the person or body represented as principal performer. If there are two or three persons or bodies so represented, enter under the heading for the first named and make added entries under the headings for the others.

Pieces of the sky
    (*Songs by various composers performed by Emmylou Harris*)
Main entry under the heading for Harris

All that jazz
    (*Various pieces by several composers performed by Fats Waller*)
Main entry under the heading for Waller

Great tenor arias
    (*Arias by various composers sung by Carlo Bergonzi with the*
    Orchestra of the Accademia di Santa Cecilia, Rome)
Main entry under the heading for Bergonzi
Added entry under the heading for the orchestra

Dancer with bruised knees / Kate & Anna McGarrigle
    (*Songs by the McGarrigle sisters and others performed by them*)
Main entry under the heading for K. McGarrigle
Added entry under the heading for A. McGarrigle

Bonaparte's retreat
    (*Folk tunes and songs by various hands performed by the band the*
    Chieftains)
Main entry under the heading for the Chieftains

Irish rebel songs
    (*Sung by Mike Barrett and Joe Kiernan*)
Main entry under the heading for Barrett
Added entry under the heading for Kiernan

21.23D. Enter under title a sound recording containing works by different persons or bodies performed by more than three principal performers or having no principal performers. For works lacking a collective title that the cataloguer wishes to treat as a unit (see 6.1G), see 21.7C.

Music of nineteenth century England
    (*Several musical pieces performed by various groups and singers*)
Main entry under title

MIXED RESPONSIBILITY IN NEW WORKS

21.24. COLLABORATION BETWEEN ARTIST AND WRITER

Enter a work that is, or appears to be, a work of collaboration between an artist and a writer under the heading for the one who is named first in the chief source of information unless the other's name is given greater prominence by the wording or the layout. Make an added entry under the heading for the one not given main entry. For instructions on texts with illustrations, see 21.11A.

> A color guide to familiar garden and field birds, eggs, and nests / by Jiří Felix ; illustrated by Květoslav Hísek
> (*A collaborative work*)
> *Main entry under the heading for Felix*
> *Added entry under the heading for Hísek*

> A Carolina rice plantation of the fifties : 30 paintings in water colour / by Alice R. Huger Smith ; narrative by Herbert Ravenel Sass ; with chapters from the unpublished memoirs of D.E. Huger Smith
> *Main entry under the heading for A. Smith*
> *Added entries under the headings for Sass and D. Smith*

> Say, is this the U.S.A. / Erskine Caldwell and Margaret Bourke-White
> (*Text by Caldwell, photographs by Bourke-White*)
> *Main entry under the heading for Caldwell*
> *Added entry under the heading for Bourke-White*

> Goodbye baby & amen : a saraband for the sixties / David Bailey & Peter Evans
> (*Photographs by Bailey, text by Evans*)
> *Main entry under the heading for Bailey*
> *Added entry under the heading for Evans*

> Cartoons / by E.W. Kemble ; limericks by G. Mayo
> *Main entry under the heading for Kemble*
> *Added entry under the heading for Mayo*

> Birds : a guide to the most familiar American birds / by Herbert S. Zim and Ira N. Gabrielson ; illustrated by James Gordon Irving
> (*A collaborative work*)
> *Main entry under the heading for Zim*
> *Added entries under the headings for Gabrielson and Irving*

21.25. REPORTS OF INTERVIEWS OR EXCHANGES

21.25A. If a report is essentially confined to the words of the person(s) interviewed or of the participants in an exchange (other than the reporter), enter under the principal participant, first named participant, or title as instructed in 21.6. Make an added entry under the heading for the reporter if he or she is openly named in the item.

> Discussion at Worksop between the Rev. R.P. Blakeney . . . and the Rev. J.B. Naghten . . . / reported verbatim by Thomas Whitehead

Main entry under the heading for Blakeney
Added entries under the headings for Naghten and Whitehead

My wartime experiences in Singapore / Mamoru Shinozaki ;
  interviewed by Lim Yoon Lin
Main entry under the heading for Shinozaki
Added entry under the heading for Lim Yoon Lin

21.25B. If a report is to a considerable extent in the words of the reporter, enter under the heading for the reporter. Make added entries under the headings for the other persons involved if there are not more than three. If there are more than three, make an added entry under the one named first.

Talks with Ralph Waldo Emerson / by Charles J. Woodbury
Main entry under the heading for Woodbury
Added entry under the heading for Emerson

Table-talk of G.B.S. : conversations on things in general between
  George Bernard Shaw and his biographer / by Archibald Henderson
Main entry under the heading for Henderson
Added entry under the heading for Shaw

Interviews impubliables / Gilbert Ganne
  (Interviews with 23 persons; none named on the title page)
Main entry under the heading for Ganne

21.26. SPIRIT COMMUNICATIONS

Enter a communication presented as having been received from a spirit under the heading for the spirit (see 22.14). Make an added entry under the heading for the medium or other person recording the communication.

Food for the million, or, Thoughts from beyond the borders of the
  material / by Theodore Parker ; through the hand of Sarah A.
  Ramsdell
Main entry under the heading for the spirit of Parker
Added entry under the heading for Ramsdell

21.27. ACADEMIC DISPUTATIONS

Enter a work written for defence in an academic disputation (according to the custom prevailing in universities before the nineteenth century and continued in some cases thereafter) under the heading for the praeses (faculty moderator) unless the authorship of the respondent, defender, etc., can be established.[6] Make an added

---

6. The designation *auctor* on the title page is not to be accepted as proof of authorship without further evidence. For works dealing with this problem, see the following: Eichler, Ferdinand. "Die Autorschaft der akademischen Disputationen" in *Sammlung bibliothekswissenschaftlicher Arbeiten*, Heft 10 (1896), pp. 24–37; Heft 11 (1898), pp. 1–40; Horn, Ewald. "Die Disputationen und Promotionen an den deutschen Universitäten, vornehmlich seit dem 16. Jahrhundert" in *Centralblatt für Bibliothekswesen*, Beiheft XI (1893); Kaufmann, Georg. "Zur Geschichte der akademischen Grade und Disputationen," ibid., XI. Jahrg. (Mai 1894), pp. ₁201₁–225; Wheatley, B.R. "On the Question of Authorship in Academical Dissertations," in Wheatley, H.B. *How to Catalogue a Library* (London : Stock, 1889), pp. 105–121.

entry under the heading for whichever of the praeses, respondent, etc., is not given main entry. *Optionally,* add the designation *praeses, respondent, defendant,* etc., as appropriate, to the headings. Do not make an added entry under the name of a person designated as an opponent.

> Principium Mosellae Ausonii, ad disputandum publice propositum /
>   praeside Conrado Samuele Schurzfleischio ; respondente M.
>   Godefrido Kupfender
> *Main entry under the heading for Schurzfleisch as praeses*
> *Added entry under the heading for Kupfender as respondent*

> Observationes circa vermes intestinales . . . / praeside . . . Ioanne
>   Quistorp ; auctor Carolus Asmund Rudolphi
>   (*Rudolphi's authorship established*)
> *Main entry under the heading for Rudolphi*
> *Added entry under the heading for Quistorp as praeses*

If no one is named as praeses, enter under (in this order of preference) the heading for (1) the proponent; (2) the defendant or respondent.

Related works

21.28. RELATED WORKS

21.28A. Scope
Apply this rule to separately catalogued works (see also 1.9) that have a relationship to another work. These include:

> continuations and sequels
> supplements
> indexes
> concordances
> incidental music to dramatic works
> cadenzas
> scenarios, screenplays, etc.
> choreographies
> librettos and other texts set to music[7]

---

7. *Alternative rule.* Enter a libretto under the heading appropriate to the musical work. Make an added entry under the heading for the librettist. If the libretto is based on another text, make a name-title added entry under the heading for the original.

> Curlew river : a parable for church performance / by William Plomer ;
>   set to music by Benjamin Britten
>   (*A libretto*)
> *Main entry under the heading for Britten*
> *Added entry under the heading for Plomer*

> Der Rosenkavalier : Komödie für Musik in 3 Aufzügen / von Hugo
>   von Hofmannsthal ; Musik von Richard Strauss
> *Main entry under the heading for Strauss*
> *Added entry under the heading for Hofmannsthal*

subseries

special numbers of serials

collections of extracts from serials

Do not apply this rule to a work that has only a subject relationship to another work.

For particular types of relationship (adaptations, revisions, translations, etc.), see 21.8–21.27.

21.28B. General rule. Enter a related work under its own heading (personal author, corporate body, or title) according to the appropriate rule in chapter 21. Make an added entry[8] (name-title or title, as appropriate) for the work to which it is related.

> An index to the Columbia edition of the works of John Milton / by
>   Frank Allen Patterson ; assisted by French Rowe Fogle
> *Main entry under the heading for Patterson*
> *Added entry under the heading for Fogle*
> *Added entry (name-title) under the heading for Milton*

> Teacher's manual / by W.D. Lewis . . . to accompany Topical studies
>   in United States history by Superintendent A.B. Blodgett
> *Main entry under the heading for Lewis*
> *Added entry (name-title) under the heading for Blodgett*

> Supplement to The conquest of Peru and Mexico by the Moguls, in
>   the xiii century . . .
>   (*Signed by John Ranking, author of the work to which the
>   supplement is related*)
> *Main entry under the heading for Ranking*
> *Added entry (name-title) for the related work*

> Supplement to Hain's Repertorium bibliographicum . . . / by
>   W.A. Copinger
> *Main entry under the heading for Copinger*
> *Added entry (name-title) under the heading for Hain*

> Ergänzungshefte zu den Blättern für Volksbibliotheken und Lesehallen
> *Main entry under title*
> *Added entry under the title of the related work*

> Cumulative book index : a world list of books in the English
>   language . . . supplementing The United States catalog
> *Main entry under title*
> *Added entry under the heading for* The United States catalog

---

If, however, a libretto is published without reference to its musical setting, enter it under the heading for the author of the libretto.

> Der Rosenkavalier : Komödie für Musik / von Hugo von Hofmannsthal
>   (*Published as a literary work*)
>   *Main entry under the heading for Hofmannsthal*

Enter a collection of librettos for works by one composer under the heading for the composer.

8. Do not make an added entry for the related work in the case of a sequel by the same author.

Élie Halévy. Histoire du peuple anglais au XIXᵉ siècle. Épilogue
(1895–1914)
Main entry under the heading for Halévy
Added entry (name-title) for the related work not required

A complete concordance to the Iliad of Homer / by Guy Lushington
Prendergast
Main entry under the heading for Prendergast
Added entry (name-title) under the heading for Homer

A complete concordance to the Holy Scriptures of the Old and New
Testament . . . / by Alexander Cruden
Main entry under the heading for Cruden
Added entry under the heading for the Bible

Astronomie topographique : complément au Traité de topographie
générale : cours professé à l'École nationale du génie rural / par
A. Carrier
Main entry under the heading for Carrier
Added entry under the heading for the author's Traité . . .

John Jasper's gatehouse : a sequel to the unfinished novel, "The
mystery of Edwin Drood," by Charles Dickens / by Edwin Harris
Main entry under the heading for Harris
Added entry (name-title) under the heading for Dickens

Over the garden wall : (Mrs. "H." and Mrs. "C." gossip, as broadcast
in "Monday night at seven") : a series of comedy episodes / by
Guy Fane
Main entry under the heading for Fane
Added entry under the heading for the radio programme

United nations : six radio dramatizations presented on "The family
hour"
(*Writer or writers unnamed*)
Main entry under title
Added entry under the heading for the radio programme

Marguerite Duras. Hiroshima mon amour : scénario et dialogues
(*A film scenario*)
Main entry under the heading for Duras
Added entry under the heading for the motion picture

Conrack
(*Filmstrip based on* The water is wide *by Pat Conroy*)
Main entry under title
Added entry (name-title) under the heading for Conroy

Art in photography : with selected examples of European and
American work / edited by Charles Holme
("*Special summer number of* 'The Studio,' *1905*")
Main entry under title
Added entries under the headings for Holme and the Studio

L'Illustration. S.M. la reine Astrid, 1905–1935
    (*"Album hors série. Juin 1936"*)
Main entry under title
Added entry under the heading for L'Illustration

Studien zur Musikwissenschaft : Beihefte der Denkmäler der
    Tonkunst in Österreich
Main entry under title
Added entry under the heading for the Denkmäler . . .

Eli Terry pillar & scroll shelf clocks / by Lockwood Barr
    (*Supplement to the* Bulletin of the National Association of Watch
    and Clock Collectors)
Main entry under the heading for Barr
Added entry under the heading for the association's Bulletin

Youth and the new world : essays from the Atlantic monthly /edited
    by Ralph Boas
Main entry under title
Added entries under the headings for Boas and the Atlantic monthly

The Penguin book of Ximenes crosswords ₍from₎ the Observer
    (*Puzzles by Ximenes originally published in the* Observer)
Main entry under the heading for Ximenes
Added entry under the heading for the Observer

Les CL Pseaumes de David escrites en diverses sortes de lettres /
    par Esther Anglois
    (*A calligraphic work related to Biblical excerpts*)
Main entry under the heading for Anglois
Added entry under the heading for the Psalms

Rosamunde : Drama / von H. v. Chézy ; mit Musik von Franz
    Schubert
    (*A musical score*)
Main entry under the heading for Schubert
Added entry (*name-title*) *under the heading for Chézy*

Cadenzas for the Flute concerto in G major (K. 313) by Mozart /
    Georges Barrère
Main entry under the heading for Barrère
Added entry (*name-title*) *under the heading for Mozart*

Walt Disney's Alice in Wonderland / Camarata Orchestra and Chorus
    (*Songs by Oliver Wallace from the motion picture; performed on
    a disc by the orchestra and chorus*)
Main entry under the heading for Wallace
Added entry under the heading for the motion picture

Curlew river : a parable for church performance / by William
    Plomer ; set to music by Benjamin Britten
    (*A libretto*)
Main entry under the heading for Plomer
Added entry (*name-title*) *under the heading for Britten*

> Der Rosenkavalier : Komödie für Musik in 3 Aufzügen / von Hugo
>   von Hofmannsthal ; Musik von Richard Strauss
>   (*A libretto*)
> *Main entry under the heading for Hofmannsthal*
> *Added entry (name-title) under the heading for Strauss*

Added entries

21.29. GENERAL RULE

21.29A. Added entries provide access to bibliographic descriptions additional to that of the main entry heading.

21.29B. Make an added entry under the heading for a person or a corporate body or under a title if some catalogue users might suppose that the description of an item would be found under that heading or title rather than under the heading or title chosen for the main entry.

21.29C. In addition, make added entries under other headings for persons and corporate bodies as instructed in 21.30.

21.29D. If, in the context of a given catalogue, added entries are required under headings and titles other than those prescribed in rule 21.30, make them.

21.29E. Construct a heading for an added entry according to the instructions in chapters 22–24. For instructions on the construction of name-title added entries, see 21.30G.

21.29F. If the reason for an added entry is not apparent from the body of the description (e.g., if a person or body used as the basis for an added entry is not named in a statement of responsibility or in the publication details), provide a note giving the name of the person or body (see 1.7B6) or the title (see 1.7B4).

21.29G. *Optionally,* use explanatory references in place of added entries in certain cases (see 26.5).

21.30. SPECIFIC RULES

21.30A. Two or more persons or bodies involved
If the following subrules refer to only one person or corporate body and two or three persons or bodies are involved in a particular instance, make added entries under the headings for each. If four or more persons or bodies are involved in a particular instance, make an added entry under the heading for the first named in the source from which the names are taken.

21.30B. Collaborators

If the main entry is under the heading for one of two or three collaborating persons or bodies, make added entries under the headings for the others.

If the main entry is under the heading for a corporate body or under a title, make added entries under the headings for one, two, or three collaborating persons or under the heading for the first named of four or more.

21.30C. Writers

Make an added entry under the heading for a prominently named writer of a work if the main entry is under the heading for another person or a corporate body or under title.

21.30D. Editors and compilers

Make an added entry under the heading for a prominently named editor or compiler of a monographic work. Make an added entry under the heading for an editor of a serial only in the rare instance when a serial is likely to be known by the editor's name.

21.30E. Corporate bodies

Make an added entry under the heading for a prominently named corporate body, unless it functions solely as distributor or manufacturer. Make an added entry under a prominently named publisher if the responsibility for the work extends beyond that of merely publishing it. In case of doubt, make an added entry.

21.30F. Other related persons or bodies

Make an added entry under the heading for a person or corporate body having a relationship to a work not treated in 21.1–21.28 if the heading provides an important access point (e.g., the addressee of a collection of letters; a person honoured by a Festschrift; a museum in which an exhibition is held).

21.30G. Related works

Make an added entry under the heading for a work to which the work being catalogued is closely related (see 21.8–21.28 for guidance in specific cases).

Make such entries in the form of the heading for the person or corporate body or the title under which the related work is, or would be, entered. If the heading is for a person or body, and the title of the related work differs from that of the work being catalogued, add the title of the related work to the heading to form a name-title added entry heading. When necessary, add the edition statement, date, etc., to the name-title added entry heading.

When appropriate, substitute a uniform title (see chapter 25) for a title proper in a name-title or title added entry heading for a related work.

21.30H. Other relationships

Make an added entry under the heading for any other name that would provide an important access point unless the relationship between the name and the work is purely that of a subject. For example, make added entries under the heading for the name of a collection from which reproductions of art works have been taken or under the heading for a collection of books upon which a bibliography is based.

When possible, formulate headings for such names by analogy with corporate name headings.

21.30J. Titles

Make an added entry under the title proper of every work entered under a personal heading, a corporate heading, or a uniform title unless:

       1) the title proper is essentially the same as the main entry heading or a reference to that heading

or 2) the title proper has been composed by the cataloguer

or 3) in a catalogue in which name-title and subject entries are interfiled, the title proper is identical with a subject heading, or a direct reference to a subject heading used for the work

or 4) a conventionalized uniform title has been used in an entry for a musical work (see 25.25–25.36)

Make an added entry also for any other title (cover title, caption title, running title, etc.) if it is significantly different from the title proper. For guidance upon what differences are significant, see 21.2A.

21.30K. Special rules on added entries in certain cases

21.30K1. Translators. Make an added entry under the heading for a translator if the main entry is under the heading for a corporate body or under title.

If the main entry is under the heading for a person, make an added entry under the heading for a translator if:

       a) the translation is in verse

or b) the translation is important in its own right

or c) the work has been translated into the same language more than once

or d) the wording of the chief source of information suggests that the translator is the author

or e) the main entry heading may be difficult for catalogue users to find (e.g., as with many oriental and medieval works)

21.30K2. Illustrators. Make an added entry under the heading for an illustrator of a work if:

       a) the illustrator's name is given equal prominence in the chief source of information with that of the person or corporate body used in the main entry heading

or b) the illustrations occupy half or more of the item

or c) the illustrations are considered to be an important feature of the work.

21.30L. Series

Make an added entry under the heading for a series for each separately catalogued work in the series if it provides a useful collocation. *Optionally,* add the numeric or other designation of each work in the series.

Do not make added entries under the heading for a series if:

1) the items in a series are related to each other only by common physical characteristics

or 2) the numbering suggests that the parts have been numbered primarily for stock control or to benefit from lower postage rates

or 3) all the parts of a series are entered under the heading for one person.

In case of doubt, make a series added entry.

21.30M. Analytical entries

Make an added entry (analytical) under the heading for a work contained within the work being catalogued (see 21.7B–21.7C, 21.13B, and 21.15A for guidance in specific cases). Make further analytical entries in accordance with the policy of the cataloguing agency. See also chapter 13.

Make such entries in the form of the heading for the person or corporate body or the title under which the work contained is, or would be, entered. Unless the entry is under title, make the added entry in the form of a name-title heading. When necessary, add the edition statement, date, etc., to the name-title or title added entry heading.

When appropriate, substitute a uniform title (see chapter 25) for a title proper in a name-title or title analytical entry heading.

Special rules

CERTAIN LEGAL PUBLICATIONS

21.31. LAWS, ETC.

21.31A. Scope

Apply this rule to legislative enactments and decrees of a political jurisdiction and decrees of a chief executive having the force of law (hereinafter referred to as laws) other than

1) administrative regulations having the force of law (see 21.32)
2) constitutions and charters (see 21.33)
3) court rules (see 21.34)
4) treaties and similar formal agreements (see 21.35)

For annotated editions of laws and commentaries, see 21.13.

21.31B. Laws of modern jurisdictions

21.31B1. Laws governing one jurisdiction. Enter laws governing one jurisdiction under the heading for the jurisdiction governed by them. Make added entries under the headings for persons and corporate bodies (other than legislative bodies) responsible for compiling and issuing the laws. Add a uniform title as instructed in 25.15A to the main entry.

The public health acts / annotated by William Golden Lumley and
　　Edmund Lumley . . .
*Main entry under the heading for the United Kingdom with uniform
　　title for the laws*
Added entries under the headings for W.G. Lumley and E. Lumley

Canada Corporations Act : chap. 53, R.S.C. 1952, as amended. —
　　2nd ed. — Don Mills, Ont. : CCH Canadian
Main entry under the heading for Canada with uniform title for the law
Added entry under the heading for CCH Canadian

Gesetz betreffend die Amortisation der Staatsschuld : auf Befehl
　　e. h. Senats der Freien und Hansestadt Hamburg publicirt den
　　29. Mai 1865
*Main entry under the heading for Hamburg with uniform title for
　　the law*

The school law of Illinois . . . / prepared by T.A. Reynolds, assistant
　　superintendent ; issued by John A. Wieland, superintendent of
　　public instruction ; amended by the Fifty-ninth General Assembly
Main entry under the heading for Illinois with uniform title for the law
*Added entries under the headings for Reynolds and the Department
　　of Public Instruction*

Building code of the city of Richmond, Virginia
*Main entry under the heading for Richmond with uniform title for
　　the code*

Byelaws for the regulation of motor hackney carriages and the drivers
　　thereof in the City of Glasgow
*Main entry under the heading for Glasgow with uniform title for the
　　byelaws*

If the laws are enacted by a jurisdiction other than that governed by them, make
an added entry under the heading for the enacting jurisdiction. Add a uniform title
as instructed in 25.15A to the added entry.

Code of the public local laws of Worcester County : (article 24 of the
　　Code of public local laws of Maryland) : comprising all the local
　　laws of the state of Maryland in force in Worcester County to
　　and inclusive of the Acts of the General Assembly of 1961 / edited
　　by Carl N. Everstine
*Main entry under the heading for Worcester County with uniform title
　　for the laws*
*Added entry under the heading for Maryland with uniform title for
　　the laws*

If the laws are decrees of a head of state, chief executive, or ruling executive body
(e.g., a junta), make an added entry under the corporate heading for the official
(see 24.20) or ruling executive body.

Notverordnungen des Reichspräsidenten
Main entry under the heading for Germany with uniform title for the
decrees
Added entry under the corporate heading for the Reichspräsident

Decretos-leyes de carácter electoral / dictados por la Junta Militar
de Gobierno ; contiene los relativos al referéndum nacional, al
procedimiento para la realización de éste, y a las reformas a la Ley
electoral . . . . — La Paz, Bolivia
Main entry under the heading for Bolivia with uniform title for the
decree laws
Added entry under the heading for the junta

21.31B2. Laws governing more than one jurisdiction. Enter a compilation of laws
governing more than one jurisdiction as a collection (see 21.7). Make added entries
under the headings for the jurisdictions governed if there are two or three. If there
are four or more jurisdictions, make an added entry under the heading for the first
one named in the chief source of information. If all the laws are enacted by a single
jurisdiction, make an added entry under the heading for the enacting jurisdiction.
Add a uniform title as instructed in 25.15A to the added entries.

Motor bus laws and regulations : a complete code of all motor bus
regulatory laws . . . / compiled and edited by John M. Meighan
Main entry under title
Added entry under the heading for Meighan

21.31B3. Bills and drafts of legislation. Enter legislative bills under the heading for
the appropriate legislative body (see 24.21). Enter other drafts of legislation as instructed in 21.1–21.7.

70th Congress, 1st session. S.2170 . . . A bill to designate a building
site for the National Conservatory of Music of America, and for
other purposes
Main entry under the heading for the Senate of the United States

Draft of an act relating to the sale of goods / by Samuel Williston
Main entry under the heading for Williston

Draft of proposed tenement house law / Commission of Immigration
and Housing of California
Main entry under the heading for the commission

21.31C. Ancient laws, certain medieval laws, customary laws, etc.
Enter the laws of ancient jurisdictions; laws of non-Western jurisdictions before
the adoption of legislative institutions based on Western models; and customary laws,
tribal laws, etc., under (in this order of preference):

1) a uniform title consisting of the title by which the law or early compilation of
   laws is known (see 25.15B)
2) the title proper of the item being catalogued.

Make added entries under the headings for compilers or enactors of such laws if they are named prominently or their names are associated with the work in reference sources.

> Lex Salica : the ten texts with the glosses and the Lex Emendata
> *Main entry under the uniform title for the* Lex Salica

> Edictum Diocletiani de pretiis rerum venalium
> *Main entry under the uniform title for the* Edictum

> The oldest code of laws in the world : the code of laws promulgated
>   by Hammurabi, King of Babylon . . .
> *Main entry under the uniform title for the laws of Hammurabi*

> Die Gesetze des Merowingerreiches, 481–714 / herausgegeben von
>   Karl August Eckhardt
> *Main entry under the title proper*
> *Added entry under the heading for Eckhardt*

> Fontes iuris romani antejustiniani, in usum scholarum ediderunt
>   S. Riccobono, J. Baviera, C. Ferrini, J. Furlani, V. Arangio-Ruiz
> *Main entry under the title proper*
> *Added entry under the heading for Riccobono*

21.32. ADMINISTRATIVE REGULATIONS, ETC.

21.32A. Administrative regulations, etc., promulgated by government agencies

21.32A1. If administrative regulations, rules, etc., are from jurisdictions in which such regulations, etc., are promulgated by government agencies or agents under authority granted by one or more laws (as is the case in the United States), enter them under the heading for the agency or agent. If the regulations, etc., are issued by an agency other than the promulgating agency, make an added entry under the heading for the issuing agency. If the regulations, etc., derive from a particular law, make an added entry under the heading and uniform title (see 25.15A) for that law.

> State of Illinois rules and regulations for recreational areas :
>   ₍Recreational Area Licensing Act rules and regulations₎. —
>   ₍Springfield₎ : Dept. of Public Health, Bureau of Environmental
>   Health, Division of Swimming Pools and Recreation, ₍1972?₎
>   (*Promulgated by the Department of Public Health*)
> *Main entry under the heading for the Department of Public Health*
> *Added entries under the headings for the Division of Swimming Pools*
>   *and Recreation and for Illinois with uniform title for the law*

21.32A2. If a law or laws and the regulations, etc., derived from it are published together, enter the item under the heading appropriate to whichever is mentioned first in the title elements. Make an added entry under the heading for the other. If only the law(s) or only the regulations, etc., are named in the title proper, enter under the heading appropriate to the one mentioned. Make an added entry under the heading for the other. If the evidence of the chief source of information is ambiguous or insufficient, enter under the heading for the law(s) and make an added entry under the heading for the regulations, etc.

Regulations and principal statutes applicable to contractors and
   subcontractors on public building and public work and on building
   and work financed in whole or in part by loans or grants from the
   United States / United States Department of Labor
   (*Includes several statutes, in whole and in part*)
   Main entry under the heading for the department
   Added entry under the heading for the United States

Gewerbesteuer-Veranlagung 1966 : Gewerbesteuergesetz und
   Gewerbesteuer-Durchführungsverordnung mit Gewerbesteuer-
   Richtlinien . . .
   (*Regulations and guidelines included were promulgated by the
   Bundesministerium der Finanzen of the Federal Republic of
   Germany*)
   *Main entry under the heading for the Federal Republic of Germany
   with uniform title for the law*
   Added entry under the heading for the ministry

21.32B. Administrative regulations, etc., that are laws

If administrative regulations, rules, etc., are from jurisdictions in which such regulations, etc., are laws (as is the case in the United Kingdom and Canada), enter them
as instructed in 21.31. Make added entries under the headings for government
agencies or agents promulgating and/or issuing them. If the regulations, etc., derive
from a particular law, make an added entry under the heading and uniform title for
that law as instructed in 25.15A.

The Building Societies (Fee) Regulations, 1976. Statutory instruments,
   1976 no. 342
   (*Promulgated by the Chief Registrar of Friendly Societies under
   authority granted by the Building Societies (Fee) Act*)
   *Main entry under the heading for the United Kingdom with uniform
   title for the regulations*
   Added entry under the heading for the Chief Registrar
   *Added entry under the heading for the United Kingdom with uniform
   title for the law*

Regulations under the Destructive Insect and Pest Act as they apply
   to the importation of plants and plant products / Department
   of Agriculture, Ottawa
   (*Promulgated by the Governor in Council*)
   *Main entry under the heading for Canada with uniform title for the
   regulations*
   *Added entries under the headings for the Governor and the
   department*
   *Added entry under the heading for Canada with uniform title for the
   law*

21.32C. Enter a collection of regulations enacted by more than one agency or agent
as a collection (see 21.7).

21.33. CONSTITUTIONS, CHARTERS, AND OTHER FUNDAMENTAL LAWS

21.33A. Enter the constitution, charter, or other fundamental law of a jurisdiction under the heading for that jurisdiction. Enter any amendments to such a document under the same heading. If the document is issued by any jurisdiction other than the one governed by it, make an added entry under the heading for the jurisdiction issuing it. Add the appropriate uniform title (see 25.15A) to the added entry if the document is a law.

> The Constitution of the United States
> *Main entry under the heading for the United States*

> . . . At a Parliament begun and holden at Westminster the first day
>   of February . . . 1866 . . . An act for the union of Canada, Nova
>   Scotia, and New Brunswick, and the government thereof . . .
> *Main entry under the heading for Canada*
> *Added entry under the heading for the United Kingdom with uniform*
>   *title for the law*

> Kongeriget Norges grundlov . . .
> *Main entry under the heading for Norway*

> Charter of the United Nations
> *Main entry under the heading for the United Nations*

> The Constitution of the state of Michigan
> *Main entry under the heading for Michigan*

> Constitución política del estado libre y soberano de Chihuahua . . .
> *Main entry under the heading for Chihuahua*

> Constitution of the state of Connecticut, and historical antecedents.
>   — ₁Hartford₁ : Office of the Secretary of the State, 1966
> *Main entry under the heading for Connecticut*
> *Added entry under the heading for the office*

> Charter of the city of Detroit : revised to April 3, 1933 / adopted
>   by the people of the city of Detroit . . .
> *Main entry under the heading for Detroit*

> Charter of the city of Nashville, Tennessee : chapter no. 246, Private
>   acts of the General Assembly of the state of Tennessee for the year
>   1947 as amended through the legislative session of 1949
> *Main entry under the heading for Nashville*
> *Added entry under the heading for Tennessee with uniform title for*
>   *the law*

> The charter granted by His Majesty King Charles II to the Governour
>   & Company of the English Colony of Connecticut
> *Main entry under the heading for Connecticut*
> *Added entry under the corporate heading for Charles II as sovereign*

21.33B. Enter the constitution, charter, or other fundamental document of a body emanating from a jurisdiction but applying to a body other than a jurisdiction as instructed in the rule applying to the type of document (e.g., if the document is a law, see 21.31). Enter any amendments to such a document under the same heading. Make an added entry under the heading for the body governed by the constitution, etc., if the main entry is not under that heading.

> Charter of the Franklin Bank of Baltimore
> (*An act of the Maryland legislature*)
> *Main entry under the heading for Maryland with uniform title for*
> *the law*
> *Added entry under the heading for the bank*

For constitutions, etc., that neither apply to, nor emanate from, a jurisdiction, see 21.1B and 21.4B.

21.33C. Drafts

If a draft of a constitution, charter, etc., is a legislative bill, enter it under the heading for the appropriate legislative body (see 24.21). Enter all other drafts of such documents as instructed in 21.1–21.7.

21.34. COURT RULES

21.34A. Enter court rules governing a single court (regardless of their official nature, e.g., laws, administrative regulations) under the heading for that court. If the rules are laws, make an added entry under the heading for the jurisdiction enacting the law and add a uniform title (see 25.15A) to the added entry. Make an added entry under the heading for the agency or agent promulgating the court rules.

> Rules of practice and procedure of United States Tax Court
> *Main entry under the heading for the court*

> Lord Chancellor's Office. The rules of the Supreme Court, 1965 . . .
> (*The rules of the English Supreme Court, promulgated by the Lord*
> *Chancellor's Office; an administrative regulation*)
> *Main entry under the heading for the court*
> *Added entry under the heading for the office*
> *Added entry under the heading for the United Kingdom with uniform*
> *title for the regulation*

21.34B. Enter a collection of rules governing more than one court of a single jurisdiction but enacted as laws of that jurisdiction as instructed in 21.31. Enter all other such collections of court rules under the heading for the agency or agent promulgating them.

Make added entries under the headings for the courts governed by the rules if there are two or three. If the rules govern four or more courts, make an added entry under the heading for the first one named in the chief source of information.

> Code de procédure civile de la province de Québec : 13–14 Elizabeth
> II chap. 80 / revisé par Lise Saintonge Poitevin . . .
> *Main entry under the heading for Québec with uniform title for the law*
> *Added entry under the heading for Poitevin*

Federal rules of appellate procedure . . .
("*Procedure in appeals to the United States Courts of Appeals . . .*
Promulgated by the United States Supreme Court")
Main entry under the heading for the Supreme Court

21.34C. Enter a collection of court rules that are the laws of more than one jurisdiction, or that are promulgated by more than one agency or agent, as a collection (see 21.7). Make an added entry under the heading for any openly named corporate body involved in the compilation unless it functions solely as a publisher.

West's California rules of court, 1975, state and federal : with
amendments received for January 1, 1975. — St. Paul, Minn. :
West Pub. Co.
(*The rules apply to numerous state and federal courts in California;
the state rules are promulgated by the California Judicial Council*)
Main entry under title
*Added entries under the headings for the Judicial Council and for the
publisher*

21.35. TREATIES, INTERGOVERNMENTAL AGREEMENTS, ETC.

21.35A. International treaties, etc.

21.35A1. Enter a treaty, or any other formal agreement, between two or three national governments[9] under (in this order of preference):

a) the heading for the government on one side if it is the only one on that side and there are two governments on the other
b) the heading for the government whose catalogue entry heading (see 24.3E) is first in English alphabetic order.

Make added entries under the headings for the other governments(s). Add a uniform title (see 25.16B1) to the main and added entries.

Convention monétaire belgo-luxembourgeoise-néerlandaise
(*A convention between the government of the Netherlands, on the
one side, and the governments of Belgium and Luxembourg on the
other side*)
*Main entry under the heading for the Netherlands with uniform title
for the treaty*
*Added entries under the headings for Belgium and Luxembourg,
each with uniform title for the treaty*

Special economic assistance : agreement between the United States
of America and Burma, effected by exchange of notes
*Main entry under the heading for Burma with uniform title for the
treaty*

---

9. The term *national governments* includes bodies exercising treaty powers such as American Indian nations and African tribal governments.

Added entry under the heading for the United States with uniform title for the treaty

Traité de paix entre le Japon et la Russie
Main entry under the heading for Japan with uniform title for the treaty
Added entry under the heading for Russia with uniform title for the treaty

... Treaty series no. 29 (1957). Convention between the governments of the United Kingdom, Belgium, and France regarding the supervision and preventive control of the African migratory locust
Main entry under the heading for Belgium with uniform title for the treaty
Added entries under the headings for France and the United Kingdom, each with uniform title for the treaty

21.35A2. Enter a treaty, or any other formal agreement, between more than three national governments under title (either the title proper or a uniform title, see 25.16B2). Make an added entry under the heading for the home government (i.e., the government of the cataloguing agency) if it is a signatory. Make an added entry under the heading for any other government publishing the item being catalogued if that government is a signatory. Make an added entry under the heading for the government named first in the chief source of information if it is neither the home government nor the publishing government. If the treaty, etc., is the product of an international conference, make an added entry under the heading for the conference. Add a uniform title (see 25.16B1) to the added entries for parties to the agreement.

The definitive treaty of peace and friendship between His Britannick Majesty, the most Christian King, and the King of Spain : concluded at Paris, the 10th day of February, 1763 : to which the King of Portugal acceded on the same day
(France, the United Kingdom, Portugal, and Spain are signatories)
Main entry under the uniform title for the treaty
Added entry under the heading for the United Kingdom with uniform title for the treaty

Universal Copyright Convention : with protocols 1, 2, and 3 : Geneva, September 6, 1952. — London : H.M.S.O., 1952
(Drawn up by the Intergovernmental Conference on Copyright; the United States and Canada are signatories)
Main entry under the uniform title for the treaty
Added entry under the heading for the United Kingdom (as publisher) with uniform title for the treaty
Added entry under the heading for Canada with uniform title for the treaty (for a Canadian cataloguing agency)
Added entry under the heading for the United States with uniform title for the treaty (for a cataloguing agency in the United States)
Added entry under the heading for the conference

21.35B. Agreements contracted by international intergovernmental bodies

Enter as instructed in 21.35A an agreement between an international intergovernmental body[10] and one or more

      1) other international intergovernmental bodies

or 2) national governments.

> Guarantee agreement, second agricultural project, between Republic of Iceland and International Bank for Reconstruction and Development
> *Main entry under the heading for Iceland with uniform title for the treaty*
> *Added entry under the heading for the bank with uniform title for the treaty*

> Agreement between the United Nations and the Food and Agriculture Organisation of the United Nations and the United Kingdom as administering power of the territories of Cyrenaica and Tripolitania regarding technical assistance for Cyrenaica and Tripolitania
> *Main entry under the heading for the Food and Agriculture Organisation with uniform title for the treaty*
> *Added entries under the headings for the United Kingdom and the United Nations, each with uniform title for the treaty*

Enter as instructed in 21.35A an agreement between an international intergovernmental body and one or more

      1) jurisdictions other than national governments

or 2) other corporate bodies.

In these cases, do not add a uniform title to the main and added entry headings.

> Project agreement (first urban sewerage project) between International Bank for Reconstruction and Development and District de Tunis
> *Main entry under the heading for the bank*
> *Added entry under the heading for the district*

> Loan agreement, paper and pulp project, between International Bank for Reconstruction and Development and Corporación de Fomento de la Producción and Compañía Manufacturera de Papeles y Cartones
> *Main entry under the heading for the bank*
> *Added entries under the headings for the corporation and the company*

Enter an agreement contracted by the member governments of an international intergovernmental body acting as individual entities rather than collectively as instructed in 21.35A.

---

10. *International intergovernmental body* means an international body created by intergovernmental action.

Agreement creating an association between the member states of the
European Free Trade Association and the Republic of Finland
. . . . — London : H.M.S.O., 1961
(*The signatories were the seven members of EFTA and Finland*)
Main entry under the uniform title for the treaty
*Added entries under the headings for the United Kingdom (as
publisher) and Finland, each with uniform title for the treaty*

21.35C. Agreements contracted by the Holy See

Enter a concordat, *modus vivendi,* convention, or other formal agreement between the Holy See and a national government or other political jurisdiction under
the party whose catalogue entry heading (see 24.3E) is first in English alphabetic
order. Make an added entry under the heading for the other party. Add a uniform
title (see 25.16B1) to the main and added entries.

Das Konkordat zwischen dem Heiligen Stuhle und dem Freistaate
Baden
*Main entry under the heading for Baden with uniform title for the
treaty*
*Added entry under the heading for the Catholic Church with uniform
title for the treaty*

Concordato celebrado entre su santidad Pío IX y el gobierno de
Ecuador
*Main entry under the heading for the Catholic Church with uniform
title for the treaty*
*Added entry under the heading for Ecuador with uniform title for
the treaty*

21.35D. Agreements contracted by jurisdictions below the national level

21.35D1. Enter an agreement between two or more jurisdictions below the national
level, or between a national government and one or more jurisdictions within its
country, as instructed in 21.6C.

Memorandum of agreement between the government of the Province
of Ontario and the government of Canada pursuant to section 4(3)
of the Anti-Inflation Act
Main entry under the heading for Ontario
Added entry under the heading for Canada

Joint agreement between the state of Maine and the Province of New
Brunswick [to maintain and foster close cooperation]
Main entry under the heading for Maine
Added entry under the heading for New Brunswick

21.35D2. Enter agreements involving jurisdictions below the national level and international intergovernmental bodies as instructed in 21.35B.

21.35D3. Enter an agreement between a national government and one or more jurisdictions below the national level outside its country as instructed in 21.35A, but do not add uniform titles to main and added entry headings.

> Protocole relatif aux échanges entre le Québec et la France en
> matière d'éducation physique, de sport et d'éducation populaire :
> pris en application de l'entente franco-québécoise du 27 février 1965
> sur un programme d'échange et de coopération dans le domaine de
> l'éducation
>
> *Main entry under the heading for France*
> *Added entry under the heading for Québec*

21.35E. Protocols, amendments, etc.

Enter a separately published protocol, amendment, extension, or other agreement ancillary to a treaty, etc., under the heading for the basic agreement. Add uniform titles as instructed in 25.16B3.

Treat a general revision of a treaty, etc., as an independent work. Make an added entry under the heading for the treaty, etc., revised if the headings differ. Add a uniform title as appropriate.

21.35F. Collections

21.35F1. If a collection of treaties, etc., consists of those contracted between two parties, enter it in the same way as a single agreement between those parties (see 21.35A1, 21.35B–21.35E). Make an added entry under the heading for an openly named compiler.

21.35F2. If a collection of treaties, etc., consists of those contracted between one party and two or more other parties, enter it under the heading for the one party. Make added entries under the headings for the other parties if there are two of them. Add a uniform title (see 25.16B1) to the main and added entries for the parties. Make an added entry under the heading for an openly named compiler.

> Treaties and other international agreements of the United States of
> America, 1776–1949 / compiled under the direction of Charles
> I. Bevans
>
> *Main entry under the heading for the United States with uniform title*
> *for the treaties*
> *Added entry under the heading for Bevans*

21.35F3. Enter any other collection of treaties, etc., as a collection (see 21.7).

21.36. COURT DECISIONS, CASES, ETC.

21.36A. Law reports

21.36A1. Reports of one court. Enter law reports of one court that are not ascribed to a reporter or reporters by name under:

a) the heading for the court if the reports are issued by or under the authority of the court

or b) title if they are not.

Make an added entry under the heading for an openly named editor or compiler. Make an added entry under the heading for the publisher if its responsibility extends beyond that of publication.

> Canada Federal Court reports / editor, Florence Rosenfeld ; assistant editor, M.J. Pierce . . .
> *Main entry under the heading for the court*
> *Added entry under the heading for the editor*

> Reports of cases argued and determined in the Court of Appeals of Arizona . . . . — St. Paul : West Pub. Co.
> (*Publisher acts in an editorial capacity*)
> *Main entry under title*
> *Added entries under the headings for the court and the publisher*

Enter reports of one court that are ascribed to a reporter or to reporters by name under the heading for the court or under the heading for the reporter or first named reporter according to whichever is used as the basis for accepted legal citation practice in the country where the court is located. If that practice is unknown or cannot be determined, enter under:

a) the heading for the court if the reports are issued by or under the authority of the court

or b) the heading for the reporter or first named reporter if they are not.

Make an added entry under the heading for the court or the reporter, whichever is not given the main entry heading. Make an added entry under the heading for an openly named editor or compiler. Make an added entry under the heading for the publisher if its responsibility extends beyond that of publication.

> Reports of cases determined in the Supreme Court of the state of California, October 23, 1969, to January 30, 1970 / Robert E. Formichi, reporter of decisions. — San Francisco : Bancroft-Whitney
> (*Cited as* California reports)
> *Main entry under the heading for the court*
> *Added entry under the heading for the reporter*

> Common bench reports : cases argued and determined in the Court of Common Pleas / ₁reported₁ by James Manning, T.C. Granger, and John Scott. — London : Benning
> (*Cited as* Manning, Granger & Scott)
> *Main entry under the heading for Manning*
> *Added entries under the headings for Granger, Scott, and the court*

21.36A2. Reports of more than one court. Enter reports of more than one court under the heading for the reporter if responsible for the reports of all the cases reported. If there is more than one reporter, apply the instructions in 21.6.

If the reporter(s) is not responsible for all the reports, enter under title. Make an added entry under the heading for the reporter named first in the chief source of information.

Make added entries under the headings for the courts if there are two or three. If there are four or more, make an added entry under the heading for the first court named in the chief source of information.

Make an added entry under the heading for an openly named editor or compiler or a corporate body involved in the publication unless it functions solely as the publisher.

> Reports of cases argued and determined in the Courts of Common
> Pleas, and Exchequer Chamber, and in the House of Lords . . . /
> ₍reported₎ by John Bernard Bosanquet and Christopher Puller . . .
> *Main entry under the heading for Bosanquet*
> *Added entries under the headings for Puller and the courts (including
> the House of Lords)*

> Australian law reports : being reports of judgments of the High Court
> of Australia and the Judicial Committee of the Privy Council and
> of state supreme courts exercising federal jurisdiction, other federal
> courts and tribunals, together with selected cases from the Supreme
> Court of the Northern Territory and reports of the Supreme Court
> of the Australian Capital Territory (authorized by the judges) /
> editor, Robert Hayes
> (*The report for each case signed by its reporter*)
> *Main entry under title*
> *Added entries under the headings for the editor and the High Court*

21.36B. Citations, digests, etc.

Enter citations to, and digests and indexes of, court reports under the heading for the person responsible for them if that person is openly named. Otherwise, enter under title. Make an added entry under the heading for an openly named corporate body involved in the publication unless it functions solely as the publisher.

> Connecticut digest, 1785 to date . . . / by Richard H. Phillips
> *Main entry under the heading for Phillips*

> Michie's digest of Virginia and West Virginia reports . . . / under
> the editorial supervision of A. Hewson Michie
> *Main entry under the heading for Michie*

> Atlantic reporter digest, 1764 to date . . . covering Atlantic reporter
> and corresponding cases in the reports of the Atlantic States . . . .
> — St. Paul, Minn. : West Pub. Co., 1939–
> *Main entry under title*
> *Added entry under the heading for the West Publishing Company*

21.36C. Particular cases

21.36C1. Proceedings in the first instance. Criminal proceedings. Enter the official proceedings and records of criminal trials, impeachments, courts-martial, etc., under

the heading for the person or body prosecuted. If more than one person or body is prosecuted, apply the instructions in 21.6C. *Optionally,* add the appropriate legal designation (e.g., *defendant, libelee*) to headings for persons or bodies prosecuted. Make an added entry under the heading for the court or other adjudicating body. Make an added entry under the heading for an openly named reporter. Do not make an added entry under the heading for the jurisdiction bringing the prosecution.

> Report of the trial of Leavitt Alley, indicted for the murder of Abijah
> Ellis, in the Supreme Judicial Court of Massachusetts / reported
> by Franklin Fiske Heard
> *Main entry under the heading for Alley as defendant*
> *Added entries under the headings for the court and Heard*

> Report of the trial of Brig. General William Hull, commanding the
> North-western Army of the United States, by a court martial held
> at Albany on Monday, 3rd January, 1814, and succeeding days /
> taken by Lieut. Col. Forbes
> *Main entry under the heading for Hull as defendant*
> *Added entries under the headings for the court-martial and for Forbes*

> Report of the case of the steamship Meteor, libelled for alleged
> violation of the Neutrality Act . . . / edited by F.V. Balch
> *Main entry under the heading for the ship as libellee*
> *Added entries under the headings for the various courts whose actions*
> *are reported and for Balch*

21.36C2. Proceedings in the first instance. Other proceedings. Enter the official proceedings and records of civil and other noncriminal proceedings in the first instance (including election cases) under the heading for the person or body bringing the action. If more than one person or body brings the action, apply the instructions in 21.6C. Make added entries under the headings for the persons or bodies on the opposing side if there are one, two, or three. If there are four or more persons or bodies on the opposing side, make an added entry under the heading for the first named, *Optionally,* add the appropriate legal designation (e.g., *plaintiff, complainant, contestant, defendant, respondent, contestee*) to the headings for parties to the action. Make an added entry under the heading for the court or other adjudicating body. Make an added entry under the heading for an openly named reporter.

> The case of William Brooks versus Ezekiel Byam and others, in equity,
> in the Circuit Court of the United States, for the First Circuit—
> District of Massachusetts
> *Main entry under the heading for Brooks as complainant*
> *Added entry under the heading for Byam as respondent*
> *Added entry under the heading for the court*

> . . . Contested election case of John A. Smith, contestant, v. Edwin
> Y. Webb, contestee, from the Ninth Congressional District of North
> Carolina, before Committee on Elections No. 2
> *Main entry under the heading for Smith as contestant*
> *Added entry under the heading for Webb as contestee*
> *Added entry under the heading for the committee*

> . . . United States Circuit Court, Western District of New York. The
> Goodwin Film and Camera Company, complainant, vs. Eastman
> Kodak Company, defendant
> *Main entry under the heading for the Goodwin Film and Camera*
> *Company as complainant*
> *Added entry under the heading for the Eastman Kodak Company*
> *as defendant*
> *Added entry under the heading for the court*

21.36C3. Appeal proceedings. Enter the official proceedings and records of appeal
proceedings in the same way as the proceedings in the first instance. *Optionally,* add
the legal designation appropriate to the appeal to that appropriate in the first instance
(e.g., *defendant-appellee, defendant-appellant*).

> United States Circuit Court of Appeals for the Second Circuit.
> October term, 1913. The Goodwin Film and Camera Company,
> complainant-appellee, vs. Eastman Kodak Company, defendant-
> appellant : transcript of record
> *Main entry under the heading for the Goodwin Film and Camera*
> *Company as complainant-appellee*
> *Added entry under the heading for the Eastman Kodak Company*
> *as defendant-appellant*
> *Added entry under the heading for the court*

21.36C4. Indictments. Enter indictments as instructed in 21.36C1.

> Copy of an indictment <No. 1>. In the Circuit Court of the United
> States in and for the Pennsylvania District of the Middle Circuit
> (*Indictment of William Duane*)
> *Main entry under the heading for Duane as defendant*
> *Added entry under the heading for the court*

21.36C5. Charges to juries. Enter a charge to a jury under the heading for the court.
Make an added entry under the heading for the judge delivering the charge. Make
added entries under the headings for the first named party on each side, except for
the jurisdiction in cases prosecuted by the jurisdiction. *Optionally,* add legal designations (see 21.36C1–21.36C3) to the added entry headings.

> The charge of Judge Patterson ₍sic₎ to the jury in the case of
> Vanhorne's lessee against Dorrance : tried at a Circuit Court for
> the United States, held at Philadelphia, April term, 1795
> (*The lessee is not named*)
> *Main entry under the heading for the court*
> *Added entry under the heading for Dorrance as defendant*
> *Added entries under the headings for Paterson and Van Horne*

21.36C6. Judicial decisions. Enter a judgement or other decision of a court in a case
under the heading for the court. Make added entries under the headings for the first
named party on each side, except for the jurisdiction in cases prosecuted by the

jurisdiction. *Optionally,* add legal designations (see 21.36C1–21.36C3) to the added entry headings.

> Freedom of the press : opinion of the Supreme Court of the United
> States in the case of Alice Lee Grosjean, supervisor of public
> accounts for the state of Louisiana, appellant, v. American Press
> Company, Inc., et al.
> *Main entry under the heading for the court*
> *Added entries under the headings for the American Press Company*
>   *as plaintiff-appellee and Grosjean as defendant-appellant*

21.36C7. Judicial opinions. Enter an opinion of a judge under the heading for the judge. Make an added entry under the heading for the first named party on each side, except for the jurisdiction in cases prosecuted by the jurisdiction. *Optionally,* add legal designations (see 21.36C1–21.36C3) to the added entry headings.

> Supreme Court of Ohio. At chambers, May 1859. Dissenting opinion
> of Hon. Milton Sutliff, one of the judges : ex parte Simeon
> Bushnell : ex parte Charles Langston : on habeas corpus
> *Main entry under the heading for Sutliff*
> *Added entry under the heading for Bushnell as defendant*

21.36C8. Records of one party. Enter a brief, plea, or other formal record of one party to a case under the heading for that party. If that party is not the one under which the proceedings of the trial would be entered (see 21.36C1–21.36C3), make an added entry under the heading for the other party. *Optionally,* add legal designations (see 21.36C1–21.36C3) to the headings for the parties to the action. Make an added entry under the heading for the lawyer concerned.

> Supreme Court of the United States. No. 132. George B. Morewood,
> John R. Morewood, Frederic R. Routh, respondents, appellants
> versus Lorenzo N. Enequist, libellant, appellee : brief for appellants
> on admiralty jurisdiction / Robert Dodge, attorney for appellants
> *Main entry under the heading for G. Morewood as respondent-*
>   *appellant*
> *Added entries under the headings for J. Morewood as respondent-*
>   *appellant, Routh as respondent-appellant, and Enequist as libellant-*
>   *appellee*
> *Added entry under the heading for Dodge*

Enter a courtroom argument presented by a lawyer under the heading for the lawyer. Make an added entry under the heading for the party represented. If that party is not the one under which the proceedings of the trial would be entered (see 21.36C1–21.36C3), make an added entry under the heading for the other party. *Optionally,* add legal designations (see 21.36C1–21.36C3) to the headings for the parties to the action.

> Argument of Franklin B. Gowen, Esq., of counsel for the
> Commonwealth in the case of the Commonwealth vs. Thomas
> Munley, indicted in the Court of Oyer and Terminer of Schuykill

> County, Pa., for the murder of Thomas Sanger . . . / stenographically
> reported by R.A. West
> *Main entry under the heading for Gowen*
> *Added entry under the heading for Munley as defendant*

21.36C9. Collections. Enter a collection of the official proceedings or records of trials as a collection (see 21.7). Make added entries under the headings for the persons or bodies who are parties to all the trials if there are not more than three persons or bodies involved. *Optionally,* add legal designations (see 21.36C1–21.36C3) to the headings for the parties.

CERTAIN RELIGIOUS PUBLICATIONS

21.37. SACRED SCRIPTURES

21.37A. Enter a work that is accepted as sacred scripture by a religious group, or part of such a work, under title. For the use of uniform titles for scriptures, see 25.17–25.18. Make an added entry under the heading for any person associated with the work.

> The Book of Mormon : an account written by the hand of Mormon
> upon plates taken from the plates of Nephi / translated by Joseph
> Smith, Jun.
> *Main entry under title*
> *Added entry under the heading for Smith*

> The Koran / translated from the Arabic by J.M. Rodwell
> *Main entry under title*
> *Added entry under the heading for Rodwell*

> The book of Isaiah . . .
> *Main entry under title*
> *Added entry under the heading for Isaiah*

21.37B. Treat harmonies of different scriptural passages as editions of the passages harmonized. Make an added entry under the heading for the harmonizer. For harmonies accompanied by commentary, see 21.13.

> The life of Our Lord / compiled from the Gospels of the four
> Evangelists and presented in the very words of the Scriptures
> as one continuous narrative by Reginald G. Ponsonby
> *Main entry under the heading for the Gospels*
> *Added entry under the heading for Ponsonby*

21.38. THEOLOGICAL CREEDS, CONFESSIONS OF FAITH, ETC.

Enter a theological creed, confession of faith, etc., accepted by more than one denominational body under the heading for the denominational body with which the edition being catalogued is associated. Make an added entry under the heading for the corporate body originally responsible for the work if its name appears in the chief source of information. If the edition is not associated with a particular denominational body, enter it under the heading for the corporate body, if any, originally responsible for the work. Otherwise, enter it under title.

> The Assembly's Shorter Catechism as used in the Presbyterian Church
>   in the United States
>   (*The catechism of the Westminster Assembly of Divines*)
> *Main entry under the heading for the church*
> *Added entry under the heading for the Westminster Assembly of*
>   *Divines*

> The Shorter Catechism of the Westminster Divines : being a facsimile
>   of the first edition . . . which was ordered to be printed by the
>   House of Commons, 14th April 1648
>   (*This edition not associated with any denominational body*)
> *Main entry under the heading for the Westminster Assembly of*
>   *Divines*

21.39. LITURGICAL WORKS

21.39A. General rule

21.39A1. Enter a liturgical work[11] under the heading for the church or denominational body to which it pertains. Add a uniform title as appropriate (see 25.19–25.23) to the main entry. If the work is special to the use of a particular body within the church (e.g., a diocese, cathedral, monastery, religious order), make an added entry under the heading for that body.

> The Book of common worship ⌈of the Church of South India⌉ as
>   authorised by the Synod 1962
> *Main entry under the heading for the church with uniform title for*
>   *the work*

> Horae diurnae Breviarii Romani ex decreto sacrosancti Concilii
>   Tridentini restituti
> *Main entry under the heading for the Catholic Church with uniform*
>   *title for the work*

> Missale ad vsum sacri et canonici Ordinis Praemonstratensis
> *Main entry under the heading for the Catholic Church with uniform*
>   *title for the work*
> *Added entry under the heading for the order*

> Common service book of the Lutheran church / authorized by the
>   United Lutheran Church in America
> *Main entry under the heading for the United Lutheran Church with*
>   *uniform title for the work*

---

11. *Liturgical works* include officially sanctioned or traditionally accepted texts of religious observance, books of obligatory prayers to be offered at stated times, and calendars and manuals of performance of religious observances.

The coronation service of Her Majesty Queen Elizabeth II . . .
*Main entry under the heading for the Church of England with uniform
title for the work*

21.39A2. Enter books of readings from sacred scriptures intended for use in a religious service as instructed in 21.39A1. However, enter single passages from sacred
scriptures used in religious services as instructed in 21.37.

Epistles and Gospels for Sundays and holy days / prepared, with the
addition of brief exegetical notes, by the Catholic Biblical
Association of America
*Main entry under the heading for the church with uniform title for
the work*

Proper lessons for the Sundays and holy days throughout the year
(*Published with* The book of common prayer . . . according to the
use of the Protestant Episcopal Church in the United States of
America)
*Main entry under the heading for the church with uniform title
for the work*

21.39A3. Enter the following types of works as instructed in the general rules
(21.1–21.7):

a) books intended for private devotions, except enter prayer books known as
"books of hours" as liturgical works
b) hymnals for congregations and choirs
c) proposals for orders of worship not officially approved
d) unofficial manuals
e) programmes of religious services
f) lectionaries without scriptural texts.

21.39B. Liturgical works of the Orthodox Eastern Church
Enter a liturgical work in the original language of the liturgy published for the use
of a national Orthodox Church or another autocephalous body within the Orthodox
Eastern Church under the heading for the specific church or body.

Trebnik. — Sofiﬁa : Sv. Sinod na Bŭlgarskata tsŭrkva
*Main entry under the heading for the Bulgarian church with uniform
title for the work*

Enter any other Orthodox liturgical work under the heading for the church as a
whole.

The ferial Menaion, or, The book of services for the twelve great
festivals and the New-Year's Day / translated from a Slavonian
edition
*Main entry under the heading for the Orthodox Eastern Church with
uniform title for the work*

344

21.39C. Jewish liturgical works

Enter a Jewish liturgical work under its title. For the use of uniform titles, see 25.21–25.22. If the work is special to the use of a particular body (association, congregation, synagogue, etc.), make an added entry under the heading for that body.

> The Jewish marriage service . . .
> *Main entry under title*

> Services of the heart : weekday, Sabbath, and festival services and
>   prayers for home and synagogue / Union of Liberal and Progressive
>   Synagogues
> *Main entry under title*
> *Added entry under the heading for the union*

CHAPTER **22**

HEADINGS FOR PERSONS

Contents

Choice of name

22.1. GENERAL RULE

22.1A. Choose, as the basis of the heading for a person, the name by which he or she is commonly known. This may be the person's real name, pseudonym, title of nobility, nickname, initials, or other appellation. For the form of the name used in headings, see 22.4–22.17.

> Caedmon
>
> William Shakespeare
>
> D.W. Griffith
> *not* David Wark Griffith
>
> Jimmy Carter
> *not* James Earl Carter
>
> Capability Brown
> *not* Lancelot Brown
>
> Anatole France
> *not* Jacques-Anatole Thibault

Ouida
not Marie Louise de la Ramée

H.D.
not Hilda Doolittle

Giorgione
not Giorgio Barbarelli

Fra Angelico
not Giovanni da Fiesole

Guido da Siena

Maria Helena
not Maria Helena Vaquinhas de Carvalho

Duke of Wellington
not Arthur Wellesley

John Julius Norwich
not Viscount Norwich

Sister Mary Hilary

Sister Mary Joseph Cahill

Queen Elizabeth II

22.1B. Determine the name by which a person is commonly known from the chief sources of information (see 1.0A) of works by that person issued in his or her language. If the person works in a nonverbal context (e.g., a painter, a sculptor) or is not known primarily as an author, determine the name by which he or she is commonly known from reference sources[1] issued in his or her language or country of residence or activity.

22.1C. Include any titles of nobility or honour (see also 22.12) or words or phrases (see also 22.8) that commonly appear in association with the name either wholly or in part. For the treatment of other terms appearing in association with the name, see 22.19B.

Sir Richard Acland

Duke of Wellington

Viscountess Astor

Fra Bartolommeo

Andrea del Castagno

Sister Mary Joseph

22.1D. Diacritical marks and hyphens

22.1D1. Accents, etc. Include accents and other diacritical marks appearing in a

---

1. When the phrase *reference sources* is used in this chapter, it includes books and articles written about a person.

name. Supply them if it is certain that they are integral to a name but have been omitted in the source from which the name is taken.

> Jacques Lefèvre d'Étaples

> Éliphas Lévi
>   (*Sometimes appears without diacritical marks*)

22.1D2. Hyphens. Retain hyphens between given names if they are used by the bearer of the name.

> Gian-Carlo Menotti

> Jean-Léon Jaurès

Include hyphens in romanized names if they are prescribed by the romanization system adopted by the cataloguing agency.

> Ch'oe Sin-dŏk

> Jung-lu

> Li Fei-kan

Omit a hyphen that joins one of a person's forenames to the surname.

> Lucien Graux
>   (*Name appears as* Lucien-Graux)

22.2. CHOICE AMONG DIFFERENT NAMES

22.2A. Predominant name

If a person is known by more than one name, choose the name by which the person is clearly most commonly known, if there is one. Otherwise, choose one name or form of name according to the following order of preference:

1) the name that appears most frequently in the person's works
2) the name that appears most frequently in reference sources
3) the latest name.

22.2B. Change of name

If a person has changed his or her name, choose the latest name or form of name unless there is reason to believe that an earlier name will persist as the name by which the person is better known. Follow the same rule for a person who has acquired and become known by a title of nobility (see also 22.6).

>   Dorothy Belle Hughes
> *not* Dorothy Belle Flanagan
>   (*Maiden name used in works before author's marriage*)

>   Sister Mary Just
> *not* Florence Didiez David
>   (*Secular name used in works before author entered religious order*)

>   Éloi-Gérard Talbot
> *not* Frère Éloi-Gérard
>   (*Name in religion, omitting surname, originally used in works*)

Akiko Yosano
not   Akiko Hō
    (*Maiden name used in works before author's marriage*)

Jacqueline Onassis
not   Jacqueline Bouvier
not   Jacqueline Kennedy
    (*Known previously under maiden and first married names*)

Ford Madox Ford
not   Ford Madox Hueffer
    (*Name changed from Hueffer to Ford*)

Muhammad Ali
not   Cassius Clay
    (*Name changed from Cassius Clay to Muhammad Ali*)

but

Benjamin Disraeli
not   Earl of Beaconsfield
    (*Title acquired and used rather late in life and after reputation
    had been established under personal name*)

22.2C. Pseudonyms

22.2C1. One pseudonym. If all the works by a person appear under one pseudonym, or if the person is predominantly identified in reference sources by one pseudonym, choose the pseudonym. <u>If the real name is known, make a reference from the real name to the pseudonym</u>.

Yukio Mishima
not   Kimitake Hiraoka

George Orwell
not   Eric Arthur Blair

Martin Ross
not   Violet Frances Martin

Nevil Shute
not   Nevil Shute Norway

For the treatment of a pseudonym used jointly by two or more persons, see 21.6D.

22.2C2. Predominant name. If the works of a person appear under several pseudonyms (or under the real name and one or more pseudonyms), choose one of those names if the person has come to be identified predominantly by that name in later editions of his or her works, in critical works, or in other reference sources[2] (in that order of preference). <u>Make references from the other names</u>.

---

2. Disregard reference sources that always enter persons under their real names.

> Anthony Boucher
> *not*   H.H. Holmes
> *not*   Herman W. Mudgett
> *not*   William Anthony Parker White
>
> Charlotte Brontë
> *not*   Currer Bell
>
> Lewis Carroll
> *not*   Charles Lutwidge Dodgson
>
> Howard Fast
> *not*   E.V. Cunningham
> *not*   Walter Ericson
>
> Shimei Futabatei
> *not*   Tatsunosuke Hasegawa
>
> Erle Stanley Gardner
> *not*   A.A. Fair
> *not*   Charles J. Kenny
>
> Stendhal
> *not*   Alceste
> *not*   Marie-Henri Beyle
> *not*   Louis-Alexandre-César Bombet

22.2C3. No predominant name. If a person using pseudonyms is not known predominantly by one name, choose as the basis for the heading for each item the name appearing in it. Make references to connect the names (see 26.2C and 26.2D).

> John Creasey
>   (*Real name used in some works*)
> Gordon Ashe
> Michael Halliday
> J.J. Marric
> Anthony Morton
> Jeremy York
>   (*Pseudonyms used in some works*)
> *Make explanatory references to and from the various headings*
>   *for Creasey as required*

22.2C4. Different names in editions of the same work. If different names appear in different editions of the same work, or if two or more names of the same person appear in one edition, choose for all editions the name most often used in editions of the work. If that cannot be determined, choose the name appearing in the latest editions of the work. Make name-title references from the other name(s).

> The croaker / John Creasey as Gordon Ashe
> *Use John Creasey as the basis for the heading. Make a name-title*
>   *reference using Gordon Ashe as the basis for the reference*
>
> The edge of terror / by Michael Halliday
>   (*Two editions published, the later under the name Jeremy York.*
>   *Both names are pseudonyms of John Creasey*)

*Use Jeremy York as the basis for the heading. Make name-title
references using Michael Halliday and John Creasey as the bases
for the references*

22.3. CHOICE AMONG DIFFERENT FORMS OF THE SAME NAME

22.3A. Fullness

If the forms of a name vary in fullness, choose the form most commonly found. As required, make references from the other forms.

> J. Barbey d'Aurevilly
> (*Most common form:* J. Barbey d'Aurevilly)
> (*Occasional form:* Jules Barbey d'Aurevilly)
> (*Rare form:* J.-A. Barbey d'Aurevilly)
>
> Morris West
> (*Most common form:* Morris West)
> (*Occasional form:* Morris L. West)
>
> Juan Valera
> (*Most common form:* Juan Valera)
> (*Occasional form:* Juan Valera y Alcalá Galiano)

If no one form predominates, choose the latest form. In case of doubt about which is the latest form, choose the fuller or fullest form.

22.3B. Language

22.3B1. Persons using more than one language. If the name of a person who has used more than one language appears in different language forms in his or her works, choose the form corresponding to the language of most of the works.

> George Mikes
> *not* György Mikes
>
> Philippe Garigue
> *not* Philip Garigue

If, however, one of the languages is Latin or Greek, apply 22.3B2.

In case of doubt, choose the form most commonly found in reference sources of the person's country of residence or activity.

For persons identified by a well-established English form of name, see 22.3B3. If the name chosen is written in a nonroman script, see 22.3C.

22.3B2. Names in vernacular and Greek or Latin forms. If a name occurs in reference sources and/or in the person's works in a Greek or Latin form as well as in a form in the person's vernacular, choose the form most commonly found in reference sources.

> Sixt Birck
> *not* Xystus Betulius

Hugo Grotius
not Hugo de Groot

Philipp Melanchthon
not Philipp Schwarzerd

Friedrich Wilhelm Ritschl
not Fridericus Ritschelius

In case of doubt, choose the Latin or Greek form for persons who were active before, or mostly before, 1400. For persons active after 1400, choose the vernacular form.

Guilelmus Arvernus
not Guillaume d'Auvergne
(*Died 1249*)

Giovanni da Imola
not Joannes de Imola
(*Died 1436*)

22.3B3. Names written in the roman alphabet established in an English form. Choose the English form of name for a person entered under given name, etc. (see 22.8) or for a Roman of classical times (see 22.9) whose name has become well established in an English form in English-language reference sources.

Saint Francis of Assisi
not San Francesco d'Assisi

Pope John XXIII
not Joannes Papa XXIII

Horace
not Quintus Horatius Flaccus

Pliny the Elder
not C. Plinius Secundus

Charles V
not Karl V
not Carlos I

King Philip II
not Rey Felipe II

John Sobieski
not Jan III Sobieski

In case of doubt, use the vernacular or Latin form.

Sainte Thérèse de Lisieux
not Saint Theresa of Lisieux

22.3B4. Other names. In all cases of names found in different language forms and not covered by 22.3B1–22.3B3, choose the form most frequently found in reference sources of the country of the person's residence or activity.

Hildegard Knef
not Hildegarde Neff

22.3C. Names written in a nonroman script[3]

22.3C1. Persons entered under given name, etc. Choose the form of name that has become well established in English-language reference sources for a person entered under given name, etc. (see 22.8) whose name is in a language written in a nonroman script. If variant English language forms are found, choose the form that occurs most frequently. As required, make references from the other forms.

> Alexander the Great
> *not* Alexandros ho Megas
>
> Avicenna
> *not* al-Ḥusayn ibn ʻAbd Allāh ibn Sīnā
>
> Empress Catherine II
> *not* Imperatrit͡sa Ekaterina II
>
> Confucius
> *not* Kʻung-tzu
>
> Homer
> *not* Homeros
> *not* Homerus
>
> Isaiah the Prophet
> *not* Yeshaʻyahu
>
> Maimonides
> *not* Moses ben Maimon
> *not* Mosheh ben Maimon
>
> Theodore Metochites
> *not* Theodōros Metochitēs
>
> Omar Khayyam
> *not* ʻUmar Khayyām
>
> King Paul I
> *not* Vasileus Paulos I

If no English romanization is found, or if no one romanization predominates, romanize the name according to the table for the language adopted by the cataloguing agency.

22.3C2. Persons entered under surname.[4] If the name of a person entered under surname (see 22.5) is written in a nonroman script, romanize the name according to the table for the language adopted by the cataloguing agency. Add vowels to names that are not vocalized. As required, make references from other romanized forms.

---

3. Systematic romanizations used in the examples in this chapter follow the tables (published by the Library of Congress in *Cataloging Service*, bulletin 118–   ) adopted jointly by the American Library Association, the Canadian Library Association, and the Library of Congress.

4. *Alternative rule.* This alternative rule may be applied selectively language by language.
Persons entered under surname. Choose the romanized form of name for a person whose name is in a language written in a nonroman script and who is entered under surname (see 22.5) that has become well established in English-language reference sources. However, in

      Jamāl ʻAbd al-Nāṣir
not Gamal Abdel Nasser

      Mosheh Dayan
not Moshe Dayan

      Evgeniĭ Evtushenko
not Yevgeny Yevtushenko

      Mordekhai Zeʼev Faiʼerberg
not Mordecai Zeev Feierberg

      P.S. Irāmaccantiran̲
not P.S. Ramachandran

      Lin Yü-tʻang
not Lin Yutang

      A.N. Skrîâbin
not A.N. Scriabin

      Yi Sŭng-man
not Syngman Rhee

If the name of a person is found only in a romanized form in his or her works, use it as found.

      Ghaoutsi Bouali
not Ghawthī Abū ʻAlī

If the person's name is found in more than one romanized form in his or her works, choose the form that occurs most frequently.

If a name is written in more than one nonroman script, romanize it according to the table for the language in which most of the works are written. As required, make references from other romanized forms.

---

the case of a person using Hebrew or Yiddish who lives in twentieth-century Palestine or Israel, prefer the romanized form appearing on items issued in Palestine or Israel.

If variant romanized forms are found in English-language reference sources, choose the form that occurs most frequently.

As required, make references from the other romanized forms.

      Lin Yutang
not Lin Yü-tʻang

      Gamal Abdel Nasser
not Jamāl ʻAbd al-Nāṣir

      P.S. Ramachandran
not P.S. Irāmaccantiran̲

      Syngman Rhee
not Yi Sŭng-man

      A.N. Scriabin
not A.N. Skrîâbin

      Yevgeny Yevtushenko
not Evgeniĭ Evtushenko

      Moshe Dayan
not Mosheh Dayan

      Mordecai Zeev Feierberg
not Mordekhai Zeʼev Faiʼerberg

'Alī Muḥammad Irtiẓā
not   'Alī Muḥammad Irtiḍā
     (*Wrote primarily in Persian but also in Arabic*)

Raghunātha Sūri
not   Irakunātasūri
     (*Wrote primarily in Sanskrit but also in Tamil*)

In case of doubt as to which of two or more languages written in the Arabic script should be used for the romanization, base the choice on the nationality of the person or the language of the area of residence or activity. If these criteria do not apply, choose (in this order of preference): Urdu, Arabic, Persian, any other language.

22.3D. Spelling

22.3D1. If variant spellings of a person's name are found and these variations are not the result of different romanizations, choose the form resulting from an official change in orthography, or, if this does not apply, choose the predominant spelling. In case of doubt, choose the spelling found in the first item catalogued. For spelling differences resulting from different romanizations, see 22.3C.

Entry element

22.4. GENERAL RULE

22.4A. If a person's name (chosen according to 22.1–22.3) consists of several parts, select as the entry element that part of the name under which the person would normally be listed in authoritative[5] alphabetic lists in his or her language or country. In applying this general rule, follow the instructions in 22.5–22.9. If, however, a person's preference is known to be different from the normal usage, follow that preference in selecting the entry element.

22.4B. Order of elements

22.4B1. If the entry element is the first element of the name, enter the name in direct order.

     Ram Gopal

22.4B2. If the first element is a surname,[6] follow it by a comma.

     Chiang, Kai-shek
       (*Name:* Chiang Kai-shek)
       (*Surname:* Chiang)

---

5. By "authoritative" alphabetic lists is meant publications of the "who's who" type, not telephone directories or similar compilations.

6. *Surname*, as used in this chapter, includes any name that is used as a family name (except in the case of Romans of classical times, see 22.9).

> **Molnár, Ferenc**
> (*Name:* Molnár Ferenc)
> (*Surname:* Molnár)
>
> **Triṇh, Vân Thanh**
> (*Name:* Triṇh Vân Thanh)
> (*Surname:* Triṇh)

22.4B3. If the entry element is not the first element of the name, transpose the elements of the name preceding the entry element. Follow the entry element by a comma.

> **Cassatt, Mary**
> (*Name:* Mary Cassatt)

22.4B4. If the entry element is the proper name in a title of nobility (see 22.6), follow it by the personal name in direct order and then by the part of the title denoting rank. Precede the personal name and the part of the title denoting rank by commas.

> **Leighton, Frederick Leighton,** *Baron*
>
> **Caradon, Hugh Foot,** *Baron*

22.5. ENTRY UNDER SURNAME

22.5A. General Rule
Enter a name containing a surname under that surname (see also 22.15A) unless subsequent rules (e.g., 22.6, 22.17, 22.28) provide for entry under a different element.

> **Bernhardt, Sarah**
>
> **Fitzgerald, Ella**
>
> **Ching, Francis K.W.**

22.5B. Element other than the first treated as a surname[7]
If the name does not contain a surname but contains an element that identifies the individual and functions as a surname, enter under this element followed by a comma and the rest of the name.

> **Hus, Jan**
>
> **Maḥfūẓ, Ḥusayn ʿAlī**
>
> **al-Bāshā, ʿAbd al-Raḥmān**
>
> **Ali, Muhammad**
> (*The American boxer*)
>
> **Kurd ʿAlī, Muḥammad**

22.5C. Compound surnames

22.5C1. Preliminary rule. The following rules deal with the entry of surnames consisting of two or more proper names (referred to as "compound surnames") and names

---

7. For Islamic names, see 22.22, 22.26C1, and 22.27.

that may or may not contain compound surnames. Apply the rules in the order given. Refer from elements of compound surnames not chosen as the entry element.

22.5C2. Preferred or established form known. Enter a name containing a compound surname under the element by which the person bearing the name prefers to be entered.[8] If this is unknown, enter the name under the element under which it is listed in reference sources[9] in the person's language or country of residence.

> **Fénelon, François de Salignac de La Mothe-**
>
> **Lloyd George, David**
> > (*Paternal surname:* George)
>
> **Machado de Assis, Joaquim Maria**
> > (*Paternal surname:* de Assis)

22.5C3. Hyphenated surnames. If the elements of a compound surname are regularly or occasionally hyphenated, enter under the first element.

> **Day-Lewis, Cecil**
>
> **Enäjärvi-Haavio, Elsa**
>
> **Chaput-Rolland, Solange**
>
> **Henry-Bordeaux, Paule**
>
> **Lykke-Seest, Hans**
>
> **Landová-Štychová, Luisa**

22.5C4. Other compound surnames, except those of married women whose surname consists of a combination of maiden name and husband's surname. Enter under the first element of the compound surname unless the person's language is Portuguese. If the person's language is Portuguese, enter under the last element.

> **Janković Mirijevski, Teodor**
>
> **Friis Møller, Kai**
>
> **Huber Noodt, Ulrich**
>
> **Johnson Smith, Geoffrey**
>
> **Hungry Wolf, Adolf**
>
> **Castres Saint Martin, Gaston**

---

8. Take regular or occasional initializing of an element preceding a surname as an indication that that element is not used as part of the surname.

> **Chavarri, Eduardo López**
> > (*Name sometimes appears as* Eduardo L. Chavarri)
>
> **Szentpál, Mária Sz.**
> > (*Name appears as* Sz. Szentpál Mária)
> > (*Husband's surname:* Szilági)
>
> **Campbell, Julia Morilla de**
> > (*Name sometimes appears as* Julia M. de Campbell)

9. Disregard reference sources that list compound surnames in a uniform style regardless of preference or customary usage.

> **Strauss und Torney, Lulu von**
>
> **Halasy Nagy, József**
>
> **Kőrösi Csoma, Sándor**
>
> **Imbriani Poerio, Matteo Renato**
>
> **Smitt Ingebretsen, Herman**
>
> **Budai Deleanu, Ion**
>
> **Cotarelo y Mori, Emilio**
>
> *but* **Silva, Ovidio Saraiva de Carvalho e**

22.5C5. Other compound surnames. Married women whose surname consists of maiden name and husband's surname. Enter under the first element of the compound surname (regardless of its nature) if the woman's language is Czech, French, Hungarian, Italian, or Spanish. In all other cases, enter under the husband's surname. For hyphenated names, see 22.5C3.

> **Semetkayné Schwanda, Magda**
>
> **Bonacci Brunamonti, Alinda**
>
> **Molina y Vedia de Bastianini, Delfina**
>
> **Figueiredo, Adelpha Silva Rodrigues de**
>
> **Stowe, Harriet Beecher**
>
> **Wang Ma, Hsi-ch'un**

22.5C6. Nature of surname uncertain. If a name has the appearance of a compound surname but its nature is not certain, treat it as a compound surname unless the language of the person is English or one of the Scandinavian languages.

If the person's language is English, enter under the last part of the name and do not refer from the preceding part unless the name has been treated as a compound surname in reference sources.

> **Adams, John Crawford**
>
> **Lee, Joseph Jenkins**

If the person's language is one of the Scandinavian languages, enter under the last part of the name and refer from the preceding part.

> **Mahrt, Haakon Bugge**
> *x* Bugge Mahrt, Haakon
>
> **Olsen, Ib Spang**
> *x* Spang Olsen, Ib

22.5C7. Place names following surnames. If a place name is hyphenated to a person's surname, follow the instructions in 22.5C3.

> **Müller-Breslau, Heinrich**

22.5C8. Words indicating relationship following surnames. Treat the words *Filho, Junior, Neto, Netto,* or *Sobrinho* following Portuguese surnames as part of the surname.

Castro Sobrinho, Antonio Ribeiro de

Marques Junior, Henrique

Omit similar terms (Jr., Sr., etc.) occurring in all other languages unless required to distinguish between two or more identical names (see 22.19B).

22.5D. Surnames with separately written prefixes

22.5D1. Articles and prepositions. If a surname includes an article or preposition or combination of the two, enter under the element most commonly used as entry element in listings in the person's language or country of residence. See the list of languages and language groups below.

If such a name is listed in a nonstandard fashion in reference sources in the person's language or country of residence, enter under the entry element used there.

If a person has used two or more languages, enter the name according to the language of most of that person's works. In case of doubt, follow the rules for English if English is one of the languages. Otherwise, if the person is known to have changed his or her country of residence, follow the rules for the language of the adopted country. As a last resort, follow the rules for the language of the name.

Specific languages and language groups:

AFRIKAANS. Enter under the prefix.

De Villiers, Anna Johanna Dorothea

Du Toit, Stephanus Johannes

Van der Post, Christiaan Willem Hendrik

Von Wielligh, Gideon Retief

CZECH AND SLOVAK. If the surname consists of a place name in the genitive case preceded by *z*, enter under the part following the prefix. Refer from the place name in the nominative case. Omit the *z* from the reference.

Žerotína, Karel z
x Žerotín, Karel

DANISH. See Scandinavian languages.

DUTCH. If the surname is Dutch, enter under the part following the prefix unless the prefix is *ver*. In that case, enter under the prefix.

Aa, Pieter van der

Beeck, Leo op de

Braak, Menno ter

Brink, Jan ten

Driessche, Albert van

Hertog, Ary den

Hoff, Jacobus Henricus van 't

Wijngaert, Frank van den

Winter, Karel de

Ver Boven, Daisy

If the name is not Dutch, enter a Netherlander under the part following the prefix and enter a Belgian according to the rules for the language of the name.

Faille, Jacob Baart de la
(*Netherlander*)

Long, Isaäc le
(*Netherlander*)

Du Jardin, Thomas
(*Belgian*)

ENGLISH. Enter under the prefix.

D'Anvers, Knightley

De Morgan, Augustus

De la Mare, Walter

Du Maurier, Daphne

Le Gallienne, Richard

Van Buren, Martin

Von Braun, Wernher

FLEMISH. See Dutch.

FRENCH. If the prefix consists of an article or of a contraction of an article and a preposition, enter under the prefix.

Le Rouge, Gustave

La Bruyère, René

Du Méril, Édélestand Pontas

Des Granges, Charles-Marc

Otherwise, enter under the part of the name following the preposition.

Aubigné, Théodore Agrippa d'

Musset, Alfred de

La Fontaine, Jean de

GERMAN. If the prefix consists of an article or of a contraction of an article and a preposition, enter under the prefix.

Am Thym, August

Aus'm Weerth, Ernst

Vom Ende, Erich

Zum Busch, Josef Paul

Zur Linde, Otto

Otherwise, enter under the part of the name following the prefix.

>**Goethe, Johann Wolfgang von**
>
>**Mühll, Peter von der**
>
>**Urff, Georg Ludwig von und zu**

Follow the same rule for German names of Dutch origin, but enter names of other foreign origin according to the rules for the language of the name.

>**De Boor, Hans Otto**
>*(Name of Dutch origin with article as prefix)*
>
>**Ten Bruggencate, Paul**
>*(Name of Dutch origin with contraction as prefix)*
>
>**Du Bois-Reymond, Emil**
>
>**Le Fort, Gertrud,** *Freiin von*

ITALIAN. Enter modern names under the prefix.

>**A Prato, Giovanni**
>
>**D'Arienzo, Nicola**
>
>**Da Ponte, Lorenzo**
>
>**De Amicis, Pietro Maria**
>
>**Del Lungo, Isidoro**
>
>**Della Volpaia, Eufrosino**
>
>**Di Costanzo, Angelo**
>
>**Li Greci, Gioacchino**
>
>**Lo Savio, Niccolò**

For medieval and early modern names, consult reference sources about whether a prefix is part of a name. If a preposition is sometimes omitted from the name, enter under the part following the preposition. *De, de', degli, dei,* and *de li* occurring in names of the period are rarely part of the surname.

>**Alberti, Antonio degli**
>
>**Anghiera, Pietro Martire d'**
>
>**Medici, Lorenzo de'**

Do not treat the preposition in an Italian title of nobility used as an entry element (see 22.6A) as a prefix.

NORWEGIAN. See Scandinavian languages.

PORTUGUESE. Enter under the part of the name following the prefix.

>**Fonseca, Martinho Augusto da**
>
>**Santos, João Adolpho dos**

ROMANIAN. Enter under the prefix unless it is *de.* In that case, enter under the part of the name following the prefix.

> **A Mariei, Vasile**
>
> **Puşcariu, Emil de**

SCANDINAVIAN LANGUAGES. Enter under the part of the name following the prefix if the prefix is of Scandinavian or German origin (except for the Dutch *de*). If the prefix is the Dutch *de* or is a prefix of another origin, enter under the prefix.

> **Hallström, Gunnar Johannes af**
>
> **Linné, Carl von**
>
> **De Geer, Gerard,** *friherre*
>
> **De la Gardie, Magnus Gabriel,** *greve*
>
> **La Cour, Jens Lassen**

SLOVAK. See Czech and Slovak.

SPANISH. If the prefix consists of an article only, enter under it.

> **Las Heras, Manuel Antonio**

Enter all other names under the part following the prefix.

> **Figueroa, Francisco de**
>
> **Casas, Bartolomé de las**
>
> **Río, Antonio del**

SWEDISH. See Scandinavian languages.

22.5D2. Other prefixes. If the prefix is not an article, or preposition, or combination of the two, enter under the prefix.

> **'Abd al-Ḥamĭd, Aḥmad**
>
> **A'Beckett, Gilbert Abbott**
>
> **Abū Zahrah, Muḥammad**
>
> **Āl Yāsĭn, Muḥammad Ḥasan**
>
> **Ap Rhys Price, Henry Edward**
>
> **Ben Maÿr, Berl**
>
> **Ó Faoláin, Seán**
>
> **FitzGerald, David**
>
> **MacDonald, William**

22.5E. Prefixes hyphenated or combined with surnames

If the prefix is regularly or occasionally hyphenated or combined with the surname, enter the name under the prefix. As required, refer from the part of the name following the prefix.

> **Tēr-Pōghosian, Petros**
>
> **Debure, Guillaume**
> > *x* Bure, Guillaume de
>
> **Fon-Lampe, A.A.**
> > *x* Lampe, A.A. fon-

22.6. ENTRY UNDER TITLE OF NOBILITY

22.6A. General rule

Enter under the proper name in a title of nobility (including courtesy titles) if the person is commonly known by that title. Apply this rule to those persons who (1) use their titles rather than their surnames in their works or (2) are listed under their titles in reference sources.[10] Follow the proper name in the title by the personal name (excluding unused forenames) in direct order and the term of rank[11] in the vernacular. Omit the surname and term of rank if the person does not use a term of rank or a substitute for it. Refer from the surname (see 26.2A3) unless the proper name in the title is the same as the surname.

> **Byron, George Gordon Byron,** *Baron*
>
> **Macaulay, Thomas Babington Macaulay,** *Baron*
>
> **Nairne, Carolina Nairne,** *Baroness*
>
> **Abrantès, Laure Junot,** *duchesse d'*
>   *x* Junot, Laure, *duchesse d'Abrantès*
>
> **Bolingbroke, Henry St. John,** *Viscount*
>   *x* St. John, Henry, *Viscount Bolingbroke*
>
> **Cavour, Camillo Benso,** *conte di*
>   *x* Benso, Camillo, *conte di Cavour*
>
> **Willoughby de Broke, Richard Greville Verney,** *Baron*
>   *x* Broke, Richard Greville Verney, *Baron Willoughby de*
>   *x* Verney, Richard Greville, *Baron Willoughby de Broke*
>
> **Winchilsea, Anne Finch,** *Countess of*
>   *x* Finch, Anne, *Countess of Winchilsea*
>
> **Monluc, Blaise de**
>   (*Name appears as Blaise de Monluc*)
>   *x* Lasseran Massencome, Blaise de, *seigneur de Monluc*
>
> **Norwich, John Julius**
>   (*Name appears as John Julius Norwich*)
>   *x* Duff Cooper, John Julius. *Viscount Norwich*
>   *x* Cooper, John Julius Duff, *Viscount Norwich*

22.6A1. Some titles in the United Kingdom peerage include a territorial designation that may or may not be an integral part of the title. If the territorial designation is an integral part of the title, include it.

> **Russell of Liverpool, Edward Frederick Langley Russell,** *Baron*

If it is not an integral part of the title, or if there is doubt that it is, omit it.

---

10. Disregard reference sources that list members of the nobility either all under title or all under surname.

11. The terms of rank in the United Kingdom peerage are Duke, Duchess, Marquess (Marquis), Marchioness, Earl, Countess, Viscount, Viscountess, Baron, and Baroness. The oldest son of a British peer often takes the next to highest title of his father during the father's lifetime.

22.6A2. Apply 22.6A to judges of the Scottish Court of Session bearing a law title beginning with the word *Lord*.

> **Kames, Henry Home,** *Lord*
> *x* Home, Henry, *Lord Kames*

22.6A3. If a person acquires a title of nobility, disclaims such a title, or acquires a new title of nobility, follow the instructions in 22.2B in choosing the name to be used as the basis for the heading.

> **Caradon, Hugh Foot,** *Baron*
> (*Previously Sir Hugh Foot*)

> **George-Brown, George Brown,** *Baron*
> (*Previously George Brown*)

> **Grigg, John**
> (*Previously Baron Altrincham; peerage disclaimed*)

> **Hailsham of St. Marylebone, Quintin Hogg,** *Baron*
> (*Originally Quintin Hogg; became Viscount Hailsham, 1950;*
> *peerage disclaimed, 1963; became Baron Hailsham of*
> *St. Marylebone, 1970*)

22.7. ENTRY UNDER ROMANIAN PATRONYMIC

Enter a person whose language is Romanian and whose name contains a patronymic with the suffix *ade* under that patronymic.

> **Heliade Rădulescu, Ioan**

22.8. ENTRY UNDER GIVEN NAME, ETC.[12]

22.8A. Enter a name that does not include a surname and that is borne by a person who is not identified by a title of nobility under the part of name under which the person is listed in reference sources. Include in the name any words or phrases denoting place of origin, domicile, occupation, or other characteristic that are commonly associated with the name in works by the person or in reference sources. Precede such words or phrases by a comma unless the name is Icelandic and the words denote a place (see 22.8C). Refer, as appropriate, from the associated words or phrases, from variant forms of the name, and from other names by which the person is known.

> **John,** *the Baptist*

> **Paulus,** *Diaconus*
> *x* Paulus, *Casinensis*
> *x* Casinensis, *Paulus*
> *x* Paulus, *Levita*
> *x* Levita, Paulus
> *x* Paulus, *Warnefridus*
> *x* Warnefridus, Paulus
> *x* Paul, *the Deacon*

---

12. For Islamic names, see 22.22, 22.26C1, and 22.27.

    x Paolo, *Diacono*

Joseph, *Nez Percé Chief*

Joannes, *Braidensis*
    x Braidensis, Joannes
    x Joannes, *de Brera*
    x Brera, Joannes de

Leonardo, *da Vinci*
    x Vinci, Leonardo da

Alexander, *of Aphrodisias*
    x Aphrodisias, Alexander of
    x Alexander, *Aphrodisiensis*
    x Alexander, *von Aphrodisias*
    x Alexandre, *d'Aphrodise*

Judah, *ha-Levi*
    x Halevi, Judah

Tsoṅ-kha-pa Blo-bzaṅ-grags-pa

22.8B. If a person with such a name is listed in reference sources by a part of the name other than the first, follow the instructions in 22.5B.

    Planudes, Maximus

    Helena, Maria

22.8C. If a name consists of one or more given names and a patronymic, enter it under the first given name, followed by the rest of the name in direct order. If the patronymic precedes the given name(s), as with Mongolian names, transpose the elements to bring the first given name into first position. If in an Icelandic name a phrase naming a place follows the patronymic, treat it as an integral part of the name. Refer from the patronymic. (See also 22.22, 22.26C1, and 22.27.)

    Snæbjörn Jónsson
        (*Given name:* Snæbjörn)
        (*Patronymic:* Jónsson)
        x Jónsson, Snæbjörn

    Steinunn Sigurðardóttir
        (*Given name:* Steinunn)
        (*Patronymic:* Sigurðardóttir)
        x Sigurðardóttir, Steinunn

    Abé Gubānā
        (*Given name:* Abé
        (*Patronymic:* Gubānā)
        x Gubānā, Abé

    Solomon Gebre Christos
        (*Given name:* Solomon)
        (*Patronymic:* Gebre Christos)
        x Gebre Christos, Solomon

Kidāna Māryām Gétāhun
> (*Given names:* Kidāna Māryām)
> (*Patronymic:* Gétāhun)
> *x* Gétāhun, Kidāna Māryām

Gabra 'Iyasus Hāyla Māryām
> (*Given names:* Gabra 'Iyasus)
> (*Patronymic:* Hāyla Māryām)
> *x* Hāyla Māryām, Gabra 'Iyasus

Isaac ben Aaron
> (*Given name:* Isaac)
> (*Patronymic:* ben Aaron)
> *x* Aaron, Isaac ben

Shirèndèv, B.
> (*Name appears as* B. Shirèndèv)
> (*Initial of patronymic:* B.)
> (*Given name:* Shirèndèv)
> *x* B. Shirèndèv

Moses ben Jacob, *of Coucy*
> (*Given name:* Moses)
> (*Patronymic:* ben Jacob)
> (*Words denoting place:* of Coucy)
> *x* Jacob, Moses ben, *of Coucy*
> *x* Jacob, *of Coucy*, Moses ben
> > (*To be made only when warranted in a particular catalogue*)

Bjarni Benediktsson frá Hofteigi
> (*Given name:* Bjarni)
> (*Patronymic:* Benediktsson)
> (*Words denoting place:* frá Hofteigi)
> *x* Benediktsson frá Hofteigi, Bjarni
> *x* Benediktsson, Bjarni
> > (*To be made only when warranted in a particular catalogue*)

22.9. ENTRY OF ROMAN NAMES

Enter a Roman living before 476 A.D. under the part of the name most commonly used as entry element in reference sources.

Lucretius Carus, Titus

Cicero, Marcus Tullius

Columella, Lucius Junius Moderatus

In case of doubt, enter the name in direct order.

Martianus Capella

22.10. ENTRY UNDER INITIALS, LETTERS, OR NUMERALS

Enter a name consisting of initials, or separate letters, or numerals, or consisting primarily of initials, under those initials, letters, or numerals in direct order. Include any typographic devices that follow the letters. Include any words or phrases associated with the initials, letters, or numerals. In the case of initials or letters, make a name-title reference from an inverted form beginning with the last letter for each item catalogued. Make a reference from any phrase associated with the initials as required. In the case of numerals, make a name-title reference from the numbers as words for each item catalogued. (See also 22.16.)

> **H.D.**
> > *x* D., H.
> > > By Avon River
> > *x* D., H.
> > > The flowering of the rod
> > ₍*etc.*₎
>
> **A. de O.**
> > *x* O., A. de
> > > Indiscretions of Dr. Carstairs
>
> **E. B—s**
> > *x* B—s, E.
> > > Lettre sur la Grèce
>
> **B . . . ,** *abbé de*
>
> **D.S.,** *Master*
> > *x* S., D., *Master*
> > *x* Master D.S.
>
> **i.e.,** *Master*
> > *x* e., i., Master
> > *x* Master i.e.
>
> **110908**
> > *x* One Hundred and Ten Thousand, Nine Hundred and Eight
> > > 'Per ardua ad astra'
> > *x* One, one, zero, nine, zero, eight
> > > 'Per ardua ad astra'

For the treatment of persons identified in their works only by predominantly non-alphabetic or nonnumeric characters or signs (e.g., *!*!* or M***), see 21.5C.

22.11. ENTRY UNDER PHRASE

22.11A. Enter in direct order a name that consists of a phrase or other appellation that does not contain a real name (whether used by the person or assigned by scholars, reference works, etc.). As required, refer from variant forms (including other language forms).

> **Dr. X**
> > *x* X, *Dr.*
>
> **Father Time**
>
> **Mr. Fixit**
>
> **Pan Painter**

Sugawara Takasue no Musume

Wu-ming-shih

Master of the Amsterdam Cabinet
    x Meister des Amsterdamer Kabinetts
    x Maître du Cabinet d'Amsterdam

Maître de Moulins
    x Master of Moulins

If, however, such a name has the appearance of a forename, forenames, or initials, and a surname, enter under the pseudosurname. Refer from the name in direct order.

Other, A.N.
    x A.N. Other

If such a name does not convey the idea of a person, add in parentheses a suitable general designation in English.

River (*Writer*)

Taj Mahal (*Musician*)

22.11B. If a phrase consists of a forename with another word or words, enter under the forename. Treat the other word or words as an addition to the name. As required, refer from the name in direct order.

Fannie, *Cousin*
    x Cousin Fannie

Jemima, *Aunt*
    x Aunt Jemima

Marcelle, *Tante*
    x Tante Marcelle

Pierre, *Chef*
    x Chef Pierre

Richard, *Poor*
    x Poor Richard

22.11C. If a phrase by which a person is commonly identified contains the name of another person, enter it in direct order. Make references to link the phrase and the heading for the other person if works by the person identified by the phrase have been ascribed to the other person.

Pseudo-Brutus
    see also **Brutus, Marcus Junius**

Brutus, Marcus Junius
    For the Greek letters erroneously attributed to this person
    see **Pseudo-Brutus**

22.11D. Enter a characterizing word or phrase, or a phrase naming another work by a person, in direct order. Omit an initial article from the heading unless it is required for grammatical reasons. Consider such a word or phrase to be the heading for a person if that person is commonly identified by it in the chief sources of information of his or her works and in reference sources. Refer, when appropriate, from the title of the other work in the form ₁*Title*₁, *Author of.*

Physician
Memoir of Bowman Henry . . . / by a physician

Author of Early impressions
The unveiled heart : a simple story / by the author of Early impressions
x Early impressions, Author of

If a person is commonly identified by a real name or another name (see 22.2A), and a word or phrase characterizing that person or including the title of another work has appeared in the chief sources of information of his or her works, refer from the word or phrase. Refer, when appropriate, from the title of the other work in the form ₁*Title*₁, *Author of.*

Bagnold, Enid
Serena Blandish, or, The difficulty of getting married / by a
lady of quality
x Lady of quality

Sassoon, Siegfried
Memoirs of an infantry officer / by the author of Memoirs of a
fox-hunting man
x Author of Memoirs of a fox-hunting man
x Memoirs of a fox-hunting man, Author of

Additions to names

GENERAL

22.12. TITLES OF NOBILITY AND TERMS OF HONOUR AND ADDRESS, ETC.

22.12A. Add to the name of a nobleman or noblewoman not entered under title (see 22.6) the title of nobility in the vernacular if the title or part of the title or a substitute for the title[13] commonly appears with the name in works by the person or in reference sources.[14] In case of doubt, add the title.

Bismarck, Otto, *Fürst von*

Nagy, Pál, *felsöbüki*

Sévigné, Marie Rabutin-Chantal, *marquise de*

---

13. United Kingdom peers (other than dukes and duchesses) usually use the terms of address *Lord* or *Lady* in place of their titles. For example, George Gordon, Baron Byron, is almost invariably referred to as Lord Byron.

14. Disregard, in this context, reference sources dealing with the nobility.

> **Johan,** *de Middelste, Graaf van Nassau-Siegen*

but

> **Buchan, John**
> (*Title* Baron Tweedsmuir *not used in the majority of his works*)

> **Campbell, Patrick**
> (*Title* Baron Glenavy *not used in his works*)

> **Visconti, Luchino**
> (*Title not used*)

22.12B. British titles of honour

Add the British titles of honour *Sir, Dame, Lord,* and *Lady* if the term commonly appears with the name in works by the person or in reference sources.[15] In case of doubt, add the term of honour.

Add the term at the end of the name if the person is entered under given name or if the person is the wife of a baronet or knight (unless she is also the daughter of a duke, duchess, marquess, marchioness, earl, or countess, see below).

> **Gregory, Augusta,** *Lady*
> (*Wife of a knight*)

Add the term before the forenames if the person is a baronet or knight, a dame of the Order of the British Empire (D.B.E.) or the Royal Victorian Order (D.R.V.O.), a younger son of a duke, duchess, marquess, or marchioness, or a daughter of a duke, duchess, marquess, marchioness, earl, or countess.

> **Hess,** *Dame* **Myra**
> (*D.B.E.*)

> **West,** *Dame* **Rebecca**
> (*D.B.E.; person identified by pseudonym*)

> **Landseer,** *Sir* **Edwin**
> (*Knight*)

> **Beecham,** *Sir* **Thomas**
> (*Baronet*)

> **Gordon,** *Lord* **George**
> (*Younger son of a duke*)

> **Greaves,** *Lady* **Rosamund**
> (*Daughter of a countess*)

> **Stanhope,** *Lady* **Hester**
> (*Daughter of an earl*)

but

> **Ayer, A.J.**
> (*Term of honour* Sir *not used in his works*)

---

15. Disregard, in this context, reference sources dealing with the nobility and gentry.

Christie, Agatha
(*Term of honour* Dame *not used in her works*)

Fraser, Antonia
(*Term of honour* Lady *not used in her works*)

22.13. SAINTS

22.13A. Add the word *Saint* after the name of a Christian saint, unless the person was a pope, emperor, empress, king, or queen, in which case follow 22.17A–22.17B.

Alban, *Saint*

Teresa, *of Avila, Saint*

Francis, *of Assisi, Saint*

John, *Climacus, Saint*

Francis Xavier, *Saint*

More, *Sir Thomas, Saint*

Seton, Elizabeth Ann, *Saint*

Arundel, Philip Howard, *Earl of, Saint*

Chantal, Jeanne-Françoise de, *Saint*
(*Not identified by title* baronne)

22.13B. Add any other suitable word or phrase necessary to distinguish between two saints.

Augustine, *Saint, Archbishop of Canterbury*

Augustine, *Saint, Bishop of Hippo*

22.14. SPIRITS
Add to a heading established for a spirit communication (see 21.26) the word (*Spirit*).

Parker, Theodore (*Spirit*)

Beethoven, Ludwig van (*Spirit*)

Espirito Universal (*Spirit*)

22.15. ADDITIONS TO NAMES ENTERED UNDER SURNAME

22.15A. If the name by which a person is known consists only of a surname, add the word or phrase associated with the name in works by the person or in reference sources. As required, refer from the name in direct order.

Deidier, *abbé*

Moses, *Grandma*
x Grandma Moses

Read, *Miss*
x Miss Read

Seuss, *Dr.*
x Dr. Seuss

If no such word or phrase exists, make additions to surnames alone only when they are needed to distinguish two or more persons with the same name (see 22.19).

22.15B. Terms of address of married women

Add the term of address of a married woman if she is identified only by her husband's name. (For the use of abbreviations, see Appendix B.2.)

> **Ward,** *Mrs.* **Humphry**

Include the enclitic *né* attached to the names of some Hungarian married women.

> **Magyary, Zoltánné**

> **Beniczkyné Bajza, Lenke**

22.15C. Do not add other titles or terms associated with names entered under surname unless they are required to distinguish between two or more persons with the same name and dates are not available (see 22.19).

22.16. ADDITIONS TO NAMES CONSISTING OF OR CONTAINING INITIALS

If part or all of a name is represented by initials and the full form is known, add the spelled out form in parentheses if necessary to distinguish between names that are otherwise identical.

Refer from the full form of the name.

If the initials occur in the inverted part of the name (forenames, etc.) or if the name consists entirely of initials, add the full form of the inverted part or of the whole name at the end of the name.

> **Smith, Russell E. (Russell Edgar)**
> *x* Smith, Russell Edgar

> **Smith, Russell E. (Russell Eugene)**
> *x* Smith, Russell Eugene

> **H.D. (Hilda Doolittle)**
> *x* Doolittle, Hilda

> **Lawrence, D.H. (David Herbert)**
> *x* Lawrence, David Herbert

If the initials occur in the entry element of the name (surnames, etc.), add the full form of the entry element at the end of the name.

> **Rodríguez H., Guadalupe (Rodríguez Hernández)**
> *x* Rodríguez Hernández, Guadalupe

Optionally, make the above additions to other names containing initials.

22.17. ADDITIONS TO NAMES ENTERED UNDER GIVEN NAME, ETC.

22.17A. Royalty

22.17A1. Add a phrase consisting of the title (in English if there is a satisfactory English equivalent) and the name of the state or people governed to the name of a monarch (emperor, empress, king, queen, ruling prince or princess, or other hereditary ruler).

> **Clovis,** *King of the Franks*
>
> **Hirohito,** *Emperor of Japan*
>
> **John,** *King of England*
>
> **Sverre,** *King of Norway*
>
> **Jean,** *Grand-Duke of Luxembourg*

22.17A2. If the name of a ruler has a roman numeral associated with it, add that numeral after the appropriate name (sometimes the first, sometimes the second, name).

> **Alfonso XIII,** *King of Spain*
>
> **Elizabeth II,** *Queen of the United Kingdom*
>
> **Victor Emmanuel II,** *King of Italy*
>
> **Gustaf I Vasa,** *King of Sweden*
>
> **Gustaf II Adolf,** *King of Sweden*
>
> **Gustaf III,** *King of Sweden*
>
> **Nicholas II,** *Emperor of Russia*

22.17A3. Do not add other epithets associated with the name. Refer from the name with the epithet.

> **Louis IX,** *King of France*
>   x Louis, *Saint, King of France*
>
> **Constantine I,** *Emperor of Rome*
>   x Constantine, *Saint*
>
> **Charles,** *Duke of Burgundy*
>   x Charles, *the Bold*
>
> **Frederick II,** *King of Prussia*
>   x Frederick, *the Great*
>
> **Suleiman I,** *Sultan of the Turks*
>   x Suleiman, *the Magnificent*

22.17A4. Add to the name of a consort of a ruler his or her title (in English if there is a satisfactory English equivalent) followed by *consort of* and the name of the ruler in the form prescribed above.

> **Philip,** *Prince, consort of Elizabeth II, Queen of the United Kingdom*
>
> **Nagako,** *Empress, consort of Hirohito, Emperor of Japan*
>
> **Albert,** *Prince Consort of Victoria, Queen of the United Kingdom*
>   (*The word* Consort *was part of the title*)
>
> **Ingrid,** *Queen, consort of Frederick IX, King of Denmark*

> **Alexandra,** *Empress, consort of Nicholas II, Emperor of Russia*
>
> **Margaret,** *Queen, consort of Malcolm III, King of Scotland*
> *not* Margaret, *of Scotland, Saint*

22.17A5. Add to the names of children and grandchildren of rulers the title (in English if there is a satisfactory English equivalent) that they bear.

> **Asahiko,** *Prince of Japan*
>
> **Carlos,** *Prince of Asturias*
>
> **Eulalia,** *Infanta of Spain*

If a child or grandchild of a ruler is known as *Prince* or *Princess* (or their equivalents in other languages) without a territorial designation, add that title (in English if there is a satisfactory English equivalent). Add any other title associated with the name, or if there is no such title, add:

> a) *daughter of, son of, granddaughter of,* or *grandson of*
> *and* b) the name and title of the parent or grandparent.

> **Margaret,** *Princess, Countess of Snowdon*
>
> **Anne,** *Princess, daughter of Elizabeth II, Queen of the United Kingdom*
>
> **Beatrix,** *Princess, daughter of Juliana, Queen of the Netherlands*
>
> **William,** *Prince, grandson of George V, King of the United Kingdom*

22.17A6. If the name by which a royal person is known includes the name of a house, dynasty, etc., or a surname, do not enter under that element (unless it is the first element), but enter the name in direct order.

> **John II Comnenus,** *Emperor of the East*
>
> **Louis Bonaparte,** *King of Holland*
>
> **Chandragupta Maurya,** *Emperor of Northern India*
>
> **Daulat Rao Sindhia,** *Maharaja of Gwalior*
>
> **Ming T'ai-tsu,** *Emperor of China*
>
> **Shuja-ud-daulah,** *Nawab Wazir of Oudh*
>
> **Yi Sejong,** *King of Korea*

22.17A7. Enter the names of members of royal houses no longer reigning or of members of reigning royal houses who have lost or renounced their thrones, and who are no longer identified as royalty, under the part of their name by which they are identified (e.g., surname (see 22.5), name of the house, dynasty, etc., treated as a surname). Add titles that they still possess or use as instructed in 22.12. Refer from the given name followed by the title as instructed in 22.17A1–22.17A5.

> **Bernadotte, Folke**
> *x* Bernadotte af Wisborg, Folke, *greve*
> *x* Folke, *Count Bernadotte of Wisborg*
> *x* Wisborg, Folke Bernadotte, *greve af*

Habsburg, Otto
     x Otto, *Archduke of Austria*

Hohenzollern, Franz Joseph, *Fürst von*
     x Franz Joseph, *Prince of Hohenzollern*

Paris, Henri, *comte de*
     x Henri, *Count of Paris*

Wied, Maximilian, *Prinz von*
     x Maximilian, *Prince of Wied*
     x Neuwied, Maximilian, *Prinz von* Wied-
     x Wied-Neuwied, Maximilian, *Prinz von*

22.17B. Popes

Add to a name identifying a pope the designation *Pope.*

    Pius XII, *Pope*

    Gregory I, *Pope*
not   Gregory, *Saint, Pope Gregory I*
not   Gregory, *the Great, Pope*

Add to a name identifying an antipope the designation *Antipope.*

    Clement VII, *Antipope*

22.17C. Bishops, etc.

If a bishop, cardinal, archbishop, metropolitan, abbot, abbess, or other high eccle-siastical official is identified by a given name, add the title (in English if there is a satisfactory English equivalent). If the person has borne more than one such title, give the one of highest rank.

Use *Archbishop* for archbishops. Use *Bishop* for all bishops other than cardinals. Use *Chorepiscopus* for persons so designated. Use *Cardinal* for cardinal-bishops, cardinal-priests, and cardinal-deacons. Add to the title of a diocesan bishop or archbishop or of a patriarch the name of the latest see, in English if there is an English form.

    Bessarion, *Cardinal*

    Dositheos, *Patriarch of Jerusalem*

    Joannes, *Bishop of Ephesus*

    Platon, *Metropolitan of Moscow*

    John, *Abbot of Ford*

    Arnaldus, *Abbot of Bonneval*

If a name of such a person has a roman numeral associated with it, add it.

    Ruricius I, *Bishop of Limoges*

If the name is of an ecclesiastical prince of the Holy Roman Empire, add *Prince-Bishop, Prince-Archbishop, Archbishop and Elector*, etc., as appropriate, and the name of the see. Add *Cardinal* also if appropriate.

> **Neithard,** *Prince-Bishop of Bamberg*
>
> **Albert,** *of Brandenburg, Archbishop and Elector of Mainz, Cardinal*

22.17D. Other persons of religious vocation

Add the title, term of address, etc., in the vernacular to all other names of persons of religious vocation entered under given name, etc. If there is more than one such term, use the one that is most often associated with the name or is considered to be more important. Use spellings found in English-language dictionaries.

> **Māhavijitāvī,** *Thera*
>
> **Nyana,** *Ledi Sayadaw*
>
> **Tathagata,** *Bhikshu*
>
> **Vivekananda,** *Swami*
>
> **Dhammatinna,** *Ashin*

If such a title, etc., has become an integral part of the name, treat it as such.

> **Kakushin Ni**
> *not* Kakushin, *Ni*
>
> **Podŏk Hwasang**
> *not* Podŏk, *Hwasang*

Add also the initials of a Christian religious order if they are regularly used by the person.

> **Anselm,** *Brother, F.S.C.*
>
> **Anselm,** *Brother, O.F.M.Cap.*
>
> **Angelico,** *fra*
>
> **Claude,** *d'Abbeville, père*
>
> **Cuthbert,** *Father, O.S.F.C.*
>
> **Mary Jeremy,** *Sister, O.P.*
>
> **Mary Loyola,** *Mother*

ADDITIONS TO DISTINGUISH IDENTICAL NAMES

22.18. DATES

Add a person's dates (birth, death, etc.) as the last element of a heading if the heading is otherwise identical to another.

Record the dates in the form given below.

Give dates in terms of the Christian era. Add *B.C.* when appropriate. Give dates from 1582 on in terms of the Gregorian calendar.[16]

---

16. The Gregorian calendar was adopted in France, Italy, Portugal, and Spain in 1582; by the Catholic states of Germany in 1583; by the United Kingdom in 1752; by Sweden in 1753; by Prussia in 1774; and by the Russian Republic in 1918. Convert dates from 1582 on from the Julian calendar to the Gregorian as set out in the following tables.

Smith, John, 1924–	*Living person*
Smith, John, 1900 Jan. 10– **Smith, John,** 1900 Mar. 2–	*Same name, same year of birth*
Smith, John, 1837–1896	*Both years known*
Smith, John, 1836 *or* 7–1896	*Year of birth uncertain as between two consecutive years*
Smith, John, 1837?–1896	*Authorities differ as to year of birth; 1837 probable*
Smith, John, *ca.* 1837–1896	*Year of birth uncertain by several years*
Smith, John, 1837–*ca.* 1896	*Year of death approximate*
Smith, John, *ca.* 1837–*ca.* 1896	*Both years approximate*
Smith, John, *b.* 1825	*Year of death unknown*
Smith, John, *d.* 1859	*Year of birth unknown*
Davies, W.H. (William Henry), 1871–1940	*Years of birth and death known*
Johnson, Carl F., *fl.* 1893-1896 **Joannes,** *Diaconus, fl.* 1226–1240	*Years of birth and death unknown. Some years of activity known. Do not use fl. dates for the twentieth century.*

Table I. The following days in December under the Julian calendar fall in January of the next year under the Gregorian calendar:

YEAR (JULIAN)	DAYS (JULIAN)
1582–1699	Dec. 22–31
1700–1799	Dec. 21–31
1800–1899	Dec. 20–31
1900–1999	Dec. 19–31

Table II. The following days in the "old style" calendar used in the British Isles fall in the next later year under the Gregorian calendar:

BRITISH ISLES (EXCEPT SCOTLAND) AND COLONIES

YEAR (OLD STYLE)	DAYS (OLD STYLE)
1582–1699	Jan. 1–31
	Feb. 1–28 [29]
	Mar. 1–24
	Dec. 22–31
1700–1750	Jan. 1–31
	Feb. 1–28 [29]
	Mar. 1–24
	Dec. 21–31
1751	Dec. 21–31

SCOTLAND

YEAR (OLD STYLE)	DAYS (OLD STYLE)
1582–1599	Jan. 1–31
	Feb. 1–28 [29]
	Mar. 1–24
	Dec. 22–31
1600–1699	Dec. 22–31
1700–1751	Dec. 21–31

Joannes, *Diaconus, 12th cent.*	*Years of birth and death unknown, years of activity unknown, century known. Do not use century dates for the twentieth century.*
Joannes, *Actuarius, 13th/14th cent.*	*Years of birth and death unknown. Particular years of activity unknown, but active in both centuries. Do not use for the twentieth century.*
Lin, Li, *chin shih* 1152	*Date at which a Chinese literary degree was conferred*

Optionally, add the dates to all personal names, even if there is no need to distinguish between headings.

22.19. DISTINGUISHING TERMS

22.19A. Names entered under given name, etc.
If dates are not available to distinguish between two or more identical names entered under given name, etc., devise a suitable brief term and add it in parentheses.

> **Johannes** (*Notary*)
>
> **Thomas** (*Anglo-Norman poet*)

22.19B. Names entered under surname
If dates are not available to distinguish between two or more identical names entered under surname, add a term of address, title of position or office, initials of an academic degree, initials denoting membership in an organization, etc., that appear with the name in works by the person or in reference sources.

> **Brown, George,** *Captain*
>
> **Brown, George,** *F.I.P.S.*
>
> **Brown, George,** *Rev.*
>
> **Valmer,** *capitaine*
>
> **Saur, Karl-Otto**
>
> **Saur, Karl-Otto,** *Jr.*

Do not use such a term if dates are available for one person and it seems likely that dates will eventually be available for the other(s).

> **Mudge, Lewis Seymour,** 1868–1945
>
> **Mudge, Lewis Seymour**
> (*Name appears as* Lewis Seymour Mudge, Jr.)

22.20. UNDIFFERENTIATED NAMES
If neither dates nor distinguishing terms are available, use the same heading for all persons with the same name.

Müller, Heinrich

80 Fotos und eine kurze Einführung in die Lage, Geschichte, und Sehenswürdigkeiten der Stadt Giessen . . .

Müller, Heinrich

Der Diebstahl im Urheberrecht . . .

Müller, Heinrich

Die Fussballregeln und ihre richtige Auslegung . . .

Müller, Heinrich

Historische Waffen . . .

Müller, Heinrich

Die Repser Burg . . .

Special rules for names in certain languages

22.21. INTRODUCTORY RULE

The preceding rules in this chapter give general guidance for personal names not written in the roman alphabet and for names in a non-European language written in the roman alphabet. For more detailed treatment of names in certain of these languages, follow the special rules given below. For more detailed treatment of names in other languages, see the IFLA International Office for UBC's survey of personal names.[17]

22.22. NAMES IN THE ARABIC ALPHABET[18]

17. *Names of Persons : National Usages for Entry in Catalogues* / compiled by the IFLA International Office for UBC. — 3rd ed. — London : The Office, 1977.

18. Major reference sources for names written in the Arabic alphabet and their treatment (note that romanization practices in these sources differ):

Babinger, Franz. *Die Geschichtsschreiber der Osmanen und ihre Werke* / von Franz Babinger ; mit einem Anhang, Osmanische Zeitrechnungen von Joachim Mayr. — Leipzig : Harrassowitz, 1927.

Brockelmann, Carl. *Geschichte der arabischen Litteratur* / von Carl Brockelmann. — 2. den Supplementbänden angepasste Aufl. — Leiden : Brill, 1943–1949.
    1.–3. Supplementband. — Leiden : Brill, 1937–1942.

Caetani, Leone. *Onomasticon Arabicum* . . . / compilato per cura di Leone Caetani e Giuseppe Gabrieli. — Roma : Casa editrice italiana, 1915.

The Encyclopaedia of Islām . . . / prepared by a number of leading orientalists ; edited by M. Th. Houtsma . . . ₍et al.₎. — Leyden : Brill, 1913–1934.
    Supplement. — Leiden : Brill, 1938.

The Encyclopaedia of Islam / prepared by a number of leading orientalists. — New ed. / edited by an editorial committee consisting of H.A.R. Gibb . . . ₍et al.₎. — Leiden : Brill, 1960–

İslâm ansiklopedisi : İslâm âlemi coğrafya, etnoğrafya ve biyografya lûgati / Beynelmilel Akademiler Birliğinin yardımı ve tanınmış müsteşriklerin iştiraki ile neşredenler M. Th. Houtsma . . . ₍et al.₎. — İstanbul : Maarif Matbaası, 1940–

Philologiae Turcicae Fundamenta . . . / una cum praestantibus Turcologis ediderunt Jean Deny . . . ₍et al.₎. — Aquis Mattiacis : Steiner, 1959–

Sezgin, Fuat. *Geschichte des arabischen Schrifttums* / von Fuat Sezgin. — Leiden : Brill, 1967–

Storey, Charles Ambrose. *Persian Literature : a Bio-bibliographical Survey* / by C. A. Storey. — London : Luzac, 1927–

22.22A. Preliminary note

The rule that follows applies only to names (regardless of their origin) originally written in the Arabic alphabet that do not contain a surname or a name performing the function of a surname. In case of doubt, assume that a name of a person active in the twentieth century includes a surname (see 22.5) and that other names do not.

22.22B. Entry element

Enter a name made up of a number of elements under the element or combination of elements by which the person is best known. Determine this from reference sources. When there is insufficient evidence available, enter under the first element. Refer from any part of the name not used as entry element if there is reason to believe that the person's name may be sought under that part. Refer as necessary from variant romanizations (see 22.3C).

22.22C. Essential elements

If the entry element is not the given name (*ism*) or a patronymic derived from the name of the father (a name usually following the given name and compounded with *ibn*), include these names unless they are not customarily used in the name by which the person is known. Include an additional name, descriptive epithet, or title of honour that is treated as part of the name if it aids in identifying the individual. Generally omit other elements of the name, particularly patronymics derived from anyone other than the father.

22.22D. Order of elements

When the elements of the name have been determined, place the best-known element or combination of elements first. Give the other elements in the following order: *khiṭāb*, *kunyah*, *ism*, patronymic, any other name. Insert a comma after the entry element unless it is the first part of the name.

KHIṬĀB (honorific compound of which the last part is typically *al-Din*)

> **Rashīd al-Dīn Ṭabīb**

> **Ṣadr al-Dīn al-Qūnawī, Muḥammad ibn Isḥāq**
> > *x* Muḥammad ibn Isḥāq al-Qūnawī, Ṣadr al-Dīn
> > *x* al-Qūnawī, Ṣadr al-Dīn Muḥammad ibn Isḥāq

KUNYAH (typically a compound with *Abū* as the first word)

> **Abū al-Barakāt Hibat Allāh ibn ʿAlī**
> > *x* Hibat Allāh ibn ʿAlī, Abū al-Barakāt

> **Abū Ḥayyān al-Tawḥīdī, ʿAlī ibn Muḥammad**
> > *x* al-Tawḥīdī, Abū Ḥayyān ʿAlī ibn Muḥammad
> > *x* ʿAlī ibn Muḥammad, Abū Ḥayyān al-Tawḥīdī

> **Abū Hurayrah**

ISM (given name)

> **ʿAlī ibn Abī Ṭalib,** *Caliph*

> **Bashshār ibn Burd**

> **Mālik ibn Anas**

Nashwān ibn Sa'īd al-Ḥimyarī
  x al-Ḥimyarī, Nashwān ibn Sa'īd

Ṭāhā Ḥusayn
  x Ḥusayn, Ṭāhā

Muḥammad Ismā'īl Pānipātī
  x Pānipātī, Muḥammad Ismā'īl

Ghulām Ḥasan Khūyihāmī
  x Khūyihāmī, Ghulām Ḥasan

Nādirah Kẖātūn
  x Kẖātūn, Nādirah

PATRONYMIC (typically a compound with *Ibn* as the first word)

Ibn Hishām, 'Abd al-Malik
  x 'Abd al-Mālik ibn Hishām

Ibn Ḥazm, 'Alī ibn Aḥmad
  x 'Alī ibn Aḥmad ibn Ḥazm

Ibn Sanā' al-Mulk, Hibat Allāh ibn Ja'far
  x Hibat Allāh ibn Ja'far ibn Sanā' al-Mulk

Ibn al-Mu'tazz, 'Abd Allāh
  x 'Abd Allāh ibn al-Mu'tazz

Ibn al-Muqaffa', 'Abd Allāh
  x 'Abd Allāh ibn al-Muqaffa'

OTHER NAMES

Laqab (descriptive epithet)

al-Jāḥiẓ, 'Amr ibn Baḥr
  x 'Amr ibn Baḥr al-Jāḥiẓ

Abū Shāmah, 'Abd al-Raḥmān ibn Ismā'īl
  x 'Abd al-Raḥmān ibn Ismā'īl Abū Shāmah

al-Kātib al-Iṣfahānī, 'Imād al-Dīn Muḥammad ibn Muḥammad
  x Muḥammad ibn Muḥammad al-Kātib al-Iṣfahānī, 'Imād al-Dīn
  x al-Iṣfahānī, 'Imād al-Dīn Muḥammad ibn Muḥammad al-Kātib

al-Qāḍī al-Fāḍil, 'Abd al-Raḥīm ibn 'Alī
  x 'Abd al-Raḥīm ibn 'Alī al-Qāḍī al-Fāḍil

Mirzā Khān Anṣārī
  x Anṣārī, Mirzā Khān

Nisbah (proper adjective ending in *ī*, indicating origin, residence, or other circumstances)

al-Bukhārī, Muḥammad ibn Ismā'īl
  x Muḥammad ibn Ismā'īl al-Bukhārī

Māzandarānī, 'Abd Allāh ibn Muḥammad
  x 'Abd Allāh ibn Muḥammad Māzandarānī

> **'Abbāsī, 'Alī Aḥmad**
> *x* 'Alī Aḥmad 'Abbāsī

> **Hilālī, Muḥammad Khān Mīr**
> *x* Muḥammad Khān Mīr Hilālī

Takhalluṣ (pen name)

> **Qā'ānī, Ḥabīb Allāh Shīrāzī**
> *x* Ḥabīb Allāh Shīrāzī Qā'ānī

> **'Ibrat, Ẓafar Ḥasan**
> *x* Ẓafar Ḥasan 'Ibrat

22.23. BURMESE AND KAREN NAMES

22.23A. Enter a Burmese or Karen name that includes a Western given name preceding the vernacular names under the vernacular names. Transpose the Western name to the end.

> **Hla Gyaw, James**
> (*Name:* James Hla Gyaw)

22.23B. Add the term of address that usually accompanies Burmese and Karen names. Add, also, any other distinguishing terms generally associated with the name. If the name of the same person is found with different terms of address, use the term of highest honour. Distinguish terms of address from the same words used as names.

> **Ba U,** *U*

> **Chit Maung,** *Saw*

> **Mya Sein,** *Daw*

> **Saw,** *U*

> **U Shan Maung,** *Maung*

> **Kaing, Katie,** *Naw*

> **Hla,** *U, Ludu*

> **Ba Yin,** *U, Hanthawaddy*

22.24. CHINESE NAMES CONTAINING A NON-CHINESE GIVEN NAME

If a name of Chinese origin contains a non-Chinese given name and the name is found in the order ₍non-Chinese given name₎ ₍Surname₎ ₍Chinese given names₎, enter the name as ₍Surname₎, ₍non-Chinese given name₎ ₍Chinese given names₎. Give all other names as instructed in 22.5.

> **Loh, Philip Fook Seng**
> (*Name appears as* Philip Loh Fook Seng)

22.25. INDIC NAMES

22.25A. Early names

Enter an Indic name borne by a person who flourished before the middle of the nineteenth century under the first word of the personal element name, ignoring honorifics and religious terms of address that may precede it (*Sri, Shri, Swami, Acharya, Muni, Bhikkhu,* etc.). For such terms as integral parts of names, see below. Do not include the enclitic *-ji* (or *-jee*) sometimes added to the personal element of the name.

Kālidāsa

Pāṇini

Īśvara Kaula

Narmadashankar Lalshankar

Enter the name of an ancient or medieval Sanskrit author or an author (usually, Jain) of a Prakrit text under the Sanskrit form of the name. Refer from any significantly different form.

Āryabhaṭa
> *x* Ārya Bhaṭa

Aśvaghoṣa
> *x* Assaghoṣa
> *x* Ashwa Ghoshu
> *x* Açvaghosha

Bhaṭṭojī Dīkṣita

Karṇapūra

Include a title (*Shri (Sri), Swami, Sastri, Acharya, Bhatta, Saraswati, Muni, Gani,* etc.) as an integral part of the name if it appears with the name in reference sources.

Narain Swami

Śaṅkarācārya

Śrīharṣa

Śrīdharasvāmin

but **Rāmānuja**
> (*Sometimes called:* Rāmānujācārya)

Enter the name of a Buddhist author of a Pali text under the Pali form of the name. Refer from any significantly different form.

Dhammakitti
> *x* Dharmakīrti

Ñāṇamoli, *Bhikkhu*

22.25B. Modern names

With the exceptions specified in 22.25B1–22.25B2 enter an Indic name of a person flourishing after the middle of the nineteenth century under the surname or the name that the person is known to have used as a surname. If there is no surname, enter under the last name.

Dutt, Romesh Chunder

Krishna Menon, V.K.

Singh, Indrajit
> (*For Sikh names ending in* Singh, *see 22.25B2*)

> Das Gupta, Hemendra Nath
>
> Shastri,[19] Lal Bahadur

22.25B1. Kannada, Malayalam, Tamil, and Telugu names. If a name in one of these languages does not contain a surname or a name known to have been used by the person who bears the name as a surname, enter under the given name. Given names in these languages are normally preceded by a place name and occasionally by the father's given name and may be followed by a caste name.

> **Kiruṣṇa Ayyaṅkār, Ṭiṭṭai**
>   (*Given name:* Kiruṣṇa
>   (*Caste name:* Ayyaṅkār)
>   (*Place name:* Ṭiṭṭai)
>
> **Sankaran Nair, C.,** *Sir*
>   (*Given name:* Sankaran)
>   (*Caste name:* Nair)
>   (*House name:* C. (Chettur))
>
> **Jōsaph, O.P.**
>   (*Given name:* Jōsaph)
>   (*Initials of place name and of father's given name:* O.P. (Oorakath Paul))
>
> **Radhakrishnan, S.**
>   (*Given name:* Radhakrishnan)
>   (*Initial of place name:* S. (Sarvepalli))

22.25B2. Sikh names. Enter a Sikh name of a person who does not use *Singh* or *Kaur* as a surname under the first of his or her names (the given name).

> **Amrit Kaur**
>
> **Mehtab Singh**

22.25B3. Religious names. Enter a modern person of religious vocation (whether Hindu, Buddhist, or Jain) under the religious name. Add the religious title.

> **Chinmayananda,** *Swami*
>
> **Ramana,** *Maharshi*
>
> **Punyavijaya,** *Muni*
>
> **Sangharakshita,** *Bhikshu*

22.26. INDONESIAN NAMES

---

19. The term *Sastri* (*Shastri*) is sometimes used as a surname, sometimes as a religious title, sometimes as an appendage to a personal name, and sometimes as a reinforcement to another surname.

22.26A. Scope

The following rules apply to names of Arabic, Chinese, Dutch, Indic, Javanese, Sumatran, Malayan, or other origin.

22.26B. Entry element

With the exceptions specified in 22.26C–22.26F enter an Indonesian name consisting of more than one element under the last element of the name. Refer from the name in direct order unless the first element is a European name.

> **Hatta, Mohammad**
> (*Compound given name*)
> *x* Mohammad Hatta

> **Djajadiningrat, Idrus Nasir**
> (*Given name plus surname*)
> *x* Idrus Nasir Djajadiningrat

> **Purbatjaraka, Purnadi**
> (*Given name plus father's name*)
> *x* Purnadi Purbatjaraka

> **Nasution, Amir Hamzah**
> (*Given name plus clan name*)
> *x* Amir Hamzah Nasution

> **Ginarsa, Ktut**
> (*Balinese name containing an element indicating seniority of children*)
> *x* Ktut Ginarsa

> **Djelantik, I Gusti Ketut**
> (*Balinese name*)
> *x* I Gusti Ketut Djelantik
> *x* Gusti Ketut Djelantik, I
> *x* Ketut Djelantik, I Gusti

> **Sani, Sitti Nuraini**
> (*Married woman's name; last element may be the husband's or the father's name*)
> *x* Sitti Nuraini Sani

> **E., Djakaria N.**
> *x* Djakaria N.E.

22.26C. Names entered under the first element

Enter the following categories of names under the first element of the name. Refer from the last element. If that element is an initial, refer also from the next to the last element.

22.26C1. Names consisting of a given name followed by an element denoting filial relationship, e.g., *bin, binti, ibni,* plus the father's name.

> **Abdullah bin Nuh**
> *x* Nuh, Abdullah bin

S. bin Umar

    x Umar, S. bin

22.26C2. Names that may be written as one word or as separate words and that begin with one of the following elements: *Adi, Budi, Djoko, Karta, Kusuma, Mangku, Noto, Prawira, Pura, Sastra, Sri, Suma, Suria,* and *Tri.* If the name of a particular person sometimes appears as one word and sometimes as separate words, use the one-word form.

Adi Waskito

    x Waskito, Adi

Adisendjaja

Sri Muljono

    x Muljono, Sri

22.26D. Names consisting of given name(s) plus adat title

Enter names that include the terms *gelar* (sometimes abbreviated as *gl.* or *glr.*) *Daeng, Datuk,* and *Sutan* under the element introduced by such words. Refer from the name in direct order.

Palindih, Rustam Sutan

    x Rustam Sutan Palindih

Batuah, Ahmad gelar Datuk

    x Ahmad gelar Datuk Batuah

Radjo Endah, Sjamsuddin Sutan

    x Sjamsuddin Sutan Radjo Endah

    x Endah, Sjamsuddin Sutan Radjo

22.26E. Names containing place names

Enter names consisting of personal names followed by a place name under the element preceding the place name. Treat the place name as an integral part of the name.

Abdullah Udjong Buloh

Daud Beureuh, Muhammad

22.26F. Names of Chinese origin

Enter names of Chinese origin that follow the normal Chinese order (surname first) under the first element of the name. Refer from the last element of the name.

Lim, Yauw Tjin

    (*Name appears as* Lim Yauw Tjin)

    x Tjin, Lim Yauw

Oei, Tjong Bo

    (*Name appears as* Oei Tjong Bo)

    x Bo, Oei Tjong

22.26G. Titles[20]

Add titles and honorific words to Indonesian names as instructed in 22.12A. Refer from the direct form of title plus name.

> **Purbatjaraka,** *Raden Mas Ngabei*
> > *x* Raden Mas Ngabei Purbatjaraka

Refer from the direct form of title plus name even when the title is not used in the heading.

> **Amrullah, Abdul Malik Karim**
> > *x* Hadji Abdul Malik Karim Amrullah
> > *x* Abdul Malik Karim Amrullah

Distingush titles used as such from the same words adopted by a person as elements of his or her name. When in doubt, treat the words as a title.

> **Rusli, Marah**
> > (*Title* Marah *used as a personal name*)
> > *x* Marah Rusli

---

20. The following list of Indonesian titles and honorific words is incomplete as only some of the more commonly used titles are listed. A few variant spellings are also noted.

adipati
anak agung (or
  agoeng) gde
anak agung (or
  agoeng) istri
andi
aria (arja, arya, arjo,
  aryo, ardjueh, arjueh)
datuk (datoek, dato,
  datok)
desak
dewa gde (or gede)
gusti (goesti)
gusti aju (gusti ayu,
  goesti ajoe)
gusti gde (goesti
  gede)
hadji (haji)

ide (ida)
ide aju (ide ayu, ide ajoe)
ide bagus (ide bagoes)
imam
marah
mas
ngabei (ngabehi,
  ngabeui)
nganten
pangeran
pedanda
raden
raden adjeng (or ajeng)
raden aju (or ayu)
raden aria (or arya)
raden mas
raden nganten

raden pandji (or panji)
raden roro
radja (raja)
ratu (ratoe, ratoh)
sidi
siti
sultan (soeltan)
susuhunan (soesoehoenan)
sutan (soetan)
tengku (tungku, teuku,
  teungku)
tjokorde (cokorde)
tjokorde (or cokorde) gde
tjokorde (or cokorde) istri
tubagus (toebagoes)
tumenggung
  (toemenggoeng)
tunku (toenkoe)

The word *gelar*, meaning "titled," often precedes Indonesian titles. The following terms of address are not to be used in headings:

> bung (boeng)—brother, when used as a term of respect
> empu (mpu)—mister
> engku (ungku)—mister
> entjik (encik che, entje, inche, tje)—mister or mistress
> ibu (boe, bu, iboe)—mother, when used as a term of respect
> njonja (yonya)—mistress
> nona—miss
> pak (pa')—father, when used as a term of respect
> tuan (toean)—mister
> wan—mister

22.27. MALAY NAMES

22.27A. Scope
The following rule applies to Malay names, including names of Arabic origin beginning with the element *al-*, borne by persons living in Malaysia, Singapore, or Brunei. Names from other ethnic groups, e.g., Ibans, Kedazans, Indians, Chinese, borne by persons living in these countries are excluded.

22.27B. General rule
Enter a Malay name under the first element of the name and refer from the last element unless it is known that the bearer of the name treats another element of the name as a surname. In that case, enter under the surname and refer from the first element.

> **A. Samad Said**
> *x* Said, A. Samad

> **Rejab F.I.**
> *x* I., Rejab F.

> **Shahnon Ahmad**
> *x* Ahmad, Shahnon

> *but* **Merican, Faridah**
> (*Surname:* Merican)
> *x* Faridah Merican

22.27C. Filial indicators
Omit words or abbreviations denoting filial relationship[21] unless consistently used by the person.

> **Adibah Amin**
> (*Sometimes found as:* Khalidah Adibah binti Haji Amin)

> *but*

> **Abdullah Sanusi bin Ahmad**

> **Siti Normin bte. Ahmad**

22.27C1. If the filial relationship is shown beyond one generation, include only the first unless more are required to distinguish between names that are otherwise identical.

> **Ali bin Ahmad**
> (*Name appears as* Ali bin Ahmad bin Hussein)
> *x* Ahmad, Ali bin
> *x* Ali bin Ahmad bin Hussein
> *x* Hussein, Ali bin Ahmad bin

---

21. Words denoting filial relationship are:
 bin (b.)—son of
 binte (bte.)—daughter of
 binti (bt.)—daughter of
 ibni—son of (royalty).

22.27D. Titles

Add after the name titles of honour, rank, or position that are commonly associated with the name. Refer from the direct form of title plus name.

>**Abdul Majid bin Zainuddin,** *Haji*
>>*x* Haji Abdul Majid bin Zainuddin
>>*x* Zainuddin, Haji Abdul Majid bin

>**Hamzah Sendut,** *Tan Sri Datuk*
>>*x* Tan Sri Datuk Hamzah Sendut
>>*x* Sendut, Tan Sri Datuk Hamzah

Omit titles appearing in the father's name.

>**Iskandar bin Muhammad Zahid,** *Raja*
>>(*Name appears as* Raja Iskandar bin Raja Muhammad Zahid)
>>*x* Raja Iskandar bin Raja Muhammad Zahid
>>*x* Zahid, Raja Iskandar bin Raja Muhammad

22.28. THAI NAMES

22.28A. General rule

Enter a Thai name under the first element. Refer from the last element, which is normally a surname.[22] Omit a term of address (e.g., *Khun, Nāi, Nāng, Nāngsāo*) unless it is a title of nobility. In case of doubt, include it.

>**Dhanit Yupho**
>>*x* Yupho, Dhanit

>**Prayut Sitthiphan**
>>*x* Sitthiphan, Prayut

>**S. Bannakit**
>>*x* Bannakit, S.

>**Maenmas Chavalit**
>>(*Married woman*)
>>*x* Chavalit, Maenmas

22.28B. Royalty

22.28B1. Add titles to the names of kings and queens of Thailand (and of consorts of kings and queens) as instructed in 22.17A.

>**Bhumibol Adulyadej,** *King of Thailand*

>**Chulalongkorn,** *King of Siam*

>**Saowaphā,** *Queen, consort of Chulalongkorn, King of Siam*

>**Thapthim,** *Čhaočhǫmmāndā, consort of Chulalongkorn, King of Siam*

22.28B2. Enter the name of a person of royal descent under the first element of the name, or latest name, that he or she uses. Add the term *Prince* or *Princess* for those

---

22. Surnames became a legal requirement for most persons in 1915.

of the ranks *Čhaofā* and *Phraʻong Čhao*. Use the initials *M.C.*, *M.R.*, and *M.L.* for *Mǫm Čhao*, *Mǫm Rātchawong*, and *Mǫm Lūang*, respectively. If the person also bears a *krom* rank, do not add it. Refer from any earlier names, together with associated ranks and titles, borne by the person.

> **Damrong Rajanubhab,** *Prince*
> > *x* Rajanubhab, Damrong, *Prince*
> > *x* Ditsawǫnkumān, *Prince*
> > *x* Damrongrāchānuphāp, *Prince*

> **Seni Pramoj,** *M.R.*
> > *x* Pramoj, Seni, *M.R.*
> > *x* Prāmōt, Sēnī, *M.R.*

22.28C. Nobility (*Khunnāng*)

22.28C1. Enter a name consisting of a title of nobility under that title in the vernacular (*rātchathinanām*). If a person has more than one title, enter under the latest. Add the given name, when ascertainable, in parentheses. Add the vernacular rank (*yot bandāsak*) associated with the title. Refer from the given name, from the surname, and from any earlier titles borne by the person.

> **Prachākitkǫrachak (Chæm),** *Phrayā*
> > *x* Chæm Bunnāk
> > *x* Bunnāk, Chæm

> **Prachákitkǫrachak (Chup),** *Phrayā*
> > *x* Chup ʻŌsathānon
> > *x* ʻŌsathānon, Chup

> **Thammasakmontrī (Sanan),** *Čhaophrayā*
> > *x* Sanan Thēphatsadin Na ʻAyutthayā
> > *x* Phaisānsinlapasāt (Sanan), *Phrayā*

22.28C2. Enter the name of the wife of a man bearing a title of nobility under her own name, followed by the husband's title and the wife's conferred rank, if any.

> **Sangīam Phrasadetsurēntharāthibǫdī,** *Thānphūying*

22.28D. Buddhist monastics, ecclesiastics, and patriarchs

22.28D1. Monastics. Enter the name of a Buddhist monastic under the Pali name in religion unless the monastic is better known under the given name. Add the monastic title *Phikkhu* to a Pali name in religion. If the monastic is better known under the given name, enter under the given name and add the rank (*samanasak*) *Phra Mahā* or *Phra Khrū*. In the latter case, refer from the Pali name in religion if known.

> **Thammasārō,** *Phikkhu*

> **Khīeo,** *Phra Mahā*
> > *x* Thammathinnō, *Phikkhu*

22.28D2. Ecclesiastics. Enter the name of a Buddhist ecclesiastic under the latest title. Add the given name in parentheses. Add also any word indicating rank. Refer from the distinctive word in the title, from the given name, and from the surname.

>**Phra Thamthatsanāchǫn (Thǫngsuk)**
>
>>*x* Thamthatsanāchǫn (Thǫngsuk), *Phra*
>>
>>*x* Thǫngsuk Sutsasǒ
>>
>>*x* Sutsasǒ, Thǫngsuk
>>
>>*x* Thǫngsuk Čhantharakhachǫn
>>
>>*x* Čhantharakhachǫn, Thǫngsuk
>>
>>*x* Sutsasa, *Thēra*

22.28D3. Supreme patriarchs. Enter the name of a supreme patriarch who is a commoner under the given name. Add *Supreme Patriarch* to the name. Refer from the surname and from any earlier names or titles by which the person is identified.

>**Plot,** *Supreme Patriarch*
>
>>*x* Phra Wannarat (Plot), *Somdet*
>>
>>*x* Phra Phrommunī (Plot)
>>
>>*x* Phra 'Ariyawongsākhatayān (Plot), *Somdet*
>>
>>*x* Plot Kittisǒphon
>>
>>*x* Kittisǒphon, Plot
>>
>>*x* Kittisǒphanǒ, *Mahāthēra*
>>
>>*x* Wannarat (Plot), *Somdet Phra*
>>
>>*x* Phrommunī (Plot), *Phra*
>>
>>*x* 'Ariyawongsākhatayān (Plot), *Somdet Phra*

Enter the name of a supreme patriarch of royal descent under the conferred name. Add the secular and ecclesiastical titles in that order. Refer from any earlier names or titles by which the person is identified.

>**Wachirayānwong,** *Prince, Supreme Patriarch*
>
>>*x* Chū'n Nopphawong, *M.R.*
>>
>>*x* Nopphawong, Chū'n, *M.R.*
>>
>>*x* Phra Sukhunkhanāphǫn (Chū'n, *M.R.*)
>>
>>*x* Phra Yānwarāphǫn (Chū'n, *M.R.*)
>>
>>*x* Sukhunkhanāphǫn (Chū'n, *M.R.*), *Phra*
>>
>>*x* Yānwarāphǫn (Chū'n, *M.R.*), *Phra*

CHAPTER 23

GEOGRAPHIC NAMES

Contents

23.1. INTRODUCTORY NOTE

The names of geographic entities (referred to throughout this chapter as "places") are used to distinguish between corporate bodies with the same name (see 24.4C);

as additions to other corporate names (e.g., conference names (see 24.7B4)); and, commonly, as headings for governments (see 24.3E).

23.2. GENERAL RULES

23.2A. English form

Use the English form of the name of a place if there is one in general use. Determine this from gazetteers and other reference sources published in English-speaking countries. In case of doubt, use the vernacular form (see 23.2B).

Austria
not Österreich

Copenhagen
not København

Florence
not Firenze

Ghent
not Gent
not Gand

Sweden
not Sverige

If the English form of the name of a place is the English name of the government that has jurisdiction over the place, use that form.

Union of Soviet Socialist Republics
not Soîuz Sovetskikh Sotsialisticheskikh Respublik
not Russia

23.2B. Vernacular form

23.2B1. Use the form in the official language of the country if there is no English form in general use.

Buenos Aires

Gorlovka

Tallinn

Livorno
not Leghorn
   (*English form no longer in general use*)

23.2B2. If the country has more than one official language, use the form most commonly found in English-language sources.

Louvain
not Leuven

Helsinki
not Helsingfors

23.3. CHANGES OF NAME

If the name of a place changes, use as many of the names as are required by:

    a) the rules on government names (24.3E)

        e.g., *use* Nyasaland *or* Malawi, *as appropriate*

or b) the rules on additions to corporate names (24.4C6) and conference names (24.7B4)

        e.g., *use* Léopoldville *or* Kinshasa, *as appropriate*

or c) other relevant rules in chapter 24.

23.4. ADDITIONS TO PLACE NAMES

23.4A. Punctuation

Make all additions to place names used as entry elements (see 24.3E) in parentheses.

> **Budapest** (*Hungary*)[1]

If the place name is being used as an addition, precede the name of a larger place by a comma.

> **Magyar Nemzeti Galeria** (*Budapest, Hungary*)[1]

23.4B. General rule

If it is necessary to distinguish between two or more places of the same name (including place names that are the same when romanized), add to each name the name of a larger place as instructed in 23.4C–23.4J. For instructions on abbreviating place names used as additions, see Appendix B.14.

Optionally, apply rules 23.4C–23.4J even if there is no need to distinguish between places.

Optionally, if the name of a state, province, or territory of Australia, Canada, or the United States; of a British county; of a constituent state of Malaysia, the U.S.S.R., or Yugoslavia; or of an island is being used as an addition (see 23.4C–23.4F), do not add to it the name of a larger geographic area.

> **Augusta** (*Ga.*)

23.4C. Places in Australia, Canada, or the United States[2]

If a place is in a state, province, or territory in Australia, Canada, or the United States, add the name of the state, province, or territory in which it is located. For places located in cities, see 23.4G.

> **Adams County** (*Ill.*)
>
> **Alexandria** (*Va.*)
>
> **Darwin** (*N.T.*)
>
> **Hull** (*Québec*)
>
> **Iowa City** (*Iowa*)
>
> **Kansas City** (*Mo.*)

---

1. This example is included solely to show the punctuation patterns. For the construction of the heading, see rules later in this chapter and chapter 24.

2. The examples in rules 23.4C–23.4J show, for purposes of illustration only, additions possible under either 23.4B general rule or 23.4B option.

    Metropolitan Toronto (*Ont.*)

    Newcastle (*N.S.W.*)

    Victoria County (*N.S.*)

23.4D. Places in the British Isles

23.4D1. Counties, etc. Add to the name of a county, region, or islands area in the British Isles used as entry element in a heading *England*, *Ireland* (for counties in the Republic of Ireland), *Northern Ireland, Scotland,* or *Wales,* as appropriate.

    Dorset (*England*)

    Clare (*Ireland*)

    Tyrone (*Northern Ireland*)

    Strathclyde (*Scotland*)

    Powys (*Wales*)

23.4D2. Other places (other than places in cities, see 23.4G). If a place is in England, Wales, or the Republic of Ireland, add the name of the county in which it is located.

    Bangor (*Gwynedd*)

    Barrow-in-Furness (*Cumbria*)

    Boston (*Lincolnshire*)

    Waterville (*Kerry*)

If a place is in Scotland, add the name of the region or islands area.

    Tarbert (*Strathclyde*)

If the name of the county, region, etc., is composed entirely of a phrase indicating orientation, add also *England* or *Scotland.*

    Birmingham (*West Midlands, England*)

    Stirling (*Central Region, Scotland*)

    Tarbert (*Western Isles, Scotland*)

If a place is in Northern Ireland, add *Northern Ireland.*

    Bangor (*Northern Ireland*)

See also 23.4F.

23.4D3. Places that bear the names of jurisdictions in the United Kingdom that have ceased to exist. If a place (other than a county) located in the United Kingdom bears a name that is also that of a jurisdiction that has ceased to exist,[3] add the name of the geographic county in which the place was located when it was a jurisdiction.

    Kelso (*Roxburghshire*)

      (*A burgh until 1975 in the geographic county of Roxburghshire;*
      now part of a district in the Borders Region of Scotland)

---

3. Certain place names ceased to be used as designations of jurisdictions on or before 1 April 1974 in England and Wales, on or before 16 May 1975 in Scotland, and on or before 1 October 1973 in Northern Ireland.

> **Pinner** (*Middlesex*)
> (*A parish until 1934 in the geographic county of Middlesex;
> now part of the London Borough of Harrow*)
>
> **Richmond** (*Surrey*)
> (*A borough until 1965 in the geographic county of Surrey;
> now part of the London Borough of Richmond-upon-Thames*)

If the jurisdiction was not part of a county, add the name of the country.

> **London** (*England*)

23.4E. Places in Malaysia, the U.S.S.R., or Yugoslavia

If a place is in a constituent state of Malaysia, the U.S.S.R., or Yugoslavia, add the name of the state.

> **George Town** (*Penang*)
>
> **Kiev** (*Ukraine*)
>
> **Split** (*Croatia*)

23.4F. Places on islands

If a place is on an island and the name of the island or island group is predominantly associated with the name of the place, add the name of the island or island group.

> **Bastia** (*Corsica*)
>
> **Mariehamn** (*Åland Islands*)
>
> **Newport** (*Isle of Wight*)
>
> **Palma** (*Majorca*)
>
> **Ramsey** (*Isle of Man*)
>
> **St. Aubin** (*Jersey*)
>
> **Southampton** (*Long Island*)

23.4G. Places in cities

If a place is in a city, add the name of the city. Refer from the name of the city followed by the name of the place.

> **Chelsea** (*London, England*)
> x London (*England*). Chelsea
>
> **11ᵉ Arrondissement** (*Paris, France*)
> x Paris (*France*). 11ᵉ Arrondissement
> x Paris (*France*). Popincourt
> x Popincourt (*Paris, France*)
>
> **Minato-ku** (*Tokyo, Japan*)
> x Tokyo (*Japan*). Minato-ku

23.4H. Other places

Add to the names of places not covered by 23.4C–23.4G the name of the country in which the place is located.

> **Formosa** (*Argentina*)
>
> **Luanda** (*Angola*)

Lucca (*Italy*)

Madras (*India*)

Monrovia (*Liberia*)

Næsby (*Denmark*)

Paris (*France*)

Toledo (*Spain*)

23.4J. Further additions

If the addition of a larger place as instructed in 23.4B–23.4H is insufficient to distinguish between two or more places with the same name, include a word or phrase commonly used to distinguish them.

Frankfurt-am-Main (*Germany*)

Frankfurt an der Oder (*Germany*)

If there is no such word or phrase, give an appropriate narrower geographical qualification before the name of the larger place.

Friedberg (*Bavaria, Germany*)

Friedberg (*Hesse, Germany*)

23.5. PLACE NAMES INCLUDING A TERM INDICATING A TYPE OF JURISDICTION

23.5A. If the first part of a place name is a term indicating a type of jurisdiction and the place is commonly listed under another element of its name in lists published in the language of the country in which it is located, omit the term indicating the type of jurisdiction.

Kerry (*Ireland*)
not County Kerry (*Ireland*)

Ostholstein (*Germany*)
not Kreis Ostholstein (*Germany*)

In all other cases include the term indicating the type of jurisdiction.

Mexico City (*Mexico*)

Città di Castello (*Italy*)

Ciudad Juárez (*Mexico*)

District of Columbia (*U.S.*)

Distrito Federal (*Brazil*)

23.5B. If a place name does not include a term indicating a type of jurisdiction and such a term is required to distinguish that place from another of the same name, follow the instructions in 24.6.

CHAPTER 24

HEADINGS FOR CORPORATE BODIES

Contents

24.1. BASIC RULE

Enter a corporate body[1] directly under the name by which it is predominantly identified, except when the rules that follow provide for entering it under the name of a higher or related body (see 24.13) or under the name of a government (see 24.18).

Determine the form of name of a corporate body from items issued by that body in its language (see also 24.3A), or, when this condition does not apply, from reference sources.[2]

If the name of a corporate body consists of or contains initials, omit or include full stops and other marks of punctuation according to the predominant usage of the body. In case of doubt, omit the full stops, etc. Do not leave a space between a full stop, etc.,

---

1. For definition, see 21.1B1.

2. When the phrase *reference sources* is used in this chapter, it includes books and articles written about a corporate body.

and an initial following it. Do not leave spaces between the letters of an initialism written without full stops, etc.

Make references from other forms of the name of a corporate body as instructed in 26.3.

3 October-Vereeniging

Aeródromo de Puerto Juárez

Aslib

Breitkopf & Härtel

British Museum

Carnegie Library of Pittsburgh

Challenger Expedition . . .[3]

Chartered Insurance Institute

Colin Buchanan and Partners

Conference "American-Allied Relations in Transition" . . .[3]

École centrale lyonnaise

G. Mendel Memorial Symposium, 1865-1965 . . .[3]

Greek Archdiocese of North and South America

Lambeth Conference . . .[3]

Light Fantastic Players

M. Robert Gomberg Memorial Committee

MEDCOM

Museum of American Folk Art

Paddington Chamber of Commerce

Radio Society of Great Britain

Real Academia de Bellas Artes de San Jorge

Royal Aeronautical Society

St. Annen-Museum

Symposium on Cognition . . .[3]

United States Catholic Conference

University of Oxford

W.H. Ross Foundation for the Study of Prevention of Blindness

World Methodist Conference . . .[3]

Yale University

---

3. For additions to the names of conferences, congresses, etc., see 24.7B.

24.1A. Romanization[4]

If the name of the body is in a language written in a nonroman script, romanize the name according to the table for that language adopted by the cataloguing agency. Refer from other romanizations as necessary.

> **Chung-kuo wen tzu kai ko wei yüan hui**
> *x* Zhongguo wenzi gaige weiyuanhui

> **Institut mezhdunarodnykh otnoshenii[5]**

> **Keihanshin Kyūkō Dentetsu Rōdō Kumiai**

24.1B. Changes of name

If the name of a corporate body has changed (including change from one language to another), establish a new heading under the new name for items appearing under that name. Refer from the old heading to the new and from the new heading to the old (see 26.3C).

> **Pennsylvania State University**
> The name of the Farmers' High School was changed in 1862 to Agricultural College of Pennsylvania; in 1874 to Pennsylvania State College; in 1953 to Pennsylvania State University.
> Works by this body are entered under the name used at the time of publication.
> *Make the same explanatory reference under the other names*

> **National Association for the Study and Prevention of Tuberculosis**
> For works by this body see also the later heading:
> **National Tuberculosis Association**

> **National Tuberculosis Association**
> For works by this body see also the earlier heading:
> **National Association for the Study and Prevention of Tuberculosis**

24.2. VARIANT NAMES. GENERAL RULES

24.2A. If a body uses variant names in items issued by it, follow the instructions in 24.2B–24.2D. Apply the special rules (24.3) as well when they are appropriate.

24.2B. If variant forms[6] of the name are found in items issued by the body, use the

---

4. *Alternative rule.* **Romanization.** If the name of the body is in a language written in a nonroman script and a romanized form appears in items issued by the body, use that romanized form as the heading. Refer as necessary from other romanizations. If more than one romanized form is found, use the form resulting from romanization according to the table adopted by the cataloguing agency for the language.

> **Zhongguo wenzi gaige weiyuanhui**
> *x* Chung-kuo wen tzu kai ko wei yüan hui

5. Systematic romanizations used in the examples in this chapter follow the tables (published by the Library of Congress in *Cataloging Service*, bulletin 118–   ) adopted jointly by the American Library Association, the Canadian Library Association, and the Library of Congress.

6. Variant forms do not include names that the body has abandoned in the past or adopted in the future. For these, see 24.1B.

name as it appears in the chief sources of information[7] as opposed to forms found elsewhere in the items.

24.2C. If variant spellings of the name appear in items issued by the body, use the form resulting from an official change in orthography, or, if this does not apply, use the predominant spelling. In case of doubt, use the spelling found in the first item catalogued.

24.2D. If variant forms appear in the chief source of information, use the form that is presented formally. If no form is presented formally, or if all forms are presented formally, use the predominant form.

If there is no predominant form, use a brief form (including an initialism or an acronym) that would differentiate between the body and others with the same or similar brief names.

> **AFL-CIO**
> *not* American Federation of Labor and Congress of Industrial Organizations
>
> **American Philosophical Society**
> *not* American Philosophical Society Held at Philadelphia for Promoting Useful Knowledge
>
> **Euratom**
> *not* European Atomic Energy Community
>
> **Kung ch'ing t'uan**
> *not* Chung-kuo kung ch'an chu i ch'ing nien t'uan
>
> **Maryknoll Sisters**
> *not* Congregation of the Maryknoll Sisters
>
> **Rateksa**
> *not* Radiobranchens tekniske og kommercielle sammenslutning
>
> **Unesco**
> *not* United Nations Educational, Scientific, and Cultural Organization

If the variant forms do not include a brief form that would differentiate two or more bodies with the same or similar brief names, use the form found in reference sources or the official form, in that order of preference.

> **Metropolitan Applied Research Center**
> (*Official name. Brief form sometimes used by the center,* MARC Corporation, *is the same as the name of another body located in New York, N.Y.*)

24.3. VARIANT NAMES. SPECIAL RULES

24.3A. Language[8]

---

7. See 1.0A.

8. *Alternative rule.* **Language.** Use a form of name in a language suitable to the users of the catalogue if the body's name is in a language that is not familiar to those users.

Japan Productivity Center
if not **Nihon Seisansei Hombu**

Union of Chambers of Commerce, Industry, and Commodity Exchanges of Turkey
if not **Türkiye Ticaret Odaları, Sanayi Odaları ve Ticaret Borsaları Birliği**

If the name appears in different languages, use the form in the official language of the body.

> **Société historique franco-américaine**
>
> *not* Franco-American Historical Society

If there is more than one official language and one of these is English, use the English form.

> **Canadian Committee on Cataloguing**
>
> *not* Comité canadien de catalogage

If English is not one of the official languages or if the official language is not known, use the form in the language predominantly used in items issued by the body.

> **Schweizerische Landesbibliothek**
>
> *not* Biblioteca nazionale svizzera
> *not* Bibliothèque nationale suisse
>> (*German is the language predominantly used by the body in its publications*)

In case of doubt, use the English, French, German, Spanish, or Russian form, in this order of preference. If none of these apply, use the form of name in the language that comes first in English alphabetic order. Refer from form(s) in other languages.

24.3B. Language. International bodies

If the name of an international body appears in English on items issued by it, use the English form. In other cases, follow 24.3A.

> **Arab League**
>
> *not* League of Arab States
> *not* Union des états arabes
> *not* Jāmiʻat al-Duwal al-ʻArabīyah

> **European Economic Community**
>
> *not* Communauté économique européenne
> *not* Europese Economische Gemeenschap
>> ₍*etc.*₎

> **International Federation of Library Associations and Institutions**
>
> *not* Fédération internationale des associations de bibliothécaires et des bibliothèques
> *not* Internationaler Verband der Bibliothekarischen Vereine und Institutionen
> *not* Mezhdunarodnai͡a federat͡sii͡a bibliotechnykh assot͡siat͡sii i uchrezhdeniĭ
>> ₍*etc.*₎

> **Nordic Association for American Studies**
>
> *not* Nordisk selskap for Amerikastudier
> *not* Nordiska sällskapet för Amerikastudier
>> ₍*etc.*₎

> **Nordisk husholdningshøjskole**
>> (*Name appears in Danish, Finnish, Icelandic, Norwegian, and Swedish*)

not Nordisk husholdshøgskole
not Nordiska hushållshögskolan
not Norrænn búsýsluháskóli
not Pohjoismainen kotitalouskorkeakoulu

24.3C. Conventional name

24.3C1. General rule. If a body is frequently identified by a conventional form of name in reference sources in its own language, use this conventional name.

> **Westminster Abbey**
> *not* Collegiate Church of St. Peter in Westminster

> **Kunstakademiet**
> *not* Det Kongelige Akademi for de skønne kunster
> *not* Det Kongelige Danske kunstakademi

24.3C2. Ancient and international bodies.[9] If the name of a body of ancient origin or of one that is international in character has become firmly established in an English form in English language usage, use this English form.

> **Benedictines**
>
> **Casablanca Conference** ...
>
> **Cluniacs**
>
> **Coptic Church**
>
> **Council of Nicaea** ...
>
> **Franciscans**
>
> **Freemasons**
>
> **Knights of Malta**
>
> **Nestorian Church**
>
> **Paris Peace Conference** ...
>
> **Poor Clares**
>
> **Royal and Select Masters**
>
> **Royal Arch Masons**
>
> **Vatican Council** ...

24.3C3. Autocephalous patriarchates, archdioceses, etc. Enter an ancient autocephalous patriarchate, archdiocese, etc., of the Eastern Church under the place by which it is identified, followed by a word or phrase designating the type of ecclesiastical jurisdiction (see 24.4C10).

---

9. Examples of bodies to which this rule applies are religious bodies, fraternal and knightly orders, church councils, and diplomatic conferences. If it is necessary to establish a heading for a diplomatic conference that has no formal name and has not yet acquired a conventional name, use the name found most commonly in periodical articles and newspaper accounts in English. If, later, another name becomes established, change the heading to that name.

      Antioch (*Jacobite patriarchate*)

      Antioch (*Orthodox patriarchate*)

      Constantinople (*Ecumenical patriarchate*)

      Cyprus (*Archdiocese*)

24.3D. Religious orders and societies

Use the best-known form of name for a religious order or society. In case of doubt, follow this order of preference:

1) the conventional name by which its members are known in English
2) the English form of name used by units of the order or society located in English-speaking countries
3) the name of the order or society in the language of the country of its origin.

      Franciscans
not Ordo Fratrum Minorum
not Order of St. Francis
not Minorites
      [*etc.*]

      Jesuits
not Societas Jesu
not Compañía de Jesús
not Society of Jesus
      [*etc.*]

      Poor Clares
not Order of St. Clare
not Clarisses
not Second Order of St. Francis
not Franciscans. *Second Order*
not Minoresses
      [*etc.*]

      Brothers of Our Lady of the Fields

      Community of the Resurrection

      Dominican Nuns of the Second Order of Perpetual Adoration
not Dominicans. *Second Order of Perpetual Adoration*

      Dominican Sisters of the Perpetual Rosary

      Sisters of the Divine Providence
not Sœurs de la divine providence

      Society of Christ the King

      Third Order Regular of St. Francis
not Franciscans. *Third Order Regular*

      Third Order Secular of St. Francis
not Franciscans. *Third Order Secular*

Divine Consciousness Light Society
not Hare Krishna Society

Zgromadzenie Służebnic Najświętszej Maryi Panny

24.3E. Governments

Use the conventional name of a government,[10] unless the official name is in common use. The conventional name of a government is the geographic name (see chapter 23) of the area (country, province, state, county, municipality, etc.) over which the government exercises jurisdiction.

France
not République française

Yugoslavia
not Socijalistička Federativna Republika Jugoslavija

Massachusetts
not Commonwealth of Massachusetts

Nottinghamshire
not County of Nottingham

Arlington
not Town of Arlington

If the official name of the government is in common use, use it.

Metropolitan Corporation of Greater Winnipeg

Greater London Council

24.3F. Conferences, congresses, meetings, etc.

24.3F1. If the variant forms of a conference name appearing in the chief source of information include a form that includes the name or abbreviation of the name of a body associated with the meeting, use this form.

FAO Hybrid Maize Meeting ...

If, however, the name or abbreviation of a name is of a body to which the meeting is subordinate (e.g., the annual meeting of an association), see 24.13.

24.3F2. If a conference has both a specific name of its own and a more general name as one of a series of conferences, use the specific name.

Symposium on Protein Metabolism ...
x Nutrition Symposium ...

Symposium on Endocrines and Nutrition ...
x Nutrition Symposium ...

---

10. The word *government* is used here to mean the totality of corporate bodies (executive, legislative, and judicial) exercising the powers of a jurisdiction. A corporate body known by the word *government*, or its equivalent in other languages, or a term with similar meaning, that is an executive element of a particular jurisdiction is treated as a government agency (see 24.18).

24.3G. Local churches, etc.

If variant forms of the name of a local church, cathedral, monastery, convent, abbey, temple, mosque, synagogue, etc., appear in the chief source of information of items issued by the body, use the predominant form. If there is no predominant form, follow this order of preference:

1) a name beginning with or consisting of the name of the person, persons, object, place, or event to which the local church, etc., is dedicated or after which it is named
2) a name beginning with a word or phrase descriptive of a type of local church, etc.
3) a name beginning with the name of the place in which the local church, etc., is situated.

For additions to names of local churches, etc., see 24.10.

      All Saints Church . . .

      Chapelle Saint-Louis . . .

      Church of the Holy Sepulchre . . .

      Duomo di Santa Maria Matricolare . . .

      Jāmi' 'Amr ibn al-'Āṣ . . .

      Hōryūji . . .

      St. Clement's Church . . .

      St. Paul's Cathedral . . .

      Temple Emanu-El . . .

      Visitation Monastery . . .

      Great Synagogue . . .

      Jüdische Reformgemeinde in Berlin

      Monasterio de Clarisas . . .

      Unitarian Universalist Church . . .

      Abtei Reichenau

      Anerley Society of the New Church

      Beechen Grove Baptist Church . . .

      English River Congregation of the Church of the Brethren

      Kölner Dom

      Parish Church of Limpsfield

      Tenafly Presbyterian Church

      Westover Church . . .

      Winchester Cathedral

Additions, omissions, and modifications

24.4. ADDITIONS

24.4A. General rule

Make additions to the names of corporate bodies as instructed in 24.4B–24.4C.

For additions to special types of corporate bodies (e.g., governments, conferences), see 24.6–24.11. Enclose in parentheses all additions required by these and other rules in this chapter.

24.4B. Names not conveying the idea of a corporate body

If the name alone does not convey the idea of a corporate body, add a general designation in English.

> **Apollo 11** (*Spacecraft*)
>
> **Bounty** (*Ship*)
>
> **Elks** (*Fraternal order*)
>
> **Friedrich Witte** (*Firm*)

24.4C. Two or more bodies with the same or similar names

24.4C1. General rule. If two or more bodies have the same name, or names so similar that they may be confused, add a word or phrase to each name as instructed in 24.4C2–24.4C10.

Do not include the additions to names of places prescribed in 24.6 when the names of those places are used to indicate the location of corporate bodies.

Optionally, apply rules 24.4C2–24.4C10 even if there is no need to distinguish between bodies.

24.4C2. Names of countries, states, provinces, etc. If a body has a character that is national, state, provincial, etc., add the name of the country, state, province, etc., in which it is located.

> **Republican Party** (*Ill.*)
>
> **Republican Party** (*Mo.*)
>
> **Sociedad Nacional de Minería** (*Chile*)
>
> **Sociedad Nacional de Minería** (*Peru*)

If such an addition does not provide sufficient identification or is inappropriate (as in the case of national, state, provincial, etc., universities of the same name serving the same country, state, province, etc.), follow the instructions in 24.4C3–24.4C10.

24.4C3. Local place names. In the case of all other bodies, add the name of the local place (see 24.4C4–24.4C7) in which the body is located or that is commonly associated with its name, unless the name of an institution, the date(s) of the body, or other designation (see 24.4C8–24.4C10) provides better identification.

In adding a local place name to a corporate heading, omit the name of the larger geographic entity (see 23.4B) if that entity is part of, or implied in, the name of the body.

> **Massachusetts Correctional Institution** (*Walpole*)
>
> *not*   Massachusetts Correctional Institution (*Walpole, Mass.*)

24.4C4. Bodies located outside the British Isles.[11] In the case of bodies located outside the British Isles (the United Kingdom and the Republic of Ireland), add the name of the smallest or most specific local political jurisdiction in which the body is located or that is commonly associated with its name (e.g., the name of the city, town, borough).

> **Loyola University** (*Chicago*)
>
> **Loyola University** (*New Orleans*)
>
> **Roosevelt Junior High School** (*Eugene*)
>
> **Roosevelt Junior High School** (*San Francisco*)
>
> **Twentieth Century Club** (*Kincaid*)
>
> **Twentieth Century Club** (*Hartford*)
>
> **York University** (*Toronto*)
>
> *not*   York University (*Downsview*)

If further distinction is necessary, give the name of a particular area within that jurisdiction, before the name of the jurisdiction.

> **St. John's Church** (*Georgetown, Washington, D.C.*)
>
> **St. John's Church** (*Lafayette Square, Washington, D.C.*)

If the body is not located in an incorporated municipality, add the geographic name that is most commonly used to specify its location (e.g., the name of an unincorporated community, the name of a city or town in the vicinity, or the name of the county).

If a body located in a specific local jurisdiction is more commonly associated with the name of another city or town or an unincorporated community in its vicinity, prefer the name of that place.

> **École française de papeterie** (*Grenoble*)
> (*School is located in St. Martin d'Hères, an incorporated suburb of Grenoble*)

24.4C5. Bodies located in the British Isles. In the case of bodies located in the British Isles, add either the name of a geographic locality or the name of the smallest or most specific jurisdiction, whichever is more commonly associated with the name of the body.

---

11. The examples shown in rules 24.4C4–24.5, 24.7–24.11, and elsewhere, with a few exceptions, omit the name of the larger geographic area in which the local place is located. The construction of these headings by a particular cataloguing agency will depend on the application of the options in chapter 23 or on the actual need for differentiation in a particular catalogue.

    Royal Hospital (*Chelsea*)

    St. Barnabas Church of England School (*Bradwell*)

    St. Peter's Church (*Hook Norton*)

    St. Peter's Church (*Sudbury*)

    Red Lion Hotel (*Newport, Gwent*)

    Red Lion Hotel (*Newport, Isle of Wight*)

24.4C6. Change of name of jurisdiction or locality. If the name of the local jurisdiction or geographic locality changes during the lifetime of the body, add the latest name in use in the lifetime of the body.

    St. Paul Lutheran Church (*Skokie*)
not St. Paul Lutheran Church (*Niles Center*)
    (*Church founded in 1881. Place name changed in 1940*)

but **Historisk samfund** (*Christiania*)
    (*Ceased to exist before Christiania became Oslo*)

24.4C7. Corporate names including a local place name. Do not add the local place name to a corporate name that includes the same local place name. If two or more such names need to be distinguished, add the name of the country, state, province, etc., in which the body is located.

    Washington County Historical Society (*Ark.*)

    Washington County Historical Society (*Md.*)

    Washington County Historical Society (*Pa.*)

24.4C8. Institutions. Add the name of an institution instead of the local place name if the institution's name is commonly associated with the name of the body. Give the name of the institution in the form and language used for it as a heading.

    Newman Club (*Brooklyn College*)
not Newman Club (*Brooklyn*)

    Newman Club (*University of Maryland*)

24.4C9. Year(s). Add the year of founding or the inclusive years of existence if the name has been used by two or more bodies that cannot be distinguished by place.

    Scientific Society of San Antonio (*1892–1894*)

    Scientific Society of San Antonio (*1904–   *)

24.4C10. Other additions. If the place, name of institution, or date(s) is insufficient or inappropriate for distinguishing between two or more bodies, add an appropriate general designation in English.

    Church of God (*Adventist*)

    Church of God (*Apostolic*)

24.5. OMISSIONS

24.5A. Initial articles

Omit initial articles unless they are required for grammatical reasons.

>   **Club** (*London*)
>
> *not* The Club (*London*)
>
>   **Français de Grande-Bretagne** (*Association*)
>
> *not* Les Français de Grande-Bretagne
>
>   **Library Association**
>
> *not* The Library Association
>
> *but*
>
>   **Der Blaue Adler** (*Association*)
>
>   **Det Norske Nobelinstitutt**

24.5B. Citations of honours

Omit phrases citing honours or orders awarded to the body.

>   **Moskovskaĭa gosudarstvennaĭa konservatoriĭa imeni P.I. Chaĭkovskogo**
>
> *not* Moskovskaĭa gosudarstvennaĭa ordena Lenina konservatoriĭa imeni
>   P.I. Chaĭkovskogo
>
>   **Moskovskiĭ khudozhestvennyĭ akademicheskiĭ teatr**
>
> *not* Moskovskiĭ khudozhestvennyĭ ordena Lenina i Trudovogo krasnogo
>   znameni akademicheskiĭ teatr

24.5C. Terms indicating incorporation and certain other terms

24.5C1. Omit adjectival terms indicating incorporation (*incorporated, E.V., ltd.,* etc.) or state ownership of a corporate body, and words or phrases designating the type of incorporated entity (*Aktiebolaget, Gesellschaft mit beschränkter Haftung, Kabushiki Kaisha, Società per azione,* etc.) unless they are an integral part of the name or are needed to make it clear that the name is that of a corporate body.

>   **American Ethnological Society**
>   *without* inc.
>
>   **Automobiltechnische Gesellschaft**
>   *without* E.V., *i.e.,* Eingetragener Verein
>
>   **Daiwa Ginkō**
>   *without* Kabushiki Kaisha
>
>   **Society of Engineers** (*London*)
>   *without* incorporated
>
>   **Thüringisches Kunstfaserwerk "Wilhelm Pieck"**
>   *without* VEB
>
>   **Compañía Internacional Editora**
>   *without* s.a.
>
> *but*
>
>   **Films Incorporated**

Nihon Genshiryoku Hatsuden Kabushiki Kaisha

Peter Davies Limited

Vickers (Aviation) Limited

24.5C2. If such a term is needed to make it clear that the name is that of a corporate body and it occurs at the beginning of the name, transpose it to the end if that is grammatically possible.

> **Elektrometall, Aktiebolaget**
> *not* Aktiebolaget Elektrometall

> **Hochbauprojektierung Karl-Marx-Stadt, VEB**
> *not* VEB Hochbauprojektierung Karl-Marx-Stadt

24.5C3. Omit an initial word or phrase in an oriental language indicating the private character of a corporate body (e.g., *Shiritsu, Ssu li*), unless the word or phrase is an integral part of the name.

> **Tan-chiang Ying yü chuan k'o hsüeh hsiao**
> *not* Ssu li Tan-chiang Ying yü chuan k'o hsüeh hsiao

> *but* **Shiritsu Daigaku Toshokan Kyōkai**

24.5C4. Omit abbreviations such as *U.S.S.* and *H.M.S.* occurring before the name of a ship.

> **Ark Royal** (*Ship*)
> *not* H.M.S. Ark Royal

24.6. GOVERNMENTS. ADDITIONS[12]

24.6A. If governments with the same name are not differentiated by 23.4, make a further addition as instructed in 24.6B–24.6D.

24.6B. Add the type of jurisdiction in English if other than a city or a town. If there is no English equivalent for the vernacular term, use the vernacular term. In case of doubt, use the vernacular term.

> **Cork** (*Cork, Ireland*)
> **Cork** (*Ireland : County*)
> **Darmstadt** (*Germany*)
> **Darmstadt** (*Germany : Landkreis*)
> **Darmstadt** (*Germany : Regierungsbezirk*)
> **Guadalajara** (*Mexico*)
> **Guadalajara** (*Spain*)

---

12. The examples shown in this rule are included solely to illustrate the use of the various additions. The construction of these headings by a particular cataloguing agency depends on the application of the options in chapter 23 or on actual need for differentiation in a particular catalogue.

> **Guadalajara** (*Spain : Province*)
>
> **Lublin** (*Poland*)
>
> **Lublin** (*Poland : Voivodeship*)
>
> **New York** (*N.Y.*)
>
> **New York** (*U.S. : State*)
>
> **Québec** (*Canada : Province*)
>
> **Québec** (*Québec*)
>
> **Québec** (*Québec : County*)
>
> **Reşiţa** (*Romania*)
>
> **Reşiţa** (*Romania : Raion*)

24.6C. If the type of jurisdiction does not provide a satisfactory distinction, add an appropriate word or phrase.

> **Germany** (*Democratic Republic*)
>
> **Germany** (*Federal Republic*)
>
> **Berlin** (*Germany : East*)
>
> **Berlin** (*Germany : West*)

24.6D. If two or more governments lay claim to jurisdiction over the same area (e.g., as with occupying powers and insurgent governments), add a suitable designation to one or each of the governments, followed by the inclusive years of its existence.

> **France**
>
> **France** (*Territory under German occupation, 1940–1944*)
>
> **Algeria**
>
> **Algeria** (*Provisional government, 1958–1962*)

24.7. CONFERENCES, CONGRESSES, MEETINGS, ETC.

24.7A. Omissions

Omit from the name of a conference, etc., words that denote its number, frequency, or year of convocation.

> **Louisiana Cancer Conference ...**
>
> *not* Biennial Louisiana Cancer Conference ...
>
> **Conference on Co-ordination of Galactic Research ...**
>
> *not* Second Conference on Co-ordination of Galactic Research ...

24.7B. Additions

24.7B1. General rule. Add to conference, etc., headings (including headings for conferences entered subordinately, see 24.13) the number of the conference, etc., the year, and the place in which it was held.

24.7B2. Number. If a conference, etc., is stated or inferred to be one of a series of numbered meetings of the same name, add the abbreviation of the ordinal number in English.

> **Conference of British Teachers of Marketing at Advanced Level**
> (*3rd* : . . .)

If the numbering is irregular, omit it from the heading. *Optionally*, provide an explanation of the irregularities in an appropriate form (e.g., a note, an information reference).

24.7B3. Date. Add the year or years in which the conference, etc., was held if the heading is for a single meeting.

> **Conference on Library Surveys** (*1965* : . . .)
>
> **Conference on Technical Information Center Administration**
> (*3rd : 1966* : . . .)
>
> **Study Institute on Special Education** (*1969–1970* : . . .)

Add specific dates if necessary to distinguish between two or more meetings.

> **Conférence agricole interalliée** (*1st : 1919 Feb. 11—15* : . . .)
>
> **Conférence agricole interalliée** (*2nd : 1919 Mar. 17–19* : . . .)

24.7B4. Location. Add the name of the local place or other location (institution, etc.) in which the conference, etc., was held. Give a local place name in the form provided for in chapter 23. Give all other locations in the nominative case in the language in which it is found in the item being catalogued.

> **Conference on Machinability** (*1965 : London*)
>
> **Symposium on Glaucoma** (*1966 : New Orleans*)
>
> **Konferentsiia po pochvovedeniiu i fiziologii kul'turnykh rastenii**
> (*1937 : Saratovskiĭ universitet*)
>
> **Workshop Conference on the Role of the Director of Medical Education
> in the Hospital** (*1959 : Chicago*)
>
> **Regional Conference on Mental Measurements of the Blind**
> (*1st : 1951 : Perkins Institution*)
>
> **Louisiana Cancer Conference** (*2nd : 1958 : New Orleans*)
>
> **International Conference on Atmospheric Emissions from Sulphate
> Pulping** (*1966 : Sanibel Island*)
>
> **International Conference on the Biology of Whales** (*1971 : Shenandoah
> National Park*)
>
> **Conference "Systematics of the Old World Monkeys"** (*1969 : Burg
> Wartenstein*)
>
> **Conference on Cancer Public Education** (*1973 : Dulles Airport*)

If the heading is for a series of conferences, do not add the location unless they were all held in the same place.

> **Hybrid Corn Industry Research Conference**

417

24.8 *Exhibitions, fairs, festivals, etc.*

If the location is part of the name of the conference, do not repeat it.

> **Arden House Conference on Medicine and Anthropology** (*1961*)
>
> **Paris Symposium on Radio Astronomy** (*1958*)

If the sessions of a conference, etc., were held in two places, add both names.

> **World Peace Congress** (*1st : 1949 : Paris and Prague*)
>
> **Institute on Diagnostic Problems in Mental Retardation** (*1957 :*
> *Long Beach State College and San Francisco State College*)

If the sessions of a conference, etc., were held in three or more places, add the first named place followed by *etc.*

> **International Geological Conference** (*15th : 1929 : Pretoria, etc.*)

24.8. EXHIBITIONS, FAIRS, FESTIVALS, ETC.

24.8A. Omissions
Omit from the name of an exhibition, fair, festival, etc., a word or words that denote its number.

24.8B. Additions
Add to headings for exhibitions, fairs, festivals, etc., the number of the exhibition, the year, and the place (as instructed in 24.7B) in which it was held. Do not add the year and/or place if they are integral parts of the name.

> **Festival of Britain** (*1951 : London*)
>
> **Biennale di Venezia** (*36th : 1972*)
>
> **World's Columbian Exposition** (*1893 : Chicago*)
>
> **Expo 67** (*Montréal*)

24.9. CHAPTERS, BRANCHES, ETC.
Add to the name of a chapter, branch, etc., that carries out the activities of a corporate body in a particular locality, the name of that locality. If the locality is part of the name of the chapter, branch, etc., do not add it.

> **Freemasons.** *Concordia Lodge, No. 13* (*Baltimore*)
>
> **Freemasons.** *United Grand Lodge* (*England*)
>
> **Knights Templar** (*Masonic order*). *Grand Commandery* (*Me.*)
>
> **Scottish Rite** (*Masonic order*). *Oriental Consistory* (*Chicago*)

If the place of activity is an institution, add the name of the institution.

> **Psi Upsilon.** *Gamma Chapter* (*Amherst College*)
>
> **Society of St. Vincent de Paul.** *Conference*[13] (*Cathedral of St. John the*
> *Baptist : Savannah*)

---

13. The term *Conference* is used by this body as the generic word for its local units.

24.10. LOCAL CHURCHES, ETC.

24.10A. If the name of a local church, etc., does not convey the idea of a church, etc., add a general designation in English.

> **Monte Cassino** (*Monastery*)

24.10B. Add to the name of a local church, etc., the name of the place or local ecclesiastical jurisdiction (parish, Pfarrei, etc.) in which it is located (see 24.4C4–24.4C6) unless the location is clear from the name itself.

> **All Saints Church** (*Birchington*)
>
> **St. Mary** (*Church : Aylesbury Vale*)
>
> **Unitarian Universalist Church** (*Silver Spring*)
>
> **Visitation Monastery** (*Waldron*)
>
> **Westover Church** (*Charles City County*)
>
> **St. James' Church** (*Bronx*)

If there are two or more local churches, etc., with the same name in the same place, add a further suitable designation.

> **St. James' Church** (*Manhattan : Catholic*)
>
> **St. James' Church** (*Manhattan : Episcopal*)

24.11. RADIO AND TELEVISION STATIONS

24.11A. If the name of a radio or television station consists solely or principally of its call letters or if its name does not convey the idea of a radio or television station, add the words *Radio station* or *Television station* and the name of the place in which the station is located.

> **HVJ** (*Radio station : Vatican City*)
>
> **WCIA** (*Television station : Champaign*)

24.11B. Add to the names of any other radio and television stations the place in which it is located unless it is an integral part of the name.

> **Radio Maroc** (*Rabat*)

but

> **Radio London**

Subordinate and related bodies

24.12. GENERAL RULE

Enter a subordinate body (other than a government agency entered under jurisdiction, see 24.18) or a related body directly under its own name (see 24.1–24.3) unless its name belongs to one or more of the types listed in 24.13. Refer to the name of a subordinate body entered independently from its name in the form of a subheading of the higher body (see 26.3A7).

Ansco
   x General Aniline and Film Corporation. *Ansco*

Association of College and Research Libraries
   x American Library Association. *Association of College and Research Libraries*

BBC Symphony Orchestra
   x British Broadcasting Corporation. *Symphony Orchestra*

Bodleian Library
   x University of Oxford. *Bodleian Library*

Congregation of the Most Holy Name of Jesus
   x Dominican Sisters. *Congregation of the Most Holy Name of Jesus*

Crane Theological School
   x Tufts University. *Crane Theological School*

Faculdade de Teologia de Lisboa
   x Universidade Católica Portuguesa. *Faculdade de Teologia de Lisboa*

Friends of IBBY
   x International Board on Books for Young People. *Friends*

Harvard Law School
   x Harvard University. *Law School*

24.13. SUBORDINATE AND RELATED BODIES ENTERED SUBORDINATELY

Enter a subordinate or related body as a subheading of the name of the body to which it is subordinate or related if its name belongs to one or more of the following types.[14] Make it a direct or indirect subheading as instructed in 24.14. Omit from the subheading the name or abbreviation of the name of the higher or related body in noun form unless this does not make sense.

TYPE 1. A name that contains a term that by definition implies that the body is part of another, e.g., department, division, section, branch.

British Broadcasting Corporation. *Engineering Division*

International Federation of Library Associations and Institutions.
   Section on Cataloguing

Stanford University. *Department of Civil Engineering*

TYPE 2. A name that contains a word normally implying administrative subordination (e.g., committee, commission), providing the name of the higher body is required for the identification of the subordinate body.

Association of State Universities and Land-Grant Colleges.
   Committee on Traffic Safety Research and Education

International Council on Social Welfare. *Canadian Committee*

---

14. Distinguish between cases in which the subordinate body's name includes the names of higher bodies from cases in which the names of higher bodies only appear in association with the subordinate body's name.

Timber Trade Federation of the United Kingdom. *Statistical Co-ordinating Committee*

National Association of Insurance Commissioners. *Securities Valuation Office*

University of Wales. *University Commission*
Name: University Commission

but **National Commission on United Methodist Higher Education**

TYPE 3. A name that has been, or is likely to be, used by another higher body for one of its subordinate or related bodies.

Bell Telephone Laboratories. *Technical Information Library*
Name: Technical Information Library

Canadian Dental Association. *Bureau of Public Information*
Name: Bureau of Public Information

Dartmouth College. *Class of 1880*

Église réformée de France. *Synode national*
Name: Synode national

International Labour Organisation. *European Regional Conference (2nd : 1968 : Geneva)*
Name: Second European Regional Conference
(Subordinate to the International Labour Organisation)

Sondley Reference Library. *Friends of the Library*
Name: Friends of the Library

TYPE 4. A name of a university faculty, school, college, institute, laboratory, etc., that simply indicates a particular field of study.

Princeton University. *Bureau of Urban Research*

Syracuse University. *College of Medicine*

University College London. *Communication Research Centre*

University of London. *School of Pharmacy*

TYPE 5. A name that includes the entire name of the higher or related body.

American Legion. *Auxiliary*
Name: American Legion Auxiliary

Auburn University. *Agricultural Experiment Station*
Name: Agricultural Experiment Station of Auburn University

Friends of the Earth. *Camden Friends of the Earth*
Name: Camden Friends of the Earth

Labour Party *(Great Britain). Conference (71st : Blackpool)*
Name: 71st Annual Conference of the Labour Party
(Activity of the Labour Party limited to Great Britain)

United Methodist Church (*U.S.*). *General Conference*
    Name: General Conference of the United Methodist Church

University of Southampton. *Mathematical Society*
    Name: Mathematical Society of the University of Southampton

University of Vermont. *Choral Union*
    Name: University of Vermont Choral Union

Yale University. *Library*
    Name: Yale University Library

but   **BBC Symphony Orchestra**
not   British Broadcasting Corporation. *Symphony Orchestra*

24.14. DIRECT OR INDIRECT SUBHEADING

Enter a body belonging to one or more of the types listed in 24.13 as a subheading of the lowest element in the hierarchy that is entered under its own name. Omit intervening elements in the hierarchy unless the name of the subordinate or related body has been, or is likely to be, used by another body entered under the name of the same higher or related body. In that case, interpose the name of the lowest element in the hierarchy that will distinguish between the bodies.

Public Library Association. *Audiovisual Committee*
    Hierarchy: American Library Association
           Public Library Association
           Audiovisual Committee

American Library Association. *Cataloging and Classification Section.*
Policy and Research Committee
    Hierarchy: American Library Association
           Resources and Technical Services Division
           Cataloging and Classification Section
           Policy and Research Committee

American Library Association. *Resources and Technical Services Division.*
Board of Directors
    Hierarchy: American Library Association
           Resources and Technical Services Division
           Board of Directors

Refer from the name in the form of a subheading of the name of its immediately superior body when the heading does not include the name of that superior body.

American Library Association. *Committee on Outreach Programs for*
Young Adults (*Ad Hoc*)
    Hierarchy: American Library Association
           Young Adult Services Division
           Committee on Outreach Programs for Young Adults
           (Ad Hoc)
    x American Library Association. *Young Adult Services Division.*
      Committee on Outreach Programs for Young Adults (*Ad Hoc*)

American Library Association. *Cataloging and Classification Section*
    Hierarchy: American Library Association
                Resources and Technical Services Division
                Cataloging and Classification Section
    x American Library Association. *Resources and Technical Services*
        Division. Cataloging and Classification Section

SPECIAL RULES

24.15. JOINT COMMITTEES, COMMISSIONS, ETC.

24.15A. Enter a body made up of representatives of two or more other bodies under its own name.

    Joint Committee on Individual Efficiency in Industry
        (*A joint committee of the Department of Scientific and Industrial*
        Research and the Medical Research Council)

    Canadian Committee on MARC
        (*A joint committee of the Association pour l'avancement des sciences et*
        des techniques de la documentation, the Canadian Library Association,
        and the National Library of Canada)

Omit the names of the parent bodies when these occur within or at the end of the name if the name of the joint unit is distinctive without them.

    Joint Committee on Bathing Places
  not Joint Committee on Bathing Places of the Conference of State
        Sanitary Engineers and the Engineering Section of the American
        Public Health Association

  but **Joint Commission of the Council for Education in World Citizenship**
        and the London International Assembly

24.15B. If the parent bodies are entered as subheadings of a common higher body, enter the joint unit as a subordinate body as instructed in 24.12–24.14.

    American Library Association. *Joint Committee to Compile a List of*
      International Subscription Agents
      (*A joint committee of the Acquisitions and Serials sections of the*
      American Library Association's Resources and Technical Services
      Division)

24.16. CONVENTIONALIZED SUBHEADINGS FOR STATE AND LOCAL ELEMENTS OF AMERICAN POLITICAL PARTIES

Give the subheading for an element of an American political party as the name of the element without any proper nouns or adjectives that are part of the name of the party or its area of activity.

    Republican Party (*Mo.*). *State Committee*
      Name: Missouri Republican State Committee

> **Republican Party** (*Ohio*). *State Executive Committee*
> *Name:* Ohio State Republican Executive Committee

> **Democratic Party** (*Tex.*). *State Convention* (*1857 : Waco*)
> *Name:* State Convention of the Democratic Party of the State of Texas

Government bodies and officials

24.17. GENERAL RULE

Enter a body created or controlled by a government under its own name (see 24.1–24.3) unless it belongs to one or more of the types listed in 24.18. However, if a body is subordinate to a higher body that is entered under its own name, formulate the heading for the subordinate body according to 24.12–24.14. Refer to the name of a government agency entered independently from its name in the form of a subheading of the name of the government (see 26.3A7).

> **American Battle Monuments Commission**
> *x* United States. *American Battle Monuments Commission*

> **Arts Council of Great Britain**
> *x* United Kingdom. *Arts Council*

> **Boundary Commission for England**
> *x* United Kingdom. *Boundary Commission for England*

> **Canada Institute for Scientific and Technical Information**
> *x* Canada. *Institute for Scientific and Technical Information*

> **Canadian National Railways**
> *x* Canada. *Canadian National Railways*

> **Consejo Superior de Investigaciones Científicas**
> *x* Spain. *Consejo Superior de Investigaciones Científicas*

> **Council on International Economic Policy**
> *x* United States. *Council on International Economic Policy*

> **Dundee Harbour Trust**
> *x* United Kingdom. *Dundee Harbour Trust*

> **University of British Columbia**
> *x* British Columbia. *University*

24.18. GOVERNMENT AGENCIES ENTERED SUBORDINATELY

Enter a government agency subordinately if it belongs to one or more of the following types. Make it a direct or indirect subheading of the heading for the government as instructed in 24.19. Omit from the subheading the name or abbreviation of the name of the government in noun form unless such an omission would result in an objectionable distortion.

> **Canada.** *Information Canada*
> *not* Canada. *Information*

TYPE 1. An agency with a name containing a term that by definition implies that the body is part of another, e.g., department, division, section, branch, and their equivalents in other languages.

Vermont. *Department of Water Resources*

Ottawa. *Department of Community Development*

United States. *Division of Wildlife Service*

TYPE 2. An agency with a name containing a word that normally implies administrative subordination (e.g., committee, commission), providing the name of the government is required for the identification of the agency.

Australia. *Bureau of Agricultural Economics*

Canada. *Royal Commission on Banking and Finance*

United Kingdom. *Royal Commission on the Press*

United Kingdom. *Central Office of Information*

United States. *Commission on Civil Rights*

United States. *Committee on Retirement Policy for Federal Personnel*

but **Royal Commission on Higher Education in New Brunswick**

TYPE 3. An agency with a name that has been, or is likely to be, used as the name of another agency, providing the name of the government is required for the identification of the agency.

Illinois. *Environmental Protection Agency*
    Name: Environmental Protection Agency

United States. *Environmental Protection Agency*
    Name: Environmental Protection Agency

Béziers. *Musée des beaux-arts*
    Name: Musée des beaux-arts

Greater London Council. *Research and Intelligence Unit*
    Name: Research and Intelligence Unit

but **Musée de Poitiers**

TYPE 4. An agency that is a ministry or similar major executive agency (i.e., one that has no other agency above it) as defined by official publications of the government in question.

United Kingdom. *Home Office*

United Kingdom. *Ministry of Defence*

Italy. *Ministero del bilancio e della programmazione economica*

United States. *National Aeronautics and Space Administration*

TYPE 5. Legislative bodies (see also 24.21).

Greenwich. *Council*

France. *Assemblée nationale*

United Kingdom. *Parliament*

United States. *Congress*

TYPE 6. Courts (see also 24.23).

> **Ontario.** *High Court of Justice*
>
> **United States.** *Supreme Court*

TYPE 7. Principal armed services (see also 24.24).

> **Canada.** *Canadian Armed Forces*
>
> **Germany.** *Heer*
>
> **United Kingdom.** *Army*
>
> **United States.** *Navy*

TYPE 8. Chiefs of state and heads of government (see also 24.20).

> **United Kingdom.** *Sovereign*
>
> **Montréal.** *Mayor*
>
> **United States.** *President*
>
> **Virginia.** *Governor*

TYPE 9. Embassies, consulates, etc. (see also 24.25).

> **Canada.** *Embassy* (*U.S.*)
>
> **United Kingdom.** *Consulate* (*New York*)

TYPE 10. Delegations to international and intergovernmental bodies (see also 24.26).

> **United Kingdom.** *Delegation to the United Nations*

24.19. DIRECT OR INDIRECT SUBHEADING

Enter an agency belonging to one or more of the types listed in 24.18 as a direct subheading of the heading for the government unless the name of the agency has been, or is likely to be, used by another agency entered under the name of the same government. In that case, add, between the name of the government and the name of the agency, the name of the lowest element in the hierarchy that will distinguish between the agencies.

> **United States.** *Office of Human Development Services*
> *Hierarchy:* United States
> Department of Health, Education, and Welfare
> Office of Human Development Services
>
> **Québec** (*Province*). *Service de l'exploration géologique*
> *Hierarchy:* Québec
> Ministère des richesses naturelles
> Direction générale des mines
> Direction de la géologie
> Service de l'exploration géologique
>
> **United States.** *Aviation Forecast Branch*
> *Hierarchy:* United States
> Department of Transportation
> Federal Aviation Administration
> Office of Aviation Policy
> Aviation Forecast Branch

United Kingdom. *Nationality and Treaty Department*
Hierarchy: United Kingdom
Foreign and Commonwealth Office
Nationality and Treaty Department

France. *Commission centrale des marchés*
Hierarchy: France
Ministère de l'économie et des finances
Commission centrale des marchés

but

United Kingdom. *Department of Employment. Solicitors Office*
Hierarchy: United Kingdom
Department of Employment
Solicitors Office

France. *Direction générale des impôts. Service de l'administration générale*
Hierarchy: France
Ministère de l'économie et des finances
Direction générale des impôts
Service de l'administration générale

Refer from the name in the form of a subheading of the name of its immediately superior body when the heading does not include the name of that superior body.

California. *Employment Data and Research Division*
Hierarchy: California
Health and Welfare Agency
Employment Development Department
Employment Data and Research Division
x California. *Employment Development Department. Employment Data and Research Division*

France. *Ministère du travail, de l'emploi et de la population. Division de la statistique et des études*
Hierarchy: France
Ministère du travail, de l'emploi et de la population
Service des études et prévisions
Division de la statistique et des études
x France. *Ministère du travail, de l'emploi et de la population. Service des études et prévisions. Division de la statistique et des études*

SPECIAL RULES

24.20. GOVERNMENT OFFICIALS

24.20A. Scope

Apply rule 24.20 only to officials of countries and other states that have existed in postmedieval times, and to officials of international intergovernmental organizations.

427

24.20B. Heads of state, etc.

The subheading for a sovereign, president, other head of state, or governor acting in an official capacity (see 21.4D) consists of the title of the office in English (unless there is no equivalent English term), the inclusive years of the reign or incumbency, and the name of the person in a brief form and in the language of the heading for that person.

> **United States.** *President (1953–1961 : Eisenhower)*
>
> **Illinois.** *Governor (1973–1977 : Walker)*
>
> **Iran.** *Shah (1941–   : Mohammed Reza Pahlavi)*
>
> **Papal States.** *Sovereign (1846–1870 : Pius IX)*

If the title varies with the sex of the incumbent, use a general term (e.g., Sovereign *not* King or Queen).

> **United Kingdom.** *Sovereign (1952–   : Elizabeth II)*
>
> **Russia.** *Sovereign (1894–1917 : Nicholas II)*
>
> **Spain.** *Sovereign (1886–1931 : Alfonso XIII)*

If there are two or more nonconsecutive periods of incumbency, use separate headings.

> **United States.** *President (1885–1889 : Cleveland)*
>
> **United States.** *President (1893–1897 : Cleveland)*

If the heading applies to more than one incumbent (see 21.4D), omit the dates and names.

> **United States.** *President*

If a heading is established for the incumbent as a person in addition to the heading as a head of state, make an explanatory reference under the heading for the head of state (see 26.3C1).

24.20C. Heads of governments and of international intergovernmental bodies

The subheading for a head of government acting in an official capacity (see 21.4D) who is not also a head of state consists of the title of the office in the vernacular. Do not include dates and names. The subheading for the head of an international intergovernmental organization (acting in an official capacity) consists of the title of the office in the language of the heading for the organization.

> **United Kingdom.** *Prime Minister*
>
> **Philadelphia.** *Mayor*
>
> **France.** *Premier ministre*
>
> **Italy.** *Presidente del Consiglio dei ministri*
>
> **United Nations.** *Secretary-General*

24.20D. Governors of dependent or occupied territories

The subheading for the governor of a colony, protectorate, etc., or of an occupied territory consists of the title of the governor in the language of the governing power as a subheading under the heading for the dependent or occupied territory.

Falkland Islands. *Governor*

Jersey. *Militärischer Befehlshaber*

Netherlands (*Territory under German occupation, 1940–1945*).
  Reichskommissar für die Besetzten Niederländischen Gebiete

Germany (*Territory under Allied occupation, 1945–1955 : U.S.
  Zone*). *Military Governor*

24.20E. Other officials

The subheading for any other official is that of the ministry or agency that the official represents.

United States. *General Accounting Office*
not   United States. *Comptroller General*

If the official is not part of a ministry, etc., or is part of one that is identified only by the title of the official, the subheading consists of that title.

United Kingdom. *Lord Privy Seal*

24.21. LEGISLATIVE BODIES

24.21A. If a legislature has more than one chamber, enter each as a subheading of the heading for the legislature.

United Kingdom. *Parliament. House of Commons*
not   United Kingdom. *House of Commons*

United Kingdom. *Parliament. House of Lords*
not   United Kingdom. *House of Lords*

24.21B. Enter committees and other subordinate units (except legislative subcommittees of the U.S. Congress) as subheadings of the legislature or of a particular chamber, as appropriate.

United States. *Congress. Joint Committee on the Library*

United States. *Congress. House of Representatives. Select Committee on
  Government Organization*

24.21C. Enter a legislative subcommittee of the U.S. Congress as a subheading of the committee to which it is subordinate.

United States. *Congress. Senate. Committee on Foreign Relations.
  Subcommittee on Canadian Affairs*
not   United States. *Congress. Senate. Subcommittee on Canadian Affairs*

24.21D. If successive legislatures are numbered consecutively, add the ordinal number and the year or years to the heading for the particular legislature or one of its chambers.

United States. *Congress (87th : 1961–1962)*

United States. *Congress (87th : 1961–1962). House of Representatives*

24.22 *Constitutional conventions*

If, in such a case, numbered sessions are involved, add the session and its number and the year or years of the session to the number of the legislature.

> **United States.** *Congress (87th, 2nd session˙: 1962)*

> **United States.** *Congress (87th, 2nd session : 1962). House of Representatives*

24.22. CONSTITUTIONAL CONVENTIONS

24.22A. Enter a constitutional convention directly under the heading for the government that convened it. Add the year or years in which it was held.

> **Germany.** *Nationalversammlung (1919–1920)*

> **Portugal.** *Assembléia Nacional Constituinte (1911)*

24.22B. If there is variation in the forms of name of constitutional conventions convened by a jurisdiction using English as an official language, use the conventionalized form *Constitutional Convention* for all the conventions. Otherwise, apply 24.2 and 24.3.

> **New Hampshire.** *Constitutional Convention (1781)*
> *not* New Hampshire. *Convention for Framing a New Constitution or Form of Government (1781)*

> **New Hampshire.** *Constitutional Convention (1889)*

> **New Hampshire.** *Constitutional Convention (1912)*
> *not* New Hampshire. *Convention to Revise the Constitution (1912)*

24.23. COURTS

24.23A. Civil and criminal courts

Enter a civil or criminal court as a subheading of the heading for the jurisdiction whose authority it exercises.

> **Vermont.** *Court of Chancery*

Omit from the name of the court the name of the place in which it sits or the area which it serves if the name of the place is grammatically separable. If such terms are required to distinguish a court from others of the same name, add them in a conventionalized form.

> **France.** *Cour d'appel (Caen)*
> *Name:* Cour d'appel de Caen

> **United Kingdom.** *Crown Court (Manchester)*
> *Name:* Manchester Crown Court

> **United States.** *Court of Appeals (2nd Circuit)*
> *Name:* United States Court of Appeals for the Second Circuit

> **United States.** *Court of Appeals (District of Columbia Circuit)*
> *Name:* United States Court of Appeals for the District of Columbia Circuit

United States. *District Court (Delaware)*
  Name: United States District Court for the District of Delaware

United States. *District Court (North Carolina : Eastern District)*
  Name: United States District Court for the Eastern District of North Carolina

United States. *District Court (Illinois : Northern District : Eastern Division)*
  Name: United States District Court for the Eastern Division of the Northern District of Illinois

California. *Municipal Court (Los Angeles Judicial District)*
  Name: Municipal Court, Los Angeles Judicial District

California. *Superior Court (San Bernardino County)*
  Name: Superior Court of the State of California in and for San Bernardino County

24.23B. Ad hoc military courts

Enter an ad hoc military court (court-martial, court of inquiry, etc.) under the heading for the particular military service. Add the surname of the defendant and the year of the trial.

United States. *Army. Court of Inquiry (Hall : 1863)*

Virginia. *Militia. Court-martial (Yancey : 1806)*

24.24. ARMED FORCES

24.24A. Armed forces at the national level

Enter a principal service of the armed forces of a government as a direct subheading of the name of the government.

Canada. *Canadian Armed Forces*

United Kingdom. *Royal Navy*

United States. *Marine Corps*[15]

United Kingdom. *Royal Marines*

Enter a component branch, command district, or military unit, large or small, as a direct subheading of the heading for the principal service of which it is a part.

United Kingdom. *Army. Royal Gloucestershire Hussars*

United Kingdom. *Royal Air Force. Central Interpretation Unit*

United Kingdom. *Royal Navy. Sea Cadet Corps*

United States. *Army. General Staff*

United States. *Army. Corps of Engineers*

United States. *Army. Far East Command*

United States. *Army. District of Mindanao*

---

15. The Marine Corps and the Royal Marines (following example) are treated as principal services.

If the component branch, etc., is numbered, follow the style of numbering found in the names (spelled out, roman numerals, or arabic numerals) and place the numbering after the name.

> **United Kingdom.** *Army. Infantry Regiment, 57th*
>
> **United States.** *Army. Infantry Division, 27th*
>
> **United States.** *Navy. Fleet, 6th*
>
> **United States.** *Army. Army, First*
>
> **United States.** *Army. Corps, IV*
>
> **United States.** *Army. Engineer Combat Battalion, 2nd*
>
> **United States.** *Army. Volunteer Cavalry, 1st*
>
> **United States.** *Navy. Torpedo Squadron 8*
>
> **Confederate States of America.** *Army. Tennessee Regiment, 1st*
>
> **France.** *Armée. Régiment de dragons, 15ᵉ*
>
> **Germany.** *Heer. Panzerdivision, 11.*
>
> **Germany.** *Luftwaffe. Jagdgeschwader 26*
>
> **Germany.** *Luftwaffe. Luftgaukommando VII*
>
> **Union of Soviet Socialist Republics.** *Armiíâ. Vozdushnaíâ armiíâ, 16.*

If the name of such a component branch, etc., begins with the name or an indication of the name, of the principal service, enter it as a direct subheading of the name of the government.

> **United States.** *Army Map Service*
>
> **United States.** *Naval Air Transport Service*

If the name of such a component branch, etc., contains but does not begin with the name or an indication of the name of the principal service, omit the name or indication of the name unless objectionable distortion would result.

> **Canada.** *Army. Royal Canadian Army Medical Corps*

24.24B. Armed forces below the national level

Enter armed forces that are controlled by governments below the national level as subheadings of the headings for such governments.

> **New York** (*State*). *Militia*
>
> **New York** (*State*). *National Guard*

Enter a component branch, etc., of such a force in a concise form as a subheading of the heading for the force.

> **New York** (*State*). *Militia. Regiment of Artillery, 9th*
> *Name:* 9th Regiment of Artillery, N.Y.S.M.
>
> **New York** (*State*). *National Guard. Coast Defense Command, 9th*

Enter a component branch, etc., of a force below the national level that has been absorbed into the national military forces as instructed in 24.24A.

> **United States.** *Army. New York Volunteers, 83rd*

> **United States.** *Army. Regiment Infantry, New York Volunteers, 9th*

24.25. EMBASSIES, CONSULATES, ETC.

Enter an embassy, consulate, legation, or other continuing office representing one country in another as a subheading of the heading for the country represented. Give the subheading in the language (see 24.3A) of the country represented. If the heading is for an embassy or legation, add the name of the country to which it is accredited. If the heading is for a consulate or other local office, add the name of the city in which it located.

> **Germany.** *Gesandtschaft (Switzerland)*

> **United Kingdom.** *Embassy (U.S.)*

> **United States.** *Legation (Bulgaria)*

> **Yugoslavia.** *Poslanstvo (U.S.)*

> **France.** *Consulat (Buenos Aires)*

> **United Kingdom.** *Consulate (Cairo)*

> **Canada.** *Embassy (Belgium)*

24.26. DELEGATIONS TO INTERNATIONAL AND INTERGOVERNMENTAL BODIES

Enter a delegation, commission, etc., representing a country in an international or intergovernmental body, conference, undertaking, etc., as a subheading of the heading for the country represented. Give the subheading in the language (see 24.3A) of the country represented. If the name of the delegation, etc., is uncertain, give the subheading as *Delegation [Mission, etc.] to* —— (or equivalent terms in the language of the country represented). Make explanatory references as necessary from the heading for the international body, etc., followed by an appropriate subheading.

> **United States.** *Mission to the United Nations*
> *Typical explanatory reference:*

> > **United Nations.** *Missions*
> > Delegations, missions, etc., from member nations to the United Nations and to its subordinate units are entered under the name of the nation followed by the name of the delegation, mission, etc.; e.g.,

> > **United States.** *Mission to the United Nations*

> > **United States.** *Delegation to the General Assembly of the United Nations*

> > **Uruguay.** *Delegación en las Naciones Unidas*

> *Make the same explanatory reference under:*
> **United Nations.** *Delegations*
> **United Nations.** *General Assembly. Delegations*
> *and wherever else it is appropriate.*

> **Mexico.** *Delegación a la Conferencia Interamericana de Consolidación de la Paz, Buenos Aires, 1936*

> **Germany.** *Reichskommission für die Weltausstellung in Chicago, 1893*

If it is uncertain that a delegation represents the government of a country, enter it under its own name.

Religious bodies and officials

24.27. RELIGIOUS BODIES AND OFFICIALS

24.27A. Councils, etc., of a single religious body

24.27A1. Enter councils, etc., of the national, regional, provincial, state, or local clergy and/or membership of a single religious body as a subheading of the heading for the religious body. When appropriate, make additions to the heading as instructed in 24.7B. (See 24.12–24.13 for general councils.)

> **Catholic Church.** *Antilles Episcopal Conference*

> **Society of Friends.** *Philadelphia Yearly Meeting*[16]

> **United Methodist Church** (*U.S.*). *Northern Illinois Conference*

24.27A2. If the name of a council, etc., of the Catholic Church is given in more than one language, use the English, Latin, French, German, or Spanish name (in that order of preference) and make appropriate references.

> **Catholic Church.** *Canadian Conference of Catholic Bishops*

> **Catholic Church.** *Concilium Plenarium Americae Latinae (1899 : Rome)*

> **Catholic Church.** *Plenary Council of Baltimore (2nd : 1866)*

24.27A3. If a council, etc., is subordinate to a particular district of the religious body, enter it as a subheading of the heading for that district (see 24.27C2–24.27C3). If the name appears in more than one language, use the name in the vernacular of the district.

> **Catholic Church.** *Province of Baltimore. Provincial Council (10th : 1869)*

> **Catholic Church.** *Province of Mexico City. Concilio Provincial (3rd : 1585)*

---

16. *Yearly Meeting* as used by the Society of Friends denotes a particular level in the structure of the society.

24.27B. Religious officials

24.27B1. Enter a religious official (bishop, abbot, patriarch, etc.) acting in an official capacity (see 21.4D1) as a subheading of the heading for the diocese, order, patriarchate, etc. (see 24.27C2–24.27C3). The subheading consists of the title in English (unless there is no equivalent English term), the inclusive years of incumbency, and the name of the person in brief form.

> **Catholic Church.** *Diocese of Campos. Bishop (1949–   : Mayer)*

> **Franciscans.** *Minister General (1947–1951 : Perantoni)*

> **Catholic Church.** *Diocese of Winchester. Bishop (1367–1404 : William, of Wykeham)*

If the heading applies to more than one incumbent (see 21.4D1), omit the dates and names.

> **Church of England.** *Diocese of Winchester. Bishop*

If a heading is established for an incumbent as a person in addition to the heading as a religious official, make an explanatory reference under the heading for the official (see 26.3C1).

24.27B2. Popes. Enter a pope acting in an official capacity (see 21.4D1) as a subheading of *Catholic Church*. The subheading consists of the word *Pope*, the inclusive years of the reign, and the pontifical name in its catalogue entry form (see 22.17B).

> **Catholic Church.** *Pope (1878–1903 : Leo XIII)*

> **Catholic Church.** *Pope (1978 : John Paul I)*

If the heading applies to more than one Pope (see 21.4D1), omit the dates and names.

> **Catholic Church.** *Pope*

If a heading is established for a pope as a person in addition to the heading as a religious official, make an explanatory reference under the heading for the official (see 26.3C1).

24.27C. Subordinate bodies

24.27C1. General rule. Except as provided in 24.27C2–24.27C4, enter subordinate religious bodies according to the instructions in 24.12–24.13. For religious orders and societies, see 24.3D.

24.27C2. Provinces, dioceses, synods, etc. Enter provinces, dioceses, synods, and other subordinate units of religious bodies having jurisdiction over geographic areas as subheadings under the heading for the religious body.

> **Church of England.** *Diocese of Ely*

> **Evangelical and Reformed Church.** *Reading Synod*

> **Evangelische Kirche der Altpreussischen Union.** *Kirchenprovinz Sachsen*

435

24.27C3 *Catholic dioceses, etc.*

> **Church of England.** *Archdeaconry of Surrey*
>
> **Nederlandse Hervormde Kerk.** *Classis Rotterdam*
>
> **Protestant Episcopal Church in the U.S.A.** *Diocese of Southern Virginia*
>
> **Russkaͭ͡a pravoslavnaͭ͡a ͭ͡serkov′.** *Moskovskaͭ͡a patriarkhiͭ͡a*
>
> **Svenska kyrkan.** *Ärkestiftet Uppsala*
>
> **Church of England.** *Woking Deanery*

24.27C3. Catholic dioceses, etc. Use an English form of name for a patriarchate, diocese, province, etc., of the Catholic Church. Give the name of the see according to the instructions in chapter 23.

> **Catholic Church.** *Archdiocese of Santiago de Cuba*
>
> **Catholic Church.** *Diocese of Uppsala*
>
> **Catholic Church.** *Diocese of Ely*
>
> **Catholic Church.** *Diocese of Hexham and Newcastle*
>
> **Catholic Church.** *Patriarchate of Alexandria of the Copts*
>
> **Catholic Church.** *Province of Québec*
>
> **Catholic Church.** *Ukrainian Catholic Archeparchy of Philadelphia*
>
> **Catholic Church.** *Vicariate Apostolic of Zamora*

Distinguish between a diocese of the Catholic Church and an ecclesiastical principality established in the Holy Roman Empire (often called *Bistum*) bearing the same name and ruled by the same bishop.

> **Catholic Church.** *Diocese of Fulda*
>
> **Fulda** (*Ecclesiastical principality*)

24.27C4. Central administrative organs of the Catholic Church (Roman Curia)
Enter the congregations, tribunals, and other central administrative organs of the Catholic Church (the Roman Curia) as subheadings of *Catholic Church.* Use the Latin form of their names. Omit any form of the word *sacer* when it is the first word of the name and make an explanatory reference (see 26.3C1) under it.

> **Catholic Church.** *Congregatio Sacrorum Rituum*
>
> **Catholic Church.** *Congregatio de Propaganda Fide*
>
> **Catholic Church.** *Rota Romana*

24.27D. Papal diplomatic missions, etc.
Enter a diplomatic mission from the Pope to a secular power as a subheading of *Catholic Church.* The subheading consists of *Apostolic Nunciature* or *Apostolic Internunciature*, as appropriate, and the name of the power to which the mission is accredited.

> **Catholic Church.** *Apostolic Internunciature* (*India*)
>
> **Catholic Church.** *Apostolic Nunciature* (*Flanders*)

The subheading for a nondiplomatic apostolic delegation consists of *Apostolic Delegation* and the name of the country or other jurisdiction in which it functions.

> **Catholic Church.** *Apostolic Delegation (U.K.)*

The subheading for any emissary of the Pope other than a nuncio, internuncio, or apostolic delegate consists of the title of the emissary (in English if there is an equivalent term; otherwise in Latin) and the name of the country or region in which the emissary functions.

> **Catholic Church.** *Legate (Colombia)*

If the country or region is not ascertained and differentiation is required, add the name of the emissary.

> **Catholic Church.** *Commissary Apostolic (Robertus Castellensis)*

UNIFORM TITLES

Contents

SPECIAL RULES FOR CERTAIN MATERIALS

Contents

25.1. USE OF UNIFORM TITLES

Uniform titles provide the means for bringing together all the catalogue entries for a work[1] when various manifestations (e.g., editions, translations) of it have appeared under various titles. They also provide identification for a work when the title by which it is known differs from the title proper of the item being catalogued. The need to use uniform titles varies from one catalogue to another and varies within one

---

1. Unless otherwise indicated, the word *work* used in this chapter includes collections and compilations catalogued as a unit.

catalogue. Base the decision whether to use uniform titles in a particular instance on:

a) how well the work is known
b) how many manifestations of the work are involved
c) whether the main entry is under title
d) whether the work was originally in another language
e) the extent to which the catalogue is used for research purposes.

Although the rules in this chapter are stated as instructions, apply them according to the policy of the cataloguing agency.

General rules

25.2. BASIC RULE

25.2A. When the manifestations (other than revised editions) of a work appear under various titles, select one title as the uniform title as instructed in 25.3–25.4.
Use a uniform title for an entry for a particular item if

1) the item bears a title proper that differs from the uniform title
or 2) the addition of another element (e.g., the name of the language of an item, see 25.5D) is required to organize the file.

Enclose the uniform title in square brackets, and give it before the title proper. If the work is entered under title, give the uniform title as the heading with square brackets. *Optionally*, record a uniform title used as main entry heading without square brackets.[2]

> **Dickens, Charles**
> [Martin Chuzzlewit]
> The life and adventures of Martin Chuzzlewit . . . 1868

> **Dickens, Charles**
> Martin Chuzzlewit . . . 1899

> **Dickens, Charles**
> [Martin Chuzzlewit]
> Martin Chuzzlewit's life and adventures . . . 1910

> **Blind date**
> Chance meeting
> (*Motion picture issued in Britain as:* Blind date. *Later issued in the U.S. as:* Chance meeting)

25.2B. Do not use a uniform title for a manifestation of a work in the same language that is a revision or updating of the original work. Relate editions not connected by

---

2. In examples in this chapter uniform titles for works entered under title are shown as headings without square brackets.

uniform titles by giving the title of the earlier edition in a note on the entry for the revision or updating (see 1.7B7, 2.7B7, etc.).

Scott, Franklin D.
The United States and Scandinavia . . . 1950

Scott, Franklin D.
Scandinavia . . . . — Rev. & enl. ed. . . . 1975
Note: Previous ed. published in 1950 as: The United States and Scandinavia

Richards, George
A treatise on the law of insurance . . . 1892

Richards, George
Richards on the law of insurance . . . . — 5th ed. / by Warren Freedman . . . 1952
("Fifth revision")
Note: First–3rd eds. published as: A treatise on the law of insurance

but

Hassenstein, Bernhard
ₗBiologische Kybernetik. Englishₗ
Information and control in the living organism . . . 1971
(*Verso of title page:* . . . English edition revised from the third German edition . . .)

25.2C. Romanization

If the title selected as the uniform title is in a language written in a nonroman script, romanize it according to the table for that language adopted by the cataloguing agency (see also 25.4C).

25.2D. Added entries and references

25.2D1. Works entered under title. If a work is entered under a uniform title, make an added entry under the title proper of the item being catalogued (see 21.30J). Refer from any other variants of the title.

25.2D2. Works entered under a personal or corporate heading. If a work is entered under a personal or corporate heading and a uniform title is used, make a name-title reference from variants of the title. Make an added entry under the title proper of the item being catalogued (see 21.30J).

INDIVIDUAL TITLES

25.3. WORKS CREATED AFTER 1500

25.3A. Use the title or form of title in the original language by which a work created after 1500 has become known through use in manifestations of the work or in reference sources. Omit an initial article only from a uniform title used as a main entry heading if it is not required for reasons of grammar (i.e., leave the initial article in all other uniform titles).

Dickens, Charles
ˌThe Pickwick papersˌ
The posthumous papers of the Pickwick Club

Whitaker's almanack
An almanack for the year of Our Lord . . .

Hemingway, Ernest
ˌThe sun also risesˌ
Fiesta . . . 1927

Shakespeare, William
ˌHamletˌ
The tragicall historie of Hamlet, Prince of Denmarke . . . 1603

Emerson, Ralph Waldo
ˌThe American scholarˌ
An oration delivered before the Phi Beta Kappa Society, at
Cambridge, August 31, 1837 . . . 1837
   (*Most subsequent editions entitled* The American scholar)

Mozart, Wolfgang Amadeus
ˌDon Giovanniˌ
Il dissoluto punito . . .

Swift, Jonathan
ˌGulliver's travelsˌ
Travels into several remote nations of the world / by Lemuel
Gulliver . . . 1726

Trial of treasure
A new and mery enterlude called the Triall of treasure . . . 1567

25.3B. If no one title in the original language is established as being the one by which
the work is best known, or in case of doubt, use the title proper of the original edition.
Omit from such titles

1) introductory phrases (e.g., "Here beginneth the tale of")
2) statements of responsibility that are a part of the title proper (see 1.1B2), if such
   an omission is grammatically permissible and if the statement is not essential to
   the meaning of the title
3) an initial article of a uniform title used as main entry heading if it is not required
   for reasons of grammar.

Gaunt, William
ˌThe pre-Raphaelite tragedyˌ
The pre-Raphaelite dream . . .

Criminal
The concrete jungle . . .
   (*Motion picture issued in Britain as*: The criminal. *Later issued in the
   U.S. as* : The concrete jungle)

Wodehouse, P.G.
ˌRing for Jeevesˌ
The return of Jeeves . . .

Norway
ₜGrundlovₜ
Kongeriget Norges Grundlov . . .

Treatyse of a galaunt
Here begynneth a treatyse of a galaũt . . . ₜ1518?ₜ

25.3C. Simultaneous publication under different titles

25.3C1. If a work is published simultaneously in the same language under two different titles, use the title of the edition published in the home country of the cataloguing agency. If the work is not published in the home country, use the title of the edition received first.

> *For a cataloguing agency in the United States*
> **Joesten, Joachim**
> Rats in the larder : the story of Nazi influence in Denmark. —
> New York . . . 1939
>
> **Joesten, Joachim**
> ₜRats in the larderₜ
> Denmark's day of doom. — London . . . 1939

25.3C2. If a work entered under the heading for a corporate body is published simultaneously in different languages and under different titles, none of which is known to be the original language or title, use as uniform title the title in the language in which the name of the corporate body is entered in the catalogue.

If there is no title in the language of the corporate heading, or if this criterion does not apply, follow the instructions in 25.3C3.

25.3C3. If any other work is published simultaneously in different languages and under different titles, none of which is known to be the original language or title, use as uniform title the title in (in this order of preference): English, French, German, Spanish, or Russian. If there is no title in one of these languages, use the title of the edition received first.

25.4. WORKS CREATED BEFORE 1501

25.4A. General rule
Use the title, or form of title, in the original language by which a work created before 1501 (other than those covered by 25.4B–25.4C and 25.14) is identified in modern reference sources. If the evidence of modern reference sources is inconclusive, use the title most frequently found in (in this order of preference):

1) modern editions
2) early editions
3) manuscript copies.

Omit initial articles if not required for reasons of grammar.

> **Avicenna**
> ₜDānishnāmah-i 'Alā'īₜ

Beowulf

Caesar, Julius
ᵢDe bello Gallicoᵢ

Chanson de Roland

Chaucer, Geoffrey
ᵢTroilus and Criseydeᵢ

Nibelungenlied

Edictum Theodorici

25.4B. Classical and Byzantine Greek works

Use a well-established English title for a work originally written in classical Greek, or a work of a Greek church father or other Byzantine writer up to 1453. If there is no such English title, use the Latin title. If there is neither a well-established English title nor a Latin title, use the Greek title.

English

Aristophanes
ᵢBirdsᵢ
not Aves
not Ornithes

Aristophanes
ᵢCloudsᵢ
not Nubes
not Nefelai

Comnena, Anna
ᵢAlexiadᵢ
not Alexias

Eusebius, *Bishop of Caesarea*
ᵢEcclesiastical historyᵢ
not Historia ecclesiastica
not Ekklēsiastikē historia

Homer
ᵢIliadᵢ
not Ilias

Homer
ᵢOdysseyᵢ
not Odyssea
not Odysseia

Plato
ᵢRepublicᵢ
not Respublica
not Politeia

Battle of the frogs and mice
not Batrachomyomachia

Latin

Apollonius, *Rhodius*
ᵢArgonauticaᵢ
not Argonautika

Aristotle
ₗMeteorologicaₗ

not Meteōrologika

Origen
ₗContra Celsiumₗ

not Kata Kelsou

Planudes, Maximus
ₗDe processione Spiritus Sanctiₗ

not Peri tēs ekporeuseōs tou Hagiou Pneumatos

Plato
ₗTheaetetusₗ

not Theaitētos

Greek

Manasses, Constantine
ₗSynopsis historikēₗ

Menander, *of Athens*
ₗGeōrgosₗ

Menander, *of Athens*
ₗPerikeiromenēₗ

Prodromus, Theodore
ₗKatamyomachiaₗ

25.4C. Anonymous works not written in Greek nor in the roman script

If the original language of an anonymous work created before 1501 is not written in Greek nor in the roman script, use an established title in English if there is one.

Arabian nights

Book of the dead

but **Slovo o polku Igoreve**

(*Published in English as* Igor's tale *and* The campaign of Igor *and* The tale of the campaign of Igor *and several other titles*)

25.5. ADDITIONS TO UNIFORM TITLES

25.5A. Make additions to uniform titles as instructed in this rule. For special additions to uniform titles for special types of material, see 25.13–25.36.

25.5B. Add in parentheses an appropriate explanatory word, brief phrase, or other designation to distinguish a uniform title used as a heading from an identical or similar heading for a person or corporate body or from an identical or similar uniform title used as a heading or reference.

Charlemagne, *Emperor*

Charlemagne *(Play)*

Guillaume, *13th cent.*

Guillaume (*Chanson de geste*)

Genesis (*Anglo-Saxon poem*)

> **Genesis** (*Book of the Bible*)
> (*Used only as a reference*)

> **Genesis** (*Middle High German poem*)

> **Genesis** (*Old Saxon poem*)

> **Adoration of the shepherds** (*Chester plays*)

> **Adoration of the shepherds** (*Coventry plays*)

> **Seven sages of Rome** (*Northern version*)

> **Seven sages of Rome** (*Southern version*)

> **King Kong** (*1933*)

> **King Kong** (*1976*)
> (*Two motion pictures with the same title*)

25.5C. Add in parentheses an appropriate designation to distinguish between identical uniform titles for works entered under the same personal or corporate heading.

> **France**
> ₁Constitution (1946)₁

> **France**
> ₁Constitution (1958)₁

25.5D. If the linguistic content of the item being catalogued is different from that of the original (e.g., a translation, a dubbed motion picture), add the name of the language of the item to the uniform title. Precede the language by a full stop.

> **Goncourt, Edmond de**
> ₁Les frères Zemganno. English₁
> The Zemganno brothers . . .
> (*An English translation of a French novel*)

> **Teorema.** *English*
> Theorem . . .
> (*An Italian motion picture dubbed in English*)

Do not add the name of the language to a uniform title for a motion picture with subtitles.

> **Jules et Jim**
> Jules and Jim . . .
> (*A French motion picture with English subtitles*)

If the language of the item is an early form of a modern language, add the name of the modern language followed by the name of the early form in parentheses, e.g., French (Old French); French (Anglo-Norman); English (Middle English).

> **Boethius**
> ₁De consolatione philosophiae. English (Middle English)₁
> Chaucer's "Boece" . . .

If an item is in two languages, name both. If one of the languages is the original language, name it second. Otherwise, name the languages in the following order:

English, French, German, Spanish, Russian, other languages in alphabetic order of their names in English. If an item is in three or more languages, use the term *Polyglot* unless the item in the original is in three or more languages (e.g., a multilateral treaty), in which case give all the languages in the order specified above.

> **Caesar, Julius**
> ₍De bello Gallico. French & Latin₎
> Les commentaires . . .

> **United States**
> ₍The Declaration of Independence. Polyglot₎
> The Declaration of Independence of the United States, in ten languages . . .

25.5E. *Optionally*, if general material designations are used (see 1.1C), add the designation at the end of the uniform title.

> **Brunhoff, Jean de**
> ₍Babar en famille. English. Sound recording₎
> Babar and his children . . .

25.6. PARTS OF A WORK[3]

25.6A. Single parts

25.6A1. If a separately catalogued part of a work has a title of its own, use the title of the part by itself as the uniform title. Make a *see* reference from the heading for the whole work and the title of the part as a subheading of the title of the whole work. Include in the title in the reference the numeric designation of the part if there is one. Give the numeric designation in arabic numerals, but omit terms such as *volume*, *part*, *tome*, etc. Substitute an explanatory reference for the *see* reference if appropriate.

> **Tolkien, J.R.R.**
> ₍The two towers₎
> *x* Tolkien, J.R.R. The lord of the rings. 2. The two towers

> **Proust, Marcel**
> ₍Du côté de chez Swann₎
> *x* Proust, Marcel. A la recherche du temps perdu. 1. Du côté de chez Swann

> **Rolland, Romain**
> ₍Mère et fils. English₎
> Mother and son . . .
> *x* Rolland, Romain. Ame enchantée. 3. Mother and son

> **Raven, Simon**
> ₍Come like shadows . . .₎[4]

---

3. Apply 25.17–25.18 to parts of the Bible and certain other sacred scriptures; apply 25.32 to parts of musical works.

4. The marks of omission in uniform titles in examples here and subsequently indicate that a further element is, or may be, required to complete the uniform title.

> *Explanatory reference:*
> **Raven, Simon**
>> Alms for oblivion
>>> For separately published novels in this series, see
>> **Raven, Simon**
>>> Come like shadows
>>> Fielding Gray
>>> Friends in low places
>>>> ₍*etc.*₎

> **Sindbad the sailor**
>> *Explanatory reference:*
>> **Arabian nights**
>>> For separately published stories from this collection, see
>> **Ali Baba**
>> **Sindbad the sailor**
>>> ₍*etc.*₎

25.6A2. If a separately catalogued part of a work is identified only by a general term (with or without a number) such as

> Preface
> Detail
>> (*For a graphic item*)
> Epilogue
> Book 1
> Part 2
> Number 1
> Band 3

use the designation of the part as a subheading of the title of the whole work. Use arabic numerals to record the number of the part.

> **Goethe, Johann Wolfgang von**
>> ₍Faust. 1. Theil. English & German₎

25.6B. Several parts

25.6B1. If the item being catalogued consists of consecutive parts of a work and the parts are numbered, use the designation of the parts in the singular as a subheading of the title of the whole work followed by the inclusive numbers of the parts. Treat them as a single part in applying 25.6B2–25.6B3.

> **Homer**
>> ₍Iliad. Book 1–6₎
>> The first six books of Homer's Iliad . . .

25.6B2. If the item consists of two unnumbered or nonconsecutively numbered parts of a work, use the uniform title (see 25.6A) of the first part as the uniform title for the item. Make a name-title added entry for the other part.

Dante Alighieri
　　[Purgatorio. English]
　　The vision of Purgatory and Paradise . . .
　Added entry under: Dante Alighieri. Paradiso. English

Homer
　　[Iliad. Book 1. English]
　　Iliad, books I and VI . . .
　Added entry under: Homer. Iliad. Book 6. English

Homer
　　[Odyssey. Book 6–14. English]
　　The Odyssey, books VI–XIV, XVII–XXIV . . .
　Added entry under: Homer. Odyssey. Book 17–24. English

25.6B3. If the item consists of three or more unnumbered or nonconsecutively numbered parts of, or of extracts from, a work, use the uniform title for the whole work followed by *Selections*.

Gibbon, Edward
　　[The history of the decline and fall of the Roman Empire. Selections]

If the item is a translation, add the subheading *Selections* following the name of the language.

Dickens, Charles
　　[Sketches by Boz. German. Selections]
　　Londoner Skizzen von Boz . . .

25.7. TWO WORKS ISSUED TOGETHER

If an item consisting of two works is entered under a personal or corporate heading, use the uniform title of the work that occurs first in the item. Make a name-title added entry using the uniform title of the second work.

Dickens, Charles
　　[Hard times]
　　Dickens' new stories . . .
　　　(*Contains* Hard times *and* Pictures from Italy)
　Added entry under: Dickens, Charles. Pictures from Italy

Gibbons, Orlando
　　[O Lord, how do my woes increase . . .]
　　Two anthems for four and five voices : from Leighton's Teares
　or lamentations . . .
　　　(*Contains* O Lord, how do my woes increase *and* O Lord, I lift my
　　　heart to thee)
　Added entry under: Gibbons, Orlando. O Lord, I lift my heart to thee

COLLECTIVE TITLES

25.8. COMPLETE WORKS

Use the collective title *Works* for an item that consists of, or purports to be, the complete works of a person, including those that are complete at the time of publication.

> **Maugham, W. Somerset**
>> ⌐Works⌐
>> Complete works . . .
>
> **Mirabeau, Honoré-Gabriel de Riqueti,** *comte de*
>> ⌐Works⌐
>> Œuvres de Mirabeau . . .

25.9. SELECTIONS

Use the collective title *Selections* for items consisting of three or more works in various forms, or in one form if the person created works in one form only, and for items consisting of extracts, etc., from the works of one person.

> **Maugham, W. Somerset**
>> ⌐Selections⌐
>> The Somerset Maugham pocket book . . .
>>> (*Contains:* Cakes and ale, The circle, Short stories, Travel sketches, Essays)
>
> **Maugham, W. Somerset**
>> ⌐Selections⌐
>> Wit and wisdom of Somerset Maugham . . .
>
> **Morris, William**
>> ⌐Selections⌐
>> Selected writings and designs . . .

25.10. WORKS IN A SINGLE FORM

Use an appropriate collective title for an item that consists of, or purports to be, the complete works of a person in one particular form.

Use the following terms as appropriate:

Correspondence	Poems
Essays	Prose works
Novels	Short stories
Plays	Speeches

If none of these terms is appropriate, use an appropriate specific collective title (e.g., Posters, Fragments). For musical works, see 25.36.

> **Maugham, W. Somerset**
>> ⌐Plays⌐
>> Collected plays . . .
>
> **Maugham, W. Somerset**
>> ⌐Short stories⌐
>> Complete short stories . . .

If the item consists of three or more but not all of the works of one person in a particular form, or of extracts, etc., from the works of one person in a particular form, add *Selections* to the collective title.

> **Maugham, W. Somerset**
>> ⌐Novels. Selections⌐
>> Selected novels . . .

Maugham, W. Somerset
ₗPlays. Selectionsₗ
Six comedies . . .

Maugham, W. Somerset
ₗShort stories. Selectionsₗ
Best short stories of W. Somerset Maugham . . .

25.11. TRANSLATIONS, ETC.

If the linguistic content of a collection or selection of the works of one person is different from that of the originals, add the name of the language to the collective title as instructed in 25.5D. If the term *Selections* is added to a collective title, add the name of the language before that term.

Maugham, W. Somerset
ₗWorks. Spanishₗ
Obras completas . . .

Archilochus
ₗFragments. Englishₗ
Archilochos / introduced, translated, and illustrated by
Michael Ayrton

Maugham, W. Somerset
ₗShort stories. Spanish. Selections
En los mares del sur . . .
(Six short stories)

25.12. UNIFORM TITLES FOR STORIES WITH MANY VERSIONS AND FOR CYCLES

25.12A. If an added entry is required for a basic story found in many versions, use the title that is established in English-language reference sources. Add the name of the language of the item being catalogued.

Le roman de Renart . . .
(First of the Reynard stories)
Added entry under: Reynard the Fox. French

The history of Reynard the Fox . . .
(Translation of a Dutch version)
Added entry under: Reynard the Fox. English

Amis and Amiloun . . .
(Thirteenth century English version of a 12th century chanson de geste)
Added entry under: Ames et Amiles. English

25.12B. Use as the uniform title for a cycle (a collection of independent early poems, romances, etc., in the same language centred on a certain person, event, object, etc.) the generally accepted title for the cycle.

> **Guillaume d'Orange** (*Chansons de geste*)
>> Guillaume d'Orange : chansons de geste des XIe et XIIe siècles . . .
>>> (*Contains:* Li coronemens Looys, Li charrois de Nymes, La prise d'Orenge, Li covenans Vivien, *and* La bataille d'Aleschans)

If the cycle is only identified by a descriptive phrase (e.g., "the Arthurian romances," "the Grail legends," "the St. Francis legends") or has no established title, enter it as instructed in 21.7.

> La Légende arthurienne . . . les plus anciens textes . . .
> *Main entry under title proper*

Special rules for certain materials

25.13. COMPOSITE MANUSCRIPTS AND MANUSCRIPT GROUPS

Use as the uniform title for a work that is, or is contained in, a composite manuscript or manuscript group (in this order of preference):

- a) a title that has been assigned to the work subsequent to its writing or compilation
- b) the name of the manuscript or manuscript group if the work is identified only by that name

> **Book of Lismore**
>
> **Dead Sea scrolls**
>
> **Tell el-Amarna tablets**

- c) the heading (see chapter 24) of the repository followed by *Manuscript* and the repository's designation for the manuscript or manuscript group. If the item being catalogued is a single manuscript in a composite manuscript, add the foliation if known.

> **British Library. Manuscript. Arundel 384**
>
> **British Library. Manuscript. Additional 15233, fol. 11–27**

Refer to the name chosen according to *a* or *b* above from the designation provided for in *c* if the manuscript or manuscript group is also identified by its designation in a repository.

> **Codex Brucianus**
> *x* Bodleian Library. Manuscript. Bruce 96

25.14. INCUNABULA

Use as the uniform title for an incunabulum the title found in standard reference sources for incunabula.

> **Victor, Sextus Aurelius**
> [De viris illustribus]
> Liber virorum illustrium . . .
>
> **Victor, Sextus Aurelius**
> [De viris illustribus]
> De rebus praeclare gestis virorum illustrium . . .

LEGAL MATERIALS

25.15. LAWS, ETC.

25.15A. Modern laws, etc.

25.15A1. Collections. Use *Laws, etc.* for complete or partial collections of legislative enactments other than compilations on a particular subject.

> **United Kingdom**
> ₍Laws, etc.₎
> Halsbury's statutes of England . . .

> **United States**
> ₍Laws, etc.₎
> United States code . . .

> **Ontario**
> ₍Laws, etc.₎
> Statutes of the Province of Ontario passed in the session held at Toronto in the twenty-third and twenty-fourth years of the reign of Her Majesty Queen Elizabeth II . . .

> **Boston**
> ₍Laws, etc.₎
> The revised ordinances of 1961 of the city of Boston . . .

If a subject compilation has a citation title (see 25.15A2), use that. Otherwise, follow the instructions in 25.3.

> **California**
> ₍Agricultural code₎
> West's California agricultural code . . .

> **United Kingdom**
> ₍Licensing acts₎
> Paterson's licensing acts. — 85th ed., 1977 / by J.N. Martin

25.15A2. Single laws, etc. Use as the uniform title for a single legislative enactment (in this order of preference):

a) the official short title or citation title
b) an unofficial short title or citation title used in legal literature
c) the official title of the enactment
d) any other official designation (e.g., the number or date).

> **United Kingdom**
> ₍Field Monuments Act 1972₎

> **New Zealand**
> ₍Copyright Act 1962₎
> *(Citation title includes date of enactment)*

> **Canada**
> ₍Canada Corporations Act₎

455

> **France**
>> ₁Code pénal₁
>
> **Argentina**
>> ₁Ley no. 20.744₁

If there are several different laws, etc., entered under the heading for the same jurisdiction and bearing the same title, add the year of promulgation.

> **United Kingdom**
>> ₁Education Act (1944)₁

25.15B. Ancient laws, certain medieval laws, customary laws, etc.

Follow the instructions in 25.3 or 25.4 for uniform titles for collections of ancient, medieval, or customary laws identified by a name or for a single ancient, medieval, or customary law.

> **Salic Law**
>> Lex Salica . . .

25.16. TREATIES, ETC.

25.16A. Collections of treaties, etc.

Use as the uniform title for a collection of treaties, etc., between two parties *Treaties, etc.* followed by the name of the other party.

> **France**
>> ₁Treaties, etc. United Kingdom₁

Use *Treaties, etc.* alone for a collection of treaties, etc., between a single party and two or more other parties.

> **United States**
>> ₁Treaties, etc.₁

If a collection of treaties, etc., signed at the same time is identified by a name, use that name followed in parentheses by the year or earliest year of signing for an item containing all the treaties, etc. For single treaties, etc., in the collection, see 25.16B. Make *see also* references from the title of the collection to the headings and/or titles of the single treaties.

> **Treaty of Utrecht** (*1713*)
>> *see also*
>
> **France**
>> ₁Treaties, etc. Prussia, 1713 . . .₁
>
> **Spain**
>> ₁Treaties, etc. United Kingdom, 1713 . . .₁
>> ₁*etc.*₁

25.16B. Single treaties, etc.

25.16B1. Two or three parties. Use a uniform title beginning *Treaties, etc.* for treaties and other agreements between two or three of the following:

a) national governments
b) international intergovernmental bodies

456

c) the Holy See

d) jurisdictions now below the national level but retaining treaty-making powers.

Add the name of the other party if there is only one party on the other side. Add the date or earliest date of signing in the form: year, abbreviated name of the month, number of the day.

Denmark
₁Treaties, etc. United Kingdom, 1966 Mar. 3₁
Agreement between the government of the United Kingdom of Great Britain and Northern Ireland and the Kingdom of Denmark relating to the delimitation of the continental shelf between the two countries : London, 3 March 1966 . . .

Netherlands
₁Treaties, etc. 1943 Oct. 21₁
Convention monétaire belgo-luxembourgeoise-néerlandaise . . .
21 oct. 1943

> (*A treaty between the Netherlands on the one side and Belgium and Luxembourg on the other*)

France
₁Treaties, etc. 1920 Aug. 10₁
Tripartite agreement between the British Empire, France, and Italy . . . : signed at Sèvres, August 10, 1920

Iceland
₁Treaties, etc. International Bank for Reconstruction and Development, 1953 Sept. 4₁
Guarantee agreement . . . between Republic of Iceland and International Bank for Reconstruction and Development : dated September 4, 1953

Baden
₁Treaties, etc. Catholic Church, 1932 Oct. 12₁
Das Konkordat zwischen dem Heiligen Stuhle und dem Freistaate Baden : vom 12. Oktober 1932

25.16B2. Four or more parties. Use as the uniform title for a treaty, etc., between four or more parties the name by which the treaty is known. Use an English name if there is one. Add, in parentheses, the year or earliest year of signing. When making added entries for individual signatories to such an agreement (see 21.35A2), formulate the uniform title as instructed in 25.16B1.

Convention Regarding the Status of Aliens (*1928*)
Convención sobre condiciones de los extranjeros : celebrada entre los Estados Unidos Mexicanos y varias naciones : firmada en la ciudad de La Habana el 20 de febrero de 1928

Treaty of Paris (*1763*)

Universal Copyright Convention (*1952*)

25.16B3. Protocols, etc. Use as the uniform title for a separately catalogued protocol, amendment, extension, or other agreement ancillary to a treaty, etc., the uniform title for the original agreement followed by *Protocols, etc.* and the date of signing (or inclusive dates if more than one protocol, etc., is involved).

> **Poland**
> ₁Treaties, etc. United Kingdom, 1948 Mar. 2. Protocols, etc., 1951 Mar. 6₁
>
> **Convention for the Protection of Human Rights and Fundamental Freedoms** *(1950). Protocols, etc., 1963 Sept. 16*

SACRED SCRIPTURES

25.17. GENERAL RULE

Use as the uniform title for a sacred scripture (see 21.37) the title by which it is most commonly identified in English-language reference sources dealing with the religious group to which the scripture belongs. If no such source is available, use general reference sources.

> **Avesta** . . .
>
> **Bible** . . .
>
> **Koran** . . .
>
> **Talmud** . . .
>
> **Tripiṭaka** . . .

For component parts of individual scriptures, see 25.18.

25.18. PARTS OF SACRED SCRIPTURES AND ADDITIONS

25.18A. Bible

25.18A1. General rule. Enter as a subheading under *Bible* any text included in the Catholic or Protestant canon.

25.18A2. Testaments. Enter the Old Testament as *O.T.* and the New Testament as *N.T.* under the heading *Bible.*

> **Bible.** *O.T.* . . .

25.18A3. Books. Enter individual books as subheadings of the appropriate testament. Use the brief citation form of the Authorized Version.

> **Bible.** *O.T. Ezra* . . .
>
> **Bible.** *N.T. Revelation* . . .

If a book is one of a numbered sequence of the same name, give its number as an ordinal arabic numeral after the name.

> **Bible.** *N.T. Corinthians, 1st* . . .

If the item is a part of a book (other than a single selection known by its title, see 25.18A7), give chapter (in roman numerals) and verse (in arabic numerals). Use inclusive numbering when necessary.

> **Bible.** *O.T. Ecclesiastes III, 1–8 . . .*

> **Bible.** *O.T. Genesis XII, 1–XXV, 11 . . .*

25.18A4. Groups of books. Enter an item consisting of one of the following groups of books under the name given here as a subheading of the appropriate testament. For other groups of books, follow the instructions in 25.18A8–25.18A9.

> **Bible.** *N.T. Catholic Epistles . . .*
> *(General epistles of James, Peter, John, and Jude)*

> **Bible.** *N.T. Corinthians . . .*
> *(1–2 Corinthians)*

> **Bible.** *N.T. Epistles . . .*
> *(All or miscellaneous epistles)*

> **Bible.** *N.T. Epistles of John . . .*
> *(1–3 John)*

> **Bible.** *N.T. Epistles of Paul . . .*

> **Bible.** *N.T. Gospels . . .*

> **Bible.** *N.T. Pastoral Epistles . . .*
> *(1–2 Timothy and Titus)*

> **Bible.** *N.T. Peter . . .*
> *(1–2 Peter)*

> **Bible.** *N.T. Thessalonians . . .*
> *(1–2 Thessalonians)*

> **Bible.** *N.T. Timothy . . .*
> *(1–2 Timothy)*

> **Bible.** *O.T. Chronicles . . .*
> *(1–2 Chronicles)*

> **Bible.** *O.T. Five Scrolls . . .*
> *(Song of Solomon, Ruth, Lamentations, Ecclesiastes, and Esther)*

> **Bible.** *O.T. Former Prophets . . .*
> *(Joshua, Judges, 1–2 Samuel, 1–2 Kings)*

> **Bible.** *O.T. Hagiographa . . .*
> *(Ruth, Chronicles, Ezra, Nehemiah, Esther, Job, Psalms, Proverbs, Ecclesiastes, Song of Solomon, Lamentations, and Daniel)*

> **Bible.** *O.T. Heptateuch . . .*
> *(Genesis, Exodus, Leviticus, Numbers, Deuteronomy, Joshua, and Judges)*

> **Bible.** *O.T. Hexateuch . . .*
> *(Genesis, Exodus, Leviticus, Numbers, Deuteronomy, and Joshua)*

> **Bible.** *O.T. Historical Books* . . .
> (*Joshua, Judges, Ruth, Samuel, Kings, Chronicles, Ezra, Nehemiah, and Esther*)

> **Bible.** *O.T. Kings* . . .
> (*1–2 Kings*)

> **Bible.** *O.T. Minor Prophets* . . .
> (*Hosea, Joel, Amos, Obadiah, Jonah, Micah, Nahum, Habakkuk, Zephaniah, Haggai, Zechariah, and Malachi*)

> **Bible.** *O.T. Pentateuch* . . .
> (*Genesis, Exodus, Leviticus, Numbers, and Deuteronomy*)

> **Bible.** *O.T. Prophets* . . .
> (*Isaiah, Jeremiah, Lamentations, Ezekiel, Daniel, Hosea, Joel, Amos, Obadiah, Jonah, Micah, Nahum, Habakkuk, Zephaniah, Haggai, Zechariah, and Malachi*)

> **Bible.** *O.T. Prophets* (*Nevi'im*) . . .
> (*Joshua, Judges, 1–2 Samuel, 1–2 Kings, Isaiah, Jeremiah, Ezekiel, and Minor Prophets*)

> **Bible.** *O.T. Samuel* . . .
> (*1–2 Samuel*)

25.18A5. Apocrypha. Enter the collection known as the Apocrypha (1–2 Esdras, Tobit, Judith, Rest of Esther, Wisdom of Solomon, Ecclesiasticus, Baruch, History of Susanna, Song of the Three Children, Bel and the Dragon, Prayer of Manasses, 1–2 Maccabees) under **Bible.** *O.T. Apocrypha.*[5] Designate an individual book as a subheading of *Apocrypha.*

> **Bible.** *O.T. Apocrypha* . . .

> **Bible.** *O.T. Apocrypha. Ecclesiasticus* . . .

> **Bible.** *O.T. Apocrypha. Maccabees, 1st* . . .

25.18A6. References. Refer, when appropriate, from the titles of individual books, variant titles of individual books, and from the names of groups of books. Refer also from these as direct subheadings of *Bible* and, in the case of variant titles, as sub-headings of the appropriate testament. Make explanatory references when necessary.

> **Bible.** *O.T. Ezra* . . .
> *x* Ezra (*Book of the Old Testament*)
> *x* Esdras (*Book 1, Vulgate*)
> *x* Bible. *Ezra*
> *x* Bible. *Esdras, 1st* (*Vulgate*)
> *x* Bible. *O.T. Esdras, 1st* (*Vulgate*)

---

5. Do not treat an edition of the Bible lacking these books as incomplete.

Bible. *O.T. Apocrypha. Esdras, 1st . . .*
  x Esdras (*Book 1, Apocrypha*)
  x Esdras (*Book 3*)
  x Bible. *Esdras, 1st (Apocrypha)*
  x Bible. *Esdras, 3rd*
  x Bible. *O.T. Esdras, 1st (Apocrypha)*
  x Bible. *O.T. Esdras, 3rd*

Bible. *O.T. Pentateuch . . .*
  x Pentateuch
  x Torah (*Pentateuch*)
  x Ḥumash
  x Bible. *Pentateuch*
  x Bible. *Torah*
  x Bible. *Ḥumash*
  x Bible. *O.T. Torah*
  x Bible. *O.T. Ḥumash*

Bible. *O.T. Prophets . . .*
  x Bible. *Prophets*

Bible. *O.T. Former Prophets . . .*
  xx Bible. *O.T. Historical Books*

Bible. *O.T. Historical Books . . .*
  xx Bible. *O.T. Former Prophets*

Bible. *O.T. Kings*
  Under this heading are found the books commonly called 1 and 2
  Kings but called 3 and 4 Kings in the Vulgate and versions based on it.
  For the books called 1 and 2 Kings in these versions, see
  Bible. *O.T. Samuel*

  Make similar explanatory references under: Bible. *O.T. Kings, 1st, and*
    Bible. *O.T. Kings, 2nd*

25.18A7. Single selections. If a single selection is commonly identified by its own title (rather than its designation as part of the Bible), use that directly as the uniform title, and refer from the form of title resulting from the application of 25.18A3.

Lord's prayer
  x Bible. *N.T. Matthew VI, 9–13*
  x Bible. *N.T. Luke XI, 2–4*

Ten commandments
  x Bible. *O.T. Exodus XX, 2–17*
  x Bible. *O.T. Deuteronomy V, 6–21*

Miserere
  x Bible. *O.T. Psalms LI*
  x Bible. *O.T. Psalms L (Vulgate)*

Enter any other single selection as instructed in 25.18A3.

  Bible. *O.T. Psalms XXIII . . .*

25.18A8. Two selections. If an item consists of two or more selections (including whole books) that can be encompassed precisely by two different uniform titles, enter under the uniform title for the first. Make an added entry under the uniform title for the second.

> **Bible.** *N.T. Gospels* . . .
>   Il Vangelo e gli Atti degli apostoli . . .
> *Added entry under:* Bible. N.T. Acts . . .

25.18A9. Other selections. Enter other selections (including miscellaneous extracts) under the most specific Bible heading. Add *Selections* after the language (see 25.18A10) and version (see 25.18A11) and before the year (see 25.18A13). If the selections are newly translated, do not include the translator's name as the version (see 25.18A11).

> **Bible.** *₁language₁ ₁version₁ Selections. ₁date₁*
>   Memorable passages from the Bible (Authorized Version) . . .

> **Bible.** *N.T. ₁language₁ ₁version₁ Selections. ₁date₁*
>   The records and letters of the Apostolic age . . .
>   (*Contains:* Acts, Epistles, *and* Revelation)

> **Bible.** *N.T. Gospels. ₁language₁ Selections. ₁date₁*
>   The message of Jesus Christ : the tradition of the early Christian communities / restored and translated into German by Martin Dibelius ; translated into English by Frederick C. Grant . . .

25.18A10. Language. Add the name of the language of the item after the designation for the Bible or part of the Bible.

> **Bible.** *English* . . .

> **Bible.** *O.T. English* . . .

> **Bible.** *O.T. Genesis. English* . . .

If the item is in two languages, add the name of:

a) the early language if one is an early language and the other modern
b) the less widely known language if both are modern languages
c) in other cases (in this order of preference):
>   the language of the text given primary emphasis in the item
>   the language named first in the chief source of information
>   the language of the chief source of information chosen according to 1.0H
>   the language of the Biblical text that appears first.

Make an added entry under the designation followed by the name of the other language.

> **Bible.** *Latin* . . .
>   La sainte Bible : texte latin et traduction française . . .
> *Added entry under:* Bible. French . . .

> **Bible.** *Kikuyu*
>   The Bible in English and Kikuyu . . .
> *Added entry under:* Bible. English . . .

If the Old Testament is in Hebrew and the New Testament is in Greek, use *Hebrew-Greek*. Make a *see also* reference from **Bible.** *O.T. Hebrew* . . . and **Bible.** *N.T. Greek* . . .
If the item is in three or more languages, use *Polyglot*.

> **Bible.** *N.T. Epistles of John. Polyglot*

25.18A11. Version. Give a brief form of the name of the version[6] following the name of the language. If the item is in three or more languages, do not add the name of the version.

> **Bible.** *Latin. Vulgate* . . .

> **Bible.** *N.T. Corinthians. English. Authorized* . . .

If the version is identified by the name of the translator, use the translator's surname. If there are two translators, hyphenate their surnames. If there are more than two, give the surname of the first followed by *et al.*

> **Bible.** *English. Lamsa* . . .

> **Bible.** *O.T. Anglo-Saxon. Ælfric* . . .

> **Bible.** *English. Smith-Goodspeed* . . .

Use *Douai* for Rheims-Douai-Challoner versions of the whole Bible. Use *Confraternity* for Confraternity-Douai-Challoner versions of the whole Bible.

> **Bible.** *English. Douai* . . .
> The Holy Bible / translated from the Latin Vulgate . . . being the
> edition published . . . at Rheims, A.D. 1582, and at Douay, 1609 ; as
> revised and corrected in 1750, according to the Clementine edition of
> the Scriptures, by Richard Challoner . . .

> **Bible.** *English. Confraternity* . . .
> The Holy Bible. — Confraternity text (Genesis to Ruth, Psalms,
> New Testament) Douay-Challoner text (remaining books of the
> Old Testament) . . .

If two versions are issued together, name the one named first in the chief source of information, or, if neither is named there, the one appearing first in the item. Make an added entry under the Bible heading naming the other version.

> **Bible.** *English. Authorized* . . .
> . . . Johnson's Worker's Bible : self-pronouncing edition of the
> Holy Scriptures arranged especially for workers, ministers, students . . .
> showing a new and simple combination of the Authorized and Revised
> versions of the Old and New Testaments . . .
> *Added entry under:* Bible. English. Revised . . .

25.18A12. Alternatives to version. If the item is in the original language, or if the version is unknown, or if the text has been altered, or if the version cannot be identified by

---

6. In connection with the Bible, the word *version* is used in its narrow sense of a translation. The version from which another version is made is ignored so far as entries and references are concerned.

name or translator, or if more than two versions are involved, use (in this order of preference):

a) the name of the manuscript or its repository designation (see 25.13) if the item is a manuscript or a reproduction, transcription, edition, or translation of a manuscript

> **Bible.** *Greek. Codex Sinaiticus*
> Bibliorum Codex Sinaiticus Petropolitanus . . .

b) the name of the person who has altered the text[7] if the altered text has no name of its own

> **Bible.** *English. Smith* . . .
> The Holy Scriptures : containing the Old and New Testaments : an inspired version of the Authorized Version / by Joseph Smith, Junior. — A new corr. ed., the Reorganized Church of Jesus Christ of Latter Day Saints . . .

c) a special name or phrase used in the chief source of information to identify the text.

> **Bible.** *English. Anchor Bible* . . .
> The Anchor Bible . . .

> **Bible.** *English. Numerical Bible* . . .
> The Numerical Bible : being a revised translation of the Holy Scriptures with expository notes : arranged, divided, and briefly characterized according to the principles of their numerical structure . . .

If none of the above applies, do not add this element.

25.18A13. Year. Add the year of publication at the end of the uniform title.

> **Bible.** *English. Revised Standard. 1959*

> **Bible.** *French. Le Maistre. 1848*

> **Bible.** *English. Revised Standard. 1961 ?*
> The Holy Bible : containing the Old and New Testaments. — Revised Standard Version . . . . — New York : Nelson, [1961 ?]

If an item is published over more than one year, add the earliest year.

> **Bible.** *Spanish. Torres Amat. 1871*
> La Sagrada Biblia / traducida . . . por Félix Torres Amat . . . 1871–1873

If an item is a facsimile reproduction, give the year of publication of the original. Make an added entry under the Bible heading with the date of the facsimile.

> **Bible.** *German. Luther. 1534*
> Biblia : das ist die gantze Heilige Schrifft / deudsch. Mart. Luth. — Leipzig : A. Foerster, 1934–1935
> (*Facsimile of an edition printed in 1534*)
> *Added entry under:* Bible. German. Luther. 1934

---

7. Do not treat a harmony of different passages of the Bible as an altered text.

25.18A14. Apocryphal books. Enter an apocryphal book (i.e., one not included in the Catholic canon nor in the Protestant Apocrypha) directly under its title. Make explanatory references from **Bible.** *Apocryphal books;* **Bible.** *O.T. Apocryphal books;* and **Bible.** *N.T. Apocryphal books.*

Enter a collection of apocryphal books as instructed in 21.7.

> **Book of jubilees**
>
> **Epistola apostolorum**
>
> **Gospel according to the Hebrews**
>
> **Bible.** *N.T. Apocryphal books*
>   For individual apocryphal books of the New Testament, see the title of the book, e.g., **Shepherd of Hermas**
>   For collections of such books, see the title of the collection, e.g., The Apocryphal New Testament.
>
> **Bible.** *O.T. Apocryphal books*
>   For individual apocryphal books of the Old Testament, see the title of the book, e.g., **Assumption of Moses**
>   For collections of such books, see the title of the collection, e.g., The Forgotten books of Eden.
>   For the Apocrypha of the Protestant Bible and its component books, see **Bible.** *O.T. Apocrypha*

25.18B. Talmud

25.18B1. Enter a particular order (*seder*) or a tractate or treatise (*masekhet*) of the Talmud as a subheading of *Talmud* or *Talmud Yerushalmi*, as appropriate. Use the form of name of these parts found in the *Encyclopaedia Judaica*.

> **Talmud.** *Ḥagigah* . . .
>   Translation of the treatise Chagigah from the Babylonian Talmud . . .

Make additions as instructed in 25.5D if the item is a translation, except that if the item consists of a translation and the original text, do not add the name of the language in the main entry uniform title, but make an added entry under a uniform title containing the name of the language of the translation.

> **Talmud Yerushalmi.** *French*
>   Le Talmud de Jérusalem / traduit pour la première fois en français . . .
>
> **Talmud**
>   New edition of the Babylonian Talmud : English translation, original text . . .
>   *Added entry under:* Talmud. English

If the item consists of selections, add *Selections* to the uniform title.

> **Talmud.** *English. Selections*
>   The Babylonian Talmud in selection / edited and translated from the original Hebrew and Aramaic by Leo Auerbach . . .

25.18B2. Use the subheading *Minor tractates* for separately published editions of those tractates. If the item consists of a single tractate, add the title of the tractate as a further subheading.

> **Talmud.** *Minor tractates*
> Seven minor tractates . . .
> *Added entry under:* Talmud. Minor tractates. English

> **Talmud.** *Minor tractates. Semaḥot. German*
> Der talmudische Tractat Ebel rabbathi, oder, S'machoth . . .

25.18C. Mishnah and Tosefta

Enter a particular order or tractate of the Mishnah or Tosefta as a subheading of *Mishnah* or *Tosefta*, as appropriate. Use the form of name found in the *Encyclopaedia Judaica*. Add the name of the language of a translation as instructed in 25.18B1.

> **Mishnah**
> Die Mischna / Text, Übersetzung, und ausführliche Erklärung . . . herausgegeben von G. Beer . . .
> *Added entry under:* Mishnah. German

> **Mishnah.** *Avot. English*
> Pirke Aboth = Sayings of the Fathers / edited, with translations and commentaries, by Isaac Unterman . . .
> > (*Text in English only*)

> **Tosefta.** *Beẓah*
> Der Tosefta-Traktat Jom Tob / Einleitung, Text, Übersetzung, und Erklärung . . . von Michael Kern . . .
> *Added entry under:* Tosefta. Beẓah. German

25.18D. References for the Talmud, Mishnah, and Tosefta

Refer from the titles of orders and tractates of the Talmud, Mishnah, and Tosefta to the uniform titles of those orders and tractates.

> **Bava kamma**
> *see*
> **Mishnah.** *Bava kamma*
> **Talmud.** *Bava kamma*
> **Talmud Yerushalmi.** *Bava kamma*
> **Tosefta.** *Bava kamma*

Make an explanatory reference from the uniform title of an order to the uniform titles of its tractates.

> **Talmud.** *Nezikin*
> For separately published tractates belonging to this order, see
> **Talmud.** ₍*name of tractate*₎, e.g., **Talmud.** *Bava kamma*

25.18E. Midrashim

25.18E1. Enter an anonymous midrash under its title. Use the form found in the *Encyclopaedia Judaica*. Add the name of the language of a translation as instructed in 25.18B1.

Mekhilta

Tanna de-Vei Eliyahu

25.18E2. Enter the *Midrash ha-gadol*, *Midrash rabbah*, and *Sifrei* under those titles. Enter any other collection of midrashim as instructed in 21.7.

25.18E3. Enter a separately published component of the *Midrash ha-gadol*, *Midrash rabbah*, or *Sifrei* under the uniform title for the collection. Add the English name of the book of the Bible with which it deals.

> **Midrash ha-gadol.** *Numbers*
>
> **Midrash rabbah.** *Ruth*
>
> **Sifrei.** *Deuteronomy*

25.18F. Buddhist scriptures

25.18F1. Enter the component divisions of the Pali canon (Abhidhammapiṭaka, Suttapiṭaka, Vinayapiṭaka) as subheadings of *Tipiṭaka*.

> **Tipiṭaka.** *Abhidhammapiṭaka*

Enter separately published parts of these component divisions as a subheading of the appropriate Piṭaka.

> **Tipiṭaka.** *Abhidhammapiṭaka. Dhātukathā*
>
> **Tipiṭaka.** *Suttapiṭaka. Khuddakanikāya. Jātaka*
>
> **Tipiṭaka.** *Vinayapiṭaka. Khandhaka. Mahāvagga*

25.18F2. Enter the component divisions of the Sanskrit canon (Abhidharmapiṭaka, Sūtrapiṭaka, Vinayapiṭaka) as subheadings of *Tripiṭaka*.

> **Tripiṭaka.** *Abhidharmapiṭaka*

Enter separately published parts of these component divisions as a subheading of the appropriate Piṭaka.

> **Tripiṭaka.** *Sūtrapiṭaka. Saddharmapundarikasūtra*
>
> **Tripiṭaka.** *Vinayapiṭaka. Prātimokṣa*

25.18F3. Refer from the titles of individually published divisions and treatises to the appropriate uniform title.

> **Jātaka**
> *see* **Tipiṭaka.** *Suttapiṭaka. Khuddakanikāya. Jātaka*
>
> **Abhidharmapiṭaka**
> *see* **Tripiṭaka.** *Abhidharmapiṭaka*

25.18G. Vedas

Enter the four standard collections of Vedas (Atharvaveda, Ṛgveda, Samaveda, Yajurveda) as subheadings of *Vedas*. If the item is a particular version of one of these collections, add the title of the version in parentheses. Make additions as appropriate as instructed in 25.5 and 25.6.

Vedas. *English. Selections*

Vedas. *Atharvaveda*

Vedas. *R̥gveda. English. Selections*

Vedas. *Sāmaveda*

Vedas. *Yajurveda (Vājasaneyīsaṃhitā). English. Selections*

25.18H. Aranyakas, Brahmanas, Upanishads

Enter a component of the Aranyakas, Brahmanas, or Upanishads as a subheading of the title of the appropriate larger collection. Make additions as appropriate as instructed in 25.5 and 25.6.

Aranyakas. *Aitareyāraṇyaka*

Brahmanas. *Adbhutabrāhmaṇa*

Upanishads. *English*

Upanishads. *Chāndogyopaniṣad*

25.18J. Jaina Āgama

Enter one of the six component collections of the Jain canon (Aṅga, Upāṅga, Prakīrṇaka, Cheda, Mūla, and Cūlikā) as a subheading of *Jaina Āgama*.

Jaina Āgama. *Aṅga*

Enter a separately titled part of a component collection as a subheading of the title for the collection.

Jaina Āgama. *Aṅga. Ācārāṅga*

25.18K. Avesta

Enter the main component parts and groups of parts of the Avesta as subheadings of *Avesta*. Use the titles by which they are identified in English-language sources. Make additions as appropriate as instructed in 25.5 and 25.6.

Avesta. *Yasna*

Avesta. *Khordah Avesta*

Enter an individually titled part of one of the main components as a subheading of the title for the main component.

Avesta. *Yasna. Gathas*

25.18L. References for Vedas, Aranyakas, Brahmanas, Upanishads, Jaina Āgama, and Avesta

Refer from the titles of parts that are entered as subheadings of the larger work.

Atharvaveda
  see **Vedas.** *Atharvaveda*

Chāndogyopaniṣad
  see **Upanishads.** *Chāndogyopaniṣad*

Aṅga
  see **Jaina Āgama** *Aṅga*

Ācārāṅga

    see **Jaina Āgama.** *Aṅga. Ācārāṅga*

Gathas

    see **Avesta.** *Yasna. Gathas*

25.18M. Koran

25.18M1. Enter a chapter (*sūrah*), one of the thirty parts (*juz'*), or a named grouping of selections of the Koran as a subheading of *Koran.* Precede the title of a chapter by *Sūrat.* Precede the title of a part by *Juz'.* Refer from *sūrah* or *juz'* numbers using *al-Sūrah* or *al-Juz'* followed by the appropriate roman numeral. Refer from the titles of established groupings of selections. Make additions as appropriate as instructed in 25.5 and 25.6.

    Koran. *Sūrat al-Baqarah*
      x Koran. *al-Sūrah II*

    Koran. *Juz' 'Amma*
      x Koran. *al-Juz' XXX*

    Koran. *al-Mu'awwidhatān*
      x al-Mu'awwidhatān

25.18M2. Enter a verse of a chapter as a subheading of Koran and add the arabic numeral of the verse to the title of the *sūrah.* Refer from the title of the verse and from the title of the verse as a subheading of Koran.

    Koran. *Sūrat al-Baqarah, 177*
      x Koran. *Āyat al-Birr*
      x Āyat al-Birr

LITURGICAL WORKS

25.19. FORM AND LANGUAGE OF TITLE OF LITURGICAL WORKS[8]

If the name of a body under which a liturgical work is entered is given in English, use as uniform title a well-established English title if there is one. Otherwise, use a brief title in the language of the liturgy.

---

8. Consult the following works in cataloguing liturgical works of the Latin and Eastern rites of the Christian church:

Attwater, Donald. *A Catholic Dictionary.* — 3rd ed. — New York : Macmillan, 1958.
Cabrol, Fernand. *Dictionnaire d'archéologie chrétienne et de liturgie.* — Paris : Letouzey et Ané, 1907–1953.
Kapsner, Oliver L. *A Manual of Cataloging Practice for Catholic Author and Title Entries.* — Washington : Catholic University of America Press, 1953.
List of Uniform Titles for Liturgical Works of the Latin Rites of the Catholic Church / recommended by the Working Group on Uniform Headings for Liturgical Works set up by the IFLA Committee on Cataloguing. — London : IFLA Committee on Cataloguing, 1975.
New Catholic Encyclopedia . . . / prepared by an editorial staff at the Catholic University of America. — New York : McGraw-Hill, [1967–1974].

Church of England
[The book of common prayer]

Catholic Church
[Missal]
(Full title in Latin: Missale Romanum)

Catholic Church
[Caeremoniale Romanum]

Catholic Church
[Ordo divini officii]
(Full title: Ordo divini officii recitandi sacrique peragendi)

Russkaĩa pravoslavnaĩa t͡serkov'
[Sluzhebnik]

Svenska kyrkan
[Handbok]

25.20. CATHOLIC LITURGICAL WORKS

25.20A. Early Catholic liturgical works

If a Catholic liturgical work compiled before the Council of Trent (1545–1563) has a close counterpart in a Tridentine work, use the Tridentine title.

Catholic Church
[Ritual . . .]
Manuale secundum vsum insignis ac preclare Ecclesie Sarū . . . 1523

If such a work has no close counterpart among Tridentine liturgical works, or in case of doubt, use the title by which the work is identified in reference sources.

Catholic Church
[Ordo Romanus primus . . .]
Ordo Romanus primus . . .
(An early work. Not the same as the later Ordo divini officii)

25.20B. The uniform title of Tridentine texts is not applicable to those post-Vatican II texts that vary in language and contents. Where such variations exist, use the individual title of each manifestation as the uniform title. Add a term to distinguish between different texts that have the same title.

Catholic Church
[Liturgy of the hours (U.S.)]

Catholic Church
[Liturgy of the hours (England)]

25.21. JEWISH LITURGICAL WORKS

Use as the uniform title for a Jewish liturgical work its name as found in the *Encyclopaedia Judaica.*

Haggadah . . .

Kinot . . .

470

25.22. VARIANT AND SPECIAL TEXTS

25.22A. If the item being catalogued contains an authorized or traditional variant or special text of a liturgical work, add in parentheses (in this order of preference):

1) the name of a special rite (e.g., a Latin rite other than the Roman rite for Catholic works; a rite other than the unmodified Ashkenazic rite for Jewish works)

> **Catholic Church**
> ₁Vesperal (Ambrosian)₁
> Liber vesperalis juxta ritum sanctae Ecclesiae Mediolanensis . . .

> **Haggadah** (*Sephardic*)
> Haggadah de Péssah : transcrite en caractères latins, prononciation rite Sépharade . . .
> (*In romanized Hebrew*)

2) the name of the place (e.g., country, diocese) or institution (e.g., monastery) in which the variant is authorized or traditional; if necessary, add both terms

> **Catholic Church**
> ₁Ordo divini officii (Trier)₁
> Directorium Diocesis Treverensis, seu, Ordo divini officii recitandi missaeque celebrandae . . .

> **Catholic Church**
> ₁Officia propria (Ireland)₁
> Officia propria sanctorum insulae Hiberniae . . .

> **Catholic Church**
> ₁Missal (St. Augustine's Abbey, Canterbury)₁
> The missal of St. Augustine's Abbey, Canterbury . . .

> **Kinot** (*Russia*)
> Seder kinot . . .
> (*In Hebrew characters*)

3) the name of the religious order for which the variant is authorized or traditional.

> **Catholic Church**
> ₁Breviary (Benedictine)₁
> Brevarium monasticum . . .

> **Catholic Church**
> ₁Missal (Dominican)₁
> Missale Dominicanum . . .

If a single term is insufficient to identify the variant text, add a second term.

> **Haggadah** (*Reform, Guggenheim*)
> Offenbacher Haggadah . . .
> (*Edited by Guggenheim*)

> **Haggadah** (*Reform, Seligmann*)
> Hagada : Liturgie für die häusliche Feier der Sederabende / in deutscher Sprache neu bearbeitet von C. Seligmann . . .

25.22B. If the uniform title is for a particular manuscript, or a reproduction of a particular manuscript, add in parentheses *Ms.* followed by (in this order of preference):

1) a brief form of the name of a particular owner if that is how the manuscript is identified

   ₁Psalter (Ms. Queen Mary)₁

2) any other name by which the manuscript is identified

   ₁Book of hours (Ms. Rohan)₁

3) a brief form of the name of the repository followed by the repository's designation.

   ₁Sacramentary (Ms. Biblioteca Vaticana. Ottoboni 356)₁

25.23. PARTS OF LITURGICAL WORKS

25.23A. If the item contains a specific liturgical observance, group of observances, or group of other texts extracted from a larger liturgical work, use as uniform title a well-established English title (if there is one) for the observance, group of observances, or other texts. Otherwise, use a brief title in the language of the liturgy. Refer from the title as a subheading of the title of the larger work.

> **Catholic Church**
> ₁Holy Week rite₁
> *x* Catholic Church. Missal. Holy Week rite

> **Protestant Episcopal Church in the U.S.A.**
> ₁Order for daily morning prayer₁
> *x* Protestant Episcopal Church in the U.S.A. The book of common
>   prayer. Order for daily morning prayer

> **Albanian Orthodox Church in America**
> ₁Liturgy of St. John Chrysostom₁
> *x* Albanian Orthodox Church in America. Euchologion. Liturgy of
>   St. John Chrysostom.

25.23B. Use as the uniform title for an Office or for a Proper of the Mass for a particular day, the term *Office* or *Mass* followed by a brief identification of the day. If the day is a saint's day, add only the saint's name in direct order and in the language of the heading for the saint. Make an explanatory reference from *Office* or *Mass* as a subheading of the larger work.

> **Catholic Church**
> ₁Office, Assumption of the Blessed Virgin Mary₁

> **Catholic Church**
>   Breviary. Offices for particular days or occasions
>   For offices for particular days or occasions, see
> **Catholic Church**
>   Office, ₁*name of day*₁, e.g.,
> **Catholic Church**
>   Office, Assumption of the Blessed Virgin Mary

> **Catholic Church**
> ₁Mass, Sainte Thérèse₁

Catholic Church
  Missal. Masses for particular days or occasions
  For Masses for particular days or occasions, see
Catholic Church
  Mass, ₁*name of day or occasion*₁, e.g.,
Catholic Church
  Mass, Sainte Thérèse

25.23C. Use as the uniform title for a numbered plainsong setting of the Ordinary of the Mass *Mass* followed by its number in the *Gradual*. Make an explanatory reference from *Ordinary* as a subheading of the *Gradual*.

Catholic Church
  ₁Mass XVI₁

Catholic Church
  Gradual. Ordinary
  For single numbered Ordinaries, see
Catholic Church
  Mass ₁*number of the Ordinary*₁, e.g.,
Catholic Church
  Mass XVI

OFFICIAL PAPAL COMMUNICATIONS, ETC.

25.24. OFFICIAL COMMUNICATIONS OF THE POPE AND THE ROMAN CURIA

25.24A. Use as the uniform title for an individual work entered under the official heading for a pope (see 21.4D1) the short title (generally the first word or words of the text) by which it is generally known and cited in the original language (usually Latin).

Catholic Church. *Pope (1963–1978 : Paul VI)*
  ₁Populorum progressio₁

25.24B. If a communication of one of the tribunals, congregations, or offices of the Roman Curia is similarly known by a short title, use it as the uniform title.

Catholic Church. *Congregatio Sancti Officii*
  ₁Lamentabili₁

MUSIC

Individual titles

25.25. GENERAL RULE
  Formulate a uniform title for a musical work as instructed in 25.26–25.36. Use the general rules 25.1–25.7 insofar as they apply to music and are not contradicted by the following rules.

25.26. DEFINITIONS

25.26A. Title

Title as used in 25.27–25.36 means the word or words that name the work exclusive of:

1) a statement of medium of performance (even if such a statement is part of a compound word—provided that the resulting word or words is the name of a type of composition)
2) key
3) serial, opus, or thematic index numbers
4) numerals (unless they are an integral part of the title)
5) date of composition
6) adjectives and epithets not part of the original title of the work.

In the following examples the title as defined above is underlined.

String quartet
Streichquartett
Symphonie no. 40
Clavierübung
Kammersymphonie
Symphonie fantastique
Carnaval op. 9
Concerto in A minor, op. 54
12 sonatas
Nocturne in F sharp minor,
    op. 15, no. 2
6 Stücke für Orchester
Fünf Orchesterstücke
Four orchestral pieces

Five little pieces for piano
Drei Gesänge
Vier Orchesterlieder, op. 22
Les deux journées
The Ten commandments
The seventh trumpet
Troisième nocturne
Mozart's favorite minuet
The celebrated Sophie waltz
Grandes études
    (*So named by the composer*)
Die Zauberflöte
War requiem

25.26B. Work

Work as used in 25.27–25.36 means:

1) a work that is a single unit intended for performance as a whole
2) a set of works with a group title (not necessarily intended for performance as a whole)
3) a group of works with a single opus number.

25.27. SELECTION OF TITLES

25.27A. Language

Use as the basis for the uniform title for a musical work the composer's original title in the language in which it was formulated. If, however, a later title in the same language is better known, use it (see also 25.1–25.4). Formulate the uniform title by applying 25.27–25.36 to the selected title.

> **Wagner, Richard**
> ₍Die Meistersinger von Nürnberg . . .₎
> The mastersingers of Nuremberg . . .

Berlioz, Hector
[La damnation de Faust . . .]
Fausts Verdammung . . .

Porter, Cole
[Gay divorce. Night and day . . .]
Nat og dag . . .

Grieg, Edvard
[Haugtussa . . .]
The mountain maid . . .

Rimskiĭ-Korsakov, N.A.
[Zolotoĭ petushok . . .]
The golden cockerel . . .

Bach, Johann Sebastian
[Präludium und Fuge . . .]
Präludium und Fuge, D-Dur für Orgel . . .

Frackenpohl, Arthur
[Rondo with fugato . . .]
Rondo with fugato . . .

Ravel, Maurice
[Introduction et allegro . . .]
Introduction et allegro . . .

25.27B. Works with titles consisting solely of the name of one type of composition[9]

If the title selected according to 25.27A consists solely of the name of one type of composition, use the accepted English form of name if there are cognate forms in English, French, German, and Italian, or if the same name is used in all these languages. Give the name in the plural (this may be a non-English plural form, e.g., divertimenti) unless the composer wrote only one work of the type.

Do not use the English form of name for works intended for concert performance called *étude*, *fantasia*, or *sinfonia concertante* or their cognates.

Boccherini, Luigi
[Quintets . . .]
Quintetto VI in sol maggiore . . .

Brahms, Johannes
[Ballades . . .]
Vier Balladen . . .

Geminiani, Francesco
[Sonatas . . .]
Sonate a violino, violone, e cembalo . . .

---

9. The name of a type of composition, as distinguished from a distinctive title, is considered to be the name of a form (concerto, symphony, trio sonata), a genre (capriccio, nocturne, intermezzo), or a generic term frequently used by different composers (movement, muziek, Stück). Other titles are generally considered to be distinctive (chamber concerto, Konzertstück, little piano suite, Übung).

> **Geminiani, Francesco**
> ₁Concerti grossi . . .₁
> Six concerti grossi for 2 violins, viola, and violoncello soli with
> strings and harpsichord . . .

> **Mozart, Wolfgang Amadeus**
> ₁Divertimenti . . .₁
> Divertimento Nr. 1 . . .

> **Chopin, Frédéric**
> ₁Études . . .₁
> Studies . . .

25.27C. Works with titles including the name of a type of composition
If all of a composer's works with titles including the name of a type of composition
are also cited as a numbered sequence of compositions of that type, use the name of
the type of composition as the uniform title.

> **Beethoven, Ludwig van**
> ₁Symphonies . . .₁
> Sinfonia eroica . . .
> > (*Also called:* Third symphony)

25.27D. Duets
Use *Duets* for works variously titled *duos*, *duets*, etc.

> **Pleyel, Ignaz Joseph**
> ₁Duets . . .₁
> Trois duos . . .

25.27E. Trio sonatas
Use *Trio sonatas* for works of the seventeenth and eighteenth centuries variously
titled *sonatas, trios, sonate a tre*, etc. These works are generally written for two treble
instruments and continuo (usually violoncello and keyboard).

> **Corelli, Arcangelo**
> ₁Trio sonatas . . .₁
> Twelve sonatas for two violins and a violoncello, with a thorough
> bass for harpsichord or organ . . .

> **Corelli, Arcangelo**
> ₁Trio sonatas . . .₁
> Zwölf Triosonaten für zwei Violinen und Basso continuo . . .

25.27F. Works with long titles
If the title is very long, use (in this order of preference):

1) a brief title by which the work is commonly identified in reference sources
2) a brief title formulated by the cataloguer.

> **Schütz, Heinrich**
> ₁Historia der Auferstehung Jesu Christi . . .₁
> Historia der frölichen und siegreichen Aufferstehung unsers einigen
> Erlösers und Seligmachers Jesu Christi . . .

Schutz, Heinrich
⌐St. John Passion . . .⌐
Historia des Leidens und Sterbens unsers Herrn und Heylandes
Jesu Christi, nach dem Evangelisten St. Johannem . . .

ADDITIONS

25.28. GENERAL RULE

Where appropriate, add the elements specified in 25.29–25.31 in the order given.

25.29. MEDIUM OF PERFORMANCE

25.29A. General rule

25.29A1. Add a statement of the medium of performance[10] if the title consists solely of the name of a type, or the names of two or more types, of composition.
⌐Sonatas, piano . . .⌐

⌐Trios, sopranos, alto, piano . . .⌐

25.29A2. Do not add a statement of the medium of performance if:

a) the medium is implied by the title

Chorale prelude
(*Implied medium: organ*)

Mass
(*Implied medium: voices, with or without accompaniment*)

Overture
(*Implied medium: orchestra*)

Songs, Lieder, etc.
(*Implied medium: solo voice with accompaniment for keyboard stringed instrument*)

Symphony
(*Implied medium: orchestra*)

If, however, the medium is other than that implied by the title, add the statement, e.g., ⌐Symphonies, organ . . .⌐.

or b) the work consists of a set of compositions for different media, or is one of a series of sets of compositions with the same title but for different media

Fesch, Willem de
⌐Sonatas . . .⌐
12 sonatas : six for a violin, with a thorough bass, several of them are proper for a German flute, and six for two violoncellos . . .

---

10. A statement of the medium of performance is a concise statement of the instrumental or vocal medium of performance, or both, for which a musical work was originally intended.

> **Monteverdi, Claudio**
> ₍Madrigals, book 1 . . .₎
> (*For 5 voices*)
>
> **Monteverdi, Claudio**
> ₍Madrigals, book 7 . . .₎
> (*For 1–6 voices and instruments*)
>
> **Monteverdi, Claudio**
> ₍Madrigals, book 8 . . .₎
> (*For 1–8 voices and instruments*)

or c) the medium was not designated by the composer

or d) the complexities of stating the medium are such that an arrangement by other identifying elements (e.g., thematic index number, opus number, etc., see 25.31) would be more useful.

> **Mozart, Wolfgang Amadeus**
> ₍Divertimenti, K. 251 . . .₎

25.29A3. Record the statement of medium of performance specifically, but do not use more than three elements (except as instructed in 25.29C). Give the elements in the following order:

a) voices

b) keyboard instrument if there is more than one nonkeyboard instrument

c) the order of other instruments in the score being catalogued.

> ₍Sonatas, violin, piano . . .₎
>
> ₍Trios, piano, clarinet, violoncello . . .₎
>
> ₍Canons, women's voices, piano . . .₎

25.29A4. If there is more than one part for a particular instrument or voice, add the appropriate arabic numeral in parentheses after the name of that instrument or voice unless the number is implied by other elements of the uniform title.

> ₍Scherzos, flutes (2), clarinets (2) . . .₎
>
> ₍Gaillards, viols (5) . . .₎

but

> ₍Quartets, violin, violas, violoncello . . .₎
>
> ₍Quartets, flutes, clarinets . . .₎

25.29B. Instrumental music intended for one performer to a part

For instrumental music intended for one performer to a part, record the medium of performance in one of, or a combination of, the following ways (in this order of preference):

1) by one of the names of certain standard chamber music combinations

2) by designation of individual instruments

3) by designation of groups of instruments.

25.29C. Standard combinations of instruments

For the following standard chamber music combinations, use the terms given in the column on the right:

COMBINATION	STATEMENT IN UNIFORM TITLE
string trio (violin, viola, violoncello)	₁Trios, strings . . .₁
string quartet (2 violins, viola, violoncello)	₁Quartets, strings . . .₁
woodwind quartet (flute, oboe, clarinet, bassoon)	₁Quartets, woodwinds . . .₁
wind quintet (flute, oboe, clarinet, horn, bassoon)	₁Quintets, winds . . .₁
piano trio (piano, violin, violoncello)	₁Trios, piano, strings . . .₁
piano quartet (piano, violin, viola, violoncello)	₁Quartets, piano, strings . . .₁
piano quintet (piano, 2 violins, viola, violoncello)	₁Quintets, piano, strings . . .₁

If the title of a work for one of these combinations does not contain the word *trio, quartet,* or *quintet,* use the name of the standard combination as given in the left column above.

> ₁Serenades, piano quartet . . .₁

For trios, quartets, and quintets for combinations other than those listed above, record the full statement of medium even if more than three different instruments must be recorded. For the order of instruments, see 25.29A3.

> ₁Quartets, violin, viola, violoncello, double bass . . .₁
>
> ₁Quartets, flute, oboe, saxophone, bassoon . . .₁
>
> ₁Quintets, piano, violin, viola, violoncello, double bass . . .₁
>
> ₁Quintets, flute, clarinets, bassoon, horn . . .₁

25.29D. Individual instruments

25.29D1. Use English terms whenever possible. Use the following list of terms as a guide in appropriate cases. When alternatives are given, use the term preferred in these cases consistently.

> cello *or* violoncello
> cor anglais *or* English horn
> double bass (*not* bass viol *or* contrabass)
> double bassoon *or* contrabassoon
> harpsichord (*not* cembalo *or* virginal)
> horn (*not* French horn)
> kettle drums *or* tympani
> recorder (*not* treble, etc., recorder)
> viol (*for sizes of viola da gamba other than bass*)
> viola da gamba (*not* bass viol *or* gamba).
> viols (*for groups of viols of different sizes*)

25.29D2. For keyboard instruments use:

> piano (*for one instrument, two hands*)
> piano, 4 hands
> pianos (2) (*for two instruments, 4 hands*)
> pianos (2), 8 hands
> organs (2)

25.29D3. Omit the following elements: (1) the designation of the key in which an instrument is pitched; (2) the terms *alto, tenor, bass*, etc.; and (3) the names of alternative instruments.

> clarinet *not* clarinet in A
> saxophone *not* alto saxophone

25.29D4. Use *continuo* for a figured bass part whether it is named as basso continuo, general bass, figured bass, thorough bass, or continuo.

Marcello, Benedetto
ₗSonatas, recorder, continuo . . .₁
XII suonate a flauto solo, con il suo basso continuo per violoncello o cembalo . . .

25.29D5. If the composition is intended for a keyboard instrument, but no particular instrument is named and the work can be played on any keyboard instrument, use *keyboard instrument*.

Gibbons, Orlando
ₗFantazias, keyboard instrument . . .₁
Fantazia of foure parts . . .

Albrechtsberger, Johann Georg
ₗFugues, keyboard instrument . . .₁
Douze fugues pour le clavecin ou l'orgue . . .

25.29E. Groups of instruments

Use the following terms for groups of instruments:

> woodwinds
> brasses
> winds (*for woodwinds and brasses*)
> percussion
> plectral instruments
> keyboard instruments
> strings
> instrumental ₗstring, wind, etc.₁ ensemble (*for four or more diverse instruments*)

ₗSextets, strings . . .₁

ₗDivertimenti, piano, woodwinds . . .₁

ₗFanfares, brasses, percussion . . .₁

ₗConcertos, instrumental ensemble . . .₁

For standard chamber music combinations, see 25.29C.

25.29F. Orchestra, etc.

For instrumental music intended for more than one performer to a part, use one of the following:

> orchestra (*for full or reduced orchestra*)
> string orchestra
> band

Ferguson, Howard
> ₍Partita, orchestra . . .₎

Hindemith, Paul
> ₍Symphonies, band . . .₎

Bartók, Béla
> ₍Concertos, orchestra . . .₎

Disregard continuo when it is part of an orchestra or string orchestra.

25.29G. Works for solo instrument(s) and accompanying ensemble

For works for one solo instrument and accompanying ensemble, use the name of the solo instrument followed by the name of the accompanying ensemble.

> ₍Rhapsodies, violin, orchestra . . .₎
>
> ₍Concertos, piano, orchestra . . .₎
>
> ₍Concertos, harpsichord, instrumental ensemble . . .₎

If such a work has two or more solo instruments, or lacks an accompanying ensemble, state the medium for the solo instruments as instructed in the preceding rules for compositions without accompaniment.

> ₍Concertos, piano trio, orchestra . . .₎
>
> ₍Concertos, woodwind quartet, string orchestra . . .₎
>
> ₍Concertos, organ . . .₎
>
> ₍Divertimenti, clarinets (2), string orchestra . . .₎
>
> ₍Sinfonie concertanti, violin, viola, orchestra . . .₎

25.29H. Vocal music

25.29H1. Solo voices. Use the following terms:

> soprano
> mezzo-soprano
> alto
> tenor
> baritone
> bass

> ₍Cantata, sopranos (2), alto, orchestra . . .₎
>
> ₍Romances, soprano, piano . . .₎

Use other terms (*high voice, countertenor,* etc.), as appropriate.

Use the following terms for two or more solo voices of different ranges whenever it is necessary to reduce the number of elements in the medium statement to three or fewer:

> mixed solo voices
> men's solo voices
> women's solo voices

Use other terms (*children's solo voices*, etc.) as appropriate. For compositions that include solo voices with chorus, give only the appropriate terms for the chorus (see 25.29H2) and the accompaniment, if any.

25.29H2. Choral music. Use the following terms:

> mixed voices
> men's voices
> women's voices
> unison voices

Use other terms (*children's voices*, etc.), as appropriate.

25.29H3. Songs, Lieder, etc. If works with the title *Songs, Lieder*, etc., are accompanied by anything other than a keyboard stringed instrument alone (see 25.29A2), add the name of the accompanying instrument(s) and *acc.* If such compositions are not accompanied, add *unacc.*

> ₁Chansons, guitar acc. . . .₁
>
> ₁Lieder, unacc. . . .₁
>
> ₁Songs, percussion acc. . . .₁

25.29J. Medium indeterminate

Do not add a statement of medium of performance to the titles of:

1) works (especially those of the Renaissance period) intended for performance by voices and/or instruments
2) instrumental chamber works for which the precise medium is not clearly defined.

> **Youll, Henry**
> ₁Canzonets₁
> Canzonets to three voices . . .

If two or more such works with the same title are entered under the same heading, record the number of parts or voices. Use *voices* to designate both vocal and instrumental parts. (See also 25.31A.)

> **Morley, Thomas**
> ₁Canzonets, voices (4)₁
> Canzonets, or, Little short songs to foure voyces . . .

> **Morley, Thomas**
> ₁Canzonets, voices (5–6)₁
> Canzonets, or, Little short aers to five and six voices . . .

> **Maschera, Florentio**
> ₁Canzoni, voices (4) . . .₁
> Libro primo de canzoni da sonare a quatro voci . . .

25.30. SKETCHES

If a work consists of a composer's sketches for a musical composition(s), add *Sketches* in parentheses to the uniform title for the completed composition(s).

> **Beethoven, Ludwig van**
> ₁Quartets, strings, no. 1–6, op. 18 (Sketches)₁
>
> **Stravinskiĭ, Igor'**
> ₁Le sacre du printemps (Sketches)₁

25.31. OTHER IDENTIFYING ELEMENTS

25.31A. Titles consisting solely of the name(s) of type(s) of composition

25.31A1. General rule. If the title consists solely of the name(s) of type(s) of composition, add as many of the following identifying elements as can readily be ascertained. Add following the statement of medium of performance and in the order given:

a) serial number
b) opus number or thematic index number
c) key.

Precede each element by a comma.

25.31A2. Serial numbers. If works with the same title and the same medium of performance are consecutively numbered, add the number.

> ₁Quartets, strings, no. 2 . . .₁
> ₁Symphonies, no. 5 . . .₁

25.31A3. Opus numbers. Include the opus number, if any, and any number within the opus, if any.

> ₁Trios, piano, strings, no. 1, op. 1, no. 1 . . .₁
> ₁Trios, piano, strings, no. 2, op. 1, no. 2 . . .₁

If there is a conflict in opus numbering among works of the same title and medium, or if the overall opus numbering of a composer's works is confused and conflicting, add to the opus number the name of the publisher originally using the number chosen. Add the publisher's name in parentheses.

> **Cambini, Giovanni Giuseppe**
> ₁Duets, flute, violin, op. 20 (Bland) . . .₁
>
> **Cambini, Giovanni Giuseppe**
> ₁Duets, flute, violin, op. 20 (LeDuc) . . .₁

25.31A4. Thematic index numbers. In the case of certain composers, use numbers assigned to the works in recognized thematic indexes. Add these numbers in the absence of, or in preference to, serial numbers and/or opus numbers. Precede the number by the initial letter(s) of the bibliographer's name (e.g., K. 453[11]) or a generally accepted abbreviation (e.g., BWV 232[12]).

---

11. Köchel, Ludwig. *Chronologisch-thematisches Verzeichnis sämtlicher Tonwerke Wolfgang Amadé Mozarts*

12. Schmieder, Wolfgang. *Thematisch-systematisches Verzeichnis der musikalischen Werke von Johann Sebastian Bach*

25.31A5. Key. Include the statement of key in the uniform title for pre-twentieth-century works. If the mode is major or minor, add the appropriate word.

> **Mendelssohn-Bartholdy, Felix**
> ₁Trios, piano, strings, no. 2, op. 66, C minor₁
> Trio, op. 66, piano, violin & violoncello . . .

> **Haydn, Joseph**
> ₁Symphonies, H. I, no. 24, D major₁
> Symphony in D major . . .

Include the statement of key in the uniform title for twentieth-century works if the key is stated prominently in the score being catalogued. If the mode is clearly major or minor, add the appropriate word.

> **Reizenstein, Franz**
> ₁Scherzo, piano, op. 20, A major₁
> Scherzo in A for pianoforte . . .

> **Reizenstein, Franz**
> ₁Trios, flute, clarinet, bassoon₁
> Trio for flute, clarinet and bassoon . . .

25.31A6. Other identifying elements. If the numeric identifying elements and key are not sufficient, or are not available, to distinguish between two or more works, add in parentheses (in this order of preference):

a) the year of completion of composition
b) the year of original publication
c) any other identifying elements (e.g., place of composition, name of first publisher)

> **Bartók, Béla**
> ₁Concertos, violin, orchestra (1938)₁

For arrangements, see 25.31B2.

25.31B. Other titles; arrangements, etc.

25.31B1. General rule. If the title does not consist solely of the name of a type, or the names of types, of composition, and there is a conflict between titles entered under the same heading, add a statement of medium of performance (see 25.29), preceded by a comma, or a descriptive word or phrase enclosed in parentheses. Use only statements of medium of performance *or* only descriptive phrases as additions to the same title.

> ₁Images, orchestra₁
>
> ₁Images, piano₁
> *not* Images (Piano work)
>
> ₁Goyescas (Opera)₁
>
> ₁Goyescas (Piano work)₁
> *not* Goyescas, piano

If one of these additions does not resolve the conflict, add one of the elements provided in 25.31A.

⌐Tu es Petrus (Motet), no. 1⌐

⌐Tu es Petrus (Motet), no. 2⌐

⌐Tu es Petrus (Offertory)⌐

25.31B2. Arrangements. If a work described as an arrangement, etc., is entered under the heading for the original composer (see 21.18B), use the uniform title for the original work and add, preceded by a semicolon, *arr.*

> **Berlioz, Hector**
> ⌐Le corsaire; arr.⌐
> The corsaire : overture for concert band / transcribed by
> Gunther Schuller . . .
> > (*Originally for orchestra*)

> **Schubert, Franz**
> ⌐Octets, woodwinds, horn, strings, D. 803, F major; arr.⌐
> Grosses Octett, op. 166 . . .
> > (*Arranged for piano, 4 hands*)

Add *arr.* also to the uniform title for a transcription by the composer.

> **Ravel, Maurice**
> ⌐Pavane pour une infante défunte; arr.⌐

25.31B3. Vocal and chorus scores. If the item being catalogued is a vocal score or a chorus score, add *vocal score* or *chorus score* to the uniform title.

> **Handel, George Frideric**
> ⌐Messiah. Vocal score . . .⌐

> **Sullivan,** *Sir* **Arthur**
> ⌐The Mikado. Chorus score . . .⌐

25.31B4. Alterations of musico-dramatic works. If the text, plot, setting, or other verbal element of a musical work is adapted or if a new text is supplied, and the title has changed, use the uniform title of the original work followed in parentheses by the title of the adaptation.

> **Strauss, Johann**
> ⌐Die Fledermaus . . .⌐
> ⌐Die Fledermaus (Champagne sec) . . .⌐
> ⌐Die Fledermaus (Gay Rosalinda) . . .⌐
> ⌐Die Fledermaus (Rosalinda) . . .⌐

> **Mozart, Wolfgang Amadeus**
> ⌐Così fan tutte (Die Dame Kobold) . . .⌐
> Die Dame Kobold (Così fan tutte) / bearbeitet von Carl
> Scheidemantel . . .
> > (*Scheidemantel substituted an entirely new libretto based on the play*
> > *by Calderón de la Barca*)

25.31B5. Librettos and song texts. If a libretto or song text is entered under the heading for the composer (see 21.28A), add *Libretto* to the uniform title for the text alone of an opera, operetta, oratorio, or the like, or *Text* or *Texts* to the uniform title for the text of a song, song-cycle, or collection of songs.

> **Verdi, Giuseppe**
> ₍La forza del destino. Libretto . . .₎

> **John, Elton**
> ₍Crocodile rock. Text . . .₎
> The words of Elton's smash hit "Crocodile rock" / Bernie Taupin . . .

25.31B6. Liturgical works. Add the name of the language of a liturgical text (Mass, Requiem, Magnificat, etc.) to the uniform title.

> **Peeters, Flor**
> ₍Missa choralis. Latin₎

> **Verdi, Giuseppe**
> ₍Requiem. English₎

25.31B7. Translations. If the text of a vocal work is a translation, add the name(s) of the language(s) as instructed in 25.5D.

> **Bizet, Georges**
> ₍Carmen. German₎
> Carmen : Oper in 4 Akten : Partitur . . .

> **Boito, Arrigo**
> ₍Mefistofele. Vocal score. English & Italian₎

> **Handel, George Frideric**
> ₍Messiah. Vocal score. Dutch & English₎

> **Lennon, John**
> ₍Let it be. French & English₎
> Let it be : en anglais et français / Lennon & McCartney . . .

PARTS OF A MUSICAL WORK

25.32. PARTS OF A MUSICAL WORK

25.32A. Single parts

25.32A1. Use as the uniform title for a separately published part of a musical work the title of the whole work followed by the designation and/or title of the part. Make a name-title reference from the heading for the composer and the title of the part if it has a specific title of its own.

> **Schumann, Robert**
> ₍Album für die Jugend. Nr. 2. Soldatenmarsch₎
> *x* Schumann, Robert. Soldatenmarsch₎

> **Verdi, Giuseppe**
> ₍Aïda. Celeste Aïda₎
> *x* Verdi, Giuseppe. Celeste Aïda

> **Brahms, Johannes**
> ₍Ungarische Tänze. Nr. 5₎

Wagner, Richard
 ₁Rienzi. Ouvertüre₁

Beethoven, Ludwig van
 ₁Symphonies, no. 1, op. 21, C major. Andante cantabile con moto₁

In the case of arrangements, add the qualification *arr.* (see 25.31B2) to any of the uniform titles provided by 25.32–25.33.

25.32A2. If a part of a musical work is designated by the same general term as other parts and lacks a number, add enough of the identifying terms as instructed in 25.29–25.31 as are necessary to distinguish the part.

 ₁Concerti ecclesiastici. Sonata, brasses, violin, continuo₁

 ₁Concerti ecclesiastici. Sonata, cornett, violin, continuo₁

25.32B. Several parts

25.32B1. Follow the instructions in 25.6B.

Brahms, Johannes
 ₁Ungarische Tänze. Nr. 5–6₁

Rossini, Gioacchino
 ₁Il barbiere di Siviglia. Largo al factotum₁
 Largo al factotum ; and, Una voce poco fa : from The barber
 of Seville . . .
 Added entry under: Rossini, Gioacchino. Il barbiere di Siviglia.
 Una voce poco fa

Schubert, Franz
 ₁Impromptus, piano, D. 899. No. 2₁
 Deux impromptus : op. 90, nos. 2 et 4 . . .
 Added entry under: Schubert, Franz. Impromptus, piano, D. 899. No. 4

Bach, Johann Sebastian
 ₁Musikalisches Opfer. Selections; arr.₁

Gounod, Charles
 ₁Faust. Hungarian. Selections₁

25.32B2. If a composer assembles a group of excerpts from a larger work and calls the group a *suite*, substitute that word for *Selections*.

Grieg, Edvard
 ₁Peer Gynt. Suite, no. 2₁

Two works published together

25.33. TWO WORKS PUBLISHED TOGETHER
 Follow the instructions in 25.7.

Schubert, Franz
 ₁Symphonies, D. 589, C major₁
 Symphony no. 6 in C major ; Symphony no. 3 in D major . . .
 Added entry under: Schubert, Franz. Symphonies, D. 200, D major

25.34. COMPLETE WORKS

Follow the instructions in 25.8.

> **Purcell, Henry**
> ₁Works₁
> The works of Henry Purcell . . .

In the case of arrangements, add the qualification *arr.* (see 25.31B2) to any of the collective uniform titles provided by 25.34–25.36.

25.35. SELECTIONS

Follow the instructions of 25.9 for a collection containing selections of various types of compositions from a composer's work that were originally composed for various instrumental and vocal media.

> **Brahms, Johannes**
> ₁Selections; arr.₁
> Brahms (simplified) : twelve favorite compositions / arranged
> for the piano . . .

25.36. WORKS OF VARIOUS TYPES FOR ONE BROAD OR SPECIFIC MEDIUM AND WORKS OF ONE TYPE FOR ONE SPECIFIC MEDIUM OR VARIOUS MEDIA

25.36A. For a collection containing works of various types in one broad medium, use the designation of that medium.

> ₁Chamber music₁
>
> ₁Choral music₁[13]
>
> ₁Instrumental music₁
>
> ₁Keyboard music₁
>
> ₁Vocal music₁[14]

For a collection containing works of various types in one specific medium, use a collective title generally appropriate to the medium.

> ₁Brass music₁
>
> ₁Orchestra music₁
>
> ₁Piano music₁
>
> ₁Piano music, 4 hands₁
>
> ₁Piano music, 2 pianos₁
>
> ₁String quartet music₁
>
> ₁Violin, piano music₁

---

13. Use *Choral music* also for collections of various types of works originally for one choral medium, with or without accompaniment.

14. Use *Vocal music* also for collections of various types of works originally for one solo voice or one combination of solo voices, with or without accompaniment.

25.36B. For a collection containing works of one type, use the name of that type. Add a statement of medium unless the medium is obvious or unless the works are for various media.

ₗConcertosₗ

ₗOperasₗ

ₗPolonaises, pianoₗ

ₗQuartets, stringsₗ

ₗSonatasₗ

ₗSonatas, violin, pianoₗ

ₗSongsₗ

25.36C. If a uniform title formulated according to 25.36A or 25.36B is for a collection that is incomplete, add *Selections* to the uniform title.

ₗInstrumental music. Selectionsₗ

ₗOrgan music. Selectionsₗ

ₗNocturnes, piano. Selectionsₗ

ₗSonatas, violin, piano. Selectionsₗ

If the selections are a consecutively numbered group, use the inclusive numbering instead of *Selections.*

Beethoven, Ludwig van
ₗSonatas, piano, no. 21-23ₗ
Sonata no. 21 in C major, op. 53 (Waldstein) ; Sonata no. 22 in F major, op. 54 ; Sonata no. 23 in F minor, op. 57 (Appassionata) . . .

Beethoven, Ludwig van
ₗSymphonies, no. 1-3ₗ
First, second, and third symphonies . . .

489

REFERENCES

Contents

26.0. INTRODUCTORY NOTES

"See" references. The function of a *see reference* is to direct the user of a catalogue from a form of the name of a person or a corporate body or the title of a work that might reasonably be sought to the form that has been chosen as a name heading or a uniform title.

"See also" references. The function of a *see also reference* is to direct the user from one name heading or uniform title to another that is related to it.

Name-title references. When a *see* or *see also reference* is made from a title that has been entered under a personal or corporate heading, it is made in the form of a *name-title reference* beginning with the personal or corporate heading followed by the title concerned.

Explanatory references. When a simple *see* or *see also reference* does not give adequate guidance to the user of the catalogue, an *explanatory reference* giving more detailed guidance is made.

Forms of references. In general the form of name of a person or corporate body from which reference is made has the same structure as it would have as a heading.

> **Gand**
> see **Ghent**

> **Guillaume d'Auvergne,** *Bishop of Paris*
> see **Guilelmus Arvernus,** *Bishop of Paris*

When reference is made to two or more different headings or titles from the same form, make one reference, listing in it all headings to which reference is being made.

> **Mahfouz, Naguib**
> *see*
> **Maḥfūẓ, Najīb,** 1882–
> **Maḥfūẓ, Najīb,** 1912–

A.B.M.
see
Associação Brasileira de Metais
Associação Brasileira de Municípios
Associação dos Bibliotecarios Municipais de São Paulo

Bava kamma
see
Mishnah. *Bava kamma*
Talmud. *Bava kamma*
Talmud Yerushalmi. *Bava kamma*
Tosefta. *Bava kamma*

Pennsylvania. *Department of Public Welfare*
see also
Pennsylvania. *Department of Public Assistance*
Pennsylvania. *Department of Welfare*

The rules in the preceding chapters in Part II have indicated particular types of references that are made in various specific circumstances; the rules in this chapter summarize the requirements for references in more general terms. In making references, bear the following points in mind:

a) There must be an entry in the catalogue under the name heading or uniform title to which any type of reference is made.

b) There should normally[1] be an entry in the catalogue under the name heading or uniform title from which a *see also* reference is made.

c) It is necessary to make a record of every reference under the name heading or uniform title to which it refers in order to make possible a correction or deletion of that reference.

d) When in doubt about making a reference, make it.

The typographic arrangement of the examples of references and the wording of the examples of explanatory references in the following rules represent only one of several methods of arranging and wording these references.

26.1. BASIC RULE

Whenever the name of a person or corporate body or the title of a work is, or may reasonably be, known under a form that is not the one used as a name heading or uniform title, refer from that form to the one that has been used. Do not make a reference, however, if the reference is so similar to the name heading or uniform title or to another reference as to be unnecessary. Use the appropriate additions to names as set out in rules 22.16, 22.18, 22.19, 23.4, 24.4, 24.6, and 25.5 to distinguish between names or titles from which references are made and other name headings or uniform titles or references.

26.2. NAMES OF PERSONS

26.2A. "See" references

---

1. *See also* references from headings under which there are as yet no entries are considered to be administratively justifiable by many libraries.

26.2A1. Different names. Refer from a name used by a person, or found in reference sources, that is different from that used in the heading for that person. (For persons entered under two or more different headings, see also 26.2C1 and 26.2D1.) Typical instances are:

Pseudonym
> **Saint-Aubin, Horace de**
> > *see* **Balzac, Honoré de**

Phrase
> **Bachelor knight**
> > *see* **Simms, W. Gilmore**

> **Author of Memoirs of a fox-hunting man**
> > *see* **Sassoon, Siegfried**

> **Memoirs of a fox-hunting man, Author of**
> > *see* **Sassoon, Siegfried**

Real name
> **Robertson, Ethel Florence Lindesay**
> > *see* **Richardson, Henry Handel**

> **Dupin, Amandine-Lucile-Aurore**, *baronne Dudevant*
> > *see* **Sand, George**

> **Dudevant, Amandine-Lucile-Aurore Dupin**, *baronne*
> > *see* **Sand, George**

> **Munro, Hector Hugh**
> > *see* **Saki**

> **Russell, George William**
> > *see* **A.E.**

Secular name
> **Gysi, Lydia**
> > *see* **Maria**, *Mother*

> **Roncalli, Angelo Giuseppe**
> > *see* **John XXIII**, *Pope*

Name in religion
> **Louis,** *Father*, 1894–
> > *see* **Biersack, Louis**

> **Louis,** *Father*, 1915–
> > *see* **Merton, Thomas**

Earlier name
> **Kouyoumdjian, Dikran**
> > *see* **Arlen, Michael**

> **Thibault, Jacques-Anatole**
> > *see* **France, Anatole**

> **Foot,** *Sir* **Hugh**
> > *see* **Caradon, Hugh Foot,** *Baron*

> **Barrett, Elizabeth**
> *see* **Browning, Elizabeth Barrett**
>
> **Richthofen, Frieda von**
> *see* **Lawrence, Frieda**
>
> **Weekley, Frieda**
> *see* **Lawrence, Frieda**
>
> **Edward VIII,** *King of the United Kingdom*
> *see* **Windsor, Edward,** *Duke of*

> *Later name*
> **Nicholls, Charlotte**
> *see* **Brontë, Charlotte**
>
> **Beaconsfield, Benjamin Disraeli,** *Earl of*
> *see* **Disraeli, Benjamin**

26.2A2. Different forms of the name. Refer from a form of name used by a person, or found in reference sources, or resulting from a different romanization of the name, if it differs significantly from the form used in the heading for that person. Always make a reference if any of the first five letters of the entry element for that form differ from the first five letters in the entry element of the heading. Typical instances are:

> *Difference in fullness of name*
> **Valera y Alcalá Galiano, Juan**
> *see* **Valera, Juan**
>
> **Schiller, Johann Christoph Friedrich von**
> *see* **Schiller, Friedrich von**
>
> **Davies, William Henry**
> *see* **Davies, W.H.**
>
> **Powell, Enoch**
> *see* **Powell, J. Enoch**
>
> **Embleton, G.A.**
> *see* **Embleton, Gerry**

> *Full name to initials used as heading*
> **Worsley, Edward**
> *see* **E.W.**

> *Different language form*
> **Domingo,** *de Guzmán*
> *see* **Dominic,** *Saint*
>
> **Jeanne,** *d'Arc, Saint*
> *see* **Joan,** *of Arc, Saint*
>
> **Terentius Afer, Publius**
> *see* **Terence**

Mikes, György
  see Mikes, George

Ó Maolruanaidh, Liam
  see Rooney, William

Meister des Amsterdamer Kabinetts
  see Master of the Amsterdam Cabinet

Different spelling
Ralegh, *Sir* Walter
  see Raleigh, *Sir* Walter

Luly, Jean
  see Lœillet, Jean Baptiste

Different romanization
Cao, Xuequin
  see Ts'ao, Hsüeh-ch'in

Dostoevsky, Anna
  see Dostoevskaîà, A.G.

Garkavi, Avraam ÎÀkovlevich
  see Harkavi, Avraham Eliyahu

26.2A3. Different entry elements. Refer from different elements of the heading for a person under which that name might reasonably be sought. Typical instances are:

Different elements of a compound name
Gould, S. Baring-
  see Baring-Gould, S.

Smith, Cecil Woodham-
  see Woodham-Smith, Cecil

Saint-Hilaire, Étienne Geoffroy
  see Geoffroy Saint-Hilaire, Étienne

Mori, Emilio Cotarelo y
  see Cotarelo y Mori, Emilio

Part of surname following a prefix
Polnay, Peter de
  see De Polnay, Peter

Balzo, Raimundo del
  see Del Balzo, Raimundo

Grunebaum, G.E. von
  see Von Grunebaum, G.E.

Annunzio, Gabriele d'
  see D'Annunzio, Gabriele

Sablière, Marguerite Hessein de La
  see La Sablière, Marguerite Hessein de

Prefix to surname used as entry element (see also 26.2D2)

Von Hofmannsthal, Hugo
see **Hofmannsthal, Hugo von**

Van de Wetering, Janwillem
see **Wetering, Janwillem van de**

Part of surname following a prefix combined with surname

Bure, Guillaume de
see **Debure, Guillaume**

First given name of person without surname when it is not entry element

Maria Helena
see **Helena, Maria**

'Alī ibn Muḥammad, Abū Ḥayyān al-Tawḥīdī
see **Abū Ḥayyān al-Tawḥīdī, 'Alī ibn Muḥammad**

'Abd al-Raḥmān al-Bāshā
see **al-Bāshā, 'Abd al-Raḥmān**

Epithet or byname

Aquinas, Thomas, *Saint*
see **Thomas,** *Aquinas, Saint*

Khayyām, Omar
see **Omar Khayyām**

Udine, Giovanni da
see **Giovanni,** *da Udine*

Last element when it is not the entry element

Barry, Jeanne Bécu, *comtesse Du*
see **Du Barry, Jeanne Bécu,** *comtesse*

Capella, Martianus
see **Martianus Capella**

al-Ḥimyarī, Nashwān ibn Sa'īd
see **Nashwān ibn Sa'īd al-Ḥimyarī**

Maung, Chit, *Saw*
see **Chit Maung,** *Saw*

Person as saint

Edward, *the Confessor, Saint*
see **Edward,** *King of England*

Constantine, *Saint*
see **Constantine I,** *Emperor of Rome*

Family name of saint

Ypes y Alvarez, Juan de
see **John of the Cross,** *Saint*

Soubirous, Marie-Bernarde
see **Bernadette,** *Saint*

Family, dynastic, etc., name of ruler
> **Bonaparte, Napoléon**
>> *see* **Napoléon I,** *Emperor of the French*

> **Bernadotte, Jean-Baptiste-Jules**
>> *see* **Charles XIV John,** *King of Sweden*

Inverted form of initials entered in direct order (see also 26.2B2)
> **C., M.**
>> *see* **M.C.**

> **E., A.L.O.**
>> *see* **A.L.O.E.**

Direct form of inverted phrase heading
> **Miss Read**
>> *see* **Read,** *Miss*

> **Dr. Seuss**
>> *see* **Seuss,** *Dr.*

Honorary titles and terms of address when sometimes used as names
> **U Kyin U**
>> *see* **Kyin U,** *U*

26.2B. Name-title references

26.2B1. If the works of a person are entered under two or more different headings, make a name-title reference when the name appearing in a particular edition of a work is not the name used as the heading for that work.

> **Ashe, Gordon**
>> The croaker
>>> *see* **Creasey, John**
>>>> (*Title page reads:* . . . ₍by₎ John Creasey as Gordon Ashe)

> **Halliday, Michael**
>> The edge of terror
>>> *see* **York, Jeremy**
>>>> (*Title page reads:* . . . by Michael Halliday. *A later edition published with the name of Jeremy York*)

26.2B2. Make a name-title reference from the inverted form of initials entered in direct order for each work entered under those initials.

> **D., H.**
>> Helidora and other poems
>>> *see* **H.D.**

> **D., H.**
>> Hymen
>>> *see* **H.D.**

> **D., H.**
>> Sea garden
>>> *see* **H.D.**

26.2B3. When two or more persons have used the same pseudonym and one or more is entered under another name, make a name-title reference from the pseudonym for each work of a person that is so entered.

> **Theophilus**
> A Burmese loneliness
> > *see* **Enriquez, Colin Metcalf**

> **Theophilus**
> A defence of the dialogue entitled, A display of God's special grace
> > *see* **Dickinson, Jonathan**

26.2B4. If a pseudonym consists of initials, a sequence of letters, or numerals, make a name-title reference from the real name for each item entered under the pseudonym. However, if the initials stand for a phrase other than a name, make a name-title reference from the phrase in direct order for each item entered under the pseudonym.

> **Garcin, Étienne**
> Le nouveau dictionnaire provençal-français
> > *see* **M.G.**
> > > *(Initials stand for Monsieur Garcin)*

> **Lawrence, Curly**
> Betty the mongoliper
> > *see* **L.B.S.C.**

> **London, Brighton & South Coast**
> Betty the mongoliper
> > *see* **L.B.S.C.**

26.2C. "See also" references

26.2C1. If the works of one person are entered under two different headings, make a *see also* reference from each heading to the other (see also 26.2D1).

> **Wright, Willard Huntington**
> > *see also* **Van Dine, S.S.**

> **Van Dine, S.S.**
> > *see also* **Wright, Willard Huntington**

26.2C2. If there are entries in the catalogue under the name of a known person and under the appellation of an unknown person involving the name of that known person, make a *see also* reference from the appellation to the name. For the reference from the name to the appellation, see 26.2D1.

> **Pseudo-Brutus**
> > *see also* **Brutus, Marcus Junius**

26.2D. Explanatory references

498

26.2D1. General rule. When more detailed guidance than a simple *see* or *see also* reference is required, make explanatory references.

> **Gustaf Adolf,** *King of Sweden*
>
> Kings of Sweden with this name are entered in a single sequence together with all kings of Sweden with the first name Gustaf, e.g.,
>
> **Gustaf I Vasa,** *King of Sweden*
> **Gustaf II Adolf,** *King of Sweden*
> **Gustaf III,** *King of Sweden*
> *Make a similar reference under* Gustaf Vasa

> **Dannay, Frederic**
>
> For works of this author written in collaboration with Manfred Lee, see
> **Queen, Ellery**
> **Queen, Ellery,** Jr.
> **Ross, Barnaby**
> *Make a similar reference under* Lee

> **Queen, Ellery**
>
> The joint pseudonym of Frederic Dannay and Manfred Lee.
> For a work written by Dannay under his earlier name, see
> **Dannay, Frederic**
> *Make a similar reference under* Ellery Queen, Jr., *and* Barnaby Ross

> **Paine, Lauran**
>
> For works of this author written under pseudonyms, see
> **Andrews, A.A.**
> **Benton, Will**
> **Bosworth, Frank**
> **Bradford, Will**
> **Bradley, Concho**
> ₍etc., as required₎

> **Bradford, Will**
>
> For works of this author written under his real name, see
> **Paine, Lauran**
> For works written under his other pseudonyms, see
> **Andrews, A.A.**
> **Benton, Will**
> **Bosworth, Frank**
> **Bradley, Concho**
> ₍etc., as required₎
> *Make similar references under the other pseudonyms*

> **Brutus, Marcus Junius**
>
> For the Greek letters erroneously attributed to this person, see
> **Pseudo-Brutus**

26.2D2. *Optionally,* make explanatory references under the various separately written prefixes of surnames to explain how names with such prefixes are entered in the catalogue.

De la

Names beginning with this prefix are also entered under *La* (e.g., La Bretèque, Pierre de) or under the name following the prefix (e.g., Torre, Marie de la)

26.3. NAMES OF CORPORATE BODIES AND GEOGRAPHIC NAMES

26.3A. "See" references

26.3A1. Different names. Refer from a name used by a body, or found in reference sources, that is significantly different from that used in the heading for that body. For references to be made in connection with changes of name, see 26.3C1. Refer from names of places that are different from the name for that place used in headings.

Common Market
   see **European Economic Community**

Order of Preachers
   see **Dominicans**

Quakers
   see **Society of Friends**

Hellas
   see **Greece**

Aix-la-Chapelle
   see **Aachen**

26.3A2. General and specific names of conferences. Refer from a general name for a conference to the specific name used as the heading.

Nutrition Symposium (*1953 : University of Toronto*)
   see **Symposium on Protein Metabolism** (*1953 : University of Toronto*)

Nutrition Symposium (*1956 : University of Michigan*)
   see **Symposium on Endocrines and Nutrition** (*1956 : University of Michigan*)

26.3A3. Different forms of the name. Refer from a form of name used by a body or for a place, or found in reference sources, or resulting from a different romanization of the name, if it differs significantly from the form used in the heading for that body or place. Typical instances are:

Different language forms
Croix-Rouge suisse
   see **Schweizerisches Rotes Kreuz**

Nations Unies
   see **United Nations**

Uffizi Gallery
   see **Galleria degli Uffizi**

500

Danmark
   see **Denmark**

Deutschland (*Bundesrepublik*)
   see **Germany** (*Federal Republic*)

Initials and acronyms not used as heading
E.E.C.
   see **European Economic Community**

G.L.C.
   see **Greater London Council**

Gestapo
   see **Germany.** *Geheime Staatspolizei*

Full names to initials or acronyms used as heading
Hertfordshire Technical Library and Information Service
   see **Hertis**

International Business Machines Corporation
   see **IBM**

European Atomic Energy Community
   see **Euratom**

Different spelling
Organization for Economic Cooperation and Development
   see **Organisation for Economic Co-operation and Development**

Rumania
   see **Romania**

Different romanization
Yaroslavsky tekhnologichesky institut
   see **Îaroslavskiĭ tekhnologicheskiĭ institut**

Pei-ching
   see **Peking**

Other variants (including shorter, fuller, and inverted forms)
American Red Cross
   see **American National Red Cross**

William Hayes Fogg Art Museum
   see **Fogg Art Museum**

United States. *State Department*
   see **United States.** *Department of State*

United Kingdom. *Army. Middlesex Regiment*
   see **United Kingdom.** *Army. Infantry Regiment, 57th*

Religious Society of Friends
   see **Society of Friends**

Friends, Society of
   see **Society of Friends**

> **Luther College**
> *see* **Dr. Martin Luther College**
>
> **Martin Luther College**
> *see* **Dr. Martin Luther College**
>
> **St. Dominic, Order of**
> *see* **Dominicans**
>
> **William and Mary, College of**
> *see* **College of William and Mary**
>
> **Victoria University of Manchester**
> *see* **University of Manchester**
>
> **Roman Catholic Church**
> *see* **Catholic Church**
>
> **Jackson (D.G.) Advertising Service**
> *see* **D.G. Jackson Advertising Service**
>
> **Jackson Advertising Service**
> *see* **D.G. Jackson Advertising Service**

26.3A4. Initials. If the filing system used in the catalogue files initials with full stops differently from those without full stops, refer from the form with full stops to a form without full stops used as a heading, and refer from a form without full stops to a form with full stops used as a heading.

> **U.N.E.S.C.O.**
> *see* **Unesco**
>
> **NAAB**
> *see* **N.A.A.B.**

In the context of such a filing system, *optionally*, refer from initials without full stops, as well as with full stops (see 26.3A3), to a full name used as a heading (see also 26.3C2).

> **NATO**
> *see* **North Atlantic Treaty Organization**
>
> **N.A.T.O.**
> *see* **North Atlantic Treaty Organization**
>
> **USA**
> *see* **United States**
>
> **U.S.A.**
> *see* **United States**

26.3A5. Numbers. If the filing system used in the catalogue files numbers expressed as words differently from numbers expressed as arabic or roman numerals, apply the following directions if a heading begins with a number or contains a number in such a position that it affects the filing of the heading:

a) If the number is expressed in numerals, refer from the form of the heading with the number expressed in words.

> **Drie October-Vereeniging**
> *see* **3 October-Vereeniging**

> **Twentieth Century Heating & Ventilating Co.**
> *see* **XXth Century Heating & Ventilating Co.**

b) If the number is expressed in words, refer from the form of the heading with the the number expressed in arabic numerals.

> **4 Corners Geological Society**
> *see* **Four Corners Geological Society**

26.3A6. Abbreviations. If the filing system used in the catalogue files abbreviated words differently from words written in full and if the heading begins with an abbreviated word or contains an abbreviated word in such a position that it affects the filing of the heading, refer from the form of the heading with the abbreviated word written in full.

> **Sankt Annen-Museum**
> *see* **St. Annen-Museum**

> **Société Saint-Jean-Baptiste de Montréal**
> *see* **Société St-Jean-Baptiste de Montréal**

26.3A7. Different forms of heading. Refer from different forms of heading under which a corporate body might reasonably be sought. Typical instances are:

Subordinate heading and its variants to name entered directly

> **American Library Association.** *American Association of School Librarians*
> *see* **American Association of School Librarians**

> **University of Oxford.** *Bodleian Library*
> *see* **Bodleian Library**

> **London School of Economics and Political Science.** *British Library of Political and Economic Science*
> *see* **British Library of Political and Economic Science**

> **London School of Economics and Political Science.** *Library*
> *see* **British Library of Political and Economic Science**

> **University of London.** *London School of Economics and Political Science*
> *see* **London School of Economics and Political Science**

> **United Kingdom.** *British Railways Board*
> *see* **British Railways Board**

> **United Kingdom.** *Foreign and Commonwealth Office. India Office Library*
> *see* **India Office Library**

> **United States.** *Tennessee Valley Authority*
> *see* **Tennessee Valley Authority**

Name and its variants in the form of subheadings under the immediately superior body when the name has been entered under a body higher than the immediately superior body

503

American Library Association. *Resources and Technical Services Division.*
Cataloging and Classification Section
see American Library Association. *Cataloging and Classification Section*

General Motors Corporation. *Fisher Body Division. Production Engineering*
Department. Engineering Pictorial Section
see General Motors Corporation. *Fisher Body Division. Engineering*
Pictorial Section

For bodies entered subordinately, the name and its variants in the form of
independent headings whenever the name does not necessarily suggest
subordinate entry
American Legion Auxiliary
see American Legion. *Auxiliary*

Task Force on Periodic Motor Vehicle Inspection
see Maryland. *Task Force on Periodic Motor Vehicle Inspection*

26.3B. "See also" references

26.3B1. Make *see also* references between independently entered but related corporate
headings:

British Ornithologists' Club
see also British Ornithologists' Union

British Ornithologists' Union
see also British Ornithologists' Club

British Iron and Steel Research Association
see also Iron and Steel Institute

Iron and Steel Institute
see also British Iron and Steel Research Association

26.3C. Explanatory references

26.3C1. General rule. When more detailed guidance than a simple *see* or *see also*
reference is required, make explanatory references. Typical instances are:

Scope of heading
Freemasons
Under subdivisions of this heading will be found publications of the
lodges, grand lodges, etc., of the basic orders of Freemasonry (also called
"craft" Masonry) in which are conferred the first three Masonic degrees.
For publications of Masonic bodies conferring degrees beyond the
first three, see
Knights Templar (*Masonic order*)
Royal and Select Masters
Royal Arch Masons
Scottish Rite (*Masonic order*)
For publications of other Masonic bodies, see their names, e.g.,
Order of the Secret Monitor

Iran. *Shah (1941–   : Mohammed Reza Pahlavi)*
Here are entered works of the Shah acting in his official capacity.
For other works, see
Mohammed Reza Pahlavi, *Shah of Iran*

Pelham Books, Ltd.
For works issued by Pelham Books, Ltd., under the designation
John Dickson, Ph.D., see **Dickson, John, Ph.D.**

When appropriate in a catalogue where verbal subject and name-title entries are interfiled, integrate the name and subject "scope" references.

References applicable to several headings
Aktiebolaget . . .
Names of corporate bodies beginning with this word are entered
under the next word in the name.

Conference . . .
Conference proceedings are entered under the name of the conference,
etc., or the title of the publication if the conference, etc., lacks a name.
Thus, see also: **Symposium . . . , Workshop . . . ,** etc.

Catholic Church. *Sacra* . . .
The word *Sacra* is omitted from the headings for administrative
bodies of the Catholic Church when it occurs at the beginning of their
names, e.g., for the Sacra Rota Romana, see **Catholic Church.** *Rota Romana.*

Headings that supersede one another
a) Simple situations (usually only two headings involved)

American Material Handling Society
see also the later heading
International Material Management Society
International Material Management Society
see also the earlier heading
American Material Handling Society
 (*A name change*)

Screen Writers' Guild
see also the later heading
Writers Guild of America, West
Radio Writers Guild
see also the later heading
Writers Guild of America, West
Writers Guild of America, West
see also the earlier headings
Radio Writers Guild
Screen Writers' Guild
 (*Merger of two bodies to form a new one*)

b) Complex situations in which more explanation is deemed necessary (usually more than two headings are involved). In each case make the same explanatory reference under each of the headings.

Complete information available

England

This heading is used for publications issued before 1536. For official publications issued 1536–1706, see **England and Wales.** For official publications issued 1707–1800, see **Great Britain.** For official publications issued 1801 to date, see **United Kingdom.**

Westminster Bank

The Westminster Bank and the National Provincial Bank merged in 1969 to form the National Westminster Bank. Works of these bodies are entered under the name used at the time of publication.

United Kingdom. *Ministry of Technology*

This ministry was set up in 1965 and incorporated the Department of Scientific and Industrial Research. It was amalgamated with the Board of Trade to form the Department of Trade and Industry in 1971. In 1974 the Department of Trade and Industry was replaced by the Department of Energy, the Department of Industry, the Department of Prices and Consumer Protection, and the Department of Trade. For works of these bodies, see their names as subheadings of **United Kingdom.**

American-Asian Educational Exchange

The American-Asian Educational Exchange was founded in 1957. In 1962 the name was changed to American Afro-Asian Educational Exchange. In 1967 the name American-Asian Educational Exchange was resumed.

Works of this body are found under the name used at the time of publication.

Incomplete information available

Zambia. *Ministry of Mines and Mining Development*

The Ministry of Mines and Mining Development was created about 1970. Works of this body are found under

Zambia. *Ministry of Mines and Mining Development*

Works of related bodies are found under the following headings:

Zambia. *Ministry of Lands and Mines*

Zambia. *Ministry of Mines*

Zambia. *Ministry of Mines and Co-operatives*

c) Multiple headings for one series of meetings. Make the same explanatory reference under each of the corporate headings involved.

Symposium on the Plasma Membrane (*1961 : New York*)

Publications of this series of meetings are found under the following headings or titles:

3rd: **Symposium on the Plasma Membrane** (*1961 : New York*)

4th: Connective tissue

5th: Differentiation and development

7th: **Symposium on Macromolecular Metabolism** (*1965: New York*)
8th: The Contractile process
9th–   : **Basic Science Symposium**

Technical Thick Film Symposium (*1st : 1967 : Palo Alto and Los Angeles*)
    Publications of this series of meetings are found under the following
headings:
Technical Thick Film Symposium (*1st : 1967 : Palo Alto and Los Angeles*)
Symposium on Hybrid Microelectronics (*2nd : 1967 : Boston*)
Hybrid Microelectronics Symposium (*3rd : 1968 : Rosmont*)
International Hybrid Microelectronics Symposium (*5th : 1970 : Beverly Hills*)

26.3C2. Acronyms. If the filing system used in the catalogue distinguishes between initials with full stops and initials without full stops, and more detailed guidance than a simple *see* reference is called for, make an explanatory reference under each form.

> **N.A.T.O.**
>   *see* **North Atlantic Treaty Organization**
>   When these initials occur in a title or other heading without spaces
> or full stops, they are treated as constituting a word.
>   *Make the same explanatory reference under* NATO

In the context of such a filing system, if the abbreviated form is not formed entirely of initial letters of the name, make the reference from the form with the letters represented as separate initials only if they might be so construed. Make a simple *see* reference if only one reference is to be made.

> **S.A.C.L.A.N.T.**
>   *see* **Supreme Allied Commander, Atlantic**
>   When these initials occur in a title or other heading without spaces
> or full stops, they are treated as constituting a word.
>   *Make the same explanatory reference under* SACLANT

26.4. UNIFORM TITLES

26.4A. "See" references

26.4A1. Different titles or variants of the title. Refer to the uniform title from the different titles and variants of the title under which a work has been published or cited in reference sources.[2] Refer from and to a name heading and title when appropriate.

> **Lied der Nibelungen**
>   *see* **Nibelungenlied**
>
> **Beethoven, Ludwig van**
>   Moonlight sonata
>   *see* **Beethoven, Ludwig van**
>   Sonatas, piano, no. 14, op. 27, no. 2, C# minor

---

2. Use an added entry, however, for the title proper of the edition being catalogued (see 21.30J).

> **Dickens, Charles**
> The personal history of David Copperfield
> *see* **Dickens, Charles**
> David Copperfield

> **Australia**
> Commonwealth of Australia Constitution act
> *see* **Australia**
> Constitution

In the case of translated titles, refer to the uniform title and the appropriate language subheading, when appropriate.

> **Red book of Hergest**
> *see* **Llyfr coch Hergest.** *English*

> **Flaubert, Gustave**
> Sentimental education
> *see* **Flaubert, Gustave**
> Éducation sentimentale. English

26.4A2. Titles of parts of a work catalogued independently. If separately published parts of works are catalogued independently, refer from the titles of such parts in the form of subheadings under the uniform title for the whole work. *Optionally*, use an explanatory reference as instructed in 26.4C2.

> **Tolkien, J.R.R.**
> The lord of the rings. 2. The two towers
> *see* **Tolkien, J.R.R.**
> The two towers

> **Proust, Marcel**
> A la recherche du temps perdu. 1. Du côté de chez Swann
> *see* **Proust, Marcel**
> Du côté de chez Swann

26.4A3. Titles of parts catalogued under the title of the whole work. If separately published parts of a work are catalogued under the uniform title of the whole work, refer from the titles of such parts, if they are distinctive, to the uniform title under which they will be found. Refer from and to a name heading and title when appropriate.

> **Old Testament**
> *see* **Bible.** *O.T.*

> **Genesis** (*Book of the Bible*)
> *see* **Bible.** *O.T. Genesis*

> **Ruth rabbah**
> *see* **Midrash rabbah.** *Ruth*

26.4A4. Collective titles. When a collection of, or a selection from, a person's works is catalogued under a conventional collective title, refer from the name and title taken from the chief source of information or found in a reference source to the name and collective title, unless the title taken from the chief source of information or found in a reference source is the same as, or very similar to, the collective title.

> **Dante Alighieri**
>> Tutte le opere
>>> *see* **Dante Alighieri**
>>>> Works

> **Andersen, H.C.**
>> Eventyr
>>> *see* **Andersen, H.C.**
>>>> Fairy tales

> **Balzac, Honoré de**
>> Due studi di donna e altri racconti
>>> *see* **Balzac, Honoré de**
>>>> Selections. Italian

26.4B. "See also" references

26.4B1. When related works, other than those that are parts of other works, are entered in the catalogue under different uniform titles, make *see also* references between them unless one or both of the references are made unnecessary by added entries. Refer from and to a name heading and title when appropriate.

> **Kerr, Orpheus C.**
>> The cloven foot
>>> *see also* **Dickens, Charles**
>>>> Edwin Drood
>>> (*The Kerr work is an adaptation of* Edwin Drood. *Added entry under Dickens makes see also reference from Dickens unnecessary*)

> **Klage**
>> *see also* **Nibelungenlied**

> **Nibelungenlied**
>> *see also* **Klage**

> **Catholic Church**
>> Breviary
>>> *see also* **Catholic Church**
>>>> Liturgy of the hours

> **Catholic Church**
>> Liturgy of the hours
>>> *see also* **Catholic Church**
>>>> Breviary

26.4C. Explanatory references

26.4C1. General rule. When more detailed guidance than a simple *see* or *see also* reference is required, make explanatory references.

Pentateuch

For the Pentateuch as a whole, see **Bible**. *O.T. Pentateuch*. For individual books of the Pentateuch, see the name of the book as a subheading of the heading for the Old Testament, e.g., **Bible**. *O.T. Genesis*.

26.4C2. Titles of parts catalogued independently. If separately published parts of a work are catalogued independently, make an explanatory reference from the name heading (when appropriate) and uniform title of the main work to any such parts.

Arabian nights

For separately published parts of this collection see

Ali Baba

Sindbad the sailor

[*etc.*]

Tolkien, J.R.R.

The lord of the rings

For the separately published parts of this work see

Tolkien, J.R.R.

The fellowship of the ring

The two towers

The return of the king

Proust, Marcel

A la recherche du temps perdu

For the separately published parts of this work see

Proust, Marcel

Du côté de chez Swann

A l'ombre des jeunes filles en fleurs

Côté de Guermantes

[*etc.*]

26.4C3. Collective titles. When the same title is used as the title proper (or the opening phrase of the title proper) of works that are assigned different uniform titles, one or more of which is a collective uniform title (cf. 25.8–25.10), refer to the latter with an appropriate explanation.

Turgenev, I.S.

Phantoms

For separate publications of this work in English, see

Turgenev, I.S.

Prizvaki. English

For collections in English beginning with this title, see

Turgenev, I.S.

Selections. English

26.5. REFERENCES INSTEAD OF ADDED ENTRIES COMMON TO MANY EDITIONS

26.5A. If a number of added entries under the same heading are required, *optionally*, replace them by appropriate references. Do this if it appears that the greater simplicity and savings in time and catalogue space offset the inconvenience to the user of the catalogue.

> Hamlet
>
> **Shakespeare, William**
>
> Editions of this work will be found under **Shakespeare, William.**
>
> Luther, Martin
>
> **Bible**
>
> For editions of the whole Bible translated by Luther, see **Bible.** *German. Luther*

26.5B. Alternatively, in such a case, make one added entry under the common heading and add a reference to the main entry.

> Hamlet
>
> **Shakespeare, William**
>
> Hamlet: an authoritative text, intellectual backgrounds, extracts from the sources, essays in criticism / William Shakespeare ; edited by Cyrus Hoy. — New York : Norton, ₁1963₁
>
> xii, 270 p. : ill. ; 21 cm. — (Norton critical editions ; N306)
>
> > For other editions, see Shakespeare, William. Hamlet

CAPITALIZATION

General rules

A.1. INITIALS AND ACRONYMS

Capitalize initials and acronyms used by corporate bodies, and appearing in headings or in bibliographic descriptions, according to the predominant usage of the body.

> AFL-CIO
>
> Unesco

A.2. HEADINGS

A.2A. General rule

Capitalize personal and corporate names used as headings and corporate names used as subheadings as instructed in the rules for the language involved. If a name begins with an article,[1] a preposition, or a contraction of an article and a preposition, capitalize it.

> **Alexander**, *of Aphrodisias*
>
> **De la Mare, Walter**
>
> **Musset, Alfred de**
>
> **Cavour, Camillo Benso,** *conte di*
>
> **Third Order Regular of St. Francis**
>
> **Société de chimie physique**
>
> **Det Norske Nobelinstitutt**
>
> **Ontario.** *High Court of Justice*

---

1. If a corporate name begins with the Arabic article *al* in any of its various orthographic forms (e.g., *al*, *el*, *es*) or the Hebrew article *ha* (*he*), lowercase it whether written separately or hyphenated with the following word. If an Arabic personal name begins with an article, follow the same rule unless it is determined that the bearer of the name treats the article as an integral part of the name; in that case, capitalize the article. If a Hebrew personal name begins with an article, always capitalize the article.

A.2B. Words or phrases characterizing persons

Capitalize a word, or the first word of a phrase, characterizing a person and used as a heading (cf. 22.11D). Capitalize proper names contained in such a phrase as instructed in the rules for the language involved; capitalize a quoted title as instructed in A.4B.

> **Physician**
>
> **Lady of quality**
>
> **Citizen of Albany**
>
> **Author of Early impressions**

A.2C. Additions to certain headings for persons

Capitalize additions to headings for persons made according to the instructions in certain rules (cf. 22.11A, 22.15A, 22.19) as instructed in the rules for the language involved. If the addition is given in parentheses (cf. 22.11A and 22.19A), capitalize the first word of the addition and any proper name.

> **Moses,** *Grandma*
>
> **Deidier,** *abbé*
>
> **Brown, George,** *Rev.*
>
> **Thomas** (*Anglo-Norman poet*)

A.2D. Additions to names of corporate bodies

Capitalize the first word of each addition to the name of a corporate body; capitalize other words in the addition as instructed in the rules for the language involved.

> **Bounty** (*Ship*)
>
> **Knights Templar** (*Masonic order*)
>
> **Regional Conference on Mental Measurement of the Blind** (*1st : 1951: Perkins Institution*)
>
> **Washington** (*U.S. : State*)

A.3. UNIFORM TITLES

A.3A. Individual uniform titles

Capitalize an individual uniform title as instructed in A.4.

A.3B. Collective uniform titles

Capitalize only the first word of a collective uniform title (cf. 25.8–25.10, 25.34–25.36).

> ₁Works₁
>
> ₁Short stories₁
>
> ₁Instrumental music₁
>
> ₁Polonaises, piano₁

A.3C. Additions to uniform titles

Capitalize the first word of each addition to an individual uniform title or a collective uniform title. Capitalize other words in an addition as instructed in the rules for the language involved.

> **Seven sages of Rome** (*Southern version*)
>
> **Guillaume** (*Chanson de geste*)
>
> **Genesis** (*Middle High German poem*)
>
> ₍Sketches by Boz. German. Selections₎
>
> ₍Poems. Selections₎
>
> ₍Goyescas (Opera)₎

In additions to uniform titles for music, lowercase words (including abbreviations) indicating medium of performance (cf. 25.29), words (including abbreviations) accompanying serial numbers and opus or thematic index numbers, and words accompanying statements of key (cf. 25.31) unless they are proper names.

> ₍Trios, piano, strings, no. 2, op. 66, C minor₎
>
> ₍Sonatas, piano, K. 457, C minor₎

A.4. TITLE AND STATEMENT OF RESPONSIBILITY AREA

A.4A. Title elements (general rule)

Capitalize the first word of the title proper, an alternative title, or a parallel title (see also A.4B below).[2] Capitalize other words, including the first word of the other title information element, as instructed in the rules for the language involved (see also A.4D). See A.19J for the capitalization of names for the Bible and its parts; A.19F for the capitalization of the names of religious creeds and confessions; and A.20 for the capitalization of names of documents.

> The materials of architecture
>
> The 1919/20 Breasted Expedition to the Near East
>
> Les misérables
>
> IV informe de gobierno
>
> Eileen Ford's A more beautiful you in 21 days
>
> Journal of polymer science
>
> The people of the state of New York, plaintiff, against the Erie Railway Company and others, defendants
>
> Sechs Partiten für Flöte
>
> Still life with bottle and grapes
>
> The Edinburgh world atlas, or, Advanced atlas of modern geography
>
> Coppélia, ou, La fille aux yeux d'émail

---

2. If a romanized title proper, alternative title, or parallel title begins with the Arabic article *al* in any of its various orthographic forms (e.g., *al*, *el*, *es*) or with the Hebrew article *ha* (*he*), lowercase it, whether written separately or hyphenated with the following word.

A.4B *Quoted titles*

Strassenkarte der Schweiz = Carte routière de la Suisse = Road map of Switzerland = Carta stradale della Svizzera

The greenwood tree : newsletter of the Somerset and Dorset Family History Society

Quo vadis? : a narrative from the time of Nero

King Henry the Eighth ; and, The tempest

A.4B. Quoted titles

Capitalize the first word of every title quoted (see also A.4D).

An interpretation of The ring and the book

Selections from the Idylls of the king

Supplement to The Oxford companion to Canadian history and literature

. . . / by the author of Memoirs of a fox-hunting man

A.4C. Titles preceded by dots, etc., indicating incompleteness

Lowercase the first word of a title if it is preceded by dots, dashes, or other symbols indicating that the beginning of the phrase from which the title was derived has been omitted.

——and master of none

A.4D. Works entered under title proper

If the first word of the title of a work entered under its title proper is an article, capitalize also the next word.

A Dictionary of American English on historical principles

The Encyclopedia of photography

The Porcupine book of verse

The Ladies advocate
  (*Anonymous*)

The International tax journal

Les Cahiers du tourisme

The Consumer education series

The Anatomical record

If, in such a case, the title (not enclosed in quotation marks) appears in a sentence written in the same language as the title, or is quoted in another title in the same language, lowercase the initial article.

"Reprinted from the Anatomical record, vol. 88, Jan.–Mar. 1944"

Songs in the opera call'd the Beggar's wedding

A Supplement to the Journal of physics and chemistry of solids

but

"In the September issue of 'The Woman's Press' "

Separate from La Revista de derecho, jurisprudencia y administración

A.4E. Certain titles of serials that have merged or been absorbed

When one serial absorbs or merges with another and incorporates that serial's title with its own, lowercase the first word of the incorporated title unless the rules for the language involved require its capitalization for another reason.

> Farm chemicals and crop life
>
> *not* Farm chemicals and Crop life

A.4F. Grammatically independent titles of supplements and sections of an item

If the title proper of an item that is supplementary to, or a section of, another item consists of two or more parts not grammatically linked (cf. 1.1B9, 12.1B3, 12.1B4), capitalize the first word of the title of the second and subsequent parts. If the title of the part is introduced by an alphabetic or a numeric designation beginning with a word, capitalize also that word.

> Faust. Part one
>
> Advanced calculus. Student handbook
>
> Journal of biosocial science. Supplement
>
> Acta Universitatis Carolinae. Philologica
>
> Progress in nuclear energy. Series 2, Reactors

A.4G. General material designation

Lowercase the words making up a general material designation.

A.4H. Statement of responsibility

In the statement of responsibility element, capitalize as instructed in the rules for the language involved all personal and corporate names; also titles of nobility, address, honour, and distinction; and initials of societies, etc., accompanying personal names. Generally, lowercase all other words.

> . . . / by Mrs. Charles H. Gibson
>
> . . . / by Alfred, Lord Tennyson
>
> . . . / International Symposium on the Cataloguing, Coding, and Statistics of Audio-Visual Materials ; organised by ISO/TC 46 Documentation in collaboration with IFLA and IFTC, 7–9 January 1976 in Strasbourg

A.5. EDITION AREA

If the first, or a subsequent, edition statement begins with a word or an abbreviation of a word, capitalize it. Capitalize other words as instructed in the rules for the language involved.

> Household ed.
>
> Facsim. ed.
>
> 1st standard ed.
>
> Neue Aufl.
>
> Rev. et corr.
>
> Wyd. 2-gie
>
> World's classics ed., New ed., rev.

A.6. MATERIAL (OR TYPE OF PUBLICATION) SPECIFIC DETAILS AREA

If the material (or type of publication) specific details area begins with a word or an abbreviation of a word, capitalize it. Capitalize other elements as instructed in the rules for the language involved.

> Scale 1:500,000
>
> Vertical exaggeration 1:5
>
> Transverse Mercator proj.
>
> Vol. 1, no. 1 (Jan./Mar. 1974)–
>
> No 1 (juil. 1970)–

A.7. PUBLICATION, DISTRIBUTION, ETC., AREA

A.7A. General rule

Capitalize the names of places, publishers, distributors, and manufacturers as instructed in the rules for the language involved. Capitalize also the shortened form of name of a publisher, distributor, etc., when used as instructed in 1.4B4.

> Montréal
>
> Coloniae Agrippinae
>
> The Hague
>
> Den Haag
>
> *but* 's-Gravenhage
>
> T. Wall and Sons
>
> Presses universitaires de France
>
> O.L.F.
>   (i.e., *Office de la langue française*)

A.7B. Initial words or abbreviations not part of a name

If an element of the area begins with a word or abbreviation not an integral part of the name of the place, publisher, distributor, manufacturer, etc., generally capitalize the word or abbreviation. Lowercase all other words or abbreviations not part of a name unless the rules for the language involved require their capitalization. Capitalize only the *s* of *s.l.*; lowercase *s.n.*

> V Praze
>
> Londini : Apud B. Fellowes
>
> Lipsiae : Sumptibus et typis B.G. Teubneri
>
> New York : Released by Beaux Arts
>
> New York : The Association
>
> Wiesbaden : In Kommission bei O. Harrassowitz
>
> Toronto : Published in association with the Pulp and Paper Institute
> of Canada by University of Toronto Press
>
> ₍S.l. : s.n.₎

A.8. PHYSICAL DESCRIPTION AREA

Capitalize trade names and certain other technical terms appearing in this area (cf. 6.5C8, 7.5B1, 8.5C12) as instructed in the rules of the language involved. Lowercase all other words, including those standing first in the area.

> leaves 81–144
>
> 1000 p. in various pagings
>
> 310 leaves of braille
>
> ill., col. maps, ports. (some col.)
>
> on 1 side of 1 sound disc (13 min.)
>
> 1 videoreel (Quadruplex) (ca. 75 min.)
>
> 12 slides : sound (3M Talking Slide), col.
>
> 14 film reels (157 min.) : Panavision

A.9. SERIES AREA

A.9A. General rule

Capitalize the title proper, parallel titles, other title information, and statements of responsibility of a series as instructed in A.4.

> Great newspapers reprinted
>
> The World of folkdances
>
> Master choruses for Lent and Easter
>
> Jeux visuels = Visual games
>
> Concertino : Werke für Schul- und Liebhaber Orchester
>
> Standard radio supersound effects. Trains
>
> Acta Universitatis Stockholmiensis. Stockholm studies in history of literature
>
> Publicación / Universidad de Chile, Departamento de Geología

A.9B. Terms used in conjunction with series numbering

Lowercase such terms as *v.*, *no.*, *reel*, *t.*, used in conjunction with the series number unless the rules for a particular language require capitalization (e.g., the German *Bd.*) Capitalize other words and alphabetic devices used as part of the numbering systems according to the usage of the item.

> Deutscher Planungsatlas ; Bd. 8
>
> Exploring careers ; group 8
>
> S266 ; block 6
>
> Music for today. Series 2 ; no. 8.
>
> Typewriting. Unit 2, Skill development ; program 1
>
> National standard reference data series ; NSRDS-NBS 5

A.10. NOTE AREA

Capitalize the first word in each note or an abbreviation beginning a note. If a note consists of more than one sentence, capitalize the first word of each subsequent sentence. Capitalize other words as instructed in the rules for the language involved.

> Title from container

> Facsim. reprint. Originally published: London : I. Walsh, ca. 1734

A.11. STANDARD NUMBERS AND TERMS OF AVAILABILITY AREA

Capitalize alphabetical elements that are part of a standard number.

> ISSN 0305-3741

Lowercase qualifiers added to a standard number or to a price. Capitalize the first word of the statement giving the terms on which the item is available if the statement appears without a price.

> ISBN 0-435-91660-2 (cased)

> ISBN 0-902573-4 : Subscribers only

> $1.00 (pbk.)

> £4.40 (complete collection). — £0.55 (individual sheets)

English language

A.12. INTRODUCTION

The rules for English-language capitalization basically follow those of the University of Chicago Press *A Manual of Style for Authors, Editors, and Copywriters*. — 12th ed., rev. — Chicago : University of Chicago Press, 1969. Certain rules that differ have been modified to conform to the requirements of bibliographic records.

A.13. PERSONAL NAMES

A.13A. General rule

Capitalize the names of persons, including names represented by initials.

> D.H. Lawrence
> H.D.
> John, the Baptist
> Benjamin Franklin
> Cecil Day-Lewis

A.13B. Names with particles

If a personal name of foreign origin includes particles, e.g., *de, des, la, l', della, von, von der,* follow the usage of the particular person with regard to capitalization of the particles; in case of doubt capitalize them.

> Daphne du Maurier; du Maurier
> Eva Le Gallienne; Le Gallienne

Mark Van Doren; Van Doren
Mazo de la Roche; de la Roche
Wernher Von Braun; Von Braun

A.13C. Titles preceding the name
Capitalize any title that immediately precedes a personal name.

Field Marshal Sir Michael Carver
Gen. Fred C. Weyand
Grandma Moses
John Henry Cardinal Newman
Pope Paul VI
President Carter
Prime Minister Pierre Trudeau
Queen Elizabeth II
Rabbi Stephen Wise
Senator Hubert H. Humphrey
Sister Mary Joseph

A.13D. Ordinal numerals following names of sovereigns and popes
Capitalize ordinal numerals used after names of sovereigns and popes to denote order of succession.

King George the Sixth
John the Twenty-third

A.13E. Titles following a name or used alone in place of a name

A.13F. Royalty and nobility
Capitalize titles of royalty and nobility.

Elizabeth II, Queen of the United Kingdom; the Queen
Charles, Prince of Wales; the Prince of Wales; the Prince
Prince Philip, Duke of Edinburgh; the Duke of Edinburgh;
    the Duke
Frank Pakenham, Earl of Longford; the Earl of Longford;
    the Earl
Sir Thomas Beecham, Bart.

A.13G. Religious titles and offices
Capitalize religious titles and offices.

His Holiness Paul VI, Pope; the Pope
Most Rev. and Rt. Hon. Frederick Donald Coggan, Archbishop
    of Canterbury; the Archbishop of Canterbury; the Archbishop
the Right Reverend Paul Moore, Bishop of New York; the
    Bishop of New York; the Bishop
the Reverend Michael O'Sullivan, Pastor of Saint Peter's
    Church; the Pastor

521

A.13H. Civil and military titles and offices

Lowercase civil and military titles and offices.

> Jimmy Carter, president of the United States; the president
>   of the United States; the president[3]
> James Callaghan, prime minister; the prime minister[3]
> the Hon. Walter Stewart Owen, lieutenant-governor of British
>   Columbia; the lieutenant-governor of British Columbia; the
>   lieutenant-governor[3]
> Edmund G. Brown, governor of California; the governor of
>   California; the governor[3]
> Warren Earl Burger, chief justice of the United States; the
>   chief justice of the United States; the chief justice
> Gen. Bernard A. Rogers, chief of staff, U.S. Army; the general
> James F. Calvert, rear admiral, USN
> Hubert H. Humphrey, senator from Minnesota, the senator
>   from Minnesota; the senator
> Kingman Brewster, ambassador to Great Britain; the
>   ambassador to Great Britain; the ambassador

A.13J. Professional titles

Generally lowercase professional titles. However, if the title is a named professorship, capitalize it.

> C.F. Harrington, chancellor of McGill University; the chancellor
> W. Carson Ryan, Kenan Professor of Education; the professor
> Robert Paul Bergman, associate professor of fine arts
> R.F. Bennett, president of the Ford Motor Company of Canada;
>   the president
> Olga Porotnikoff, secretary, IFLA Committee (Section) on
>   Cataloguing

A.13K. Certain other terms following names

Capitalize the names or abbreviations of academic degrees, honours, religious orders, etc.

> Father Brendan Malley, S.J.
> C.D. Needham, Fellow of the Library Association
> R.C. Strong, Ph.D., F.S.A.
> Ralph Damian Goggens, Order of Preachers

Capitalize the words *esquire*, *junior*, and *senior* (and their abbreviations) following a name.

> John Mytton, Esq.
> John D. Rockefeller, Jr.

---

3. Capitalize such words as *president*, *prime minister*, and *governor* as instructed in A.18B when they designate the office rather than a particular person occupying the office.

A.13L. Titles of honour and respect
Capitalize titles of honour and respect.

> Her Majesty
> His Royal Highness
> His Holiness
> Your Excellency
> Your Grace
> Your Honour

A.13M. Epithets
Capitalize an epithet occurring with, or used in place of, a personal name.

> the Iron Chancellor
> Old Hickory
> the Autocrat of the Breakfast Table
> Bonnie Prince Charlie
> Light Horse Harry Lee
> Jerome H. (Dizzy) Dean
> Abraham Lincoln, the Great Emancipator

A.13N. Personifications
Capitalize a personification of an abstraction or a thing.

> A dialogue between Death and a beautiful lady
> Let Fame sound the trumpet

A.14. NAMES OF RACES, ETC.
Capitalize the names of peoples, races, tribes, and ethnic and linguistic groups.

African	Polynesian
Celt	Scandinavian
German	Slav
Hottentot	Teutonic
Mongol	Yoruba

A.15. PLACE NAMES

A.15A. Geographic features, regions, etc.
Capitalize the names of geographic features, regions, etc. Lowercase a descriptive adjective not part of an accepted name.

> Arctic Circle
> Arctic Ocean
> Asia; Asian continent
> Atlantic; South Atlantic; southern Atlantic
> Central America; central European (*but* Central Europe
>   when referring to the political entity)

Cheviot Hills
the Continent (i.e. Europe); continental Europe; the
    European continent; Continental customs
East; the Orient; Far East(ern); Near East(ern); Middle
    East(ern); Eastern customs; oriental (adjective); eastern
    Europe (but Eastern Europe when referring to the political
    division); the East (U.S.)
Great Lakes
Great Slave Lake
Isthmus of Suez
Mackenzie River
Mississippi Delta
North Temperate Zone
Sea of Marmara
South America; South American continent
Southeast Asia; southeastern, southern, central Asia
Strait of Dover
Tropic of Capricorn; the tropics
the West, Far West, Middle West, Midwest (U.S.); western,
    far western, Midwestern

A.15B. Political divisions

Capitalize the names of political divisions, e.g., a country, state, province, city. Capitalize such a word as *empire, kingdom, state, country,* and *city* following a proper name if it is a commonly accepted part of the name. Capitalize such a word when preceding the proper name only when it is determined that it is a part of the full name of a political division. Lowercase such a word when used alone to indicate a political division.

Austrian Empire; the empire
Canada; Dominion of Canada
Eleventh Congressional District; the congressional district
New York City; the city of New York
Simcoe County; the county
Sixth Precinct; the precinct
United Kingdom; the kingdom of Great Britain
Washington State; the state of Washington

A.15C. Popular names

Capitalize popular and legendary names of places.

Atlantis
Bay Area (San Francisco)
Belgravia (London)
Benelux countries
the Channel (English Channel)
City of Brotherly Love
Erin
Eternal City

Foggy Bottom (Washington, D.C.)
Latin Quarter (Paris)
New World; Old World
the Nutmeg State
Old Dominion (Virginia)
Panhandle (Texas; Oklahoma)
the Potteries (England)
South Seas
the States (i.e., the U.S.)
the Village (New York)
West End (London)

A.16. NAMES OF STRUCTURES, STREETS, ETC.

Capitalize the names of buildings, monuments, and other structures; and the names of roads and streets. Lowercase such words as *avenue, bridge, hotel,* and *park* when they are used alone. See A.18E for the capitalization of names of buildings in which religious bodies meet.

the Capitol (Washington, D.C.)
Central Park (New York); the park
Cleopatra's Needle (London; New York)
Drury Lane Theatre; the theatre
Forty-second Street
Hoover Dam; the dam
Iroquois Lock
Jacques Cartier Bridge; the bridge
Oxford Circus (London); the circus
Pyramid of the Sun; the pyramid
Royal Air Force Memorial
Tower of the Winds (Athens)

A.17. DERIVATIVES OF PROPER NAMES

Lowercase words derived from personal or place names when they are used with a specialized meaning.

angstrom unit	italicize
arabic numbers	malapropism
bikini	melba toast
bourbon whiskey	nile green
burnt sienna	raglan sleeves
cologne	roman type
diesel engine	timothy grass
hamburger	

A.18. NAMES OF CORPORATE BODIES

A.18A. International organizations and alliances

Capitalize the names of international organizations and alliances.

Central Treaty Organization
Common Market

European Coal and Steel Community
Hanseatic League; Hansa
Holy Alliance
International Monetary Fund
Little Entente
North Atlantic Treaty Organization; NATO
Organization of African Unity
Triple Alliance, 1882
United Nations; UN; United Nations Security Council;
  the Security Council; the council
World Health Organization; WHO

A.18B. Government bodies

Capitalize the full names of legislative and judicial bodies; administrative departments, bureaus, and offices; armed forces (armies, navies, air forces, and their regiments, battalions, companies, fleets, etc.); and accepted shortened forms of their names. Lowercase other incomplete designations, except abbreviations, and adjectives derived from the names.

Agency for International Development; AID; the agency
Atlantic Fleet
Canadian Armed Forces
Canadian Citizenship Branch; the branch
Central Office of Information; the office
Circuit Court of the United States; the federal Circuit Court
Commission on Post-Secondary Education in Ontario; the
  commission
Congress; the Ninety-fifth Congress; congressional
Court of Appeals of the State of Colorado; the court of appeals
Department of State; State Department; the department
District Court for the Southern District of New York;
  district court
Division of Education for the Disadvantaged; the division
Domestic Council Committee on Illegal Aliens; the committee
Federal Court of Canada; the federal court
First Army; the First; the army
First Infantry Division; the division
House of Commons; the Commons
House of Representatives; the House; the lower house of
  Congress
Juvenile and Domestic Relations Court; juvenile court;
  domestic relations court
Ministry of Agriculture, Fisheries, and Food; the ministry
Parliament; parliamentary
Peace Corps
President of the United States (i.e., the office)
Prime Minister (i.e., the office)
Queen's Bench Division of the High Court of Justice
Queen's Own Cameron Highlanders of Canada

Royal Air Force
Royal Canadian Army Medical Corps
Royal Gloucestershire Hussars
Twentieth Air Force
Twenty-first Regiment of U.S. Infantry
United States Court of Appeals for the Second Circuit; court
    of appeals
United States Navy

A.18C. Political parties

Capitalize the name of political parties and their members.

Communist Party; Communist(s)
Labour Party; Labourite(s)
Nazi Party; Nazi(s)
Democratic Party; Democrat(s)
Social Credit Party of Canada

A.18D. Political and economic systems

Lowercase names of political and economic systems or schools of thought and their proponents unless the name is derived from a proper noun. Generally lowercase names of political groups other than parties.

anarchism	mugwumps
capitalism	nationalism
egalitarianism	right wing
fascism	socialist bloc
farm bloc	*but*
independent(s)	Benthamism
mercantilism	Keynesianism
monarchism	Marxism

A.18E. Other corporate bodies

Capitalize the names of institutions, associations, conferences, companies, religious denominations and orders, local churches, etc. (see A.19D for the names of religions), and their departments and divisions. Lowercase the article *the* preceding the name, even when a part of the official name. Lowercase generic words such as *society*, *company*, *conference*, when used alone.

Abbey of Mont Saint-Michel
American Library Association
the Board of Regents of the University of California; the board of
    regents; the board; the regents
Boy Scouts of America; a Boy Scout; a Scout
Canadian National Railways
Catholic Church
Church of England
Christian Brothers
Church of the Redeemer
Congregation Anshe Mizrach
Council of Trent

527

> Fifty-second Annual Meeting of the American Historical
>   Association; the annual meeting of the association
> First Baptist Church
> First Council of Constantinople; Second General Council
> Garrick Club; the club
> General Council of the United Church of Canada
> General Foods Corporation
> Green Bay Packers; the Packers; the team
> Independent Order of Odd Fellows; IOOF; an Odd Fellow
> Iowa Falls High School; the high school
> Lambeth Conference
> London Natural History Society; the society
> League of Women Voters; the league
> Metro-Goldwyn-Mayer, Inc.
> Midwest Baptist Conference
> Monastery of the Visitation
> Mosque of Sidi Okba
> National Bank of New Zealand, Ltd.
> National Dance Theatre Company of Jamaica
> Order of Preachers
> Presbyterian Church in Canada
> Reference Section of the Canadian Library Association; the section
> Roman Catholic Church
> Second Vatican Council; Vatican II
> Society of Jesus; Jesuits; a Jesuit
> Synod of Whitby
> Temple Israel
> Textile Workers Union of America; the union
> Toronto Symphony Orchestra
> United Methodist Church
> Young Men's Christian Association; YMCA; the association

A.18F. Plural generic terms

Capitalize a plural generic term when it precedes the distinctive nouns in two or more proper names; lowercase the generic term when it follows them.

> Atlantic and Pacific oceans
> Authorized and Revised versions
> Industry and Trade departments
> Lakes Erie and Ontario
> Saints Constantine and Helen

A.19. RELIGIOUS NAMES AND TERMS

A.19A. Deities

Capitalize the names of God, terms referring to the Christian Trinity, and the names of other deities.

Adonai	Mars
Allah	Messiah (Jesus Christ)
the Almighty	Minerva
Astarte	the Omnipotent
Brahma	Prince of Peace
Christ	Providence
the Father	Son of God
the First Cause	Son of Man
Hera	the Supreme Being
Holy Ghost; Holy Spirit	Vishnu
Jehovah	the Word
King of Kings	Yahweh
Lamb of God	Zeus
Lord	

A.19A1. Lowercase pronouns referring to the names of deities unless capitalization is necessary to avoid ambiguity.

> God as I understand him
> The appearance of Christ after his resurrection

but

> God gives man what He wills
> Trust Him who doeth all things well

A.19A2. Lowercase most derivative words, both adjectives and nouns.

> God's fatherhood, kingship, omnipotence
> Jesus' sonship
> godlike
> messianic hope
> christological; *but* Christology, Christlike, Christian

A.19B. Names of Satan

Capitalize words specifically denoting Satan.

> the Devil
> Father of Lies
> His Satanic Majesty
> Lucifer
> Prince of Darkness

but

> a devil
> the devils
> the devil's advocate

A.19C. Revered persons

Capitalize appellations of revered persons such as prophets, apostles, and saints.

the Apostle to the Gentiles	the Blessed Virgin
the Baptist	Buddha
the Beloved Apostle	the Fathers; church fathers

Messiah (Jewish)	the Prophet (Mohammed)
Mother of God	the Twelve
our Lady	the Virgin (Mary)

A.19D. Religions

Capitalize the names of religions, sects, and the names of specific religious movements. Capitalize also the names of their members and adjectives derived from their names. See A.18E for the names of denominations, orders, local churches, etc.

Anglicanism; an Anglican; Anglican communion
Arianism; Arian heresy
Buddhism; a Buddhist; Buddhist ideas
Catholicism; a Catholic
Christian Science; a Christian Scientist
Dissenter
Essene; the Essenes
Gnosticism; a Gnostic; the Gnostic heresy
Islam; Islamic; Muslim
Judaism; Orthodox Judaism; Reform Judaism; an Orthodox Jew
Lutheranism; a Lutheran
Mormonism; Mormon; the Mormon church
Protestantism; a Protestant
Roman Catholicism; a Roman Catholic
Shinto
Sufi; Sufism
Theosophy; Theosophist
Vedanta
Zen; Zen Buddhism

A.19E. Religious events and concepts

Capitalize the names of major Biblical and religious events and concepts.

Armageddon	the Hegira
the Assumption of the Virgin	the Immaculate Conception
the Captivity (Babylonian)	Judgement Day
the Creation	the Last Supper
the Crucifixion	Redemption
the Enlightenment (Buddhism)	the Second Advent

A.19F. Creeds and confessions

Capitalize the name of particular creeds and confessions.

Augsburg Confession
Nicene Creed
the Thirty-nine Articles

A.19H. The Eucharist

Capitalize terms referring to the Eucharist.

Communion	the Lord's Supper
the Divine Liturgy	the Mass
Holy Communion	

A.19J. The Bible

Capitalize names for the Bible, its divisions and groups of books, and individual books.

Holy Bible	Apocrypha
Holy Scriptures	Five Scrolls
Sacred Scriptures	Historical Books
New Testament; Old Testament	Minor Prophets
New Covenant	Pentateuch
Gospels	Genesis
Acts of the Apostles	History of Susanna
Apocalypse of John	Song of Songs
Epistles of Paul	

A.19J1. Capitalize the word *book* when it refers to the entire Bible; otherwise, lower-case it.

the Book

but

the book of Proverbs
the book of the Prophet Isaiah
the second book of Kings

A.19K. Special selections from the Bible

Capitalize the first word of the names of special selections from the Bible that are commonly referred to by specific names.

the Beatitudes	the Nunc dimittis
the Decalogue	the Shema
the Lord's prayer	the Sermon on the mount
the Miserere	the Ten commandments

A.19L. Versions of the Bible

Capitalize the names of versions of the Bible.

Authorized Version	New English Bible
Confraternity Version	Septuagint
Jerusalem Bible	Vulgate
New American Standard Bible	

A.20. NAMES OF DOCUMENTS

Capitalize the formal, or conventional, names of such documents as charters, constitutions, legislative acts and bills, pacts, plans, statements of policy, and treaties.

Articles of Confederation
Atlantic Charter
Bill of Rights
British North America Act
Canada Corporations Act; the act
Civil Rights Act of 1964
Concordat of Worms

Constitution of Virginia; the constitution
Declaration of Independence
Fourteenth Amendment (U.S. Constitution)
Magna Charta
Marshall Plan; the plan
Reform Bill
Third Five Year Plan (India)
Treaty of Versailles; the treaty
Universal Copyright Convention; the convention
Webster-Ashburton Treaty

A.21. NAMES OF HISTORICAL AND CULTURAL EVENTS AND PERIODS

Capitalize the names of historical and cultural events and major historical and cultural periods.

Age of Discovery	Norman Conquest
Battle of Dunkirk	Operation Deep Freeze
Boxer Rebellion	Reformation
Dark Ages	Second Battle of the Marne
Elizabethan Age	Second World War
French Revolution	Siege of Leningrad
Grand National Steeplechase	Thirty Years' War
Middle Ages	World War I
New Deal	

A.22. DECORATIONS, MEDALS, ETC.

Capitalize the names of particular decorations, medals, and awards.

Bronze Star Medal
Carnegie Medal
Congressional Medal of Honor
Distinguished Conduct Medal
Iron Cross
Victoria Cross

A.23. NAMES OF CALENDAR DIVISIONS

Capitalize the names of the months of the year and the days of the week. Lowercase the names of the seasons.

January
Monday
winter

A.24. NAMES OF HOLIDAYS

Capitalize the names of secular and religious holidays and religious seasons.

Advent	Feast of the Annunciation
Boxing Day	Labor Day
Christmas Day	Lent
Dominion Day	Saint Patrick's Day
Epiphany	Thanksgiving Day

A.25. SCIENTIFIC NAMES OF PLANTS AND ANIMALS

Capitalize the name of a phylum, class, order, family, or genus, and names of intermediate groupings, e.g., subclasses. Lowercase the name of a species or subspecies even if it is derived from a proper name. Lowercase English derivatives of scientific names.

> Arthropoda (phylum)
> Insecta (class)
> Pterygota (subclass)
> Lepidoptera (order)
> Papilionidae (family)
> Papilioninae (subfamily)
> Papilio (genus)
> Papilio oregonius (species)
>
> *but* arthropod (from *Arthropoda*)

A.26. GEOLOGIC TERMS

Capitalize the distinctive word in the names of geologic eras, periods, etc. Lowercase such words as *era* and *period*; also such modifiers as *early*, *middle*, or *late* when used only descriptively.

> Eocene epoch
> Jurassic period
> Lower Triassic period
> Mesozoic period
>
> *but*
>
> the early Miocene
> the late Eocene

A.27. ASTRONOMICAL TERMS

Capitalize the names of planets and their satellites, stars, constellations, asteroids, etc. Lowercase the words *sun*, *moon*, and *earth* except, in the case of *earth*, when the word is used in conjunction with the names of other planets (e.g., The planet Mars lies between the Earth and Jupiter).

> Alpha Centauri
> Betelgeuse
> Canis Major *or* Larger Dog
> Cygnus *or* Swan
> Mercury
> the Milky Way
> Polaris *or* North Star
> Sirius *or* Dog Star
> Ursa Minor *or* Little Bear *or* Little Dipper
> Venus

A.28. SOIL NAMES

Capitalize the names of the twenty-four soil classifications.

Alpine Meadow	Half Bog
Chernozem	Prairie

A.29. TRADE NAMES

Capitalize trade names, variety names, and market grades. Lowercase common nouns following such names.

> Aylesbury duckling (variety)
> Black Leaf 40 (trade name)
> Choice lamb (market grade)
> Formica (trade name)
> Orlon (trade name)
> Polaroid film (trade name)
> Red Radiance rose (variety)
> Yellow Stained cotton (market grade)

A.30. CERTAIN LETTERS USED AS WORDS OR PARTS OF COMPOUNDS

Capitalize the pronoun *I* and the interjection *O*. Capitalize single letters used as part of a compound word whether or not hyphenated.

> A major   vitamin B
> H-bomb   X ray
> U-boat

A.31. HYPHENATED COMPOUNDS

A.31A. If the rules require the capitalization of a hyphenated compound, in addition to capitalizing the first part, capitalize the second also if it is a noun or a proper adjective or if it has the same force as the first part.

> Twentieth-Century   Blue-Black
> Basket-Maker   Secretary-Treasurer

A.31B. Lowercase the second part if it modifies the first part or if the two parts constitute a single word.

> French-speaking   Twenty-five
> Small-sized   Co-ordinate

A.32. HYPHENATED PREFIXES

Lowercase a prefix joined by a hyphen to a capitalized word unless other rules require its capitalization.

> ex-President Roosevelt   trans-Siberian
> pre-Cambrian   un-American

Foreign languages

A.33. GENERAL RULE

Apply the rules for the capitalization of English to the capitalization of a foreign language unless a contrary rule is provided in a section below treating that language or unless the romanization table for the language adopted by the cataloguing agency provides otherwise.

A.34. CAPITALIZATION OF ROMANIZED HEADINGS AND TITLES

Capitalize words in romanized headings and titles, as far as possible, in accordance with the instructions in A.33 above. If the language has no system of capitalization, capitalize the first word of a title or a sentence and the first word of the name of a corporate body or a subdivision of a corporate body. Capitalize proper names according to English usage.

A.35. BULGARIAN

A.35A. Proper names and their derivatives

A.35A1. Lowercase names of peoples, races, and residents of specific localities.

българин; софиянец; семит

A.35A2. Lowercase names of religions and their adherents.

будизъм; християнство; лютеранец

A.35A3. Lowercase proper adjectives.

софийски улици

A.35B. Names of regions, localities, and geographic features, including streets, parks, etc.

Capitalize the first word unless it is a common noun. Capitalize other words only if they are proper nouns.

Орлово гнездо; Бряг на слоновата кост; Стара Загора; Охридско езеро; село Белица; Червеният площад; ул. Шипка

A.35C. Names of countries and administrative divisions

Capitalize the first word and proper nouns in names of countries and administrative subdivisions.

Обединена арабска република; Народна република България; Софийска област; Министерство на селскостопанското производство

A.35D. Names of corporate bodies

Capitalize only the first word and proper nouns in the names of corporate bodies.

Българска комунистическа партия; Организация на обединените народи; Държавна библиотека "Васил Коларов"; Български червен кръст

A.35E. Titles of persons

A.35E1. Capitalize the title "свети" and titles of royalty, high government officials, and high ecclesiastical officials if they are followed by a name.

Министър Даскалов; Свети Климент

A.35E2. Capitalize any title occurring in conjunction with the name of a well-known personage.

> Отец Паисий; Хаджи Димитър; Бачо Киро

A.35E3. Generally lowercase other titles.

> министър; крал; отец; професор; отец Борис

A.35F. Personal pronouns

A.35F1. Lowercase the pronoun "аз."

A.35F2. Capitalize the pronouns "Вие (Вий)," "Ви," "Вас," and "Вам" when used in formal address.

A.35G. Names of calendar divisions
Lowercase the names of days of the week and of months.

A.35H. Names of historic events, etc.
Capitalize the first word and proper nouns in the names of historic events, etc.

> Първата световна война; Великата октомврийска социалистическа революция; Възраждането; Битката при Косово поле

A.36. CZECH (BOHEMIAN)

A.36A. Proper nouns and their derivatives

A.36A1. Capitalize only the distinctive word in geographic names consisting of a distinctive word and a generic word: *Tichý oceán.*

A.36A2. Capitalize the first word and any other word that is a derivative of a proper name in names of streets: *U invalidovny; Na růžku; Na Smetance.*

A.36B. Names of corporate bodies

A.36B1. Generally capitalize only the first word in names of corporate bodies: *Československá republika; Česká akademie věd a umění; Bratří čeští; Milosrdní bratří.*

A.36B2. Lowercase names of branches of schools, conservatories, universities, ministries, and departments of government: *ministerstvo školství; závodní rada.*

A.36C. Titles of persons
Lowercase all titles of persons: *doktor; král; ministr; svatý.*

A.36D. Personal pronouns

A.36D1. Lowercase the pronoun *já.*

A.36D2. Capitalize the pronouns of formal address: *Ty, Tvůj, Tobĕ; Vy, Vám; Vás, Váš.*

A.36E. Names of calendar divisions
Lowercase the names of days of the week and of months.

DANISH. *See* Scandinavian languages.

A.37. DUTCH

A.37A. First words

A.37A1. If the first word of a sentence or the first word of a proper name consists of a single letter only, lowercase it and capitalize the next word: *'s Avonds is het koud; 'k Weet niet wat hij zegt; 's-Gravenhage.*

A.37A2. Capitalize the first word of a sentence if it is the interjection *O*, the pronoun *U*, or a letter referring to a letter of the alphabet as such (e.g., *A is een aapje*).

A.37B. Particles in personal names
Capitalize the name particles *de, ten, van*, if not preceded by the Christian name.

A.37C. Personal pronouns

A.37C1. Lowercase the pronoun *ik*.

A.37C2. Generally capitalize the pronouns *U, Uw*, and *Gij* in personal correspondence.

A.37D. Names of calendar divisions
Lowercase the names of days of the week and of months.

A.38. FINNISH

A.38A. Names of corporate bodies

A.38A1. Capitalize only the first word and proper nouns in names of state and local government agencies, courts, and church bodies: *Erillinen komppania Kontula; Helsingin kaupunginkirjasto; Kauppa- ja teollisuusministeriö; Kirkon ulkomaanasiain toimikunta; Korkein oikeus; Suomen Unesco-toimikunta.*

A.38A2. Capitalize only the first word and proper nouns in names of scientific and economic institutions of the state: *Kansallismuseon esihistoriallinen osasto; Geodeettinen laitos; Helsingin yliopisto.* Exceptions: *Suomen Akatemia; Suomen Pankki.*

A.38A3. In the names of other institutions, societies and firms, follow the usage of the body; if the usage is not known, capitalize all words.

A.38B. Names of buildings
Capitalize only proper nouns in the names of buildings; *kaupungintalo; Helsingin kulttuuritalo.*

A.39. FRENCH

A.39A. Proper names and their derivatives

A.39A1. Lowercase names of members of religious groups, sects, religious orders, political and other organizations, names of religions, and names of languages: *les jésuites; les démocrates; le bouddhisme; l'anglais* (the English language).

A.39A2. Lowercase adjectives derived from names of members of religious groups, sects, religious orders, political and other organizations, names of religions, names of languages, geographical names, and adjectives denoting nationality: *la religion catholique; la région alpine; le peuple français.*

A.39A3. Capitalize nouns denoting nationality: *les Français.*

A.39A4. Lowercase a common noun used as a generic word in a geographic name: *la mer du Nord; l'île aux Oiseaux.*

A.39B. Name of corporate bodies

A.39B1. Capitalize the first word, any adjectives preceding the first noun, the first noun, and all proper nouns in the names of corporate bodies: *Société de chimie physique; Grand Orchestre symphonique de la R.T.B; Église réformée de France.* Notable exceptions: *Société des Nations; Nations Unies.*

A.39B2. Capitalize the nouns and adjectives in hyphenated corporate names: *le Théâtre-Français.*

A.39C. Particles in names of persons
Capitalize prefixes of French names consisting of an article or a contraction of an article and a preposition: *La Fontaine; Du Cange.*

A.39D. Titles of persons

A.39D1. Lowercase titles designating rank or office: *le roi; le ministre; le pape Léon X.*

A.39D2. Capitalize titles of address and titles of respectful address or reference: *Monsieur; Mme de Lafayette; Son Éminence, Sa Majesté le roi de France.*

A.39D3. Lowercase the word *saint* (*sainte, etc.*) when it refers exclusively to a person; otherwise capitalize it: *saint Thomas More;* but *la cathédrale Saint-Lambert; l'été de la Saint-Martin.*

A.39E. Personal pronouns
Lowercase the pronoun *je.*

A.39F. Names of calendar divisions
Lowercase the names of days of the week and of months.

A.39G. Miscellaneous

A.39G1. Lowercase the word *rue* and its synonyms: *rue de la Nation; avenue de l'Opéra.*

A.39G2. Lowercase the word *église* when it indicates a building: *l'église Notre-Dame;* capitalize the word when it refers to the Church as an institution.

A.39G3. Capitalize the word *état* when denoting the nation: *le Conseil d'État.*

A.40. GERMAN

A.40A. Nouns

Capitalize all nouns and words used as nouns: *das Buch; das Geben; die Armen; das intime Du* (reference to the word *du*).

A.40B. Proper names and their derivatives

A.40B1. Generally lowercase proper adjectives: *die deutsche Sprache.*

A.40B2. Capitalize adjectives derived from personal names when used in their original meaning: *die Lutherische Übersetzung; die Platonischen Dialoge.* Lowercase such adjectives when they are used descriptively: *die lutherische Kirche; die platonische Liebe.*

A.40B3. Capitalize indeclinable adjectives derived from geographic names (ending in *er*): *Schweizer Ware; die Zürcher Bürger.*

A.40B4. Capitalize adjectives, pronouns and numerals used as parts of a name or title: *Alexander der Grosse; das Schweizerische Konsulat; Seine Excellenz; Friedrich der Zweite; Bund der Technischen Angestellten und Beamten; der Erste der Klasse* (expressing rank). See also A.40D2 below.

A.40C. Pronouns

A.40C1. Lowercase the pronoun *ich.*

A.40C2. Capitalize the following pronouns, including their inflected forms when used in correspondence: *Du, Ihr; Dein, Euer.*

A.40C3. Capitalize the pronouns *Sie* and *Ihr* and their inflected forms when used in formal address and in correspondence.

A.40D. Miscellaneous

Lowercase the following categories:

1) pronouns (see also A.40C above): *jemand, ein jeder, der eine . . . der andere, etwas anderes, die übrigen*

A.41A *Proper nouns and their derivatives* (*Hungarian*)

2) numerals (see also A.40B4 above): *die beiden, alle drei, der vierte* (indicating numerical order)
3) adverbs: *mittags, anfangs, morgen, montags, aufs neue, fürs erste, im voraus*
4) verbal phrases: *not tun, schuld sein, haushalten, preisgeben, teilhaben, wundernehmen, ausser acht lassen, zuteil werden, zumute sein*
5) adjectives modifying nouns that are implied if the noun has been expressed elsewhere in the same sentence: *Hier ist die beste Arbeit, dort die schlechteste.*

A.41. HUNGARIAN

A.41A. Proper nouns and their derivatives

A.41A1. Lowercase nouns denoting nationality: *az oroszok.*

A.41A2. Lowercase adjectives derived from proper nouns: *budapesti.*

A.41B. Titles of persons

A.41B1. Capitalize titles used in direct address: *Felséges Uram.*

A.41B2. Lowercase titles of nobility, including those consisting of an adjectival term derived from place of origin, etc.: *gróf Teleki Pál; körmendi Frim Jakab.*

A.41C. Personal pronouns

A.41C1. Lowercase the pronoun *én.*

A.41C2. Capitalize pronouns used in formal address: *Maga.*

A.41D. Names of calendar divisions
Lowercase the names of days of the week and of months.

A.42. ITALIAN

A.42A. Proper names and their derivatives

A.42A1. Lowercase names of members of religious groups, sects, religious orders, political and other organizations, names of religions, and names of languages: *i protestanti; i benedettini; un democratico; il buddhismo; il francese* (the French language).

A.42A2. Lowercase adjectives derived from names of members of religious groups, sects, religious orders, political and other organizations, names of religions, names of languages, geographical and personal names, and adjectives denoting nationality: *la religione cattolica; la flora alpina; il popolo italiano; iconografia dantesca.*

A.42A3. Capitalize nouns denoting nationality: *gl'Italiani.*

540

A.42B. Names of corporate bodies

Generally capitalize only the first word, proper nouns, religious terms, and the word following an adjective denoting royal or pontifical privilege in the names of corporate bodies: *Istituto nazionale di fisica nucleare; Accademia nazionale de Santa Cecilia; Università cattolica del Sacro Cuore; Pontificio Seminario francese; Chiesa evangelica italiana*. Notable exceptions: *Società delle Nazioni; Nazioni Unite; Croce Rossa*.

A.42C. Titles of persons

A.42C1. Lowercase titles of persons except for ceremonious titles of respectful address or reference consisting of a possessive pronoun and a noun expressing an abstract quality: *signora; il signor Donati; il duca d'Aosta; Umberto I, re d'Italia;* but *Sua Santità; Sua Altezza Reale il principe Umberto; le LL. MM. il re e la regina*.

A.42C2. Lowercase the word *san* (*santo*, etc.) when referring exclusively to a person; capitalize it when it is abbreviated and when it is an integral part of the name of a place, a building, etc.: *san Francesco d'Assisi;* but *S. Girolamo; Castel Sant'Angelo*.

A.42D. Personal pronouns

A.42D1. Lowercase the pronoun *io*.

A.42D2. Capitalize the pronouns of formal address: *Ella; Lei; Loro*.

A.42E. Names of calendar divisions

Lowercase the names of days of the week and of months.

A.42F. Names of centuries

Capitalize the names of centuries: *il Cinquecento; il Seicento;* but *il sedicesimo secolo*.

A.42G. Miscellaneous

A.42G1. Lowercase the word *via* and its synonyms: *via Vittorio Veneto; corso Umberto I*.

A.42G2. Lowercase the word *chiesa* when it indicates a building: *la chiesa di S. Maria degli Angeli;* capitalize the word when it refers to the Church as an institution.

A.42G3. Capitalize the word *stato* when denoting the nation: *Consiglio di Stato*.

A.43. LATIN

Capitalize Latin according to the rules for the capitalization of English.

NORWEGIAN. *See* Scandinavian languages.

A.44. POLISH

A.44A. Proper names and their derivatives

A.44A1. Lowercase names of residents of cities and towns: *warszawianin*.

A.44A2. Lowercase adjectives derived from proper names: *mickiewiczowski.*

A.44A3. Lowercase names of religions and their adherents and names of members of religious orders: *katolicyzm; katolik; mahometanin; jezuici.*

A.44A4. Capitalize each part of a compound geographic name unless the distinctive word is in nominative case and can stand alone; in that case capitalize only the distinctive word: *Morze Bałtyckie;* but *jezioro Narocz.*

A.44A5. Lowercase geographic names applied to wines, dances, etc.: *tokaj; krakowiak.*

A.44A6. Lowercase names of administrative districts and geographic adjectives: *województwo poznańskie; diecezja łomżyńska.*

A.44B. Names of corporate bodies
Capitalize all words except conjunctions and prepositions in the names of corporate bodies: *Towarzystwo Naukowe w Toruniu; Ewangelicko-Augsburski Kościół.*

A.44C. Titles of persons
Lowercase titles of persons except in direct address: *papież; król; święty.*

A.44D. Personal pronouns

A.44D1. Lowercase the pronoun *ja.*

A.44D2. Capitalize the pronouns of formal address: *Ty, Tobie, Twój; On, Ona, Jego, Jej, Jemu; Wy, Wam, Was.*

A.44E. Names of calendar divisions
Lowercase the names of days of the week and of months.

A.44F. Names of historic events, etc.
Lowercase names of historic events and wars: *pokój wersalski; wojna siedmioletnia.*

A.45. PORTUGUESE

A.45A. Derivatives of proper names
Lowercase derivatives of proper names unless used substantively: *os homens alemães* but *os Alemães.*

A.45B. Titles of persons
Generally, lowercase names of positions, posts, or hierarchical dignitaries and words that designate titles: *o arcebispo de Braja; o duque de Caxias: o presidente da Republica.* By exception, capitalize such words to indicate special deference and whenever the title follows a term of address: *Senhor Professor; Sr. Prof.; Sua Excelencia o Presidente da Republica.*

A.45C. Personal pronouns

Lowercase the pronoun *eu*.

A.45D. Religious terms

Capitalize the word *igreja* when referring to the Church as an institution.

A.45E. Names of calendar divisions

Lowercase the names of days of the week and of months.

A.46. RUSSIAN

A.46A. Proper names and their derivatives

A.46A1. Lowercase particles, prepositions, and conjunctions forming part of a proper name, except when they are connected to the following part of the name by a hyphen.

фон Клаузевиц; ван Бетховен; Ван-Гог

A.46A2. Lowercase names of peoples, races, and residents of specific localities.

араб; таджик; москвичи

A.46A3. Lowercase the names of religions and their adherents.

католицизм; католик

A.46A4. Lowercase proper nouns that are parts of adverbs.

по-пушкински

A.46B. Names of regions, localities, and geographic features, including streets, parks, etc.

A.46B1. Lowercase a common noun forming part of a geographic name.

мыс Горн; остров Рудольфа; канал Москва-Волга

A.46B2. Capitalize a common noun forming an integral part of a name.

Кривой Рог; Белая Церковь; Богемский Лес

A.46B3. Capitalize the common noun if it is a foreign word that has not become a part of the Russian language.

Рю-де-ла-Пе (Рю—meaning street, Пе—meaning peace); Сыр-Дарья (Дарья—meaning river)

A.46B4. Lowercase the title or rank of the person in whose honour a place is named.

остров королевы Виктории; мыс капитана Джеральда

A.46B5. Lowercase adjectives derived from geographic names.

московские улицы

A.46B6. Lowercase geographic names applied to wines, species of animals, birds, etc.

мадера; херес; сенбернар

A.46C. Names of countries and administrative divisions

A.46C1. Capitalize the first word in the commonly accepted names of groups of countries.

Балканские страны

A.46C2. Capitalize nonofficial but commonly accepted names of countries, cities, and territorial divisions.

Советский Союз; Страна Советов; Приуралье; Белокаменная
(for Moscow)

A.46C3. Capitalize administrative divisions of the USSR as follows:

a) Capitalize every word in the names of republics and autonomous republics.

Башкирская Автономная Советская Социалистическая Республика

b) Capitalize only the first word in the names of provinces, autonomous provinces, territories, regions, and village soviets.

Алма-Атинская область; Приморский край; Коми-Пермяцкий национальный округ; Егоршинский район; Краснинский сельсовет

c) Capitalize every word in the names of the highest Soviet and non-Russian governmental units and Communist Party organizations except those in parentheses and the word "партия."

Верховный Совет СССР (also of the Union republics and autonomous republics); Совет Союза, Совет Национальностей; Всесоюзная Коммунистическая партия (большевиков); Рейхстаг; Конгресс США; Правительствующий Сенат

d) Capitalize only the first word and proper nouns in the names of other governmental units.

Государственная плановая комиссия СССР; Народный комиссариат иностранных дел; Военный совет Закавказского военного округа

e) Lowercase the names of bureaus when used in the plural and when used in a general sense.

советы народных комиссаров; народный комиссариат

f) Always capitalize the word "Совет" in "Совет депутатов трудящихся."

Загорский районный Совет депутатов трудящихся

544

A.46D. Names of corporate bodies

A.46D1. Capitalize only the first word and proper nouns in names of corporate bodies.

>Академия наук СССР; Книжная палата; Профессиональный союз работников высшей школы и научных учреждений; Дом книги

A.46D2. If part of the name of a corporate body is in quotation marks, capitalize only the first word and proper nouns within the quotation marks.

>завод "Фрезер"; совхоз "Путь к социализму"

A.46D3. If a corporate body is also known by a part of its name, capitalize the first word of the part when it appears in conjunction with the full name.

>Государственный ордена Ленина академический Большой театр (Большой театр)

A.46D4. Lowercase the following words in the names of congresses, conferences, etc.

>съезд; конференция; сессия; пленум

A.46D5. Lowercase the word "совет" when used to refer to the council of a society or institution.

A.46E. Titles of persons

Capitalize the titles of the highest government officials.

>Председатель Совета Народных Комиссаров; Маршал Советского Союза

A.46F. Pronouns

A.46F1. Lowercase the pronoun "я".

A.46F2. Capitalize the pronouns of formal address.

>Вы; Вам; Вас

A.46G. Names of calendar divisions

Lowercase the names of days of the week and of months.

A.46H. Names of historic events. etc.

A.46H1. Capitalize the first word, the distinctive word, and proper nouns in the names of historic periods and events.

>Великая Октябрьская социалистическая революция; Возрождение; Третья республика; Парижская коммуна; Кровавое воскресенье; Ленский расстрел; Бородинский бой

A.46H2. Lowercase the names of the five-year plans.

>третья сталинская пятилетка; *but* соревнование имени Третьей Сталинской Пятилетки

A.46H3. Lowercase the word "война" in the names of wars.

Франко-Прусская война; Русско-Японская война; Великая
Отечественная война; Отечественная война

A.47. SCANDINAVIAN LANGUAGES

A.47A. Derivatives of proper names
Lowercase adjectives derived from proper nouns: *europeisk; københavnsk; luthersk; svensk.*

A.47B. Names of corporate bodies
Generally, capitalize the first word and the word following an adjective denoting royal privilege in the names of corporate bodies; capitalize other words, such as proper nouns, according to the appropriate rule of capitalization: *Kungl. Universitet i Lund; Ministeriet for kulturelle anliggender; Selskabet for dansk skolehistorie.*

A.47C. Compound names
Generally, capitalize only the first word of a compound name, other than a compound personal name: *Förenta staterna; Kronborg slot; Norske kirke.*

A.47D. Titles of persons
Generally, lowercase titles of persons: *fru Nielsen; kong Haakon VII; Gustav, prins av Vasa.*

A.47E. Personal pronouns

A.47E1. In Danish, lowercase the pronoun *jeg;* capitalize the pronouns of formal address: *De; Dem; Deres;* also capitalize the familiar form *I* (you) to distinguish it from *i* (in).

A.47E2. In Norwegian, lowercase the pronoun *jeg;* capitalize the pronouns of formal address: *De; Dem; Deres; Dykk; Dykkar.*

A.47E3. In Swedish, lowercase the pronoun *jag;* capitalize the pronouns *Ni, Eder,* and *Er* in correspondence.

A.47F. Names of calendar divisions
Lowercase the names of days of the week, of months, and of holidays: *jul; nyår.*

A.48. SERBO-CROATIAN (ROMAN AND CYRILLIC ALPHABETS)

A.48A. Proper names and their derivatives

A.48A1. Lowercase names of peoples and races: *bijelac; crnac; semit.*

A.48A2. Lowercase proper adjectives: *srpskohrvatski jezik.*

A.48A3. Lowercase names of religions and their adherents: *katoličanstvo; katolik.*

A.48B. Names of regions, localities, and geographic features, including streets, parks, etc.

Capitalize only the first word and proper nouns: *Tetovska kotlina; Velika Morava; Bliski istok; Ulica bosanska; Ulica Branka Radičevića; Trg žrtava fašizma; Park bratstva i jedinstva.*

A.48C. Names of administrative divisions of countries

Lowercase names of administrative divisions of countries: *primorsko-krajiška oblast; zagrebački kotar.*

A.48D. Names of corporate bodies

Capitalize only the first word and proper nouns in the names of corporate bodies: *Jugoslovenska akademija znanosti i umjetnosti; Udruženje književnika Srbije; Hrvatsko narodno kazalište u Zagrebu; Savez komunista Jugoslavije; Centralni komitet Saveza komunista Jugoslavije.*

A.48E. Titles of persons

Lowercase all titles of persons: *predsednik Tito; kralj Georg; ministar; sveti Petar.* However, capitalize the word *sveti* when it appears in the name of a holiday (see A. 48H2).

A.48F. Personal pronouns

A.48F1. Lowercase the pronoun *ja.*

A.48I F2. Capitalize the pronouns of formal address: *Ti, Tvoj, Ti; Vi, Vam, Vas, Vaš.*

A.48G. Names of calendar divisions

Lowercase names of days of the week and of months.

A.48H. Names of historic events, holidays, etc.

A.48H1. Capitalize only proper nouns in the names of historic periods and events: *kameno doba; srednji vijek; oktobarska revolucija; boj na Mišaru; prvi srpski ustanak.*

A.48H2. Capitalize the first word and proper nouns in the names of holidays: *Božić; Veliki četvrtak; Nova godina; Sveti Petar.*

A.49. SLOVAK

Capitalize Slovak according to the rules for the capitalization of Czech.

A.50. SLOVENIAN

A.50A. Proper names and their derivatives

A.50A1. Lowercase names of peoples and races: *arijec; semit; črnec.*

A.50A2. Capitalize only the distinctive words in the names of nationalities that consist of more than one word: *severni Korejec; zahodni Nemec.*

A.50A3. Lowercase proper adjectives: *slovenski jezik.*

A.50A4. Lowercase the names of religions and their adherents: *katolicizem; katoličan.*

A.50B. Names of regions, localities, and geographic features, including streets, parks, etc.
Capitalize only the first word and proper nouns: *Ziljska dolina; Novo mesto; Škofja Loka; Daljni vzhod; Otok kraljice Viktorije; Rtič dobrega upanja; Ulica stare pravde.*

A.50C. Names of countries and administrative divisions
Capitalize the first word and proper nouns in the names of countries and administrative subdivisions: *Federativna socialistična republika Jugoslavija; Združene države Amerike.*

A.50D. Names of corporate bodies
Capitalize the first word and proper nouns in the names of corporate bodies: *Društvo slovenskih književnikov; Državna založba Slovenije.*

A.50E. Titles of persons
Lowercase all titles of persons: *predsednik; sekretar; doktor; maršal Tito; kralj Matjaž; sveti Peter.* However, capitalize the word *sveti* when it appears in the name of a holiday (see A.50H).

A.50F. Personal pronouns

A.50F1. Lowercase the pronoun *jaz.*

A.50F2. Capitalize the pronouns of formal address: *Ti, Tebe, Tebi, s Teboj; Vidva, Vidve, Vaju, Vama; Vi, Vas, Vam, z Vami.*

A.50G. Names of calendar divisions
Lowercase the names of days of the week and of months.

A.50H. Names of historic events, holidays, etc.
Capitalize only proper nouns in the names of historic events, holidays, etc.: *ledena doba; renesansa; francoska revolucija; boj na Mišaru; prva srbska vstaja; božič; velika noč; Sveti Peter.*

A.51. SPANISH

A.51A. Derivatives of proper names

A.51A1. Lowercase derivatives of proper names: *las mujeres colombianas.*

A.51A2. Lowercase adjectives used substantively: *los franceses.*

A.51B. Titles of persons

A.51B1. Capitalize titles of honor and address only when they are abbreviated: *señor, Sr.; doctor, Dr.; general, Gral.*

A.51B2. Capitalize *Su Excelencia, Su Majestad*, etc., when used alone, whether written out or abbreviated. Lowercase these words when they are used with a name or another title: *su majestad Juan Carlos; su majestad el Rey.*

A.51C. Personal pronouns

A.51C1. Lowercase the pronoun *yo*.

A.51C2. Capitalize the pronouns of formal address: *Vd., Vds. (Ud., Uds.)*

A.51D. Religious terms
Capitalize the word *iglesia* when it refers to the Church as an institution.

A.51E. Names of calendar divisions
Lowercase the names of days of the week and of months.

A.51F. Questions within a sentence
Generally lowercase the first word of a question occurring within a sentence: *Cuando viene la noche ¿ cómo se puede ver?*

SWEDISH. *See* Scandinavian languages.

A.52. UKRAINIAN
Capitalize Ukrainian according to the rules for the capitalization of Russian.

ABBREVIATIONS

B.1. Use abbreviations in catalogue records as instructed in rules B.2–B.8 below. In the case of words abbreviated by the cataloguer, use the abbreviations prescribed in B.9–B.15 below.

B.2. Use the following categories of abbreviations in headings:

    a) those that are integral parts of the heading, e.g., *St.* (Saint), if the person or corporate body uses the abbreviation

    b) designations of function, e.g., *comp.*, if they are used (cf. 21.0D)

    c) certain names of larger places added to the name of another place (cf. 23.4) or to the name of a corporate body (cf. 24.4C2)

    d) certain terms used with dates, e.g., *b., fl.* (cf. 22.18)

    e) distinguishing terms added to names of persons, if they are abbreviated in the source from which they are taken (cf. 22.15B, 22.19B)

B.3. Use the following categories of abbreviations in uniform titles, including uniform titles used as headings:

    a) those that are integral parts of the title

    b) designations of parts of a work as instructed in a particular rule, e.g., *N.T.* (New Testament) (cf. 25.18A2)

B.4. Use the following categories of abbreviations in the title and statement of responsibility area and the statement of responsibility element in the edition area; also use them in titles and statements of responsibility in the series area and in contents notes:

    a) those found in the prescribed sources of information for the particular area

    b) *i.e., et al.*, and their equivalents in nonroman scripts (cf. 1.0F, 1.1F5)

B.5. Use abbreviations elsewhere in the catalogue entry, subject to the limitations specified in footnotes to section B.9 below. Do not use them if the brevity of the statement makes them unnecessary or if the resulting statement might not be clear. Do not use single letter abbreviations to begin a note. Do not abbreviate words in quoted notes.

B.6. Use an abbreviation for the corresponding word in another language if the abbreviation commonly used in that language has the same spelling. In case of doubt, do not use the abbreviation.

B.7. Use a prescribed abbreviation for the last part of a compound word, e.g., Textausg. for Textausgabe.

B.8. In inflected languages, use the abbreviation of a word given in the following lists in the nominative case for an inflected form of that word. If, however, the abbreviation includes the final letter(s) of the word, modify the abbreviation to show the final letter(s) of the inflected form, e.g., литература, лит-ра; литературы, лит-ры.

B.9. GENERAL ABBREVIATIONS

TERM	ABBREVIATION	TERM	ABBREVIATION
årgang	årg.	bind	bd.
aastakäik	aastak	black and white	b&w
Abdruck	Abdr.	bogtrykkeri	bogtr.
abgedruckt	abgedr.	boktrykkeri	boktr.
Abteilung, Abtheilung	Abt.	book	bk.
accompaniment	acc.	born	b.
afdeling	afd.	bővített	böv.
aflevering	afl.	broj	br.
altitude	alt. [1]	Brother, -s	Bro., Bros. [4]
alto	A [2]	Buchdrucker,	
and	& [3]	Buchdruckerei	Buchdr.
and others	et al.	Buchhandlung	Buchh.
Anno Domini	A.D.	bulletin	bull.
approximately	approx.	bytes per inch	bpi
argraffiad	arg.	capitolo	cap.
arranged	arr.	část	č.
arranger	arr.	centimetre, -s	cm.
átdolgozott	átdolg.	century	cent. [5]
Auflage	Aufl.	cetekan	cet.
augmenté, -e	augm.	chapter	ch.
augmented	augm.	circa	ca.
aumentada	aum.	číslo	čís.
aumentato	aum.	colored, coloured	col.
Ausgabe	Ausg.	Compagnia	Cia.
avdeling	avd.	Compagnie	Cie
Bändchen	Bdchn.	Compañía	Cía.
Bände	Bde.	Company	Co.
Band	Bd.	compare	cf.
band	bd.	compiler	comp.
baritone	Bar [2]	confer	cf.
bass	B [2]	copyright	c
Before Christ	B.C.	Corporation	Corp.
binary coded decimal	BCD	corrected	corr.

1. Use only in recording mathematical data in entries for cartographic materials.
2. Use only in notes to indicate voice range of vocal works.
3. Use only in uniform titles in listing languages.
4. Use only in names of firms and other corporate bodies.
5. Use in headings and in indicating the period when a manuscript was probably written.

TERM	ABBREVIATION	TERM	ABBREVIATION
corretto, -a	corr.	id est	i.e.
corrigé, -e	corr.	Idus	Id.
część	cz.	illustration, -s	ill.
deel	d.	illustrator	ill.[6]
del (Danish, Norwegian, and Swedish)	d.	imienia	im.
département	dép.	imprenta	impr.
Department	Dept.	imprimerie	impr.
diameter	diam.	inch, -es	in.
died	d.	inches per second	ips
diena	d.	including	incl.
djilid	djil.	Incorporated	Inc.[8]
document	doc.	introduction	introd.
dopunjeno	dop.	izdája	izd.
drukarnia	druk.	izmenjeno	izm.
edition, -s	ed., eds.	jaargang	jaarg.
édition	éd.	Jahrgang	Jahrg.
editor	ed. [6]	javitott	jav.
enlarged	enl.	jilid	jil.
equinox	eq. [7]	Kalendae	Kal.
ergänzt	erg.	kiadás	kiad.
erweitert	erw.	kilometre, -s	km.
establecimiento tipográfico	estab. tip.	kniha	kn.
et alii	et al.	knjiga	knj.
et cetera	etc.	kötet	köt.
évfolyam	évf.	księgarnia	księg.
facsimile, -s	facsim., facsims.	leto	l.
fascicle	fasc.	librairie	libr.
fascicule	fasc.	Lieferung	Lfg.
flourished	fl.	Limited	Ltd.[8]
folio	fol.	livraison	livr.
following	ff.	maatschappij	mij.
foot, feet	ft.	manuscript, -s	ms., mss.
frame, -s	fr.	mėnuo	mėn.
frames per second	fps	metai	m.
fratelli	f.lli[8]	mezzo-soprano	Mz [9]
Gebrüder	Gebr.[8]	miesięcznik	mies.
gedruckt	gedr.	millimetre, -s	mm.
genealogical	geneal.	minute, -s	min.
godina	g.	miscellaneous	misc.
government	govt.	monophonic	mono.
Government Printing Office	G.P.O.	Nachfolger	Nachf.[8]
Handschrift, -en	Hs., Hss.	nakład	nakł.
Her (His) Majesty's Stationery Office	H.M.S.O.	nakladatelství	nakl.
Hermanos	Hnos.[8]	naukowy	nauk.
hour, -s	hr.	neue Folge	n. F.
		new series	new ser.
		New Testament	N.T.
		no name (of publisher)	s.n.
		no place (of publication)	s.l.
		Nonae	Non.

6. Use only in a heading as a designation of function (see 21.0D).

7. Use only in recording mathematical data in entries for cartographic materials.

8. Use only in names of firms and other corporate bodies.

9. Use only in notes to indicate voice range of vocal works.

TERM	ABBREVIATION	TERM	ABBREVIATION
nouveau, nouvelle	nouv.	revisé, -e	rev.
number, -s	no.	revised	rev.
numbered	numb.	revolutions per minute	rpm
numer	nr.	revu, -e	rev.
numero (Finnish)	n:o	riveduto	riv.
numéro (French)	no	ročník	roč.
numero (Italian)	n.	rocznik	rocz.
número (Spanish)	no.	rok	r.
Nummer	Nr.	rozszerzone	rozsz.
nummer	nr.	second, -s	sec.
nuovamente	nuov.	série	sér.
odbitka	odb.	series	ser.
oddział	oddz.	sešit	seš.
Old Testament	O.T.	signature	sig.
omarbeidet	omarb.	silent	si.
oplag	opl.	sine loco	s.l.
opplag	oppl.	sine nomine	s.n.
opracowane	oprac.	skład główny	skł. gł.
opus	op.	soprano	S[13]
otisk	ot.	sound	sd.
page, -s	p.	stabilimento	
paperback	pbk.	tipográfico	stab. tip.
part, -s	pt., pts.[10]	stereophonic	stereo.
parte	pt.	številka	št.
partie, -s	ptie, pties	stronica	str.
photographs, -s	photo., photos.	superintendent	supt.
plate number	pl. no.	Superintendent of	
poprawione	popr.	Documents	Supt. of Docs.
portrait, -s	port., ports.	supplement	suppl.
posthumous	posth.	svazek	sv.
predelan	pred.	szám	sz.
preface	pref.	tahun	th.
preliminary	prelim.	talleres gráficos	tall. gráf.
printing	print.[11]	Teil, Theil	T.
privately printed	priv. print.	tenor	T[13]
projection	proj.[12]	tipografía, tipográfica	tip.
proširen	proš.	tiskárna	tisk.
przekład	przekł.	title page	t.p.
przerobione	przerob.	tjetakan	tjet.
pseudonym	pseud.	tome	t.
publishing	pub.	tomo	t.
quadraphonic	quad.	towarzystwo	tow.
redakcja	red.	translator	tr.
refondu, -e	ref.	typographical	typog.
réimpression	réimpr.	typographie,	
report	rept.	typographique	typ.
reprinted	repr.	udarbejdet	udarb.
reproduced	reprod.	udgave	udg.
reviderade	revid.	udgivet	udg.

---

10. Do not use in recording the extent of the item in the case of musical works.

11. Do not use in recording the date of printing in the publication, distribution, etc., area (cf. 1.4F6, 2.4G2).

12. Use only in recording mathematical data in entries for cartographic materials.

13. Use only in notes to indicate voice range of vocal works.

B.10 *Cyrillic abbreviations*

TERM	ABBREVIATION	TERM	ABBREVIATION
uitgaaf	uit.	verbesserte	verb.
uitgegeven	uitg.	vermehrte	verm.
uitgevers	uitg.	volume, -s	v., vol.,[14] vols.[14]
umgearbeitet	umgearb.	vuosikerta	vuosik.
unaccompanied	unacc.	vydání	vyd.
Universitäts-Buchdrucker,		wydanie	wyd.
Universitäts-Buchdruck-		wydawnictwo	wydawn.
erei	Univ.-Buchdr.	wydział	wydz.
upplaga	uppl.	založba	zal.
utarbeidet	utarb.	zeszyt	zesz.
utgave	utg.	zväzok	zv.
utgiven	utg.	zvezek	zv.
uzupełnione	uzup.		

B.10. CYRILLIC ABBREVIATIONS

TERM	ABBREVIATION	TERM	ABBREVIATION
без имена	б.и.	железнодорожный	жел-дор.
без имени	б.и.	заглавие	загл.
без імені	б.і.	и другие	и др.
без места	б.м.	и так далее	и т. д.
без месца	б.м.	и тому подобное	и т. п.
без міста	б.м.	издание	изд.
без място	б.м.	издательство	изд-во
видання	вид.	имени	им.
видавництво	вид-во	Императорский	Имп.
відповідальний	відп.	институт	ин-т
военный	воен.	исправленный	испр.
всероссийский	всерос.	исследовательский	иссл.
всесоюзный	всес.	інститут	ін-т
вступление, всту-		књига	књ.
пительный	вступ.	книгоиздательство	кн-во
выдавецтва	выд-ва	книга	кн.
выпуск	вып.	комитет	ком-т
географический	геогр.	литература	лит-ра
геологический	геол.	література	літ-ра
главный	глав.	медицинский	мед.
год	г.	музыкальный	муз.
головний	гол.	народный	нар.
городской	гор.	науковий	наук.
государственный	гос.	научный	науч.
губернский	губ.	областной	обл.
державний	держ.	оборонный	обор.
дзяржаўны	дзярж.	обработанный	обраб.
диссертация	дисс.	общество	об-во
дополненный	доп.	ответственный	отв.
държавен	држ.	отделение	отд-ние
държавен	държ.	палітычны	паліт.
друкарня	друк.	педагогический	педагог.
електричний	електр.	переработанный	перер.
енергетичний	енерг.	пересмотренный	пересм.

---

14. Use at the beginning of a statement and before a roman numeral.

TERM	ABBREVIATION	TERM	ABBREVIATION
полиграфический	полигр.	текстильный	текстил.
политический	полит.	теоретический	теорет.
політичний	політ.	технический	техн.
предисловие	предисл.	типография	тип.
переработен	прер.	типо-литография	типо-лит.
промышленность	промышл.	товариство	т-во
радянський	рад.	товарищество	т-во
редакция	ред.	том	т.
рік	р.	транспортный	трансп.
рэдакцыя	рэд.	украинский	укр.
селскостопански	сел.-стоп.	университетский	унив.
сельскохозяйствен- ный	с.-х.	управление учебный	упр. учеб.
сільськогоспо- дарський	с.-г.	финансовый химический	фин. хим.
скорочений	скор.	хімічний	хім.
советский	сов.	художественный	худож.
сокращенный	сокр.	центральный	центр.
социалистический	социалист.	часть	ч.
социальный	соц.	экономический	экон.
статистический	стат.	электрический	электр.
страница	стр.	энергетический	энерг.
строительный	строит.	юридический	юрид.

B.11. GREEK ABBREVIATIONS

TERM	ABBREVIATION	TERM	ABBREVIATION
Ἀδελφοί	Ἀφοί	ἐπηυξημένη	ἐπηυξ.
ἀναθεωρημένη	ἀναθ.	καὶ ἄλλοι	κ.ἄ.
ἄνευ ὀνόματος	ἄ.ὀ.	μέρος	μέρ.
ἄνευ τόπου	ἄ.τ.	Πανεπιστήμιον	Παν.
ἀριθμός	ἀρ.	Σύλλογος	Σύλλ.
βελτιωμένη	βελτ.	τεῦχος	τεῦχ.
δελτίον	δελτ.	τμῆμα	τμ.
δηλαδή	δηλ.	τόμος	τ.
ἔκδοσις	ἔκδ.	Τυπογραφεῖον	Τυπογρ.
Ἐκδοτικός Οἶκος	Ἐκδοτ. Οἶκος		

B.12. HEBREW ALPHABET ABBREVIATIONS

TERM	ABBREVIATION	TERM	ABBREVIATION
אויסגאבע	אויסג.	חסר מוציא לאור	חמו"ל
אויפלאגע	אויפל.	חסר מקום	ח"מ
און אנדערע	א"א	טייל	טל.
אן ארט	א"א	טעות דפוס	ט"ד
אן פֿאָרלאָג	אפֿ"ג	יארגאנג	יארג.
באַנד	בד.	מהדורה	מהד'
גליון	גל'	מספר	מס'
דאָס הייסט	ד"ה	נומער	נום.
זאת אומרת	ז"א	פֿאַרבעסערטע	פֿאַרב.
חוברת	חוב'	פֿאַרמערטע	פֿאַרמ.

555

B.13. ABBREVIATIONS TO BE USED IN CITING BIBLIOGRAPHIC SOURCES OF DATA

Use common, self-explanatory abbreviations of the type listed below in citing the source of data used in the catalogue entry, so long as the use of abbreviations does not obscure the language of the source cited.

TERM	ABBREVIATION	TERM	ABBREVIATION
American	Amer.	directory	direct.
annuaire	ann.	encyclopedia	encycl.
annuario	ann.	English	Engl.
anuario	an.	history	hist.
bibliography	bibl.	Katalog	Kat.
biography	biog.	literature	lit.
British	Brit.	littérature	litt.
catalog, catalogue	cat.	museum	mus.
cyclopedia	cycl.	national	nat.
diccionario	dicc.	report	rept.
dictionary	dict.		

B.14. ABBREVIATIONS OF NAMES OF CERTAIN COUNTRIES, THE STATES OF AUSTRALIA AND THE UNITED STATES, THE PROVINCES OF CANADA, AND THE TERRITORIES OF AUSTRALIA, CANADA AND THE UNITED STATES

Use the following abbreviations of place names, other than the names of cities and towns, as additions to certain other place names (cf. 23.4), as additions to names of certain corporate bodies (cf. 24.4C), as additions to the name of the place of publication or distribution in the place of publication, distribution, etc., area (cf. 1.4C3), and in notes. Do not abbreviate names omitted from the list.

TERM	ABBREVIATION	TERM	ABBREVIATION
Alabama	Ala.	Minnesota	Minn.
Alberta	Alta.	Mississippi	Miss.
Arizona	Ariz.	Missouri	Mo.
Arkansas	Ark.	Montana	Mont.
Australian Capital		Nebraska	Neb.
Territory	A.C.T.	Nevada	Nev.
British Columbia	B.C.	New Brunswick	N.B.
California	Calif.	New Hampshire	N.H.
Colorado	Colo.	New Jersey	N.J.
Connecticut	Conn.	New Mexico	N.M.
Delaware	Del.	New South Wales	N.S.W.
District of Columbia	D.C.	New York	N.Y.
Distrito Federal	D.F.	New Zealand	N.Z.
Florida	Fla.	Newfoundland	Nfld.
Georgia	Ga.	North Carolina	N.C.
Illinois	Ill.	North Dakota	N.D.
Indiana	Ind.	Northern Territory	N.T.
Kansas	Kan.	Northwest Territories	N.W.T.
Kentucky	Ky.	Nova Scotia	N.S.
Louisiana	La.	Oklahoma	Okla.
Maine	Me.	Ontario	Ont.
Manitoba	Man.	Oregon	Or.
Maryland	Md.	Pennsylvania	Pa.
Massachusetts	Mass.	Prince Edward Island	P.E.I.
Michigan	Mich.	Puerto Rico	P.R.

TERM	ABBREVIATION	TERM	ABBREVIATION
Queensland	Qld.	Union of Soviet Socialist	
Rhode Island	R.I.	Republics	U.S.S.R.
Russian Soviet Federated		United Kingdom	U.K.
Socialist		United States	U.S.
Republic	R.S.F.S.R.	Vermont	Vt.
Saskatchewan	Sask.	Victorïa	Vic.
South Australia	S. Aust.	Virgin Islands	V.I.
South Carolina	S.C.	Virginia	Va.
South Dakota	S.D.	Washington	Wash.
Tasmania	Tas.	West Virginia	W. Va.
Tennessee	Tenn.	Western Australia	W.A.
Territory of Hawaii	T.H.	Wisconsin	Wis.
Texas	Tex.	Wyoming	Wyo.
		Yukon Territory	Yukon

B.15. ABBREVIATIONS OF THE NAMES OF THE MONTHS

BELORUSSIAN	BULGARIAN	CZECH	DANISH
студз.	ян.	led.	jan.
лют.	февр.	ún.	febr.
сак.	март	břez.	marts
крас.	април	dub.	april
май	май	květ.	maj
чэрв.	юни	červ.	juni
ліп.	юли	červen.	juli
жнівень	авг.	srp.	aug.
верас.	септ.	září	sept.
кастр.	окт.	říj.	okt.
ліст.	ноем.	list.	nov.
снеж.	дек.	pros.	dec.

DUTCH	ENGLISH	ESTONIAN	FRENCH
jan.	Jan.	jaan.	janv.
feb.	Feb.	veebr.	févr.
maart	Mar.	märts	mars
apr.	Apr.	apr.	avril
mei	May	mai	mai
juni	June	juuni	juin
juli	July	juuli	juil.
aug.	Aug.	aug.	août
sept.	Sept.	sept.	sept.
oct.	Oct.	okt.	oct.
nov.	Nov.	nov.	nov.
dec.	Dec.	dets.	déc.

B.15 Abbreviations of the names of the months

GERMAN	GREEK, MODERN	HUNGARIAN	INDONESIAN AND MALAYSIAN
Jan. (Jän.)	'Ιαν.	jan.	Jan. (Djan.)
Feb.	Φεβρ.	feb.	Peb.
März	Μάρτ.	márc.	Mrt.
Apr.	'Απρ.	ápr.	Apr.
Mai	Μάϊος	máj.	Mei (Mai)
Juni	'Ιούν.	jun.	Juni (Djuni)
Juli	'Ιούλ.	jul.	Juli (Djuli)
Aug.	Αὔγ.	aug.	Ag.
Sept.	Σεπτ.	szept.	Sept.
Okt.	'Οκτ.	okt.	Okt.
Nov.	Νοέμ.	nov.	Nop.
Dez.	Δεκ.	dec.	Des.

ITALIAN	LATIN	LATVIAN	LITHUANIAN
genn.	Ian.	jan.	saus.
febbr.	Febr.	feb.	vas.
mar.	Mart.	marts	kovas
apr.	Apr.	apr.	bal.
magg.	Mai.	maijs	geg.
giugno	Iun.	junijs	birž.
luglio	Iul.	julijs	liepa
ag.	Aug.	aug.	rugp.
sett.	Sept.	sept.	rugs.
ott.	Oct.	okt.	spalis
nov.	Nov.	nov.	lapkr.
dic.	Dec.	dec.	gr.

NORWEGIAN	POLISH	PORTUGUESE	ROMANIAN
jan.	stycz.	jan.	Ian.
febr.	luty	fev.	Feb.
mars	mar.	março	Mar.
april	kwiec.	abril	Apr.
mai	maj	maio	Mai
juni	czerw.	junho	Iunie
juli	lip.	julho	Iulie
aug.	sierp.	agosto	Aug.
sept.	wrzes.	set.	Sept.
okt.	paźdz.	out.	Oct.
nov.	listop.	nov.	Noem.
des.	grudz.	dez.	Dec.

RUSSIAN	SERBO-CROATIAN		SLOVAK	
янв.	jaн.	siječ.	l'ad.	jan.
февр.	фебр.	velj.	ún.	feb.
март (мартъ)	март	ožuj.	brez.	mar.
апр.	април	trav.	dub.	apr.
май	мај	svib.	kvet.	máj.
июнь (iюнь)	jуни	lip.	červ.	jún
июль (iюль)	jули	srp.	červen.	júl
авг.	ауг.	kol.	srp.	aug.
сент.	септ.	ruj.	zári.	sept.
окт.	окт.	list.	ruj.	okt.
ноябрь	нов.	stud.	list.	nov.
дек.	дец.	pros.	pros.	dec.

SLOVENIAN	SPANISH	SWEDISH	UKRAINIAN	WELSH
jan.	enero	jan.	січ.	Ion.
feb.	feb.	febr.	лют.	Chwe.
mar.	marzo	mars	бер.	Mawr.
apr.	abr.	april	квіт.	Ebr.
maj	mayo	maj	трав.	Mai
jun.	jun.	juni	чер.	Meh.
iul.	jul.	juli	лип.	Gorf.
avg.	agosto	aug.	серп.	Awst
sept.	sept. (set.)	sept.	вер.	Medi
okt.	oct.	okt.	жовт.	Hyd.
nov.	nov.	nov.	лист.	Tach.
dec.	dic.	dec.	груд.	Rhag.

Abbreviations of the names of the months in languages not listed above may be used if they appear in style manuals for the language concerned.

APPENDIX C

NUMERALS

C.0. INTRODUCTORY RULE

Apply the following rules to all items published after 1820. Apply them also to items published before 1821 unless rules 2.12–2.18 instruct otherwise.

C.1. ARABIC VS. ROMAN

C.1A. Retain the roman numeral in headings for persons identified by roman numerals (e.g., rulers, popes) and in headings for corporate bodies whose names include roman numerals unless, in the case of a corporate body, a particular rule instructs otherwise (cf. 24.7B2).

> **John XXIII,** *Pope*
>
> **XXth Century Heating & Ventilating Co.**

C.1B. Retain roman numerals in uniform titles that are integral parts of the name of the work. In the case of numerals used to identify particular parts of a work, follow instructions of the appropriate rule (cf. 25.6A2, 25.18A3).

> **Sancho II y el cerco de Zamora**

C.1C. Substitute arabic numerals for roman in the following areas of the bibliographic description:

1) in the edition or issue statement in the edition area
2) in the material (or type of publication) specific details area unless a particular rule directs otherwise (cf. 3.3B2) or unless C.1D applies
3) in the date of publication, distribution, etc., in the publication, distribution, etc., area.

> , 1971
> *not* , MCMLXXI

4) in the other physical details element of the physical description area
5) in the series numbering in the series area unless C.1D applies.

C.1D. Retain roman numerals if the substitution of arabic numerals makes the statement less clear; for example, when roman and arabic numerals are used in conjunction to distinguish the volume, section, series, or other group from the number, part, or other division of that group.

> (The Washington papers ; vol. IV, 36)

C.1E. When roman numerals are retained, write them in capitals except those used in paging or page references and those appearing in lowercase in the chief source of information or in quoted notes. Use lowercase roman numerals in paging or page references even though capitals appear in the item.

> xliii, 289 p.

C.2. ARABIC VS. NUMERALS SPELLED OUT

C.2A. Retain spelled-out numerals in the names of corporate bodies unless a particular rule instructs otherwise (cf. 24.7B2).

> **Four Corners Geological Society**

C.2B. Retain spelled-out numerals in uniform titles that are integral parts of the name of the work. In the case of numerals used to identify particular parts of a work, follow the instructions of the appropriate rule (cf. 25.6A2, 25.18A3).

> **Quinze joies de mariage**

C.2C. Substitute arabic numerals for spelled-out numerals in the following areas of the bibliographic description:

1) in the edition or issue statement in the edition area
2) in the material (or type of publication) specific details area unless a particular rule directs otherwise (cf. 3.3B2)
3) in the date of publication, distribution, etc., element in the publication, distribution, etc., area, unless a particular rule directs otherwise (cf. 1.4F1)
4) in the physical description area
5) in the series numbering in the series area.

C.3. NUMERALS BEGINNING NOTES

Spell out a numeral that is the first word of a note that is not quoted.

> First ed. published in 1954
> Four no. a year, 1931; 5 no. a year, 1932–1934

C.4. ORIENTAL NUMERALS

C.4A. Substitute roman numerals or Western-style arabic numerals for numerals in the vernacular in the cataloguing of Arabic alphabet, Far Eastern, Greek, Hebrew, Indic, etc., materials as instructed in the following rules.

C.4B. Use roman numerals in romanized headings for persons identified by numerals (e.g., rulers).

C.4C. Substitute Western-style arabic numerals for vernacular numerals in romanized headings for corporate bodies and in uniform titles.

> **Thawrat 25 Māyū, 1969**
>
> **al-Lajnah al-ʿUlyā li-Iḥtifālāt 14 Tammūz**

C.4D. Substitute Western-style arabic numerals in the following areas of the bibliographic description:

1) in the edition or issue statement element in the edition area
2) in the material (or type of publication) specific details area unless a particular rule directs otherwise (cf. 3.3B2)
3) in the date of publication, distribution, etc., element of the publication, distribution, etc., area
4) in the physical description area
5) in the series numbering in the series area.

C.4E. Consider inclusive dates and other numbers to be a single unit in languages that are read from right to left, e.g., 1960–1965, not 1965–1960. Add punctuation following the unit at the left, e.g., .1973–1976.

C.5. INCLUSIVE NUMBERS

Give inclusive numbers in full, e.g., p. 117–128, 1967–1972.

C.6. ALTERNATIVE DATES

When alternative dates of birth or death are given in headings for persons (cf. 22.18), word the second of the alternatives as it is spoken, e.g., 1506 *or* 7; 1819 *or* 20; 1899 *or* 1900. In all other cases, repeat all of the digits common to the two numbers, e.g., 1971 *or* 1972.

C.7. ORDINAL NUMERALS

C.7A. In the case of English-language items, record ordinal numerals in the form 1st, 2nd, 3rd, 4th, etc.

C.7B. In the case of other languages, follow the usage of the language if ascertainable,[1] e.g., French, 1er, 1ère, 2e, 3e, etc.; German, 1., 2., 3., etc.; Italian, 1o, 1a, 2o, 2a, 3o, 3a, etc.

C.7C. For Chinese, Japanese, and Korean items, accompany the arabic numeral by the character indicating that the numeral is ordinal.

C.7D. If the usage of a language cannot be ascertained, use the form 1., 2., 3., etc.

---

1. The following publication is a useful source for the form of ordinal numerals in European languages:

> Allen, C.G. *A Manual of European Languages for Librarians* / C.G. Allen. — London ; New York : Bowker, 1975.

GLOSSARY

In this glossary are definitions of most of the technical bibliographic and cataloguing terms, including those relating to the field of nonbook materials, used in these rules. The terms have been defined only within the context of the rules. For definitions of other terms, consult the standard glossaries of bibliographic and library terms or technical dictionaries.

Access point. A name, term, code, etc., under which a bibliographic record may be searched and identified. *See also* Heading.

Adaptation (Music). A musical work that represents a distinct alteration of another work (e.g., a free transcription), a work that paraphrases parts of various works or the general style of another composer, or a work that is merely based on other music (e.g., variations on a theme). *See also* Arrangement (Music).

Added entry. An entry, additional to the main entry, by which an item is represented in a catalogue; a secondary entry. *See also* Main entry.

Added title page. A title page preceding or following the title page chosen as the basis for the description of the item. It may be more general, as a series title page, or equally general, as a title page in another language.

Alternative title. The second part of a title proper that consists of two parts, each of which is a title; the parts are joined by the word *or* or its equivalent in another language, e.g., *The tempest, or, The enchanted island.*

Analytical entry. An entry for a part of an item for which a comprehensive entry has been made.

Analytical note. The statement in an analytical entry relating the part being analyzed to the comprehensive work of which it is a part.

Anonymous. Of unknown authorship.

Architectural rendering. A pictorial representation of a building intended to show, before it has been built, how the building will look when completed.

Area. A major section of the bibliographic description, comprising data of a particular category or set of categories.

Arrangement (Music). A musical work, or a portion thereof, rewritten for a medium of performance different from that for which the work was originally intended; also, a simplified version of a work for the same medium of performance. *See also* Adaptation (Music).

Art original. The original two- or three-dimensional work of art (other than an art print (q.v.) or a photograph) created by the artist, e.g., a painting, a drawing, or sculpture, as contrasted with a reproduction of it.

Art print. An engraving, etching, lithograph, woodcut, etc., printed from the plate prepared by the artist.

Art reproduction. A mechanically reproduced copy of a work of art, generally as one of a commercial edition.

Artefact. Any object made or modified by man.

Atlas. A volume of maps, plates, engravings, tables, etc., with or without descriptive letter-press. It may be an independent publication or it may have been issued to accompany one or more volumes of text.

Audiorecording. *See* Sound recording.

Author. *See* Personal author.

Author-title added entry. *See* Name-title added entry.

Author-title reference. *See* Name-title reference.

Binder's title. The title lettered on the cover of an item by a binder, as distinguished from the title on the publisher's original cover.

Broadsheet. *See* Broadside.

Broadside. A separately published piece of paper, printed on one side only and intended to be read unfolded; usually intended to be posted, publicly distributed, or sold, e.g., proclamations, handbills, ballad-sheets, news-sheets. *See also* Sheet.

Caption title. The title of a work given at the beginning of the first page of the text or, in the case of a musical score, immediately above the opening bars of the music.

Cartographic material. Any material representing, in whole or in part, the earth or any celestial body at any scale; includes two- and three-dimensional maps and plans; aeronautical, navigational, and celestial charts; globes; block diagrams; sections; aerial, satellite, and space photographs; atlases; bird's-eye views, etc.

Case binding. A method of binding in which a hard cover is made wholly separately from the book and later attached to it.

Cased. *See* Case binding.

Catalogue. 1. A list of library materials contained in a collection, a library, or a group of libraries, arranged according to some definite plan. 2. In a wider sense, a list of materials prepared for a particular purpose, e.g., an exhibition catalogue, a sales catalogue.

Chart. 1. An opaque sheet that exhibits data in graphic or tabular form, e.g., a wall chart. 2. In cartography, a special-purpose map generally designed for the use of navigators (e.g., an aeronautical chart, a nautical chart), although the word is also used to designate other types of special purpose maps, e.g., a celestial chart (i.e., a "star map").

Chief source of information. The source of bibliographic data to be given first preference as the source from which a bibliographic description (or portion thereof) is prepared.

Chinese style. *See* Traditional format (Oriental books).

Chorus score. A score of a vocal work showing only the chorus parts, with accompaniment, if any, arranged for keyboard instrument. *See also* Vocal score.

Cinefilm. *See* Motion picture.

Close score. A score of vocal music in which the separate parts are written on two staves, as with hymns.

Codebook (Machine-readable data files). A manual that describes the organization and content of one or more data files.

Collaborator. One who works with one or more associates to produce a work; all may make the same kind of contribution, as in the case of shared responsibility (cf. 21.6), or they may make different kinds of contributions, as in the case of collaboration between an artist and a writer (cf. 21.24). *See also* Joint author, Mixed responsibility, Shared responsibility.

Collection. If by one author: three or more independent works or parts of works published together. If by more than one author: two or more independent works or parts of works published together and not written for the same occasion or for the publication in hand.

Collective title. A title proper that is an inclusive title for an item containing several works. *See also* Uniform title 2.

Colophon. A statement at the end of an item giving information about one or more of the following: the title, author(s), publisher, printer, date of publication or printing; it may include other information.

Coloured illustration. An illustration in two or more colours.

Compiler. One who produces a collection by selecting and putting together matter from the works of various persons or bodies. Also, one who selects and puts together in one publication matter from the works of one person or body. (Cf. Editor.)

Compiler (Machine-readable data files). A computer program that converts each program statement of the source program into many machine-language instructions.

Compound surname. A surname consisting of two or more proper names, often connected by a hyphen, conjunction, or preposition.

Condensed score. The score of an orchestral or band work reduced to two, three, or four staves as required.

Conference. 1. A meeting of individuals or representatives of various bodies for the purpose of discussing and acting on topics of common interest. 2. A meeting of representatives of a corporate body that constitutes its legislative or governing body.

Continuation. 1. A supplement (q.v.). 2. A part issued in continuance of a monograph, a serial, or a series.

Conventional name. A name, other than the real or official name, by which a corporate body, place, or thing has come to be known.

Conventional title. *See* Uniform title.

Corporate body. An organization or group of persons that is identified by a particular name and that acts, or may act, as an entity. Typical examples of corporate bodies are associations, institutions, business firms, nonprofit enterprises, governments, government agencies, religious bodies, local churches, and conferences.

Cover title. A title printed on the original cover of an item. *See also* Binder's title, Spine title.

Cross-reference. *See* Reference.

Data set name. In certain computer systems, the name that the software recognizes as the identifier of a given machine-readable data file.

Diorama. A three-dimensional representation of a scene created by placing objects, figures, etc., in front of a two-dimensional painted background.

Distributor. An agent or agency that has exclusive or shared marketing rights for an item.

Double leaf. A leaf of double size with a fold at the fore edge or at the top edge of the book. *See also* Traditional format (Oriental books).

Edition. 1. In the case of books and booklike materials, all those copies of an item produced from substantially the same type image, whether by direct contact or by photographic methods. 2. In the case of nonbook materials, all the copies of an item produced from one master copy and issued by a particular publishing agency or a group of such agencies. Provided the foregoing conditions are fulfilled, a change of identity of the distributing body or bodies does not constitute a change of edition. *See also* Facsimile reproduction, Impression, Issue, Reprint.

Editor. One who prepares for publication an item not his own. The editorial labour may be limited to the preparation of the item for the manufacturer, or it may include supervision of the manufacturing, revision (restitution) or elucidation of the text, and the addition of an introduction, notes, and other critical matter. For certain works it may involve the technical direction of a staff of persons engaged in writing or compiling the text. (Cf. Compiler.)

Element. A word, phrase, or group of characters representing a distinct unit of bibliographic information and forming part of an area (q.v.) of the description.

Engineering drawing. *See* Technical drawing.

Entry. A record of an item in a catalogue. *See also* Heading.

Entry word. The word by which an entry is primarily arranged in the catalogue, usually the first word (other than an article) of the heading. (Cf. Heading.)

Explanatory reference. An elaborated *see* or *see also* reference that explains the circumstances under which the headings involved should be consulted.

Explicit. A statement at the end of the text of a manuscript or early printed book, or at the end of one of its divisions, indicating its conclusion and sometimes giving the author's name and the title of the work.

Facsimile reproduction. A reproduction that has as its chief purpose to simulate the physical appearance of the original work as well as to provide an exact replica of the text.

Fascicle. One of the temporary divisions of a work that, for convenience in printing or publication, is issued in small installments, usually incomplete in themselves; they do not necessarily coincide with any formal division of the work into parts, etc. Usually the fascicle is protected by temporary paper wrappers and may or may not be numbered. A fascicle is distinguished from a part (q.v.) by being a temporary division of a work rather than a formal component unit.

Filing title. *See* Uniform title.

Filmstrip. A length of film containing a succession of images intended for projection one at a time, with or without recorded sound.

Flash card. A card or other opaque material printed with words, numerals, or pictures and designed for rapid display.

Format. In its widest sense, any particular physical presentation of an item.

Format (Machine-readable data files). A predetermined order or arrangement of data in a record.

Format (Texts). The number of times the printed sheet has been folded to make the leaves of a book, e.g., folio (one fold giving two leaves), quarto (two folds giving four leaves), etc.

Full score. *See* Score.

Game. A set of materials designed for play according to prescribed rules.

General material designation. A term indicating the broad class of material to which an item belongs, e.g., sound recording. *See also* Specific material designation.

Globe. The model of a celestial body, usually the earth or the celestial sphere, depicted on the surface of a sphere.

Graphic. A two-dimensional representation whether opaque (e.g., art originals and reproductions, flash cards, photographs, technical drawings) or intended to be viewed, or projected without motion, by means of an optical device (e.g., filmstrips, stereographs, slides).

Half title. A brief title of a publication appearing on a leaf preceding the title page.

Harmony (Bible). 1. An arrangement of passages of the Bible on the same topic into parallel columns so that similarities and differences are readily compared. 2. An interweaving of such passages into a continuous text.

Heading. A name, word, or phrase placed at the head of a catalogue entry to provide an access point in the catalogue.

Impression. All those copies of an edition printed at one time. *See also* Issue, Reprint.

Incipit. The opening words of a manuscript or early printed book, or of one of its divisions. It frequently includes the word *incipit* or its equivalent in another language. An incipit at the beginning of a work often contains the name of the author and the title of the work.

Internal user label. *See* Label.

International intergovernmental body. An international body created by intergovernmental action.

International Standard Book Number (ISBN). *See* Standard number.

International Standard Serial Number (ISSN). *See* Standard number.

Issue. 1. In the case of books and booklike materials, those copies of an edition forming a distinct group that is distinguished from other copies of the edition by more or less slight but well-defined variations; most commonly a new impression for which corrections or revisions have been incorporated into the original type image. 2. In the case of nonbook materials, those copies of an edition of an item forming a distinct group that is distinguished from other copies by well-defined variations. *See also* Impression, Reprint.

Item. A document or set of documents in any physical form, published, issued, or treated as an entity, and as such forming the basis for a single bibliographic description.

Jacket (Sound disc). *See* Sleeve.

Japanese style. *See* Traditional format (Oriental books).

Joint author. A person who collaborates with one or more other persons to produce a work in relation to which the collaborators perform the same function. *See also* Shared responsibility.

Key-title. The unique name assigned to a serial by the International Serials Data System (ISDS).

Kit. An item containing two or more categories of material, no one of which is identifiable as the predominant constituent of the item; also designated *multimedia item* (q.v.).

Label (Machine-readable data files). A machine-readable identifier containing alphanumeric characters, which frequently provides information about the contents of a volume or a file.

Leaf. One of the units into which the original sheet or half sheet of paper, parchment, etc., is folded to form part of a book; each leaf consists of two pages, one on each side, either or both of which may be blank.

Logical record. In the context of machine-readable data, a group of words, characters, or bytes identified as a unit on the basis of content function and use rather than on physical attributes.

Machine-readable data file (MRDF). A body of information coded by methods that require the use of a machine (typically but not always a computer) for processing. Examples include files stored on magnetic tape, punched cards, aperture cards, disk packs, etc.

Macroform. A generic term for any medium, transparent or opaque, bearing images large enough to be easily read by the naked eye. *See also* Microform.

Main entry. The complete catalogue record of an item, presented in the form by which the entity is to be uniformly identified and cited. The main entry may include the tracings of all other headings under which the record is to be represented in the catalogue. *See also* Added entry.

Main heading. The first part of a heading that includes a subheading.

Manuscript. A writing made by hand (including musical scores), typescripts, and inscriptions on clay tablets, stone, etc.

Map. A representation, normally to scale and on a flat medium, of a selection of material or abstract features on, or in relation to, the surface of the earth or of another celestial body. *See also* Chart 2, Plan 2.

Masthead. The statement of title, ownership, editors, etc., of a newspaper or periodical; although its location is variable, in the case of newspapers it is commonly found on the editorial page or at the top of page one, and, in the case of periodicals, on the contents page.

Mechanical drawing. *See* Technical drawing.

Microfiche. A sheet of film bearing a number of microimages in a two-dimensional array.

Microfilm. A length of film bearing a number of microimages in linear array.

Microform. A generic term for any medium, transparent or opaque, bearing microimages. *See also* Macroform.

Microopaque. A sheet of opaque material bearing a number of microimages in a two-dimensional array.

Microscope slide. A slide designed for holding a minute object to be viewed through a microscope or by a microprojector.

Miniature score. A musical score not primarily intended for performance use, with type reduced in size.

Mixed authorship. *See* Mixed responsibility.

Mixed responsibility. A work of mixed responsibility is one in which different persons or bodies contribute to its intellectual or artistic content by performing different kinds of activities (e.g., adapting or illustrating a work written by another person). *See also* Shared responsibility.

Mock-up. A representation of a device or process that may be modified for training or analysis to emphasize a particular part or function; it usually has movable parts that can be manipulated.

Model. A three-dimensional representation of a real thing, either of the exact size of the original or to scale.

Monograph. A nonserial item, i.e., an item either complete in one part or complete, or intended to be completed, in a finite number of separate parts.

Monographic series. *See* Series 1.

Motion picture. A length of film, with or without recorded sound, bearing a sequence of images that create the illusion of movement when projected in rapid succession.

Multifile item. A bibliographic entity that consists of more than one machine-readable data file.

Multimedia item. An item containing two or more categories of material, no one of which is identifiable as the predominant constituent of the item; also designated *kit* (q.v.).

Multipart item. A monograph complete, or intended to be completed, in a finite number of separate parts. *See also* Multifile item.

Multivolume monograph. *See* Multipart item.

Name-title added entry. An added entry consisting of the name of a person or corporate body and the title of an item.

Name-title reference. A reference in which the refer-from line, the refer-to line, or both consist of the name of a person or a corporate body and the title of an item.

Object. A three-dimensional artefact (or replica of an artefact) or a specimen of a naturally occurring entity. *See also* Realia.

Object program. The computer-language program prepared by an assembler or a compiler after acting on a programmer-written source program.

Other title information. Any title borne by an item other than the title proper or parallel titles; also any phrase appearing in conjunction with the title proper, parallel titles, or other titles, indicative of the character, contents, etc., of the item or the motives for, or occasion of, its production or publication. The term includes subtitles, *avant-titres*, etc., but does not include variations on the title proper (e.g., spine titles, sleeve titles, etc.).

Overhead projectual. *See* Transparency.

Overlay. A transparent sheet containing matter that, when superimposed on another sheet, modifies the data on the latter.

Parallel title. The title proper in another language and/or script.

Part. 1. One of the subordinate units into which an item has been divided by the author, publisher, or manufacturer. In the case of printed monographs, generally synonymous with *volume* (q.v.); it is distinguished from a fascicle (q.v.) by being a component unit rather than a temporary division of a work. 2. As used in the physical description area, the word *part* designates bibliographic units intended to be bound several to a volume (cf. Part (Music)).

Part (Music). The music for one of the participating voices or instruments in a musical work; the written or printed copy of such a part for the use of a performer, designated in the physical description area by the word *part*.

Patronymic. A name derived from the given name of the father, often by the addition of a suffix.

Personal author. The person chiefly responsible for the creation of the intellectual or artistic content of a work. (*See* 21.1A1 for a gloss on this definition.)

Phonorecord. *See* Sound recording.

Photocopy. A macroform photoreproduction produced directly on opaque material by radiant energy through contact or projection.

Piano [violin, etc.] conductor part. The part of an ensemble work for a particular instrument with cues for the other instruments; intended for the use of the person who plays the instrument and also conducts the performance of the work.

Piano score. A reduction of an orchestral score to a version for piano, on two staves.

Picture. A two-dimensional visual representation accessible to the naked eye and generally on an opaque backing. Used when a more specific term (e.g., art original, photograph, study print) is not appropriate.

Plan. 1. A drawing showing relative positions on a horizontal plane, e.g., relative positions of parts of a building, a landscape design; the arrangement of furniture in a room or building; a graphic presentation of a military or naval plan. 2. In cartography, a large-scale, detailed map or chart with a minimum of generalization.

Plate. A leaf containing illustrative matter, with or without explanatory text, that does not form part of either the preliminary or the main sequences of pages or leaves.

Portfolio. A container for holding loose materials, e.g., paintings, drawings, papers, unbound sections of a book, and similar materials, consisting of two covers joined together at the back; the covers are usually tied with tapes at the fore edge, top, and bottom.

Praeses. The faculty moderator of an academic disputation, who normally proposed a thesis and participated in the ensuing disputation.

Predominant name. The name or form of name of a person or corporate body that appears most frequently (1) in the person's works or works issued by the corporate body; or (2) in reference sources, in that order of preference.

Preliminaries. The title page or title pages of an item, together with the verso of each title page, any pages preceding the title page(s), and the cover.

Printing. *See* Facsimile reproduction, Impression, Issue, Reprint.

Producer (Motion pictures). The person with final responsibility for the making of a motion picture, including business aspects, management of the production, and the commercial success of the film.

Production company (Motion pictures). The company or other organization that determines the content and form of a motion picture and is responsible for its manufacture or production. If there is, in addition, a sponsor, the production company is normally responsible only for the manufacture or production of the motion picture.

Program file. A machine-readable data file that contains the instructions that control the operation of a computer so that it performs the tasks required to produce the desired result.

Programming language. A language in which computer programs are written.

Pseudonym. A name assumed by an author to conceal or obscure his or her identity.

Radiograph. A photograph produced by the passage of radiation, such as X rays, gamma rays, or neutrons, through an opaque object.

Realia. Actual objects (artefacts, specimens) as opposed to replicas. *See also* Object.

Recto. 1. The right-hand page of a book, usually bearing an odd page number. 2. The side of a printed sheet intended to be read first.

Reference. A direction from one heading or entry to another.

Reference source. Any publication from which authoritative information may be obtained. Not limited to reference works.

Reissue. *See* Issue, Reprint.

Related body. A corporate body that has a relation to another body other than that of hierarchical subordination, e.g., one that is founded but not controlled by another body; one that only receives financial support from another body; one that provides financial and/or other types of assistance to another body, such as "friends" groups; one whose members have also membership in or an association with another body, such as employees' associations and alumni associations.

Related music. *See* Adaptation (Music).

Releasing agent. The agent or agency responsible for the initial distribution of a motion picture.

Reprint. 1. A new printing of an item made from the original type image, commonly by photographic methods. The printing may reproduce the original exactly (an impression (q.v.)) or it may contain more or less slight but well-defined variations (an issue (q.v.)). 2. A new edition with substantially unchanged text. *See also* Facsimile reproduction.

Respondent (Academic disputations). A candidate for a degree who, in an academic disputation, defends or opposes a thesis proposed by the praeses (q.v.); also called the defendant.

Romanization. Conversion of names or text not written in the roman alphabet to roman-alphabet form.

Running title. The title, or abbreviated title, of the book repeated at the head of each page or at the head of the versos.

Score. A series of staves on which all the different instrumental and/or vocal parts of a musical work are written, one under the other in vertical alignment, so that the parts may be read simultaneously. *See also* Chorus score, Close score, Condensed score, Miniature score, Part (Music), Piano [violin, etc.] conductor part, Piano score, Short score, Vocal score.

Secondary entry. *See* Added entry.

Section (Serials). A separately published part of a serial, usually representing a particular subject category within the larger serial and identified by a designation that may be a topic, or an alphabetical or numerical designation, or a combination of these. *See also* Subseries.

Sequel. A literary or other imaginative work that is complete in itself but continues an earlier work.

Serial. A publication in any medium issued in successive parts bearing numerical or chronological designations and intended to be continued indefinitely. Serials include periodicals; newspapers; annuals (reports, yearbooks, etc.); the journals, memoirs, proceedings, transactions, etc., of societies; and numbered monographic series. *See also* Series 1.

Series. 1. A group of separate items related to one another by the fact that each item bears, in addition to its own title proper, a collective title applying to the group as a whole. The individual items may or may not be numbered. 2. Each of two or more volumes of essays, lectures, articles, or other writings, similar in character and issued in sequence, e.g., Lowell's *Among my books*, second series. 3. A separately numbered sequence of volumes within a series or serial, e.g., *Notes and queries*, 1st series, 2nd series, etc.

Shared authorship. *See* Shared responsibility.

Shared responsibility. Collaboration between two or more persons or bodies performing the same kind of activity in the creation of the content of an item. The contribution of each may form a separate and distinct part of the item, or the contribution of each may not be separable from that of the others. *See also* Joint author, Mixed responsibility.

Sheet. As used in the physical description area, a single piece of paper other than a broadside (q.v.), with manuscript or printed matter on one or both sides.

Short score. A sketch made by a composer for an ensemble work, with the main features of the composition set out on a few staves. *See also* Close score, Condensed score.

Sine loco (s.l.). Without place, i.e., without the name of the place of publication.

Sine nomine (s.n.). Without name, i.e., without the name of the publisher.

Sleeve. A protective envelope for a sound disc, made of cardboard or paper.

Slide. Transparent material on which there is a two-dimensional image, usually held in a mount, and designed for use in a projector or viewer.

Sound recording. A recording on which sound vibrations have been registered by mechanical or electrical means so that the sound may be reproduced.

Specific material designation. A term indicating the special class of material (usually the class of physical object) to which an item belongs, e.g., sound disc. *See also* General material designation.

Spine title. The title that appears on the spine of an item. *See also* Binder's title.

Standard number. The International Standard Number (ISN), e.g., International Standard Book Number (ISBN), International Standard Serial Number (ISSN), or any other internationally agreed upon standard number, that uniquely identifies an item.

Standard title. *See* Uniform title.

Statement (Machine-readable data files). A meaningful expression or generalized instruction in a computer program.

Statement of responsibility. A statement, transcribed from the item being described, relating to persons responsible for the intellectual or artistic content of the item, to corporate bodies from which the content emanates, or to persons or corporate bodies responsible for the performance of the content of the item.

Subordinate body. A corporate body that forms an integral part of a larger body in relation to which it holds an inferior hierarchical rank.

Subseries. A series within a series; that is, a series which always appears in conjunction with another, usually more comprehensive, series of which it forms a section. Its title may or may not be dependent on the title of the main series. *See also* Section (Serials).

Supplement. An item, usually issued separately, that complements one already published by bringing up-to-date or otherwise continuing the original or by containing a special feature not included in the original; the supplement has a formal relationship with the original as expressed by common authorship, a common title or subtitle, and/or a stated intention to continue or supplement the original. *See also* Sequel.

Supplied title. In the case of an item that has no title proper on the chief source of information or its substitute, the title provided by the cataloguer. It may be taken from elsewhere in the item itself or from a reference source, or it may be composed by the cataloguer.

Technical drawing. A cross section, detail, diagram, elevation, perspective, plan, working plan, etc., made for use in an engineering or other technical context. *See also* Architectural rendering.

Text. 1. A term used as a general material designation to designate printed material accessible to the naked eye (e.g., a book, a pamphlet, or a broadside). 2. The words of a song, song cycle, or, in the plural, a collection of songs.

Thematic index. A list of a composer's works, usually arranged in chronological order or by categories, with the theme given for each composition or for each section of large compositions.

Title. A word, phrase, character, or group of characters, normally appearing in an item, naming the item or the work contained in it. *See also* Alternative title, Caption title, Cover title, Half title, Running title, Spine title, Supplied title, Title proper, Uniform title.

Title frame. A frame containing written or printed material not part of the subject content of the item.

Title page. A page at the beginning of an item bearing the title proper and usually, though not necessarily, the statement of responsibility and the data relating to publication. The leaf bearing the title page is commonly called the *title page* although properly called the *title leaf*. *See also* Added title page.

Title proper. The chief name of an item, including any alternative title but excluding parallel titles and other title information.

Tracing. 1. The record of the headings under which an item is represented in the catalogue. 2. The record of the references that have been made to a name or to the title of an item that is represented in the catalogue.

Traditional format (Oriental books). Format of books consisting of double leaves with folds at the fore edge and with free edges sewn together to make a fascicle. Usually several fascicles are contained in a cloth-covered case.

Trailer. A short motion picture film consisting of selected scenes from a film to be shown at a future date, used to advertise that film.

Transcription (Music). *See* Adaptation (Music), Arrangement (Music).

Translator. One who renders from one language into another, or from an older form of a language into the modern form, more or less closely following the original.

Transparency. A sheet of transparent material bearing an image and designed for use with an overhead projector or a light box. It may be mounted in a frame.

Uniform title. 1. The particular title by which a work that has appeared under varying titles is to be identified for cataloguing purposes. 2. A conventional collective title used to collocate publications of an author, composer, or corporate body containing several works or extracts, etc., from several works, e.g., complete works, several works in a particular literary or musical form.

Version (Bible). A particular translation of the Bible or any of its parts. (For the broader use of this term for other works, to designate a type of adaptation, cf. 21.10.)

Verso. 1. The left-hand page of a book, usually bearing an even page number. 2. The side of a printed sheet intended to be read second.

Videorecording. A recording on which visual images, usually in motion and accompanied by sound, have been registered; designed for playback by means of a television set.

Vocal score. A score showing all vocal parts, with accompaniment, if any, arranged for keyboard instrument. *See also* Chorus score.

Volume. 1. In the bibliographic sense, a major division of a work, regardless of its designation by the publisher, distinguished from other major divisions of the same work by having its own inclusive title page,[1] half title, cover title, or portfolio title, and usually independent pagination, foliation, or signatures. This major bibliographic unit may include various title pages and/or paginations. 2. In the material sense, all that is contained in one binding, portfolio, etc., whether as originally issued or as bound after issue.[2] The volume as a material unit may not coincide with the volume as a bibliographic unit.

Volume (Machine-readable data files). A physical unit of external storage such as a disk, a reel of magnetic tape.

---

1. The most general title page, half title, or cover title is the determining factor in deciding what constitutes a bibliographic volume, e.g., a reissue in one binding, with a general title page, of a work previously issued in two or more bibliographic volumes is considered to be one bibliographic volume even though the reissue includes the title pages of the original volumes.

2. Such a composite volume bound by or for an individual owner may contain either two or more bibliographic volumes of the same work or two or more works published independently.

INDEX

Compiled by K. G. B. BAKEWELL

The index covers the rules (including introductions to the rules) and appendices, but not examples or works cited in any of the rules or appendices. All index entries refer to rule numbers. *App. D* indicates that a term is defined in Appendix D (Glossary), which begins on page 563.

As the rules are based upon bibliographic conditions rather than specific cases, kinds of work have been indexed only when actually named in a rule (e.g., concordances and other kinds of related works named in Rule 21.28). There is no entry under *Encyclopedias, Directories*, etc. because they could represent several bibliographic conditions.

Rules for description have been indexed only to the general chapter (chapter 1) unless there is an amplification or amendment in a later chapter dealing with the description of a specific kind of material.

The index is arranged according to *ALA Rules for Filing Catalog Cards* / prepared by the ALA Editorial Committee's Subcommittee on the ALA Rules for Filing Catalog Cards ; Pauline A. Seely, chairman and editor. — 2nd ed. — Chicago : American Library Association, 1968.

Abbreviations used in the index

App.	Appendix
n	footnote

Index

Abridgements, 21.12
Absorbed serials, *see* Mergers of serials
Academic degrees, honours, etc.
 added to identical personal names, 22.19B
 capitalization, App. A.13K
 omission from statement of responsibility, 1.1F7
Academic disputations, 21.27
Academic dissertations, *see* Dissertations
Accents
 description of item, 1.0G
 personal names, 22.1D1
Access points
 choice, 21
 definition, App. D
 see also Headings
Access, restrictions on
 to machine-readable data files, 9.7B14
 to manuscripts, 4.7B14
Accession, year of, *see* Date(s) of
 accession or ownership
Accompaniments, added (musical works), 21.21
Accompanying instruments (songs, Lieder, etc.), 25.29H3
Accompanying material
 general rules, 1.5E
 notes on, 1.7B11
 with specific materials:
  cartographic materials, 3.5E, 3.7B11
  graphic materials, 8.5E, 8.7B11
   accompanying material as source of information, 8.0B1, 8.0B2
  machine-readable data files, 9.5D, 9.7B11
  manuscripts, 4.7B11
  microforms, 11.5E, 11.7B11
  motion pictures and videorecordings, 7.5E, 7.7B11
   accompanying material as source of information, 7.0B1, 7.0B2
  music, 5.5E, 5.7B11
  printed monographs, 2.5E, 2.7B11
  serials, 12.5E, 12.7B11
  sound recordings, 6.5E, 6.7B11
   accompanying material as source of information, 6.0B
  three-dimensional artefacts and realia, 10.5E, 10.7B11
   accompanying material as source of information, 10.0B1
Account books, manuscript, without title, 4.1B2
Acetate film base (motion pictures and video recordings), 7.7B10(e)
Acharya (early Indic names), 22.25A
Acoustic recordings, notes on, 6.7B10
Acquisition, source of (manuscripts), 4.7B7
Acronyms
 corporate names
  capitalization, App. A.1
  explanatory references, 26.3C2
  preferred form, 24.2D

presentation and spacing, 24.1
 "see" references, 26.3A3, 26.3A4
 serial titles, 12.1E1
Actors and actresses, *see* Performers
Acts, legislative, *see* Bills; Laws, etc.
Ad hoc events, *see* Events; Exhibitions, fairs, festivals, etc.; Expeditions
Ad hoc military courts, 24.23B
Adaptations
 art works, 21.16
 definition, App. D
 musical works, 21.18C
 musico-dramatic works (uniform titles), 25.31B4
 notes on, 1.7B2
 texts, 21.10
Adat title (Indonesian names), 22.26D
Added accompaniments, etc. (musical works), 21.21
Added entries, 21.29–21.30
 definition, 21.0A, App. D
 replaced by references, 21.29G, 26.5
 uniform titles, 25.2D
Added title page, 1.0H
 definition, App. D
 see also Variations in title
Additional titles, *see* Other title information
Additions
 to date of publication, distribution, etc., 1.4F2, 1.4F4, 1.4F5
 to headings
  conferences, etc., 24.7B
  corporate names, 24.4
   capitalization, App. A.2D
  embassies, consulates, etc., 24.25
  exhibitions, fairs, festivals, etc., 24.8B
  government names, 24.6
  introductory note, 20.3
  personal names, *see* Personal names, additions to
  place names, 23.4
  radio and television stations, 24.11
 to name of publisher, distributor, etc., 1.4E1
 to place of publication, distribution, etc., 1.4C2–1.4C4, 1.4C7
  early printed monographs, 2.16C
 to series title, 1.6H3
 to standard number or terms of availability, 1.8E
 to statement of projection, cartographic materials, 3.3C2
 to statements of responsibility, 1.1F8
 to title (early printed monographs), 2.14D
 to uniform titles, 25.5
  capitalization, App. A.3C
 see also type of addition (e.g., Date)
Address of publisher, distributor, etc., 1.4C7
 early printed monographs, 2.16C
Address, terms of, *see* Terms of address
Address, titles of, *see* Titles of honour, nobility, address, etc.

574

Index

British Isles
  corporate bodies located in, addition of
    place name, 24.4C5
  localities in, added to place names, 23.4D
  see also United Kingdom
British peerage, explanation of, 22.6A n11,
  22.12A n13
British titles of honour, added to personal
  names, 22.12B
Broadsheets, *see* Broadsides
Broadsides (broadsheets)
  definition, App. D
  description, 2.5B1, 2.5B18
  early printed items, 2.17A
  for other rules see Printed monographs
Buddhist names, 22.25A, 22.25B
  ecclesiastics, 22.28D2
  monastics, 22.28D1
  supreme patriarchs, 22.28D3
Buddhist scriptures, 25.18F
Budi (Indonesian names), 22.26C2
Buildings, capitalization, App. A.16
  Finnish language, App. A.38B
Bulgarian language, capitalization,
  App. A.35
Bulls, papal, 21.4D1
Burmese names, 22.23
Business firms, *see* Corporate bodies
"By the author of . . . ," 22.11D
Bynames, *see* Given names, etc.; Words or
  phrases
Byzantine Greek works (uniform titles),
  25.4B

Cadenzas, 21.28
Calendar divisions
  abbreviations, App. B.15
  capitalization, App. A.23
    Bulgarian language, App. A.35G
    Czech language, App. A.36E
    Dutch language, App. A.37D
    French language, App. A.39F
    Hungarian language, App. A.41D
    Italian language, App. A.42E
    Polish language, App. A.44E
    Portuguese language, App. A.45E
    Russian language, App. A.46G
    Scandinavian languages, App. A.47F
    Serbo-Croatian language, App. A.48G
    Slovenian language, App. A.50G
    Spanish language, App. A.51E
Calendars, Gregorian and Julian, *see*
  Gregorian calendar
Calendars, liturgical, *see* Liturgical works
Canadian place names
  abbreviations, App. B.14
  additions to, 23.4C
Capitalization, App. A
  roman numerals, App. C.1E
Caption, as source of information
  early printed monographs, 2.13
  music, 5.0B
  printed monographs, 2.0B
  serials, 12.0B1

Caption title
  added entries, 21.30J
  definition, App. D
Carbon copies, manuscript, notes on, 4.7B1
Cardinals, *see* Bishops, etc.
Cards, number of (graphic materials), in
  contents note, 8.7B18
Cartographers as personal authors, 21.1A1
Cartographic materials, 3
  collections, 3.0J
  coordinates and equinox, 3.3D
  definition, 3.0A, App. D
  edition area, 3.2
  general material designation, 1.1C1, 3.1C
  in microform
    mathematical data, 11.3A
    sources of information for special
      data, 11.0B2
  mathematical data area, 3.3
  note area, 3.7
  physical description area, 3.5
  projection, 3.3C
  publication, distribution, etc., area, 3.4
  scale, *see* Scale
  series area, 3.6
  sources of information, 3.0B
  specific material designation, 3.5B
  standard number and terms of
    availability area, 3.8
  title and statement of responsibility
    area, 3.1
Cartridges, film, *see* Film cartridges
Cartridges, microfilm
  specific material designation, 11.5B1
  for other rules see Microforms
Cartridges, sound, *see* Sound cartridges
Case binding, definition, App. D
Cases, court, 21.36
Cases for printed monographs (description),
  2.5B1, 2.5B18
Cassettes, film, *see* Film cassettes
Cassettes, microform
  specific material designation, 11.5B1
  for other rules see Microforms
Cassettes, sound, *see* Sound cassettes
Cast (motion pictures and video recordings,
  sound recordings, etc.), *see* Performers
Catalogue, definition, App. D
Cathedrals, 24.3G; *see also* Churches
Catholic Church
  apostolic delegations, 24.27D
  concordats, 21.35C
  councils, etc., 24.27A2
  dioceses, etc., 24.27C3
  liturgical works (uniform titles), 25.20
  Mass (uniform titles), 25.23B–25.23C
  see also Holy See; Liturgical works;
    Popes; Religious orders
Celestial charts
  declination, 3.3D2
  magnitude, 3.7B8
  specific material designation, 3.5B1
  for other rules see Cartographic materials

Index

Codebooks
  accompanying machine-readable data
    files, 9.5D2, 9.5D3
    ISBN, 9.7B11
  definition, App. D
Collaborations, *see* Shared responsibility
Collaborators
  added entries, 21.30B
  artists and writers, 21.24
  definition, App. D
  machine-readable data files, 9.7B6
  see also Mixed responsibility; Shared
    responsibility
Collation
  ancient, medieval, and Renaissance
    manuscripts, 4.7B22
  see also Physical description area
Collections, 21.7
  added entries, 21.30H
  definition, 21.7A, App. D
  of administrative regulations, 21.32C
  of ancient, medieval, or customary laws
    (uniform titles), 25.15B
  of cartographic materials, 3.0J
  of court proceedings, 21.36C9
  of court rules, 21.34B
  of laws governing more than one
    jurisdiction, 21.31B2
  of laws (uniform titles), 25.15A1
  of manuscripts
    accompanying material, 4.7B11
    dimensions, 4.5D2
    lack of title, 4.1B2
    notes, 4.7B1
    statement of extent, 4.5B2
  of Midrashim, 25.18E2
  of musical excerpts, 21.19B1
  of musical settings of songs, etc., 21.19C
  of official communications, 21.4D1
  of official communications and other
    works, 21.4D3
  of pamphlets, assembled by library,
    sources of information, 1.0A2
  of songs (uniform titles), 25.31B5
  of translations, 21.14B
  of treaties, etc., 21.35F
    uniform titles, 25.16A
  with collective title, 21.7B
  without collective title, 21.7C
  see also Collective title; Contents notes;
    Selections; "With" notes
Collective title
  as title proper (printed monographs),
    2.1B2
  capitalization, App. A.3B
  collections with, 21.7B
  complete works, 25.8
  cycles, 25.12B
  definition, App. D
  explanatory references to, 26.4C3
  lack of, 1.1G
    cartographic materials, 3.1G
      extent, 3.5B4
    collections, 21.7C

  edition statements, 1.2B6
  general material designation, 1.1C2
  microforms, 11.1G
    extent, 11.5B2
  motion pictures and video recordings,
    7.1G
    extent, 7.5B3
  notes of separately published items,
    see "With" notes
  sound recordings, 6.1G
    duration of individual parts, 6.7B10
    extent, 6.5B3
  music, 25.34–25.36
  "see" references, 26.4A4
  uniform titles, 25.8–25.12
Collectors of field material (sound
  recordings), 6.1F1
Colleges of universities, 24.13 (type 4)
Colon, use of, *see* Punctuation of
  description
Colophon
  as source of information
    early printed monographs, 2.13
    music, 5.0B
    printed monographs, 2.0B
    serials, 12.0B1
  definition, App. D
Colour
  art prints, 8.5C2
  art reproductions, 8.5C3
  cartographic materials, 3.5C1, 3.5C3
  filmslips and filmstrips, 8.5C4
  flash cards, 8.5C5
  flip charts, 8.5C6
  microforms, 11.5C3
  motion pictures and videorecordings,
    7.5C1, 7.5C4
  photographs and transparencies, 8.5C7
  pictures, 8.5C8
  postcards, 8.5C9
  posters, 8.5C10
  slides, 8.5C12
  stereographs, 8.5C13
  study prints, 8.5C14
  three-dimensional artefacts and realia,
    10.5C2
  transparencies, 8.5C16
  wall charts, 8.5C17
Colour printing (early printed monographs),
  2.18E
Colour process or recording system
  (motion pictures and videorecordings),
  7.7B10(c)
Colour separation films, 7.7B10(d)
Coloured illustrations (printed
  monographs), 2.5C3
  definition, App. D
Colouring, hand (early printed
  monographs), 2.18F
Columns, number of
  ancient, medieval, and Renaissance
    manuscripts, 4.5B1
  early printed monographs, 2.17A, 2.18E
  see also Pagination

580

Index

Karta (Indonesian names), 22.26C2
Key (music)
  added to uniform titles, 25.31A5
  capitalization of accompanying words,
    App. A.3C
  as part of title proper, 5.1B2
  omitted from uniform titles when
    designating pitch of musical
    instruments, 25.29D3
Key-titles of serials, 1.8C, 12.8C
  definition, App. D
  facsimiles, 1.11E
Keyboard instruments, terms for (uniform
    titles), 25.29D2, 25.29D5
Khiṭāb (names in Arabic alphabet), 22.22D
Khun (Thai names), 22.28A
Khunnāng (Thai names), 22.28C
Kings, *see* Royalty
Kits
  definition, App. D
  extent, 1.10C2
  general material designation, 1.1C1,
    1.1C4, 1.10C1, 2.1C2
  notes, 1.10C3
  see also Mixed material items;
    Multimedia items
Knightly orders, 24.3C2 n9
Knights, additions to personal names,
    22.12B
Koran (uniform titles), 25.18M
Korean language, ordinal numerals in,
    App. C.7C
Krom ranks (Thai names), 22.28B2
Kunyah (names in Arabic alphabet), 22.22D
Kusuma (Indonesian names), 22.26C2

Lab kits, 1.1C1 n1
Labels (machine-readable data files)
  as sources of information, 9.0B1
  definition, App. D
Labels (sound recordings), as sources of
    information, 6.0B1
Laboratories (subordinate corporate
    bodies), 24.13 (type 4)
Lack of title, *see* Collective title, lack of;
    Title proper, lack of
Lady added to personal names, 22.12B
Language
  added to uniform titles, 25.5D
    Bible, 25.18A10
    Mishnah or Tosefta, 25.18C
    musical liturgical works, 25.31B6
    stories with many versions, 25.12A
    translations, 25.11
    translations of vocal works, 25.31B7
  notes on, 1.7B2
    cartographic materials, 3.7B2
    graphic materials, 8.7B2
    machine-readable data files, 9.7B2
    manuscripts, 4.7B2
    microforms, 11.7B2
    motion pictures and videorecordings,
      7.7B2
    music, 5.7B2

    printed monographs, 2.7B2
    serials, 12.7B2, 12.7B7(h)
    sound recordings, 6.7B2
  of description, 1.0E
    chief source of information in more
      than one language or script, 1.0H
    edition statement, 1.2B5
      serials, 12.2B1(d)
      see also Multilingual edition
        statements
    other title information, 1.1E5
    publication, distribution, etc., area,
      1.4B5
    title proper, 1.1B8
  of headings
    administrative offices of the Roman
      Curia, 24.27C4
    Catholic Church councils, 24.27A2
    Catholic dioceses, etc., 24.27C3
    corporate names
      change of name, 24.1B
      "see" references, 26.3A3
      variant forms, 24.3A
    international bodies, 24.3B
    papal diplomatic missions, etc., 24.27D
    personal names, 22.3B
      "see" references, 26.2A2
    place names, 23.2
      "see" references, 26.3A3
    religious orders and societies, 24.3D
  of uniform titles
    liturgical works, 25.19
    Midrashim, 25.18E1
    music, 25.27A, 25.27B
    sacred scriptures, 25.17
    Talmud, 25.18B1
    works created after 1500, 25.3
    works created before 1501, 25.4
  preferences in AACR 2, 0.12
  see also Multilingual . . .
Languages, capitalization
  French language, App. A.39A1–A.39A2
  Italian language, App. A.42A1–A.42A2
Laqab (names in Arabic alphabet),
    22.22D
Latin capitals, transcription (early printed
    monographs), 2.14E
Latin language, capitalization, App. A.43
Latin v. vernacular form of personal
    names, 22.3B2
Latitude (cartographic materials), 3.3D1
Law reports, 21.36A
Laws, etc.
  capitalization, App. A.20
  definition, 21.31A
  entry, 21.31
  uniform titles, 25.15
  see also Administrative regulations, etc.;
    Constitutions; Court decisions,
    cases, etc.; Court rules; Treaties
Leases without title, 4.1B2
Leaves, definition, App. D; *for rules see*
    Pagination
Lectionaries (liturgical works), *see* Readings
    from sacred scriptures

names consisting of surname alone or
surname with word or phrase,
22.15
romanization of names, 22.3C2
in entry under title of nobility, 22.6A
in names of royal persons, 22.17A6
references from
Buddhist supreme patriarchs, 22.28D3
Thai names, 22.28A, 22.28C1
with prefixes, *see* Prefixes, surnames with
Suspension of publication (serials),
12.7B8
Sutan (Indonesian names),22 .26D
Swami (early Indic names), 22.25A
Swedish, *see* Scandinavian languages
Symbols
at beginning of titles, capitalization of
words following, App. A.4C
in edition statement, 1.2B2
in statements of responsibility, 1.1F9
in title proper, 1.1B1
replacement of, 1.0E
Symposia, *see* Conferences; Corporate
bodies
Synagogues, 24.3G
Synods, official messages to, entry, 21.4D1
Synods (regional units of certain religious
bodies), headings, 24.27C2
Systems analysts (machine-readable data
files), 9.7B6

Table books (specific material designation,
music), 5.5B1
Table talk, 21.25
Tables
not illustrations, 2.5C1
notes on, 2.7B18
Tables, genealogical (illustrative matter,
printed monographs), 2.5C2
Takhallus (names in Arabic alphabet),
22.22D
Talmud
references, 25.18D
uniform titles, 25.18B
Tamil names, 22.25B1
Tape reels, sound, *see* Sound tape reels
Tapes
chief source of information, 6.0B1
number of tracks, 6.5C1, 6.5C6
playing speed, 6.5C3
width, 6.5D4
for other rules see Sound recordings
Tapestries, *see* Art works
Technical drawings
definition, App. D
dimensions, 8.5D6
general material designation, 1.1C1
reproduction method, 8.5C15
specific material designation, 8.5B1
for other rules see Graphic materials
Telegrams without title, 4.1B2
Television stations, additions to, 24.11
Telugu names, 22.25B1
Temples, 24.3G

Tenor
abbreviation for, 5.7B1
omitted from uniform titles when
distinguishing musical instruments,
25.29D3
Terminology of ACCR 2, 0.2
Terms indicating incorporation (corporate
names)
omission, 24.5C
transposition, 24.5C2
Terms of address
added to identical names entered under
surname, 22.19B
Burmese and Karen names, 22.23B
capitalization in statement of
responsibility, App. A.4H
early Indic names, 22.25A
married women, 22.15B
"see" references, 26.2A3
Thai names, 22.28A
Terms of availability, 1.8D
additions to, 1.8E
capitalization, App. A.11
facsimiles, etc., 1.11E
Terrestrial remote sensing image
specific material designation, 3.5B1
for other rules see Cartographic materials
Territorial designations
added to place names, 23.4
in titles of nobility, 22.6A1
Territories, occupied, governors of, 24.20D
Testaments (Bible, uniform titles), 25.18A2
Texts
adaptations, 21.10
as sources of information
accompanying graphic materials,
8.0B1, 8.0B2
accompanying motion pictures and
videorecordings, 7.0B1
accompanying sound recordings, 6.0B
accompanying three-dimensional
artefacts and realia, 10.0B1
definition, App. D
general material designation, 1.1C1
illustrated, 21.11
in two languages with pages numbered
in opposite directions, 2.5B15
modifications of, 21.10–21.15
of religious observances, *see* Liturgical
works
opening words of (early printed
monographs), as title proper, 2.14A
revisions, 21.12
with biographical/critical material, 21.15
with commentary, 21.13
with music, notes on language, 5.7B2
Thai names, 22.28
Thematic index numbers
added to uniform titles (music),
25.31A1, 25.31A4
capitalization of accompanying words,
App. A.3C
definition, App. D
Theological creeds, 21.38
Theses, *see* Dissertations

Index

Third level of description, 1.0D3
  parallel titles, 1.1D2
Thorough bass (uniform titles), 25.29D4
Three-dimensional artefacts and realia, 10
  colour, 10.5C2
  definition, 10.0A
  edition area, 10.2
  general material designation, 10.1C
  material, 10.5C1
  note area, 10.7
  physical description area, 10.5
  publication, distribution, etc., area, 10.4
  series area, 10.6
  sources of information, 10.0B
  specific material designations, 10.5B
  standard number and terms of availability
      area, 10.8
  title and statement of responsibility
      area, 10.1
Three-dimensional cartographic materials
  scale, 3.3B8
  for other rules see Cartographic materials
Tipiṭaka, 25.18F1
Title
  added entries under, 21.30J
  changes in, *see* Title proper, changes in
  definition, App. D
  entry under, *see* Title entry
  facsimiles, etc., 1.11B
  music, definition, 25.26A
  preceded by dots, capitalization,
      App. A.4C
  references, 26.4
  variations in, *see* Variations in title
  see also Alternative titles; Caption title;
      Collective title; Cover title; Half
      title; Other title information;
      Running titles; Spine title; Title
      proper; Uniform titles
Title and statement of responsibility
      area, 1.1
  abbreviations, App. B.4
  capitalization, App. A.4
  cartographic materials, 3.1
    sources of information, 3.0B3
  graphic materials, 8.1
    sources of information, 8.0B2
  machine-readable data files, 9.1
    sources of information, 9.0B2
  manuscripts, 4.1
    sources of information, 4.0B2
  microforms, 11.1
    sources of information, 11.0B2
  motion pictures and videorecordings, 7.1
    sources of information, 7.0B2
  music, 5.1
    sources of information, 5.0B
  printed monographs, 2.1
    sources of information, 2.0B2
  serials, 12.1
    sources of information, 12.0B1
  sound recordings, 6.1
    sources of information, 6.0B2
  three-dimensional artefacts and realia,
      10.1
    sources of information, 10.0B2

Title cards (aperture cards) as sources of
      information, 11.0B1
Title entry, 21.1C
  adaptations of music, 21.18C
  adaptations of texts, 21.10
  capitalization, App. A.4D
  citations, digests, etc. of court reports,
      21.36B
  reports of interviews or exchanges, 21.25
  sacred scriptures, 21.37
  sound recordings, 21.23D
  theological creeds, etc., 21.38
  treaties, intergovernmental agreements,
      etc., 21.35A2
  works of shared responsibility, 21.6C2
  works of unknown or uncertain
      authorship, 21.5
Title frames
  definition, App. D
  graphic material, 8.5B2
  microforms, 11.0B1
Title of position or office added to identical
      names, 22.19B
Title page
  as source of information, 1.0A1
    early printed monographs, 2.13
    music, 5.0B1, 5.0B2
    printed monographs, 2.0B
    serials, 12.0B1
  definition, App. D
  lack of (early printed monographs),
      2.14A
  lost, 1.0A2
  several title pages, 1.0H
Title proper, 1.1B
  capitalization, App. A.4A
  cartographic materials, 3.1B, 3.7B3
  changes in, 21.2
    serials, 12.3B3, 21.2C
  definition, App. D
  early printed monographs, 2.14, 2.18B
  explanatory addition, 1.1E6
  graphic materials, 8.1B, 8.7B3
  in two or more languages or scripts, 1.1B8
  lack of, 1.1B7
    graphic materials, 8.1B2
    machine-readable data files, 9.1B3
    manuscripts, 4.1B2
    motion pictures and videorecordings,
        7.1B2
    music, 5.1B3
    nonprocessed sound recordings, 6.11B
      sound recordings, 6.1B2
    see also Collective title, lack of
  machine-readable data files, 9.1B, 9.7B3
  manuscripts, 4.1B, 4.7B3
  motion pictures and videorecordings,
      7.1B, 7.7B3
  music, 5.1B, 5.7B3
  printed monographs, 2.1B, 2.7B3
  serials, 12.1B, 12.7B3
  series, *see* Series statements
  sound recordings, 6.1B, 6.7B3
  source of, in notes, 1.7B3
  supplements or sections of other items,
      1.1B9

works entered under, *see* Title entry

Titles of honour, nobility, address, etc.
  capitalization
    Bulgarian language, App. A.35E
    Czech language, App. A.36C
    following names or used alone,
      App. A.13E
    French language, App. A.39D
    Hungarian language, App. A.41B
    in statement of responsibility,
      App. A.4H
    Italian language, App. A.42C
    Polish language, App. A.44C
    Portuguese language, App. A.45B
    preceding names, App. A.13C
    Russian language, App. A.46B4
    Scandinavian languages, App. A.47D
    Slovenian language, App. A.50E
    Spanish language, App. A.51B
    titles of honour and respect,
      App. A.13L
  change of personal names, 22.2B
  entry under, 22.6
    order of elements, 22.4B4
  in headings for personal names, 22.1C,
    22.12A, 22.12B
    early Indic names, 22.25A
    Indonesian names, 22.26G
    Malay names, 22.27D
    names entered under given name, etc.,
      22.17
    names in Arabic alphabet,
      22.22C–22.22D
    Thai names, 22.28A, 22.28C
  in statements of responsibility, 1.1F7

Topographic drawings
  specific material designation, 3.5B1
  for other rules see Cartographic materials

Topographic prints
  specific material designation, 3.5B1
  for other rules see Cartographic materials

Tosefta, 25.18C–25.18D

Towns, *see* Cities, towns, etc.

Tracings, definition, App. D

Track configuration (sound track films),
  6.5C1, 6.5C5

Tracks, number of (sound recordings),
  6.5C1, 6.5C6

Trade names
  capitalization, App. A.29
    physical description area, App. A.8
  machine-readable data files, 9.7B10
  sound recordings, 6.4D2–6.4D3
  stereographs, 8.5B1
  videorecordings, 7.5B1

Traditional format (oriental books), 2.5B12
  definition, App. D

Trailers, film
  definition, App. D
  other title information, 7.1E2
  for other rules see Motion pictures and
    video recordings

Transcription of title, *see* Title and
  statement of responsibility area;
  Title proper

Transcripts (manuscripts), notes, 4.7B1

Transcripts (musical works), *see*
  Adaptations; Arrangements

Translations
  entry, 21.14
  language, in description, 1.0H
  notes on, 1.7B2
  "see" references, 26.4A1
  serials, 12.7B7(a)
  uniform titles, 25.5D
    Bible, 25.18A10–25.18A12
    collections, 25.11
    Midrashim, 25.18E1
    selections, 25.6B3
    Talmud, 25.18B1
    vocal works, 25.31B7

Translators
  added entries, 21.30K1
  Bible, names added to uniform titles,
    25.18A11
  definition, App. D
  designation in added entries, 21.0D

Transliteration, *see* Romanization

Transparencies
  colour, 8.5C16
  definition, App. D
  dimensions, 8.5D4
  general material designation, 1.1C1
  multipart, 8.5B5
  not designed for projection, 8.5C7
  overlays, 8.5B4
  specific material designation, 8.5B1
  for other rules see Graphic materials

Transposition
  Burmese and Karen names, 22.23A
  elements of personal names, 22.4B3
  statement of responsibility, 1.1F3
  terms indicating incorporation (corporate
    bodies), 24.5C2

Treaties, intergovernmental agreements, etc.
  capitalization, App. A.20
  entry, 21.35
  uniform titles, 25.16

Tri (Indonesian names), 22.26C2

Trials, 21.36

Tribal laws, 21.31C

Tribes, *see* Races

Tribunals of the Roman Curia, 24.27C4

Tridentine liturgical texts, uniform titles,
  25.20A

Trinity (Christian), capitalization,
  App. A.19A

Trio sonatas, uniform titles, 25.27E

Trios, uniform titles. 25.27E

Tripiṭaka, 25.18F2

Two-dimensional art originals, *see* Graphic
  materials

Two-dimensional cartographic materials
  dimensions, 3.5D1
  for other rules see Cartographic materials

Two or more places of publication,
  publishers, etc., 1.4B8

Two-way paging, 2.5B15

Two works issued together, uniform titles,
  25.7

Type measurements (early printed
  monographs), 2.18E